| S5<br>FUSED<br>SENTENCES<br>426 | S6<br>COMMA<br>SPLICE<br>427 |
|---|---|
| S11<br>EXCESSIVE<br>COORDINATION<br>440 | S12<br>ILLOGICAL<br>SUBORDINATION<br>441 |

| W03<br>VAGUE<br>PRONOUNS<br>447 | W04<br>AWKWARD<br>SEPARATION<br>449 | W05<br>MISPLACED<br>EMPHASIS<br>451 | W06<br>USE AND ABUSE OF<br>PASSIVE<br>454 |
|---|---|---|---|

| G1<br>PARTS OF<br>SPEECH<br>457 | G2<br>WRONG<br>PRINCIPAL PART<br>465 | G3<br>TENSE<br>FORMS<br>469 | G4<br>CASE<br>479 | G5<br>AGREEMENT<br>(SUBJECT—VERB)<br>485 |
|---|---|---|---|---|
| G6<br>AGREEMENT<br>(PRONOUNS)<br>491 | G7<br>FAULTY<br>COMPLEMENT<br>495 | G8<br>FAULTY<br>MODIFIER<br>498 | G9<br>FAULTY<br>CONNECTIVE<br>500 | G10<br>FAULTY<br>COMPARISON<br>501 |

| P2<br>MISUSE OF<br>COMMA<br>512 | P3<br>USES OF<br>SEMICOLON<br>514 | P4<br>MISUSE OF<br>SEMICOLON<br>515 | P5<br>THE<br>PERIOD<br>516 | P6<br>QUESTION AND<br>EXCLAMATION MARKS<br>517 |
|---|---|---|---|---|
| P8<br>QUOTATION<br>MARKS<br>519 | P9<br>PUNCTUATION WITH<br>QUOTATION MARKS<br>520 | P10<br>THE<br>APOSTROPHE<br>522 | P11<br>ELLIPSIS AND<br>DASH<br>523 | P12<br>PARENTHESES<br>AND BRACKETS<br>525 |

| ital<br>ITALICS<br>550 | no<br>NUMBERS<br>551 | gloss<br>GLOSSARY<br>556 |
|---|---|---|

*second edition*

# WRITING WITH A PURPOSE

HOUGHTON MIFFLIN COMPANY

James M. McCrimmon/The University of Illinois

# A FIRST COURSE IN COLLEGE COMPOSITION

The Riverside Press Cambridge

The Riverside Press

Cambridge, Massachusetts

Printed in the U.S.A.

# CONTENTS ✱

*confusion of stylistic levels (179), the specific word: contrast
of specific and general words (181), sensory words (184),
figurative language: metaphors and similes (186), allusions
(188), personification (188), inappropriate figures (189),
the unspoiled word (190), exercises (192).*

# PART TWO: SPECIAL ASSIGNMENTS

# PREFACE

This second edition of *Writing With a Purpose* is largely indebted to instructors who have used the first edition and have suggested changes to make its use by students more efficient. Of these changes, the most extensive are the reorganization of the grammatical conventions into a form better suited to student reference, the condensation of the treatment of diction and its inclusion in Part One as part of the composition process, a rewriting of the chapter on vocabulary to provide illustrations from the three most popular college dictionaries and to give greater emphasis to the techniques of vocabulary building, a more detailed treatment of bibliography and documentation and more attention to notetaking in the chapter on the research paper, a new presentation of the material on argument, and a general revision of the exercises in various chapters. Although much of the text has been rewritten, the basic theme of purpose, the attitude towards linguistic conventions, and the major emphases of the first edition have not been changed.

This book is written in the belief that the most useful approach to the problems of composition is through a serious concern with purpose. A clear grasp of his intention becomes the only criterion by which a writer can wisely choose between alternatives — between one form of organization and another, between different patterns of development, between formal and informal styles, between alternative usages in diction, grammar, and mechanics. These choices cannot intelligently be made apart from some frame of reference. The writer's knowledge of his purpose is that frame, and his decisions are wise or unwise as they are or are not appropriate to his purpose.

To say that writing should have a controlling purpose is to say something that is more obvious to the instructor than to the student. Except in an elementary sense, the notion of purpose is foreign to most students of freshman composition. They have had little experience in analyzing a writing problem or in thinking out what they want to do before they begin to write. Their concern with organization has hitherto been rudimentary or mechanical. Because of the emphasis on "correct" and "incorrect" writing in their previous training, they tend to look upon the conventions of grammar as absolutes and to regard questions of diction as choices between "proper" and "improper" words. In short, they have not yet developed enough self-confidence to understand that within certain limits they are not only free, but have an obligation to make their own judgments about what forms and usages are appropriate to their particular needs.

The emphasis on purpose in this book attempts to give the student a point of view from which he can see his writing problems in perspective. That emphasis hopes to achieve three related objectives. First, it seeks to make writing a more deliberate act, to free the student from the frustration of trying to get a result without first knowing clearly what result he wishes, and thus it helps to give him a sense of control over what he writes. Second, it tries to make him linguistically more mature by showing him that usage is relative, and thus it encourages him to adopt a more discriminating attitude toward his linguistic decisions.

Third, the failure of composition courses to develop a concern with purpose contributes to the common student notion that the problems of composition are the problems of the composition course, and that once the course has been passed the problems are left behind. However much English instructors may regret it, a good many conscientious students see little relationship between "theme writing" and the kind of workaday communication required by essay-type examinations, reports on supplementary reading for various courses, and the demands of specialized writing courses, such as report writing. The tradition that "composition" is a special, impractical kind of writing dies hard, and perhaps those of us who teach composition are not entirely guiltless of keeping it alive. Be that as it may, the logic of making freshman composition a requirement would seem to dictate that the success of the course should be judged by the quality of the writing a student does in his other courses. Some way, therefore, must be found to make the student aware that writing a "theme" is merely a convenient way of gaining experience, skill, and confidence in using the writing process. A concern with purpose, by subordinating types of writing to an analysis of the particular needs of particular assignments, is one way to make the work of the composition class carry over into other courses and writing assignments.

This theme of purpose has been developed through each of the three main sections of the book. Part One deals with the writing process from the choice of subject through restriction, organization, and detailed development to the composition of paragraphs and sentences and the choice of diction. Although the emphasis is on exposition, the techniques apply to all kinds of writing. Part Two applies the composition process to a series of special assignments — research papers, summaries, essay-type examinations, critical reviews, and so on. Part Three explains and provides practice in using the conventions of grammar and mechanics. This part is intended primarily for students who need remedial assistance in making the conventions of educated usage habitual. For ease of reference, the correction chart on the inside back cover identifies common errors and the pages dealing with them.

A word should be said here about the chapter on argument and persuasion. The decision to make purpose the theme of the book made the conventional fourfold classification of writing unnecessary. Therefore Exposition, Narration, Description, and Argument are not considered as special types of writing. Effective argument, however, requires some attention to analysis of issues and to the evaluation of authorities, evidence, and reasoning, as well as to techniques of composition. For this reason, the study of argument has been presented in Part Two as a special assignment.

In the selected bibliography following this preface I have listed those works which I have found most helpful. I should like to acknowledge here a special obligation to Professor C. C. Fries's *American English Grammar* in my treatment of grammar, and to Dr. S. I. Hayakawa's *Language in Thought and Action* in my discussion of meaning. I owe thanks to those authors and publishers identified in the footnotes for permission to reprint illustrative material. To the many students whose work I have used as examples I am deeply grateful. For reasons which will at times be obvious, I have decided as an editorial policy not to identify student writers unless their work was taken from a published source, such as the *Green Caldron*. The one exception to this policy is the identification of the student author of the sample research paper in Chapter 14.

For their contributions during the preparation of the first edition I wish to re-express my gratitude to Professor George A. Gullette of North Carolina State University, to Professors Sarah S. Bissell and Ruby T. Scott of the University of Toledo, and to Professor Robert Y. Robb of Wayne University. For many helpful suggestions about revision I am indebted to Professors Homer Combs of Kansas State College, William Coyle of

Wittenburg College, Kenneth Forward of the University of Nebraska, Ernest Gray of the University of Toledo, Lee S. Hultzén of the University of Illinois, Robert S. Hunting and Howard A. Burton of Purdue University, Bryson L. Jaynes and F. A. Dudley of the State College of Washington, G. Edward Jones of Louisiana Polytechnic Institute, Franklin T. McCann of Alabama Polytechnic Institute, Dorles Parshall of Lyons Township Junior College, and M. L. Shane of South Dakota State College. For examples of student writing, good and bad, I owe thanks to Dr. James Clay of Iowa State Teachers College and to Arthur Flemings, Walter Draper, and A. Tress Lundman of the University of Illinois.

To the following people I owe more than this acknowledgment will reveal: to Professors Robert H. Moore of The George Washington University, Joshua McClennen of the University of Michigan, and George D. Stout of Washington University for page by page criticisms of the first edition; to Professor Leo Hughes of the University of Texas for a thorough criticism of the original chapters on diction; to Professor William V. Jackson of the University of Illinois who read the chapter on the use of the library; to Professor Thomas E. Ratcliffe, Jr., Reference Librarian of the University of Illinois, who brought up to date the pages on reference works; to Professor Lucius Garvin of the University of Maryland who read the chapter on argument; and to Professor James B. McMillan of the University of Alabama who read all of Part III. It is understood, of course, that my thanks to these critics involves them in no responsibility for whatever deficiencies remain in the book.

JAMES M. MCCRIMMON
URBANA, ILLINOIS

# BIBLIOGRAPHY

The following works have been most helpful in the preparation of this book:

Aiken, Janet R. *Commonsense Grammar*. New York: Thomas Y. Crowell Company, 1936. A readable and stimulating introduction to the common problems of grammar.

Baugh, Albert C. *A History of the English Language*. New York: D. Appleton-Century Company, 1935. The standard history.

Bloomfield, Leonard. *Language*. New York: Henry Holt and Company, 1938. A scholarly introduction to the science of linguistics.

Curme, George O. *Syntax*. Boston: D. C. Heath and Company, 1931. With *Parts of Speech and Accidence* (see below), the most complete grammar of current English.

Curme, George O. *Parts of Speech and Accidence*. Boston: D. C. Heath and Company, 1935. See *Syntax*, above.

Fries, C. C. *American English Grammar*. New York: D. Appleton-Century Company, 1940. Not so comprehensive a work as Curme's, but more up-to-date. The best example available of the use of the scientific method in the study of American grammar.

Hayakawa, S. I. *Language in Action*. New York: Harcourt, Brace and Company, 1940. The most popular introduction to general semantics. The revised edition, 1949, is entitled, *Language, Thought, and Action*.

Hixon, J. C., and I. Colodny. *Word Ways*. New York: American Book Company, 1939. An excellent handbook on the vocabulary of English.

Horwill, H. W. *A Dictionary of Modern American Usage*, 2nd edition. Oxford University Press, 1944. The American counterpart to Fowler's *Dictionary of Modern English Usage*, but less prescriptive in purpose and tone than Fowler's work.

Jesperson, Otto. *Growth and Structure of the English Language,* 4th edition. New York: D. Appleton and Company, 1929. A detailed account of the evolution of English.

Kennedy, A. G. *Current English.* Boston: Ginn and Company, 1935. A comprehensive summary of the knowledge of current English, containing an extremely useful bibliography.

Kenyon, J. S., and T. A. Knott. *A Pronouncing Dictionary of American English.* Springfield, Mass.: G. & C. Merriam Company, 1944. The standard dictionary of American pronunciation.

Krapp, G. P. *The Knowledge of English.* New York: Henry Holt and Company, 1927. Contains a series of analyses of the backgrounds of idiomatic English.

Lee, I. J. *Language Habits in Human Affairs.* New York: Harper and Brothers, 1941. A readable introduction to general semantics, unusually rich in illustrative material.

Marckwardt, A. H., and F. G. Walcott. *Facts About Current English Usage.* New York: D. Appleton-Century Company, 1938. An analysis of dictionary judgments on the 239 constructions originally comprising the Sterling A. Leonard study of usage.

Ogden, C. K., and I. A. Richards. *The Meaning of Meaning,* 3rd edition. New York: Harcourt, Brace and Company, 1930. Along with Alfred Korzybski's *Science and Sanity* one of the most influential of the works on semantics. Most undergraduates will find Hayakawa and Lee (above) easier to read and more rewarding.

*Oxford English Dictionary.* Oxford: Clarendon Press, 1888-1928, *Supplement,* 1933. The most complete and authoritative study of the historical development of English words and their meanings.

Perrin, P. G. *Writer's Guide and Index to English.* Chicago: Scott, Foresman and Company, 1950. Comprehensively applies the results of linguistic scholarship to the work in college composition. Like Kennedy's *Current English,* an excellent summary of the facts of current usage.

Pooley, R. C. *Teaching English Usage.* New York: D. Appleton-Century Company, 1946. Contains an excellent discussion of the most common problems of usage.

Robertson, Stuart. *The Development of Modern English,* revised by Frederic G. Cassidy. New York: Prentice-Hall, 1954. A series of studies in the historical backgrounds of modern English.

**PART ONE  \*  THE PROCESS OF COMPOSITION**

# 1

## INTRODUCTION

THROUGHOUT this book you will find one dominant assertion recurring in various forms: *All effective writing is controlled by the writer's purpose.* Except possibly when making a memorandum for himself, a writer is always addressing readers. He is trying to do something to those readers: to inform or convince or delight them, to explain something to them, or to make them see or feel what he has experienced. Each of these general purposes will exert its own influence on the selection and presentation of his material.

For example, two papers by the same author will differ considerably in content, organization, and style if one is written to provide students with a factual summary of the football team's record during the season and the other to praise the team for its fine work. In each paper the writer will select that particular material which his intention requires and will present it in a style that suits his purpose.

Writing does not take place in a vacuum. When well done, it is always an attempt by one person to communicate to others those ideas, facts, or impressions that build up to the result *which the writer has intended to achieve.* The writer, therefore, must always begin with a clear sense of purpose. This means that before he starts to write he must give careful attention to two related questions: "What *precisely* do I want to do?" and "How can I best do it?" Answering these questions properly is the first step toward writing well.

These two questions are so closely related that a writer will sometimes know *what* he wants to do only when he has decided *how* he wants to do it. A simple analogy will illustrate. Imagine an expert golfer facing a twenty-foot putt on a rolling green. What is his purpose? To say that he wants to sink his putt is to describe his purpose in terms too general to be helpful. For him, the important decision is *how* the shot should be played. Therefore he studies the contour of the green, observes the grain and texture of the grass, and plans the course he wants his ball to follow. Only when he has thought out his problem in this way can he be said to know what he wants to do. His precise purpose, then, is to stroke the ball in such a way that it will follow the contour of the green in a *predetermined* path to the cup.

In much the same way a writer must try to understand what it means to make his writing do what he wants it to do. This means, first, that he must know precisely what his purpose is and, second, that he must realize how particular decisions about choice of material, organization, development, style, diction, and grammar will help or hinder that purpose. Those requirements are neither simple nor easy. Sometimes they impose a discipline from which the writer has an understandable desire to escape. But taking the easy way out and running away from that discipline often exacts a heavy price, as some of the illustrative student essays used later in this chapter will show.

A poor sense of purpose in student writing usually reveals itself on one of three levels. At the worst, the writer shows no sense of purpose at all. Because he has no clear idea what he wants to do, he has no one path to follow, and his ideas meander through the assignment and follow no consistent direction. We can call such writing *directionless*. Usually such a writer literally has no idea what is going to happen when he begins to write. He simply puts down whatever occurs to him at the moment, in a desperate effort to say *something* on the assigned subject, no matter what. Because his thinking is not continuous, his writing is directionless. It goes forward a little in one direction, stops, veers off in another, and turns again. The following student essay is a fair example of writing without direction.

## MY FIRST IMPRESSIONS OF THE UNIVERSITY

I knew this was one of the biggest universities in the country, but I never understood till I arrived on campus just how big it really is. When I first came here I was so scared that I felt like returning home, but then I convinced myself that I was being silly. After all, if thousands of other people could stand it, why couldn't I?

After looking around for a while I went to what would be my home for at least a semester. When I got to the door I saw a light seeping out from under it. I was scared again. I was going to meet my roommate. Cautiously I opened the door and looked in. He was lying in bed reading. It was now or never. I went in. We quickly became friends.

The next morning we got up and went to eat breakfast. After eating breakfast, we went off together to explore the campus.

Since Fred, my roommate, was especially interested in gymnastics, we went to the Old Gymnasium, where we worked out for a few minutes on the sidehorse. I tried to do some of the stunts he showed me, but I was no good at them. I like to watch gymnastic meets, but my sport is basketball. I am looking forward to the basketball season, and I hope I will be lucky enough to make the freshman squad.

When we got tired of walking around the campus we returned to our room. Fred turned out to be a swell companion. Getting to know him has helped me to overcome the loneliness that I first felt when I came to this huge campus.

Each of the five paragraphs in this essay goes in a different direction. The first starts off to explain how the size of the university made the student feel insignificant, lonely, and homesick. That general impression could have been developed into an effective essay, had the student stayed with it and shown us in detail how lonely and insecure he was. But instead, he changed direction in the second paragraph in order to report his first meeting with his roommate. That subject, too, could have been developed into a good essay; but, again, the writer stopped just as he was getting nicely started. He turned away from that first meeting, with all the evidence it could have provided of a new and satisfying companion-ship growing out of the loneliness of both boys, to record the unim-portant detail that they had breakfast together before making a tour of the campus. Then the tour is interrupted before it gets well started by a digression on gymnastics and basketball. When that is over, so is the tour, without mention of any building except the Old Gymnasium. The total result is a communication which goes in no consistent direction and has no effect on a reader except to leave him wondering what the writer was trying to do.

The answer, of course, is that the writer did not know. He was just trying to get enough words on paper to satisfy an assignment. Because he had no clear sense of purpose, he had no control over what he wrote. As he thought of his first meeting with Fred, their breakfast together, and their workout in the Old Gymnasium, he wrote a little about each, without considering what relation these events had to the subject implied in his title. In all this meandering, no goal is quite reached. We never really feel the impact of the boy's loneliness; we get no clear picture of Fred's personality; we learn nothing about the campus except that it is big. What we get is a hodge-podge of material which has not been shaped into any unified structure. This is purposeless writing at its worst.

On a second level is writing which is not quite without direction but is *unselective*. The writer *knows*, in a general way, what he wants to do, and his writing does move in a single direction. But because he fails to distinguish between relevant and irrelevant details, his work lacks purposeful emphasis. It does not focus on any one point but treats all details as though they were equally important to the purpose. This weakness is especially common in student accounts of vacation trips. The following paper is a fair sample.

## A Fishing Trip

Even though my extent of travel is somewhat limited, I have had some very interesting and educational trips. My first venture from home took place a few years ago when some friends asked me to accompany them to Canada on a two-weeks' fishing trip. I must admit that at the time I knew nothing about fishing but I had all the enthusiasm to learn.

It was a bright, sunny day when we left Columbus in a tightly packed car for Sparrow Lake, Canada. Along the way we stopped at Niagara Falls to see one of nature's beautiful creations, and then continued to drive what seemed to be an endless distance. At last we arrived in Orillia, Canada, bought a few necessary supplies, and drove several miles down a typical washboard road till we arrived at our destination.

As I think back, I can still see that huge old brick home standing on top of the hill — not a tree around. After unpacking our clothes, and eating one of those delicious home cooked dinners, we sat around and talked to all the new people, and then prepared for a good night's sleep in preparation for the busy day ahead of us.

From that day on, most of our time was spent in the boat on the lake trying to catch muskies. Even though our luck was pretty good I just couldn't learn to like that rod and reel sport. Consequently I was bribed into steering the boat.

I found my pleasures in the evening, after dinner, in swimming and playing tennis. Many of us used to row boats into the deeper part of the lake, dive, swim around, climb into the boat and row back to shore. I met many new friends and I am still writing to them.

I fully understand that a good fisherman could not imagine such a story, but it is a true one nevertheless. I'm sure I'll not accept another invitation to go on a fishing trip.

What is the main point of this composition? The title suggests that the emphasis will be on fishing, and the opening and closing paragraphs — always important parts of an essay — support that expectation. But all the fishing the student actually did is dismissed in the three short sentences of the fourth paragraph. The rest of the paper describes other details — the stop at Niagara Falls, the stop for groceries, the washboard road, the brick house on the top of the hill, and so on. What happened was that, having determined to write about her fishing trip, the student began at the beginning and mentioned almost everything she remembered about the whole vacation. As a result, the original purpose of the essay almost gets lost. The emphasis that should have been placed on one aspect of the trip is dispersed through many. This lack of concentration leaves the reader dissatisfied. He was given an implied promise, and that promise was not kept.

Had this student been more concerned about her purpose in writing, she might have decided that what she really wanted to do was to show that muskie-fishing is an overrated sport and that she found it dull.

With that purpose in mind, she might have felt that the best way to develop the paper was to contrast the excitement she had expected with the boredom she actually felt. The question where to begin would then have been solved almost automatically. She would have ignored the stop at Niagara Falls, the old brick house, the home-cooked food. She might even have ignored the pleasures of the evening, though she could legitimately have used them as a contrast to the dullness of fishing. Along with this omission of irrelevant detail she might have done more to emphasize the unpleasantness of fishing by providing illustrative details. In short, a little thought about what she wanted her writing to do would have given her a unified essay, perhaps something like this:

## A Fishing Trip? No Thanks!

Although I had never been on a fishing trip, I had seen how much pleasure Dad always got from his annual fishing vacation and I had imagined that fishing, especially for muskies, must be thrilling. Therefore, when some friends invited me to accompany them on a two-weeks' fishing trip to Sparrow Lake, Canada, Lair of the Big Muskies, I jumped at the chance. I was so eager to fish that the necessary preparations and the long, tedious car trip were severe tests of my patience. When we finally reached our cabin, late at night, I had difficulty getting to sleep. Visions of successful catches chased each other through my head. Had I known what I know now, I would have slept soundly — and late.

From the first day at the lake, most of our time was spent in the boat trying to catch muskies. We would get up before daylight, slosh some cold water on our faces, and prepare breakfast on a capricious kerosene stove. By the time it was light enough to bait a hook we would be pushing off from the wharf. Usually we would fish until noon, take an hour out for lunch, and try again until evening. Once we took sandwiches and a thermos of coffee with us and ate lunch in the boat, after rinsing our fishy hands in the lake. Once was enough. After that, we girls insisted on being put ashore to prepare lunch.

The prerequisite for comfortable fishing, I found, is the right kind of anatomy. I didn't have it. Even three cushions, piled one on top of another, only partially modified the hardness of the boat seat. I am sure that if God had intended the human frame to be subjected to five or six continuous hours on a narrow, wooden plank, He would have designed it differently. The slimy business of baiting the hook and of unhooking a fish when I was unfortunate enough to catch one, I could usually delegate to the men. But I never found a way of getting somebody to sit for me.

I admit that muskie-fishing has its exciting moments — the sudden thrill of a hard strike, those delicious seconds when you wait for the muskie to turn the bait in his mouth before you set the hook, his final desperate dive as you bring him near the boat, the first gleam of his greenish-white body as you pull him close to the surface, and the pistol shot that finally dispatches him. But those moments are paid for by hours of boredom and discomfort, when you sit, cold and wet, with nothing to do but fend off the persistent horse fly that is enamored of your knuckles. Even the thrill of landing a big one soon descends to an anticlimax as you spend a frustrating fifteen minutes trying to pry or cut the hooks from his vicious mouth or fumbling with numbed fingers to untangle the line, now hopelessly snarled in the contents of the spilled tackle box.

And when all this dreary routine is over, and your line is paying out freely from the side of the boat, what is there to look forward to? At best, the same thing over again — and all this for a fish which is hardly fit to eat. Do you blame me for deciding that if I had to be involved in such foolishness I would confine my efforts to steering the boat? That way I could save my disposition and what was left of my fingernails.

There are three things to observe about this revision. First, it eliminates everything which in the original version detracted from the purpose of the essay, and so is more unified. Second, it gives the illustrative details necessary to show why the girl disliked muskie fishing, and so brings about a fuller and clearer development of her purpose. Third, although the revised version covers less territory, it is actually longer. In reducing the scope of the subject, the writer has discovered more to write about. For students who have difficulty writing more than a couple of hundred words on any subject, this result is worth noticing. We shall deal with it more thoroughly in Chapter 5, but it is worth mentioning in passing that the more clearly a writer understands his purpose, the less trouble he has in finding something to say. His sense of purpose actually suggests the illustrative details he needs.

Failures of purpose on yet a third level are subtler still, and are usually the result of faulty analysis of the assignment. When a writer fails to see that the situation imposes certain restrictions or requires him to deal with the subject in a particular way, he cannot do what the situation requires of him. He may have a clear sense of what he wants to do, and his writing may follow a consistent direction and show a discriminating selection of details, but if he is not sensitive to the demands of the situation, what he writes will not be appropriate. We can call his writing *uncritical* or *insensitive*.

Common examples of insensitive writing are found in answers to essay-type examinations. Often a student fails to read a question carefully enough to understand what is required of him. If he is asked to "compare and contrast," he should not describe the two things separately without establishing a comparison or a contrast between them, nor should he summarize an argument when asked to "evaluate" it. Such errors are discussed and illustrated in Chapter 12. At this stage of our work we can illustrate this kind of insensitive or uncritical writing by an assignment in persuasion.

Imagine a writer faced with the following problem:

Suppose you have a sister, seventeen years old and about to begin her senior year in high school. She is very much in love with a boy of nineteen, a sophomore in college, who is about to be drafted and expects to be sent abroad. They want to get married now. His parents have given their consent; yours object to an immediate marriage because they feel that your sister is too young, that she ought to finish high school and delay the wedding until the boy gets out of service, in about two years. Although your mother has explained her objections fully, your sister is not persuaded. Indeed, she is seriously thinking of eloping. But before doing so, she writes asking your advice. Write your reply to her in the form of a letter.

Let us suppose that the writer agrees with his parents and wants to persuade his sister to delay marriage until the boy has completed his military service. This supposition establishes the general purpose of the letter he will write, but there are elements in the situation which will affect both the content and the tone of his reply. The first task of the writer, then, is to analyze the situation and discover these elements. His analysis might go like this:

1. The fact that my sister is postponing elopement until she hears from me is a sign that she is still willing to listen to reason. She evidently considers elopement as a last resort. My main effort, therefore, should be to persuade her not to elope, since elopement would end all consideration of her problem. The more I can get her to delay, the wiser her decision is likely to be and the less strain it will impose on both families.
2. My sister's appeal for advice suggests that she trusts me to be sympathetic with her problem. Nothing I say must destroy that confidence. Above all, I must not take a superior attitude or lecture her. The tone of my letter will be as important as my advice.
3. Obviously my sister believes (a) that she is mature enough to marry and (b) that her love for the boy is the real thing, not merely an adolescent infatuation. In her present disturbed state, contradicting her is sure to cause resentment and may hasten rather than delay an elopement. The question to be dealt with is *when* she should marry the boy, not *whether* she should marry him.
4. Since I have an obligation to my parents, too, I must not take sides with her against my mother, nor give the impression that I think mother entirely right and sister entirely wrong. My job is to lessen, not increase, family tension. If I can get sister to look objectively at mother's advice, she may be influenced by it more than she now seems to be.
5. Since sister probably knows all the stock arguments against hasty marriages, there is no point in my repeating them. The thing to do is to find the one argument that will best persuade my sister, and to concentrate on that.

This is a great deal of analysis for a single letter, but the problem requires no less. Unless the writer is willing to think out his problem in some such way as this, *before he writes a single word*, he is not prepared to write. If he plunges into a hasty answer, he runs the danger of producing a letter as bad as this one:

Dear Rhoda:

You are much too young to get married. At seventeen you simply haven't had enough experience with boys to decide to tie your whole life to one of them. So the first question you should ask yourself is, "Am I really in love with Ted or is it just a plain case of infatuation?" If you married Ted what would you do when he was shipped abroad? Sit around night after night twiddling your thumbs while the other girls were having fun on dates? What would you do if you had a baby? If you married Ted now you would be leaving school, your parents, your friends, everything that you have always liked. Are you willing to give up all this just for a few extra months of married life? And then what?

To add to these, Rhoda, you know that doing something more or less behind your parents' back and without their consent would never leave you with a clear conscience. Mother and Dad have always done what was best for you, and it is really quite selfish of you to go against their wishes now. Even if their reasons seem a bit old-fashioned, you ought to recognize that they are older and wiser than you.

Rhoda, I am sure that if you read this carefully and think about it, you will make the right decision. I'm looking forward to having you as the maid of honor at my wedding next summer. You haven't forgotten that I was in the same predicament a few years ago. I listened to sensible advice, and the outcome has pleased everyone. Don't disappoint me with your decision.

Love,

*Alice*

Without regard to the soundness of Alice's advice, what do you think of the tone of her letter? How would you feel if you were in Rhoda's situation and the sister you had counted on to understand and sympathize with your problem had written you this letter? How would you react to her suggestion that you were being foolish, that your love was merely the infatuation of an inexperienced girl, and that your unwillingness to follow your parents' advice was sheer selfishness? Would you be persuaded or repelled by the way Alice presents her advice and the smug example of her own conduct?

Contrast the tone and content of this letter with the following:

Dear Janie:

I wish I knew what was the wise thing to tell you, but I don't. Every time I try to look at your problem as an outsider would look at it, I realize that I am not an outsider and I feel the conflict and uncertainty that I know you must have felt. About all I am really sure of is that you will finally do what you honestly think is best for you and Bill and your future together, and that, whatever that is, it will not really weaken the love that Mom and Dad and I have for you.

But, dear, don't be bitter about Mom and Dad. The advice they have given you is the advice any responsible parent would have to give a 17-year old daughter. It is the advice you would have to give if you were in their place. Whether it is wise advice or not, only the future can show. You have the right to reject it, but don't reject it in anger. After all, Mom wants you to marry Bill, and she wants your marriage to be successful. She is simply trying to make sure that your marriage gets off to the best possible start. Even if you think she is mistaken, you can hardly blame her for feeling as she does.

The chief trouble with eloping is the effect it may have on the friendship between Bill's parents and ours. Bill's mother doesn't want an elopement any more than Mom does. She wants you to have a church wedding, and I am sure that if you talk with her about eloping she will tell you it is not the best answer. If you eloped, she would feel that Mom had driven you to it, and Mom and Dad would feel that Bill's family had encouraged you.  This would cause a rift between the families that would make your marriage more difficult than it needs to be.  I think that in eloping you would be running away from a problem that you and Bill should settle before you get married.  I am sure that you and Mom together can find a better solution.

What I wonder most about is whether you and Bill will not some day regret your leaving high school without graduating.  By the time Bill returns from abroad you may have a family and it will be difficult for you to return to high school.  Yet, in the circles in which Bill will be moving after he graduates from college, a wife without even a high school diploma is going to be at a disadvantage.  It would not make things easier for you if you felt educationally inferior to him and to the wives of his associates.  Wouldn't you be more useful to Bill's future and to that of your children if you finished high school and perhaps had a year of college?

I realize, Janie, that you and Bill are very much in love and I'm sure you are both mature enough to face the responsibilities of marriage.  The only question I have is whether you will both later have to pay too much for the few months of companionship you will have before Bill goes overseas.  I don't know the answer to that question, but I am sure that you and Bill will have the wisdom and patience to consider it carefully.  I know that if you do you will not act impulsively and that Mom and Dad will finally respect your decision, whatever it is.

All my love,

Jo

Because this letter is more sympathetic, and because it considers the question from the reader's point of view, it has a far better chance than the first one of persuading the girl not to elope. Alice's advice may be quite sound, though it is probably merely a summary of what her parents have already said. But Alice does not see, as Jo does, how the situation must affect both the content and the tone of the letter. This is another way of saying that Alice is less sensitive than Jo and that her letter shows this lack of sensitivity. But it is important to recognize that Alice's mistakes were made before she began to write. They are a result of her failure to analyze the situation carefully in order to clarify her own purpose in writing.

Obviously, it is not only in writing that planning is important. In all fields of endeavor success is usually a result of careful, often painstaking preparation. A concern with purpose is important no matter what you do. The following news report is one of many illustrations of this truth.

### Danger for a Living [1]

Audiences at the forthcoming movie, "The Boss," will watch a machine-gun killing in which the three victims, handcuffed together, go pinwheeling over one another down a long flight of marble steps and fall dead in the street. This takes 45 seconds. Staging it, however, took two full days of rehearsal.

"The main problem," says Paul Stader, the stuntman who plotted the job, "was to get in the right positions at the start. After that, we knew the momentum would do the rest for us."

Stader and two other stuntmen, Saul Gorss and Harvey Parry, spent hours "walking-through" the fall, marking their body-contact positions on the steps as they went. Then, with their hips, knees, and elbows trussed in hidden pads, they ran through it fast. On the day of filming, the steel handcuffs snapped in two on the way down. The second take was perfect. Each of the three stuntmen pocketed $500, plus an extra $200 for the second fall, and went home.

There is probably no habit more useful to form at the beginning of your college career than the habit of asking yourself before you begin a piece of writing, "What exactly do I want to do in this paper?" The question will usually be easier to ask than to answer, for the answer may require you to plan your paper in detail. But if you face the question squarely and refuse to stop with a superficial answer, you will derive three very practical advantages: you will be able to avoid many of the false starts and pencil-chewing periods that make writing a frustrating ordeal for many people; you will be able to exert a firmer control over what you do write; and you will have a point of view which will serve as a guide through the complex of decisions that must be made at every stage of the writing. Let us consider these advantages.

[1] Reprinted by permission of *Newsweek* from the issue of August 13, 1956. Copyright, 1956, by *Newsweek*.

Many students find it hard to get started on a writing assignment. They make a dozen desperate beginnings, hopeful that each succeeding one will turn out well. But after an hour or two they have little to show for their efforts except a full wastebasket and a short temper. Now, when the ideas that a writer is dealing with are difficult, or when the writing problem is unusually subtle, some of these false starts are understandable. Even experienced writers make them. But too often the student's trouble is that he is trying to substitute the physical activity of pounding a typewriter or pushing a pen for the more exacting effort of thinking. Writing is a product of thought, not a substitute for it. A student who tears up enough experimental pages will, it is true, often learn from his failures what it is that he wants to do. But he could get the same results more pleasantly and probably more quickly by thinking out his problem before trying to write about it. A half-hour's walk, during which he concentrated on getting clear in his mind exactly what he wanted to do, might give him the whole pattern of his paper and make the actual writing unexpectedly painless.

Second, a student who clearly understands his purpose is not likely to be trapped by an accidental sequence of ideas, for he will recognize when he is going astray. A good deal of writing is censorship — keeping irrelevant thoughts out of the paper. Many of the ideas that arise in our minds have little relation to the purpose of our writing, and the habit of following impromptu ideas may result in a jumble of pointless remarks. A student who knows his purpose can detect and reject any idea that interferes with his intention. But a student who has no practical understanding of what he is trying to do has no standard by which to distinguish good ideas from bad. He has therefore little control over what he writes and is likely to put down anything that comes to mind.

Finally, a student with a clear sense of purpose has a point of view which gives him a consistent approach to all the problems of composition. Every writer, whether he is aware of it or not, is continuously facing the choice between alternatives. At successive stages of his work he must make decisions between alternative forms of organization, illustration, style, diction, and grammar. If he has no adequate sense of purpose, his successive choices are likely to work against each other, making his writing awkward or confused. He may vary between a too-formal and a too-informal style, between pompous diction and inappropriate slang, or between pedantic and informal grammar. If, on the other hand, he understands the implications of what he is trying to do, his choices are more likely to be harmonious. His writing will be all of a piece. It will have unity of style as well as unity of subject.

# 2

\* \* \* \* \*

# CHOOSING

# A SUBJECT

CAUTIOUS DELIBERATION in choosing a subject to write about is a sign of wisdom, but some students waste valuable time worrying unprofitably. Like the philosophical donkey who starved to death surrounded by haystacks because he could not decide where to begin, such students spend hours rejecting subjects, any one of which might be developed into an acceptable paper, and finally retreat behind the excuse that they have nothing to write about.

This complaint cannot be taken very seriously. College students have not been living in a vacuum. Every instructor knows that they have been living moderately active lives, surrounded by hundreds of other people, in a world that is forever forcing its worries, disasters, hopes, and triumphs on their consciousness. He knows also that good writing is not confined to subjects far away and long ago, that the everyday events of ordinary living can be recorded freshly and effectively by a student who knows how to make use of them.

As a simple illustration of this assertion, consider the following student essay:

### SOCIAL PRESSURE

"Ginneeeeeee! Phone. It's a man."

"For me?" Anticipating a date, I dashed down the stairs of the dormitory to the phone booth.

"Hello."

"Hello, Ginny? This is Steven Conn. How would you like to go to the movies with me Friday night?"

"O.K."

"I'll be over to the house about 7:30 then?"

"All right."

"Good night."

15

I went back to my room and the girls who were congregated there wanted to know who, what, when, where, how, as they always did after a phone call from a male.

"It was Steve Conn. I'm going to the movies Friday night with him."

My roommate and Elsie, one of our best friends, exchanged meaningful looks. They grinned a little, then burst out laughing. Belligerently, I demanded to know why they were laughing. All they could manage to say was, "Steve Conn!" and off they went again into gales of laughter. I stamped my foot and insisted that they stop laughing and tell me why my going out with Steve was such a wonderful joke. Realizing that I was in earnest, they stopped laughing. Elsie offered an explanation. "Ginny, you just can't go out with him! He's such a queer. He can hardly talk English and he lisps. Besides he's only about five feet five. Everybody laughs at him. The guy's just a freak, that's all. You'll have to call him and tell him you can't go."

"I shall do no such thing!" I snatched up my books and stamped downstairs to the study room. But I couldn't study. All I could think of was the kids' reaction to my forthcoming date with Steve. Steve was a German refugee. His English was faulty, and besides he had a slight speech impediment which added to his language difficulties. At times he was absolutely incoherent and was forced to resort to gestures. He was quite ugly, had small eyes obscured by thick glasses, a large nose and mouth, and bushy hair. His figure was short and squat; his clothes illfitting and worn. Neither the students nor the faculty liked him, for besides being a foreigner and an unpleasant looking one at that, he always interrupted class discussions to ask stupid questions. There were so many things that he didn't understand that everyone had grown impatient with him. Nearly everyone found him distasteful and avoided him as much as possible. He sat next to me in English, and because I was kind to him I suppose he decided to ask me for a date. I couldn't have refused him, for my heart went out to him. He was such a pathetic creature. I began to hate the girls for tormenting me, and I determined that not only should I go out with Steve, but I should do it proudly.

The days preceding the Friday date were a horror. The girls called me "Stevie's gal" and affected lisps and German accents every time I came around. By Friday the entire house knew that I was going out with Steve Conn; they thought it a huge joke. When he came to call for me, there was much snickering and remark-passing. The girl at the desk called up, "Ginneeeee, Stevie's here." A general giggle resulted.

Everybody on campus attended the Friday night movies, and as we started toward the auditorium the usual crowds filled the sidewalk. I suggested that we take a roundabout way to avoid the mob. But crowds didn't usually bother me! I was suddenly aware that the kids had won. I just didn't want people to see me with Steve. The rest of the evening I suffered. We sat back in a dark corner of the auditorium. I hoped fervently that no one would notice us. After the movies, I assured Steve that I didn't want anything to eat. I couldn't go in the Bee Hive with him. We returned to the house in the same roundabout way that we had gone. As I was saying good night to him on the porch, he asked me whether I had a date for Saturday. I said "Yes," hurriedly. It was a lie; I didn't have a date, but I knew I couldn't go out with him again. We said good night and with a sigh I went into the house. I had been defeated. I hated myself for being so weak, but it was no use; I couldn't fight so much opposition. The opinion of my house mates ruled me, and I knew it. I have not since doubted that social pressure is a potent force in determining individual action.

Nothing in this incident lies outside the experience of a normal student. Long before we have reached college age, we have all learned how much we are influenced by the attitudes of our friends. Even if an individual student had never experienced the particular sort of pressure this essay illustrates, he could still develop the idea expressed in the concluding sentence with evidence of his own. All he would have to do would be to keep the last sentence in mind and think out its im- plications in his own life. He could not then fail to uncover enough material for several essays.

Any student who feels that he has nothing to write about should sit down for an hour or two some evening early in the semester and make an inventory of subjects which could be drawn up merely from his own experience. The more he analyzes his experience, the more writing possibilities he will find in it. Consider how many topics come out of the following general areas of experience.

| *The student's total experience:* | *Topics derived from his experience:* |
|---|---|
| *family* | Life with father — On being the oldest (or youngest) child — Mother's pet peeves — The worst day in our family — Are sisters (brothers) worth while? — The mother's part in making a successful family life — Democracy in the family — Family reunions |
| *friends* | Fair weather friends — The best friend I ever had — Vacation friendships — Friends I have forgotten — And I thought she was my friend — That gang in high school — Are friends closer than parents? |
| *neighborhood* | The people next door — Death comes to our street — Hallowe'en in our block — The neighborhood bully — How the neighbors have changed — The importance of the right neighborhood — Community events — The best fire our neighborhood ever had |
| *hobbies and recreations* | What stamp collecting teaches — When the hunting season opens — Overhauling the family car — A trunk- ful of scrapbooks — Keeping up with the movie stars — Why save autographs? — The best sport of all |
| *hopes and ambitions* | New Year's resolutions — What I'd really like to do with my life — The chance that college offers — How much money is enough? — Marriage or a career? — The house |

I'd like to build — What every man (woman) wants most — How mottoes have reflected my successive ambitions

*fears and prejudices*
Childhood fears — The things I still fear — The kind of man (woman) I detest — The origin of a prejudice — The worst kind of hurt — What I don't like about big cities

*relations with people*
What makes us self-conscious? — These things used to embarrass me — How my attitude toward boys (girls) has changed — Things parents forget — On being called upon to recite in class — People I envy — How important are the social graces? — What do people find to talk about on dates? — Does anyone really know us?

*knowledge of how to do things*
How to test a second-hand car — How to handle a skid — How to tell good music from bad — The part the orchestra leader plays — How to win radio contests — How not to argue — How to borrow the family car — What a balanced diet means — The best way to pay a compliment

Many students overlook good topics because they fail to see that what they consider a single experience is really a series of experiences, any one of which might make an effective paper. Some students will write papers in which they summarize a week's visit to New York in three or four hundred words. If they could learn to see that such a visit is a complex event which includes a great many topics, they might understand that their problem was not how to say enough to fill a single essay, but how to pick out that phase of the total experience which seemed to promise the best essay. Often the surest way to do this is to make a list of the most prominent or interesting features of the trip or other experience. Look how "A Trip to New York" breaks down into twenty different topics:

*The trip east*
Driving through Pennsylvania
Highways that invite speeding
Billboard advertising as a cause of accidents
A contrast in motels

*In New York*
Coming into a large city: first impressions
The New York skyline
Driving in New York City
My first subway ride
The view from the Empire State Building
Rockefeller Center — A city within a city
Chinatown
Harlem
The Great White Way
The Battery
My first sight of ocean liners

Eating in an automat
Inside the Stock Exchange
Shopping in New York
A night at a play
Are New Yorkers always in a hurry?

Any student about to write an essay on his vacation trip would have fewer worries about subject matter if he broke down his general topic in this manner. Moreover, such a list will protect the student against one of the greatest weaknesses of college writing — the habit of presenting complex experiences in such general terms that the work communicates almost nothing to a reader. For example, had the girl who wrote the paper about fishing (page 6) made such a list, she might have avoided the temptation to cram a series of unrelated experiences into a paper which should have been confined to a single experience.

## Restricting the Subject

The very act of thinking out a general subject by breaking it into its parts carries us into the second stage of determining the purpose of an essay. When we broke down the subject, "A Trip to New York," into its sub-topics we were restricting it. Sometimes the restricted topic was still broad (Chinatown, for example). Sometimes (Rockefeller Center — A City Within a City) the restriction was so complete that it pretty clearly established the purpose of any paper written on the topic.

Restricting a subject not only reduces it to a scope that can be dealt with in a short paper; it also creates a channel through which the author's ideas may flow. In other words, it helps him to discover his purpose. For instance, suppose that at the beginning of the term you are asked to write a paper on your impressions of the university. As you recall these impressions you find they are a chaotic jumble of often unrelated observations. If you were to put them down in note form in the order in which they occur to you, you might get some such hodge-podge as this:

Many more students here than in high school. Appearance of the campus. Architecture. Lack of snobbishness in upper classmen. Variety of students. Experience at first freshman smoker. Difficulty of finding way to classes. Helpfulness of old timers. Many pretty girls. Some not so pretty. Faculty seems quite young. Class procedure different from high school. Instructors less formal. Being addressed as Mr. and Miss makes students feel more mature. Park on other side of creek makes pleasant addition to campus. Tennis courts conveniently located.

Suppose that you recognize how chaotic these impressions are, and so you begin to think about your dominant or over-all impression of university life. As you do this, it occurs to you that college life is really quite different from what you had expected. You begin to see that your ideas about college had largely been formed from the movies and from occasional football games. You therefore decide to write a paper showing that college is not as Hollywood shows it. Now you not only have a basic idea that you want to develop but you also have a principle of selection that leads you to choose certain impressions and reject others. You have restricted your subject by taking a particular point of view toward it. Perhaps you write a paper something like this:

## So This Is College

Although I had never been on a college campus until I enrolled here a week ago, I had gained a pretty clear notion of college life from the movies. A college, I thought, was a cluster of ancient, ivy-covered buildings, populated by beautiful coeds, broad-shouldered athletes, and gray-bearded or bald-headed professors, most of whom were notoriously absent-minded. Perhaps there are such colleges, but after one week on this campus I am forced to admit that this is not one of them.

This university bears little resemblance to a Hollywood campus. That doesn't necessarily mean that our campus is unattractive. True enough, that straggling little stand of ivy clinging so desperately to the back of the science building is not impressive. But I like the neatness of the well-kept lawns, I am impressed by the fine job of landscaping that has been done, and I am glad that whoever laid out the parking lot behind University Hall was artist enough to work it into the general scheme. And though there isn't any Hollywood lake on which to go canoeing on moonlit nights, the park on the other side of the creek, with its fine shade trees, will probably be a satisfactory substitute.

The students I have seen and talked with do not fit into the movie pattern. Perhaps the inevitable Joe College will make his appearance in time, and no doubt some of the girls I have met would be as glamorous as movie starlets if they dressed as Hollywood coeds do. But dressed as they are, they seem pretty much like the girls you would expect to see wherever several hundreds of them are brought together. A little more mature, perhaps, than the girls I knew in high school, a bit smoother, and a lot quieter, but still very much the same.

I am impressed, however, with the friendliness of students here. I had expected upper classmen to look down their noses at lowly freshmen. That is how it is in the movies. Here, not only do upper classmen fail to display any superiority towards the newcomers, but, if my experience is typical, they often go out of their way to be helpful. During the first few days I had difficulty finding my way around the buildings. Classrooms and offices had the habit of being elsewhere when I was due to appear in them. At first I didn't like to advertise my confusion, but

I soon found that older students sensed my plight and were glad to direct me. In fact, I am beginning to think that one good way to make friends around here is to stand in the halls and look lost.

Perhaps it would be wiser not to mention it, but the faculty seems to me to be farthest removed from the Hollywood ideal. I have yet to see my first graybeard, and so far none of my instructors has shown any of the traditional signs of absent-mindedness. On the contrary, faculty members here look about as human and undistinguished as the men and women you might see at a convention of realtors or advertisers. I like the way they address students as "Mr." and "Miss." Perhaps that is a concession to Hollywood, but it is a refreshing change from high school. I also like the informality of their classroom procedure. I have one instructor whose grammar is as informal as his habit of sitting on the edge of the desk. That sort of thing just isn't done in the movies.

First impressions may not always be true impressions. It may be that before the semester is over I will want to take back all that I have said in this paper. But, whatever my feelings may be then, right now I am sure of one thing: whatever college is like, it is not what it is in the movies.

If you compare this essay with the list of jottings out of which it grew, you will see that the purposeful restriction of the subject not only excluded many impressions in that first list; it also brought forth new ones to support the contention that college life is not what the movies show it to be. This happens often. Once a writer has his purpose clearly in mind, he has so concentrated his thinking that needed facts and illustrations come to mind of their own accord. By clarifying his purpose he makes his thinking more efficient.

Students are often tempted to restrict an autobiographical subject merely by cutting the time it covers — that is, by confining themselves to a single year of their lives or to a particular summer vacation. Such restriction is often more obvious than useful. The goal of restriction is to get a topic which can be completely developed in a single paper. Usually simple restriction in time does not achieve that goal. On the other hand, a paper may deal with several years of the writer's life and still be thoroughly restricted, as long as the author is selecting from these years only those experiences that have a clear connection with his main idea. Consider, for example, the following essay written by a University of Wisconsin student:

### I Know the Value of Money [1]

My parents wanted me to grow up independent, capable of managing my possessions and my life. So when I was still a child, they began their training which has accomplished just the object they had in view.

On my twelfth birthday Mother and Daddy sat me down for a talk

[1] From "I Know the Value of Money," by Jean R. McDuffie. Copyright by *Parents' Magazine,* May, 1941. Reprinted by permission.

which I shall always remember. "It isn't just age that makes a person wise and capable," they told me. "Nor is it having lots of money and a fine social position. Knowing your own mind, your own affairs, and the value of money is one of the greatest things to which a person can aspire, and this is what we want to teach you."

So with $15 a month for my very own I began my life as a person within myself. With that money, $10 of which I got from Daddy the first of the month, and $5 from Mother on the fifteenth, I had to take care of all my expenses, clothes included. It was rather difficult at first, buying all my own things, but any important article I brought home and had Mother put on the final approval.

Fifteen dollars seemed enormous to me, but I soon discovered that I couldn't persist in eating sweets and ice creams to any great extent if I wanted to be dressed as well as the other girls and have my clothes in repair. Money just didn't go anywhere near that far. I was lucky to have a considerably well stocked wardrobe when I started out, for I didn't have to worry about needing such a thing as a coat, which would have been a little too expensive for me to know how to budget.

My parents took care of the expense of my school books, so I was relieved of that large burden. A typical monthly account for me from the ages of 12 to 14 was as follows:

| | |
|---|---|
| Clothes | $10 |
| Cleaning and repair | 2 |
| Spending | 3 |
| | $15 |

Through those years, my father was making a comparatively small salary, and I couldn't have had more even if it was merited. So when I was 14 years old and Daddy was given a raise, my allowance underwent a similar change.

As prices of wearing apparel went up considerably at that time, my family felt I needed a little more to make ends meet, so I was given $5 more, making my monthly allotment $20. Despite clothes being more expensive, I contrived to buy fewer, thereby spending only slightly more for this item than I had in the previous two years.

I also learned to sew, and made four or five summer dresses each year, which carried me through the brunt of the season at a greatly reduced cost. By doing this I was able to have more during the winter, for I prodigiously saved whatever I could. From the time I was 14 until I reached 17, my expenses were:

| | |
|---|---|
| Clothes | $13 |
| Cleaning and repair | 2 |
| Spending | 5 |
| | $20 |

Daddy usually gave me a heavy coat at the beginning of the winter, and that was supposed to last clear through, but when I found I needed another for spring or fall, as a rule I bought one on the installment plan, paying $5 a month for it until the bill was paid. Only once did I have a charge account, and that was responsible for the only time I slipped up on my obligations.

There was a small all-purpose shop near where we lived, and there I did most of my shopping. For Christmas, I had many friends, aside from my family, to whom I wished to give presents.

Wanting to try my luck at a charge account some months before December, I opened one at the shop and proceeded to charge everything I bought. The end of the first month my pocketbook permitted the payment, but on the conclusion of the second month it was slightly in the reverse.

I wasn't a bit worried, for I figured I could stint through December and settle at the close of that month. There I didn't reckon with the Yuletide spirit, for when my bill came the second of January, I was $50 in debt. That was the only time I was forced to seek family aid. Daddy gave me $35 for a Christmas present and I added $15 to finish the charge account once and for all. . . .

When I was 17 . . . I began to want more substantial articles. I saw a beautiful radio one day for $65, and nothing would do but I should have it. Have it I did, on the installment plan, and I thought I would never finish paying for it. To bolster my depleted pocketbook, I undertook to teach ballroom dancing lessons in the recreation room of our home. . . .

Making my own decisions was wonderful. My parents never gave me any advice on any of them. When I asked their opinions they simply discussed the case from both sides, leaving the ultimate issue to my own discretion. . . . As a result, I have learned how and where to shop to get the most for the smallest sum. I know good quality from poor, and I am sure that when I marry, no matter how little money my husband may have, I will be able to get along on it and handle it efficiently.

My parents wanted me to grow up independent, capable of managing my possessions and my life. They have accomplished their purpose.

Here is an excellent example of purposeful restriction. The author knew exactly what she wanted to do. She wanted to show her readers that she knew the value of money by showing them in detail how she learned its value. That purpose required her to report her talk with her parents on her twelfth birthday. It also required her to show, through the years, her struggles to achieve financial responsibility: her temptations and mistakes, the need to supplement her income when she wanted things she could not afford, the determined way her parents forced her to make her own decisions. Her restricted purpose kept the paper unified. It acted as a safeguard against wandering into incidents which, however interesting, had no immediate connection with the title of her essay.

## Stating the Purpose

When a student successfully restricts his subject, he has usually come to a decision about purpose. For example, restricting such a general subject as "A Trip to New York" to the specific topic, "Rockefeller Center — A City Within a City," commits the writer, through his choice of title, to discussing Rockefeller Center from a particular point of view. That point of view will control the selection of his material. Of all the things he might say about Rockefeller Center he will select only those that show how it is a city in itself.

A good title, therefore, will often so restrict the topic that it implies the purpose of the paper. Such titles as "How to Win Radio Contests," "The Part the Conductor Plays in the Orchestra," and "What to Do in Case of Serious Burns" are rudimentary statements of purpose. For short papers they will sometimes be enough to guide the student in the decisions he must make about selecting and presenting his material. For long papers, it will usually be wise to go one step further — to make a formal statement of the purpose which the title implies.

### Purpose Statements: The Thesis

For many student essays the most useful — and the most exacting — kind of purpose statement is the *thesis*.[2] A thesis is a single sentence, *preferably a simple sentence,* which expresses the basic idea which the paper is to develop. Just as a composer first announces his musical theme and then develops or elaborates it through the rest of the composition, so the writer may state the purpose of his paper in a sentence and then develop it. The thesis is to the whole paper what the topic sentence or topic idea is to the paragraph. The following sentences might serve either as topic sentences for paragraphs or as theses for whole essays:

> The first requirement of a good speaker is a sense of confidence.
>
> Final examinations encourage cramming.
>
> All stories to the contrary, women drive as carefully as men.

A good thesis is *restricted, unified,* and *precise.* To be restricted, it must indicate which of several approaches to the subject the writer will take. It thus limits the scope of the paper to what can be properly discussed in the space available. For example, such a thesis as "There are serious objections to compulsory national health insurance" does not specify what objections the author is going to present. To discuss all the objections in detail would take several thousand words. The easy way is to state those that come readily to mind and discuss them super-

---

[2] The word *thesis* is used to avoid any ambiguity which might result from the use of the commoner word *theme.*

ficially. Notice that the following theses clearly say which particular objection the writer will discuss, and thus limit him to something he may do fairly thoroughly in 500 to 1000 words.

Compulsory national health insurance would encourage hypochondriacs to monopolize a doctor's time.

Compulsory national health insurance would destroy the friendly relationship that now exists between doctors and their patients.

Compulsory national health insurance would reduce the doctor's incentive to keep abreast of new medical discoveries.

Compulsory national health insurance would increase, rather than decrease, the number of man hours lost through sickness.

Compulsory national health insurance has always cost much more than its supporters estimated it would cost.

All five of these theses, and several more, lay hidden under the general, unrestricted statement that "There are serious objections to compulsory national health insurance." The unrestricted thesis gives the reader no real clue to what the author plans to do, and often makes the writer think his purpose is clear when he has little more than a general subject and perhaps a title. An unrestricted thesis invites vague thinking, meandering organization, and superficiality.

A good thesis is unified as well as restricted. To be unified, it must commit the writer to deal with only one dominant idea. Such a thesis as "The United Nations Organization has major weaknesses and cannot prevent a major war" requires the writer to do two things, not one. He must (1) demonstrate the weaknesses and (2) prove that the UN cannot prevent a major war. A paper with this double purpose will almost certainly fall into two parts having little connection with each other. If the writer believes that these two points are related — perhaps that one results from the other — he should show that relation in his thesis: "The organization of the UN makes it incapable of preventing a war between major powers." This thesis restricts the discussion to those features of organization which make the UN powerless to avert a major war and thus fuses the two parts into a unified purpose statement.

In the following theses the lack of unity at the left is removed in the revision at the right:

| | |
|---|---|
| Printing has had a long and complex history, during which it has brought about social and cultural reforms. | The development of printing has brought about social and cultural reforms. |
| Fraternities have grown rapidly in this country and fulfill a social need. | Fraternities have grown rapidly in this country because they fulfill a social need. |

In the first of these pairs, the thesis at the left requires the writer to do two things: first, to recount the history of printing — a big job in itself — and then to show the social and cultural reforms which have come from printing. The revision rules out much of the history and restricts the writer to the single task of showing how certain social and cultural improvements were made possible by advances in printing. Similarly, the first statement about fraternities would make two papers — one a history, the other a justification. The revision requires the writer to select evidence from the history to show that fraternities have flourished because they were useful. A paper with this thesis will be an argument which draws evidence from the social value which fraternities have demonstrated.

Note that the two revised statements express a logical relationship between two parts of a subject at first unrelated. In these examples the relationship is one of cause and effect. To find such a relationship is "to have an idea" — to perceive a truth or gain an understanding. This idea gives direction to your thinking and so shapes your writing.

Finally, a thesis should be precise. It should be phrased in words which permit only one interpretation. Especially it should avoid words and phrases which are so general that they convey no exact meaning. For example, such statements as

My home town is one of the most interesting towns in the state.

Winston Churchill has had a colorful career.

are useless as statements of purpose because the key words "interesting" and "colorful" could mean almost anything and hence exert no real control over what the writer does. A student who sets out to show that his home town is "interesting" is almost sure to end with an essay "about" his home town; one who intends to show that Churchill has had a colorful career is likely to write "about" Churchill's life. Any student who intends to write "about" a subject has not yet established his purpose. He has merely lulled himself into a false sense of achievement by the vagueness of his own words.

Avoid figures of speech in a thesis. Metaphors and similes can be vivid and expressive within a composition, or even in a title, but in a thesis they can easily hide a confusion that might be exposed in a more literal statement. For example, consider this: "Where instructors are concerned, all that glitters is not gold." Does the sentence mean that the most entertaining instructors are not always the most helpful, or that the most accomplished scholars are not always the best teachers? Or does it merely mean that instructors are not always what they seem to be? The statement does not communicate a clear purpose. It may seem apt or impressive, but in a thesis clarity is more important than effect.

The unsatisfactory theses we have been studying all suffer from failure to define purpose clearly. We saw in Chapter 1 that a serious concern with purpose requires a discipline which a writer will often wish to escape. A student who escapes it by writing a statement of purpose which is unrestricted, not unified, or vague will fail to guide the development of his paper and will deceive only himself. He gains nothing by such self-deception. It is always wiser to thrash out the basic decision about purpose once and for all in the purpose statement.

Can you identify the weaknesses of the following purpose statements and suggest how they might be revised? Watch especially figures of speech and vague words in key positions.

1. Hockey is an exciting game.
2. Eisenhower was a greater general than Napoleon.
3. The fall of Corregidor was America's darkest hour.
4. The atomic bomb is the most powerful instrument of destruction ever devised and there is no adequate defense against it.
5. During my senior year in high school I had some very interesting and educational trips.
6. This essay will deal with the advisability of working one's way through college.
7. The study of foreign languages is an excellent discipline.
8. The evils of professionalism in college athletics should be considered.
9. The forthcoming conference with Russia may pave the way to ending the cold war, but we better not count our chickens before they are hatched.
10. The life of Abraham Lincoln should be an inspiration to all of us.

## Purpose Statements: Other Forms

A thesis is a statement of the basic *idea* of an essay. Many quite purposeful compositions, however, do not develop an idea, but present information or impressions. They may explain a process, give directions, or describe a person, place, or event. Such purposes require you to report what you see or know. They are concerned with facts rather than with ideas, and they do not require a thesis.

For example, if you want to explain the operation of a Diesel engine or summarize the events leading to the Boston Tea Party, your paper will not have a dominant idea, although it will have a clear purpose. Any attempt to pretend it has a thesis by writing some such statement as "The operation of the Diesel engine is complex" or "The background of the Boston Tea Party is interesting" would waste time and distort your real intention. For you are concerned not with the complexity of the Diesel engine but with its mode of operation, and you have no intention of proving that the events leading up to the Boston Tea Party were "interesting" but only of showing what they were.

Although an essay may not have a dominant idea, it must have a purpose, and putting that purpose down on paper will be helpful. Notice how the following statements make the purpose clear and thus help toward efficient development:

> In this paper I want to recreate the incident in which a rattler crawled over me. I don't just want to summarize the incident. I want to make the reader see what I saw and feel what I felt.

> I intend to illustrate the four most common kinds of changes in the meanings of words by tracing the evolution of *lady, gossip, boycott,* and *acorn.*

> This paper will explain how the New York Fair Employment Practices Commission works by reporting two case histories: one in which there was discrimination, and one in which there was not.

These statements not only record purpose but also suggest how the paper will be developed. Each is, in effect, a basic plan for the paper. A writer who can state his purpose so explicitly has taken a long step in planning the development of his essay.

## Summary

This chapter may be summarized briefly as four pieces of advice:

1. When, in choosing a subject, you find yourself flitting from topic to topic, pick the likeliest one and concentrate on it until you see its implications. Remember that in the long run the subject you choose is less important than what you do with it.

2. If your subject is general, restrict it, either by breaking it into its parts (*A Trip to New York*) or by adopting a point of view — an opinion or a judgment toward it (*Rockefeller Center — A City Within a City*). Restriction from a point of view will determine your purpose more quickly.

3. When you are satisfied that your topic is sufficiently restricted, establish your purpose by writing a thesis or other purpose statement. Make sure that this statement is restricted, unified, and precise.

4. If your paper is not going to develop a dominant idea, express its purpose in the form that best suggests its development.

Finally, the paper "So This Is College" and the discussion concerning it (pages 20–21) will, if reread in the light of the whole chapter, provide a practical demonstration of the whole process of purposefully restricting a subject and developing a thesis.

## Exercises

**A.** The following list of topics is designed to serve two purposes: first, to suggest possible subjects to any student who finds such suggestions useful; second, to provide a common body of material for such class exercises and impromptu essays as the instructor wishes to assign.

From each of the first three parts of the following list, select one topic. Restrict each topic by phrasing a title which suggests the point of view you intend to take toward the topic. Finally, expand your title into a clear statement of purpose. If your instructor wishes, these statements may be written on the board and subjected to class criticism.

## I. Subjects from Personal Experience

### A. *Reminiscences*

1. My first encounter with education
2. How I learned the value of money
3. Circus days
4. Rugged individualist — aged 12
5. My first date
6. My struggle for self-confidence
7. Birthdays used to be fun
8. The disadvantages of being 17
9. All children are vandals
10. My experience with the English language
11. Factory job
12. An adventure in business
13. What music has meant to me
14. What parents forget
15. Thank you, Dad!
16. Learning the hard way
17. First impressions of college
18. Life in an army camp
19. Winter in the country
20. My son won't make those mistakes

### B. *Descriptions of people*

1. My parents
2. The black sheep
3. He was more than a coach
4. High school big shot
5. Toughest kid in the block
6. A teacher I won't forget
7. Social climber
8. Freshman Romeo
9. A self-made man
10. The bravest man I ever knew
11. Top sergeants I have known
12. G.I. Joe
13. My favorite relative
14. The greatest champion of them all
15. Small time politician
16. A typical American
17. The man (or woman) I'd like to be
18. People I cannot stand

### C. *Descriptions of places*

1. The county seat on Saturday night
2. County fair
3. My corner of the South
4. The ideal vacation spot
5. Yellowstone National Park
6. Rockefeller Center
7. Niagara Falls
8. Washington, D. C.
9. The city of tomorrow
10. My home town

D. *Descriptions of events*

1. My most embarrassing experience
2. It couldn't happen, but it did
3. I witness an accident
4. A storm to remember
5. A terrifying experience
6. The best World's Series
7. A defeat that hurt
8. A lie that backfired
9. A case of stage fright
10. Mother knew best

## II. Subjects Suggested by Your Reading

1. On reading the newspapers
2. The inspiration of biographies
3. History through the novel
4. Life in pioneer times
5. Religious persecution
6. Great inventions
7. Great moments in history
8. The conquest of disease
9. The history of sport
10. Splitting the atom
11. Public Opinion Polls
12. Li'l Abner — the all-American numbskull
13. The background of an election
14. The Bible as history
15. The Bible as a way of life
16. Poets vs. scientists
17. The struggle for world peace
18. The power of ideas
19. My favorite poet
20. The reality of fiction

## III. Subjects Based on Your Knowledge of How to Do Things

1. What my hobby has taught me
2. You don't need money to travel
3. The art of outdoor cooking
4. Working your way through college
5. Being a good hostess
6. Farming at a profit
7. How to take an examination
8. What every salesman must learn
9. How the public is fooled
10. Editing a paper
11. Photography is an art
12. Football is a science
13. What the professional sees
14. Fun with a fly rod
15. How to get along with the opposite sex
16. If I were in high school again
17. Behind the scenes in student elections
18. How to give a party
19. The dangers of night fishing
20. Be your own interior decorator

## IV Subjects Dealing with Your Own Opinions and Beliefs

1. Do fraternities (sororities) do more harm than good?
2. Is an honor system practicable?
3. Does compulsory attendance protect the student?
4. What do students expect from college?
5. What does the college graduate owe society?
6. Should college football be emphasized less?

7. Should college football be subsidized?
8. Are student elections democratic?
9. Is faculty supervision of student activities necessary?
10. Does college education influence religious beliefs?
11. Do science and religion conflict?
12. How vital a force is the church today?
13. How democratic is the United States?
14. How free is free enterprise?
15. Is capitalism efficient?
16. Should colleges be propagandists for democracy?
17. Have we lived up to the constitution?
18. What do we mean when we say that all men are born free and equal?
19. The Fair Deal in retrospect
20. Roosevelt's place in history
21. What was World War II about?
22. Could the Korean War have been avoided?
23. Can the nations outlaw war?
24. Is the UN another League of Nations?
25. Imperialism at home and abroad
26. What does Russia want?
27. The case for or against strikes
28. Socialized medicine
29. Compulsory military service
30. Is lobbying justifiable?
31. Should movies be censored?
32. In defense of Hollywood
33. Radio commercials — necessity or nuisance?
34. Do newspapers distort the news?
35. Should there be any limits to freedom of expression?
36. What do we mean by tolerance?

**B.** The two papers which follow were written by different students to satisfy the assignment: "Write a 500-word essay in which you present a picture of your experience with the English language." Read both essays and answer the questions which follow them.

## My Experience with the English Language

My experience with the English language began in my cradle with the customary baby talk. In grade school and high school I had the preliminary grammar and literature training. During my junior year in high school I entered into several "High School Forums." In writing my paper on the topic scheduled I found that I didn't know the English language as well as I thought I had. There was extensive required reading in the library, and usually those outside books contained words of four or five syllables and took half a line in spelling. This is where I first began to understand the value of a dictionary. I believe that since I have become acquainted with the dictionary I have learned more about vocabulary, pronunciation, and articulation. Actual experience with the study of words is of such great value that I have tried to train myself to use the dictionary often.

I have had some speech training which helped me a great deal in my English training. I remember during one program I slaughtered the English language. Since then I have tried to become aware of what I am saying.

## My Mother Done Tole Me

I suppose it must have been some rather humiliating revelation of mine that led my mother to place me across her lap one day early in my life, hold me with one hand and spank me with the other, at the same time explaining that little boys should be seen and not heard. "Don't you know," she said crossly, "that everybody has just so many words to speak in his life, and if you use them all up now you won't have any left when you're a man? That's why you mustn't talk so much now. You must save all your words for the time when you really have something to say."

I had accepted everything that my mother had ever told me before; so I accepted this, too — accepted it and heeded it until I was thirteen years old and learned that the physical principle underlying speech production recognized no limitations upon either the quantity or length of words used by a human being. It is true that during those years I wondered many times how it was possible for mother to have been so taciturn in her youth, and father so verbose; for in their frequent discussions mother seemed oblivious of any word quota and father all too keenly aware of it. But I never seriously doubted mother until a junior high school instructor, Miss Conlin, Piano-legs Conlin as we called her, unfolded to me the scientific basis of speech.

Perhaps that seven year embargo has influenced my use of English more than any other factor. I endeavored to make up for lost time by talking at every opportunity at school and at home. Not content with that, I determined to increase my truncated vocabulary. I spent many painful hours culling polysyllabic enormities from the biggest dictionaries our public library boasted, and actually used them, undismayed by the laughter that greeted my mispronunciations, until I could both utter and understand them without more than a few seconds' distress. From thirteen to sixteen I was probably my family's chief source of amusement as I manfully strove to raise my level of speech to more sublime realms and revenge myself for mother's deceit.

I realize now that I was a pedantic prig, insufferable in my attitude and incomprehensible in my usage, with extreme youth my only saving grace. To me the purpose of speech was to impress rather than to inform; and the use of sesquipedalian words, albeit inappropriate and inexact, offered the best means of achieving that purpose. I was a freshman in college before I appreciated how sadly mistaken I had been, that communication was the destined goal of speech, and that, though my instructors' vocabularies easily exceeded mine, they always managed to make themselves clear without calling on any of my favorites unless such words were an inevitable choice.

Today I have partially curbed my juvenile megalomania, but privately I still retain an inveterate fondness for the biggies, and when exacerbated beyond endurance I am likely to utilize a string of expletives representing more than half a decade's labor. Occasionally, too, the sheer admiration and reverent devotion I have for such words make me unwilling to see them fall into desuetude. Thus impelled, I write them as I have in this paper. But if that weakness is regrettable now, it was deplorable five years ago. Let us hope that by the time I graduate it will have vanished entirely.

## Questions

1. Which of the two papers above gives the clearer picture of the student's experience with the English language? Write a paragraph to justify your verdict.

2. Does either of the papers show restriction of the general subject as it was given in the assignment? If so, what is the nature of the restriction — a restricted topic or a restricted viewpoint? Discuss the nature of the restriction in a short paragraph.

3. Does either paper contain a thesis? If no thesis is explicitly stated, is one implied? Write out any thesis you can discover, either stated or implied, in either paper.

4. Make a rough estimate of the length of each paper by counting the number of words in four or five lines, finding the average number of words in a line, and multiplying that average by the number of lines.

5. How do you explain the difference in the length of the papers? Do you think that one student had more unusual experiences than the other and therefore had more to write about, or do you see any relation between the length of each paper and the amount of restriction it reveals? Write a short paragraph developing an answer to this question.

6. Consider the diction in the second paper. Are the big words out of place? Are they attempts to show off? Or are they justified by the author's purpose? Write a short paragraph discussing the appropriateness of the diction.

# 3

\* 
\* **ORGANIZATION:**
\* **INFORMAL**
\* **PATTERNS**
\*

ONCE THE PURPOSE is clear, the next step is to decide what structural plan or pattern to follow. The amount of planning necessary will depend on the complexity of the writing problem. We saw in Chapter 2 that sometimes a clear statement of purpose will do all that is needed to plot the organization of an essay. At other times an informal plan is helpful. For long and complex writings, such as term or research papers, the best plan is usually a formal outline. This chapter will deal with informal patterns of organization; the formal planning represented by an outline will be discussed in Chapter 4.

In one of his ballads Kipling observed that

> There are nine and ninety ways of constructing tribal lays,
> And every single one of them is right.

There are as many ways of shaping a purpose statement into an essay. The best way is the one that best enables you, as the writer, to carry out your purpose. This chapter will try to give you background for making wise choices by discussing two common and useful patterns for expository or explanatory writing — *illustrative organization* and *analytical organization.*

## *Illustrative Organization*

Illustrative organization, as the name implies, explains a purpose statement by illustrating it. The means of illustrating may vary, though as you will see, they tend to follow the pattern of *statement, explanation,* and *example.* This is the simplest of all expository patterns and one of the most useful. If you master it you will have learned a method of organization which can often be used in impromptu essays or speeches, in answers to essay-type examination questions, in paragraphs of longer papers, even in conversation. We can illustrate the pattern by a paragraph analysis of a short essay.

### IT IS NEVER TOO COLD TO SNOW

Too cold to snow?

As winter grips many parts of the world in sub-freezing temperatures, this age-old "true or false" poser bobs up to test the lore of weather-wise amateurs. It never gets too cold to snow, but it frequently gets too cold for snow to fall in "flakes."

Flakes fall when the air through which they pass is 32° Fahrenheit or slightly lower. At this temperature the air usually holds enough moisture to allow the flakes to become fat and mat together, and the fall is likely to be heavy.

As the temperature sinks lower, the air becomes drier, the snowfall lighter and more powdery. At temperatures below zero a heavy fall of snow is rare. The snow that does fall takes the form of ice spicules, ice needles, or fills the air with fine glittering diamondlike dust. The air at these subzero temperatures is too dry to produce flakes.

Snow has fallen in Little America with the thermometer at 65 below zero. Alaska temperatures well under 50 below have produced snow. In Eastern Siberia, temperatures which average under 40 below have been accompanied by snow. Verkhoyansk — the coldest spot in the world — with a recorded winter temperature of 94 below zero, is within this Siberian section where snowfall is apt to be light, but where snow can and does fall.[1]

*Title:* Explicitly states the thesis of the article.

¶1. Restates the thesis as a question.

¶2. The first sentence asserts the pertinence of the question and gains attention. The second sentence restates the thesis and sets up the distinction on which the answer to the opening question depends.

¶'s 3 – 4. In these two paragraphs the author considers the sub-question, "Does it ever get too cold for snowflakes?" To answer this question he must show (*a*) how flakes are formed, and (*b*) why flakes do not form at low temperatures. He does (*a*) in paragraph 3 and (*b*) in paragraph 4.

¶5. So far the author has been concerned with a theoretical explanation. Now he gives a series of examples to show the theory in practice.

From this analysis we can describe the structure of the essay as follows:

1. Thesis stated (in the title and opening question).
2. Thesis restated in fuller form (¶2).

[1] Copyright 1945 by the *World Almanac.* Reprinted by permission.

3. Thesis explained in detail (¶'s 3 – 4).
4. Examples (¶5).

This is the illustrative pattern. Its minimum components are *statement of thesis, explanation of thesis, examples of thesis*. But here are possible variations: Key terms in the thesis may be defined. The thesis may be restated more than once at the beginning of the essay or it may not be restated at all. Instead of a series of examples, a single example may be given, or a series of short examples may be followed by a long one. And a final restatement of the thesis may be added as a conclusion. But the core of the pattern is *statement – explanation – example*. Notice how it is used in the following student essay:

*Title hints at thesis.*

## MORE THAN A SPORT

*Thesis stated:*
*Football prepares a young man for citizenship by teaching him to cooperate with others.*

Football is more than a sport. It is an invaluable teacher. In teaching a young man to cooperate with his fellows on the practice field and in scheduled games, it also shows him the necessity of team-work in society. It prepares him to be a better citizen and person.

*Thesis explained in part by showing interdependency of individual and team.*

The novice player first learns that football is not a one-man game, that he is but one member of an eleven-man team, and that in every play, either defensive or offensive, he has a particular job to do. If he fails to do it, the team suffers. If his task is to block the opposing right end, that job must be done. And he must do it alone, for every other man on the team has his own assignment in the play. The ends, tackles, guards, backfield men, and center must do their individual tasks if the play is to succeed.

*Example.*

While Red Grange was making football history at the University of Illinois in the 1920's, he monopolized sports stories about the Illini. He was "headline stuff," as the newspapermen put it, and the general public came to believe that he was a miracle man on the playing field. Certainly his long runs through tough opposition suggested superman football ability. But football players everywhere knew better. They knew that Grange's starring role was made possible by the cooperation of ten teammates on the field. A modest fellow, Red admitted it, readily bestowing praise on his fellow Illini, particularly on two expert blocking backs, Wally McIlwaine and Earl Britton, who bowled over opposing backfield men once he had passed the line of scrimmage. The famed Galloping Ghost of the Gridiron said, "Only crack team-work enabled me to make my touchdown runs." He knew the value of cooperation. When Red's teammates fell down on the job, he failed too and was stopped for no gain or thrown for a loss.

*Thesis restated and enlarged to include carryover of cooperation from football to citizenship, ending with final restatement of thesis in concluding sentence.*

Wherever football is played in the United States, on sand-lot, high school field, college gridiron or in professional stadium, the players learn the invaluable rough-and-tumble lesson that only by the cooperation of each man can the team win. It is a lesson they do not forget on the field. Off the field, they duly remember it. In society, the former player does not look upon himself as a lone wolf who has the right to create his individual moral code and observe his individual social laws. He understands his place in the scheme of things; he knows he is a member of society and must conduct himself as such. He realizes that only by cooperating, not shying off as a lone wolf, can he do his share in making society what it should be — the protector and benefactor of all. The man who has played football knows that team-work is essential in modern living and that every citizen must do his part if the nation is to prosper. So he has little difficulty in adjusting himself to his role in family life and in the business world, and to his duties as a citizen in city, state and nation. In short, his football training helps make him a better citizen and person.

Structurally, the main differences between this essay and "It's Never Too Cold to Snow" are that here the writer uses a single sustained example instead of several shorter ones, and after the example he restates and further explains his thesis. The basic pattern is still statement-explanation-example.

The order of statements in the illustrative pattern is thus from general to specific. The most general statement in the essay, the thesis, usually comes first. The next step is to make its meaning more specific by explaining or clarifying it. The third step makes the thesis still more specific by limiting it to a particular example or series of examples. With the example, the illustration is complete; the meaning of the thesis is fully spelled out. In a sense, then, the whole explanation comes to a focus at the illustration. Hence the name of the pattern.

## Means of Specifying

With this view of the pattern as a whole, let us look more closely at the ways of working it out. Although any means may be used which give a satisfactory result, the most common are *clarifying statement, causal explanation, examples, comparison,* and *contrast.*

**Clarifying Statement.** The clarifying statement advances the general meaning of the thesis one step in the direction of specific statement. It usually does so by qualifying the thesis, that is, by showing in what particular sense it is to be understood. Notice how the following statements clarify by making the thesis more specific.

| *Thesis* | *Clarifying Statement* |
|---|---|
| It never gets too cold to snow. | It never gets too cold to snow, but it frequently gets too cold for snow to fall in "flakes." |
| Football is more than a sport. | It is an invaluable teacher. In teaching a young man to cooperate with his fellows . . . it also shows him the necessity of team-work in society. It prepares him to be a better citizen and person. |
| It is a good thing that we learn to speak as children. | If the learning were postponed until we were adults, most of us would be too discouraged by the difficulties to persevere in the task. |
| The intellectual outlook of the masses remains much the same as it was in primitive times. | Anthropologists have described the primitive mind as characterized chiefly by an all-pervading supernaturalism, lack of precise and logical thinking, credulity, and an ignorance of scientific methods and results. Judged by these standards, it is obvious that the great majority of moderns are still overwhelmingly primitive in their ways of thinking. |

Notice that the last example defines a key term and then restates the thesis in the light of the definition. This is common practice when the meaning of the thesis depends on a particular interpretation of a word. Sometimes a writer will simply give a "dictionary definition"; occasionally he may explain a word by showing what it is not, or by ruling out meanings that would distort his purpose; frequently he will define a word by showing the special sense in which he is using it. The two definitions reprinted below combine all three methods:

colloquial . . . belonging to the words, phrases, and idioms characteristic of conversation and informal writing; the label [Colloq.] is used throughout this dictionary in this sense, and does not indicate substandard or illiterate usage. . . .[2]

If you try to arrive at a proper and watertight definition of exactly what an amateur is, you will wind up considerably confused. The dic-

[2] From *Webster's New World Dictionary of the American Language*, College Edition. Copyright 1957 by The World Publishing Company.

tionary says that an amateur is one who is not rated as a professional, and that a professional is one, generally, who has competed in a sport for a stake or purse, or gate money, or with a professional for a prize, or who has taught or trained in sports or athletics for pay. To this, modern amateur governing bodies have added that a professional is also anyone who capitalizes his athletic skill or name, directly or indirectly, for pay. But the exigencies of modern sports still leave considerable room for doubt and argument. The American sportswriter comes much closer to it. He defines an amateur as a guy who won't take a check.

But it seems to me, from my experience in watching and dealing with amateurs over a long period of years, that too much latitude is permitted even in the last critical definition. In my book, an amateur golfer is one who goes out to his club on a Sunday morning and dubs around between eighty and a hundred and ten. An amateur tennis-player is a gentleman or lady who appears on the courts week-ends and hopes he or she won't get too many shots on the backhand, which is always weak. And an amateur runner is a commuter running for the 8:13 out of Larchmont, or Port Washington, and catching it. Otherwise I do not know of any genuine amateurs in the United States of America.[3]

**Causal Explanation.** When the thesis states an effect of some cause, the best explanation is usually one that shows how the effect came about. This was the method used in paragraphs 3 and 4 of "It's Never Too Cold to Snow," and the causal explanation there given was so necessary that the thesis could not have been adequately developed without it. You can test this assertion by placing a piece of paper over those two paragraphs and seeing what you have left. You will find that the key statement "it frequently gets too cold for snow to fall in 'flakes'" loses much of its meaning when the causal explanation is omitted.

Notice how the causal explanations in the following selections help to specify the meaning of the italicized theses.

> *Frontier towns burned like tinder.* The board streets and sidewalks, the open frame buildings, the lack of water pressure and fire-fighting apparatus made them terribly vulnerable . . . The very ground they rested upon, built up of sawdust, slabs and refuse from the mills, was inflammable. . . .[4]

> *What we know of prenatal development makes all this* [attempts to mould the unborn child's character by the conduct of the mother during pregnancy] *seem utterly impossible.* How could such extremely complex influences pass from the mother to the child? There is no connection between their nervous systems. Even the blood vessels of mother and child do not join directly. They lie side by side and the chemicals are interchanged through the walls by a process that we call osmosis. An emo-

---

[3] From Paul Gallico, *Farewell to Sport.* Copyright 1937, 1938 by Paul Gallico. Reprinted by permission of Alfred A. Knopf, Inc.

[4] From *The Long Ships Passing,* by Walter Havighurst. Copyright, 1942, by The Macmillan Company. Reprinted by permission of the publishers.

tional shock to the mother will affect her child, because it changes the activity of her glands and so the chemistry of her blood. Any chemical change in the mother's blood will affect the child — for better or worse. But we cannot see how a liking for mathematics or poetic genius can be dissolved in the blood and produce a similar liking or genius in the child.[5]

**Examples.** We have seen that the example completes the explanation and is the clinching device in the illustrative pattern. But to do its job, an example must be clear, and it must be relevant. An unclear example will do more harm than good, for, coming near the end of the explanation, it may confuse the reader and undo all that was done earlier. Similarly, an irrelevant example will make the reader wonder how it illustrates the explanation and doubt whether he properly understood the explanation. The example, then, must be clearly appropriate to its purpose.

Whether to use a single sustained example or a series of short ones depends on whether the idea needs one detailed illustration or a variety of brief general ones. The following selection rightly confines itself to short examples, because the thesis requires a quantity of examples, none of which is any more important than the others.

Seven is supposedly one of the most powerful numbers. Wherever superstition involving numbers exists — and that includes the entire world — seven plays a prominent part. In East India, for instance, the natives refuse to work six days and rest the seventh. They believe that would be calamitous. Instead, they rest on the eighth day, missionaries notwithstanding. To the Hebrews seven was a sacred number. The Bible is full of the number seven. God made the earth in six days and rested on the seventh. Likewise, "there were seven years of plenty, and seven years of famine; Jacob served Laban seven years for Leah and seven for Rachael, and his children mourned for him seven days at his death. There was a whole complex of sevens involved in the fall of Jericho — on the seventh day the city was encompassed seven times by seven priests bearing seven trumpets. Balaam demanded seven altars, with seven bullocks and seven rams; Elijah sent his servant seven times to look for rain; and Elisha healed Naaman of leprosy by making him wash seven times in Jordan. Later we find Jesus casting out seven demons from Mary, speaking seven words from the cross, and commanding his followers to forgive their enemies, not seven times, but seventy times seven." The Greeks, too, considered seven lucky as did (and do) many other races. Our week is based on this same belief in the potency of the number seven.[6]

On the other hand, a single sustained example can explain a point

[5] From *Psychology You Can Use,* by William H. Roberts. Copyright 1943 by Harcourt, Brace and Company, Inc. Reprinted by permission of the publishers.

[6] Carol Stewart, "Seven Come Eleven." From *The Green Caldron: A Magazine of Freshman Writing* (December, 1950), published at the University of Illinois, Urbana, Illinois. Copyright, 1950, by Charles W. Roberts. Reprinted by permission.

in considerable detail. The single example of Red Grange in "More Than a Sport" conveys the author's complex ideas about the values of football better than a series of short, undeveloped examples could have done.

The use of a single example is less desirable when the thesis is attempting to show a trend or a generalization, since the reader may doubt that the example is typical. Consider the following student essay.

> The modern trend toward youthful participation in religious service is a step toward a higher level of maturity for our young people. By active association with a religious group they experience the ethical and spiritual values they were taught in childhood; they are awakened to a new understanding of their future responsibility as adult members of a community.
>
> To illustrate this trend, I am going to cite the example of the temple youth group of which I was a member while in high school. This group actually conducted its own Sabbath services apart from the regular congregation. Teenagers were in charge of reading the prayers; teenagers sang in the choir; teenagers were responsible for obtaining good speakers each week to give the sermon. The whole service was conducted for young people by young people.
>
> During the service the prayers were explained to make their full meaning clear to the congregation. In preparing to give a prayer, a boy had to understand its implications and to realize his responsibility for helping others to see these implications. When a girl lighted the Sabbath candles and blessed them with an ancient prayer, she became conscious that she was helping to carry the light of past truth into the present and future and she felt a bond with all ages of humanity.
>
> After the services the group discussed topics of interest viewed in the light of ethical values. These discussions were stimulating and thought-provoking; they made for a keener awareness of the problems in the world around us. The young participants in these discussions learned to think for themselves and at the same time gained knowledge of the individual's needs in relation to the needs of society.

The opening paragraph of this essay states the thesis so generally that illustration is necessary. The example clearly explains how participation in religious service gives young people a sense of maturity and responsibility. But is one illustration enough to establish a trend? Do we have evidence that this is a typical religious activity, or is it a special case? A reader is likely to feel this doubt. To give evidence of a trend the writer should have cited a number of examples, though she could have developed only one of them. When the thesis states a quantitative generalization, a number of examples are needed, though they need not all be developed.

When it is hard to decide whether to use one example or many, the natural compromise is to combine both methods — to use several very short ones and a final longer and more detailed one. Notice this combination in the following selection:

*Thesis*

The historian is wise if . . . he concedes the eternal presence of the irrational and the inexplicable.

*Clarifying Statement*

It is a recognition which encourages intellectual humility. I venture to think, too, that our sense of the mystery and variousness of life is enlarged, when we realize that the very great may spring from the very small. How does Edmund Burke put it? — "A common soldier, a child, a girl at the door of an inn, have changed the face of fortune, and almost of Nature."

*Series of Short Examples*

History is full of these momentous trifles — the accident which kills or preserves life in some figure of destiny; the weather on some critical battlefield, like the fog at Lutzen or the snow at Towton; the change of wind which brings two fleets to a decisive action; the severe winter of 1788 which produces the famine of 1789, and thereby perhaps the French Revolution; the birth or death of a child; a sudden idea which results in some potent invention.

*Sustained Example*

Let me give you an instance from the most recent history. The success of Turkish Nationalism under Kemal was due to the complete rout of the Greek armies in 1922 in Asia Minor. That ill-omened Greek campaign was largely due to the restoration in 1920 of King Constantine, which led to the Western Allies dissociating themselves from Greek policy and leaving Greece to her own devices. King Constantine was recalled as a consequence of a general election when M. Venizelos was defeated, and that election was held because young King Alexander, the protégé of the Allies, died early in the autumn of 1920. The cause of his death was blood-poisoning due to the bite of a pet monkey in the palace gardens. I cannot better Mr. Churchill's comment: "A quarter of a million persons died of that monkey's bite." [7]

**Comparison (Analogy).** Sometimes a subject can best be explained if compared with another, which the reader is presumably familiar with. The author of the following paragraph helps us understand the structure of music by comparing it with that of language.

Music has often been compared with language itself, and the comparison is quite legitimate. While it combines easily with actual language, it also speaks a language of its own, which it has become a platitude to call universal. To understand the significance of the organizing factors of rhythm, melody, harmony, tone color and form, the analogy of a familiar language is helpful. Music has its own alphabet, of only seven letters, as compared with the twenty-six of the English alphabet. Each

[7] John Buchan, *The Causal and the Casual in History.* Copyright by Cambridge University Press, publishers. Reprinted by permission.

of these letters represents a note, and just as certain letters are complete words in themselves, so certain notes may stand alone, with the force of a whole word. Generally, however, a note of music implies a certain harmony, and in most modern music the notes take the form of actual chords. So it may be said that a chord in music is analogous to a word in language. Several words form a phrase, and several phrases a complete sentence, and the same thing is true in music. Measured music corresponds to poetry, while the old unmeasured plain-song might be compared with prose. The relationship of modern music to free verse at once becomes apparent, and impressionism, expressionism, cubism and futurism can all be found in music as well as the other arts.[8]

A common form of comparison is *analogy*, which allows a writer to discuss complex events or ideas by comparing them with simpler ones. As the parables of Jesus illustrate, this kind of comparison is helpful in explaining complex or difficult ideas. Development by analogy is a favorite pattern with philosophers and scientists when they try to explain new concepts to non-technical readers. Notice how Sir James Jeans uses an explanatory analogy to develop the idea of his first paragraph — that any prediction about the behavior of atoms is statistical, and may have no bearing on the behavior of individual atoms.

These and other considerations to which we shall return below . . . have led many physicists to suppose that there is no determination in events in which atoms and electrons are involved singly, and that the apparent determinism in large-scale events is only of a statistical nature. When we are dealing with atoms and electrons in crowds, the mathematical law of averages imposes the determinism which physical laws have failed to provide.

We can illustrate the concept by analogous situation in the large-scale world. If we spin a half-penny, nothing within our knowledge may be able to decide whether it will come down heads or tails, yet if we throw up a million tons of half-pence, we know there will be 500,000 tons of heads and 500,000 tons of tails. The experiment may be repeated indefinitely, and will always give the same result. We may be tempted to instance it as evidence of the uniformity of nature, and to infer the action of an underlying law of causation: in actual fact it is an instance only of the operation of the purely mathematical laws of chance.

Yet the number of half-pence in a million tons is nothing in comparison with the number of atoms in even the smallest piece of matter with which the earlier physicists could experiment. It is easy to see how the illusion of determinacy — if it is an illusion — crept into science.[9]

What is the usefulness of this analogy? We know that the law of averages predicts a theoretical probability that a tossed coin will turn

[8] From Sigmund Spaeth's *The Art of Enjoying Music,* copyright, 1933, by Sigmund Spaeth. Reprinted by permission of the McGraw-Hill Book Company.
[9] From Sir James Jeans' *The Mysterious Universe.* Reprinted by permission of the Cambridge University Press.

up heads as often as tails. We also know that this theoretical probability is quite untrustworthy in determining the toss of a particular coin. By discussing atoms and electrons in terms of coins, the author uses our experience to help him convey his meaning. He is thus able to develop a thesis which is probably too difficult to be understood readily by general readers without the use of analogy.

**Contrast.** In writing which describes, explains, or analyzes, the use of contrast often helps the development of the purpose. The simplest kind of contrast deals first with one of the contrasted elements and then with the other. The pattern of such contrast is suggested in the following brief selection:

> No two branches of mathematics present a greater contrast than arithmetic and the *Theory of Numbers.* . . .
> Arithmetic is the foundation of all mathematics, pure or applied. It is the most useful of all sciences, and there is, probably, no other branch of human knowledge which is more widely spread among the masses.
> On the other hand, the theory of numbers is the branch of mathematics which has found the least number of applications. Not only has it so far remained without influence on technical progress, but even in the domain of pure mathematics it has always occupied an isolated position, only loosely connected with the general body of the science.[10]

The following is a fuller development by simple contrast. The writer's purpose is to show the value of planning in teaching by contrasting an instructor who had planned exactly what he wanted to do with one who had not.

> I once took a course in "World History" which ran through an entire year. The instructor in the first semester was supposed to begin with the dawn of time, proceed from one mountain peak to another, and finish with the fall of Rome in 476 A.D. He set off at top speed the first day and did not remove his seven-league boots during the semester, with the result that we arrived — somewhat breathless — on the last day of class just in time to view the smoking ruins. From the first it was clear (1) that he had decided exactly how many days could safely be spent on each period, and (2) that he had mastered the materials himself. Whenever the students showed a tendency to get off the main track he herded them back onto it. He drove the class, quietly but relentlessly; if an unexpected event deprived us of an hour's time, he merely gave the screw another twist. I know he had a schedule — not only from his occasional comments about where the class should be at a given point in the semester but because he one day dropped it on the floor! Although he did push us a good deal, there was no confusion and no cramming of

[10] From Tobias Danzig, *Number: The Language of Science.* Copyright, 1930, 1933, and 1939, by The Macmillan Company. Used by permission of The Macmillan Company, Publishers.

facts into an inadequate amount of time. He had such good mastery of the data that he could concentrate upon what was vital for our under-standing. By having a schedule and sticking to it he gave his students precisely the overview of "World History" that was advertised in the catalog.

The second semester was a distinct contrast. We dawdled along, got completely lost in one cul-de-sac after another, loitered to admire Charle-magne, spent a whole week with the popes at Avignon, worked out an interesting but time-consuming project on social organization under feudal conditions, and suddenly found ourselves — a week before the final exami-nations — centuries away from the announced objective. The teacher tried to crowd all the remaining events of history up to the present into a week, but she was so unprepared herself that she did not know what to omit and what to include. The result was a hodgepodge, delivered under conditions of considerable mental and emotional stress. This second teacher had obviously no large plan whatever, although — with the ex-ception of the last few days — her daily preparation was excellent. The classwork was not only good but stimulating; the difficulty was that she had no scheme for the semester as a unit.[11]

The pattern of such a contrast is very simple, since all that is re-quired is to finish discussing one element before beginning the other. The alternative is to deal with both elements at once — to contrast A and B by showing first one of their differences, then another and an-other until the total contrast is completed. Observe how this is done in the following selection:

Death is at all times solemn, but never so much so as at sea. A man dies on shore; his body remains with his friends, and "the mourners go about the streets"; but when a man falls overboard at sea and is lost, there is a suddenness in the event, and a difficulty in realizing it, which give to it an air of awful mystery. A man dies on shore — you follow his body to the grave, and a stone marks the spot. You are often prepared for the event. There is always something which helps you to realize it when it happens, and to recall it when it has passed. A man is shot down by your side in battle, and the mangled body remains an *object,* and a *real evidence;* but at sea, the man is near you — at your side — you hear his voice, and in an instant he is gone, and nothing but a *vacancy* shows his loss. Then, too, at sea — to use a homely but expressive phrase — you *miss* a man so much. A dozen men are shut up together in a little bark, upon the wide, wide sea, and for months and months see no forms and hear no voices but their own and one is suddenly taken from among them, and they miss him at every turn. It is like losing a limb. There are no new faces or new scenes to fill up the gap. There is always an empty berth in the forecastle, and one man wanting when the small night watch is mustered. There is one less to take the wheel and one less to lay out

---

[11] Luella Cole, *The Background for College Teaching* (Copyright 1940 by Farrar & Rinehart), pp. 354–355. Reprinted by permission of Rinehart & Company, Inc.

with you upon the yard. You miss his form, and the sound of his voice, for habit had made them almost necessary to you, and each of your senses feels the loss.[12]

Notice how this pattern binds the passage together. The details are presented in interlocking contrast: a detail of death on land followed immediately by a detail of death at sea, then a second contrasting pair, and so on. This pattern has two advantages over the simpler one: first, it establishes each point of contrast as it is presented and does not require the reader to hold the description of A in mind until he finishes B; second, it tends to produce more integrated writing, since all the details are woven together and there is little opportunity of introducing irrelevant details. Especially for extended or highly detailed contrasts, where the burden on the reader is considerable, this second method is clearer and easier to follow.

## Analytical Organization

Analysis is the process of breaking a thing into its parts in order to understand how it is put together or to see how it functions. Analytical organization, sometimes called organization by division, is the method of breaking the total purpose statement into its parts and taking up each part in succession. Thus the student author of "So This Is College" broke his total subject, *college,* into three parts, *the campus, the students,* and *the faculty,* and dealt with each in turn. By showing his readers that the campus, the students, and the faculty were not as the movies represent them, he accomplished his purpose, which was to show that college life is not as Hollywood pictures it.

To use a mathematical metaphor, we may say that in analytical organization the thesis or purpose statement is *factored,* and each factor is then explained in detail. Sometimes the factors are enumerated or even explicitly stated in the thesis. For example, the following thesis reveals that the discussion will have three parts:

> The definition of war and peace may be approached from three different points of view. The first is deceptively clear, the second is significantly vague, and the third becomes clear only in perspective.

You can see that the organization of an essay with this thesis must fall into three divisions. First, the writer must discuss the distinction between war and peace, which he feels is deceptively clear. Second, he

---

[12] Richard Henry Dana, *Two Years Before the Mast.* Reprinted by permission of Houghton Mifflin Company, publishers.

must take up the one which is significantly vague. Finally, he must tell us what distinction is clear only in perspective. When he has explained each of these three factors, he has explained his thesis. Notice the structure of his essay:

THE DISTINCTION BETWEEN WAR AND PEACE [13]

*Thesis stated,*
*with three*
*factors indicated*

The definition of war and peace may be approached from three different points of view. The first is deceptively clear, the second is significantly vague, and the third becomes clear only in perspective.

*First factor — the*
*legal distinction*

First, there is the legal aspect of the difference between war and peace. This is deceptively clear. In December 1941 Japan attacked the United States and declared war upon this country and Great Britain, and immediately thereafter Germany and Italy declared war upon the United States. In each case the United States reciprocated. The joint resolution declaring war upon Japan was adopted by Congress on the 8th of December and was signed by the President at 4:10 p.m. Eastern War Time. Under the Constitution of the United States, that was, for the American people, the legal change to war in place of peace. But by the time that signature became effective, every United States battleship based upon Pearl Harbor was already out of action. The legal inception of war did not correspond with the moment of war's physical impact, much less with its substantive reality. Yet that definite day, December 8, 1941, will be set down in all the books of history as the date for America's entry into the war. It corresponds with the legal status, but with no other; this is why, though it is clear, it is nonetheless deceptive. . . .

The legal distinction between war and peace is not without significance; property rights and many interests are modified by it. But relative to the total pattern of life as affected by war, this excessively precise legal distinction is vastly less important than the political aspect.

*Second factor —*
*the political*
*distinction*

By contrast, the political distinction between war and peace is significantly vague. People talk about the "white" war which preceded the "red" war. They refer to the economic war which preceded the battles. They speak of the "long armistice" between the Treaty of Versailles and the outbreak of this war, as though

[13] From *Strategy of Peace*, by Henry M. Wriston. Reprinted by permission of the World Peace Foundation.

there never was an interval of genuine peace. Some regard the recent war as beginning in 1931 at the time of the Manchurian incident and the development of the Stimson Doctrine. Others say war began in 1934 when Japan denounced the Washington treaties. Still others think it started in 1935 when Italy attacked Ethiopia and defeated the concept of sanctions. Others would connect it with the German occupation of the Rhineland in 1936. Every person has his favorite time, some suggesting the civil war in Spain, others the *Anschluss,* yet others the Sudeten crisis. Each of those claims has a plausible basis. It is obvious that every act of aggression was part of a maturing crisis; the declaration of war is only a culminating step which completes the development.

Defining the state of war politically, therefore, is like inquiring when some functional disorder took on serious pathological qualities. It may start as some mild or benign affliction, but slowly or swiftly by unperceived degrees develop to a point where it menaces life itself. At what moment in that tragic sequence did the disease begin?

Peace comes politically in the same way as war itself. The peace treaty, whatever its legal effects, does not ensure political peace. Genuine peace, if it is ever achieved, will come through many channels over many long years. It will be a wise man indeed who can set a precise date upon which others, equally well informed, will agree.

*Third factor — the military distinction*

The third distinction between war and peace is military; it is clear only in long perspective. This last was called a global war, and many insist it was one war. But common sense makes it obvious that so long as the Soviet Union was not at war with Japan or the United States with Finland, the statement that there was a single war was imprecise.

The same difficulty appears when the chronology of the war is examined. The use of force began with the Manchurian incident in 1931. The later phase of the war in China began in 1937. Fighting took place in Africa in 1935 with the conquest of Ethiopia, and on the continent of Europe with the occupation of Albania in the spring of 1939. In the period since the declaration of war by Great Britain against Germany on September 3, 1939, some thirty-five other nations have declared war and others have severed diplomatic relations with the Axis. Denmark and Norway, Belgium and the Netherlands, Italy, the Balkan States, the Soviet Union, Finland, Japan and the United States all became involved in the fighting at different times. . . .

Such military facts are characteristic of all war. The Hundred Years' War between France and Britain was by no means a period of uninterrupted fighting; the name could be applied to the era only in retrospect. Similarly, the Napoleonic wars were interrupted by truces, by reversal of alliances, and by treaties of peace which proved temporary. Yet in the long perspective the whole period had a certain unity; the successive phases of the lengthy series of struggles are now regarded as constituting one war. Those are illustrations of what is meant by the assertion that the military aspects of war and peace are comprehensible only in perspective.

*Final restatement of thesis in light of discussion of all three factors*

War is a legal, political, and military fact; its appearance is different when observed from those various points of view. Since the distinction between peace and war is legally clear, politically vague, and militarily plain only in perspective, the effort to roll all three types of description into one has resulted in confusion of thought.

This essay is a clear example of analytical development. If we summarize its structure we see how simple it really is:

1. Statement of the thesis to be developed, with the factors indicated.
2. Full explanation of each factor in turn.
3. Restatement of thesis as concluding summary.

## Combined Analytical and Illustrative Organization

So far we have considered these two major patterns — illustrative and analytical — as completely distinct; but in actual practice, most papers which develop a thesis by analysis also use illustration. The analytical division merely sets up the main units of the paper. As these are taken up in turn, each is likely to be developed by illustration. For example, if you re-read "The Distinction Between War and Peace," you will see that after the thesis is broken into its three factors — the legal, political, and military distinctions — each of these is developed by illustration. That is a very common pattern. One way of describing it is to say that each factor of the thesis becomes a subthesis which is then developed by statement, explanation, example, and restatement. This combination of analytical division and illustration is shown in the following essay, in which the italicized thesis in the opening sentence is broken into five factors — politics, law, property, sex, and education — each of which is then developed by illustration.

*Thesis stated.*

*Key word, "primitive," defined, and thesis restated in light of the definition.*

In contrasting our material culture with the mental life of Americans today, *it is useful at the outset to emphasize the fact that the intellectual outlook of the masses remains much the same as it was in primitive times.* Anthropologists have described the primitive mind as characterized chiefly by an all-pervading super-naturalism, lack of precise and logical thinking, credulity, and an ignorance of scientific methods and results. Judged by these standards, it is obvious that the great majority of moderns are still overwhelmingly primitive in their ways of thinking. . . .

*Transitional sentence leading to division of thesis.*
*1st factor. Subthesis 1 explained.*

We may now consider more specifically the archaic nature of the prevailing opinions and institutions in contemporary society. *Our political opinions and institutions represent a mosaic compounded of*: (1) The veneration of the state derived from the oriental emperor worship; (2) Roman legalism and the conception of secular omnipotence; (3) the classical obsession with the merits of monarchy, aristocracy, and democracy; (4) archaic views of representative government that developed between the sixteenth century and the eighteenth; (5) seventeenth and eighteenth century doctrines of natural rights; and (6) the eighteenth-century view of the perfectability of man, linked up with the nineteenth-century enthusiasm for democracy. While there is much vital political doctrine expounded by modern thinkers, this has found but slight adoption in practice, and there has been singularly little effort to adapt our political institutions to the needs of an urban, industrial age. . . .

*Subthesis restated.*

*2nd factor. Subthesis 2 stated and explained,*

*Law, likewise, is founded upon ancient theories and practices.* It is still based primarily upon oriental usages and conceptions, the formulations of the Roman jurists, the precedents of the English common law, and the eighteenth-century natural law. Very little progress indeed has been made in the way of introducing the historical and sociological point of view in the reconstruction of juristic theory and practice in America. We attempt to regulate a twentieth-century civilization by applying to it legal concepts and methods that have changed but little since the year 1700. The rules of legal evidence are hopelessly out of date and confused. . . . Even in the field of insanity, where the conventional legal conception of the free moral agent is in part suspended, the test for insanity is strictly legal and not medical. In a

*and illustrated by example.*

the classical languages embody the flower of secular learning and represent the most exquisite form of literary expression. . . . Education in the natural and social sciences and in technology has not been regarded as relatively important or respectable, and occupies nothing like so great a part in our educational system as the older currents in our curriculum. As Professor Kallen has observed, education today is more of a distraction from life than a preparation for it. Few of *and restated.* the real problems involved in living intelligently and successfully in an urban and industrial society are touched upon vitally in our educational system, from the kindergarten to the graduate school. . . .

The discussion above enables us to comment intelligently upon the frequent assertion that we are living in a scientific age. The fact is, of course, that we are not doing anything of the sort. *Restatement of thesis* *We are living in an era in which our opinions and* *with reference to all 5* *institutions are overwhelmingly the product of* *factors.* *contributions from the prescientific era.* . . . Not infrequently persons who are most exacting in their demands for the most recent provisions in *Clarifying* plumbing, the best medical attention, the most *restatement* efficient and up-to-date automobiles, and the rest, are found at the same time defending classical or medieval civilization as the ideal period of human development. . . . In short, the real problem *Final restatement of* facing modern civilization is to make this actually *whole thesis.* a scientific age, that is, one in which we would not only insist upon contemporaneous bathtubs but also upon contemporaneous intellectual attitudes and assumptions.[14]

We can briefly summarize the organization of this essay as follows:

1. Thesis stated, defined, restated.
2. First factor (political thinking) explained in detail and then restated in general terms.
3. Second factor (legal thinking) stated, clarified, and illustrated by example.
4. Third factor (attitude toward property) stated, clarified, restated.
5. Fourth factor (sex mores) stated, clarified, restated.
6. Fifth factor (education) stated, clarified, restated.
7. Total thesis restated, clarified, and restated again.

[14] Condensed from *The History of Western Civilization*, Vol. 2, by Harry Elmer Barnes, copyright, 1935, by Harcourt, Brace and Company, Inc.

notorious case in Ohio — that of Mr. Remus —
witnessed the amusing spectacle of a group
learned and logical physicians branding the
fendant as legally sane but medically and socia
quite irresponsible.

*3rd factor. Subthesis 3*
*stated and explained,*

*Our attitudes and usages with respect to pro*
*erty are equally full of primitive vestiges.* Th
notion of the unique sanctity of property is i
part an outgrowth of primitive mysticism and
superstition. Our contemporary view of property
rights is a compound of ancient legalism and the
prevailing sixteenth and seventeenth century Prot-
estant views of God's approval of thrift and profit.
To these have been added the seventeenth and
eighteenth century notion that the chief purpose
of the state and legal institutions is to protect

*and restated.*

private property. . . . There is little or nothing in
present-day American conceptions of property
rights that cannot be discovered explicitly or implicitly in the writings of John Locke.

*4th factor. Subthesis 4*
*stated and explained,*

*We have been especially reluctant to bring the*
*control of sex and the family into harmony with*
*contemporary scientific and esthetic considera-*
*tions.* Our sex mores and family institutions embody: (1) a primitive reaction to the mystery of
sex and of women in particular; (2) Hebraic ux-
oriousness and conceptions of patriarchal male
domination; (3) patristic and medieval views regarding the baseness of sex and sex temptation,
especially as offered by women; (4) the medieval
esteem for virginity in women; (5) the sacra-
mental view of marriage, which leads us to regard
marriage as a theological rather than a social
issue; (6) the property views of the early bour-
geois; and (7) the Kantian rationalization of
personal inadequacy and inexperience. There is

*and restated.*

hardly a single item in the sex mores of a conventionally respectable American today that squares
with either science or esthetics.

*5th factor. Subthesis 5*
*stated and explained,*

*Our educational system has changed but little*
*as compared with the vast alteration in our way*
*of living.* Certain basic strains in our educational
doctrine are derived from the oriental and medieval notion that the chief purpose of education is
to make clear to man the will of the gods or of
God. From the Greeks and Romans came the
high esteem for training in rhetoric and argumen-
tation as the prime essential of a successful career
in politics. Humanism contributed the view that

## *Review Exercises*

**A.** As a review of Chapter 3, study and describe the organizational pattern of the following essays. First explain the overall structure of each essay; then make a paragraph analysis to show the relationship of the separate paragraphs to that overall structure. Be especially careful about the second essay. It was written impromptu in a 50-minute class period and its organization is not as neat as it seems to be.

### *(1)*

Umpiring is by its very nature an arbitrary and dictatorial calling. An umpire is 1) rrright!, 2) the boss. In fact, it can't very well be any other way. But within this seemingly inflexible framework there are certain tacit agreements that, while they may upset the purists, are no more than practical applications of mercy and reason to justice.

As surely as an umpire's word is law, on the next 10 close plays you see at first base where the ball clearly beats the runner, the umpire is going to call the runner out and everybody will be satisfied. Just as surely, they shouldn't be. In at least seven out of 10 of those plays the runner will be safe — definitely and unassailably safe. The reason: the first baseman took his foot off the bag a split second before either ball or runner got to him.

The observation was first made to me by an accredited, card-carrying umpire in the Open Classification Pacific Coast League. When he said it, I should have been shocked. I was a fellow umpire working in the same league. I wasn't shocked though, and now that I have had time to think it over I probably know the reason why. Watch first base closely and you will probably figure it out too. And the same applies to the steal down to second, and quite frequently to the double play.

Take the steal. The catcher's peg gets down there first, the tag is on, and the umpire's right fist makes the short pumping motion that means out. Yet the chances are excellent the man was not out. The umpire knows it, the second baseman knows it, even the runner knows it — but does not, for reasons I will get to in a second, protest.

For "tag" in this instance is a misnomer for the tagging motion. The rules state that the ball must make contact with the sliding runner. Common sense states that it had better not.

Similarly, in the case of the double play, the rule book has it that the baseman must be on the base and in possession of the ball simultaneously to effect the force at second. But if you think umpires always insist on strict compliance with this regulation, you must suspect us of a sadistic streak even baser than the one you accord us as a matter of course. Because the rule book, although fundamentally an admirable document, offers no provision for the first baseman who, as a consequence of his thorough lawfulness, has his foot maimed by descending spikes. Nor does it make mention of what or how often the wife and children of the shortstop (or second baseman) eat while he hobbles around on severed tendons.[15]

[15] From Gil Stratton's "Umpires Ever Wrong? Sure but with a Purpose," *Sports Illustrated*, August 6, 1956. Copyright, 1956, by Time, Inc. Reprinted by permission.

(2)

### THIS SEMESTER IN RETROSPECT

This semester, my first at college, has had tremendous significance for me, for it has deepened my understanding, broadened my thought, and heightened my consciousness of life.

From dormitory life I have learned much in respect to my relationships with other people. I slowly realized that I must accept my friends for what they are and not expect too much from them. When my friend Ruthie (from the room next to mine) was thoughtless one day, my first reaction was hurt bewilderment, but it soon dawned on me that since I am certainly not an angel all the time, I shouldn't be surprised at other people's imperfections. Now I don't expect too much from my friends so that, when they are especially thoughtful, I feel the joy of unexpected pleasure in our friendship.

My roommate Mary Lou has taught me an excellent lesson in courage and perseverance. She is a polio victim, fifty per cent paralyzed, yet she meets the great challenges of her life with cheerfulness, fortitude, and an amazing sense of humor. This valiant and sensible attitude of hers makes my problems, which at times used to seem overwhelming, now appear trivial.

Being in the school of music has forced me, through much agony of introspection and thought, to crystallize my feelings about what is important in life. When I was a senior in high school I could hardly wait for the time when I would be specializing in music and taking courses almost all of which would be related to this field of interest. But after five months of being in such a professional school, I have come to the conclusion that there is much more to life than music and that in order to become a well-educated and well-balanced person, I must take courses in many different fields of interest. The college atmosphere has caused me to become aware of the manifold aspects of life and thought, many of which were formerly unknown to me.

However, the most thrilling part of my growth this semester has been the valuable experience of really being on my own for the first time in my life. At home my life was planned for me and expertly guided by my wise and well-meaning parents. But in the process of becoming an adult I must be able to think for myself. Little things, like making my own doctor's appointment for the first time, have proved exciting to me. With experience I have gained more and more capability in making decisions and in becoming a more self-sufficient and effective person. The big decision, which I made myself, to transfer to the school of liberal arts, was made possible only by the practice which I have been allowed this semester in making the smaller decisions of everyday life.

My growth as a person this term has exceeded my expectations in its dimensions. The college years are ones of great change and development. I am looking forward to even greater growth in the semesters to come.

**B.** The two selections that follow deal with the same subject. The first is a student essay written from the author's personal experience; the second is part of a book in which a professional author is presenting the evidence of his research to awaken the public to the waste of our national resources. Keeping these differences in mind, first identify the theses of the selections, noticing the unusual position of the student thesis; then contrast the use of example in both selections; finally consider what each writer would have gained or lost, in relation to his purpose, had he followed the method of the other.

### A FARM [16]

I saw a picture of a farm today. It was a hill farm, with a long, winding road leading up to a big, lonely house set back in a grove of maple trees. The roof of the house was starting to cave in, and the yard was overgrown with cockleburs and jimson weeds. An old apple orchard behind the house was a wild tangle of underbrush and dead trees. A ruined barn and a gullied field completed the desolate view. The farm was dead.

It had once been a gay, prosperous place, with its widespread fields presenting a glittering patchwork pattern of green and yellow to the sky, and its wood offering a cool haven from the hot fields. Its inclined fields had lent it a quiet charm. It was a small boy's dream world and a grown man's paradise.

The first owner of the farm came in 1884 and built the big house and the barn. The nine inches of Marshall clay loam which covered the rolling fields made him forget their steepness, and he cropped the farm heavily, farming it exactly as he would a flat farm. The years were kind to him. His place came to be known as the best farm in the region. Year after year, he grew thirty-bushel wheat and eighty-bushel corn on the rich fields. He became the richest and, by men's standards, the most successful farmer in the area. But long before he moved to town his plows were turning up the red subsoil in his fields.

The next farmer fared worse at the hands of nature. Erosion had reduced the nine inches of topsoil to barely three inches, and the gullies were getting too large to farm across. If he had been a thinking man, he would have considered the decision which faced him at this time. He could do one of two things. First, he could convert to pasture and hayland farming, thus saving his soil and increasing his future profits, although the first few years would necessarily be a little lean. Second, he could keep on farming in the manner of the first owner, planting grain every year, without giving a thought to conserving soil or planting cover crops. The first choice led to permanent prosperity; the second led to more immediate profits and a ruined farm. Perhaps the farmer did not realize the choice before him. At any rate, he either took or just drifted into the latter choice, and traveled down the road to financial ruin.

After the bank took over the mortgaged farm in 1924, there followed a

[16] James B. Allen, "A Farm." From *The Green Caldron: A Magazine of Freshman Writing* (October, 1954), published at the University of Illinois, Urbana, Illinois. Copyright, 1954, by Charles W. Roberts. Reprinted by permission.

long succession of tenant farmers, who struggled vainly to wrest a living from the barren hills.

The nine inches of topsoil was gone, and with it the last vestige of prosperity. Two generations of farmers had ruined the farm. It lay a barren, weed-grown place, unclaimed by any taxpayer, its big ruined house the only sign of former wealth. From glittering prosperity to irredeemable poverty in forty years! Such is the story of the old farm on the hillside.

The Johnson farm is typical of many in the United States. It represents a little greed, a great deal of ignorance, and not a little stupidity. It is the product of men who call the soil "dirt" and despise it as a thing good only for making money. Until all men realize that "soil" and "life" are synonymous, there will always be farms like the Johnson place.

## The Land Runs to the Sea [17]

The most obvious result of deforestation, overgrazing, and bad farming methods is soil erosion. American civilization, founded on nine inches of topsoil, has now lost one-third of this soil. Dr. Hugh H. Bennett, testifying before a Congressional committee in 1939 said, "In the short life of this country we have essentially destroyed 282,000,000 acres of land, crop and rangeland. Erosion is destructively active on 775,000,000 additional acres. About 100,000,000 acres of cropland, much of it representing the best cropland we have is finished in this country. We cannot restore it.

"It takes nature from 300 to 1000 years or more to bring back a single inch of topsoil and we sometimes lose that much topsoil as the result of a single rain, if it is an especially heavy torrential type of rain. . . ."

During the past hundred years the Potomac River has carried more than half a billion tons of soil past Washington, or about seventy-five tons of soil from each of the 7,400,000 acres that make up the drainage basin above Washington. Some of the land is in woods and some is so steep and stony that it has never been cultivated. Accordingly, the actual per acre loss on the cultivated land is much greater than indicated.

Since early colonial days, erosion has removed from one-fourth to three-fourths of the best part of the crop-producing topsoil from more than five million acres of the complete Potomac River drainage basin. In addition, from three-fourths to all of the topsoil has been eroded from another 221,000 acres. Small wonder that the deep harbor into which came ocean-going ships from the seven seas has filled with silt and is now the site of the Lincoln Memorial.

It was estimated by the Soil Conservation Service that approximately 5,500,000 tons of sediment would flow by Washington in 1947. This, in spite of the fact that twenty soil conservation districts have been organized on the Potomac watershed. These districts embrace almost 87 per cent of the basin's land. With the help of Soil Conservation Service tech-

[17] From William Vogt's *Road to Survival*. Reprinted by permission of William Sloane Associates, Inc., publishers.

nicians, supervisors, and farmers, there have already been worked out almost 55,000 complete conservation farm plans, which provide for the acre-by-acre treatment of almost 1,000,000 acres. Yet five and a half million tons of earth a year go down the river. And this is merely one rather small stream.

At the head of Chesapeake Bay, 85,000,000 cubic yards of sediment were deposited between 1846 and 1938; the average depth of water over an area of 32 square miles was reduced 2½ feet! At the site of two Maryland ports, once open to overseas trade, the mooring posts are more than two miles from navigable water. In the seventeenth century ocean-going vessels sailed up the creek to Piscataway, Maryland; the depth of the water at the creek's entrance is now about two feet. The decadence of the countryside about Port Tobacco, reported by Craven's traveler, also contributed to the silting and abandonment of many ports on Chesapeake Bay. Port Tobacco is, itself, now a mile from tidewater.

Though during the past hundred years the federal government has spent about $17,000,000 digging out the port of Baltimore, the depth of water under its Hanover Street Bridge fell from seventeen feet to six inches by 1924.

**C.** Using whatever means of specifying seems best, or a combination of means if you prefer, select one of the following terms and explain what it means to you.

| | |
|---|---|
| bigotry | courtesy |
| brashness | immaturity |
| courage | independence |

morality

**D.** Select one of the following statements and develop it into a short essay through these three stages: (1) a general explanation, (2) a series of short examples, (3) a sustained example.

What they told me about college is true.
A kind answer turns away wrath.
A blind date is always a risk.
Honesty may sometimes be a difficult policy.
Young brothers (or sisters) are pests.

**E.** By means of contrast or comparison or both, develop one of the following topics into a short paper.

Two Kinds of Teachers
Mother and Dad
The Contradictions of Adolescence
High School and College Instruction
The Best Team in Baseball
My Growth During the Last Three
(or Five) Years

**F.** Select any person you know well (it may be yourself) and write a thesis stating what that person most needs to get from his total college experience. (Examples: *I hope my college experiences will cure me of the habit of jumping at conclusions; My roommate needs to learn that charming helplessness may attract a man but it won't hold him.*) Analyze the thesis into its parts and develop each part fully.

# 4

\*
\*
\* **O U T L I N I N G**
\*
\*

FOR MOST college writing the kind of purposeful planning discussed in Chapters 2 and 3 will be sufficient. But for long papers — especially for research and term papers — you should draw up the plan of the paper in the form of an outline. Outlining is not basically different from the analytical organization discussed in Chapter 3. A slight change in the form of the marginal comments to the essays on war and peace and on primitive thinking would have converted these comments into outlines. In moving from a study of informal patterns of organization to a study of outlining we are simply moving toward a more formal and detailed statement of the structural pattern.

## The Uses of an Outline

A formal outline has four uses: it helps a writer to clarify his purpose and organize his material to achieve that purpose; it offers a convenient way of testing the proposed organization of an essay; it may occasionally serve as a complete communication in itself; and it may be used as an aid to efficient reading.

### Outlining to Determine Purpose

In practice, most of us often begin to outline before we fully understand what we want to do. We go through a period of preliminary outlining during which we are not really drawing up a plan for the paper we will finally write but are feeling our way toward our purpose. We use the outline as a tool to help us clarify our thoughts, somewhat like the housewife who finds out how she wants her furniture arranged by moving it about the room. Like the housewife, we could save ourselves a good deal of trouble if we could see, without all this experimenting, how our material should be organized, but these experimental outlines are often a necessary means of thinking out our purpose so that we can proceed to the final outline.

Let us illustrate. Suppose you are asked to write a term paper on the characteristics of superior college students. Assume that you have done the necessary reading and have acquired a collection of notes, including statistical evidence, case histories, academic and professional records of superior students, and comparisons of superior and inferior students. As you study these notes (grouping similar kinds of information together) you decide that superior college students show certain characteristics, which you list as follows:

1. They make a rapid survey before reading a chapter.
2. They associate what they learn in one course with work in another.
3. They study alone.
4. They tend to be non-social.
5. They are more introverted than other students.
6. They notice the headings in the text books.
7. They are more self-conscious than other students.
8. They are younger than most students.
9. They are relatively indifferent to the opposite sex.
10. They are less assertive, but more independent.
11. They take a slightly lighter schedule.
12. They are persistent.
13. They recite to themselves.
14. They clear up any point they do not understand before going on to another.
15. They spend a little more time than the average in study.
16. They are happy in college.
17. They participate in more extracurricular activities, but mostly in clubs in which the interest is intellectual rather than social.
18. They usually have abilities necessary for success in their chosen profession.[1]

As you study these characteristics you begin to see that some of them are related; so you begin to group them under what seem to be topic headings, which at first may look something like this:

> Study habits
> Age
> Personality traits
> Social characteristics

But on reconsidering these headings you see that what you have to say about age could be dismissed in a sentence and that the two dominant

---

[1] For these characteristics I am indebted to Luella Cole's *The Background for College Teaching* (Copyright by Farrar & Rinehart, Inc., New York, 1940), p. 396. Reprinted by permission of Rinehart & Company.

topics seem to be study habits and personality traits. You therefore set these up as headings and group specific characteristics under them as follows:

| Personality Traits | Study Habits |
|---|---|
| non-social | spend more time on studies |
| introvertive | study alone |
| self-conscious | notice headings of textbooks |
| indifferent to opposite sex | make rapid survey before reading |
| persistent | recite to themselves |
| less assertive, more independent | clear up one point before moving on to another |
| (?) participate in more extracurricular activities, but of intellectual type | associate what they learn in one course with what they learn in another |
| | (?) take slightly lighter schedules |

You put a question mark before some of the items because you feel that they do not fit too well under their headings, and you see that a pattern is beginning to emerge. Indeed, at this point you are tempted to draft as your thesis: "Superior college students have characteristic personality traits and study habits." But you recognize that if that is all you are going to show you might as well hand in your list of characteristics, since they show all that your thesis asserts.

As you study your material again, you begin to see a variety of possibilities. You could write a paper to show that the superiority of college students is determined by academic rather than by social success. But since that seems self-evident, you reject it. You try "Although superior students are happy in college, they are not socially successful." That seems better, but you realize that it puts too much emphasis on the personality traits and not enough on study habits; so you try again. Finally, you decide that if you wrote an essay to show that superior students are better adjusted in their academic than in their social activities, you could get a unified paper which would allow you to use most of your material. So you begin to draft an outline which emerges like this:

what article about

Thesis: Superior college students are better adjusted to their academic than to their social environment.
  I. They are well adjusted to their academic environment.
     A. They have efficient study habits.
     B. They supplement their class work with intellectual extracurricular activities.
     C. They are happy in college.
  II. They are less well adjusted to their social environment.
     A. They are introverted and self-conscious.
     B. They are non-social.
     C. They are relatively indifferent to the opposite sex.

At this point, assuming that you have the details in your notes to develop these sentences, you have the basic organization of your paper completed. You may still subdivide some of your headings. For example, the study habits might be subdivided, and different non-social attitudes might be recognized. But these are refinements. The basic structure has been established.

### Outlining To Test Organization

A badly organized paper will not be thoroughly successful, no matter how well it is written in other ways. Therefore if there are flaws in the organization you plan to use, it will be wise to detect them before beginning the first draft. Since the outline serves as a sort of X-ray picture of the skeleton of a piece of writing, it offers a convenient and reliable test of organization and allows a change of plans before it is too late.

Examine the following outline, made by an instructor from a student research paper which had been turned in without an outline. The purpose statement was taken from the opening paragraph which, as far as the instructor could judge, was designed to set up the thesis of the paper. The remaining ten paragraphs dealt successively with the topics labeled by the capital letters in the outline. The topics opposite the Roman numerals were provided by the instructor to show the main divisions of the paper.

reason for writing article NEW CURES FOR CANCER

Purpose statement: To show the advances made in the control and cure
                              of cancer during recent times.
  I.  The history of cancer
      A.  Among the early Egyptians
      B.  Among the ancient Greeks and Romans
      C.  Down to the nineteenth century
  II. The causes of cancer
      A.  External irritation
      B.  Internal irritation
      C.  Inherited tendencies
  III. Recent remedies
      A.  Cysteine disulphide
      B.  Surgery
      C.  X-rays and radium
      D.  Preventive care

We do not have to look very closely at this outline to see serious defects in the structure of the paper. If it is to deal with recent advances in the control and cure of cancer, then the history and causes of cancer are irrelevant, and two thirds of the paper has no relation to this purpose. Conversely, if this student does not intend to deal with recent developments in the treatment of cancer, she should not suggest that purpose in her opening paragraph. Finally, if we reject this purpose, no other is evident in the outline, except the vague intention to write *about* cancer. We can be sure that the paper will be a purposeless development of an unrestricted subject.

The moral of this example is not merely that the organization of this paper is poor, but that its weaknesses are at once revealed by the outline. Had the writer been able to study this outline before she began to write, she might have foreseen these weaknesses and so avoided them. Considering the time it took her to gather material and write her paper, a little more time spent on an outline would have been wise insurance against failure.

Because drawing up a sound outline is a rigorous exercise in logic, students sometimes try to escape the discipline it imposes. Every instructor is familiar with the student request, "Can't I write the outline *after* I write the paper? It's a lot easier that way." This is much like asking, "Can't I study the road map after I have made the trip?" or "Can't I prepare the blueprint after I have built the house?" Such a request misinterprets the function of an outline, which is to sketch out a plan and a procedure. Once the paper has been successfully written, the plan is not needed. It is true that, as one writes, he may make organizational changes he did not foresee when he made the outline, and there is no reason why he should not do so. But if a paper requires careful planning, this should be done before the basic structure is obscured by illustrations and other details.

### Outlining as Complete Communication

In addition to the uses so far considered, an outline sometimes serves as a communication in its own right. College assignments, including examination questions, sometimes specify an outline as the final product. Sometimes an outline is required instead of a summary to show that the student has mastered the content of an essay or a lecture. Occasionally, as an exercise in organization, an instructor will ask his students to arrange material in logical outline form without developing the outline into an essay.

### Outlining as a Reading Aid

Much of your college work will consist of digesting the contents of books and essays and being able to explain and discuss what you have read. When material is complex — as it often is on such subjects as economics, history, literary criticism, philosophy, and political science — the discipline of reducing it to outline form has two advantages: it forces you to watch carefully what the author is doing and how he is doing it, and it gives you, in a form convenient for review, a digest of the basic content. In both these ways the outline is to the essay what a map is to a city. It is an efficient and streamlined device for understanding the total structure and the relations among parts.

The following outline reduces a long article to a form which permits a quick review of the original. Even without reading the article you can tell from the outline what the author was saying. It is quite probable that on the evidence of the outline alone you could answer an examination question on the advantages of gas as a weapon of war.

### Chemical Warfare

*Thesis:* Gas is the ideal weapon of war.
I. The ideal weapon is one which does not necessarily destroy but nevertheless is effective in subduing the opponent.
  A. The direct object of war is to force the enemy into submission, not to kill him.
  B. The ideal weapon has the following characteristics:
    1. It should be simple to manufacture in peace or war and its production should not affect prosperity.
    2. Its nature should be unknown to the enemy.
    3. It should be capable of incapacitating, but the incapacitation should not be permanent.
    4. It should permit an established defense against it, one known in advance and prepared for by the side using the weapon.
    5. It should inflict no permanent damage upon property.
II. Gas meets the requirements of the ideal weapon.
  A. The chemical industry does not require any expensive conversion to manufacture war gas.
    1. The facilities for production exist and are in use in peacetime industry.
    2. The cost of production is less than that of other weapons of war, and the product can be quickly and cheaply converted to peacetime uses.
  B. The enemy cannot provide efficient protection against a gas attack.
    1. Preparations for a gas attack cannot be so effectively reconnoitered as preparations for air, artillery, or tank attacks.
    2. Even when a gas attack is anticipated, uncertainty about the type of gas to be used makes defense difficult.
      a. Different types of gas require different defenses.
      b. The attack may shift from one form of gas to another.
      c. The use of masks as a defense must be confined to short periods or morale and efficiency of troops will suffer.
  C. Gas attacks can be controlled to achieve a specified degree of incapacitation.
    1. Death, incapacity to work or fight, or morale-sapping irritation may be obtained by controlling the concentration of the gas.

    2. The results desired can be achieved at once or after a period of latency, depending on which effect best suits the plans of the attackers.

  D. Gas permits a defense by the army using it.

    1. The attacking force can be equipped with masks and protective clothing to allow them to advance in gassed areas.

    2. The defense against a specific plan could be worked out in advance and incorporated in the plan of attack.

  E. Gas inflicts no permanent damage on property.

    1. Contaminated areas may be decontaminated by the use of chemicals.

    2. Even if no decontamination is used, the effects of the gas wear off in time.

Such an outline allows you to summarize both the content and the structure of the original article. It is therefore a useful device whenever the material to be studied is difficult or important enough to warrant the time outlining takes. The following are the steps involved in preparing a reading outline:

1. Read the essay to form a general impression of its purpose and structure. Pay particular attention to the opening paragraphs, which usually state the intention or thesis, and to any headings which may give you a clue to the units of organization.

2. Determine the writer's purpose by picking out his thesis. If none is explicitly stated, formulate the purpose which is implied.

3. Determine the main divisions of the essay and mark them I, II, III, etc. Sometimes the author will have marked these divisions for you. If the essay is well constructed each of these parts should constitute a major unit of the outline.

4. Express the purpose of each of these major units as a topic heading or a subthesis. Test these headings to see whether they logically develop the main purpose statement.

5. After you have done all this, consider whether the headings established in 4 above should be subdivided. If they should, break each of them, in turn, into its parts and mark these parts A, B, C, etc. If still further subdivision is required, mark the new subdivisions 1, 2, 3, etc.

6. Check the completed outline against the original essay to see that it adequately reveals its structure and content.

This process may be simply illustrated by outlining the essay on the distinction between war and peace (page 47). A first reading shows that the thesis is stated in the first paragraph and is then broken into three factors. Each factor — the legal, political, and military distinctions between peace and war — is then discussed in a major division of the essay. The outline, then, consists of the thesis and three subtheses — I, II, and III, though subtopics can be added if more detail is desired. Similarly, an outline of the selection on pages 50–52 would consist of

the thesis ("The intellectual outlook of modern life is essentially primitive"), five major divisions which apply the thesis to politics, law,
property rights, sex and family life, and education, and a sixth which
sums up the argument.

The outline, then, has four main uses — as a tool for clarifying purpose, as a test of organization, as an independent communication, and
as a reading aid. The ability to organize material is essential to good
work in many college courses, and the student who develops it early
in his college career will work more efficiently because of it.

## Topic and Sentence Outlines

A *topic outline* is one in which the headings are single words or
phrases, not complete sentences. The outline on cancer cures on page
62 and the following example are topic outlines.

### THE DIVISIONS OF FEDERAL AUTHORITY

*Purpose:* To show the main divisions of the federal government.
  I. The Executive
     A. The President
     B. The Cabinet
     C. Appointed authorities
  II. The Legislature
     A. The House of Representatives
     B. The Senate
  III. The Judiciary
     A. The Federal Courts
     B. The Supreme Court

The *sentence* outline has already been illustrated on pages 64–65
and on page 61. There each entry is a complete sentence.

Of the two forms, the topic outline is the more popular. Although it
need not be less logical or precise than a sentence outline, most students
find it easier to handle. In general, it is the more convenient form to use
when the purpose of the outline cannot be expressed as a thesis — that
is, when the outline does not develop one dominant idea. When the
outline does contain a thesis the sentence outline is usually the better
form to use, since it provides a clearer and usually a fuller plan of
development. Notice how the following sentence outline spells out the
meaning of the thesis through three logical and related steps.

WHAT HYBRID SEED CORN HAS DONE FOR FARMERS

*Thesis:* The use of hybrid seed corn has raised the standard of living of the American farmer.

   I. The use of hybrid seed corn has increased the production of corn.
     A. It has increased the yield per acre.
     B. It has decreased the loss due to disease and weather conditions.

  II. The use of hybrid seed has brought about new markets for corn.
     A. The nature of the hybrid seed industry has encouraged successful exploration of new uses for corn.
     B. As a result of new industrial uses the market for corn has been greatly expanded.

 III. The combination of increased production and an expanded market has raised the farmer's standard of living.
     A. It has increased his annual net income.
     B. It has provided more leisure time by allowing the farmer to purchase time-saving machinery.
     C. The combination of more money and more free time has made the farmer eager and able to provide comforts and conveniences in his home.

Here the development of the thesis is carried beyond the mere blocking out of the material to be presented. The thesis is factored into its logical subtheses, each of which, in turn, is subdivided. As a result the whole outline is knit tightly together and there is little chance for the writer to stray from his purpose.

## The Conventions of Outlining

A complete outline consists of three parts: the title, the purpose statement, and the body of the outline. The main divisions of the body are represented by Roman numerals; their divisions, in turn, are marked by capital letters. Successive subdivisions are indicated by Arabic numerals, small letters, Arabic numerals in parentheses, and small letters in parentheses. These symbols follow a progressive system of indention so that the relation and relative importance of topics may be seen at a glance.

Title

Purpose statement (or thesis) ...........................................
  I. ...................................................................
    A. ...............................................................
      1. .............................................................
        a. ...........................................................
          (1) .........................................................
            (a) .......................................................
            (b) .......................................................
          (2) .........................................................
        b. ...........................................................
        c. ...........................................................
      2. .............................................................
      3. .............................................................
    B. ...............................................................
      1. .............................................................
      2. .............................................................
  II. ..................................................................
    A. ...............................................................
    B. ...............................................................
    C. ...............................................................

There are two conventions that cannot be revealed by this model. First, different levels of division must not be confused. To represent main headings as subheadings or vice versa would misrepresent the logical division of the material and could mislead the student when he writes his paper. Contrast the two erroneous outlines that follow with the correct one on page 66.

I. The Executive
  A. The President
  B. The Supreme Court
II. The Legislature
  A. The House of Representatives
  B. The Senate

I. The Legislature
II. The Senate
III. The President
IV. The Judiciary

At the left, listing the Supreme Court as a division of the executive authority distorts the organization of the government into two divisions, not three. At the right, the failure to recognize the Senate as a division of the legislature has resulted in what looks like four main branches of government. A paper developed from either outline would probably be unsatisfactory, since to avoid the confusion which the outlines invite, the writer would have to plan his material more effectively while writing than he could do when devoting all his attention to organization.

The second convention not illustrated in the abstract outline is the use of parallel structure. So far as possible the form of all entries in an outline should be consistent. Topic and sentence headings should not both be used in the same outline. In addition, parallel grammatical constructions throughout a topic outline make it easier to see whether the outline is actually logical. Notice below that the outline at the left obscures the equality of the topics by shifting from prepositional to infinitive phrases, while the one at the right is clearer because the entries are parallel.

| *Why I Came to College* | *Why I Came to College* |
|---|---|
| I. For economic reasons | I. To improve my economic status |
| II. In order to improve myself socially | II. To develop social poise |
| III. To make myself a cultured person | III. To make myself a cultured person |
| IV. For fun | IV. To enjoy college activities |

You may have noticed that neither the abstract outline on page 68, nor any of the outlines presented earlier, includes entries for Introduction, Body, and Conclusion. These headings are common in high school outlines and have some usefulness, since most essays have an introduction and a conclusion. But these are not aspects of the purpose statement and need not appear in the outline. If a student wishes introductory and concluding paragraphs, he may write them when he writes the paper. Their content, however, seldom appears in the outline.

## Shaping the Outline

How easily you can shape your outline will depend on how clearly you have your purpose in mind. If you are still not sure what you want to do, you will probably have to experiment, much as we did on pages 60–61. You will probably have to list your information, as we listed the characteristics of superior students, group similar pieces of information together, organize these groups into major units, and finally determine what these units show. Until you have done these things you are not ready to begin the final outline, since you do not yet know to what end you are trying to organize your material.

Once you have a clear statement of purpose, it is best to lay out the main divisions of your outline before you worry about subdivisions. First establish all the Roman numerals, then break each Roman numeral into its capital letters, and so on. This way you will keep better control of your outline: you will not be likely to distort the organization by developing some headings too much and others too little. Since any change in the main headings will probably require changes in the subheadings, too early attention to subheadings may be time wasted.

Let us assume that a writer wishes to show the development of military aviation by contrasting the part it played in World Wars I and II. His purpose immediately suggests the basic contrast in his paper, and hence the two Roman numerals of his outline.

*Stage 1.*
    I. Aviation in World War I
   II. Aviation in World War II

The next step is to break these Roman numerals into their main divisions.

*Stage 2.*
    I. Aviation in World War I
      A. The nature of the early airplane
      B. The uses of aviation
      C. The reputation of aviation
   II. Aviation in World War II
      A. The nature of the modern airplane
      B. The uses of aviation
      C. The reputation of aviation

These subdivisions establish the basic plan of the paper. But the outline is still too general to be a useful blueprint. The development must be carried forward another stage, first to test the plan, and second to make it really useful.

*Purpose:* To show the development of military aviation by contrasting the roles it played in World Wars I and II.

*Stage 3.*
*(Completed topic outline)*

    I. Aviation in World War I
      A. The nature of the early airplane
        1. Its flimsy construction
        2. Its insignificant pay load
        3. Its mechanical unreliability
      B. The uses of aviation
        1. Short range reconnaissance
        2. Crude bombing
        3. Spectacular but insignificant aerial duels
      C. The reputation of aviation
        1. Generally ignored by military authorities
        2. Regarded as an expensive novelty by public
   II. Aviation in World War II
      A. The nature of the modern airplane
        1. Variety of construction to suit purposes
          a. Light, medium, and heavy bombers
          b. Pursuit ships
          c. Transports
          d. Training craft
        2. Structural capacities
          a. Range of flight
          b. Load capacity
          c. Armament and firepower

B. The uses of aviation
   1. Offensive uses
      a. Long range mass and precision bombing
      b. Preliminary bombardment before attack
      c. Long range reconnaissance
      d. Supply
      e. Transport
   2. Defensive uses
      a. Break-up of enemy concentrations
      b. Harassing of enemy movements
      c. Air cover for ships and troops
      d. Submarine reconnaissance
      e. Evacuation of personnel
      f. Interception of enemy planes
C. The reputation of aviation
   1. Regarded as decisive factor by military authorities
   2. Regarded by troops as aristocratic branch of the services
   3. Highly favored by public opinion
   4. Considered as co-equal with army and navy at end of war

The outline is now a complete plan for a long paper. There is still work to be done in developing these headings into an essay by explanation and illustrative details, but the outline has established the whole structure of the essay. The chances are that the plan might not have been so completely or so consistently worked out had the writer not proceeded methodically through the first two stages before attempting the third.

## Testing the Outline

When a careful outline is required, try to avoid finishing it at a single sitting. Second thoughts are often better than first, and the time spent on the outline of a long paper is so small compared with the total time of composition that you can usually afford to reconsider your plan many times before you begin to write. It is often wise to test the outline by asking yourself the following questions:

1. Is the thesis or purpose statement satisfactory?
2. Is there a logical and clear relationship among the parts of the outline?
3. Is the outline sufficiently developed to be really useful?
Let us consider these questions.

### Is the Purpose Statement (Thesis) Satisfactory?

Since the whole outline develops the purpose statement, an unsatisfactory statement invites trouble all along the way. As we have seen, the statement of purpose should be restricted, unified, and precise. A faulty purpose statement will probably lead to a badly organized or a pointless paper. A rigorous checking of the purpose statement is therefore the first and most important step in testing the usefulness of a tentative outline.

As an additional illustration of what may develop from an unsatisfactory statement, consider the following:

> The purpose of this paper is to provide a better understanding of the American Indian by revealing a few facts about his everyday life and customs.

The author of this statement has not really clarified his purpose, and any paper he writes is likely to be superficial. Why does he think that "a few facts" about the everyday life and customs of the Indian will help us to understand him better? What kind of facts? What will be his criterion for using some facts and omitting others? When we look at his outline we see, as his purpose statement suggests, that he is simply going to write a purposeless paper "about" the American Indian.

    I. The Indian religion differs from the white man's.
       A. The Indian religion is complicated.
       B. His conception of the supernatural has a strong influence on his everyday life.
   II. The Indian medicine man is one of the most important people in the tribe.
       A. The training of the medicine man begins at an early age.
  III. Dancing is of great importance in the life of the Indian.
       A. There are many classes of dancing.
       B. The instruments used to accompany the dancers are of a wide variation.
  IV. The education of the Indian was not very extensive.
       A. There were several Indian colleges built.
   V. The government of the Indian was simple.
       A. There were four divisions in the government.

Do you see that the vagueness of the purpose statement encouraged the student to tack on anything that had any connection with his general subject? The only purpose of this outline is to string together enough information to bring the paper up to the required length. This example, of course, is an unusually bad one, but it shows what can happen when a student bases an outline on fuzzy or pointless statement of purpose.

### Is There A Clear Relationship Among the Parts of the Outline?

In a good outline the relationship among the parts is clear. One should be able to see how each Roman numeral brings out an important aspect of the purpose statement and how each subdivision helps to develop its main heading. If there is any doubt about the relation of any heading to the purpose statement, that heading is either poorly stated or is a potential trouble spot in the organization. Whatever the reason, the difficulty should be removed before beginning to write.

Notice how clear is the relation among all parts of the following outline. Each Roman numeral shows a clear relation to the thesis, each capital letter is a logical division of its Roman numeral. No entry in the outline fails to advance the purpose, and each introduces, at its proper place, a significant part of the argument. You can be confident that the paper written from this outline will be coherent and closely-reasoned.

*Thesis:* The age at which a citizen may vote should be reduced to 18.
  I. The present age limit has no logical justification.
    A. It has no relation to physical maturity.
    B. It has no relation to intellectual maturity.
    C. It has no relation to economic maturity.
  II. Whatever justification the present age limit once had has been removed by changed conditions.
    A. In the last war we were forced to draft 18-year-olds because they made the best soldiers.
    B. The draft necessitates a change in the voting age if we are to respect the political maxim that the responsibilities of citizenship presuppose the privileges of citizenship.
  III. The objections against reducing the age limit, like the objections against female suffrage, are based on unsupported assertions.
    A. It was asserted that women would use the vote foolishly, but the facts have disproved that assertion.
    B. It is asserted that 18-year-olds neither care about voting nor will take the trouble to make themselves politically informed, but the facts do not support that assertion.
  IV. The argument that there has to be some minimum age begs the question, since reducing the age limit does not abolish it.
  V. Reducing the age limit would broaden the base of our democracy, a consequence which has been traditionally desirable.

A good way to test an outline is to ask yourself, for every entry, whether it "points back" to the one it is developing. Do the Roman-numeral entries point back to the thesis or purpose statement? Do those with capital letters point back to the main headings? Notice below how A, B, and C all point back to I, the contention that the present age limit for voting has no logical justification.

  I. The present age limit has no logical justification.
    A. It has no relation to physical maturity.
    B. It has no relation to intellectual maturity.
    C. It has no relation to economic maturity.

### Is the Outline Sufficiently Developed?

If an outline is a blueprint for a paper, it must be detailed enough to be really useful. For example, if we had stopped at either Stage 1 or Stage 2 of the outline on military aviation (page 70), we would still have been left with a good deal of organizing to do while writing the paper. The more problems of organization you can solve in the outline, the freer you will be later to concentrate on the problems of composition. A review of the preliminary outlines on the superior student (pages 60–61) will show how true this is.

### Can Each Entry in the Outline be Developed in Detail?

An outline is a plan, not a finished essay, and each entry should be fully developed when the essay is written. Every instructor has known students who construct outlines containing entries for which they have no material, so that all they have to say about these entries is what they have already said in the outline. *Every entry in an outline should be adequately developed, and no entry should appear unless the author intends to develop it.* There can be no rigid rule about how much development each entry should receive. Sometimes a single entry will require two or three paragraphs in the essay; occasionally several minor entries may be dealt with in a single paragraph. For inexperienced writers, a useful rule of thumb is that each entry will usually be developed into at least one paragraph.

## Summary

1. The ability to outline is useful: (*a*) as a tool for clarifying and developing purpose; (*b*) as a means of testing the proposed organization of a paper; (*c*) as a complete communication; (*d*) as a reading aid.

2. In a topic outline the entries are expressed in words or phrases; in a sentence outline each entry is a complete sentence. The topic outline is best for an essay which is not going to develop a dominant idea; when the paper is going to develop an idea (thesis), the sentence outline is preferable. In practice, most sentence outlines evolve out of preliminary topic outlines.

3. The conventions of outlining require that all headings be marked with an appropriate symbol and indented to show the degree of division. They also require that the outline distinguish major and minor divisions and keep the grammatical structure of all headings parallel.

4. In preparing an outline, finish the major divisions before you touch minor ones. Do the Roman numerals before you begin the capital letters, and the capitals before the Arabic numerals. This will insure that you work out the outline in a series of stages.

parallelism

5. When you think your outline is complete, test it by considering the following questions: (*a*) Is the purpose statement satisfactory? (*b*) Is there a logical and clear relationship between the purpose statement and each main division, and between the main and minor entries? Do the Roman numerals point back to the thesis, and the capital letters to the Roman numerals? (*c*) Is the outline sufficiently developed to be thoroughly useful? (*d*) Can each entry be adequately developed in the final essay?

## Exercises

**A.** In each of the following pairs of outlines one version is the student's original; the other is his revision after a conference with his instructor. Study each pair carefully, identify the revised version, and explain in a short report the reasons for the revisions.

(1)

To show how the Tennessee Valley will benefit by the various projects carried on by TVA

I. Production of fertilizer to aid agriculture
 A. Prevention of erosion
II. Production of cheap electricity
 A. Electrical appliances will be encouraged in every household
 B. Electric power will attract great industries to the valley
III. The goal of TVA is to provide a more assured existence for everyone in the valley
 A. Housing plans for model communities
 B. Development of waterways to stimulate tourist trade
 C. Government instruction in practical subjects
IV. Federal government justified in creating TVA

To show the means by which TVA hopes to improve economic and living conditions in the Tennessee Valley

I. Agricultural improvements
 A. Prevention of erosion
 B. Production of cheap fertilizer
 C. Government advice to farmers
II. Industrial improvements
 A. Attraction of large industries through supply of cheap electric power
 B. Promotion of local industries through government instruction
 C. Development of waterways to stimulate tourist trade
III. Improvements in living conditions
 A. Development of model communities
 B. Increased housing facilities
 C. Extensive use of electrical appliances in all homes

(2)

To show Elizabeth's contribution to the development of the English Navy

I. Condition of navy prior to Elizabeth's reign
   A. Its size compared with first rate navies
   B. Its lack of government support
   C. Its inefficient use

II. Elizabeth's support of the "Sea Dogs" — Drake, Frobisher, Howard, Raleigh, and Grenville
   A. Political and economic reasons for her support
   B. Nature and extent of her support

III. Results of Elizabeth's support of Sea Dogs
   A. Economic rivalry with Spain
   B. Defeat of Armada and new prestige of English navy
   C. Extensive shipbuilding program to forestall Spanish retaliation
   D. More efficient design for ships
   E. Improved theory of naval warfare
   F. Foundation of English naval tradition

IV. Summary of condition of navy at end of Elizabeth's reign in contrast to condition described in I above

To show Elizabeth's contribution to the development of the English Navy

I. Condition of navy prior to Elizabeth's reign
   A. Navy relatively small in comparison with other first rate powers
   B. Inadequate government attention to fleet

II. Development of naval warfare during the period
   A. Importance of battle with Spanish Armada
      1. Types of warfare used by both sides
      2. Defeat of Armada a turning point in English naval history
   B. Brief description of offensive and defensive forces of English navy
      1. Classification of ships as to size and armament
      2. Location of forces
   C. Work of Elizabethan Sea Dogs
      1. Influence upon Elizabeth
      2. Sea Dog fighting tactics
         a. Work of Drake
         b. Treatment of Spanish ships

III. Comparison of formation and battle tactics of Elizabethan and modern navies
   A. Factors of formation and battle tactics
   B. Closing paragraph

**B.** The following student outline looks good but is completely useless as a controlling plan for a long essay. All its weaknesses have their origin in the thesis. Study the outline carefully. Apply the tests for the thesis and for the relation among parts. Discuss the outline in class.

*Thesis:* The Munich Conference was in reality a political poker game.
   I. Hitler held three tens in the game.
      A. The ten of clubs was manpower.
         1. Hitler had much power and made the men join the Nazi party.

2. The children that were born were brought up to love war and were therefore confirmed Nazis.

B. The ten of hearts was morale of the people.
1. Austria had been taken seemingly without bloodshed.
2. The rich industrialists were backing Hitler because they were jealous of the money and the power that the Jews were accumulating.

C. The ten of diamonds was air power.
1. Hitler had more planes, he said, than England, France, and Czechoslovakia together.
2. England was not all out for war at this time and had less planes than did Hitler.

II. England held a pair of aces but was bluffed out because she wanted peace so badly.

A. The ace of spades was finance.
1. Hitler was using all his money for war preparations.
2. The English knew that they could get financial help from the United States if necessary.

B. The ace of hearts was sea power.
1. Germany and England made an agreement that Germany was to have 35% as much sea power as England.
2. Hitler had built 250 submarines which was against the Treaty of Versailles, but England let him go because they were afraid of war.

III. France held a pair of fives.

A. The five of clubs was foreign relations.
1. England would have entered the war on the side of France although neither country was prepared for war.
2. Czechoslovakia would not have had to bow down to Hitler if France and England had not sold her out.

B. The five of spades was the poor government of France.
1. The government of France accepted the ultimatum of Germany in regard to Czechoslovakia although they had not been delegated to do so.
2. France undermined the Czech government by telling them to wait; they did, until it was too late.

**C.** Fit the following statements into their appropriate place in the framework that follows and supply statements for I and II. Since the order of statements under I and II may vary, put first the statement which has the lowest number. Thus the statements under I should be arranged with the first appropriate statement opposite A, the next opposite B, and so on.

F 1. Speed of air travel is its major advantage.
A 2. Fear has been the greatest deterrent to passenger travel by air.
A 3. Time and cost to airport is another deterrent.
F 4. Frequency of service has stimulated growth.

A 5. Advance reservation has been a drawback.

A 6. Baggage limitation is an inconvenience to commercial travellers.

F 7. There is a probable saving in the cost of air travel.

A 8. Air sickness and other discomforts are still prevalent to some degree.

A 9. Cancellations of flights are still too high to satisfy the traveling public.

*Thesis:* The growth of air passenger travel has been affected by both favorable and adverse factors.

    I. ...................................................

        A. ...............................................

        B. ...............................................

        C. ...............................................

    II. ...................................................

        A. ...............................................

        B. ...............................................

        C. ...............................................

        D. ...............................................

        E. ...............................................

        F. ...............................................

**D.** The purpose statement and Roman numerals of a student outline are given below. Under them are statements that comprise the capital letters and Arabic numerals. From these two sets of data, reconstruct the complete outline. It is not important that all students agree in the order of every statement. Some statements could fit under I or II or both, and you will have to decide how you will treat them. This is a normal problem in outlining.

The purpose of my paper is to reveal what the plastic surgeons are doing to restore function and improve the appearance of scarred and wounded veterans of World War II.

    I. The primary aim of the plastic surgeon is to restore function.

    II. The plastic surgeon is also interested in improving the appearance of scarred and wounded veterans.

F 1. The hands and arms are among the first portions of the body to be restored.

A 2. The plastic surgeon can rebuild an entire new face for the patient.

A 3. Noses are rebuilt to enable patients to breathe and to improve appearance.

F 4. New eyelids are made to protect eyes.

F 5. Leg and arm stumps may be made healthy and alive by plastic surgery before artificial limbs are applied.

A 6. Scars that make veterans hideous are removed.

A 7. Patients are restored to their former likeness as nearly as possible.

A 8. Ears are restored by plastic surgery.

F 9. New tendons are put into fingers so they can move.

A 10. Skin grafts are done on burns that are too noticeable.

F. 11. Thumb and forefinger are most important to save so hand can function.

F. 12. Lower jaws are rebuilt so that veteran can eat, drink, and speak naturally.

F. 13. Entire forearms are rebuilt by plastic surgery.

A. 14. Scars that are opened and undermined, then sewed together, heal neatly without scarring.

F. 15. Hands are most important for veteran to help himself.

F. 16. Surgeons connect live tissue to paralyzed area to heal it almost without a defect.

# 5

\*

\*   **P U R P O S E F U L**

\*

\*   **D E T A I L S**

\*

Once you have determined the purpose and structure of your essay, you have completed the "rough work" of composition. From then on your problem is similar to that of a portrait painter who has blocked out the head he is about to paint and has all the features in their right places and proportions. His next job is to bring out the details of these features so as to make the portrait lifelike. So your task, after you have worked out the purpose and structural pattern of your paper, is to fill in the details which will transform your plan into a finished composition. To do that successfully you must be aware of two things: first, the need for detailed development; second, the distinction between details which actually help to achieve your purpose and those which merely pad your writing without improving it.

## Detailed Versus General Statement

Let us begin by contrasting an undeveloped and a well developed account of the same experience:

### A Terrifying Experience

One fine day a friend and I went fishing. After we had fished for several hours I felt tired. Since my friend was not willing to quit I decided to take a nap until he was ready to go home; so I stretched out on the ground and soon fell asleep.

I was awakened by my friend's voice close at hand. He warned me not to move, that a rattlesnake was crawling towards me, and that if I lay still it would probably pass by and not hurt me.

At first I thought he was joking, but I soon realized the wisdom of his advice; so I closed my eyes and lay still. Soon I felt the snake's clammy body on my arm. I was terribly scared, but I had enough sense to remain motionless. I could feel the snake crawl slowly across my body and once when I opened my eyes I could see him looking at me. Then, after what seemed ages, he moved on.

I must have fainted, because the next thing I remember my friend was shaking me. He said I looked like a ghost, and the way I felt he was probably right.

Before you go on to the next version, stop a minute. The author's purpose in this paper was to reproduce for his readers an experience which must indeed have been terrifying. If he has succeeded, you, as the reader, should have shared as much of that experience as it is possible to transmit in writing. Have you done so? Has the writer done all he could to make you feel what he felt while the snake was crawling over him? Try to answer this question before you read the second version.

It was a perfect afternoon, grand fishing weather, and Mack and I had had splendid luck in the morning, each having caught four fine bass. Now the sun was just touching the top of the east wall of Apple River Canyon, which is really not a canyon although the natives call it that. It was late afternoon, and I do not believe I ever saw the fast-running water sparkle more, or the rocks of the canyon reflect their reds and blues more brilliantly. Just above the rapids Mack was slowly "whipping" his fly on the surface of a quiet, deep pond that was nestled close against the steep rock wall. I was tired of fishing; so, in order to enjoy the west rays of the sun, I clambered up the wall toward a small shelf that hung over the water. After carefully laying down my rod, I stretched out to rest before starting the long walk back to camp.

I had dozed a few minutes, when that silent sixth sense which all people who sleep in the wilderness have, made me wake up suddenly, but without moving. I lay thus for a very short time, when I heard the voice of Mack, who apparently was below and to the left of me.

"Listen, Joe," he cautioned quietly, "don't be alarmed at what I am going to say, and under no circumstances must you move a muscle of your body, or ask me why you must not."

He spoke quietly, reassuringly, but what he said was as sharp and cold as ice-water. It was something like being told that an executioner's squad you were facing had only blank bullets in its guns. Obeying this tone in his voice, I remained perfectly motionless, and he spoke again.

"Now listen carefully, and again, don't move," he warned. "There is a rattlesnake about a foot from you, and slowly approaching you. You will be perfectly safe if you don't move. Perhaps he will crawl around you, but he will not strike if you do not move. I shall not speak again, because it might frighten him."

My muscles tensed; the blood rushed to my face; I wanted to jump and run, anything to get out of there. The thought flashed through my mind that perhaps my companion was joking, but almost the minute it entered, I knew that no one, speaking the way he did, could be joking. Lord! What could I do? If I could only see the snake, perhaps I could kill it, but I dared not move. Thus I waited, unable to analyze my feelings, almost sure of certain death if I moved. I closed my eyes and waited. Suddenly I felt something on the biceps of my right arm — a queer light touch, clinging for an instant — and then the smooth glide of an oily body. I could feel the muscles of the snake's body slowly contract, then relax as it slid smoothly, oh, how smoothly across my naked arm. Again and again that body contracted, and again and again it relaxed. At last I saw a flat, V-shaped head, with two glistening, black protruding buttons. A thin, pointed, sickening yellow tongue slipped out, then in, accompanied by a sound like that of escaping steam. Slowly, slowly it advanced, the rounded spots on its back and sides drawing together and then stretching to their length as it moved slowly forward. When it was about in the middle of my chest, it paused, slowly turned its head toward me, and fixed its cold, boring eyes in my direction. Now I could not have moved had I wished; I was fascinated. So he remained, darting his tongue out and in. Finally he slowly, very slowly, turned his head, and again moved forward. Once more I had to see and feel the slow contraction, relaxation, contraction, relaxation. The body began to narrow, the spots grew smaller, the cracks on his revolting greenish-white stomach grew closer together and more minute. At last the slender, whipping tail appeared on my chest, and then so slowly slid along until . . .

My head felt so queer; up and down, up and down it went. Why, my face was all wet! I weakly shoved at the bronzed arm that shook me, and asked, "What's the matter?"

"God! and only a couple of minutes!" I heard a voice filter into my brain. "Wonderful! I don't think I could have let a rattler crawl across me. Lord! but you're clammy, and look at your muscles and veins. Your face looks like a dead man's." [1]

The first version, of course, has all the benefit of surprise. Yet there can be no doubt which is the more effective. The first account tells you about the experience; the second makes you live it. The second snake is real. You can see its markings, feel the contraction of its muscles, see that thin tongue flashing. You can see the cracks on the greenish-white belly. And when the thin tail finally slides off Joe's chest you are almost as relieved as he was.

A comparison of these two versions will show just how the second achieves its effect. It is clear that this effect comes from skillful use of details, but what constitutes this "skillful use"? Suppose you conduct a little experiment. Take a sheet of paper and rule it down the middle. On one side note details from the first version; on the other side put the same detail as it is expressed in the second version. Here are some samples:

[1] Joe Daly, "Too Close." From *The Green Caldron: A Magazine of Freshman Writing* (October, 1934), published at the University of Illinois, Urbana, Illinois. Reprinted by permission.

| *First Version* | *Second Version* |
|---|---|
| One fine day | It was a perfect afternoon. . . . I do not believe that I ever saw the fast-running water sparkle more, or the rocks of the canyon reflect their reds and blues more brilliantly. |
| A friend | Mack |
| I stretched out on the ground. | I clambered up the wall toward a small shelf that hung over the water. After carefully laying down my rod I stretched out to rest. |
| He warned me **not** to move. | He spoke quietly, reassuringly, but what he said was as sharp and cold as ice-water. It was something like being told that an executioner's squad you were facing had only blank bullets in its guns. |
| I was terribly scared. | My muscles tensed; the blood rushed to my head; I wanted to jump and run . . . Lord! What could I do? If I could only see the snake, perhaps I could kill it, but I dared not move. Thus I waited, unable to analyze my feelings, almost sure of certain death if I moved. |
| Soon I felt the snake's clammy body on my arm. | Suddenly I felt something on the biceps of my right arm — a queer, light touch, clinging for an instant — and then the smooth glide of an oily body. |

If you make this comparison conscientiously, you will learn more about how to use details than you are likely to learn from pages of advice. You will learn that there is a vast difference between recreating an experience and merely summarizing it. You will see that the second account gives a clear picture of the event and that the author is concerned with bringing out all its significant details, whereas in the first version the writer has not called up the scene before him and expects the reader to do what is essentially the writer's responsibility — that is, to create the scene and the event in his imagination.

You will also learn from this comparison that one by-product of detailed writing is greater length. For students who find it hard to develop any paper beyond a few hundred words this discovery should be a boon. You will not be tempted to say, "That's all there is to tell. I can't make it any longer unless I pad it." You will understand that supplying details to bring out the implications of general statements is not padding but the essence of successful communication.

Finally, you will notice that a hackneyed word or phrase does not get the effect obtained by fresher and sharper diction. Contrast, for example, "I felt the snake's clammy body on my arm" with "I felt something on the biceps of my right arm — a queer, light touch, clinging for an instant — and then the smooth glide of an oily body." The difference between these two statements is not that the second writer knows more words than the first. The real difference is that one writer communicates the details by which the reader can recreate the experience, while the other does not. The first writer did not lack words; he lacked the willingness to live the experience over again so that his reader might live it with him.

## Choosing Effective Details

Well-chosen details make writing more meaningful by making it more specific. Details are the illustrative materials with which a writer develops his general statements so as to convey their full significance to a reader. The materials may be actions, ideas, sense-impressions, emotional attitudes, factual information, statistical data — they may be almost anything. All that matters is that they be chosen to create deliberate effects and that they do create these effects.

Let us look at a series of writing assignments, considering what details are needed to fulfill these assignments, and then showing the result when the appropriate details have been provided.

**Assignment A**

A writer wishes to praise the mayor for his conduct of the city government. Selecting the details in this assignment is easy, since their function is to itemize or enumerate the specific accomplishments of the mayor's administration.

> Morrison's accomplishments have reached far beyond delousing the city of underworld parasites. He drove through a $50,000,000 public-works program and bond issue which will provide a new union station, a new civic center, new express highways and streets — and incidentally eliminate 144 dangerous grade crossings. His administration lopped off deadheads, reducing city payrolls by 600; established the first real pension fund for city employees; saved the municipality $500,000 annually by centralizing purchasing, and — miracle of miracles in boss-ridden New Orleans — inaugurated open meetings of the city council where municipal business is transacted at announced times each week in front of any citizen who wants to watch. An overdraft of $1,000,000, inherited from his predecessor, Robert S. Maestri, has been wiped out and a $1,500,000 surplus rolled up.[2]

**Assignment B**

A writer wishes to describe a room in such a way as to characterize the man who lives in it. That man is an unpleasant and pathetic personality who is both morbidly self-centered and shy. The details, then,

[2] From Ralph Wallace, "Chap Morrison — Mayor," *Forum*, May, 1948, p. 271.

must be selected to bring out these qualities. The writer must select from all the details of the room only those that reveal the man's exaggerated concern with himself, and his shyness. Here is the description:

It was an overcrowded museum of everything connected with himself, the fantastic monument to a singularly uninteresting past. Little space remained on the walls between enlarged snapshots of Mr. Wallace at all ages — baby pictures and photographs of choir-outings and army groups in which he figured — and an assortment of framed certificates proving that he had joined the Derry branch of the Primrose League in 1909, maintained an unbroken attendance at choir practice in the same town during 1911, and completed a course in first-aid, prior to taking out a druggist's license to sell patent medicines as well as groceries in 1912. In that year he had also moved over the border to Kildooey; several photographs testified to this, all were dated and bore explanations: "Day of Arrival. R. J. W. approaching shop," "R. J. W. by Kildooey bridge. The first Sunday." . . . The few inches of the wall-space which remained, round about eye-level, had been filled by tacked-up showcards; on these were gummed a series of apparently pointless souvenirs. "A pretty seashell. Picked up by R. J. W. at Drumross Head, Whitsun, 1913," or a piece of bog-oak, "Found by R. J. W. on a walk near Kilcar, August bank Holiday, 1913." In group-photographs, where other people had crowded nearer the camera, partly eclipsing him, he had identified himself with an arrow or a cross as well as his initials, lest he should fail to be recognized by the unknown spectator for whom this display was arranged. There were many pictures in which he was only half visible; a burning diffidence seemed to keep him always hanging about the outskirts of any little assembly, so that he was easily pushed aside. No other names and initials were given in his records of days gone by. And into this house, Bridie had said, no one but himself came, from month's end to month's end. While none at all ever came willingly, without a business intention.[3]

## Assignment C

A writer wishes to explain the time-lag between the onset of a rainstorm and the flooding of the rivers. Essentially the answer is that the dry earth is capable of absorbing a great deal of water and that the rivers will not begin to flood until the earth is saturated. What kind of details does he need? Those that will show the actual mechanics of absorption — the means by which the rain is soaked up. His real purpose is to spell out the meaning of the general statement, "dry ground absorbs water." He can do that only by showing the rain actually being absorbed.

*strong attraction* *soggy*

By deep affinity, every grain of dust drew water to itself. The punky dryness of rotting logs grew slowly sodden. In the thickets of blackberry, and toyon, and poison oak, the dead leaves lay deep; beneath these rested

*Evergreen bush*

[3] From E. A. Robertson, *The Signpost*. Copyright, 1944, by Eileen A. Robertson Turner. Used by permission of The Macmillan Company.

*pick out words saying dry ground picking up water.*

the half rotted leaves and twigs of older years, and still deeper the mould of generations. This porous mass sucked moisture like a stiff sponge, and paradoxically the life-giving water even woke to new vigor the very processes of decay.

*seemingly contradictory qualities*

Still more, the living vegetation sucked in and held the rain. How many bucketfuls to change from black to green all the moss upon the rocks? How many tank-cars to wet all the pine-needles and all the oak leaves? How many trains of tank-cars to uncurl all the blades of grass upon all the hills? Leaves shrunken to conserve moisture expanded and grew heavy; drooping shoots stood up stiff and vigorous. The very cells expanded, and the protoplasm for its subtle chemistry absorbed to itself countless tons of water.

*dull grayish brown*

Even animal life drew in the water. Cattle and horses grew dark beneath the downpour. The fleeces of the sheep were heavy. Deer in the forest glades changed from dun to brown. Through the tunnels of ants and beetles the moisture seeped downward. The channels of earthworms were as millions of conduits. The myriad far-ranging burrows of gophers and ground-squirrels took the trickles deeper still. Then at last following

*openings*

the fissures of the earth itself the seeping moisture from the surface reached ground which was no longer dry, and began to join that great fluctuating reservoir of the waters which are beneath the earth.

Until all this should be fully achieved, the river was low. As well expect water to stand in a sieve as streams to run high before the land itself was satisfied.[4]

## Assignment D

A housewife who was a victim of the notorious radio scare when Orson Welles broadcast his realistic version of *The War of the Worlds* was asked to report her experience to a psychologist who was studying the hysteria created by the broadcast. What was her purpose? It was to re-create as well as possible what she actually did, thought, and said when she heard the program. She had to recall the details which would reveal her fear and confusion. Here is her report:

We listened getting more and more excited. We all felt the world was coming to an end. Then we heard "Get gas masks!" That was the part that got me. I thought I was going crazy. It's a wonder my heart didn't fail me because I'm nervous anyway. I felt if the gas was on, I wanted to be together with my husband and nephew so we could all die together. So I ran out of the house. I guess I didn't know what I was doing. I stood on the corner waiting for a bus and I thought every car that came along was a bus and I ran out to get it. People saw how excited I was and tried to quiet me, but I kept saying over and over again to everybody I met: "Don't you know New Jersey is destroyed by the Germans — it's on the radio." I was all excited and I knew that Hitler didn't appreciate President Roosevelt's telegram a couple of weeks ago.

---

4 From *Storm* by George R. Stewart. Copyright, 1941, by George R. Stewart. Reprinted by permission of Random House, Inc.

While the U.S. thought everything was settled, they came down unexpected. The Germans are so wise they were in something like a balloon and when the balloon landed — that's when they announced the explosion — the Germans landed. When I got home my husband wasn't there so I rushed in next door and warned the neighbors that the world was coming to an end. My aunt was there and she tried to quiet me and said, "If God is coming that way, we just have to wait — go home and be quiet — don't be excited." I went home. My knees were shaking so, I could hardly walk up the stairs. I found my nephew had come home and gone to bed. I woke him up. I looked in the ice-box and saw some chicken left from Sunday dinner that I was saving for Monday night dinner. I said to my nephew, "We may as well eat this chicken — we won't be here in the morning." Then my husband came in. When I told him about it, he wasn't as excited as I was, but he thought it was the end of the world coming, too. He turned on our radio to WOR. It was eleven o'clock and we heard it announced that it was only a play. It sure felt good — just like a burden was lifted off me.[5]  *STOP*

## Assignment E

A writer intends to elaborate the thesis that leading one's own life in America requires more social courage than most of us have. What kind of details are required? Obviously those that show people being forced by social pressure into a pattern which they would not adopt voluntarily and which destroys their individuality. The range of such details is wide. We have already seen one example in the essay, "Social Pressure," in Chapter 2. In the following selection the writer has used clothes as his examples, and contrasts the individuality of English clothes with the standardized dress of Americans:

Americans pride themselves on their courage and individuality and brag of the frontier virtues, but the fact is we are the most cowardly race in the world socially. Read Emerson's essay on *Self-Reliance* and ask yourself honestly how much you dare to be yourself. He has been called the most essentially American of our authors, but would he be so today? . . . Take the matter of clothes as a simple touchstone of individuality. Every American woman who goes to London is either shocked, interested, or amused by the variety of women's dress there. Most of it, except sport clothes, is, I admit, extremely bad, but the point is that a woman dresses just as she pleases. Little girls may have long black stockings or legs bare to their full length; older women may have skirts that display the knee or drag the ground; hats of the latest mode from Paris, or from Regent Street when Victoria was a girl. Watching the passing crowd on the Broad Walk is like turning the pages of *Punch* for half a century. A man may wear any headgear from a golf cap to a pearl satin "topper." Compare this, for example, with New York and the mass antics of the Stock Exchange where if a man wears a straw hat beyond the day ap-

[5] From Hadley Cantril's *The Invasion From Mars,* Copyright 1940 by Princeton University Press. Reprinted by permission.

Atlantic City

Eng, Mag, of humor

pointed by his fellows they smash it down over his eyes, and where he is not safe from similar moronic hoodlumism even in the streets. . . . One has to fight to be oneself in America as in no other country I know. Not only are most Americans anxious to conform to the standards of the majority, but that majority, and the advertisers, insist that they shall.[6]

It will be obvious from these five assignments that the main source of details for most kinds of writing which students will do in composition courses is the writer's personal observation. For some assignments we may obtain our materials from special reading, but mostly we reproduce them from personal experience. We may report our experience directly, as when we describe a scene or a person we are looking at. Or we may review — "see again" — the details in our memories. However we do it, our task as writers is to give the reader the details which he needs to understand what we wish to tell him.

## Purposeful Selection of Details

Details are not good in themselves; they are good when they help the writer make himself clear to the reader. Hence they must be selected to fit the writer's purpose. Details which have no relation to that purpose will be worse than useless; for the concrete quality which makes them effective when well chosen will make them conspicuous or even misleading when they are inappropriate or irrelevant.

The selections presented so far in this chapter have illustrated purposeful use of details. But look at this paragraph:

> Perhaps the best vantage-point from which I may view the sights of the town is the platform of the depot. The Chicago local stops daily and the mail clerks heave the mail into the baggage car and pull the wagon back to the express room. After the local has left, the switch engine begins shunting the box cars in the yards, and my eyes idly turn to look down the quiet street. A small theater can be seen across the street. The name of the feature is printed on the canopy. In front of the hotel which stands next door can be seen the usual crowd. People lean over the bridge over the creek. The creek would lead you beneath the hotel and various business houses to the gas plant. From this coal gas plant issues black smoke. The fireman regularly stokes the fires in the huge ovens. The smell of gas and coal tar prevails in the entire area around the gas plant.

This paragraph is full of details, but what are they supposed to do? As far as we can tell, the paragraph starts out to describe the town as it is seen from the railroad platform, but instead of selecting descriptive

---

[6] From James T. Adams, *Our Business Civilization.* Copyright, 1929, by Albert & Charles Boni, Inc. Reprinted by permission of the publishers.

details for that purpose, the writer lets his attention wander, and he records any detail that comes to mind. The loading of the mail car and the shunting of the box cars are pictorial, but they do not describe the town. Even when the writer does turn his attention to the town, he fails in two ways. First, he selects too few details to give a clear picture, for he mentions only the theater, the crowd before the hotel, and the people leaning over the bridge. Second, he drifts into irrelevant details — the course of the creek and the stoking of the ovens, neither of which is evident from the station platform. The result is an incoherent paragraph which fails to do its job.

In the following paragraph most of the details are wisely chosen to bring out England's veneration of her past, but those in italics have no relation to that purpose and are awkward digressions:

> England's veneration for the past is revealed in a myriad of trifling ceremonies and customs, some glorious, some, at least to a foreigner, amusingly old-fashioned. It is seen in the pomp and pageantry with which England loves to invest its public ceremonies — the opening of parliament, the patriarchal royal carriage, the Lord Mayor's barge, the Beef-eater's pike, the vintner's procession, *the lamp-lighter, the communal and unsanitary drinking fountains, the lack of refrigeration in meat and fish shops, and the fruit and vegetable stalls with their wares exposed to the flies and the dirt of the city.* It is seen, especially, in the profusion of monuments that flourish in the cities. London is full of memorials to people and events that seem insignificant today. Westminster Abbey is crammed with statues, plaques, and busts of heroes long dead and comfortably forgotten. A few of the monuments may be pushed obscurely into a corner, but none is ever discarded. Year after year new relics are crowded in upon the old as the nation adds to its memories.

The inappropriate details have slipped into the writing because the writer failed to keep his purpose clearly in mind. His thesis committed him to present only those details which illustrated pomp and pageantry. But his mind wandered, for part of one long sentence, from ancient ceremonials to inefficiency and unsanitary conditions.

## Revision for Greater Detail

In Chapter 2 the essay, "So This Is College," was quoted to show that when a writer has his purpose clearly in mind his thinking is so concentrated that the details he needs come crowding in upon him as he writes. For the most part, experienced writers seldom have to dig hard in their memories for the details they will use; their chief problem is rather to choose from the wealth of details at their disposal those which will give the best results.

But inexperienced writers may profit by studying their first drafts with a view to adding details wherever the writing seems too general. This does not mean that the insertion of detail is a separate step in the composition of an essay; but revision need not be confined to improvements in grammar, punctuation, and diction. If the first draft can be improved by adding details which increase vividness or improve clarity, they should be added. The following paragraphs illustrate. The parenthetical numbers at the left show where the correspondingly numbered details at the right should be inserted during revision.

Many of the girls on this campus seem eager to make themselves as unattractive as possible. Their dress is slovenly. (1) They are indifferent about personal grooming. (2) They act as though being a coed requires them to dress and look as though they were working in a glue factory.

1. Sloppy jeans for skirts; bare legs and old saddle shoes instead of hose and pumps; form-fitting sweaters replaced by shapeless sweat shirts.
2. Stringy, unbarbered hair; shiny noses; untended nails.

An income of $5,500 in 1957 meant no more than a $3,200 income in 1941 or a $2,900 income in 1939. Food costs had increased considerably. (1) Clothing was much more expensive. (2) The cost of medical care had risen sharply. (3) Considering similar increases in all commodities, statisticians have estimated that from 1939 to 1957 the cost of living rose 157%.

1. Meat up 24 cents a pound; butter up 39 cents; milk rose 11 cents, eggs 25.
2. Wardrobe that cost $542 in 1941 cost $992 in 1957.
3. Visit to doctor's office rose from $2 to as much as $10.

During my undergraduate years I worked at a variety of occupations. (1) In taking these jobs I was concerned only about making enough money to meet my college expenses, but I now realize that the experience I got from working was a useful supplement to my academic education. (2)

1. Door-to-door salesman, inspector in a shovel factory; bellboy, elevator operator, night-switchboard operator, hospital orderly.
2. Taught me the value of money, gave me a sense of independence and confidence, gave me an insight into the hopes, fears, and attitudes of various kinds of people, and helped me to understand how to get along with them.

Sometimes the details may be added in a separate paragraph which illustrates the ideas expressed in general terms in the first paragraph. Here is an example:

Playgoing [in the Elizabethan period] was not the orderly activity that it is today. We go to the theatre quietly, to listen attentively to a half-literary exercise. The Elizabethans went to the public theatres boisterously, with little reverence or consideration for dramatist or actor, the dandies anxious to show themselves superior to the entertainment by which they were passing idle hours, aiming at *conspicuous* attendance, and the groundlings in the pit offering vociferous approval or disapproval at every opportunity.

If this is all the author has to say about the Elizabethan audience he has left his task only half done. From this description we get no real picture of the audience. We need more details: what kind of people went to the theater; what did they do during the play; in what ways were they inconsiderate and irreverent; and how did they make themselves conspicuous? When these details are added the picture of the audience comes into sharp focus:

> The flag flying over the building to signify "a play is on" brought, indeed, a strange audience: a pit crowd of apprentices playing "hookey," town idlers, a few shameless women, travellers intent on seeing the sights, fighters off duty, seafarers ashore, etc.; and above in the balconies students and poets and a few shrewd burghers or minor court hangers-on (perhaps with ladies, who dared come only under masculine protection); and on the stage itself the fops and beaux and noblemen, as anxious to be seen as to see, interrupting the action if they willed, smoking and talking and displaying their figures and their finery. To this queer mixture of cultured and uneducated, of lowly and exalted, of those who came for love of drama and those who came to show their superiority, the Elizabethan drama was shaped. No doubt about this vigorous audience enjoying spirited verse or swift action. No doubt about its vociferous reaction if the lines or the action became too slow or too tame. Coarseness went down agreeably, but literary fineness might kill comedy or tragedy. If anything on the stage bored, the audience took to the dice or cards; and always there was much drinking of ale and widespread eating of fruits and sweets.[7]

We know now what the author meant by his first paragraph. But it took the details of the second paragraph to make us understand. Had these details not been added, the author would have stopped short of achieving his purpose. Perhaps these samples will help you see that if you can detect a too-general statement in your first draft you can rewrite the passage to provide more detailed development.

As an exercise in revision to provide details, take the first paragraph of the purposeless essay on page 4:

> I knew this was one of the biggest universities in the country, but I never understood till I arrived on campus just how big it really is. When I first came here I was so scared that I felt like returning home. . . .

[7] From Sheldon Cheney's *The Theatre*, Copyright 1929 by Longmans, Green and Co. Reprinted by permission of Longmans, Green and Co.

Two kinds of details are needed, those to illustrate bigness, and those to show loneliness or insecurity. If your college is large, select from your own experience details to show how big it is and use them to expand the first sentence into an essay. If your college is small, jot down from experience details which illustrate loneliness or the kind of "scaredness" the boy was talking about, and use these details to develop the second sentence into an essay.

## Exercises

**A.** Without attempting to incorporate them in a piece of writing, list the details you would use if you were describing any three of the following. Actually study the subject before preparing your list.

1. Your room
2. Your roommate
3. A contrast of two instructors
4. The campus

5. The college paper
6. Your favorite eating place
7. A recent social event
8. Your work in composition

**B.** Choose one of these subjects and develop it into a fair-sized paragraph.

**C.** Suppose you are writing to a friend who intends to come to college next year. Supply the necessary details so that he will fully understand what you mean by the following general statements:

1. Freshman week is exciting.
2. Registration is the world's worst headache.
3. There is likely to be a good deal of confusion during the first week of classes.
4. College professors are not a special breed of people.
5. Methods of teaching vary with the instructors.
6. Assignments are going to take longer than they did in high school.
7. I have already had some useful advice from upper classmen.
8. College life isn't all work.

**D.** In the following passage all the details have been numbered. In a short report, first list the numbers of those details which you consider appropriate to the writer's purpose; then list those which you consider inappropriate; finally explain why you consider each item in the second list inappropriate.

If a sociologist of the year 2500 were to write a history of the Victorian society solely on linguistic evidence, he would have to conclude that its members enjoyed a special dispensation from the usual laws of nature. (1) Men did not die; they passed away, or went to their rest, or answered the last summons, or slept with their fathers, or met their Maker, or did something equally romantic. (2) Transportation, without the aid of the airplane, the automobile, electricity, or the diesel engine, was still primitive. (3) Except for the daily newspapers, the means of communication were scarcely different from what they had been in Shakespeare's day, since there was neither radio nor telephone to flash messages around the world in a few seconds. (4) Men did not spit or sweat; they expectorated and perspired. (5) Women had no legs, only limbs. (6) They were not allowed to vote or to hold public office. (7) Only lower-class babies were born; the others were issued into the world or came to bless the home. (8) Pregnancy was unknown; instead the mothers passed through an interesting (or delicate) condition before their little strangers were deposited by the stork. (9) Labor unions were struggling into existence, but the Anti-Combinations Act, which made it a penal offense for any two workmen to talk together about ways of increasing their wages or improving their working conditions, forced the unions underground. (10) Thanks to such men as Darwin, Huxley, Galton, and Lyell, science was beginning to dominate thought, but the poets, especially Tennyson, were afraid of it and of its repercussions on the stability of religious beliefs. (11) Polite members of society did not put on their clothes, eat, or go to bed; rather they dressed, dined, and retired. (12) Flowers, food, and breath did not smell; they emitted an odor. (13) Bellies were nonexistent among animals, with the embarrassing exception of the whale, which had indelicately been given a belly in the Biblical account of Jonah's misfortunes — probably as a result of faulty translation. The only abdominal organ was the stomach. (14) Anyone who did not belong to the Church of England was considered a nonconformist and was often subject to economic and political discrimination.

**E.** The following selection is a brilliant example of the effective use of details. Read it carefully, with special attention to (*a*) the kinds of details used — actions, sights, sounds, etc., (*b*) the appropriateness of specific details to the author's purpose at the moment, (*c*) the most memorable details in the whole article.

### R.M.S. TITANIC [8]

The sea was surging into the Titanic's hold. At 12:20 the water burst into the seamen's quarters through a collapsed fore and aft wooden bulkhead. Pumps strained in the engine-rooms — men and machinery making a futile fight against the sea. Steadily the water rose.

The boats were swung out — slowly; for the deckhands were late in reaching their stations, there had been no boat drill, and many of the crew did not know to what boats they were assigned. Orders were

[8] From Hanson Baldwin's *R.M.S. Titanic* (Harper's Magazine, January, 1934). Copyright, Hanson W. Baldwin, 1934. Reprinted by permission of Willis Kingsley Wing.

shouted; the safety valves had lifted, and steam was blowing off in a great rushing roar. In the chart house Fourth Officer Boxhall bent above a chart, working rapidly with pencil and dividers.

12:25 A.M. Boxhall's position is sent out to a fleet of vessels: "Come at once; we have struck a berg."

To the Cunarder Carpathia (Arthur Henry Rostron, Master, New York to Liverpool, fifty-eight miles away): "It's a CQD, old man. Position 41-46 N.; 50-14 W."

The blue spark dancing: "Sinking; cannot hear for noise of steam."

12:30 A.M. The word is passed: "Women and children in the boats." Stewards finish waking their passengers below; life-preservers are tied on; some men smile at the precaution. "The Titanic is unsinkable." The Mt. Temple starts for the Titanic; the Carpathia, with a doublewatch in her stokeholds, radios, "Coming hard." The CQD changes the course of many ships — but not of one; the operator of the Californian, nearby, has just put down his ear-phones and turned in.

The CQD flashes over land and sea from Cape Race to New York; newspaper city rooms leap to life and presses whir.

On the Titanic, water creeps over the bulkhead between No. 5 and 6 firerooms. She is going down by the head; the engineers — fighting a losing battle — are forced back foot by foot by the rising water. Down the promenade deck, Happy Jock Hume, the bandsman, runs with his instrument.

12:45 A.M. Murdoch, in charge on the starboard side, eyes tragic, but calm and cool, orders boat No. 7 lowered. The women hang back; they want no boat-ride on an ice-strewn sea; the Titanic is unsinkable. The men encourage them, explain that this is just a precautionary measure: "We'll see you again at breakfast." There is little confusion; passengers stream slowly to the boat deck. In the steerage the immigrants chatter excitedly.

A sudden sharp hiss — a streaked flare against the night; Boxhall sends a rocket toward the sky. It explodes, and a parachute of white stars lights up the icy sea. "God! Rockets!" The band plays ragtime.

No. 8 is lowered, and No. 5. Ismay, still in dressing gown, calls for women and children, handles lines, stumbles in the way of an officer, is told to "get the hell out of here." Third Officer Pitman takes charge of No. 5; as he swings into the boat Murdoch grasps his hand. "Good-by and good luck old man."

No. 6 goes over the side. There are only twenty-eight people in a life-boat with a capacity of sixty-five.

A light stabs from the bridge; Boxhall is calling in Morse flashes, again and again, to a strange ship stopped in the ice jam five to ten miles away. Another rocket drops its shower of sparks above the ice-strewn sea and the dying ship.

1:00 A.M. Slowly the water creeps higher; the fore ports of the Titanic are dipping into the sea. Rope squeaks through blocks; lifeboats drop jerkily seaward. Through the shouting on the decks comes the sound of the band playing ragtime.

The "Millionaires' Special" leaves the ship — boat No. 1 with a capacity of forty people, carries only Sir Cosmo and Lady Duff Gordon and ten others. Aft, the frightened immigrants mill and jostle and rush for a boat. An officer's fist flies out; three shots are fired in the air, and the panic is quelled. . . . Four Chinese sneak unseen into a boat and hide in its bottom.

1:20 A.M. Water is coming into No. 4 boiler room. Stokers slice and shovel as water laps about their ankles — steam for the dynamos, steam for the dancing spark! As the water rises, great ash hoes rake the flaming coals from the furnaces. Safety valves open; the stokers retreat aft, and the water-tight doors clang shut behind them.

The rockets fling their splendor toward the stars. The boats are more heavily loaded now, for the passengers know the Titanic is sinking. Women cling and sob. The great screws aft are rising clear of the sea. Half-filled boats are ordered to come alongside the cargo ports and take on more passengers, but the ports are never opened — and the boats are never filled. Others pull for the steamer's light miles away but never reach it; the lights disappear, the unknown ship steams off.

The water rises and the band plays ragtime.

1:30 A.M. Lightoller is getting the port boats off; Murdoch the starboard. As one boat is lowered into the sea a boat officer fires his gun along the ship's side to stop a rush from the lower decks. A woman tries to take her Great Dane into a boat with her; she is refused and steps out of the boat to die with her dog. Millet's "little smile which played on his lips all through the voyage" plays no more; his lips are grim, but he waves good-by and brings wraps for the women.

Benjamin Guggenheim, in evening clothes, smiles and says, "We've dressed up in our best and are prepared to go down like gentlemen."

1:40 A.M. Boat 14 is clear, then 13, 16, 15 and C. The lights still shine, but the Baltic hears the blue spark say, "Engine-room getting flooded."

The Olympic signals, "Am lighting up all possible boilers as fast as can."

Major Butt helps women into the last boat and waves good-by to them. Mrs. Straus puts her foot on the gunwale of a lifeboat, then she draws back and goes to her husband: "We have been together many years; where you go I will go." Colonel John Jacob Astor puts his young wife in a lifeboat, steps back, taps cigarette on fingernail: "Good-by, dearie; I'll join you later."

1:45 A.M. The foredeck is under water, the fo'c'sle head almost awash; the great stern is lifted high toward the bright stars; and still the band plays. Mr. and Mrs. Harris approach a lifeboat arm in arm.

Officer: "Ladies first, please."

Harris bows, smiles, steps back: "Of course, certainly; ladies first."

Boxhall fires the last rocket, then leaves in charge of boat No. 2.

2:00 A.M. She is dying now; her bow goes deeper, her stern higher. But there must be steam. Below in the stokeholds the sweaty firemen keep steam up for the flaring lights and the dancing spark. The glowing coals slide and tumble over the slanted grate bars; the sea pounds behind that yielding bulkhead. But the spark dances on.

The Asian hears Phillips try the new signal — SOS.

Boat No. 4 has left now; boat D leaves ten minutes later. Jacques Futrelle clasps his wife: "For God's sake, go! It's your last chance; go!" Madame Futrelle is half-forced into the boat. It clears the side.

There are about 660 people in the boats, and 1,500 still on the sinking Titanic.

On top of the officers' quarters men work frantically to get the two collapsibles stowed there over the side. Water is over the forward part of A deck now; it surges up the companionways toward the boat deck. In the radio shack, Bride has slipped a coat and lifejacket about Phillips as the first operator sits hunched over his key, sending — still sending — "41-46 N.; 50-14 W. CQD — CQD — SOS — SOS — "

The captain's tired white face appears at the radio-room door: "Men, you have done your full duty. You can do no more. Now, it's every man for himself." The captain disappears — back to his sinking bridge, where Painter, his personal steward, stands quietly waiting for orders. The spark dances on. Bride turns his back and goes into the inner cabin. As he does so, a stoker, grimed with coal, mad with fear, steals into the shack and reaches for the lifejacket on Phillips' back. Bride wheels about and brains him with a wrench.

2:10 A.M. Below decks the steam is still holding, though the pressure is falling — rapidly. In the gymnasium on the boat deck the athletic instructor watches quietly as two gentlemen ride the bicycles and another swings casually at the punching bag. Mail clerks stagger up the boat-deck stairways, dragging soaked mail sacks. The spark still dances. The band still plays — but not ragtime:

> Nearer my God to Thee,
> Nearer to Thee . . .

A few men take up the refrain; others kneel on the slanting decks to pray. Many run and scramble aft, where hundreds are clinging above the silent screws on the great uptilted stern. The spark still dances and the lights still flare; the engineers are on the job. The hymn comes to its close. Bandmaster Hartley, Yorkshireman violinist, taps his bow against a bulkhead, calls for "Autumn" as the water curls about his feet, and the eight musicians brace themselves against the ship's slant. People are leaping from the decks into the nearby water — the icy water. A woman cries, "Oh, save me!" A man answers, "Good lady, save yourself. Only God can save you now." The band plays "Autumn":

> God of Mercy and Compassion!
> Look with pity on my pain . . .

The water creeps over the bridge where the Titanic's master stands; heavily he steps out to meet it.

2:17 A.M. Men run about blackened decks; leap into the night; are swept into the sea by the curling wave which licks up the Titanic's length. Lightoller does not leave the ship; the ship leaves him; there are hundreds like him, but only a few who live to tell of it. The funnels still swim above the water, but the ship is climbing into the perpendicular; the bridge is under and most of the foremast; the great stern rises like a squat leviathan. Men swim away from the sinking ship; others drop from the stern.

The band plays in the darkness, the water lapping upwards:

> Hold me up in mighty waters
> Keep my eyes on things above,
> Righteousness, divine atonement,
> Peace and everlas. . . .

The forward funnel snaps and crashes into the sea; its steel tons hammer out of existence swimmers struggling in the freezing water. Streams of sparks, of smoke and steam, burst from the after funnels. The ship upends to 50 to 60 degrees.

Down in the black abyss of the stokeholds, of the engine-rooms, where the dynamos have whirred at long last to a stop, the stokers and the engineers are reeling against hot metal, the rising waters clutching at their knees. The boilers, the engine cylinders, rip from their bed plates; crash through bulkheads; rumble — steel against steel.

The Titanic stands on end, poised briefly for the plunge. Slowly she slides to her grave — slowly at first, and then more quickly — quickly — quickly.

2:20 A.M. The greatest ship in the world has sunk. From the calm, dark waters, where the floating lifeboats move, there goes up, in the white wake of her passing, "one long continuous moan."

# 6

**PARAGRAPHS:**

**COMPOSITIONS**

**IN MINIATURE**

A PARAGRAPH requires the same process of composition as a whole essay, though in smaller scope. An essay must have a purpose; so must a paragraph. The purpose of the essay is stated in the *thesis,* that of the paragraph in the *topic sentence.* An essay must have a pattern of development, its organization; likewise a paragraph has its order. An essay must be developed in enough detail to make its general statements meaningful; so must a paragraph. In short, a paragraph is an essay in miniature.

## Four Requirements of Good Paragraphs

A good paragraph makes clear the meaning of its topic or idea. A paragraph intended to develop a unit of an outline or to elaborate a factor of the thesis should devote itself to that task and should not stop until it has satisfactorily completed it. Its chance of succeeding will depend on how well it observes four requirements: *completeness, unity, order,* and *coherence.*

### Completeness

Detailed development is just as important in a paragraph as in a whole composition — indeed, no essay can be rounded out unless its paragraphs are. For example, look at this student essay:

### WHY I CAME TO COLLEGE

My chief reason for coming to college was to prepare myself for a position that would allow me to have a larger income than I would be likely to obtain as a high school graduate. There is no question that college graduates make more money.

Another reason for coming to college was to provide myself with a cultural background that would help me to make a more satisfying use of my leisure time.

A third reason for coming to college was to increase my social experience. Getting along with people is important, and college teaches a man to be a good mixer.

This selection is little more than an outline; each paragraph merely adds a second general statement to the topic sentence. If the function of a paragraph is to drive home the meaning of the topic sentence, then the three units of this paper can scarcely be called paragraphs at all.

The habit of confining a paragraph to a general judgment, without evidence, illustration, or support of any kind, is a major weakness of much college writing. If the author of this paper believes that a college education will improve his economic and social position, he should show his reasons for thinking so. Notice how much more complete are the paragraphs of the revised version.

## WHY I CAME TO COLLEGE

My chief reason for coming to college was to prepare myself for a position that would allow me to have a larger income than I would be likely to obtain as a high school graduate. Even though some high school graduates make reasonably good wages these days, their economic opportunities are limited in two ways: without a college degree they are not eligible for most of the good jobs, and without a degree they have less chance of promotion. I want to be an engineer. If I graduate with an engineering degree, I can expect within fifteen years of graduation to have a responsible position in management at a salary between eight and twelve thousand dollars. If I have only a high school diploma, about the most I can eventually hope for is to become a foreman at five or six thousand dollars. There is no question that in my field college graduates make more money.

Another reason for coming to college was to provide myself with a cultural background that would help me to make a more satisfying use of my leisure time. I won't be an engineer 24 hours a day. When I come home from the plant or office I expect to take an interest in what is going on in state and national politics. I expect to take an active part in community affairs. I expect to read good books, listen to good music, and engage in good talk with my wife and friends. I will owe it to myself, my wife, and my children to provide the kind of home environment in which these interests receive attention. By providing me with a wide variety of interests, college should make it easier for me to escape the limitations of my job, no matter how interesting or significant that job may be.

A third reason for coming to college was to increase my social experience. An engineer works as much with men as he does with machines. He must know how to get the cooperation of workmen, how to deal with labor leaders and government officials, how to express his ideas to management, how to represent his company in public. The ability to mix easily with people is therefore important to him. A college education, by giving him four years of intimate association with people from all parts of the country and from all walks of life, teaches a man to understand and get along with people.

This revision applies to the paragraph the lesson of Chapter 5, the use of purposeful details. If a student has learned that lesson well, his paragraphing is not likely to be incomplete. If he finds, when he revises the first draft of his paper, that any particular paragraph is too general, he can rewrite it and add the necessary details, as they were added in the revision above. In actual composition, a student who appreciates the need for detailed development of a statement is likely to think of illustrative details as he first writes, but if he does not, he has a chance to add them during revision.

### Unity

Since a paragraph develops a topic sentence, stated or implied, there should be nothing in it which does not clearly serve that end. This is the principle of unity. A unified paragraph makes clear reading. One which digresses or drifts away from its topic puts extra demands on the reader and sometimes thwarts him in his efforts to follow the writer's purpose.

Unified paragraphs stick to their purpose. You have already seen (page 89) how the intrusion of inappropriate details disrupted the unity of one paragraph. The following paragraph also has an obvious digression.

It is a good thing that we learn to speak as children. If the learning were postponed until we were adults most of us would be too discouraged by the difficulties to persevere in the task. *Perhaps, in that event, our political campaigns would be conducted in sign language and our radio broadcasters would be required to learn the Morse code.* We take a child's learning to talk for granted, and not infrequently parents grow worried when their four-year-old stumbles over his consonants or becomes snarled in his syntax. Yet compared with the intellectual achievement of learning to talk, the discovery of the theory of relativity is a trifling accomplishment.

Clearly the author started with the idea that learning to speak is man's greatest intellectual achievement. But as he wrote he became interested in the possible consequences of our not learning to speak, and in an uncritical moment he introduced the italicized sentence. If he really wants to develop this idea — and it could be an entertaining one — he should save it for a new paragraph. But he should not let it intrude here, where it doesn't belong.

The paragraph below digresses even more flagrantly.

In order to bring about harmony in our economy, Congress must force unions to become more responsible. This is no reactionary proposal. It is made in the interests of labor itself. Organized labor is an asset to the economy of a nation. One has only to read of the conditions that prevailed in mills and mines and factories during the last century to understand what the lot of the workingman would be like if he were deprived of his right to unite with his fellow workers to force concessions from entrepreneurs whose short-sighted irresponsibility has been nourished on *laissez-faire*.

This writer begins by accusing labor unions of being irresponsible and concludes by asserting the irresponsibility of management. The ability to see both sides of a question is valuable, but a writer who fails to make up his mind what side he is on before he begins his paragraph (or essay) merely transmits his confusion to his reader. The result, in this case, is a "broken-backed" paragraph

Here is one more example:

During the war years Churchill became the very symbol of British determination and endurance. For many of us in the United States he was John Bull in person. When he addressed Congress, shortly after our entry into the war, his speech was enthusiastically cheered. He pointed out that if his father, instead of his mother, had been an American, he might have been speaking that day as a member of Congress. One can well imagine such an event, for there is something typically American about Churchill and his ideals.

Notice how this paragraph drifts into a contradiction. The first sentence states the topic and the second begins the development. Then the author refers to Churchill's speech before Congress. The only justification for mentioning that speech would be to illustrate the way Churchill symbolized the British people. But the writer becomes more interested in the speech than in the use he is supposed to be making of it; so when he recalls Churchill's reference to his American mother, he begins to see in Churchill a typically American figure. This is the kind of thing that all too often happens to a writer who makes up his mind as he goes along.

The only cure for such paragraphs is complete rewriting. The author must begin again, but first he must get clear in his own mind what one idea he wants to develop in the paragraph. It will be a useful discipline for him to set down the topic sentence at the beginning of the paragraph and to keep his eye on it while he writes. That will help him to resist intruding ideas which seem interesting or important but which have nothing to do with his immediate purpose.

## Orderly Movement

If the paragraph is to be an organic unit its movement should follow some clear order. There are several different ways in which the material of paragraphs may be arranged. But while there may be no one inevitable order for a given paragraph, certainly some orders will be more effective than others.

Consider the following:

(1) We all know that if we "burn" chalk the result is quick-lime. (2) There are a great many other ways of showing that chalk is essentially nothing but carbonic acid and quick-lime. (3) Chemists enunciate the result of all the experiments which prove this, by stating that chalk is almost wholly composed of carbonate of lime. (4) By the procedure of burning we see the lime, but we do not see the carbonic acid. (5) If, on the other hand, you were to powder a little chalk and drop it into a good deal of strong vinegar, there would be a great bubbling and fizzing, and, finally, a clear liquid, in which no sign of chalk would appear. (6) Here you see the carbonic acid in the bubbles; the lime, dissolved in the vinegar, vanishes from sight. (7) Chalk, in fact, is a compound of carbonic acid gas, and lime, and when you make it very hot the carbonic acid flies away and the lime is left.

This paragraph is fully developed and unified. But a careful reader might notice a certain jerkiness in its development. Rereading, he would observe that the sequence of ideas in the paragraph is as follows:

1. A statement about a specific experiment — burning.
2. A statement about other experiments.
3. A conclusion drawn from all experiments.
4. A second statement about burning.
5. A statement about a specific experiment — dissolving.
6. A second statement about that experiment.
7. Another statement essentially about burning.

He would then understand what had bothered him on the first reading: the author should have grouped the statements about burning in the first part of the paragraph, those about dissolving in the second part, and finally should have drawn the general conclusion about all such experiments. This is exactly what T. H. Huxley did in the paragraph from which our scrambled version was taken.

We all know that if we "burn" chalk the result is quick-lime. Chalk, in fact, is a compound of carbonic acid gas, and lime, and when you make it very hot the carbonic acid flies away and the lime is left. By this method of procedure we see the lime, but we do not see the carbonic acid. If, on the other hand, you were to powder a little chalk and drop it into a good deal of strong vinegar, there would be a great bubbling and fizzing, and, finally, a clear liquid, in which no sign of chalk would appear. Here you see the carbonic acid in the bubbles; the lime, dissolved in the vinegar, vanishes from sight. There are a great many other ways of showing that chalk is essentially nothing but carbonic acid and quick-lime. Chemists enunciate the result of all the experiments that prove this, by stating that chalk is almost wholly composed of "carbonate of lime." [1]

We have said that order in a paragraph is like organization in an essay. The patterns of organization we studied in Chapter 3 also apply to paragraphs. Thus a topic sentence may be developed by clarifying statement, causal explanation, example, comparison, contrast, or analytical division. But because the paragraph is smaller in scope than the essay, it may be simpler to consider paragraph order as *direction*. We shall therefore discuss it in terms of five directional patterns: (1) from one time to the next, (2) from one space to an adjoining space, (3) from particular statements to a general statement or conclusion, (4) from a general statement to particular statements, (5) from question to answer or from effect to cause.

**1. Time.** A time, or chronological, order is the natural order of narration and is commonly used in explaining the steps in a process. Events are recorded in the order in which they occur — first, second, next, and so on to the last. Thus if you were telling a story or giving directions on how to reach a certain destination or how to bake a cake, the natural order would be a time order. Here is an illustration.

> While I jacked the fore end of the car up, and cleared away the snow from under it, Dan built a fire about a foot in front of the radiator to keep the car and us from freezing to death and to furnish light for the operation. The wheel correction was surprisingly easy; we were ready to leave again in a few minutes. Then we discovered that it would be more difficult to get out of the lane than it had been to get in. Because of the density of the timber there was no way of turning around without serious risk of getting stuck, and the whirling snow made the visibility poor everywhere except directly within the beams of the head lights. Dan therefore very carefully directed my backing; yet in spite of this I bumped several small pines which retaliated by dumping their burden of snow on top of the car. The Plymouth was little more than a snow drift on wheels by the time we reached the highway.[2]

**2. Space.** A space order is useful when the writer wishes to report what he sees. The movement of the paragraph thus follows the movement of his eyes. That movement must have some continuity which a reader can recognize and follow. It need not start at the far left and move

[1] From T. H. Huxley, "A Piece of Chalk," *Collected Essays.* The Macmillan Company, publishers.

[2] Charles R. Goldman, "Luck and Wheels." From *The Green Caldron: A Magazine of Freshman Writing* (November, 1949), published at the University of Illinois, Urbana, Illinois. Copyright, 1949, by Charles W. Roberts. Reprinted by permission.

steadily to the far right, or vice versa, since in any view an observer's gaze is likely to be drawn quickly to the most conspicuous object. But there should be some logical or natural progression from one descriptive detail to the next. It may be very confusing to flit haphazardly from left to right, then center to left again. Notice that the following paragraph begins with a front view, then moves right, down, and to the rear. This order reflects the relative conspicuousness of the objects described.

> I seated myself in the barber chair, which was only a rickety, straight-backed affair made of bamboo placed on a wooden box in the center of the room. Directly in front of this throne hung a dingy, blurred mirror, suspended by ropes from the roof. To my right stood a square table, upon which rested the barber's only tools — a pair of clippers, a dirty-looking comb, and a razor. As I cast my eyes downward, I was somewhat surprised to find that the floor was still in its natural state — dirt. It also showed evidence that hair had been cut here before. I noticed now for the first time an opening at the rear, over which a piece of gray material was draped. Evidently this archway led into the living quarters of the barber.[3]

3. **Particular to General.** A common order in expository paragraphs is from a succession of particular statements to the general statement or conclusion to which the particulars lead. Huxley used this order (page 102) when he began a paragraph by describing an experiment which shows that chalk contains lime, related a second experiment to show that chalk also contains carbonic acid, and finally stated the conclusion that chalk is composed of carbonate of lime. By this order the reader is led to the conclusion through details of evidence or illustration. Hence the order is often called *inductive,* from the Latin word meaning to "lead in."

A paragraph so organized will have the topic sentence at or near the end. Notice how the author of the following paragraph leads up to his topic sentence, that logic is fun.

> If you enjoy working out the strategy of games, tit-tat-toe or poker or chess; if you are interested in the frog who jumped up three feet and fell back two in getting out of a well, or in the fly buzzing between the noses of two approaching cyclists, or in the farmer who left land to his three sons; if you have been captivated by codes and ciphers or are interested in cross-word puzzles; if you like to fool around with numbers; if music appeals to you by the sense of form which it expresses — then you will enjoy logic. You ought to be warned, perhaps. Those who take up logic get glassy-eyed and absent-minded. They join a fanatical cult. But they

---

[3] James Hiser, "Filipino Barber Shop." From *The Green Caldron: A Magazine of Freshman Writing* (December, 1946), published at the University of Illinois, Urbana, Illinois. Copyright, 1946, by Charles W. Roberts. Reprinted by permission.

have a good time. Theirs is one of the most durable, absorbing and inexpensive of pleasures. *Logic is fun.*[4]

**4. General to Particular.** The most popular order for expository paragraphs is just the reverse of the one above. It begins with a general statement, then moves to particulars which explain or illustrate, or persuade the reader to accept the generalization. This order is similar to the illustrative pattern for developing an essay (see page 37). In effect, the topic sentence at or near the beginning of the paragraph states the purpose, and the subsequent sentences illustrate it. In the paragraph that follows, the italicized topic sentence is developed by three sentences, each of which adds an illustration.

*Beauty is the quality which makes to endure.* In a house that I know, I have noticed a block of spermaceti lying about closets and mantel-pieces, for twenty years together, simply because the tallow-man gave it the form of a rabbit; and, I suppose, it may continue to be lugged about unchanged for a century. Let an artist scrawl a few lines or figures on the back of a letter, and that scrap of paper is rescued from danger, is put in portfolio, is framed and glazed, and, in proportion to the beauty of the lines drawn, will be kept for centuries. Burns writes a copy of verses, and sends them to a newspaper, and the human race take charge of them that they shall not perish.[5]

In the next paragraph the topic sentence is followed by the details of evidence which spell out the meaning of the general statement that America has been going suburban.

*America has been going suburban.* The city moving out and the country moving in have met and mingled in this new melting pot — the urban belt. According to the latest United States census, the suburban population increased approximately thirty per cent between 1930 and 1940, against little more than seven per cent for the country as a whole. In the decade between 1920 and 1930, the suburbs grew five times faster than the rural districts and three times faster than the cities they encompassed. Already fifty-eight per cent of the people in this country live in metropolitan areas, with a disproportionate number in nineteen centers such as Greater New York, Chicagoland, and Greater Los Angeles. Small towns, the traditional citadels of American provincialism, have become enveloped in some metropolitan area or another, and have become citified. Highway 67 is now the extension of Main Street, and the corner grocery has given place to the A. & P.[6]

[4] From Roger W. Holmes' *The Rhyme of Reason,* copyright, 1944, with permission of Appleton-Century-Crofts, Inc.
[5] Emerson, "Beauty."
[6] From Carl von Rhode's "The Suburban Mind," *Harper's Magazine,* April, 1946. Reprinted by permission of *Harper's Magazine.*

For the reader, this general-to-particular order (sometimes called *deductive*) has the great advantage that it announces the topic at the beginning and thus makes it easy to see the relation of each new sentence to the topic as the paragraph proceeds. For the writer, it has the advantage of holding his purpose clearly before him so that he is less likely to introduce irrelevant material or wander off on a digression.

Two variations of this general-to-particular order deserve special notice. The first is the paragraph that not only begins but also ends with a general statement. Until the last sentence, such a paragraph follows a general-to-particular order, then the topic idea is restated, usually in different words, to provide a concluding sentence. You saw this pattern in Chapter 3. The following paragraph also shows it.

*Most disputes about whether or not men are stronger than women are meaningless because the disputants fail to consider that the word "stronger" may mean many things.* Most men can surpass most women in lifting heavy weights, in striking an object (say a baseball or an opponent's jaw), in running, jumping, or doing heavy physical labor. But the statistics indicate that most women live longer than most men, that they have a better chance of resisting disease, that they can beat men at operations requiring finger-dexterity and the ability to work accurately under monotonous conditions. On this kind of evidence it would be legitimate to argue that women are stronger than men. The truth is that each sex can surpass the other in certain kinds of activities. *To say that one is stronger than the other is to indulge in an argument which would not arise if the word "stronger" were more sharply defined.*

A second variation is the paragraph which deliberately reverses its movement. It usually begins with a topic sentence that states or implies a qualification or a contrast. The first half of the paragraph develops one phase of the idea, and the second half qualifies what has been said. Usually the point of reversal is indicated by a transitional connective, such as *but, on the other hand, nevertheless, still,* or *yet.* For example:

*The statement that the German people were ultimately responsible for the war is a half truth which encourages a convenient oversimplification.* It is true that Hitler was the constitutionally appointed leader of the German nation and that, despite individual protests, his policies, as long as they were successful, had the approval, or at least the acquiescence, of the German voters. *But* in the world in which we live no man, no nation causes war. To fix any ultimate responsibility for World War II we must go beyond Hitler and the Nazi ideology; we must look before Munich and the invasion of Poland. And the farther we look the more clearly we will see that the roots of war were world wide, and that no nation was guiltless of nourishing them.

The italicized topic sentence suggests that (1) the German people were responsible for the war, (2) other people were also responsible. The next sentence supports the suggestion of German guilt. Then at the transitional *But* the paragraph begins to reverse itself and to move toward the conclusion that all nations were involved in the responsibility for the war.

A word of caution is necessary about this kind of paragraph movement. In the hands of an inexperienced writer, a reversed paragraph may easily become disunified, and may end, like those we saw on pages 100–101, by saying the opposite of what the author intended. To be successful, the reversal must be deliberate. The author must be aware at the outset that he intends to qualify his opening statement within the paragraph, and the topic sentence should be phrased to reveal that intention. Unless these conditions are observed, it will often be safer to break the paragraph in two at the point of transition. For example:

> The statement that the German people were ultimately responsible for the war is a half truth which encourages a convenient oversimplification. It is true that Hitler was the constitutionally appointed leader of the German nation and that, despite individual protests, his policies, as long as they were successful, had the approval or at least the acquiescence of the German voters.
>
> But in the world in which we live no man, no nation causes war. To fix any ultimate responsibility for World War II we must look beyond Hitler and the Nazi ideology; we must look before Munich and the invasion of Poland. And the farther we look the more clearly we will see that the roots of war were world wide, and that no nation was guiltless of nourishing them.

**5. Question to Answer, Effect to Cause.** Less common than any of the orders we have considered so far is the paragraph that begins with a question and moves toward the answer, or begins with an effect and moves toward the cause. Such a paragraph usually has no explicit topic sentence, since the answer to the question or the cause of the effect is explained by the paragraph as a whole. But the opening question, problem, or dilemma announces the purpose of the paragraph clearly if implicitly.

The following example moves from question to answer:

> *And when is water boiling?* It can be said, with few people to argue the point, that water boils at two hundred and twelve degrees Fahrenheit. Myself, I would say that when it bubbles with large energetic bubbles, and looks ready to hop from the kettle, and makes a rocky rather than a murmuring noise, and sends off a great deal of steam, it is boiling.[7]

[7] From M. F. K. Fisher's *How To Cook A Wolf.* Copyright, 1942, by M. F. K. Fisher. Reprinted by permission of the publishers, Duell, Sloan and Pearce, Inc.

The next paragraph first states a result, then gives the cause:

*When Basil Rathbone was handed a scenario titled: "The Monster," he gave it back to Paramount without reading it.* A wise man in the studio retitled it "Destiny" and sent the same script back to Rathbone. He read it, liked it, and assured me on the set that it is not a horror picture. "I'm through with horror and villainy," says Basil, "a man has only so many villains in him, and I've played all mine." [8]

The following table will summarize the types of paragraph movement we have been discussing:

### Time order
(A chain of events recorded in the order in which they occurred. Paragraph begins with the first event and ends with the last one. Usually no topic sentence.)

Event 1
Event 2
Event 3, and so on.

### Space order
(Sentences in paragraph move from one area to the next as these areas are viewed, in turn, by the writer. Movement may be in any direction but must be easy to follow. Usually no topic sentence.)

left-right, front-rear, up-down, or any logical movement from one space to the next.

### Particular to general (inductive)
(From a series of explanatory or illustrative statements to the conclusion drawn from them. Topic sentence at or near end of paragraph.)

Details leading up to concluding topic sentence.

### General to particular (deductive)
(From general statement to supporting details which explain, illustrate, or prove it. Topic sentence at or near beginning of paragraph.)

Conclusion or general statement followed by details of explanation or proof.

(*Variation 1.* Topic sentence restated as conclusion at end of paragraph.)

Details

[8] From Sheilah Graham's column, *Chicago Daily News*, March 6, 1940. Reprinted by permission of the *Chicago Daily News* and The Bell Syndicate, Inc.

(*Variation 2.* Topic sentence implies qualification or contrast which requires paragraph to develop first one phase then the other of topic sentence. Point of reversal indicated by transitional connective: *but, yet, still, on the other hand.*)

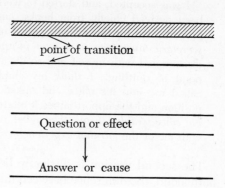

point of transition

*Question-answer, Effect-cause* (Paragraph begins with question or effect, then answers the question or shows the cause. Usually no topic sentence.)

Question or effect

Answer or cause

## Coherence

Literally, the word *cohere* means to hold together. A paragraph is said to have coherence when its sentences are woven together or flow into each other. If a paragraph is coherent, the reader moves easily from one sentence to the next without feeling that there are gaps in the thought, puzzling jumps, or points not made. If a paragraph lacks coherence, the reader will feel that the sentence, not the paragraph, is the unit of writing, that he is reading a collection of separate statements rather than an integrated discussion.

### Coherence Within the Paragraph.

A paragraph which lacks unity or orderly movement will not be coherent, since a reader cannot move easily from one sentence to the next if the second sentence has no clear relation to the first. But coherence is not simply a matter of unity and consistent order. Consider the following paragraph:

> (1) I was accepted and started work. (2) My experience had been derived chiefly from books. (3) I was not prepared for the difficult period of adjustment. (4) I soon became discouraged with myself and so dissatisfied with my job that I was on the point of quitting. (5) My employer must have sensed this. (6) He called me into his office and talked to me about the duties of my position and the opportunities for advancement. (7) I realized that there was nothing wrong with me or the job and I decided to stay.

This paragraph is fairly well developed, it is unified, it follows an orderly development; yet it is a poor paragraph. The writer's ideas do not flow from one sentence to the next. Rather, they seem to come out in a series of jolts and jerks, because the connecting links between them are not expressed. The sentences are not knitted together, so that the reader is forced to tackle each one separately, and in hunting the connections, he loses the flow and continuity which a more carefully constructed paragraph would provide.

Now look at the same paragraph slightly altered:

I was accepted, and started to work. *Until that time* my experience had been derived chiefly from books, *and unfortunately* those books had not prepared me for the difficult period of adjustment *that every inexperienced secretary must face in a new position. Consequently* I soon became so discouraged with myself and so dissatisfied with the job that I was on the point of quitting. *I think* my employer must have sensed this, *for* he called me into his office and talked to me *both* about the duties of my position and the opportunities it offered for advancement. *That talk helped me considerably. From then on,* I realized that there was nothing wrong with me or the job *that experience could not cure,* and I decided to stay.

The second version is distinctly better than the first, and if you read both aloud, the difference between them will be still more obvious. Why? The content is substantially the same, the diction is scarcely changed and the second version is only slightly more fully developed than the first. The general answer is that the second paragraph is more coherent because the author has provided transitions — bridges — between the thoughts expressed in the original sentences. These transitions are created by two means: sometimes by filling a small gap in the thought, thus providing better continuity of statement; sometimes by the addition of connecting words and phrases which tie sentences together.

**Transition Through Continuity of Thought.** A writer who looks upon a paragraph as a unit developing a single topic, who consequently composes a whole paragraph at a time, is not likely to write paragraphs seriously lacking in coherence. Most incoherent passages are a result of thinking in single sentences rather than whole paragraphs. When a writer works that way, he is likely to write one sentence, stop, think a minute, write a second sentence, stop, and continue in a series of jerks and pauses. Paragraphs developed in this way are almost sure to be weak in coherence, for the writer is starting afresh at every new sentence. He loses the feeling of continuity with the last sentence before he begins the next one. Consequently, he is likely to omit significant links or details of thought and thus leave gaps in his writing.

For example, when the author of the incoherent paragraph stopped between sentences 1 and 2, she left out a small but important detail of her thought. She was contrasting her previous experience with her new one and she needed somewhere to make the point that *now* her experience was changing. In the revised version the phrase "Until that time" supplies the necessary clue. Similarly, when she wrote that she was not prepared "for the difficult period of adjustment," she had in mind a particular adjustment, the kind that must be made "in a new position." But her original statement omitted that link in her thought. Again, she skipped a thought between sentences 6 and 7. She was helped by her talk with her employer. By failing to record that fact, she ran the talk and its result too closely together. In the revised paragraph the italicized sentence provides the missing detail and thus gives a fuller statement of what she meant.

Finally, she omitted a necessary idea in her last sentence. There *was* something wrong with her, but nothing "that experience could not cure." The revision, by providing these omitted details, makes the paragraph more completely reflect all that was in the writer's mind.

**Transition Through Related Sentence Patterns.** A writer who thinks in sentences rather than in paragraphs often finds it hard to keep a consistent grammatical pattern running through a paragraph. In the example cited, the author herself is the subject of five sentences and her employer the subject of the other two. The following example is much less consistent:

> Although writing a research paper is a difficult assignment, many students make it more difficult than it need be because of inefficient work habits. The work on the paper is too often postponed until it is too late to do a decent job of it. Failure to find out at the beginning of the study whether sufficient material is available in the library often invites serious difficulty. Many students tackle the topic in detail before they have formed a general notion of the topic. It is unwise to begin reading the first book available and to plunge into fine points before the student has learned to understand the topic as a whole. The habit of taking notes too soon is inefficient. Students should postpone notetaking until they have decided what kind of information they need. It is also a mistake to quote a paragraph in its entirety. The notes should consist of the factual information taken from the paragraph.

Because this paragraph was obviously developed one sentence at a time, the writer failed to maintain any consistent point of view toward his material. He changes from active to passive voice, from a personal to an impersonal subject, and he uses seven different subjects for the nine sentences of his paragraph. As a result there is no grammatical consistency within the paragraph, and it reads as jerkily as it was composed.

Notice the improvement in this version:

> Although writing a research paper is a difficult assignment, many students make it more difficult than it need be because of inefficient working habits. Too often they postpone work on the paper until it is too late to do a respectable job of it. Often they invite avoidable difficulty by failure to find out at the beginning of their study whether sufficient material is available in the library. Instead of developing a general notion of the topic before tackling it in detail, they begin with the first convenient book and plunge into fine points before they see the topic as a whole. They take more notes than are necessary because they begin to take notes before they have decided what kind of information they need, and because they do not pick out the factual information in a paragraph but quote the paragraph in its entirety.

The biggest change here is that the noun *students* or its pronoun *they* has been made the subject of every sentence. This not only eliminates unnecessary and awkward shifting but allows the writer's purpose to develop easily and steadily through successive sentences.

It is of course not necessary that every sentence in a paragraph have the same subject. Changes of subject within a paragraph are often necessary or wise. But when arbitrary changes destroy coherence, revision to avoid these shifts will often greatly improve the paragraph.

**Coherence Through Pronoun Reference.** Since a pronoun refers to an antecedent, the use of a pronoun in one sentence to point back to an antecedent in the one before is a simple and natural connecting device. Notice how the alternating use of pronoun and antecedent provides effective transitions in the following sentences:

> In the history of the American film no other single personality has so endeared himself to the world as Charlie Chaplin. His presence is as much alive as ever in the thousands of 16 mm. revivals of his work. Every generation takes him to its heart anew. As with all great characters one sees in Chaplin what one brings to him.[9]

The use of pronouns often allows a writer to keep his subject running through the paragraph without falling into monotonous repetition. Notice how this is done in the following paragraph, in which nominative, possessive, and objective forms of the same pronoun bind the sentences together by inconspicuous repetition.

> He was a monster of conceit. Never for one moment did he look at the world or at people, except in relation to himself. He was not only the most important person in the world, to himself; in his own eyes he was the only person who existed. He believed himself to be one of the greatest dramatists in the world, one of the greatest thinkers, and one of the greatest composers. To hear him talk, he was Shakespeare, and Beethoven, and Plato rolled into one. . . .[10]

**Transitional Markers.** These are words or phrases placed at or near the beginning of a sentence or clause to signal to the reader the relationship between the new sentence and the one before it. The commonest of these markers are the simple connectives *and, or, nor, but, for,* which serve as bridges over which the reader may easily pass from one sentence or clause to the next. Others — sometimes called transitional connectives — indicate the direction which the new sentence is about to take

---

[9] From *The Rise of The American Film* by Lewis Jacobs, copyright, 1939, by Lewis Jacobs. Reprinted by permission of Harcourt, Brace and Company, Inc.

[10] The subject of this description is later identified as Richard Wagner, the famous German composer. Reprinted from *Of Men and Music* by permission of Simon and Schuster, publishers. Copyright, 1937, by Deems Taylor.

and so prepare the reader for what is to follow. The commonest transitional connectives may be classified as follows:

1. To introduce an illustration: *thus, for example, for instance, to illustrate.*

2. To add another phase of the same idea: *secondly, in the second place, next, moreover, in addition, similarly, again, also, finally.*

3. To point a contrast or qualification: *on the other hand, nevertheless, despite this fact, on the contrary, still, however.*

4. To indicate a conclusion or result: *therefore, in conclusion, to sum up, consequently, as a result, accordingly, in other words.*

You have already seen a few of these transitional markers used in the revised versions of both faulty paragraphs discussed in the preceding pages. Here is another illustration.

> Such a controlling purpose, of course, limits the appeal of the book, and probably this work will have a greater attraction for the layman than for the professional historian. *Moreover,* it always runs the risk of producing a book which, because of its lack of any unifying theme, is merely another book about the subject with which it deals. There are, *indeed,* moments when one feels that the author has not sufficiently resisted the temptation to add another story merely because it is a good story, without concerning himself too much about the relationship of the story to the theme that he is developing. *Thus* the chapter dealing with Strang's kingdom on Beaver Island hardly escapes being an eight page digression, since it has no other claim to being an integral part of the story of the development of the Great Lakes than the fact that Beaver Island happened to be located in Lake Michigan. The story, of course, is interesting, *but* like a cuckoo in a sea-gull's nest, it would be more at home in other quarters.

To see the value of the connectives in this paragraph, one need only read it again and omit them.

The following paragraphs use various transitional devices:

> The good educator is very serious but also very sensible. And somewhere in his soul there is a saving lightness. He understands, to begin with, the meaning of a recent remark: "Not everything can be learned." Some things are never taught; they are simply known. Other things cannot in the nature of things be known, either by student or by teacher. And then there is that endless series of knowable things only a few of which can be bestowed upon the student during the fragment of his life he spends in school.[11]

The transitional devices in this paragraph are the connectives *And* and *And then,* the pronouns *he* and *his* pointing back to the antecedent *educator,* and the connecting relationship between the words *every-*

[11] From Mark Van Doren, *Liberal Education.* Copyright 1943 by Henry Holt and Company, publishers. Reprinted by permission.

*thing, Some things,* and *Other things.* Still a subtler linking is achieved by the words *learned . . . taught . . . known . . . knowable.*

|  |  |
|---|---|
| *Deliberate*<br>*repetition*<br><br>*Deliberate*<br>*repetition*<br><br>*Interconnection*<br>*of pronouns and*<br>*antecedents* | In a world in which the leaders of war democracies are the Daladiers and Chamberlains and Churchills, *we have reason to be proud of* Lincoln. *We have reason to be proud* that *with every opportunity* of setting up a dictatorship, he did not *succumb; with every opportunity* of betraying democratic values under the guise of war necessity, he did not *succumb.* . . . I have no intention of saying that Lincoln was wholly consistent in the strength of his humanism. . . . Yet there never was a time when it was more important for us than now to know the capacity of a democracy to turn up *greatness* of Lincoln's sort from its humblest sons — a *greatness* that will survive the grime and savagery of war.[12] |

All the transitional devices we have discussed are used in this paragraph. Lincoln, although his name is seldom the actual subject of a sentence, is referred to in almost every sentence and thus gives the paragraph a continuity of subject; the pronoun references help tie the paragraph together; the purposeful repetition of similar phrasing in the first half of the paragraph strengthens the coherence; and the transitional connective *Yet* links the last sentence with the one preceding it.

**Coherence Between Paragraphs.** We have been thinking of the single paragraph as a unit. But it is, of course, only one of several units in the larger scheme of the whole paper. Just as there should be coherence *within* the paragraph, so there should be coherence *between* paragraphs.

In an analytical paper which is well organized, the relationship between paragraphs will be clear, for the reader will be following the thesis of the paper and, especially if the topic sentence appears at the beginning of each paragraph, he will have no trouble seeing the relationship of each new paragraph to what has gone before. For example, each of the paragraphs of "Why I Came to College" (page 99) begins with a topic sentence which points back to an implied thesis. If we set the topic sentences under the thesis we can see clearly how, by pointing to the three factors of the thesis, each topic sentence relates its paragraph to the purpose of the essay.

|  |  |
|---|---|
| *Thesis* | My reasons for coming to college were threefold: to improve my earning power, to provide myself with a cultural background that would help me to make a satisfying use of my leisure time, and to increase my social experience. |

[12] From Max Lerner's review of Sandburg's *Abraham Lincoln: The War Years.* Reprinted by permission of the *New Republic.*

| | |
|---|---|
| *Topic Sentence, ¶1:*<br>*first factor of thesis.* | My chief reason for coming to college was to prepare myself for a position that would allow me to have a larger income than I would be likely to obtain as a high school graduate. . . . |
| *Topic sentence, ¶2:*<br>*second factor of thesis.* | Another reason for coming to college was to provide myself with a cultural background that would help me to make a more satisfying use of my leisure time. . . . |
| *Topic sentence, ¶3:*<br>*third factor of thesis.* | A third reason for coming to college was to increase my social experience. . . . |

The clear relationship of each topic sentence to the thesis creates the effect of "signposting" each paragraph, of informing the reader in advance what each is going to do, what part of the thesis it is going to develop. Such signposts serve the double purpose of setting off each paragraph as a structural unit of the essay and of providing transitions between paragraphs. Notice the signposts in the next selection.

The politicians tell us, "you must educate the masses because they are going to be masters." The clergy join in the cry for education, for they affirm that the people are drifting away from the church and chapel into the broadest infidelity. The manufacturers and the capitalists swell the chorus lustily. They declare that ignorance makes bad workmen. . . . And a few voices are lifted up in favor of the doctrine that the masses should be educated because they are men and women with unlimited capacities for being, doing, and suffering, and that it is as true now, as ever it was, that the people perish for lack of knowledge.

These members of the minority, with whom I confess I have a good deal of sympathy, . . . question if it be wise to tell people that you will do for them, out of the fear of their power, what you have left undone, so long as your only motive was compassion for their weakness and their sorrows. And if ignorance of everything which it is needful a ruler should know is likely to do so much harm in the governing classes of the future, why is it, they ask reasonably enough, that such ignorance in the governing classes of the past had not been viewed with equal horror? . . .

Again, this sceptical minority asks the clergy to think whether it is really want of education which keeps the masses away from their ministrations — whether the most completely educated men are not as open to reproach on this score as the workmen; and whether, perchance, this may not indicate that it is not education which lies at the bottom of this matter?

Once more, these people, whom there is no pleasing, venture to doubt whether the glory, which rests upon being able to undersell all the rest of the world, is a very safe kind of glory — whether we may not purchase it too dear; especially if we allow education, which ought to be directed to the making of men, to be diverted into a process of manufacturing human tools, wonderfully adroit in the exercise of some technical industry, but good for nothing else.

(And finally,) (these people) inquire whether it is the masses alone who need a reformed and improved education. . . . They seem to think that the noble foundations of our old universities are hardly fulfilling their functions. . . . And while as zealous for education as the rest, they affirm that if the education of the richer classes were such as to fit them to be the leaders and the governors of the poorer; and if the education of the poorer classes were such as to enable them to appreciate really wise guidance and good governance, the politicians need not fear mob-law, nor the clergy lament their want of flocks, nor the capitalists prognosticate the annihilation of the prosperity of the country.[13]

As the circled expressions show, Huxley uses two sets of transitional devices: the signposts *Again, Once more, Finally* to mark the transition from one paragraph to the next; and the references *These members of the minority, this sceptical minority, these people,* each of which points back to the people holding the opinion described at the end of the first paragraph.

**Transitional Paragraphs.** Occasionally a whole short paragraph may be used as a transition. Such a paragraph always occurs at a point at which the author has finished one main unit of his composition and is about to start another. The transitional paragraph may be used in several ways. It may sum up what has been said before beginning the next unit. It may introduce one or more illustrations of a point already made. Or it may state what the writer intends to do next. The following paragraphs illustrate these uses:

To sum up before beginning the next unit:

Before we begin to analyze the merits of this proposal, let us sum up what we have already established. We have shown that the proposed program has several times been offered to the American people and has always been rejected. We have shown that the proponents of the program have attempted to manufacture a need which does not exist. We have further shown that the program is being advocated by diverse groups which have nothing in common except a conviction that what is best for their special interests must also be best for the country.

To introduce a series of illustrations:

The point that I have been making is necessarily abstract. In order to make it more concrete, let me cite three illustrations, all of which are drawn from common experience.

[13] From T. H. Huxley, *Collected Essays*. The Macmillan Company, publishers.

To show what the writer intends to do next:

> Now, you may admit all these things and yet inquire what can be done about them without sacrificing values that have become precious to us all. Since I realize that this question is a just one, I shall outline briefly the organization of the University of Utopia. It will be seen that not all the features of this university are new and original. At Wisconsin, Harvard, Swarthmore, and numerous other places, many phases of its plan have been tried and have succeeded. Much of the rest of the program has been under discussion at the University of Chicago and elsewhere for some years.[14]

These transitional paragraphs connect what has gone before with what is to follow. In addition, each is a sort of aside to the reader in which the writer shows the connection between parts of his work. The transitional paragraph, then, links larger units as a transitional word or phrase connects sentences or paragraphs.

## Assignments in Paragraphing

As a practical application of what we have been saying, let us take three assignments and work them out as finished paragraphs. For each we shall first state the problem, then analyze it, and finally present one possible solution.

There will be one objection to this procedure. In going about the assignment so deliberately we will exaggerate the procedure which a writer actually uses. An experienced writer seldom goes about writing a paragraph as methodically as we shall do. His decisions about its content and form are usually made only when he has determined the whole purpose of his work. Because he sees his essay as a whole, the paragraph is not for him an individual assignment; it is a part of the whole, and its content, form, and relation to other paragraphs are determined by his original choice of purpose. But just as football players profit from studying a picture of a game in slow motion, so we may profit from slowing down the process of composition.

### Assignment A

A rewrite man in a newspaper office is to write a single paragraph to go with a series of pictures about the survivors rescued from a sinking Italian liner by the *Ile de France*. Reports coming to his desk have given him the following information, arranged in no meaningful order.

1. Some survivors angry over lost possessions.
2. Some nearly undressed.

[14] From R. M. Hutchins, "The University of Utopia," in *The Yale Review*. Copyright, 1931, by Yale University Press.

3. The *Ile* finished rescue operations with her decks full of survivors.
4. They were stupefied by shock and exhaustion.
5. Some were rejoicing at finding relatives thought to be lost.
6. *Ile* proceeded to New York at full speed to land survivors.
7. Some dressed in oddments.
8. Some hysterical in relief.
9. *Ile* radioed that she was reversing course to return to New York.
10. Some survivors in anguish over missing relatives.

The writer's first step is to organize these notes in some logical order. He first separates the ten notes into two groups: one group (3, 6, 9) dealing with the ship, the other with the condition of the survivors. Since the first group tells what the ship did, and since she did these things one after the other, he puts these three notes in chronological order and expresses them in a sentence, perhaps something like this:

> When the *Ile* finished rescue operations, with her decks full of survivors, she radioed that she was reversing her course and proceeding at full speed to New York.

The remaining seven notes also fall into two groups: those about dress (2, 7) and those about emotional state (1, 4, 5, 8, 10). The two details about dress seem to form a contrast. He puts them down thus:

> Some were dressed in oddments; some were nearly undressed.

Of the first five notes about emotional state, two deal with feelings about relatives:

> Some were in anguish over missing relatives; some were rejoicing at finding relatives thought to be lost.

Since details about relatives have greater human interest than those about possessions, the writer puts them in the most emphatic position in the paragraph — at the end. At this stage the paragraph looks like this:

> When the *Ile* finished rescue operations, with her decks full of survivors, she radioed that she was reversing her course and proceeding at full speed to New York. Some of the survivors were dressed in oddments; some were nearly undressed. They were stupefied by shock and exhaustion. Some were hysterical in relief. Some were angry over lost possessions. Some were in anguish over missing relatives. Some were rejoicing at finding relatives thought to be lost.

The organization of the paragraph is now complete, but the style is still crude and jerky. More transition is needed between sentences 1 and 2. The rest of the paragraph is just a collection of sentences which have not been shaped into a coherent pattern. The writer has to decide what effect he wants to produce with these sentences. Does he want to emphasize a contrast? If so, perhaps he should use a *some . . . others* pattern to set up contrasting details in parallel form. Or does he want a series of details adding up to a general impression? If so, what impression? Here is how he solved his problem:

> When the *Ile* finished her rescue operation, she radioed that she was reversing course, full speed, to land the survivors in New York. Her decks were full of human beings caught up in the emotional complexity of deliverance from great peril. Some dressed in oddments, some nearly undressed, they were stupefied by shock and exhaustion, or sometimes hysterical in relief. Some were angry over lost possessions, others in anguish over missing relatives. And for some there was wild rejoicing when those lost were miraculously found again.[15]

Notice how this paragraph transmutes the raw notes into a compact, tightly-knit unit. Just how the writer actually composed the paragraph, we do not know; though we can guess that he did not proceed quite so methodically from notes to organization to rough draft to finished paragraph. But even if he went from notes to final paragraph in one step, he went through the process illustrated here — which is, after all, the process of composition. His experience simply allowed him to do quickly and efficiently what a less experienced writer would have to do slowly step by step.

### Assignment B

An economist wishes to explain to an ordinary reader that social scientists have, in many respects, a more difficult job than physical scientists. He wants to open his essay with a paragraph which will both establish his purpose and attract the reader's attention. How should he go about writing this paragraph?

Of the various possibilities open to him, here are some:

1. He can state his purpose as a topic sentence and explain it by enumerating the economist's difficulties. If he does this, his introductory paragraph will summarize the whole essay. If he were writing for other economists or for physicists, that might be a satisfactory procedure, but an ordinary reader would probably find the paragraph difficult and uninteresting.
2. He can state his purpose in a topic sentence and then illustrate it by contrasting details, as in the pattern shown on page 45. This may be a little better than the first way, for the contrasting details are likely

[15] From *Life*, August 6, 1956. Copyright, 1956, by Time, Inc. Reprinted by permission.

to be more specific than a list of the difficulties. But it still requires the reader to get the gist of the essay from the first paragraph.

3. He can begin with an illustration showing a social scientist at work and the problems he faces. This opening will be more interesting than the others. It will also be concrete. But probably all the difficulties cannot be shown in a single paragraph, and how is the reader to know that a physical scientist does not have to cope with similar ones?

None of these answers is just right. What the writer needs is a solution that will allow him to contrast the conditions under which physical and social scientists work without actually presenting these conditions. Perhaps an analogy would help. If he could find a well-known example of two groups operating under conditions which gave one group an advantage, he could perhaps make his purpose clear without having to present a mass of detail in the introductory paragraph. See how he solved his problem.

> In discussing the relative difficulties of analysis which the exact and inexact sciences face, let me begin with an analogy. Would you agree that swimmers are less skillful athletes than runners because swimmers do not move as fast as runners? You probably would not. You would quickly point out that water offers greater resistance to swimmers than the air and ground do to runners. Agreed, that is just the point. In seeking to solve their problems, the social scientists encounter greater resistance than the physical scientists. By that I do not mean to belittle the great accomplishments of physical scientists who have been able, for example, to determine the structure of the atom without seeing it. That is a tremendous achievement; yet in many ways it is not so difficult as what the social scientists are expected to do. The conditions under which the social scientists must work would drive a physical scientist frantic. Here are five of those conditions. He can make few experiments; he cannot measure the results accurately; he cannot control the conditions surrounding the experiments; he is often expected to get quick results with slow-acting economic forces; and he must work with people, not with inanimate objects. Let us look at these conditions more closely.[16]

This paragraph combines analogy and analytical division. The analogy not only creates the reader interest which the writer wants, but it also gives a quick illustration of his purpose. The division establishes the factors or subtheses which the rest of the essay will illustrate. It thus leads the reader into the serious discussion of the succeeding paragraphs.

### Assignment C

A student is writing a research paper, on the thesis that Thomas

[16] From "Are Social Scientists Backward?" by Donald L. Kemmerer, in the *American Association of University Professors Bulletin,* Autumn, 1948.

Jefferson's writings are characterized by habits of careful research and independent thinking. As one illustration of this thesis she wants to cite Jefferson's work, *The Life and Morals of Jesus of Nazareth*. Here is the material she has in her notes.

1. T. J. pasted Greek, Latin, French, and English texts of New Testament side by side.
2. T. J. thought the Bible should be read critically, like any other book.
3. T. J. accepted or rejected stories about Jesus on the basis of their agreement with natural laws. Thus the teachings of Jesus OK, but miracles out. Anything that had to be explained by revelation also out.
4. "I think that every Christian sect gives a great handle to atheism by their general dogma that, without revelation, there would not be sufficient proof of the being of God" — Letter to Adams
5. T. J. considered Christianity purest system of morality known.

If this student simply strings these notes together in the form of a paragraph (as students sometimes do), this is the kind of product she will have:

Jefferson could read Greek, Latin, French, and English, so he pasted texts of the New Testament in these languages side by side. He thought that the Bible should be read critically, like any other book; so he accepted those stories about Jesus which agreed with natural laws, and rejected those that did not. He kept the teachings of Jesus but rejected the miracles. He also rejected anything that had to be explained by revelation. "I think," he wrote in a letter to Adams, "that every Christian sect gives a great handle to atheism by their general dogma that, without revelation, there would not be sufficient proof of the being of God." Jefferson considered Christianity the purest system of morality known.

Notice the weaknesses of this paragraph:

1. Although it discusses a book mentioned in a preceding paragraph, it does nothing to show a relation with that paragraph or any other. It needs some transitional sentence or phrase to tie it to what went before.
2. What is the purpose of the paragraph? We know from the description of the assignment that the writer wants to illustrate Jefferson's habits of careful research and independent thinking. The information does illustrate these habits, but the significance of the details would be made clearer by stating their purpose as the topic sentence.
3. While the repetition of "He" does provide a natural coherence within the paragraph, pronoun reference alone is not enough to weave the sentences into a coherent pattern. The lack of variety in sentence structure and the lack of transition between the first two sentences and between the last two gives the impression that the paragraph is merely a collection of sentences, which of course it is.

4. The last sentence seems to have no relation to the rest of the paragraph. If it is not a digression, its function should be indicated.

Now contrast the unsatisfactory paragraph with the one the student actually wrote:

> The actual writing of the book was controlled by two disciplines: careful collection and comparison of the evidence, and the acceptance or rejection of it on the basis of reason rather than authority. To compare the evidence, Jefferson pasted texts from the New Testament in Greek, Latin, French, and English in columns side by side. As he was proficient in all four languages he felt that he could come closer to the true meanings of the words by reading them in this way. To ensure that reason rather than the authority of tradition would guide him, he followed his own advice that the Bible should be read critically, like any other book. Accordingly, he accepted those stories which revealed the teachings of Jesus, and rejected stories of miracles, which, he felt, had no real relation to these teachings. He also rejected those passages which had to be supported by revelation. "I think," he wrote in a letter to Adams, "that every Christian sect gives a great handle to atheism by their general dogma that, without revelation, there would not be sufficient proof of the being of God." The result was a work which emphasized what Jefferson considered the purest system of morality known and toned down or omitted incidents which required a supernatural explanation.

Notice:

1. The topic sentence which states the purpose of the paragraph (and so gives point to all that follows) and also refers to the preceding paragraph by the phrase "The actual writing of the book."
2. The explanation of why Jefferson pasted the four different texts side by side. This explanation is necessary to illustrate the thoroughness of his working habits.
3. The clearer explanation of his selection and rejection of material ("To ensure that reason rather than authority . . ."). This explanation helps to bind together four sentences which, in the unsatisfactory version, were connected only by a common subject.
4. The concluding sentence, which not only shows the pertinence of what previously looked like a digression but also, by showing Jefferson's emphasis, sums up the content of the whole paragraph.
5. The more pleasing effect obtained by slight but significant variations in the basic sentence pattern.
6. Finally, the fact that in shaping her notes into a paragraph the writer was doing a creative piece of composition. She was making something from her material, giving form to the information she had acquired, not just presenting it unedited.

## Exercises

**A.** Study each of the following paragraphs and come to class prepared to answer the following questions:

1. What is the topic sentence? If none is explicitly stated, can you provide a sentence which expresses the topic idea?
2. What is the order of development of the paragraph — time, space, particular-to-general, general-to-particular, question to answer or effect to cause?
3. What transitional devices are used to keep the paragraph coherent?

### (1)

Chalk is almost wholly composed of carbonate of lime, a compound of lime and carbonic acid gas. The existence of both elements may easily be demonstrated by simple experiments. If a small quantity of powdered chalk is dropped into a good deal of strong vinegar, a great bubbling and fizzing will ensue and finally there will remain a clear liquid containing no trace of lime. The bubbles can be identified as carbonic acid gas. The lime has dissolved completely in the vinegar. But if, in a second experiment, chalk is burned, only the lime remains, the gas having been driven off by the heat. [Compare the order of this paragraph with the second paragraph on the same subject on page 102.]

### (2)

In the year 1830 a French customs official unearthed, in the valley of the Somme, strange implements of flint now recognized by the learned as the weapons with which the men of the Old Stone Age made war. These stones are called *coups de poing*, or "blows of the fist," for one end was rounded to be grasped in the hand, while the other end was pointed for persuasion. With these modest tools of death, it seems, Neanderthal men from what is now Germany, and Cro-Magnon men from what is now France, fought fifty thousand years ago for the mastery of the continent, and, after a day of lusty battle, left perhaps a score of dead on the field. Twenty years ago, modern Germans and modern Frenchmen fought again, in that same valley, for that same prize, with magnificent tools of death that killed ten thousand men in a day. One art alone has made indisputable progress in history and that is the art of war.[17]

### (3)

The purist claims to base his case on cultivated usage, but even this claim is largely specious, for cultivated usage is by no means wholly on his side. Such usage may eschew the double negative; it may separate *sit* from *set;* but there is a large proportion of the purist's dictums which it fails to justify. Take the business of *It's me,* for example. Cultivated

[17] Will Durant, "Why Men Fight," *The Saturday Evening Post,* July 10, 1937. Reprinted by permission of the author and the Curtis Publishing Company.

conversational practice is very definitely against *It is I* (see for example the analysis of this locution in Leonard's *Current English Usage*) and yet the purist declines to budge from his championing of the latter phrasing. As a matter of fact, *It is I* is only a third in a series of changes from Old English *Ic eom hit* (*I am it*) down through Chaucer's *It am I* to the present, fourth stage, *It's me.* To be historically consistent the purist should go back to Old English. To be grammatically consistent he should accept the fourth change to *It's me,* a change which has taken place in actual fact.[18]

## (4)

Yes, you may say, but if fraternities and sororities should be abolished, wouldn't students organize other cliques and clubs? I admit they would, but such groups would be formed in a normal natural way. Students would be judged on their merits and find their own level. A boy or girl would not be relegated to a fixed position in campus society during the first days of school, as is provided under smug Panhellenic rules, merely because of the prestige or bank account of his parents, or because of the way he flipped a cigarette or handled a cup of tea.[19]

## (5)

If I were a freshman (again) I should determine to do some one line of work well. As I remember, I was principally concerned in "getting through." I think I was not quite so modest in my scholastic ambitions as the young fellow who told me not long ago that a "pass" was as good as one hundred per cent to him, but at least I was not so much concerned about doing my best in some one line of work as I wish now I had been. Practically every college man, every freshman included, is rushed with his work. He takes more "hours" than he should, or he neglects to prepare the assignments at the proper time, so that when his work is done it is done hastily. Nine out of ten freshmen are behind with assigned work. I have known fellows even to go as far as to argue that it is an excellent practice to get behind, for then if one is to catch up he must force himself to do a large amount of work in a short time. I grant that this may be a good thing, but work done under such conditions usually shows all the earmarks of slovenliness and superficiality. There are many subjects in which I think it would be sufficient to merely do good work, but at least in one subject I wish I had made it a point to take time to give the matter careful thought, and to do it as well as it was possible for me to do.[20]

[18] From Janet Rankin Aiken's *Commonsense Grammar.* Copyright, 1936, by Janet Rankin Aiken. Reprinted by permission of the publishers, Thomas Y. Crowell Company.

[19] From Mrs. Glenn Frank's "Heartache on the Campus," *Woman's Home Companion,* April, 1945. Reprinted by permission of the *Woman's Home Companion.*

[20] Thomas Arkle Clark, "If I Were a Freshman Again." From *The American College Magazine* for July, 1910.

(6)

One day a girl brought me a composition that had been corrected and returned. On the two pages that it occupied there was a total of 127 corrections. I could not get any coherent picture from such a complete mess, so I tabulated the errors according to type. Out of the 127 mistakes, 92 came from wrong punctuation. There were no errors of capitalization or grammar. Two sentences were incomplete, 19 were far too long and involved, 8 contained wrong references, and 6 lacked parallelism. The girl had another composition to write at once. I told her to go to work on it, but to concentrate on the avoidance of a single error — the long, loose-jointed sentences. In fact, I was so sure from the analysis that her key mistake was mere length that I instructed her to use not over fifteen words per sentence. She promised to keep within this limit and went into an adjoining laboratory. I did not see the finished product, but I know she went directly to class where she handed in her work, and I know she got no help from anyone. The total length of this second composition was about twenty words more than the first, but when it came back there were only eight errors — one incomplete sentence, three errors in spelling and four unnecessary commas. All of the mistakes the girl had made earlier had been pyramided upon the single error of trying to write sentences that were too long. Naturally, this girl still needed to learn how to write sentences that were of greater length than fifteen words, but the situation was much clarified for all concerned by this isolation of the key difficulty.[21]

(7)

creative

Some of the current coinages show a considerable ingenuity, e.g., *klim,* the name of a powdered milk, which is simply *milk* backward; *flit,* a spray for obnoxious insects, suggesting very forcibly their precipitate departure; *rem,* a cough cure, obviously based on *remedy; jonteel,* a perfume, from the French *gentile; toncan,* a brand of sheet-iron, produced by reversing the syllables of *Canton,* the town in Ohio where it is made. . . . Many trade-names embody efforts to state claims for the product without colliding with the legal prohibition of descriptive terms, e.g., *holeproof, eversharp, interwoven, softee,* and *klingtite.*[22]

(8)

From the point of view of the ordinary citizen, democracy is both the easiest and most difficult form of government. It is the easiest because it permits each citizen a high degree of freedom. In a democracy, more than in any other form of government, he remains his own man — free to think, talk, and worship as he pleases, and, within wide limits, free to carve out for himself whatever kind of profession or career seems to him most lucrative or most satisfying. Yet these privileges are not purchased

[21] From Luella Cole's *The Backgrounds for College Teaching* (Copyright 1940 by Farrar & Rinehart). Reprinted by permission of Rinehart & Company, Inc.

[22] From H. L. Mencken, *Supplement I: The American Language.* Copyright, 1945, by Alfred A. Knopf, publisher.

without a price. For a democracy makes heavy demands of each citizen. It places upon him the responsibility of being continually informed of the needs not only of his own country but of the whole world. It requires him to weigh and decide which of several conflicting policies will best meet these needs. It demands that he distinguish between the interests of special groups and the general welfare, and between immediate and long range interests. It insists that he learn to observe the will of the majority without ignoring the rights of minorities. And it constantly requires of him the difficult task of seeing the implications of economic, political, and social theories and of sensing the effect that these implications will have in the lives of his grandchildren.

### (9)

I remember once hearing a rhythmic noise coming from a Salteaux wigwam. Peering under the wigwam covering I saw a young girl rocking a cradle. The cradle was made of a strip of bark slung from a pole resting on two forked sticks driven into the ground near the fire. At first I thought the noises came from the baby, but I soon realized that it was only the dry bearing of stick on crotch that made the weird and agonizing squeaks.[23]

### (10)

Below them lay a little semicircular green cove. At its deepest indentation a full brook splashed into the lake. The curving, shining channel led back up to a large white frame house shaped like an L with the long side facing the wide water. It stood in dazzling brightness and its reflecting white sides gave it so clean and luminous a quality that sight of it seemed almost unbearable in the intense clarity. The effect was the stronger for the softness of the atmosphere that lay upon the lake. Out there was blueness and a misty blending of light and air. Here the sun seemed to have sent a straight shaft down to illumine the objects within a sharply defined circle. In the center stood the tall white house, and on the edges but still within the light squatted weathered gray log cabins. Beyond the circle other cabins, many of them, were indistinct in the blurred distance. Where the upward slope of the shore ended on a high plateau a grove of towering hickories dispelled the light and seemed to keep it from spilling outside the circle.[24]

**B.** Study the following selection to observe both the internal development of the paragraphs and the way they are related to each other. Then summarize the selection in a single paragraph which opens with a topic sentence. Finally, compare your paragraph with the original and decide whether, considering that he was writing for ordinary readers, the writer was wise to take five paragraphs to say what you said in one.

What makes an airplane fly is not its engine nor its propeller. Nor is

---

[23] From *Canoes* by Terence T. Quirke. Copyright, 1952, by the University of Illinois Press. Reprinted by permission.
[24] From *Genesee Fever*, by Carl Carmer. Copyright, 1941, by Carl Carmer. Reprinted by permission of the author.

it, as many people think, some mysterious knack of the pilot, nor some ingenious gadget inside. What makes an airplane fly is simply its shape. This may sound absurd, but gliders do fly without engines and model airplanes do fly without pilots. As for the insides of an airplane, they are disappointing for they are mostly hollow. No, what keeps an airplane up is its shape — the impact of the air upon its shape. Whittle that shape out of wood, or cast it out of iron, or fashion it, for that matter, out of chocolate and throw the thing into the air. It will behave like an airplane. It will *be* an airplane.

This — that its shape is what counts — is what makes the airplane so beautiful. It also makes it easy to understand. You don't have to open it up and look at "the works" inside as one has to do with a watch, a refrigerator or an automobile. An airplane's outside appearance is its "works." If you want to understand it, simply have a look.

Look at the wing. It holds the airplane up entirely by its shape. A wing is nothing but an air deflector, curved so and set at such an angle that it will catch the air and push it down. The air, resisting, pushes back up against the wing's bottom surface and that gives it some lift. At the same time — and this is more important — the wing also creates a lack of air on its top surface because of the way it is curved there. Thus it sucks air down from above. That air, resisting, sucks back upward on the wing's top surface and this is what gives the wing most of its lift. . . .

It is simple. If flight seems just the same a little miraculous and, to many people, still a little unsound, it is not because the natural law involved is at all strange. The law is the old one of action and reaction: if you push against *anything*, that thing resists and pushes back against you. As the gun pushes the bullet forward, the bullet kicks the gun backward making it recoil. What seems so strange about flying is merely that the thing we work against is air. And air is strange stuff. Because we cannot see it, we think of it as nothing. Because we cannot pinch it between our fingers, we think of it as empty space. And thus an airplane seems to sit up there in empty space, held up by nothing.

Actually, air is real stuff, just as real as water. It has density and body. It is a thick and slightly sticky fluid, molasses-like, though very thin molasses. Its tendency to stick to the skin of an airplane causes much headache to the engineers. It has weight. A cubic yard of air (a bathtubful) weighs about 2 lb. Thus if we could only see air, all the mystery would go out of flying at once. We could then see the fierce attack with which the wing smashes into that stuff. We could see the terrific downward wallop which the wing gives to thousands of pounds of air every minute. And we could see that everywhere in the wake of an airplane, the air is in downward flow and keeps swirling and eddying for many minutes when the airplane itself is already miles farther on.[25]

C. The following unorganized information is about amounts of money spent during a national political convention and during a Presidential campaign. First, select information concerning convention expenses and

[25] From "Why an Airplane Flies," by Wolfgang Langewiesche, in *Life*, May 17, 1943. Copyright by Wolfgang Langewiesche. Reprinted by permission of the author.

write a paragraph explaining and illustrating the thesis that a convention is a big business enterprise for the city that gets it. Then follow the same procedure for the campaign. Finally write an introductory paragraph and provide the necessary transition to shape the finished work into a three-paragraph essay developing a thesis. You may provide illustrative material of your own and you may omit some of the information provided here. Unless otherwise stated, the figures are estimates for 1956.[26]

1. One manufacturing company does $100,000 worth of business in campaign buttons.

2. The Yellow Cab Company in San Francisco expected to clear an extra $10,000 a day on convention business.

3. In 1952 delegates from both parties and their friends spent $5 million for food, hotel rooms, and recreation.

4. Airplane companies collected about $2.5 million for chartered flights during the campaign.

5. Rent for campaign quarters in Los Angeles alone cost about $750 a month for each major candidate; staffing the headquarters required another $35,000.

6. The cost of a single coast-to-coast run for a campaign train is about $46,000, not counting food and refreshments.

7. During the campaign, radio and television do about $20 million worth of business.

8. Delegates to the convention, their families, and friends spend about $170 for each person.

9. To obtain the 1956 conventions, Chicago and San Francisco each paid $250,000. This money was paid by merchants.

10. One Chicago jeweler expected to sell $225,000 worth of campaign jewelry.

11. There is a substantial business in novelties — ball-point pens, auto stickers, bumper strips, campaign wrappers, and so on.

12. Newspaper circulation increases 5 to 15 per cent during the campaign.

**D.** From the material supplied on page 60, supplemented by your experience with other students, write a substantial paragraph developing the topic sentence: *Inferior students could help themselves by adopting the study habits used by superior students.*

**E.** From your work in another course, select a technical term and explain it clearly to your classmates in a paragraph which moves from dictionary definition to clarifying statement to example.

**F.** Without actually writing it, plan a three-paragraph essay dealing with the things that most surprise you about college. Then indicate the

[26] Data taken from "Cashing in on Campaigning," *Newsweek*, August 13, 1956.

structure of the essay you have been planning, either by an outline or an informal pattern.

**G.** Select any three of the following statements. Use each of them as the topic sentence of a paragraph. Develop the paragraph so that it is complete, unified, and coherent.

1. The transition from high school to college life is a difficult one.
2. Essentially, college is a place in which students learn from each other.
3. Student activities belong to the students.
4. The educational value of fraternity bull sessions is greatly overrated.
5. There is a significant distinction between self-confidence and conceit.
6. Much adolescent shyness is sheer egotism.
7. What is college spirit?
8. There never yet was a self-made man.
9. It is easier to confess our sins than our weaknesses.

# 7

## ✳ EFFECTIVE
## ✳
## ✳ SENTENCES
## ✳
## ✳

---

TRULY EFFECTIVE SENTENCES — those which are neat and sure as well as accurate — are probably more often rewritten than written. Inexperienced writers, especially, do not always find the best expression of their thoughts in a first draft, but have to work over what they have written once it is down on paper. For this reason, much of this chapter applies more to revision than to the first draft. Yet practice at getting your sentences right finally is the best preparation for learning to get them right at the first try.

The chief characteristics of effective sentences are *clarity, consistency, economy,* and *variety.* These are not separate virtues. Clear sentences are likely to be consistent, economical, and varied; conversely, unclear ones are often inconsistent and wordy. For ease of discussion, however, we shall take up these characteristics one by one.

## *Clarity*

Most unclear sentences fail because the writer has not kept his reader in mind. Obviously, a writer who is confused about his own meaning is not likely to convey it clearly to anyone else. But merely knowing what one wants to say is no guarantee of clarity. The writer must always remember that unless he expresses himself in ways which will be as clear to the reader as they are to him, his meaning may be misunderstood or not understood at all.

In practice, this requirement is not so difficult as it may seem, because both the writer and the reader have grown up with the same system of language conventions. Therefore, if the writer follows the system, the reader will respond as he is supposed to. When sentences are unclear, the writer usually is not following the conventions. He is making the wrong signals, and the reader is likely to become either confused or irritated.

The most common specific causes of unclear sentences are inadequate punctuation, confused pronoun reference, and misleading word order.

### Inadequate Punctuation

The following is from a letter written by a physician to an insurance company in answer to the question whether there was any active tuberculosis in the family of an applicant:

> In none of this period has there been any active, open tuberculosis in any member of the family, with the exception of his younger sister, none of the family have had any chronic illness of any kind.

If you were an officer of the insurance company and had to charge a higher premium if there was active tuberculosis in the family, which rate would you charge, and how would you justify your decision on the evidence of this letter?

The confusion in this letter comes chiefly from the fact that two sentences have been written as one. When the reader, recognizing the error, tries to break the sentences apart, he cannot tell to which sentence the all-important phrase — "with the exception of his younger sister" — belongs. Remember, there was no doubt in the doctor's mind. He knew the facts, and he had no intention of misleading or confusing the insurance company. But his failure to see his answer as his reader would see it caused him to assume that what was clear to him would be equally clear to others. Had he detected the ambiguity before he mailed the letter, he could have corrected it simply by separating the two sentences by a period, as the conventions of punctuation require him to do.

> In none of this period has there been any active, open tuberculosis in any member of the family. With the exception of his younger sister, none of the family have had any chronic illness of any kind.[1]

In the following sentences poor punctuation may invite misinterpretation on the first reading. Can you revise the punctuation so as to remove any possible confusion? [2]

1. I had to make a ground check of the radio, the mechanics and their helpers had to check the instruments and fill the gas tanks.

2. I asked him, before you arrived, I wanted to know what happened.

3. They have been unable to find an apartment since he returned from service they have been living with their parents.

4. Throughout the game was hopelessly one-sided.

---

[1] For additional exercises on this kind of error, see the *Comma Splice,* pages 427–430.

[2] For additional exercises, see pages 504 ff.

5. She did not care for movies meant little to her.

6. There has been no significant change in his condition since the accident he has been conscious for only a few minutes.

7. Mother was very pleased when your letter came she was so happy she cried.

8. None of the brothers was willing to show much sympathy for his action was not only mean but reflected on the whole chapter.

9. When we started to eat the dog, after a few timid advances, came over beside us.

10. She broke her wrist and her right ankle was discolored and swollen.

## Confused Pronoun Reference

You have seen that using pronouns which point back to nouns in earlier sentences is one way to make a paragraph coherent. But a pronoun which has no clear antecedent, which points ambiguously to several, or is too far away from its antecedent may create an awkward, ludicrous, or confusing sentence. Observe how the following sentences are improved when they are revised to make the pronoun reference clearer.

| *Confusing Reference* | *Clear Reference* |
|---|---|
| My coat was too shabby to wear to the dance. He lent me his because it looked so bad. | He lent me his coat to wear to the dance because mine was shabby. |
| I lived on a farm and drank unpasteurized milk. Now that I am older, I wouldn't do that. | When I lived on a farm I drank unpasteurized milk. I wouldn't drink it now. |
| Parents are hopelessly prejudiced in favor of their children when they are small. They are really not much better than savages, but they think of them as angels. | Although small children are not much better than savages, their parents regard them as angels. |

Any writer may be trapped into a confused pronoun reference when he is writing a first draft, but really awkward references are so easy to detect that there is little excuse for not discovering and correcting them in revision. You should have no difficulty removing the confused pronoun references in the following sentences.[3]

1. Students ought to have conferences with their instructors frequently, and if they need help with their work they should give it to them.

2. Her sister met her at the station and she ran to her and embraced her.

3. James Stewart did a wonderful job of acting, and by looking so much like Glenn Miller it made the movie seem almost as if he was playing the role.

[3] For additional exercises, see *Ambiguous Modifiers*, pages 446–447, and *Vague Pronoun Reference*, pages 447–449.

4. Young men who go to war must leave their homes and friends. But if they love them, they will help to make the parting easy.

5. Four people were killed when the car missed the curve. There are several dangerous curves on that road and this one crashed into a viaduct.

6. I ate venison for the first time at their house, which I found to have a very strong flavor.

7. No one would make such a statement about our President unless he was trying to undermine our democracy.

8. In this story the two brothers quarrel and their wives take sides with them. Then their children become involved in the quarrel. When they see what is happening to them they decide they had better have a reconciliation.

## Misleading Word Order

The basic convention of English word order is that related elements be kept as close together as possible. Thus a modifier should be kept close to the word it modifies. Unless this convention is observed, the reference of a modifier may be misleading, as it is in the following examples.[4]

| Misleading Word Order | Explanation | Improved Word Order |
|---|---|---|
| I was born on a small farm where I lived until I was ten. I grew up observing how the different vegetables and fruits grew *without any special effort.* | *The italicized phrase is intended to modify* observing, *but its position suggests that it modifies* grew. *It should be put as close to* observing *as possible.* | I was born on a small farm where I lived until I was ten. I grew up observing, *without any special effort,* how the different vegetables and fruits grew. |
| The prosecution revealed that she had planned to kill him *repeatedly.* | Repeatedly *is intended to modify* had planned. *This order suggests that it modifies* to kill. | The prosecution revealed that she had *repeatedly* planned to kill him. |
| Today a woman is not required to promise to love, honor and obey her husband *in many marriage ceremonies.* | *The position of the italicized phrase is awkward because it allows an important idea to dangle at the end of the sentence and also permits an unintended meaning. The revision at the right cannot be misinterpreted.* | *Many marriage ceremonies* no longer require the woman to promise to love, honor, and obey her husband. |

[4] For additional exercises, see *Ambiguous Modifiers,* pages 446–447.

Revise the following sentences to correct any misleading word order.

1. The man who was nominated to the cabinet post said he would sell his stock in any company that might receive government contracts as soon as his appointment was confirmed by the Senate.
2. The athletic office announced that all tickets had been sold for the homecoming game on August 15.
3. The coach said that the movie of last week's game would be shown while dessert was being served.
4. According to the police, a car had been found in a downtown garage fitting the description of the getaway car.
5. The kitten jumped into her lap as she sat on the sofa and purred contentedly.
6. This was the only English course I received credit for because of my leaving college for active service.

## Consistency

All sentences follow conventional patterns. The writer is free to choose the pattern that best suits his purpose, but once he has committed himself to a particular pattern he is expected to follow it consistently until he has finished the sentence. If he does not, if he leads the reader to expect one pattern and then shifts to another, the reader will accuse him of clumsiness.

Two types of sentence patterns are most likely to cause errors of this kind. These are the *parallel* (or *balanced*) sentence and the *periodic* sentence.

### The Parallel Sentence

A parallel sentence is one in which two or more parts expressing ideas of equal importance are presented in similar grammatical forms. The pattern of the parallel sentence can be seen in the following examples.

1. Speak softly and carry a big stick.

This sentence consists of two main clauses connected by the conjunction *and*. The clauses might be thought of as opposite sides of a balance, with the conjunction serving as the fulcrum. In its present form the sentence is balanced. If, however, it is written,

Speak softly and you should carry a big stick.

the balance is destroyed. The two parts of the sentence are no longer parallel, since the verbs are in different moods and one has an expressed subject while the other has not.

2. I do not want to see him or to talk to him.

The parallelism of this sentence becomes apparent when we set it up thus,

I do not want

to see him

or

to talk to him.

We see that the two infinitive phrases which complete the verb are parallel in structure. If we write the sentence,

I do not want to *see* him or *talking* to him.

we destroy the parallelism. But notice that the omission of the second *to* in the original sentence would not affect the grammatical construction for that *to* would be understood as following the first one even if not expressed.

3. He was encouraged to persevere by the wishes of his parents, the advice of his teachers, and the hopes of his friends.

In this sentence a series of phrases, all similar in form, complete the preposition *by*, thus:

He was encouraged to persevere by

the wishes of his parents,

the advice of his teachers,

and

the hopes of his friends.

The parallelism of these phrases would be destroyed if the sentence had been written:

He was encouraged to persevere by

*the wishes* of his parents,

*the advice* of his teachers,

and

*to justify* his friends' hopes.

On the evidence of these examples we can say that *in a parallel sentence, elements similar in idea and grammatical function should be similar in form*. The elements may be main clauses, subordinate clauses, phrases, or single words; they may act as subjects, verbs, complements, or modifiers; they may be balanced in pairs (as they are in examples 1 and 2), or they may constitute a series (example 3). But, whatever their nature, they show a regularity of structure and rhythm which constitutes a recognizable pattern.

When well written, the parallel sentence can be a very effective pattern because it can say so much — and say it so neatly — in such small space. Notice how much the student author of the following paragraphs packs into some seventy-five words by her use of the parallel sentence.

A man who had this quality [of quiet gentleness] could be large or small, serious or light-hearted, quiet or loquacious, but in his relations with others he would be gentle and understanding.

If he had it, he would love without demanding love in return, he would hold firm convictions without being dogmatic, he would criticize without being caustic, he would sympathize without being patronizing, and he would be constantly awake to the feelings of others.

When a writer begins what is evidently a parallel construction, his readers expect him to continue it. If halfway through the sentence he introduces elements which are not parallel with those that went before, he strikes a discord in the reader's ear. If he begins a series with a noun, he must continue with nouns. If he begins with infinitives, he must stick to infinitives. If he uses a simple conjunction (*and, or, nor, but*), the reader will assume that the part of the sentence just after the conjunction will be parallel to the part just before it.

These requirements sometimes put quite a strain on an inexperienced writer who has started a parallel sentence, perhaps without realizing it, and who is more concerned with getting his thought on paper than with observing conventions. No such strain exists when that writer is revising. It should not be too difficult to revise the following sentences so as to make similar elements parallel in form.[5]

1. We knew that he was lying but being unable to prove it because of lack of evidence.

2. The instructor said that we would take up the chapter at the next meeting of the class and for us to study it carefully before then.

3. Only some comic books are a bad influence. Many teach children that crime does not pay and to provide wholesome entertainment.

4. He said that girls are fickle, frivolous, and he was crazy about them.

5. If I understand you correctly, you're saying that what poetry does is to give an individual a sense of harmony, a sense of fulfillment, make him more complete or feel more significant.

6. Every engineer who has expectations of becoming an executive some day and not be just a machinist should learn to speak and write well.

7. The new secretary has already demonstrated his ability to win the confidence of congressmen, to deal frankly with the press without saying more than he should, and how to get wholehearted cooperation from his subordinates.

8. This writer says that athletic scholarships are unnecessary, unethical, and create a false sense of values in the boys who receive them.

[5] For additional exercises, see *Faulty Parallelism*, pages 430–432.

9. We subscribe to some of the leading periodicals, such as *Reader's Digest, Time,* and a few women's magazines.

## The Periodic Sentence

Another troublesome construction is the periodic sentence. A periodic sentence is one in which the main thought is not completed until the end. Such a sentence frequently opens with a subordinate clause, a long introductory phrase, or a series of modifying elements. The following sentence from *Time's* review of *Henry V* is a good example:

1. To find the "kind of poetic country" he wanted, and to avoid such chance anachronisms as air raids (the picture was made in Britain during the war), Olivier shot the battle sequence in Ireland.

In normal order, this sentence would begin with the main clause — *Olivier shot the battle sequence in Ireland.* By inverting the normal order, the writer produces a sentence with a stronger ending, but one which requires the reader to hold the modifying phrases in mind until he reaches the main statement.

In the examples below, the main clauses have been italicized.

2. While he would not make any definite commitment, and wants to consult his father before talking with you, *I think he is going to buy.*
3. Showing a great deal more power than we had expected, *the team ran up three victories in succession.*
4. Thwarted in his attempts to enlist the support of his colleagues against the measure, *the senator threatened to filibuster.*

Periodic sentences which open with phrases (examples 1, 3, and 4) often lead to inconsistent constructions. In such sentences the reader usually expects the introductory phrase to modify the subject of the main clause. If the phrase does not do so, it is said to be a *dangling modifier.* Thus, in the sentence, "Slamming the door behind her, their marriage was at an end," there is nothing in the main clause for the opening phrase to modify, so it seems to modify "marriage." Had the sentence been written,

Slamming the door behind her, Mary walked out of his life.

the phrase would have modified *Mary* and would not have been left dangling.

The introductory modifiers most likely to be left dangling are participial phrases, infinitive phrases, and elliptical clauses. A participial phrase usually opens with a present or a past participle — *slamming, having slammed, deserting, deserted.*[6] An infinitive phrase is built on the in-

---

[6] For an explanation of participles and infinitives, see pages 420–423.

finitive form of the verb — *to do, to speak, to try.* An elliptical clause is one in which significant parts have been omitted but are implied — *When tired* for *When I am tired, While reading* for *While I was reading.*

An introductory dangling modifier is usually revised by (1) rewording the main clause so that the opening phrase may modify its subject, (2) converting the phrase into a subordinate clause, or (3) expanding an elliptical clause to provide its missing elements. These methods are illustrated below.

| *Dangling Modifiers* | *Explanation* | *Revised Form* |
|---|---|---|
| Seeing the policeman out of the corner of one eye, my car came to a dead stop at the intersection. | *Since the participle* Seeing *seems to modify* car, *revise the main clause to give it a subject which* Seeing *may logically modify.* | Seeing the policeman out of the corner of one eye, I brought my car to a full stop at the intersection. |
| Having spilled paint all over the carpet, my wife was annoyed with me. | *Who spilled the paint? Grammar suggests the wife; the sense suggests the husband. Make grammar and sense agree by changing the participial phrase to a clause.* | When I spilled the paint all over the carpet my wife was annoyed with me. |
| To make sure that your paper is well organized, an outline will help. | *The sentence is not ambiguous but it is awkward, since the infinitive has nothing to modify. Keep the same subject throughout the sentence as at the right.* | To make sure that your paper is well organized you should make an outline. |
| When not yet five, my father began daily batting practice with me in our backyard. | *When not yet five is an elliptical clause meaning* When I was not yet five. *To make it refer to the boy rather than his father, insert the missing elements.* | When I was not yet five, my father began daily batting practice with me in our backyard. |

The dangling modifiers in the following sentences may be revised by whichever method seems best: [7]

---

[7] For additional exercises, see *Dangling Modifiers,* pages 432–435.

1. While standing on the corner, two cars collided in the intersection.
2. Eating our lunch, the child watched us hungrily.
3. Having lost all his money gambling, his girl broke off their engagement.
4. When in the eighth grade, my parents moved to California.
5. Lying in the hammock, the big elm looked diseased.
6. Refreshed by a shower and a good meal, the remaining 200 miles seemed an easy jaunt.
7. Looking out the kitchen window, the grass needed cutting.
8. After failing algebra, Dad began a twenty-minute drill session each evening after supper.

## Grammatical Consistency

A writer is also expected to be consistent in his use of grammatical forms. He is expected to keep his tenses consistent; to make subjects and verbs agree in number and person; to make pronouns agree with their antecedents in gender, number, and person; to spell words and punctuate sentences in accordance with established practice — in short, to follow the recognized conventions of educated usage. Since a complete review of these conventions would lead us afield from the purpose of this chapter, we shall confine ourselves here to inconsistent pronoun references and leave other grammatical inconsistencies to Part Three.

One common kind of inconsistency is the unnecessary and awkward shuttling between a personal and an impersonal subject or between first, second, and third person pronouns. Look at the following excerpt from a student theme.

If *one* has developed good English usage through listening to eloquent speakers and has read worthy material, *they* will be able to speak correct English. One of the best ways to keep *your* speaking and writing up to a high standard is to keep away from inferior styles and stay on a level with which *you* are familiar.

This student would have done well to take her own advice. If, instead of shifting the subject from *one* to *they* to *you,* she had kept to the informal *you* throughout, her paragraph would have been more consistent.

It is not difficult, once you see how such shifting bothers a reader, to catch any examples of it in your first draft. Which pronoun you choose will depend on how formal you want to be. The impersonal *one* is more formal than most student composition requires, and it sounds stilted when used repeatedly in a paragraph. For this reason the shift from *one* or *one's* to *he, his,* or *him* (whichever case is appropriate) has become acceptable even to fastidious readers. With this exception you should stick consistently with the pronoun you have decided to use.

Inconsistency in the person of the pronoun usually goes hand in hand with unnecessary shifts in subject, with shifts from active to passive voice, and with changes from a formal to an informal style. All these inconsistencies are reflected in the following sentences. Can you correct them? [8]

1. No matter what one does for a woman like that, you just can't please her.
2. The paragraph begins with a topic sentence and tells what is to be explained, and after that he sticks right to the topic.
3. When you get a good grade on an important quiz, one's morale is definitely improved.
4. No one knows how large the cave is, but they are hoping it will be larger than was originally thought.
5. A person feels that he could write a good answer on a question but not enough time is allowed for the examination, so you just do what can be done quickly.
6. The hand-drawn maps show very little detail but is used chiefly in finding the target, as they are very closely marked on these maps.
7. I am sure that you are aware that a person can change his or her name if they so desire.
8. I like the first description better than the other two. I think it is written more clearly, so that you can actually imagine what it looks like. One can mentally picture Rockefeller Center, the offices, the elevators, and the people.
9. When you are writing your research paper, a typewriter is desired but not required.
10. Each state was to set up its own commission which shall make its selection of eligibility on the basis of intellectual capacity and financial need, but the stipend to the student is not to exceed eight hundred dollars or to exceed four years.

## *Economy*

Contrast the two following sentences:

1. If there were an imaginary race of people, all the members of which had this characteristic in common, that, because of some defect in their physiological structure, they were not able to perceive any of the colors which we see, except blue, there is every reason for believing that this race of people would probably not be able to extract from their experience a law to the effect that blue was the only color which they were able to see.
2. If a race of people had the physiological defect of being able to see only the color blue, they would hardly be able to formulate the rule that they saw only blue.

These two sentences say exactly the same thing. But the first says it in eighty words and the second says it more clearly in thirty-two. The

[8] For additional exercises, see *Shifts in Subjects and Verbs*, pages 435–438.

wordiness of the first sentence creates no literary merit lacking in the second sentence, nor does it allow fuller development or qualification of meaning. The first sentence simply contains forty-eight words which in no way help communication. Rather, they take extra effort from the reader without adding meaning.

Wordiness is one of the worst weaknesses in writing. For the reader, it can often be worse than grammatical errors, misspellings, and other lapses from educated usage. Bad grammar may irritate him but it will only occasionally obscure meaning. But sustained wordiness puts a heavy burden on the reader and may baffle him completely.

In student writing the chief causes of wordiness are (1) misguided attempts at a literary style, and (2) failure to eliminate useless words in revision.

## Pretentious Diction

Good writing is first of all clear. "Literary" flourishes that make the reader's task harder are worse than useless; they are harmful. Consider this excerpt from a student paper:

> It was fortunate, or unfortunate, depending on the circumstances and the evaluation thereof, that I had no formulated or precise conceptions when I left high school and commenced work as a telegraphist in the Public Service. While on duty one evening, a colleague, who was interested in weight lifting, allowed me to peruse a book on the subject entitled *Big Arms,* by Bob Hoffman. Not yet having realized my latent interest in athletic endeavors, I was surprised at the manner in which the book held my interest. This I only realized after a while. It was that book which stimulated me to make a purchase of a weight-lifting set, and despite the inhibiting influences of long work hours, little sleep and irregular meals, to exercise in my free moments.

It would be hard to imagine a less successful paragraph, yet this student has something to say: that his interest in weight-lifting stems from a book which a fellow worker in the telegraph office once lent him. That is not a difficult idea to express. Yet the student's inability — or unwillingness — to put it down in simple language traps him into a pretentious style and smothers his thought with words, many of them inappropriate and most of them unnecessary. The revision that follows has no special literary merit, except the greatest merit of all — it expresses a simple observation in suitable and concise language.

> I became interested in weight-lifting while I was working as a telegraphist. One of my office mates, who was enthusiastic about the sport, lent me a book called *Big Arms,* by Bob Hoffman. That book so stimulated me that I bought a weight-lifting set and began to exercise in every spare moment.

The second version has less than half as many words as the first; yet it includes everything that bears on the writer's purpose. It contains no distinguished diction, but none is required. The big words of the original version ("evaluation thereof," "formulated or precise conceptions," "commenced," "colleague," and "latent interest in athletic endeavors") are liabilities in such a paragraph. The second version is not only more concise; it is much more effective.

A student who feels that "lofty" diction helps to create a literary style should read successful modern writers. Many of our best plays, poems, short stories, articles, and essays are simply and informally written. Indeed, to write simply is a better test of literary ability than most students realize, for it is easy to use pretentious diction, but quite hard to present a complex idea or a moving experience in simple, natural language. There is a great deal of truth in the playwright Sheridan's comment that "easy writing's curst hard reading" — and it is equally true that hard writing makes for easy reading. Readability is one good test of writing, and good, readable prose is often the fruit of careful revision. That is why we said at the beginning of this chapter that truly effective sentences are probably more often rewritten than written.

The following contrasted sentences further illustrate how a "pretentious" style obscures meaning. In so far as they can be translated, the student sentences at the left have been revised into the more natural statements at the right.

| *Pretentious and Obscure* | *Clearer* |
| --- | --- |
| As I grew older I became more interested in the different fields of occupation and what they had to offer me as far as choosing a life's occupation was concerned. | As I grew older I began to examine more carefully the relative advantages of different professions. |
| Our educational system is not lacking in any way as to its purpose of helping one to prepare oneself for the requirements of a future career. | Education succeeds in preparing us for our future careers. |
| Trusting that I have imparted the fact that I, too, have dreamed the same dreams that girls always do, I deem it best to conclude this version of my innermost fancies. | I end this description of my reveries with the hope that they reveal me as a normal girl. |
| I found myself stepping from the rather casual high school life into a world of serious, studious adults. The three months' interlude between classes was hardly enough to adapt oneself to the new environment. The transitory extent of those ninety-six days was astonishing, and soon those of us who chose a higher degree of education found ourselves among unfamiliar gray walls. | The summer vacation was all too short to prepare me to bridge the gap between the adolescent level of high school and the adult level of college. |

The following sentences are pretentious and obscure. Try to decide what they were intended to say and rewrite them in plain English.

1. Concerning my own sojourn within the portals of higher education, I have spent a little more than a semester in college.

2. Although I cannot truthfully say that I was acclaimed during my high school career as a prodigy, being what is generally known as an average student, I was able to survive the rigors of four years of academic pursuits and to achieve graduation without ever having received a single failing grade in any subject.

3. The ideas put forth are misleading, however exact, and could only be used if the entire selection were modified to include only those suggestions for improvement of only several of the large scope of ideas enumerated.

4. Due to the present accessibility of all types of comics to our youth of today, they are exerting an ever-increasing adverse influence upon our youth. The evil is additionally malignant because it is exerted on our youth during their most formative years.

5. In a youth the mind is also young and tends to do most which is exciting and adventurous. Comic books can destroy the legacy for the support of a good and moral foundation in children.

6. Usually his expectations are fulfilled, for the gentleman he is introduced to does understand very well the various phrases, selections of words, and grammatical structures, that otherwise might not be understood by a person whose geographical location of his home was not what his was.

7. She participated in several excursions undertaken by our class to the local museums and other institutions of cultural interest and was always a factor in the livelihood.

8. The quest for equipment of lighter dimensions has launched a complete reconsideration of many electrical theories in the attempt to reduce the density of the particular element of which the theory is back of.

9. One of the many reasons the affirmative speaker is more persuasive than the negative is because the reasoning involved by the former is founded upon concrete principles.

10. This trend was due to the non-production of cars during the war, the lack of gasoline available for non-military functions during the war, and the many veterans who were in demand of cars at this time.

## Useless Words

If you have ever composed a telegram you have had a valuable lesson in cutting out words not necessary to your message. Such ruthless pruning is neither necessary nor advisable in most college writing. But often a single word will do the work of two or three, and a short phrase may replace a long clause without hurting style or meaning.

The three most common means of reducing wordiness are excision substitution, and direct statement. *Excision* means pruning out useless words. Here are two examples:

1. Cutting out a purposeless introductory phrase. The words to be cut out are enclosed in parentheses.

(With reference to the relationship between the laws of today and the laws of ancient times,) *I think that the author is wrong in stating that the laws of today are based on ancient laws.*

2. Cutting out deadwood [9] within the body of the sentence.

*I* (only) *hope I get as much* (benefit) *out of* (my years of) *college* (work and study) *as I got from* (the four years I spent in) *high school.*

*Substitution* is the replacing of a wordy expression by an economical one.

1. Substituting one word for a phrase:

I took an academic line of subjects.
I took an academic *course.*

2. Substituting a phrase for a clause:

She is the girl who is wearing a blue dress.
She is the girl *in blue.*

3. Substituting a simple sentence for a compound or complex sentence:

He married the former Jane Smith; she is his third wife.
The former Jane Smith is his third wife.

They live in Eau Claire, which is in Wisconsin.
They live in Eau Claire, Wisconsin.

*Direct statement* is explicit statement. It says, rather than implies, what the author means, and it avoids *circumlocutions* — words or phrases which shy away from clear statement through timidity, false modesty, or literary affectation. Contrast these pairs of sentences:

I was so sick that I released the contents of my stomach.
I was so sick that I vomited.

He was — shall we say? — in an inebriated condition.
He was drunk.

I find myself not in complete agreement with Dr. Jones.
I don't completely agree with Dr. Jones.

In the following contrasts, the sentences at the right are not just shorter but clearer and more precise. At the left, important ideas, such as logical subjects, are often put into modifying phrases, so that the

---

[9] Professor Perrin, from whom I have borrowed this term, defines *deadwood* as "a lazy word or phrase that adds nothing to the meaning of the sentence." *Writer's Guide and Index to English,* p. 284.

structure of the sentence does not reflect the structure of the thought. At the right this does not happen.

| *Wordy* | *Economical* |
|---|---|
| Dealing with the idea about the use of property in ancient times and the use of property today, I think it is about the same. | The uses of property have not changed during the centuries. |
| All persons should strive to develop a usage of good English. | Everyone should try to use good English. |
| I believe to some extent, about the same as the author in his attitude toward crime and criminal tendencies. | I agree with the author's attitude toward crime and criminal tendencies. |
| In the way of college mathematics, I have had College Algebra, Trigonometry, and Analytical Geometry. | I have had College Algebra, Trigonometry, and Analytical Geometry. |
| I was born in the city of Bangor. It is located in the state of Maine. | I was born in Bangor, Maine. |
| In regard to specific influences on my speech and writing, I might say that there has been nothing outstanding to influence either. It has been gradual all the way along. In other words, I've had nothing to overcome, such as, impediments in speech, accent, or influence of foreign tongue being used in the family. The latter being rather impossible since the fact exists that my ancestors came over in the Mayflower. | There have been no significant influences on my use of English. I have had no speech impediments, and, as a descendant of an old American family, I have not been exposed to a foreign language at home. |

Rewrite the following sentences for greater economy of statement:

1. I will be available for an interview whenever time will see fit for you.
2. This was done under the direction of Mr. Russell Osborne, to whom you may refer to for reference.
3. Of course, as time goes by there is being made much improvement in sanitary and medical matters.
4. The need for a practical education cannot be denied, just to go on living requires it. But to do more than just exist there is something more required, and that something more is a liberal education.
5. Skin grafts usually require two weeks to take. That is, it takes that time for skin to grow to the area to be repaired. The preliminary treatment of some burns may take as long as four weeks. That is just getting them in condition for a graft. The actual graft itself may take months to complete. It depends, of course, on the degree of the burn and the area to be treated.
6. Take, for example, the price of meat. If there are two stores, one selling meat for one price, and the other selling for a lower price, which

one would sell the most meat? The answer is not difficult to guess. Of course it would be the one which sold the meat at a lower price.

7. What high school did to me to overcome this feeling of inferiority is something about which I can only state my opinions, not knowing whether or not they are true.

8. He learns the dangers and uses of his equipment and how to take care of any situation that may arise through the use of his equipment.

9. Many of my friends in the business world who work in the same field, that is child psychology, have told me that they know of many cases where juvenile delinquents admit to reading comics excessively, and it is the opinion of these psychologists that comics cause a definite impression in the minds of the readers.

10. I think that they gave a very poor demonstration of what they could do, as far as the acting abilities. I know some of the actors and actresses, and I have also seen them in other productions. So that is the reason I know they could have done better.

## *Variety*

Sentences may be clear, consistent, and economical, yet still be ineffective if they are monotonously alike in length and structure. Examine the following, for instance:

Shakespeare's *Chronicle History of Henry the Fifth* is a drama of kinghood and war. It is essentially a play about a young king's coming of age. Henry V had been an irresponsible young prince before his accession to the crown. He had to prove his worthiness as king by leading his army in war. He invaded France and captured Harfleur, and then tried to withdraw his troops to Calais. He and his men were confronted by a numerically superior French army at Agincourt. In a famous passage in Shakespeare's play, Henry urges his soldiers on to an incredible victory. The superior mobility and firepower of the English proved too much for the heavily armored French.

As you have probably noticed, all the sentences in this paragraph are similar in length and pattern. With one exception, the word order is subject, verb, complement; and the number of words is respectively 14, 12, 14, 15, 15, 14, 16, 16.

This much similarity may not become monotonous in a single paragraph, but a 500-word essay in this style could be quite tedious. A writer, like a baseball pitcher, is more effective with a change of pace, and varied sentences are more effective than those that plod along in constant lengths and patterns.

But a word of caution is necessary at this point. *Too much variety may be as bad as none at all.* The subject-verb-complement pattern is the favorite order of English sentences, and a student who strives too hard to avoid it may end up with an affected and unnatural style or he may fall into the kind of inconsistencies that we considered earlier in this chapter. If you keep this caution in mind, the following discussion of ways to obtain variety will be helpful.

### Inversion

The normal order of the elements in a sentence is subject-verb-complement, with modifying phrases and clauses following the elements they modify. Inversion is a deliberate departure from this order. Thus, instead of saying *They who only stand and wait also serve,* Milton gained in rhythm and force by placing the subordinate clause at the end of the sentence — *They also serve who only stand and wait.*

The following sentences contrast normal and inverted word order:

| Normal | Explanation | Inverted |
|---|---|---|
| The Elizabethan drama was shaped to this queer mixture of cultured and uneducated, of lowly and exalted, of those who came for love of drama and those who came to show their superiority. | *In normal order, phrases modifying the main clause follow it. In the inverted sentence the modifying phrases come at the beginning. Since a place of major emphasis in an English sentence is the beginning, this inversion gives added emphasis to the description of the audience.* | To this queer mixture of cultured and uneducated, of lowly and exalted, of those who came for love of drama and those who came to show their superiority, the Elizabethan drama was shaped. |
| The audience took to dice or cards if anything on the stage bored; and there was always much drinking of ale and eating of fruits and sweets. | *On each side of the semicolon is an independent sentence. The first is inverted at the right by placing the subordinate clause before the main clause; the second shows normal order in both versions.* | If anything on the stage bored, the audience took to dice or cards; and always there was much drinking of ale and eating of fruits and sweets. |
| The dead leaves lay deep in the thickets of blackberry, and toyon, and poison oak. | *The normal order at the left is inverted at the right by placing the modifying phrase before the main clause.* | In the thickets of blackberry, and toyon, and poison oak, the dead leaves lay deep. |

From the discussion on pages 137–138 you will recognize the first and third versions at the right as periodic sentences. When a sentence is continued after the main thought has been expressed — as at the left — it is called a loose sentence. The term is unfortunate, since it suggests carelessness. Actually, the loose sentence is normal, and the name is not used in a derogatory sense.

Many sentences are not strictly either loose or periodic but have characteristics of both types. The example that follows begins as a periodic but ends as a loose sentence.

> After all the promises he had given us, he stayed away from the party, without even offering the courtesy of an excuse.

Such a sentence we may call a mixed sentence. Again the name is used without derogatory connotations.

Most sentences are loose or mixed. Indeed, an overfondness for periodic sentences makes writing seem affected or self-conscious. But the change of pace that comes from a combination of loose, mixed, and periodic sentences is often effective. Notice the variation in the following:

> (*Loose*) Three times too has earthquake spread ruin in California since the Charleston disaster of fifty years ago. (*Periodic*) Stalking down the coast like a hungry cat, it sprang upon San Francisco in 1906, Santa Barbara in 1925, and Long Beach in 1933. (*Loose*) The deadliest quake in the history of Europe laid low the city of Messina in 1908 and claimed the lives of more than a hundred thousand. (*Mixed*) Within the same brief span of years the demon fell upon India, South America, the West Indies, and China, with terrible destruction of life and property.
>
> (*Periodic*) Although such disasters have been all too frequent, they record but a few of the shocks that have racked the globe in fifty years. (*Mixed*) Many earthquakes are happily lost beneath the sea; many others, like the Montana quake of 1925, though severe enough to wreck great cities, are centered in areas of sparse population. And many another is so slight that only the delicate seismograph can detect it. (*Periodic*) Yet so marked is the earth's infirmity, so false the concept of *terra firma*, that a perceptible trembling of the ground is felt at some place on the globe during every hour of the day and night.[10]

## Subordination

To understand *subordination* you must also understand its opposite, *coordination*. Statements are coordinate when they are logically and grammatically equal or parallel. Thus the clauses in Caesar's famous statement, "I came, I saw, I conquered," are coordinate main clauses. Had Caesar written, "Having come and seen, I conquered," he would have reduced the first two clauses to a participial phrase, thus making them grammatically subordinate to the final clause, though coordinate with each other. Subordination, then, is a reduction in grammatical

[10] From *Autobiography of Earth*, by John Hogdon Bradley; copyright, 1935, by Coward-McCann, Inc.

rank so as to make the subordinated expression dependent on something else.

Monotonous sentences are likely to suffer from too much coordination. They tend to express as main clauses or independent sentences many ideas which could better be presented in phrases or subordinate clauses. The result is not only monotony of sentence pattern, but wordiness and lack of emphasis. A wise use of subordination lets a writer emphasize what is important, play down what is minor, and express his thoughts more succinctly. Whenever you find yourself writing too many *and's, but's,* or *for's,* pause and take thought. It may be a sign you are not subordinating minor ideas to main ones.

In the following examples the versions at the right have been revised by subordination:

| *Over-coordination* | *Explanation* | *Subordination* |
|---|---|---|
| They approached even closer to our hiding place, and we felt increasingly sure we would be discovered. | *Italicized main clause of loose sentence is subordinated at right, creating a periodic sentence.* | As they approached even closer to our hiding place we felt increasingly sure we would be discovered. |
| Rider attended Oxford and there he met young Sebastian Flyte and the two boys became friends. *Sebastian was the youngest son of the Marquis of Marchmain.* | *Italicized sentence subordinated to modifying phrase at right, achieving greater economy.* | At Oxford Rider became friendly with Sebastian Flyte, *the youngest son of the Marquis of Marchmain.* |
| John Stuart Mill *was born in 1806 and died in 1873.* He was famous as a child prodigy, *but his fame continued throughout his life. He was a logician, a political economist, and a man of letters.* He was one of the most influential thinkers of the nineteenth century. | *Except for subject, first sentence is subordinated as dates in parentheses. Second italicized main clause is reduced to subordinate clause. Third italicized main clause is reduced to a modifying phrase.* | John Stuart Mill (1806–1873) was a child prodigy *whose fame did not cease at maturity. As a logician, political economist, and man of letters,* he was one of the most influential thinkers of the nineteenth century. |

Study the following contrasted versions carefully and come to class prepared to explain in detail the means by which the original version was revised.[11]

[11] For additional exercises, see *Excessive Coordination,* pages 440–441.

| Original | Revised |
|---|---|
| The Levenford of Dr. Cronin's book is really the town of Dumbarton. It is one of the oldest towns in Scotland. It was the most important town north of the Tweed at the time of the Anglo-Saxon invasion, and was called Alcluyd. The Pict chieftains gathered there when they were preparing to swoop down into England in search of plunder; and they always returned there to divide the spoils of victory. The town stands at the gateway to the highlands and has been the field of many battles. Its great island rock has served successively as a fortress for Picts, Romans, Northmen, Jacobites, and Royalists. It has often served as a refuge for the townspeople whenever they were attacked by superior forces. They would retreat to the rock, as the Athenians retreated to their ships, until an opportunity presented itself for overthrowing the invaders. | Dumbarton, the Levenford of Dr. Cronin's book, is one of the oldest towns in Scotland. At the time of the Saxon invasion, Alcluyd, as it was then called, was the only town of any importance north of the Tweed. It was there that the Pict chieftains gathered before swooping down into England in search of plunder, and there that they returned to divide the spoils of victory. Standing as it does at the gateway of the highlands, the town has been the field of many battles, and the great island rock of Dumbarton has served successively as the fortress of Picts, Romans, Northmen, Jacobites, and Royalists. When attacked by superior forces, the townspeople, like the Athenians deserting their city for the ships, would seek refuge in this great rock and bide their time until an opportunity for overthrowing the invaders should arise. |

## Summary

Efforts to make sentences as effective as possible are more often the work of revision than of the first draft. Here are some of the questions you should consider when you come to revise your work:

1. Will the sentences be clear to a reader?

*a.* Is the sentence structure clear? Have two sentences been written as one, or one sentence as two? Can the reader see at the first reading the relationship between the elements of a sentence? Does the punctuation bring out this relationship?

*b.* Are the pronoun references clear? Do the pronouns refer to specific antecedents so that there can be no doubt in the reader's mind to what they refer?

*c.* Is the word order clear? Would the sentence be less awkward or ambiguous if modifying words or phrases were transferred to another position?

2. Are the sentences structurally and grammatically consistent?

*a.* Are the elements in a parallel sentence as uniform as they can be made? If in doubt, read the sentence aloud and test the regularity of rhythm which is one of the characteristics of a parallel structure.

*b.* Do introductory phrases correctly modify an element of the following main clause, or are they left dangling? Watch particularly participial and infinitive phrases and elliptical clauses.

*c.* Is the sentence grammatically consistent? Do subjects agree with verbs, and pronouns with antecedents, so far as they can? Are the tenses as consistent as it is possible to make them? Is there any unnecessary shifting between personal and impersonal pronouns or between active and passive voice?

3.   Would the writing be improved by greater economy?

*a.*   Do attempts at a "pretentious" style result in wordiness?

*b.*   Is there any deadwood that might be pruned out of the sentences?

*c.*   Could sentences be stated more directly to avoid circumlocutions or lack of emphasis?

*d.*   Would the subordination of main clauses to subordinate clauses or phrases tighten up the sentences? Could a single word or a short phrase be substituted for a long phrase or a clause?

4.   Are the sentence patterns sufficiently varied?

*a.*   Are all the sentences of the same length? Do they tend to follow an unchanging order of subject-verb-complement, or are they pleasantly varied?

*b.*   Could you get greater variety by changing some loose sentences into periodic or mixed sentences?

*c.*   Would the sentences become more emphatic if modifiers were transferred out of normal order?

*d.*   Do the sentences show too much coordination? Would the pattern become more varied if several simple sentences were combined, through subordination, into a complex sentence?

## Exercises

**A.** The following sentences from student essays reveal a variety of deficiencies. Some are unclear, some inconsistent, some wordy, and some combine two or three of these faults. Decide what is wrong with each and revise it.

1. In card games, the reason that certain cards are higher in value is that the players have all placed the value for each card in their minds and in a particular card game, the values in each person's mind for each card should be the same.

2. Inevitably, marriage will cost him money. A home of some sort, food and clothing, and, of course, heat, light, etc.

3. The opponents of compulsory fair employment laws point to the average person and ask if they would like to be told whom to hire.

4. My greatest thrills were attained in a two-hour fight with a hundred-pound tarpon. They are memories you can never forget.

5. After reading the selection from Mr. Barnes's *History of Western Civilization*, it is agreed that the intellectual outlook of the masses remains much the same as it was in primitive times.

6. About my writing after I leave the service is still undecided.

7. Employers and owners of restaurants today have a problem of getting proper help for both their kitchens as well as for waiting on tables.

8. As Dr. Wertham points out in his many examples, such as policemen having to stand guard in classes because the children were affected by the use of comics to the point of causing violence in class. Also examples where a teen-age boy had killed another boy because he had become addicted to comic books.

9. Upon asking many of those guilty of crimes whether they read comic books or not, the answer was usually yes.

10. Also under this plan any doctor who loses the value of his practice is paid a compensation. By losing the value of his practice is meant, that by going into the proposed health service or by being prohibited from transferring his practice to another doctor, because of the grounds that there may be too many doctors in a particular area.

11. The typical occupation of the adults I have been with are the professional people, and also a great many people of the laboring class.

12. Naturally, having been to college and graduating from high school, it has given me a better grasp than others who have not been so fortunate.

13. After a person is found to have a positive reaction to the patch test an x-ray of the chest is advised. This is also to ascertain whether a person has any activity in their lungs. Not everyone with a positive reaction has activity in their lungs, but all positive reactions without activity are advised to have an x-ray at least once a year.

14. By keeping up with these daily quizzes will allow you to master each part of the work as it comes along.

15. Having finished our pie and coffee the tires were checked and the tank filled up.

16. A person's race or religion should have nothing to do with their getting a job.

17. I started in by cleaning ten cases of beer up that they had already done away with and then standing around and watching the circus animals perform.

18. The picture started with a good opening and a happy ending.

19. If we were to make a survey we would find the relationship between our youngsters reading good books to be very low in comparison to the youngsters reading comics.

20. An estimate of the prevalence of disability is much more than realized.

21. Writing is one of the best ways of expressing yourself, and if you use good English it will reflect favorably on your character and will present a good impression of you to anyone who reads your writing.

22. In plotting a course the navigator or fighter pilot uses math in so many ways that it would be an impossible task for him to perform without the use of math.

23. I agree very disappointingly with Dr. Wertham when he says that there are many child and teen-age delinquents today. Perhaps even more so than ever before.

24. Before any state receives such aid, they must prove to the Office of Education that they are unable to raise the needed amount of money by their own means, such as income taxes, bonds, levying a sales tax, etc.

25. For example, a man would rather put ten dollars towards paying for his car, that all of the members of his family could enjoy, than to go to a doctor and sit for ten minutes and be told that he should exercise daily for the same ten dollars.

26. Besides having twenty guests at our house for the weekend, each girl was required to sell fifty programs, so you see that the weekend was bound to be hectic.

27. The framework of the house is wooden, but the walls between the rooms and the floor are of straw. It has been woven together to make it strong and durable.

28. By the statement, knowing the will of God, I take it to mean that a person acquired a sense of what is right and what is wrong.

29. At the completion of the piles being driven in we then set the floor forms.

30. Unless a person went to college, or unless his work included writing, I don't believe many of us developed our English by writing.

31. Being in good humor will keep one out of quarrels. This does not mean agreeing to everything someone else says in order to keep peace. However, you are not likely to lose your head and bicker needlessly if you grin and shrug your shoulders at the problem. A grin is contagious. Let's use it.

32. We are really not using the modern mind when electrocuting or hanging a criminal. Of course, we could not let them go free to harm others.

33. Most of my life has been spent in contact with the middle class of people. The majority of these people being employed in factories.

34. Speaking of the movie as a whole, I like it very much. There are, however, a couple of exceptions. I don't think very much of the way it opened. It pictured Mr. Ziegfeld, played by William Powell, in heaven. He was reminiscing of the Ziegfeld Follies of past years. He was wishing he could put just one more Follies on. If he could, he would make it the greatest he had ever produced. He goes on dreaming of the stars he would use in the picture and of the beautiful costumes and elaborate scenes he would have. Then continues a series of scenes with these stars, in which each one contributes their share.

35. The author is trying to show us that our educational system is not entirely adequate. Our educational program is designed to give us basic knowledge of many subjects of our choice, but they sometimes fail to explain how it is applied to real life. Then, because we do not know how to apply it, it is of no use to us. The conditions under which we work

and live are constantly changing and new cases arise that have never been dealt with before, so we are lost.

**B.** The following essay, written impromptu in a 50-minute class period, could have been greatly improved by more varied sentence structure and less wordiness. Edit the paper to make it a more satisfying composition.

### THIS SEMESTER IN RETROSPECT

This semester is my first semester in college. For me it has been a hard period of adjustment. Having to learn to live with others and having to learn to get along on my own in classes has helped me to grow into an adult student.

The adjustment of learning to live with others and without my parents beside me was hard to make. I came to the University not knowing anyone. I moved into a sorority house which was full of girls I barely remembered from last spring's Rush Week. The girls were all very nice to me and did their best to make me feel at home. I tried to be just as friendly as they were, but I didn't know any of them intimately and so I kept to myself quite a bit.

As school began, however, I became more friendly with the girls. Naturally, they were a poor substitute for my parents whom I had depended on when I was at home. These girls had lives of their own to lead and my feelings didn't touch them deeply, although they did seem interested in my affairs.

Now, at the end of my first semester, I have found the girls in my house to be my sisters. We seem like one big family. I like to walk into the house in the evening and see them relaxing and I like their warm smiles and friendly "hellos." I appreciate the time they are willing to spend to help when I feel low and can't get my lessons. I feel as though I've known them for years instead of just a few months. I can honestly say that I have profited a great deal from the experience of learning to live with others and away from my parents.

Another adjustment which faced me was the fact that I had to go to school with what seemed to be myriads of people. The classes were filled with people I had never seen and the instructors hardly even noticed me. I was terribly frightened. I would have long thinking periods when I would almost talk myself into going back to the shelter of my parents. But there was something in me, pride I guess, which wouldn't let me leave. This little bit of pride kept driving me on to prove to my classmates, instructor, and mostly to myself that I was no dumbbell and that I could do things well.

This proof of my ability to at least keep up with others has given me the self-assurance to keep going on in this place of strangers. In fact, now the strangers aren't really strangers. I don't know most of the students I see, but I like to see them on the campus. The spirit which they give makes me feel good all over. Another great feeling is to see and hear foreign students on the campus. I've thought to myself in my moodier moments that if people have the courage to come to this university from a foreign country, then surely I can have the courage to get through. They have more handicaps to overcome because of their descent than I do coming from the United States.

I still have a lot to learn and even more self-confidence to establish. Final exams are beginning to bother me and at times I get panicky. If I can just do as well to overcome these feelings, as I have tried to in the past, I'm sure I'll get much more pleasure and satisfaction out of college life.

College life is a challenge and I know it has helped me immensely to become more serious and grown-up in my thoughts and actions.

# 8

# R I G H T   W O R D S

---

THE ENGLISH WRITER Jonathan Swift defined good writing as the art of putting "proper words in proper places." Although this definition tremendously oversimplifies the process of composition, it does stress the fact that words are the units with which a writer works. Words are the essence of communication, even of communication to oneself. The writer thinks with words just as he writes with them, and neither his thinking nor his writing can be efficient unless his words are accurate. A concern about right words, therefore, is not just a matter of choosing imposing or arresting words. It is a matter of ordering experience, evaluating it, and communicating the results.

## How Words Work

**Symbols and Referents.** Words are symbols for experience. They represent what we see, hear, feel, smell, taste, and do, and the attitudes and thoughts which we derive from these experiences. The word is not the experience itself. We cannot drink the word "water," ride in the word "car," or refresh our bodies with the word "sleep." But we can use words to "stand for" these experiences. Therefore we say that the word is a *symbol* for the experience. The thing to which the word refers — water, car, sleep — is called the *referent*.

The relationship between a word and its referent is a mental one. The word makes us "think of" the referent. Thus the word "book" makes you think of something like this thing you are reading. In the sentence, "The President will speak on television tonight," a number of connected symbols make us think of a number of related referents. We think of a particular person who will perform a definite action through a certain medium at a specified time. By means of this thinking we are able to anticipate an event that will take place in the future and

at a considerable distance. Similarly, the statement "Christ was cruci-
fied," makes us think of an event that happened in a far-off country
nearly two thousand years ago. By words, therefore, we are able to
draw on the experience of people in all ages and in all places and to
use that experience to plan for the future. In a sense, then, words give
us a degree of control over time and space by giving us a means of
thinking about events in other times and places.

**Context.** Since the relation between a word and its referent is a mental
one, we can think of different referents for the same word. Thus a
*spring* may be a season, a source of drinking water, or a metal bar or
coil. This multiple use of the same word allows us to describe a limitless
number of experiences with a limited number of words. The people
to whom we are speaking or writing can usually tell which meaning
we have in mind by noticing the whole statement or situation in which
we use the word — "I'll be glad when spring comes"; "Fill this bottle
at the spring"; "The car has a broken spring." The whole statement or
situation in which the word is used is called its *context*.

In practice we learn the meanings of words by their contexts.
When we are learning our language we do not meet the word "run" by
itself; we always meet it in some situation — a man running for a bus,
a child running a temperature, a quarterback running a team, and so on.
We learn the meanings of "run" by learning the contexts in which it is
used. This is exactly how the writers of dictionaries get their definitions.
They gather sample contexts and write the definitions to describe them,
so that when a dictionary lists different meanings for the word "spring,"
it is recording the contexts in which "spring" most frequently occurs.

**The Principle of Usage.** We can sum up this discussion by saying that:
(1) the only meanings a word has are those that exist in the minds of
people who use it; (2) a word is always used in some situation or
context; (3) the context shows how a word is being used, or what it
means. The general principle explaining these three conditions is called
the *principle of usage,* which states that the meanings of a word are
determined by the ways speakers and writers *generally* use it. This
principle could be applied to uneducated as well as to educated usage
and to local as well as national uses, but we are concerned here only
with the meanings generally given a word by educated people throughout the United States. The study of uneducated usage, or of the dialects
of particular regions, lies outside the scope of this book. For our purposes, the principle of usage explains how the dictionary meanings of
words are established.

The principle of usage has two important corollaries. First, a word
has no *intrinsic* meaning, that is, no meaning of its own apart from the
uses people give it. Second, the current meanings of a word will change

if users accept the changes. As a consequence of these corollaries, the vocabulary of our language is ceaselessly changing, as old words die out or are given new meanings, and as new words are adopted.

Many words have quite different meanings from those they once had. "Wench" once meant a child and had no unpleasant associations; "buxom" was once complimentary, so much so that a fifteenth century writer could use it to refer to the Virgin Mary; "manufacture" meant "to make by hand," but when goods came to be machine-made we retained the old name for the new process; "lingerie," when imported from France, meant "linen goods," but its most popular use today has nothing to do with linen; "quarantine" has long since lost its original Italian meaning of "forty days."

In addition, the language is steadily acquiring new words to describe new discoveries or events. Quite apart from slang, which comes and goes with the seasons, what would Abraham Lincoln make of such words as *airport, auto, basketball, blitz, carburetor, dentifrice, gyroscope, motel, movie star, nuclear fission, radar, television, world series,* and thousands of others? Yet all these additions and changes are normal signs of growth. There is nothing static about the meanings of words in a living language.

### Denotation and Connotation

We have seen that words mean whatever users agree to make them mean, that many of them have had different meanings at different stages of their histories, and that their present meanings vary with the contexts in which they are used. It is nevertheless possible to generalize these meanings into two main types. Consider these two sentences:

> Who is that *girl* with Bill?
> Who is that *wench* with Bill?

Both italicized words point to the same person — a relatively young female. But, in addition, "wench" suggests unpleasant associations; it not only points to a person but also expresses the speaker's attitude toward that person. We contrast these two uses by saying that here the meaning of "girl" is a *denotation* — the physical referent which it denotes — and that the meaning of "wench" is a *connotation* — a compound of physical referent and an attitude of the speaker or writer toward that referent.

The distinction, then, between denotations and connotations is that the latter reveal attitudes about an object or event but the former do not. These attitudes may be favorable or unfavorable. In "That is a cute hat" and "That is an absurd hat," the word "hat" is used denotatively in both sentences, but "cute" has favorable and "absurd" unfavorable connotations. Some words, such as *cute, brave, efficient, fame, glory, hope,* and *valuable* usually have only favorable connotations. Others, such as *absurd, callous, hate, idiotic, lust, treason,* and *vicious* have usually only unfavorable connotations. Still others have favorable connotations in some contexts but unfavorable ones in others. Compare, for example, *free enterprise* and *free speech* with *free thinker* and *free love,* or a *fat check* with a *fat girl.*

The denotative and connotative uses of words are sometimes referred to as *scientific* and *poetic* uses. These descriptions remind us that a writer's purpose determines his diction. A writer who is interested only in providing information will tend to use words at a denotative level. Since clarity of communication — clear pointing to specific facts — is his main aim, he cannot afford to let his readers make all sorts of private interpretations; therefore he tries to restrict interpretation by choosing words and contexts which are relatively free from connotations.

The following paragraph is a good example of scientific writing at a popular level. Notice that the words point to things, not to attitudes, and that the diction makes no attempt to create either favorable or unfavorable responses in the mind of the reader.

> When a beam of sunlight enters a darkened room with dust in it, one can see the beam of light clearly defined as the light is scattered from the dust particles. The more dust particles in the room, the more the light is scattered; and if there is a real cloud of dust, the light is scattered so much that one can hardly see beyond it. The same thing happens to the beams from the headlights of a car in a fog. The small particles of water making up the fog in the air scatter the light that shines on them. The denser the fog, the more the light is scattered, the less of it gets through the fog, and the less one can see through a fog with even the most powerful beam of light. By measuring the fraction of the incident light that goes straight through the fog and the fraction that is scattered by the fog particles, one can estimate the number of water droplets in the fog — or the number of dust particles in the air. This method is accurate for determining the number of fine particles in a cloudy suspension in air or in water and is used frequently in analytical chemistry.[1]

The poet, in contrast with the scientist, is more concerned with creating emotional responses than with conveying information. His poetry may contain facts, may even be highly informative. But since his chief desire is to stimulate the imagination, he makes greater use of figurative language and of connotations which invite emotional responses. As the following passage illustrates, a poet who failed to do this would be most disappointing:

> The use of emotionally toned words is not, of course, always to be condemned. They are always harmful when we are trying to think clearly

[1] From *Explaining the Atom,* by Selig Hecht, copyright, 1947, by The Viking Press, Inc.

on a disputable point of fact. In poetry, on the other hand, they have a perfectly proper place, because in poetry (as in some kinds of prose) the arousing of suitable emotions is an important part of the purpose for which the words are used.

In "The Eve of St. Agnes," Keats has written:

> Full on this casement shone the wintry moon,
> And threw warm gules on Madeline's fair breast.

These are beautiful lines. Let us notice how much of their beauty follows from the proper choice of emotionally colored words and how completely it is lost if these words are replaced by neutral ones. The words with strikingly emotional meanings are *casement, gules, Madeline, fair,* and *breast. Casement* means simply a kind of window with emotional and romantic associations. *Gules* is the heraldic name for red, with the suggestion of romance which accompanies all heraldry. *Madeline* is simply a girl's name, but one calling out favorable emotions absent from a relatively plain and straightforward name. *Fair* simply means, in objective fact, that her skin was white or uncolored — a necessary condition for the colors of the window to show — but also *fair* implies warm emotional preference for an uncolored skin rather than one which is yellow, purple, black, or any of the other colors which skin might be. *Breast* has also similar emotional meanings, and the aim of scientific description might have been equally well obtained if it had been replaced by such a neutral word as *chest.*

Let us now try the experiment of keeping these two lines in a metrical form, but replacing all the emotionally colored words by neutral ones, while making as few other changes as possible. We may write:

> Full on this window shone the wintry moon,
> Making red marks on Jane's uncolored chest.

No one will doubt that all of its poetic value has been knocked out of the passage by these changes. Yet the lines still mean the same in external fact; they still have the same objective meaning. It is only the emotional meaning which has been destroyed.[2]

## Exercises

**A.** Suppose you were editing a dictionary and had to write definitions of "man" and "make up" from the following contexts. For each entry, write as many definitions as your samples require. Then check your dictionary to see if it records your definitions. If it does not, what does that prove?

[2] Reprinted from *How to Think Straight,* by Robert H. Thouless. Copyright, 1939, by Simon and Schuster, Inc. Canadian copyright, Hodder and Stoughton, Ltd., publishers.

*Man:*

1. Man was made to mourn.
2. He was her man, but he done her wrong.
3. Man the boats!
4. He is his own man; he takes orders from nobody.
5. Man, but I'm tired!
6. A man has a deeper voice than a woman.
7. Come on, be a man!

*Make up:*

1. I'll be with you as soon as I make up my face.
2. You must make up the test that you missed.
3. Make up your mind!
4. You make up the beds while I do the dishes.
5. This is a serious quarrel; I'm afraid they won't make up.

**B.** Decide from the context whether the italicized words are being used denotatively or connotatively. If they are being used connotatively, are the connotations favorable or unfavorable?

1. The *baby* is *asleep.*
2. I wish you would not *baby* her so much.
3. The *shortstop* was *asleep* on that play.
4. She was wearing a *red* dress.
5. He talks like a *red.*
6. Such *slander* makes me see *red.*
7. I thought the room was *colorful,* but my wife said it was *gaudy.*
8. My girl is always *cold* to me when I have a *cold.*
9. He *used* the money to buy a car and he *used* his friends to keep up the payments.
10. The *critics* disagreed about his acting in that *scene.* Some said he gave a *sophisticated performance;* others said he *catered to vulgarity.*
11. Even her worst *critics* were embarrassed by the *scene* she made on that occasion.
12. It was a *dark* night, and a night for *dark* deeds.
13. The surgeon cut the damaged *nerve.* It takes *nerve* to make that first parachute jump. What a *nerve* that woman has!
14. He said he was a man of *firm purpose,* but his wife said he was just *selfishly stubborn.*
15. The difference between *a boyish prank* and *an act of vandalism* depends on whether it is your children or the neighbors' who do the mischief.
16. He is a *wolf* and his wife is a *cat.*
17. I am *portly,* my wife is *chubby;* but Bill and his wife are *obese.*
18. Mary said he was *shy;* I thought he was *sullen.*

## The Accurate Word

Words are not right or wrong in themselves but as they succeed or fail to do what a writer wants them to do in a particular situation. But in any context the right word has certain characteristics: it must be *accurate;* it must be *appropriate;* it should be as *specific* as possible; it may be *figurative;* and it should be *unspoiled.* The rest of this chapter will deal with each of these qualities in turn.

If a word is to say what it was intended to say, it must have the right denotation and the right connotation. It must refer the reader accurately to the things and ideas which the writer wishes to communicate, and it must express only those attitudes which he intends to express.

Failure to use words accurately is usually a result of one of four kinds of difficulty: (1) confusion of words that look or sound alike; (2) confusion of a word with its antonym, or opposite; (3) failure to discriminate among synonyms, or words with the same general meaning; (4) failure to appreciate connotations.

**Confusion of Similar Forms.** Many words, including some very common ones, look or sound so much alike that they are often confused. Sometimes (as in *accept-except, affect-effect, causal-casual, compliment-complement, principal-principle,* and *stationary-stationery*) the error can be one of spelling more than of meaning. Sometimes (as in *contemptible-contemptuous, detracted-distracted, disinterested-uninterested, practicable-practical,* and *persecute-prosecute*) the writer has not had enough experience with both forms to distinguish their separate uses. He may understand each form from the context when he meets it in reading, but he does not know the words well enough to put them into a context of his own making.

Most conscientious students easily clear up a confusion of similar forms once it has been pointed out to them: between *causal* and *casual,* for instance, or *persecute* and *prosecute.* It is also helpful to study a list of pairs most likely to be confused (see page 542) and to check the troublesome ones for further study. The following sentences will provide you with a partial check list.

First select the appropriate word; then use the other word in a sentence of your own.

1. She makes all her own clothes. She is quite (adapt, adept) at tailoring.
2. Often the seeds are (born, borne) by the wind for several miles.
3. The organization passed a resolution (censoring, censuring) the movie.
4. This is the second marriage for both of them. Each of them was (formally, formerly) divorced.
5. The chairman said the question was (irrelevant, irreverent) to the discussion.
6. Both runners returned to their (respectful, respective) bases.
7. The rain has made the grass grow (luxuriantly, luxuriously).
8. The (moral, morale) of the troops was badly (affected, effected).

9. The lady should always (precede, proceed) the gentleman.

10. The noise made by the construction workers (detracted, distracted) the class.

11. The lecture was boring. I was completely (disinterested, uninterested) in what the speaker said.

12. There is no truth in her story. It is all a (figment, fragment) of her imagination.

13. I have never had such a (grisly, gristly) experience.

14. The President was asked to issue an (official, officious) explanation.

15. The conditions of the contest were (prescribed, proscribed).

16. His speeches are full of Biblical (allusions, illusions).

17. Did you ever hear such an illogical argument? His reasoning was completely (fallacious, fictitious).

18. I thought it was a very (credible, credulous) explanation.

**Confusion of Contrasted Terms (Antonyms).** Pairs like *up-down, good-bad, black-white* contrast opposites. When such terms are in our active vocabulary they cause little trouble, but when they are in our recognition vocabulary only, we are likely to confuse them.[3] Thus we may know that *port* and *starboard* designate opposite sides of a ship, but we may forget which is which. Or we may know that a curved lens has a *concave* and a *convex* side, but not remember which side curves inward. Again, we may learn that the two basic types of reasoning are *deductive* and *inductive* and that one goes from a general statement to a particular conclusion and the other goes from particular to general. But we may still say *inductive* for *deductive*.

Such contrasted terms are confusing chiefly when they are new to us. If we had considerable experience with ships and lenses and types of reasoning, the word pairs would be as familiar to us as *east-west, offense-defense, pleasure-pain.* Therefore the more quickly we gain experience with them, the sooner we shall use them confidently. Sometimes we can get real help from the etymology (origin of a word) in a good dictionary (see, for example, *starboard*). Sometimes we can fix the distinction in our memory by associating one of the words with something we already know — for example, a cave curves inward; therefore a concave surface will curve in towards the center. But usually we learn to use words only by using them, even though our first attempts may be a bit uncertain and may require repeated use of a dictionary.

The following contrasted terms are often misused. Go over the list and check those you cannot confidently use in a sentence or two. Then consult your dictionary for their definitions. Finally, use the words in sentences which clearly reveal their meanings.

---

[3] The active vocabulary consists of the words we actually use in speaking or writing; the recognition vocabulary consists of those words we understand when we meet them in context though we do not use them in our own writing or speaking. See pages 214–227.

absolute — relative
abstract — concrete
abstruse — obvious
affinity — antipathy
analysis — synthesis
antagonist — protagonist
antonym — synonym
bullish — bearish
concord — discord
condemn — condone
coordinate — subordinate
emigrant — immigrant
expert — layman
explicit — implicit

extrovert — introvert
homogeneous — heterogeneous
horizontal — vertical
laconic — talkative
native — alien
ornate — plain
reticent — forward
stimulate — enervate
suave — brusque
surfeit — starve
temerity — timidity
transparent — opaque
urban — rural
zenith — nadir

**Failure to Discriminate Synonyms.** Synonyms are words which have the same general meaning. Often, however, two words which are roughly synonymous will have important differences in particular contexts. For example, "comely," "handsome," and "pretty" all have the same general meaning, but we would not talk of a "pretty" man or a "comely" dress, and while a girl could be either "comely" or "pretty" we would not usually call her "handsome" until she was middle-aged. Since a desk dictionary does not always discriminate among synonyms, the best way to be sure that a particular word fits its context is to consult a dictionary of synonyms (see pages 209–210).

In the following list all the words in a line have the same general meaning as the italicized word at the left; yet these words cannot always be used interchangeably. Can you distinguish their differences by showing how they would affect the meaning of the phrase if they were substituted for the italicized word?

To *accuse* someone of a crime: charge, incriminate, indict.
To *adore* a girl: be infatuated with, dote upon, idolize.
An *angry* remark: annoyed, belligerent, indignant, wrathful.
A *calm* repose: placating, serene, unruffled.
A *careful* answer: cautious, circumspect, painstaking, deliberate.
To *ask* for a favor: coax, demand, plead, wheedle.
To *provide* an answer: betray, disclose, supply, divulge.
An *embarrassed* speaker: abashed, disturbed, flustered, nervous.
A *dirty* room: disordered, filthy, messy, squalid.
To *hesitate* to act: dawdle, falter, procrastinate, vacillate.
To *incite* a riot: encourage, foment, instigate, lead.
An *indifferent* response: apathetic, detached, impartial, unconcerned.
To *nullify* a gain: annul, cancel, invalidate, repudiate.
A constant *pain:* ache, pang, twinge.
To *punish* a child: chastise, cuff, discipline, spank.
*Quarrelsome* neighbors: belligerent, contentious, litigious.
To *reprimand* an offender: admonish, chide, rebuke, scold.

A *strange* costume: odd, outlandish, unconventional, quaint.
A *tired* man: exhausted, sleepy, weary, worn-out.
A *witty* answer: amusing, humorous, ironic, satirical.

**Failure to Recognize Connotations.** Words may have similar denotations but quite different connotations. Thus "cheap" and "inexpensive" have the same denotation, but "a cheap dress" and "an inexpensive dress" are not synonymous phrases, since to many readers the unpleasant connotations of "cheap" will suggest an unflattering description. The following verses provide a humorous illustration of the difference between favorable and unfavorable connotations.

> Call a woman a kitten, but never a cat;
> You can call her a mouse, cannot call her a rat;
> Call a woman a chicken, but never a hen;
> Or you surely will not be her caller again.
>
> You can call her a duck, cannot call her a goose;
> You can call her a deer, but never a moose;
> You can call her a lamb, but never a sheep;
> Economic she likes, but you can't call her cheap.
>
> You can say she's a vision, can't say she's a sight;
> And no woman is skinny, she's slender and slight;
> If she should burn you up, say she sets you afire,
> And you'll always be welcome, you tricky old liar.[4]

Most of the nouns in this jingle are used in figurative rather than literal senses, but as the adjectives "skinny," "slender," and "slight" in the last verse show, the connotative use of words is not confined to figures of speech.[5] Any word which, in a particular context, implies approval or disapproval of the thing it denotes is being used connotatively. If the writer wants to suggest these attitudes, his words do what he wishes and he is using them accurately. But if he suggests connotations which he did not intend, his diction is inaccurate.

The choice of words with the right connotations, or with none at all, is often difficult, even for professional writers. It is especially so for students because it requires a good deal of sophistication about the uses of words. Often the final choice is best made in revision, when the bulk of the composition is completed and the writer is free to concentrate on the finer details. He may then examine his diction to see that it says exactly what he wants it to say, neither more nor less. If he finds he is using connotative words when he should not, or words with connotations which he did not intend, he can revise his diction to make it carry out his purpose.

[4] John E. Donovan, "Semantics," *The Saturday Evening Post,* July 13, 1946. Reprinted by permission of Mrs. Gertrude D. Crane and *The Saturday Evening Post.*
[5] For a discussion of the figurative use of words, see pages 186–190.

The paragraph below is modified from a serious but popular book on science. In the original, the words were chosen for their denotations, as the author's purpose required. In this version, connotative words have been added within the parentheses. Select the word or phrase which best fits the context and justify your choice.

Take a shallow long vessel, place it on a table or floor so that it is absolutely level, fill it with water to the rim, and put across it a wire that will (brush, kiss, lean upon, press upon, touch) the surface of the water. If you now drop a (short, small, trifling, wee) droplet of some (high-grade, pure, unadulterated) oil on one side of the wire, the oil will (reach out, scatter, spread, stretch) all over that part of the (body, mass, skin, surface) of the water that is on the side of the wire on which you have (dashed, dropped, flipped, secreted) the oil. If you now (edge, move, shove, skim) your wire along the rim of the vessel, away from the oil, the (coating, layer, mantle, skin) of oil will (crawl, drift, run, spread), following the wire and becoming thinner and thinner, and its thickness must ultimately become equal to the diameter of a single oil molecule. Any further (agitation, manipulation, motion, pushing) of the wire after this thinness is achieved will result in the (breaking up, decimating, lacerating, ripping apart) of the continuous oil surface and the (designing, erection, construction, formation) of water holes. Knowing the amount of oil you (cast, laid, put, spilled) on the water, and the maximum area over which it can spread without breaking up, you can (calculate, count, guess, imagine, predict) easily the diameter of a single molecule.[6]

## The Appropriate Word

### (Levels of Usage)

#### Social Levels: Standard and Nonstandard English

Words not only point to things and to attitudes; they also reflect the social level of the person using them. Thus, "I have no money" and "I ain't got no money" refer to the same financial condition. One is just as clear as the other; but the connotations of the second statement invite the judgment that the speaker is not very well educated. We distinguish between these two uses by saying that the first is *standard English* and the second is *nonstandard English*.

Standard English is a class dialect. It may be defined as the speech of those who enjoy a favored economic and social status in our society, and since this class may be roughly described as the educated class, we may say that standard English is the way that educated people speak and write. It is, therefore, the kind of English written and spoken by business executives, lawyers, doctors, ministers, teachers, writers, editors,

---

[6] From *One Two Three . . . Infinity,* by George Gamow. Copyright, 1947, by The Viking Press. Reprinted by permission.

artists, engineers, and other professional people, and, of course, by their wives. All these comprise a small minority of the total users of the language.

Nonstandard English is the speech of the great majority of the users of the language. It is the language of the farm, the factory, the mine, the lumber camp, the railroad, and, in general, of those occupations which do not require what we call "higher education." It is essentially a spoken rather than a written language, but it is often imitated in writing by novelists, dramatists, and short-story writers when they are representing characters who would be expected to use nonstandard English. It is occasionally used by educated people for humorous effects.

Standard English is more expressive than nonstandard. The latter serves well enough the purposes for which it is commonly used, but it has a limited vocabulary, especially for terms referring to ideas, and its grammar is simple. So it can express many complex thoughts poorly if at all. Yet the strongest objection to it is social. Indeed, the use of nonstandard expressions is usually taken as a sure sign of inferior social background, and the unlucky speaker is handicapped in his struggle for economic and social advancement. This is one reason why teachers try so hard to weed nonstandard expressions out of student speech and writing. Colleges are preparing students to take their places on the economic and social levels at which standard English is spoken and written. Therefore college students are committed to study and use it, and to avoid expressions which are nonstandard. Save in special assignments (chiefly fiction) in which the writer must represent uneducated speech, *nonstandard English has no place in college writing.*

### Stylistic Levels: Formal, Informal, Colloquial

Standard English may be *formal, informal,* or *colloquial.* Each of these levels is appropriate to particular purposes, and when it is appropriate, it is correct. The differences between the levels are essentially stylistic. Just as different social occasions call for different styles of clothing, so different writing purposes require different styles of writing. The writer's obligation is to select the style appropriate to his particular purpose.

Before we can profitably discuss these styles, it will be necessary to consider five classes of words into which the vocabularies of educated people can be divided. These are *popular words, learned words, idiomatic diction, colloquialisms,* and *slang.*

**Learned and Popular Words.** In English, as in other languages, a great part of the total vocabulary consists of words which are common to the speech of educated and uneducated speakers alike. These words are the basic elements of our language. They are indispensable for everyday communication, and by means of them people from widely different social levels are able to speak a common language. These are called *popular words;* they belong to the whole populace.

Contrasted with these are words which we read more often than we hear, and write more often than we speak — words more widely used by educated than by uneducated people, and more likely to be used on formal than on informal occasions. These we call *learned words.* The distinction can be illustrated by contrasting some pairs which have roughly the same meaning.

| *Popular* | *Learned* | *Popular* | *Learned* |
|-----------|-----------|-----------|-----------|
| agree | concur | lying | mendacious |
| beggar | mendicant | make easy | facilitate |
| behead | decapitate | near (in time) | imminent |
| break | fracture | prove | verify |
| clear | lucid | queer | eccentric |
| end | terminate | secret | cryptic, esoteric |
| fat | corpulent | surrender | capitulate |
| hair-do | coiffure | truth | veracity |

Learned words are usually imported by educated people from a foreign language and, at first, retain their foreign pronunciations, meanings, and grammatical forms. If they become so useful that they pass into the vocabulary of all classes, they lose their foreign characteristics and become Anglicized or naturalized — that is, treated as native words. They lose their foreign pronunciations (*cottage, garage, lieutenant*), give up their foreign grammatical features (*gymnasia* and *indices* become *gymnasiums* and *indexes*), and acquire new meanings (*curfew, lingerie, quarantine*). In the process of being naturalized they usually pass through a transitional stage when both the foreign and the naturalized uses are common (*data are — data is; detoúr — détour; flair* meaning "capacity to detect" and also "having a knack for"). When the new uses begin to be popular they are often denounced as "mistakes," but when the process of naturalization is complete, the learned words, in their new uses, become part of the popular vocabulary.

**Idiomatic Diction.** Every language contains a host of expressions which are not subject to logical analysis but are so characteristic that until one has learned to use them naturally he has not mastered the language. These expressions are called idioms. Unless one has learned the language as a native, they are often difficult to use. For example, a foreigner who has learned what *hard* and *up* mean in English will still be puzzled by the phrase *hard up.* A Frenchman to whom the greeting "How do you carry yourself?" seems the most natural kind of expression will be puzzled by "How do you do?" Yet the only real difference between these two salutations is that one is the French way of talking and the other is the English way. Each is natural to the people who use it. Each is an idiomatic expression.

Because idioms are traditional rather than logical, they can be learned only by experience, not by rule. There is, for example, no rule that will tell us in advance what verbs will govern what prepositions. We say aim *at,* abide *by,* account *for,* arise *from,* and adhere *to.* The meaning of a verb may be no clue to its meaning in an idiomatic verb-adverb combination. A dictionary definition of *get* will be of little use in such phrases as *get ahead, get by, get over.* It is this arbitrary nature of idioms that causes trouble.

The following list illustrates common English idioms.

| | | |
|---|---|---|
| all in all | fight shy of | meddle with |
| at any rate | get a move on | mull over |
| be taken in | get away with | nice and cold |
| by and large | get behind | off and on |
| call off | get off | pull through |
| call up | get on | put up with |
| catch fire | hard and fast | right away |
| come in handy | in any event | set about |
| do away with | keep up | set up |
| do up | kill off | strike a bargain |
| down and out | look down on | take heed |
| drink up | look over | tear down |
| eat away | look up to | tear out |
| eat up | make no bones about | tear up |
| every now and then | make out | watch out |
| fall sick | make up | wind up |

You will notice that these idioms are mostly made up of popular words. They are used by all classes of people and are common to both standard and nonstandard speech. Often a particular idiom may be replaced by a more learned word. Thus "periodically" may be used for "every now and then" and "eradicate" for "rub out." As we shall see later, whether such substitution is advisable will depend on the formality or informality of the style.

**Colloquialisms.** The word *colloquial* is defined by the *American College Dictionary* as "characteristic of or appropriate to ordinary or familiar conversation rather than formal speech or writing." It does not mean here, as it is sometimes taken to mean, "incorrect," "slovenly," or "undesirable." Its closest synonym is "conversational." A colloquialism, therefore, is any word or expression which might appropriately be used in conversation among educated people.

This definition of *colloquial* makes it a broader term than *popular words* or *idiom.* Colloquialisms include popular words and idiomatic constructions; they also include learned words with popular meanings (the use of *alibi* to mean *excuse*, for example), and constructions which are not strictly idioms, especially abbreviated or clipped forms of more formal words, such as *ad* for *advertisement*. The following are illustrations:

| | | |
|---|---|---|
| aggravate (annoy) | fix (predicament) | outside of (aside from) |
| anyway (at any rate) | folks | out loud (aloud) |
| auto | heap (a great deal) | over with (completed) |
| awfully (very) | it's me | party (person) |
| back of (behind) | kind (sort) of | peeve (annoy) |
| bank on (rely on) | like (as though) | phone |
| bust (failure) | locate (settle) | plenty (adv.) |
| cute | lot(s) of | reason is because |
| enthuse | mad (angry) | show (movie) |
| expect (suppose) | math | show (chance) |
| exam | mean (nasty) | sure (certainly) |
| fellow | mighty (very) | terribly |

**Slang.** The *Oxford Dictionary* defines slang as "a language of a highly colloquial type." Notice that the adjective is *colloquial*, not *vulgar, incorrect,* or *nonstandard*. There may be specific slang words which are confined to standard or to nonstandard speakers, but slang is used at all social levels. Its use is less frequent and more discriminating among educated speakers, but, though a college president would usually avoid slang in a public address, he might well use it in many informal speech situations.

Slang has its origin in a desire to be vivid and original. People, especially young people, are constantly experimenting with language, using old words in unconventional ways and, very rarely, coining new words. Many slang expressions are borrowed from the specialized vocabularies of particular occupations or recreations and put into general use —*brass, goldbrick, snafu* (army), *ham* (theater), *on the beam* (radio), *southpaw* (baseball), *behind the eight ball* (pool), *raise the ante* (poker). Most of them are figurative uses of expressions in the general vocabulary with literal meanings — *flat tire, wet blanket, blow a fuse, corn, dope, lemon, lid*.

If these adaptations serve a useful purpose, they may survive and, in time, be accepted as established usage. For example, the words *bus, cab, canter, hoax,* and *mob* were once slang terms but are now acceptable even in formal English; the clipped forms *auto, phone, taxi,* and the words *enthuse, mad* (angry), and *show* (movie) were once slang but are now classified as colloquial; and such current slang as *kids, liable* (likely), *sick* (disgusted), *swell* (good), and *windbag* are so common that their recognition as colloquialisms seems certain.

The great majority of slang terms, however, soon depreciate in value.

The freshness that made them effective at first is soon worn off by over-use, and what was once creative becomes lazy borrowing. This is the chief reason why instructors often object to slang in college writing. If the slang words were carefully chosen and if they were appropriate to the style of the paper, they might be effective. But if slang were so chosen, there would be much less of it in student compositions.

Let us now return to the formal, informal, and colloquial styles.

## Formal Style

Formal English is primarily a written style, though it is occasionally used in public lectures of a serious or ceremonial nature. Its chief characteristics are (1) relatively long and involved sentences, with frequent rhetorical devices such as the parallel and the periodic sentence (see pages 134–138); (2) an extensive vocabulary which makes a liberal use of learned words and avoids abbreviations, contractions, colloquialisms, and slang; (3) conservative grammatical usage which tends to observe distinctions often ignored at a less formal level; (4) an impersonal tone; and (5) a serious and dignified attitude toward the subject and the reader.

The following paragraph is moderately formal:

There are, indeed, other objects of desire that if attained leave nothing but restlessness, and dissatisfaction behind them. These are the objects pursued by fools. That such objects ever attract us is a proof of the disorganization of our nature, which drives us in contrary directions and is at war with itself. If we had attained anything like steadiness of thought or fixity of character, if we knew ourselves, we should know also our inalienable satisfactions. To say that all goods become worthless in possession is either a piece of superficial satire that intentionally denies the normal in order to make the abnormal seem more shocking, or else it is a confession of frivolity, a confession that, as an idiot never learns to distinguish reality amid the phantasms of his brain, so we have never learned to distinguish true goods amid our extravagances of whim and passion. That true goods exist is nevertheless a fact of moral experience. "A thing of beauty is a joy forever"; a great affection, a clear thought, a profound and well-tried faith are eternal possessions. And this is not merely a fact, to be asserted upon the authority of those who know it by experience. It is a psychological necessity. While we retain the same senses, we must get the same impressions from the same objects; while we keep our instincts and passions, we must pursue the same goods; while we have the same powers of imagination, we must experience the same delight in their exercise. Age brings about, of course, variation in all these particulars, and the susceptibility of two individuals is never exactly similar. But the eventual decay of our personal energies does not destroy the natural value of objects, so long as the same will embodies itself in other minds, and human nature subsists in the world. The sun is not now unreal because each one of us, in succession, and all of us in the end, must close our eyes upon it; and yet the sun exists for us only because we perceive it. The ideal has the same conditions of being, but has this advantage over the sun, that we cannot know if its light is ever destined to fail us.[7]

Notice the style of this passage. The tone is serious and dignified. The diction (*objects of desire, disorganization of our nature, inalienable satisfaction, etc.*) tends to be learned. The sentence structure is frequently inverted, and there are many long sentences. The whole expression, as the following contrasted excerpts show, is far removed from the style in which the same ideas would be expressed in conversation or in informal writing.

| *Formal* | *Informal* |
|---|---|
| There are, indeed, other objects of desire that if attained leave nothing but restlessness and dissatisfaction behind them. These are the objects pursued by fools. That such objects ever attract us is a proof of the disorganization of our nature, which drives us in contrary directions and is at war with itself. If we had attained anything like steadiness of thought or fixity of character, if we knew ourselves, we should also know our inalienable satisfactions. | We all have foolish desires. We want things which do not satisfy us when we get them. The fact that we want these things is evidence of our inconsistent nature. We are subject to conflicting desires and want to go in opposite directions at the same time. If we had a clearer understanding of our own needs and purposes, we would know what course was best for us. |

Translating a formal style into an informal one sacrifices dignity and eloquence in order to achieve ease, informality, and clearer communication to a wider audience. Whether we gain or lose by such translation will depend partly on how great is the need for clearer communication and partly on how skillfully the formal style is handled. In the hands of a skillful writer a formal style may be immensely eloquent. If we destroy that eloquence, we remove much — perhaps most — of what the writer has to tell us.

But not all purposes require eloquence. It would be a serious mistake to use an exalted style on a subject which did not merit it. Much of the writing you will do in college will require only clear and concise statement. And, as we shall presently see, some very effective writing can be done in a style less formal than that of the paragraph quoted above.

## Colloquial Style

A colloquial style is fundamentally the style used by educated people

[7] From *The Sense of Beauty,* by George Santayana, copyright, 1896, 1936, by Charles Scribner's Sons. Reprinted by permission of Charles Scribner's Sons.

when speaking informally to their social equals. It is basically a spoken rather than a written style, but it is often used by writers dealing popularly with subjects which are not too serious or dignified.

The characteristics of a colloquial style are (1) relatively short simple sentences, often grammatically incomplete, with few rhetorical devices; (2) a generous use of contractions (*I'll, we've, didn't, can't*), clipped words (*cab, exams, phone*), and the omission of relative pronouns (*who, which, that*) which would be retained in a formal style; (3) a vocabulary marked by general avoidance of learned words and by inclusion of some less objectionable slang terms; (4) a simplified grammatical structure which leans heavily on idiomatic constructions and sometimes ignores the fine distinctions of formal grammar; and (5) a personal or familiar tone, by which the writer tries to create the impression of speaking intimately to the reader.

Here is an example:

> You're going to paint that picturesque old barn. All right. One vertical line (better use charcoal) will place the corner of the barn, another line the base. A couple of lines for the trunk of the tree, and maybe a branch or two. Then a line to indicate the horizon — whatever divides the sky from whatever meets it (tree, barn, hill). That's all! No leaves, doorknobs, cats, mice, or daffodils. It's the painting that's fun, and any time wasted in getting into a mess of details is to be deplored. As we start to paint, anything resembling a real drawing on our canvas is purely accidental. . . .
>
> Now squeeze out little blobs of color on your palette, and a big blob of white. And take a look at that sky. It is, let's say, cloudless. And it really is blue. Still not as blue as Uncle Ed's shirt. Take a half of a butter ball of white on your palette knife and plaster it on the front of your palette. Careful now! Just a pinch of blue and mix with the white until there are no streaks. Not blue enough? All right, just a tiny bit more — but easy! Satisfied? Dip your brush in the turpentine, then in the paint and slap it on! Boldly — never mind if you slop over the barn a bit.[8]

Notice, first, the sentence structure. The twenty-two sentences average only ten words in length and half of them are not full sentences but fragments, a kind of structure that almost never occurs in formal writing and only rarely in informal writing, although it is quite common in speech. Notice also the simplicity of the diction and the frequent use of contractions. Finally, notice the intimate tone. It is as though the writer were looking over the reader's shoulder and telling him what to do. The whole effort in these paragraphs is to talk simply, directly, and familiarly to the reader. These are the characteristics of a colloquial style.

[8] Joseph Alger, "Get in There and Paint." From *Recreation,* November, 1944. Reprinted by permission of the National Recreation Association.

The potential strength of a formal style lies in its eloquence and state-liness. The potential strength of a colloquial style lies in its simplicity, its liveliness, and its wider appeal. In the hands of an incompetent writer both styles may fail to do the best they can. The dignity of a formal style may degenerate into pompousness, its eloquence into vague wordiness. Its tone may be stuffy rather than serious. The colloquial style, too, may be abused. Instead of being lively, it may merely be slovenly; instead of familiar, merely crude. Both styles have potential weaknesses.

### Informal Style

The informal style tries to avoid the dangers of both these extremes and to exploit the broad middle way between. Its sentence patterns are less involved than those of formal English without being as loose or fragmentary as those of colloquial English. It avoids the nice re-quirements of formal grammar without being dominated by conversa-tional usages. It may occasionally use learned words, but it prefers idio-matic expressions and words which are easy rather than impressive. Its tone may have the seriousness of the formal style without its dignity, and the informality of the colloquial style without its easygoing familiar-ity. In short, it is to a formal and a colloquial style what a business suit is to evening clothes and a slacks-and-sweater combination. The following paragraphs illustrate an informal style.

> A man in whom I have complete trust once looked me in the eye and told me he had seen a snake, when alarmed, open its mouth and allow its six young to crawl down its throat out of sight, and when danger was past, permit them to reappear. Now cannibal snakes which subsist wholly on their fellows (once or twice removed) are not rare. A nearsighted parent black snake might conceivably, tempted by the pangs of hunger, devour one of its own offspring, but I cannot believe in the willful use by an infant serpent of its mother's acid-filled tummy as a shelter.
>
> A strange thing about nature fakes is that they are almost always gone one better by actual truths. The snake-swallowing sanctuary idea be-comes a minor stunt when compared with certain common tropical fish, which look like little perch. If you want to see sheer magic, tap on the glass of an aquarium which holds a mother, father, and one hundred (count them) tiny young. The moment after an alarm, there will be only two fish visible; every youngster being snugly hidden within the mouth of a parent. When danger is over, the whole mob is gently spewed forth, rolling head over tail to form a dense, orderly cloud around and behind their parents.[9]

This passage compromises the differences between the formal and the colloquial. The sentences are longer and more complex than those in

[9] From "Nature in False Face," by William Beebe in *Collier's*, January 29, 1944, Reprinted by permission of author and publishers.

our colloquial example, but shorter and simpler than those in the formal one. There are no sentence fragments, although an occasional one may be found in informal writing. With the possible exception of "subsist" and "devour," there are no learned words, and no colloquialisms except "fakes," "tummy," and "stunts." Nearly all the diction is drawn from the popular vocabulary. In one sentence the reader is addressed directly as "you," but the author makes no attempt to establish the kind of over-the-shoulder intimacy we noticed in the painting instructions.

Since the informal style is really a range lying between formal and colloquial, some samples will be more formal and some more colloquial than others. This broad range makes it the most useful all-purpose style. In the informal range comes much narration and description, many reports of events, most nontechnical exposition, and critical and argumentative papers addressed to general readers. Most of the modern novels, essays, stories, magazine and newspaper articles you read will be written at an informal level. Most of the lectures and speeches you listen to and many of the textbooks you study — including this one — are informal. The following selections illustrate the wide uses of this style.

### Light Verse

Jenny kissed me when we met,
Jumping from the chair she sat in;
Time, you thief, who love to get
Sweets into your list, put that in:
Say I'm weary, say I'm sad,
Say that health and wealth have missed me,
Say I'm growing old, but add,
Jenny kissed me! [10]

### Serious Poetry

When I, the People, learn to remember, when I, the people,
use the lessons of yesterday and no longer forget
who robbed me last year, who played me for a fool —
then there will be no speaker in all the world say
the name: "The People," with any fleck of a sneer in
his voice or any far-off smile of derision.[11]

### Political Statement

Suppose my neighbor's house catches fire and I have a length of garden hose four or five hundred feet away. If he can take this garden hose and connect it up with his hydrant, I may help him to put out the fire. Now what do I do? I don't say to him before that operation, "Neighbor, my garden hose cost me fifteen dollars; you have to pay me fifteen dollars

[10] Leigh Hunt.
[11] Carl Sandburg, "I Am the People, the Mob." Copyright, 1916, by Henry Holt and Company, Inc. Copyright, 1943, by Carl Sandburg. Reprinted by permission.

for it." No! What is the transaction that goes on? I don't want fifteen dollars — I want my garden hose back after the fire is over.[12]

### Scientific Statement

Why do we speak of atoms? Why do we say that matter is made up of a host of atoms? Objects like the table and the chair, and substances like iron and sugar, appear to be continuous. Water looks as if it were continuous, and so does the glass that contains it; otherwise the water would come through the glass. . . .

Simple and common experiences can give the answer. Ordinary table salt dissolves and disappears when put into water. So does sugar in coffee, and so do hundreds of common substances when placed in water or other liquids. . . .

All this tells us that appearance is not reality; that what we see is only a superficial continuity of matter; that fundamentally there are innumerable holes in all substances, even the most solid. We explain these holes by supposing them to be the space between the ultimate small particles, the atoms, that compose matter.[13]

### Newspaper Report

No war is being fought this week anywhere in the world. No soldier is diving for his life into any foxhole or rice paddy. No messenger is carrying notification of a battlefield casualty to anybody's wife or mother.

When the statesmen at Geneva agreed to a cease-fire in Indo-China, they put a stop to the last of a series of wars which started with Mussolini's invasion of Ethiopia in 1934 and raged continuously for the next twenty years.

Yet the return of world peace was not joyous. No bells were rung, and no confetti was spilled. Like Leon Blum, who had been premier of France just before Munich, western statesmen were half relieved, half ashamed.[14]

### Editorial

Do you know that hobbyhorses are now hard to come by? I don't mean the sort that you and I ride but the old-fashioned kind which has a head at one end of a stick and is very suitable for use either in the nursery or the back yard.

Perhaps the fact is not very important in itself. But the reason why the toy shops no longer stock the horses is. That reason — as given by S. H., *The New Yorker's* shopper who keeps an eye out for the little amenities of life — is simply this: the playschool consultants have decided that a hobbyhorse "does not develop the group spirit." . . .

Here is a straw in the wind if there ever was one, and the warm winds (sometimes called hot air) which blow lustily around the child psycholo-

[12] Franklin D. Roosevelt introducing the Lend-Lease program at a press conference on December 17, 1940.

[13] Selig Hecht, *Explaining the Atom*. Copyright, 1947, by Selig Hecht. Reprinted by permission of The Viking Press, Inc.

[14] Reprinted by permission of *Newsweek* from the issue of August 2, 1954. Copyright, 1954, by *Newsweek*.

gists are full of straws. . . . Nowadays even "self expression" is routinized. My young friend tells me that if you don't want to fingerpaint when the others do, that is just too bad. "Do what you want" is the rule. But you jolly well better want what you ought to want and what you ought to want is what others "at your age level" are supposed to want.[15]

### College Lecture

Our minds thus grow in spots; and like grease-spots, the spots spread. But we let them spread as little as possible: we keep unaltered as much of our old knowledge, as many of our old prejudices and beliefs, as we can. We patch and tinker more than we renew. The novelty soaks in; it stains the ancient mass; but it is also tinged by what absorbs it. . . . It happens relatively seldom that the new fact is added *raw*. More usually it is embedded cooked, as one might say, or stewed down in the sauce of the old.[16]

### Correspondence

Dear Ike:

Now that we have all signed in Berlin I suppose we shall soon begin to run our own affairs. I would like, before this happens, to say what a privilege and an honor it has been to serve under you. I owe much to your wise guidance and kindly forbearance. I know my own faults very well and I do not suppose I am an easy subordinate; I like to go my own way.

But you have kept me on the rails in difficult and stormy times, and have taught me much.

For all this I am very grateful. And I thank you for all you have done for me.

> Your very devoted friend,
> Monty [17]

Few, if any, of your college assignments will require any other than an informal style. Once you understand this you will be more likely to avoid those twin plagues of college composition: the pretentious writing that we saw illustrated in Chapter 7 and the over-colloquial writing which sacrifices the conventions of sentence structure and diction to a striving for conversational usages in assignments which do not call for them.

The table on page 178 summarizes this discussion of formal, informal, and colloquial styles.

[15] Joseph Wood Krutch, "Little Man on a Horse," *The Saturday Review*, July 24, 1954. Copyright, 1954, by *The Saturday Review*. Reprinted by permission of author and publishers.

[16] From *Pragmatism*, by William James. Copyright, 1907, by William James. Reprinted by permission of Longmans, Green & Co., Inc.

[17] From *Crusade in Europe*, by Dwight D. Eisenhower. Copyright, 1948, by Doubleday & Company, Inc. Reprinted by permission of the publishers.

LEVELS OF STANDARD ENGLISH USAGE *

| STYLISTIC LEVELS | LINGUISTIC CHARACTERISTICS | REPRESENTATIVE USES |
|---|---|---|
| *Formal*<br><br>(more often written than spoken) | 1. Relatively long sentences, complex in structure, employing many rhetorical devices.<br>2. Extensive vocabulary, numerous "learned" words.<br>3. General avoidance of abbreviations, contractions, omitted relative pronouns, and other colloquial shortcuts.<br>4. Conservative grammatical usage which observes distinctions generally ignored in popular speech.<br>5. Impersonal tone and dignified attitude towards subject and reader. | 1. Books and articles on scholarly or technical subjects, written for experts in the field.<br>2. "Belles-lettres": novels, essays, stories, poems, written for highly educated readers.<br>3. Prepared serious or ceremonial addresses to restricted audiences. |
| *Informal*<br><br>(both written and spoken, the general level of educated writing and of educated, deliberate speech) | Overlaps formal and colloquial styles, but avoids the extremes of both. | 1. Books and articles on important subjects, but for general readers.<br>2. Most novels, essays, poems, magazine and newspaper articles and editorials.<br>3. Most college writing.<br>4. Most speeches to general audiences; the deliberate conversation of educated speakers in formal speech situations. |
| *Colloquial or Conversational*<br><br>(more often spoken than written) | 1. Short sentences, simple in structure, usually in subject-verb-complement order, few rhetorical devices.<br>2. Many contractions, abbreviations, clipped words; tendency to omit relative pronouns and other constructions not necessary to meaning.<br>3. Few "learned" words, many idiomatic expressions, the use of less objectionable slang. | 1. Light, chatty writing for general readers.<br>2. Dialogue in fiction, and any writing which attempts to catch the rhythms of conversation.<br>3. The letters of educated people to intimate friends.<br>4. Almost all the conversation of educated people when they are at ease. |

* This table is indebted to a similar table in Perrin's *Writer's Guide and Index to English*. The differences between Professor Perrin's table and this one arise out of differences of classification.

## Confusion of Stylistic Levels

A writer should choose the stylistic level most appropriate to his purpose, and he should stay with it. Words which are too formal or too colloquial for their context are discordant, or even ludicrous, and call attention to the writer's lack of sureness. Notice the misfit diction in the following passage from an essay in which a student is relating how his service in the Marines helped to free him from the domination of his twin brother.

> I was never allowed to fight my own battles, for he was at my side and would step in and pound the hell out of my diabolical enemies. This, too, contributed to my shyness.
>
> During the terminating days of my high-school career I came to the conclusion that life in the Marine Corps would cure me of this bad attribute. I quickly told my brother. His eyes seemed to be glaring like a dragon's. He then told me, "I am going to join the army and you shall do such also."

The lapses here are clear enough. Except in some kinds of dialogue, the use of profanity is almost never justifiable in college writing. If it is used at all, the whole style of the paper must be so obviously colloquial that the profanity does not call attention to itself. Yet here is profanity in one paragraph and learned words like *terminating* and *attribute* in the next. These two levels of usage, however justifiable either might be alone, are impossibly inconsistent in the same paper. Other choices of diction are almost as bad. The description of the brother's eyes "glaring like a dragon's" is a trite and far-fetched metaphor, and his words "you shall do such also" are overformal and comically unidiomatic. What the brother would probably say is, "I'm going to join the army, and so are you."

Incongruous diction will be most conspicuous in writing which is clearly formal or clearly colloquial, as may be shown by substituting inappropriate diction in a passage quoted earlier.

> There are, indeed, other objects of desire that if *got* leave nothing but restlessness and *griping* behind them. These are the objects pursued by fools. That such objects ever attract us is a proof of the *cussedness* of our nature, which drives us in contrary directions and is at war with itself. If we had attained anything like steadiness of thought or fixity of character, if we knew ourselves, we should know also *what's good for us*. To say that all goods become worthless in possession is either a piece of *half-baked bunk* that intentionally denies the normal in order to make the abnormal seem more shocking, or else it is a confession of frivolity, a confession that, as an idiot never learns *what the score is,* so we have never learned to distinguish true goods amid our extravagances of whim and passion. That true goods exist is nevertheless a fact of moral experience. "A thing of beauty is a joy forever"; a great *yen,* a *bright idea,* a profound and well-tried faith, are eternal possessions. And this is not merely

a fact, to be asserted upon the *say-so* of those who know it by experience. It is a psychological necessity.

There are contexts in which *got, griping, cussedness, what's good for us, what the score is, yen, bright idea,* and *say-so* might be appropriate, but this paragraph is not one of them. These colloquial and slang expressions are as conspicuously out of place in a formal style as a ukelele in a symphony orchestra.

Conversely, the italicized learned words in the following colloquial selection are hopelessly out of tone.

Have you ever tried to quit smoking? It's quite simple. I know. I have *achieved abstinence* thousands of times already. In fact, I quit every day. I awaken in the morning — my nose and throat dry and parched. Then, I decide to *renounce all further association with the weed.* But it's a terrible vice over which I no longer have any control. I've got to have a smoke. Just one. Then I'll *refrain from further indulgence* the rest of the day. Just one to take care of my terrible longing. I can go without food, without drink. But I must have a cigarette. Just one.

So I smoke one before going to school. Only that one. I promise myself, I'm not going to smoke any more today. I'll leave my cigarettes home today. Yeh, that's what I'll do. And since I have no cigarettes, I *shall be unable to make even a momentary concession to appetite.*

The formal expressions in this passage are just as awkward as the colloquialisms in the preceding one.

In the following paragraph some of the bracketed words harmonize with the context and some are either too formal or too informal. Underline the expression you would have chosen had you written the paragraph, circle others which would be acceptable even though they are not your first choice, and cross out those which would be completely unacceptable.

When George Bernard Shaw was [composing, writing, batting out] *Pygmalion,* he had in one scene to make an extremely [discriminating, meticulous, nice, subtle, tricky] choice of diction. His hero, a speech expert, had, as the result of a [bet, wager, sporting proposition], guaranteed to [change, make over, transform, transmogrify] a dirty, ignorant, [foul-mouthed, dirty-talking, profane] girl of the slums into a beautiful and refined lady. With the aid of baths, cosmetics, and costumes it was easy to make her look like a lady. The real [arduous undertaking, difficulty, stumper] lay in getting her to [orate, gab, speak] like one. The speech professor put her through a [grueling, hard, tough, difficult] course of instruction. When he felt that, although not perfect, she could [masquerade, pass, get by] as a lady if she [canalized, constricted, kept] her conversation within narrow limits, he arranged to have her attend a tea at his mother's [domicile, joint, house, place of residence]. By following his instructions carefully and by [adhering, sticking] to the speeches she had [brushed-up on, conned, memorized, got by heart], she was able to [carry-off, execute, get by, swing] the impersonation, stiffly but satisfactorily. Finally, as she [got up to go, gave indications of betaking her departure, rose to go], a young aristocrat who [had fallen for her, was enamored of her presence, had found her most attractive] offered to walk home with her. Since such a [proposal, proposition, overture] had not been anticipated, no [canned, pat, preconceived, ready-made] answer had been provided for it. Shaw's problem then, was to put into her [oral cavity, mouth, trap] an answer that would [betray, give away, tip off, divulge] both the economic and linguistic level from which she had sprung. She must, in the fewest possible words, refuse to walk home because she thought that no one who was attempting to pass as a lady would [acquiesce, agree, condescend, stoop] to anything less than a taxi-ride, and to refuse in terms that were both profane and in the uneducated idiom of her slum environment. The speech Shaw gave her was: "Me walk? Not bloody likely!"

## The Specific Word

"Specific" is the opposite of "general." A specific word points to a particular referent — a particular person, object, or event; a general word points to a group or class of referents. Thus "Adlai Stevenson," "Mickey Mantle," "the present heavyweight champion," "the apple tree beside my garage," and "last night's rain" indicate particular referents. But "politician," "baseball player," "pugilist," "tree," and "rain" indicate group referents. The general term, therefore, includes a number of specific terms, as "red" includes "carmine," "coral," "crimson," "maroon," "rose," "scarlet," "vermilion," and so on, and as "Midwest" includes "Michigan," "Minnesota," "Illinois," "Indiana," "Iowa," and several other states.

Actually the contrast between "specific" and "general" is relative. A term may be specific in contrast to one word, but general in contrast to another. We can show this relativity by the following table.

| Very General | Less General | More Specific | Quite Specific |
|---|---|---|---|
| athlete | baseball player | Yankee outfielder | Mickey Mantle |
| college student | freshman | member of Dr. Jones's composition section | Bill Mason |
| vegetation | tree | apple tree | The apple tree beside my garage |
| criminal | thief | pickpocket | The man who stole my wallet |

As you can see, the words in the middle columns are more specific than those at the far left, but more general than those at the far right.

The more general words are, the harder it will be for a reader to see precisely what a writer intends them to mean. For example, "The man was making preparations for a journey" is such a general statement that we get only a vague idea of what the man was doing. He may have been making hotel reservations, buying a railroad ticket, having his car tuned up, arranging for someone to handle his business affairs, or packing a suitcase. We cannot tell which, because the phrase "making preparations for a journey" does not communicate specifically.

Notice below how the specific diction at the right communicates meaning which is obscured by the general diction at the left.

| General | Specific |
|---|---|
| He is an accomplished athlete. | He is a top-flight golfer. |
| He drives an old car. | He drives a 1950 Buick. |
| The boy has a serious disease. | The boy has diphtheria. |
| I have been reading a Shakespearean play. | I have been reading *Macbeth*. |
| Her grades at midsemester were unsatisfactory. | She received two failing grades and a D at midsemester. |
| After the strenuous activities of the day, I did not feel like dancing. | After playing 36 holes of golf, I did not feel like dancing. |
| In the past, girls in rural communities had no facilities for bathing except those offered by some neighboring stream. In such circumstances a bathing suit was not always a necessity, but if one was worn it was likely to consist of nothing more than some discarded article of clothing tailored to fit the occasion. Women in urban areas seldom owned their own costumes. Only those who moved in the more wealthy and sophisticated social circles had private bathing suits. The usual practice was to wear a rented one. This distinction no longer exists. Now the modern country girl owns a bathing suit similar to those worn at fashionable beaches in the East. | Twenty years ago if the farmer's daughter went swimming she swam in the crick below the pasture, and if she wore a bathing suit, which was not as customary as you may think, it was likely to be a pair of her brother's outgrown overalls trimmed with scissors as her discretion might suggest. Her cousin in such a town as Great Bend (Kansas) rented a shapeless gray cotton suit at an amusement park. Only the Banker's daughter, who had been to a finishing school, had a bathing suit of her own. There are no such distinctions now; all women have bathing suits, and they are exactly like those worn at Hyannis, Southampton, and Narragansett Pier.[18] |

The last example shows you that the more specific diction is, the more pictorial it is likely to be. "A pair of her brother's outgrown over-

---

[18] Bernard De Voto, "Main Street Twenty Years After," *Harper's Magazine*, November, 1940. Reprinted by permission of *Harper's Magazine*.

alls trimmed with scissors" makes a clearer picture than "some discarded article of clothing tailored to fit the occasion." "The crick below the pasture" is easier to visualize than "some neighboring stream." "Her cousin in . . . Great Bend (Kansas)" instead of "Women in urban areas" and "the Banker's daughter" in place of "those who moved in the more wealthy and sophisticated social circles" provide sharper identification.

To find the most telling specific word or phrase takes thought, and too many students are willing to take the easy way out and use "utility words" instead. Of these words, Professor Kennedy says, "Any long used and well-developed language accumulates ultimately a supply of general utility words which have such broad meaning and general application that they can be utilized in a great many different ways with no special change of meaning." [19] These, as their name implies, are useful words. In conversation, their general meaning is often sharpened by tone of voice, facial expression, or gesture. Their discreet use in writing needs no defense, but when a writer uses them to excess, his work is likely to be colorless and inexact, as the following sentences show.

1. It had been an *awful* day and we felt *awfully* tired.
2. It was such a *nice thing* to do. It made me feel *grand*.
3. It was a *strange sensation* to see the *queer* look on his face.

The italicized words in these sentences are so vague, could mean so many different things, that the sentences simply fail to communicate any precise meaning. They reveal either fuzzy or lazy thinking and should never be allowed to get beyond the first draft. The way to revise them is, first, to sharpen the idea to be expressed and, second, to choose words specific enough to express it exactly. The following revisions make the original sentences more meaningful.

### (1)
After such a frustrating day we felt emotionally exhausted.
*Or,* It had been a day of repeated shocks which had finally left us numb.
*Or,* We had been under such a strain all day that we were on the point of collapse.

### (2)
It was such a friendly gesture that I felt immediately at home.
*Or,* It was such a generous remark that it brought tears to my eyes.
*Or,* It was flattery, of course, but I flushed with happiness.

### (3)
It was pathetic to watch the hurt in his eyes.
*Or,* It was amusing to observe his evident embarrassment.
*Or,* The vindictiveness of his look terrified me.

[19] *Current English* (Ginn and Company, 1935), p. 552.

The following sentences are vague because of the italicized general utility words. Even though you may not always know exactly what the writer intended to say, can you revise the sentences to give them some specific meaning?

1. It gave me a *funny feeling* to hear him say that another war was inevitable.

2. It was an *awful* trip. The car *acted up*. It rained *like everything* and the roads were *terrible*. Altogether we had a *fierce* time of it.

3. That kind of publicity is always *bad business* for an *organization*, and the boys in our chapter felt *pretty bad* about it.

4. His wife always is a *smooth dresser*. Today she wore a *lovely outfit*. It was a *nice shade of blue*. She also wore a *cute little* white hat with a matching blue ribbon.

5. She has a *marvelous figure* and *gorgeous* red hair.

6. The homecoming party was a *terrific success*. The decorations and the refreshments were *wonderful*, and everybody thought the favors were *swell*. It was the *sort of affair* I'll remember for years.

7. When I said that, a *peculiar light* came into his eyes and I had a *queer sensation* that I had said the wrong thing.

**Sensory Words.** A number of specific words refer to sensory experiences, to what we see, hear, touch, taste, and smell. Because these words call up sensory images, they are particularly effective in description. In the following list, some words could fit into more than one sensory category.

*Touch:* chill, clammy, cold, corrugated, grainy, gritty, harsh, jarring, knobby, moist, nubby, numb, plushy, rough, satiny, slimy, slithering, smooth, sting, tingle, tickly, velvety.

*Taste:* bland, biting, bitter, brackish, briny, metallic, minty, nutty, peppery, salty, sour, spicy, sweet, tainted, vinegary, yeasty.

*Smell:* acrid, fetid, greasy, mouldy, musky, musty, pungent, putrid, rancid, rank, reek, stench, sulphurous, woodsy.

*Sound:* bellow, blare, buzz, chatter, chime, clang, clatter, clink, crackle, crash, creak, gurgle, hiss, hum, murmur, pop, purr, rattle, rustle, screech, snap, splash, squeak, swish, tinkle, whine, whisper.

*Sight:* blaze, bleary, bloody, burnished, chalky, dappled, ebony, flame, flash, flicker, florid, foggy, gaudy, glare, glitter, glossy, glow, golden, grimy, haze, inky, leaden, lurid, muddy, roiled, sallow, shadow, smudged, spark, streak, tawny, turbid.

Sensory words help the reader feel the experience that the writer is recording. If you reread the two versions of the rattlesnake incident on pages 80–82 you will see that much of the detail in the second version is expressed in words that appeal to the senses and so make it easy for the reader to re-live the incident in his imagination. Notice how the following description makes the reader feel, hear, see, and smell the details of ploughing.

The ploughing, now in full swing, enveloped him in a vague, slow-moving whirl of things. Underneath him was the jarring, jolting, trembling machine; not a clod was turned, not an obstacle encountered, that he did not receive the swift impression of it through all his body; the very friction of the damp soil, sliding incessantly from the shiny surface of the shears, seemed to reproduce itself in his finger-tips and along the back of his head. He heard the horse-hoofs by the myriads crushing down easily, deeply, into the loam, the prolonged clinking of trace-chains, the working of the smooth brown flanks in the harness, the clatter of wooden hames, the champing of bits, the click of iron shoes against pebbles, the brittle stubble of the surface ground crackling and snapping as the furrows turned, the sonorous, steady breaths wrenched from the deep, labouring chests, strap-bound, shining with sweat, and all along the line the voices of the men talking to the horses. Everywhere there were visions of glossy brown backs, straining, heaving, swollen with muscle; harness streaked with specks of froth, broad, cup-shaped hoofs, heavy with brown loam; men's faces red with tan, blue overalls spotted with axle-grease; muscled hands, the knuckles whitened in their grip on the reins, and through it all the ammoniacal smell of the horses, the bitter reek of perspiration of beasts and men, the aroma of warm leather, the scent of dead stubble — and stronger and more penetrating than everything else, the heavy, enervating odour of the upturned, living earth.[20]

Now notice what happens to the paragraph when most of the sensory words are removed.

He abandoned himself to his ploughing to such an extent that he became a part of the total process and identified himself with the machine beneath him. He could detect the resistance of the damp soil to the impact of the plough, and whenever an obstacle of any sort was encountered, he felt the repercussion in his own body. He was conscious too of the noises that the team and the harness produced as the work continued, and of the appearance of the horses and their immediate environment. All around him was a confusion of sensory impressions, the strongest of which was the odor of the horses and the characteristic smell of upturned earth.

Do you agree that the rewritten paragraph is merely a flat and lifeless summary of the original?

Our stress on the value of specific words should not imply that general diction is never desirable. For example, when you are asked to summarize a 5000-word essay in 500 words, your purpose is to state the central thought of the essay, not its illustrative detail, and your summary has to be more general than the original. Moreover, a writer will not always intend to be specific. His statement may depend not on a set of particular facts but on a broad or universal truth. Whether a subject should be treated generally or specifically is part of the decision about purpose. An excellent illustration is the writing of the Declaration of Independence.

The committee appointed to write the Declaration had a double duty to perform. It had, in the same document, to make a general statement of the relationship between free people and their governors and a particular statement of the abuses which George III had committed against the Colonies. The first part of the Declaration is necessarily, and wisely, general:

> We hold these truths to be self-evident, that all men are created equal, that they are endowed by their Creator with certain unalienable rights. . . . That to secure these rights, Governments are instituted among Men, deriving their just powers from the consent of the governed. . . .

These remarks could apply to any nation, and have been interpreted by other nations as applying to them. The second part is more specific:

> For quartering large bodies of troops among us. . . .
> For cutting off our Trade with all parts of the world:
> For imposing taxes on us without our Consent:
> For depriving us in many cases of the benefit of Trial by Jury. . . .

These charges refer to particular acts of a particular monarch. This makes this part of the Declaration less valuable as a universal inspiration, but more informative as a statement of why the Colonies renounced their allegiance to George III.

The contrast between the two parts of the Declaration shows that there is a time to be general and a time to be specific. Your own analysis of the nature of your assignment should guide you in your choice, but you should know that the emphasis which college instructors place upon specific diction arises from the fact that much college writing is more general than it need be.

## Figurative Language

Figurative language communicates by analogy. One thing is likened to another, usually familiar, and the comparison invites the imagination to visualize the similarity. For example, a scientist wishes to describe the structure of an atom for lay readers. Knowing that they will be familiar with the pattern of the solar system — the elliptical rotation of planets round the sun — he can give a quick, easily visualized description of the atom:

> An atom is a submicroscopic solar system in which electrons, like tiny planets, swing in their orbits around a central nucleus.

An atomic system is not a solar system, and electrons are not planets, but the structural similarity is close enough so that the comparison is informative and vivid.

The commonest figures of speech are metaphors, similes, allusions, and personification.

## Metaphors and Similes

Both metaphor and simile compare two things, but the former says they are the same, whereas the latter, usually by inserting *as* or *like,* merely says they are similar. Metaphor says the atom *is* a submicroscopic solar system; simile says it is *like* one. Here are other examples:

| *Metaphors* | *Similes* |
|---|---|
| The sky was a vast black blanket riddled with tiny star holes. | The star-dotted sky was like a vast black blanket riddled with tiny holes. |
| The moon was a ghostly galleon tossed upon cloudy seas. | As fresh he was as is the month of May. |
| Marriage had modified his conception of her. Once she had been his lovely wild rose; now she was the thorn in his flesh. | Like summer tempest came her tears. |
| Mussolini's attack on France was not only a stab in the back. It was a stab with a pocket-knife by a small boy who was taking advantage of the fact that his victim's arms had already been securely tied. | The judge's head oscillated from one side of the net to the other, for all the world like the pendulum of a grandfather clock. |
| | Her death destroyed all that was meaningful in his existence. Thereafter his life was like a building which had been gutted by fire. |

The effectiveness of metaphors and similes lies in their power to suggest ideas too complex or abstruse to be easily communicated in literal terms. They picture vividly in a few words what would be less effectively described in many. Consider how the following figure of speech describes abstract and complex phenomena in terms which a reader will at least think he understands:

> Life's but a walking shadow, a poor player
> That struts and frets his hour upon the stage
> And then is heard no more. It is a tale
> Told by an idiot, full of sound and fury,
> Signifying nothing.

One might write a long essay on the insignificance of life without driving the point home as thoroughly as Shakespeare did in this triple metaphor in which Macbeth sees his own life as unsubstantial as a shadow, as unreal as a poor play, and as meaningless as a madman's babbling.

Many words and phrases no longer thought of as figures of speech were originally metaphors and similes. Thus *foil* and *parry* derive from the sport of fencing; *checkmate* was a metaphor from chess; *rosy red* and *sapphire blue* were similes, as were *dirt cheap* and *silver hair*. At *bay* once described a hunted animal when it finally turned to face the baying hounds; a *crestfallen* cock was one which had been injured in a fight; and an *alarm* was a call to arms. Many other expressions retain their metaphorical appearances, but are so common that we no longer think of them as figures of speech — expressions such as the mouth of a river, the face of a clock, the front (originally "forehead") of a house, the brow of a hill, the top of the morning.

### Allusions

Allusions are figures of speech which suggest a similarity between people, places, or events, real or imaginary, as in "the Babe Ruth of bowling," "the Athens of the Midwest," "a dog-in-the-manger attitude."

Like metaphors and similes, allusions are vivid and memorable short cuts. Instead of trying to describe the bewilderment of a football crowd watching a strong team beaten by a weak one, a writer may suggest their stunned surprise by saying, "The crowd couldn't have been more shocked if the Christians had started to eat the lions." Or he may sum up a story of world suffering as "the Gethsemane of our age."

Allusions must be used with care. When successful, they not only communicate effectively but also give the reader the pleasure of recognition. But if the reader does not recognize an allusion, it will mean nothing to him and may annoy him. Rather than blame his own ignorance, he will then label the allusion "pedantic" — that is, so erudite that no "normal" reader should be expected to understand it. For this reason, a writer should always be reasonably sure that his allusions will be familiar to the audience he is writing for.

### Personification

Personification is the device of endowing animals, inanimate objects, abstractions, and events with human qualities and abilities:

> The eagle, perched on his mountain throne, surveyed the far reaches of his kingdom.
> Truth, crushed to earth, will rise again.
> The flames ate hungrily at the wooden foundations.
> The once proud trees bent meekly before the storm.
> All around, the forest united in a conspiracy against them.
> Her clothes not only invited attention, they commanded it.

Personification, like metaphor, simile, and allusion, implies and pictures a similarity. But whereas metaphor may compare any two things, one of the elements of a personification must be a human characteristic. The subject must be described in terms of human actions, attitudes, feelings, or responses.

### Inappropriate Figures

The power of figures of speech to call up vivid images in our minds sometimes leads an uncritical writer into trouble. For if the figures are inappropriate, they may call up images which are ludicrous or incredible. The student who described his brother's eyes as "glaring like a dragon's" (page 179) was writing without thinking. If he had asked himself, "Is this really the way he looked?" he might have realized that his simile was neither fresh nor appropriate. Obviously the exaggerated image of ferocity did not occur to the student or he would not have used it. This habit of using figurative language without visualizing its probable effect often results in confused imagery like this:

> When spring comes, the face of old Mother Earth is arrayed in garments of breath-taking beauty.
>
> Efforts to help the veterans were sidetracked by a bog of red tape.
>
> The President's ill-advised action has thrown the ship of state into low gear, and unless congressmen wipe out party lines and carry the ball as a team, it may take the country months to get back on an even keel.

The beauty of spring has often been compared to that of a woman's face, or to a woman's clothes; but telescoping the two images suggests a face wearing clothes, and is merely funny. Sidetracked efforts is a common enough metaphor, but to mix this railroad image with that of a bog, and then with red tape, shows that the writer was not visualizing. The third sentence, more chaotic still, mixes images of a ship, a car, some lines that can be erased (chalk or pencil lines?), a football team, and a ship again — all in one blurred comparison! Mixed images, like shifts in sentence structure (pages 134–139), show what comes of changing purpose halfway through a sentence. They also show what comes of using words because they "sound good," not because of what a reader will get from them.

Similes, too, may go wrong if images are mixed inappropriately.

> He felt as uncomfortable and out of place in the room full of ladies as a wolf in a sheepfold.
>
> The huge rock went crashing down the hill like a lover rushing to meet his beloved.

Far-fetched similes like these invite the reader to see unlikely similarities which are difficult to imagine. It is hard, for instance, to think of a wolf being uncomfortable in a sheepfold, or to picture a rock crashing downhill in the same mood and manner as a lover going to meet his lass. A reader is more likely to laugh at such a comparison than to take it seriously.

Identify the following figures of speech. If you consider any of them inappropriate, explain why.

1. The grades that a student makes are not the only yardstick for his academic success.

2. I saw Eternity the other night
   Like a great ring of pure and endless light.

3. The great liner acknowledged the acclaim of the passing tugs with dignified blasts of her horn.

4. We expected Bill to win the debate in his rebuttal, but, like Casey at the bat, he fumbled every chance.

5. All afternoon this pigskin Proteus consistently eluded his All-American opponent.

6. Life like a dome of many colored glass
   Stains the white radiance of eternity.

7. Drivers who drink keep Charon working overtime.

8. Into this great forest the hand of man had never set foot.

9. His words fanned the flame of her indignation and caused it to boil over.

10. Along the river bank the willows were whispering in the wind.

11. I cannot praise a fugitive and cloistered virtue . . . that never sallies out and sees her adversary, but slinks out of the race, where that immortal garland is to be run for, not without dust and heat.

12. Like the foolish virgins in the Bible the politicians have been asleep at the switch and have allowed a glorious opportunity to go down the drain.

13. The trouble with arguing with your wife is that, even if you win, it's a Pyrrhic victory.

14. Can Honour's voice provoke the silent dust,
    Or Flattery soothe the dull cold ear of death?

15. For anyone who has slept in one of those hammocks the bed of Procrustes would have no terrors.

## The Unspoiled Word

The terms *trite, hackneyed, shopworn, threadbare* are used to describe expressions which have been spoiled by overuse. Just as cloth may lose its luster and fruit its texture by excessive and careless handling, so words may lose their value by being used too much. Trite words, like most slang, were once fresh and crisp. Such phrases as "a calculated risk," "a near miss," "a moral victory," and such figures of speech as "blind as a bat," "busy as a bee," "close as a clam," "safe as the bank" were once forceful expressions, but they have lost the freshness which once made them effective and are now little more than conspicuous utility words, common in casual conversation, but undesirable in any writing in which the choice of diction is important.

The worst thing about trite diction is the way it stops thought. A writer who cannot resist the temptation to use a ready-made phrase instead of fashioning his own thought into words soon has no thought except the stereotyped comment which his trite diction suggests. Consequently his ideas and observations follow set patterns: any change in personnel becomes a "shakeup"; all hopes become "fond," "foolish," or "forlorn"; standard procedure for making a suggestion is to "drop a hint"; defeats are "crushing"; changes in the existing system are "noble experiments" or "dangerous departures"; unexpected occurrences are "bolts from the blue"; and people who "sow wild oats" always have to "pay the piper" even though they are "as poor as churchmice." The result is a kind of automat-thinking in which the writer puts in a trite phrase and pulls out a platitude.

Triteness can be cut out in revision, and should be. But the best way to keep it out of your writing is to keep your diction specific. As long as you strive to use words that point to specific referents you have a control over your diction that will protect you from triteness. Or, to put this differently, as long as you are thinking about what you want your writing to do, you are likely to use clear, fresh words to convey your meaning. Any considerable use of trite words in a paragraph is usually a sign that the writer stopped thinking during that paragraph. Notice how the writer of the following essay fails to provide the illustrative detail and specific diction necessary to make her thoughts clear, and resorts instead to trite statements which serve as escapes from thinking. Underline every trite expression you detect in the paper.

To be taken out of a little world, high school, and placed on a large university campus was a big step in my life. From the first day I arrived at the University, I changed. I could no longer be "mother's little girl" and run to her for advice on what to do about this and how to do that. I had to change.

I am, from all outward appearances, the same person I was when I left home in September and yet, I'm not. Being with people who are more mature has helped me grow up. I've developed a more grown-up idea of life. I've had to make decisions and judgments I've never before been faced with. I've had to give my own opinions and as the old saying goes, "fend for myself." Life isn't a bower of roses, and I've learned it. I've learned to think more seriously of why I'm at school and what I'm deriving from it. Am I doing my best down here? If not, I'd better get busy. People depend on me and I've had to shoulder responsibility. I've grown up a lot. I'm on my own. I have to be able to prove to myself and my parents I can take my place in the world.

Money doesn't grow on trees and how well I've learned that. What a rude awakening, when I finally realized all the odd change I used to ask for at home wasn't with me at school. I had thought my allowance was an enormous amount and, before I knew it, it was gone. College has taught me "a penny saved is a penny earned." I've learned to live within my allowance and have some left to store in my bank for a rainy day.

College has helped me to become a more mature person who has the ability to make decisions for herself. It's not all in the books, what you learn at college. It's in your every day existence with different people and situations that gives you something more, perhaps it helps you grow up a little. It's made me a better person and more able to cope with any situation which is to come.

# Review Exercises

**A.** Substitute the right word or phrase for the italicized words in the following sentences.

1. Only two of the employees had *excess* to the vault.
2. The reprimand had no *affect* on him.
3. The picture was *adopted* from a magazine story.
4. The reporter could *illicit* no further information from the senator.
5. The mammoth is no longer *exempt*.
6. I think his *conscious* is hurting him.
7. She was dressed in one of her sister's *customs*.
8. He cited a supreme court judgment as an *instant*.
9. Before setting off on the canoe trip we carefully *chartered* our course.
10. His left leg was *factored* below the knee.
11. Without a reservation you will not be able to get a *birth* on the train.
12. These angles are said to be *complimentary*.
13. For Pete's sake, Jim, *extinguish* the light.
14. I like to talk to small, *homely* audiences.
15. He is the fairest umpire in the league. His decisions are always completely *indifferent*.
16. For sheer *veracity* I've never seen such a fight.
17. Even their mannerisms were *of a similitude*.
18. The tramp knocked him down, rifled his pockets, and *absconded with* his watch.
19. The minister told the congregation that in his estimation the issue was a *fifty-fifty proposition*.
20. The jury recommended a light sentence because of *attenuating* circumstances.
21. Tomorrow we are to take scholastic *attitude* tests.
22. *Sensual* perception means learning about things through your senses.
23. Stop worrying about it. Just *discharge* the whole thing from your mind.
24. At least you ought to listen to the *corresponding* side of the question.
25. The convention chairman pleaded with the delegates to avoid *concord*.

26. The best salesmen have easy, outgoing, *introvertive* personalities.

27. In evident anger, the speaker said that his opponent's attitude would be *condoned* by all fair-minded people.

28. A *transparent* window provides some light but keeps anyone from looking into the office.

29. The altitude of a triangle is equal to a line drawn *horizontally* from the apex to the base.

30. Before we left, Dad gave us *implicit* instructions about how to conduct ourselves.

**B.** Study the diction of the following story from the point of view of its appropriateness to the characters, then write a short report explaining and illustrating your findings.

## INTERRUPTIONS, INTERRUPTIONS [21]

"This seat taken?" Mr. Stacey asked hurriedly, glancing back at the crowd struggling down the aisle.

The man with the book glanced up briefly. "No."

Mr. Stacey stretched his stubby figure, shoved his bag into the overhead rack, and sank into the vacant seat. "Boy, was I lucky!" he observed.

"Yes," responded the other, abstractedly.

Mr. Stacey permitted himself a slight chortle. "Yes, sir, guess I was the early bird, all right, all right. Like to read?"

"Yes," said the other.

"Me, too," Mr. Stacey said, gratified at their kindred tastes. "Only I don't get much time for it. Always interruptions, interruptions. That way with you?"

The other glanced up while turning a page. "Yes," he said and turned back to his book.

"Yes, sir," Mr. Stacey continued musingly, "don't guess I've read a whole book for several years. Just can't get the time." He reached into his pocket. "Have a smoke?"

"No."

"Mind if I do?" Mr. Stacey asked considerately.

"No," said the other, his eyes going back to the beginning of a paragraph.

"Remember once," Mr. Stacey said, "feller gave me a Mexican cigarette. Boy, was that something! I don't see how anybody can smoke 'em. Just cigar scrapings and chocolate; what a taste! Yes, sir, give me an American cigarette every time. Sure you won't have one?"

"Yes."

"That's America for you," Mr. Stacey declared, holding up his cigarette. "Best cigarette, best everything. Greatest country in the world. We've got our problems, all right, but we'll lick 'em. Won the war, now we'll win the peace. Yes, sir, I'm a one-hundred-per-cent believer in America."

[21] Edgar Brooke, "Interruptions, Interruptions," *Collier's*, February, 1948. Reprinted by permission of *Collier's* and Ann Watkins, Inc.

The man lowered his book and considered for a moment. "Which America?" he asked.

"Beg pardon?" Mr. Stacey said.

"I asked," the other repeated, "which America?"

"I don't get you," Mr. Stacey said. "You mean North America? The United States?"

"Weren't you referring to the United States?"

"Yes — that's right," Mr. Stacey said with relief.

"Well, which United States?"

Mr. Stacey's mystification was complete. For a wild moment he glanced around to assure himself that he was in his right mind, on the right train.

"Look," he said uncertainly, "we aren't connecting. I don't know what you're talking about."

"Why," said the other quietly, "I'm simply asking you to which United States you were referring."

The pale, soft hands of confusion fumbled over Mr. Stacey's brain. His eyes took on a hunted look.

"Listen," he exclaimed, "there isn't but *one* United States. It's all around us. We're in it right now."

"Ah," said the other, "but are there not many United States — or, if you prefer, many Americas?"

"Look," Mr. Stacey said, "imagine we are in a plane flying over the Mississippi, halfway between Chicago and Miami. High, you see, so high that we can see from Canada to Mexico, from Maine to California. That's America. That's the United States. That's what I'm talking about."

"Very clear," said the other, and Mr. Stacey sighed. "But, there is a difficulty. By the time our plane reached the ground again, the America which we viewed from the air would be a different America."

"How's that?" Mr. Stacey was startled.

"By the same reasoning," the other continued evenly, "America is not the same as it was when this train departed from New York. The change, in all likelihood, has been slight, but still, unquestionably, change has occurred. So, that America of the recent past and the one of this precise instant are not the same."

"What's happened to it?" Mr. Stacey asked dully. He involuntarily glanced out of the window at the landscape passing at blurring speed.

"Happened to it?" said the man. "If all the human beings in the world were to undertake together the problem of measuring all the minute changes — psychological, physical, human, social, cultural, economic — which have occurred in America since we left New York, they would fail ignominiously."

"That so?" said Mr. Stacey.

"Again," the man proceeded remorselessly, "America may be viewed as the embodiment of a political concept, framed by the Declaration of Independence and the Constitution, and evolving through the years under such influences as the activities of political parties, Supreme Court decisions, governmental changes effected by vested interests operating through lobbies, and so forth, with the result that 'America' as a political concept is seen to be an ever-changing one. Then, there is the historical America, by which we mean the land and the people, and the story of all that has happened here since our forefathers landed on these shores — the opening of the West, the Civil War, the growth of cities, and so on. There is yet another America — the member-state of an anarchic world community, in which we see our country playing a role analogous to that of one of the original thirteen colonies before the Union was formed, attempting to act as if complete independence of all other countries were possible in a world community which has already inextricably bound our interests, responsibilities and destinies together. There are, of course, still other Americas, as you are doubtless fully aware. So," and he turned full upon Mr. Stacey, "I ask: Which America?"

"What America?" Mr. Stacey replied blankly.

"Precisely," said the other, "which America — or, if you prefer, *what* America do you have in mind?"

"If you don't mind," said Mr. Stacey feebly, "let's skip it."

"Skip it?" said the man. "Very well, but which?"

"Which what?" Mr. Stacey mumbled thickly.

"America," the other replied, lifting his eyebrows in surprise.

A dizziness passed over Mr. Stacey. He wiped his face with his hand. He began to climb lumberingly to his feet. "Very interesting, but if you don't mind," he said heavily, "think I'll go and have a beer. You understand. Some other time, maybe."

"Not at all," said the other. "Perhaps we can take it up again."

In the diner, the steward ushered Mr. Stacey to a chair beside a sharp-faced woman eating a salad. He ordered a beer and methodically reviewed the puzzling conversation. It began to make sense now. This fellow had simply given him the brush-off. Mr. Stacey was nettled. But — it must be admitted that the guy did a fancy job. In fact, a superduper job. Not only that, the guy was a really deep thinker. Possibly a college professor. Well, he was not the one to harbor a grudge. Mr. Stacey smiled wryly. Yes, sir, that was one for the books. He took a long satisfying draw on his beer. As he lowered the glass, he glanced at the woman beside him and found her looking with distaste and disapproval at the beer bottle.

"Hope you don't mind my having this beer," Mr. Stacey said politely. "Like with smoking, I like to consider the other fellow."

"Well," the woman said with a cold semblance of a smile. "I shan't pretend that I approve of drinking in any form. But you are within your legal rights, of course." She paused and added primly, "Not that I approve of those either. I sometimes wonder where America is headed."

With great deliberation, Mr. Stacey poured the rest of the beer into his glass, lighted a cigarette, turned slightly toward her and said, "Which America?"

**C.** Write as many specific words as you think of for each of the following italicized general words. You may interpret the general word in any way you please or in more than one way. For example, for "call" you might specify the calls of different animals — "bark," "bellow," "bleat," etc. — or human calls — "cry," "roar," "yell," etc. What is important is not how you interpret the general term but how many specific terms you can draw from it. To get you started, three specific words are suggested in each example.

1. *Clever:* artful, bright, cunning . . .
2. *collection:* armada, band, bevy . . .
3. *concise:* brief, compact, terse . . .
4. *dog:* cur, hound, mongrel . . .
5. *dress:* costume, gown, robe . . .
6. *eat:* devour, gorge, nibble . . .
7. *falsehood:* deception, fraud, sham . . .
8. *happy:* gay, glad, jovial . . .
9. *inflexible:* firm, stubborn, unyielding . . .
10. *noise:* clang, din, hubbub . . .
11. *quick:* agile, brisk, nimble . . .
12. *refuge:* asylum, haven, retreat . . .
13. *road:* boulevard, path, street . . .
14. *shameless:* barefaced, brazen, wanton . . .
15. *slight:* flimsy, slender, trivial . . .
16. *small:* petite, short, tiny . . .
17. *stupid:* dull, obtuse, moronic . . .
18. *talkative:* chatty, garrulous, loquacious . . .
19. *walk:* limp, march, saunter . . .
20. *wet:* drenched, moist, saturated . . .

**D.** Some of the following figures of speech are effective; some are not. Study them; then write a brief report in which you identify each figure and explain why you judge it effective or ineffective.

1. Once the "phony war" was over and the German invasion of the Lowlands had begun, Hitler had committed himself irrevocably. In a very real sense he had crossed his Rubicon.

2. Physically they were as alike as two peas in a pod, but intellectually they were as different as day and night.

3. The facts were presented in all their stark nakedness and their implications hit us like a bolt from the blue.

4. She was as cute as a bug's ear and he looked like something the cat had dragged in. They made a strange pair: a lily of the valley and a disheveled dockweed.

5. The hydrogen bomb may yet prove to be another Frankenstein.

6. He had hoped to live until his granddaughter graduated from college, but the Grim Reaper mowed him down.

7. You shall not press down upon the brow of labor this crown of thorns. You shall not crucify mankind upon a cross of gold.

8. Even as a young man, this colossus of industry, this Napoleon of finance, was recognized as a budding business genius.

9. Such appears to me, king, this present life of man on earth in comparison with the time which is unknown to us, as though you were sitting at

the banquet with your leaders and thanes in winter and the fire was lighted and the hall warmed, and it rained and snowed and stormed outside; and there would come a sparrow and quickly fly through the house, come in through one door and go out through the other. Now in the time that he is inside he is not touched by the storm of winter; but that is only the twinkling of an eye and the least interval, and at once he comes from winter back to winter again. So this life of man appears save for but a little while; what goes before or what follows after we do not know.

10. But at my back I always hear
Time's winged chariot hurrying near.

**E.** In the light of all that has been said in this chapter about words, study the following selections and write a report in which you explain whatever virtues or defects you find in each passage.

## (1)

Rhoda was not a slim girl. As she skipped her way to school, her flesh bobbed and jiggled like jelly. Her arms were like long balloons, her short sleeves biting deeply into the thick flesh of her upper arms. Her chin was lost in the folds of fat that covered her neck. This lent her a bulldog appearance — as though she had no neck at all. Her legs were hardly legs at all — but rather little stumps of thick fatty tissue. When she moved, one could hardly say that she walked or ran. Rather — she seemed to undulate. The movement looked more like that of an amoeba putting forth a pseudopodium, the rest of the mass flowing into the projection of the ectoplasm. No. Rhoda was not a slim girl.

## (2)

Man seeks many vantage points to observe the beauty of nature. He scales mountains, climbs a knoll; in short, he surmounts many obstacles to better his view of nature's splendid fantasy. There is one mode, however, that surpasses all others. It is cruising some swift stream in a canoe.

From the canoe the woodsman, the hunter, the fisherman can better appreciate the bold strokes, the chromatic hues, or the somber tints of Mother Nature's brush more readily, more easily than their uninitiated brethren. In fact, they are a part of nature, integrated into the composition of that cacophony of color, sound, and aroma that constitutes the varied paradise.

Pick your canoe. Regardless of make it is a thing of beauty — a true esperanto in which to enjoy this paradise. Kneel in it. Look up about you. Breathe deep. Aye, and hearken well, also. Now dip your blade into the liquid azureness about you. But easily, for the freeness from parasitic resistance of your craft requires not the task of other water-borne craft. Glide away from the earthen bounds that previously handicapped your acuteness. Straighten out in midstream and settle into the rhythm of paddling.

## (3)

Suppose it were perfectly certain that the life and fortune of every one of us would, one day or another, depend upon his winning or losing a game at chess. Don't you think that we should all consider it to be a primary duty to learn at least the names and the moves of the pieces; to have a notion of a gambit, and a keen eye for all the means of giving and getting out of check? Do you not think that we should look with a disapprobation amounting to scorn, upon the father who allowed his son, or the state which allowed its members, to grow up without knowing a pawn from a knight?

Yet it is a very plain and elementary truth that the life, the fortune, and the happiness of every one of us, and, more or less, of those who are connected with us, do depend upon our knowing something of the rules of a game infinitely more difficult and complicated than chess. It is a game which has been played for untold ages, every man and woman of us being one of the two players in a game of his or her own. The chessboard is the world, the pieces are the phenomena of the universe, the rules of the game are what we call the laws of nature. The player on the other side is hidden from us. We know that his play is always fair, just, and patient. But also we know, to our cost, that he never overlooks a mistake, or makes the smallest allowance for ignorance. To the man who plays well, the highest stakes are paid, with that sort of overflowing generosity with which the strong shows delight in strength. And one who plays ill is checkmated — without haste, but without remorse.

## (4)

Every morning at eight o'clock and again in the afternoon a certain ancient, small, and very feminine-looking steamer, the S.S. *Goldenrod,* affectionately called the *Rod* for short, used to glide across the peaceful river to stop at the little landing and pick up a bag of mail and a passenger or two, and perhaps some article of freight. I used to like to watch the *Rod* lying against the wharf over there. She seemed to like it, and she would linger fifteen minutes or so before she glided back across the smooth bosom of the river to our old yellow steamboat landing, where she took on the rest of her passengers and mail and freight for the bold trip she made every day clear across the wide Bay of Belfast. The *Rod* was a dowdy ridiculous old lady, creaking terribly in every joint, yet she always had her gloves on and her bonnet at a jaunty angle as she went careening across the Bay, bouncing ridiculously and showing her petticoats, or else primly gliding with an air of intense propriety and self-satisfaction, according to the wind.

The *Goldenrod* was not by any means the largest and most impressive ship that ever came in or out of Castine. Our harbor is very deep, so deep and spacious that a whole fleet of battleships can anchor there. But for some reason battleships and great private yachts were not, in my time, particularly interested in coming to visit us. On the Fourth of July once, I remember, a battleship came and lay in the harbor and gave us a gala celebration. And usually once or twice during every summer I used to be waked up by hearing an early morning shout of excitement ring through the house, exclaiming "Look out the window! The *Corsair* has come in!" Then feeling a great thrill of snobbish joy I would run to the window to drink in the sight of that inhabitant of the great world of fashion and power, lying at anchor within the circle of the round Brooks-ville hills. But she never stayed. We had nothing to hold her, no resident multi-millionaires, no diplomatic society. At last even the Rockland steamer, the S.S. *Pemaquid,* affectionately called the *Quid* for short, gave up coming any more because her passengers grew fewer and fewer, and after that the *Rod,* and the sardine boats, and the Dennetts' motorboats taking us across to the islands on picnics and painting excursions and faithfully rescuing us in thunderstorms, and the handful of small sailboats belonging to the summer colony, were all the craft we were used to seeing in our deep, beautiful, forgotten harbor.[22]

## (5)

When things get so balled up that the people of a country have to cut loose from some other country, and go it on their own hook, without ask-ing no permission from nobody, excepting maybe God Almighty, then they ought to let everybody know why they done it, so that everybody can see they are on the level, and not trying to put nothing over on no-body.

All we got to say on this proposition is this: first, you and me is as good as anybody else, and maybe a damn sight better; second, nobody ain't got no right to take away none of our rights; every man has got a right to live, to come and go as he pleases, and to have a good time however he likes, so long as he don't interfere with nobody else. That any government that don't give a man these rights ain't worth a damn; also, people ought to choose the kind of government they want themselves, and nobody else ought to have no say in the matter.[23]

[22] From *The Little Locksmith,* by Katharine Butler Hathaway. Copyright, 1942, 1943, by Coward-McCann, Inc.

[23] From *The American Language,* 3rd ed., by H. L. Mencken. Copyright, 1924, by Alfred A. Knopf, Inc., publishers.

PART TWO　　　✱　SPECIAL ASSIGNMENTS

# 9

## USING A

## DICTIONARY

To MAKE the best use of your dictionary, you should understand both its scope and its limitations. A good dictionary is much more than a guide to spelling, pronunciation, and meanings. It is also less than the absolute and infallible authority some people think it is. To understand the real value of a dictionary you must know what it is intended to do and how it does that.

### What Dictionaries Are, and Are Not

Kinds of Dictionaries. Dictionaries are of two main kinds, general and specialized. A general dictionary, which is the type usually thought of as "the dictionary," records information about words in general use among educated speakers and writers. It does not limit its vocabulary to any special field, but neither does it include highly technical, scientific, or professional terms. Specialized dictionaries are confined to restricted fields or purposes — law, medicine, philosophy, pronunciation, dialects, slang, and so on. A list of some of the commonest specialized dictionaries is given in Chapter 13 on "Using the Library."

General dictionaries come in unabridged, desk, and pocket sizes. Unabridged dictionaries, because of their completeness, are the best sources of information about words in the general vocabulary. But because they are too big and expensive for most students, they are primarily library reference works. You should, however, become acquainted with them as supplements to your personal dictionary. The best known (in alphabetical order) are:

A *Dictionary of American English,* 4 vols., University of Chicago Press, Chicago.

*New Standard Dictionary of the English Language,* Funk and Wagnalls, New York.

*The Oxford English Dictionary,* 10 vols. and Supplement, Clarendon Press, Oxford.

*Webster's New International Dictionary of the English Language, Second Edition,* G. & C. Merriam Co., Springfield, Mass.

Pocket dictionaries are useful because they can be carried in one's pocket and be used as an ever-present reference to the spelling, pronunciation, and meanings of words. But the information they contain is so limited that they are not satisfactory as the only dictionary a student owns.

For the college student, the best all-purpose dictionary is a desk dictionary. Although the best of these contain less than a quarter of the entries in an unabridged dictionary, they are so well edited that they provide nearly all the information one is likely to need about words. Consequently, when instructors require a "college-level" dictionary, they mean a desk dictionary.

The best known desk dictionaries (in alphabetical order) are:

*The American College Dictionary,* Harper & Brothers, New York.

*College Standard Dictionary,* Funk and Wagnalls, New York.

*The Concise Oxford Dictionary* (one volume) and *The Shorter Oxford Dictionary* (two volumes), Clarendon Press, Oxford.

*The Thorndike-Barnhart Comprehensive Desk Dictionary,* Doubleday & Co., New York.

*Webster's New Collegiate Dictionary,* G. & C. Merriam Co., Springfield, Mass.

*Webster's New World Dictionary,* The World Publishing Company, Cleveland.

*Winston's Simplified Dictionary,* John C. Winston Company, Chicago.

(Three of these dictionaries are so popular that we will often refer to them in this chapter by their initials: *ACD* for *The American College Dictionary, NCD* for *Webster's New Collegiate Dictionary,* and *NWD* for *Webster's New World Dictionary.*)

**The Date of a Dictionary.** The date of a dictionary is more important than many of its users realize. Since English is a living language, continuously adding new words, dropping others, and suffering changes in meanings and pronunciations, an old dictionary may be as outmoded a description of current usage as a ten-year-old photograph is of your appearance today. It is false economy, therefore, to try to save a few dollars by using an old dictionary that somebody else no longer wants or uses.

Moreover, there may be little relationship between the date on the title page and the date at which the work on the dictionary was done. Not all "new editions" are new throughout. They may be merely reissues of older dictionaries or reprints with minor revisions. Usually your instructor will recommend one or a number of satisfactory dictionaries. If you are given a completely free choice, a good policy is to select the latest edition of one of the popular desk dictionaries already identified.

**The Authority of the Dictionary.** A dictionary is a record of established, educated usage. It shows, among other things, the spellings, pronunciations, and meanings which educated people have given to words. It is an indispensable guide for words with which we have had little personal experience. It is a most reliable guide to the usage of the past. When it is used to settle controversies about today's usage, it has two limitations: it is necessarily incomplete; and it is necessarily somewhat behind the pace of an ever-changing language.

The incompleteness of a dictionary is intentional. Even the most extensive unabridged dictionary is deliberately restricted. Not only does it make no attempt to cover all special fields, but its definitions cannot indicate all the finely shaded meanings which a word may be given in different contexts. For reasons of space, a dictionary must restrict itself to those meanings which most frequently occur.

## The Contents of Desk Dictionaries

The quickest way to become acquainted with the contents of your dictionary is to study its table of contents. When you do, you may be surprised to learn that the book contains useful information about a variety of subjects: biographical data about famous persons, the population of cities, the location and size of American colleges and universities, the forms used in addressing public officials, proofreader's marks, standard signs and symbols, tables of weights and measures, and many other kinds of information.

In general, the contents fall into three parts: the front matter, the dictionary proper, and the supplements or appendixes. The front matter contains much important introductory and explanatory material. You should at least skim over this material, paying special attention to the "Guide to Pronunciation" and to any parts that may help you to use the dictionary efficiently. The supplementary material can usually be identified from the table of contents, but the *ACD* and the *NWD* record information about people and places in alphabetical order within the dictionary proper, not in an appendix.

Check the table of contents of your dictionary and answer the following questions:

1. What sections of the front matter may help you to use your dictionary more effectively?

2. What is the standard of pronunciation and what is the editors' attitude toward less formal pronunciations?

3. In what order are the definitions arranged?

4. How does your dictionary indicate that a particular entry is still considered a foreign word?

5. What kinds of information are provided in the supplements or appendixes?

6. If biographical and geographical data are not contained in an appendix, are they provided within the dictionary proper? If in doubt, look up *Hangchow, Indonesia,* and *Mussolini.*

Our main concern, however, is with the dictionary proper — 1000 to 1700 pages of information about words. The kinds of information it provides can best be seen by studying a representative entry: [1]

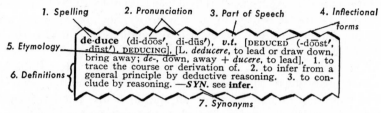

1. Spelling     2. Pronunciation     3. Part of Speech     4. Inflectional forms

5. Etymology

6. Definitions

de·duce (di-dōōs′, di-dūs′), v.t. [DEDUCED (-dōōst′, -dūst′), DEDUCING], [L. deducere, to lead or draw down, bring away; de-, down, away + ducere, to lead], 1. to trace the course or derivation of. 2. to infer from a general principle by deductive reasoning. 3. to conclude by reasoning. —SYN. see infer.

7. Synonyms

**1. Spelling:** The centered period between the syllables shows how the word may be divided, if necessary. If the word is usually capitalized (*Negro*) or hyphenated (*self-centered*) or if two words are written with a space between them (*cross section*) or solid (*setback*), the vocabulary entry provides that information. If more than one spelling is acceptable (*sextet, sextette*), the variant spelling is indicated, usually in the same entry but sometimes separately. When two spellings are listed, the first is said to be "preferred." But different dictionaries sometimes prefer different spellings, and the preference means only that in the samples studied by the editors one spelling occurred more frequently than the other. Do not conclude that the spelling which is not preferred is in any way less acceptable. If one is the American spelling and the other the British, that fact is usually noted.

**2. Pronunciation:** The pronunciation given in a general dictionary is the sound the word is given when pronounced by itself, as in a spelling test, or in careful platform delivery. In their introductory explanations most reliable dictionary editors point out that less formal pronunciations are accepted in the conversation of educated people. A general dictionary, therefore, is useful for pronunciation when a reader wishes to know the pronunciation of a word with which he is not familiar. A strongly stressed syllable is marked with a heavy accent mark (′), a weaker stress with a lighter accent (′). Because the symbols used to represent pronunciation are likely to seem a bit strange at first, you should, until you are familiar with them, check their values in the "Guide to Pronunciation." Both the *ACD* and the *NWD* make this task easier by providing a brief key at the bottom of each right-hand page. The *NCD* has a simplified **pronunciation key on the inside covers.**

**3. Part of Speech:** Since a word may be used in several parts of speech, the labeling of each entry as a noun (*n*), transitive verb (*v.t.*), intransitive verb (*v.i.*), and so on is helpful in avoiding confusion among different grammatical functions of a word.

**4. Inflectional Forms:** Only those inflectional forms that are considered "irregular" are cited in a dictionary. Thus the *-s* plural form of a

[1] Copyright 1957 by The World Publishing Company.

noun is not usually given, nor are the past tense and present participle forms ending in *-ed* and *-ing*. Irregular inflectional forms are listed after the part of speech. Thus in *deduce,* the past tense is formed by adding only *-d,* not *-ed,* and the final *-e* is dropped before the *-ing* of the present participle.

5. **Etymology:** Etymologies — the sources of words — are recorded in square brackets, either (as in the *NCD* and the *NWD*) immediately after the part of speech, or (as in the *ACD*) after the definitions. Thus *deduce* was borrowed directly from the Latin combination *de* + *ducere.* When a word is borrowed from one language through the agency of another, as when a Latin word comes through French, that fact is shown. For example, the *NCD* lists the etymology of *pardon* as follows:

OF. *pardoner,* fr. LL. *perdonare,* fr. L. *per* through, thoroughly + *donare* to give.

This means that our word *pardon* was borrowed from the Old French *pardoner,* which, in turn, came from the Low (or Late) Latin *perdonare,* which originally came from the Latin combination *per donare.* The abbreviations for the various languages will be less troublesome than they seem here, partly because they can quickly be identified in the "List of Abbreviations" given in the front matter, and partly because the more common abbreviations occur so frequently that you will soon become familiar with them. The most common are L. (Latin), Gr. (Greek), F. (French), G. (German), N. (Norse), O. (Old, as in Old English — OE., Old French — OF., Old Norse — ON.), LL. (Late or Low Latin), and ME. (Middle English). When no etymology is given, the word is derived from an earlier entry, where the etymology has already been given. Thus the etymology of *cockerel* is the same as that of *cock,* and the etymology of *deathbed* has already been explained under *bed* and *death.*

6. **Definitions:** Since different dictionaries record their definitions in different orders, it is important that you learn from the front matter what order your dictionary uses. The *ACD* lists definitions in order of frequency, with the most used meaning first. The *NCD* uses a historical order, with the oldest meaning first. Except for definitions accompanied by a usage label (see next paragraph), the *NWD* also uses a historical order.

The order of meanings should never be taken to imply that some meanings are preferred to others. All recorded meanings should be interpreted as conventional uses of a word unless the definition is accompanied by a usage label which limits that meaning to a particular area, group, or situation. Thus the label *U.S.* or *Brit.* shows that a usage is American or British, not common to both. *Colloq.* (or *Colloquial*) shows that a definition is acceptable only in conversation or informal writing. Labels such as *Chem., Law, Mil.* (chemistry, law, or military affairs) indicate technical usage. If any label is not self-explanatory, its meaning may be checked in the "List of Abbreviations."

**7. Synonyms and Antonyms:** A synonym is a word having the same general meaning as the vocabulary entry. An antonym is a word having the opposite meaning. In a desk dictionary, only some entries show synonyms and antonyms. For fuller treatment, consult a specialized dictionary such as *Webster's Dictionary of Synonyms.*

**8. Foreign Words:** Different dictionaries use different means to indicate that a word or phrase (*Gestalt, bon voyage*) is still classified as a foreign expression in English. Since it is conventional in print to italicize (and in writing to underline) such words, this information is sometimes useful. The *ACD* gives the nationality of words in italics immediately after the part of speech. The *NCD* and the *NWD* place a special symbol before the vocabulary entry — ‖ in the *NCD* and ‡ in the *NWD.*

It will be useful to spell out the information given in a simple entry from each of the leading desk dictionaries.

From the *ACD:* [2]

**lyre** (līr), *n.* **1.** a musical instrument of ancient Greece, consisting of a sound box (usually a turtle shell), with two curving arms carrying a cross bar (yoke) from which strings are stretched to the body, used to accompany the voice in singing and recitation. **2.** (*cap.*) *Astron.* Lyra. [ME *lire*, t. OF, t. L: m. *lyra*, t. Gk.]

Woman playing an ancient Greek lyre

The noun *lyre*, pronounced to rhyme with *fire*, as the key at the bottom of the next dictionary page shows, is used in two ways: when spelled with a small letter it is the name of an ancient Greek musical instrument; when spelled with a capital, it is used in astronomy as a variant spelling of the constellation Lyra. The word came into Middle English with the spelling *lire* from an Old French form which had been taken from a modification of the Latin *lyra*, which the Romans had originally borrowed from the Greek. Thus the word came from the Greek through Latin and Old French into English.

From the *NCD:* [3]

**fi·du′cial** (fĭ·dū′shǎl), *adj.* [L. *fiducia* trust, confidence.] **1.** Founded on faith or trust, esp. religious beliefs. **2.** Having the nature of a trust; fiduciary. **3.** *Physics, etc.* Taken as a standard of reference; as, a *fiducial* line, point, etc. — **fi·du′cial·ly,** *adv.*

The adjective *fiducial* is a three-syllable word with the accent on the second syllable. As we learn from the pronunciation key on the inside cover (also from the more comprehensive "Guide to Pronunciation" in the front matter), the first *i* is pronounced like the *i* of *cabin* or *ill; u* is long as in *use,* and the last syllable rhymes with the second syllable of *martial.* The word came into English directly from the Latin *fiducia,* meaning *trust* or *confidence.* Of the two general meanings shown in definitions 1 and 2, definition 1 was the earlier. Definition 3, as the usage label shows, is confined to the sciences. The adverbial form, except for the *-ly* ending, has the same spelling and pronunciation.

From the *NWD:* [4]

> ‡**ka·mi·ka·ze** (kä′mi-kä′zi), *n.* [Japan., lit., divine wind < *kami,* (Shinto) god or goddess + *kaze,* the wind], 1. a suicide attack by a Japanese airplane pilot in World War II. 2. the airplane or pilot in such an attack.

The noun *kamikaze* is a four-syllable word with the main stress on the third syllable and a secondary stress on the first. The key to pronunciation at the bottom of the dictionary page shows that the first and third vowels are pronounced like the *a* in *car* and the second and fourth vowels like the *i* in *is.* The symbol before the entry shows that the word is considered foreign, and the etymology tells us it is Japanese. In Japan its literal meaning (divine wind) is a compound of the word for divinity in the Shinto religion and the Japanese word for wind. It was first used in English to denote the kind of attack explained in definition 1 and was later extended to include the agent of the attack, the plane or the pilot.

For each of the following words write out all the information provided by the entry in your dictionary:

| | | |
|---|---|---|
| autocrat | divan | harridan |
| bawl | esprit de corps | illiterate |
| cherub | fluster | non sequitur |

## Dictionary of Synonyms

A dictionary of synonyms groups together words essentially similar in meaning and distinguishes the particular differences in their uses. Thus *Webster's Dictionary of Synonyms* lists after the first meaning of *nice* the synonyms: *dainty, fastidious, finical, particular, fussy, squeamish, pernickety,* and then goes on to distinguish between the connotations of these words. Then comes a series of analogous words ("near

4 Copyright 1957 by The World Publishing Company.

synonyms"), then a series of contrasted words ("near antonyms"), and finally a series of antonyms, words with meanings the very opposite of *nice*.

Because a dictionary of synonyms makes no attempt to record the whole general vocabulary of the language, it can afford a more thorough treatment of synonyms than is possible in a general dictionary. It is therefore the best reference source when you wish an answer to either of two questions: How do two or more words of the same general meaning differ in denotation or connotation in actual use? What other words might be substituted for a particular word? The following entry illustrates:[5]

> **dwarf,** *n.* **1** Dwarf, pygmy, midget, manikin (*or* manni-
> kin), homunculus (*or* homuncle, homuncule), runt come
> into comparison when they mean a person of diminutive
> size. **Dwarf** is the general term not only for a human be-
> ing but for any animal or plant that is far below the
> normal size of the species: often, but not necessarily, the
> term suggests stunted development. "His [the fool's]
> value was trebled in the eyes of the king by the fact of
> his being also a *dwarf* and a cripple" (*Poe*). **Pygmy,** in
> earliest use, was applied to one of a race (or races) of
> fabled dwarfs mentioned by Homer and others, and now
> is applied especially to one of a dwarf people found in
> central Africa. The term carries a stronger connotation
> of diminutiveness and a weaker suggestion of arrested
> development than *dwarf;* when used generally in refer-
> ence to a person, it often implies tininess (often relative
> tininess), sometimes in body but more often in intellect.
> "To him all the men I ever knew were *pygmies*. He was
> an intellectual giant" (*Byron*). **Midget** stresses abnormal
> diminutiveness but, unlike *dwarf,* carries little suggestion
> of malformation or deformity, the term is applied usually
> to a tiny but otherwise shapely person exhibited in a
> circus or employed in place of a child in theatrical per-
> formances; as, P. T. Barnum's famous *midget,* Tom
> Thumb. **Manikin** is often applied contemptuously not
> only to a dwarf but to any human being who for one
> reason or another seems despicably small or weak. "Can
> it be fancied that Diety ever vindictively Made in his
> image a *mannikin* merely to madden it?" (*Poe*). **Homun-
> culus** usually suggests even greater diminutiveness and
> often greater perfection in form than *midget:* it is the
> specific term for an exceedingly small artificial human
> being such as was supposedly developed by Paracelsus, a
> famous Renaissance alchemist; it is also applied, as
> a technical term, to the human fetus. **Runt,** usually a
> contemptuous designation, applies to a dwarf or under-
> sized person, especially to one who is conspicuously puny
> or undeveloped or, occasionally, to one who is thick as
> well as short. "I always did admire a good, sizable, stout
> man. I hate a *runt*" (*McClure's Mag.*). The term is also
> applied to an animal, especially a domestic animal, small
> of its kind; and, dialectally in the United States, it is
> applied specifically to the undersized one of a litter, as of
> pigs.

[5] By permission. From *Webster's Dictionary of Synonyms,* copyright 1942, 1951 by G. & C. Merriam Co.

# Thesaurus

A *thesaurus* is a special kind of word book which records under a single entry all words expressing the general notion of that entry. The most popular of such works is Roget's (pronounced Rojay's) *Thesaurus of English Words and Phrases*. The simplest way to use this work is to check the general word in the index, observe the section number of its entry, and consult that section in the main part of the book. Thus if you want to find words referring to the ideas of *disobedience* and *obedience*, you look in the index, learn that these words are entered in sections 742–743, turn to these sections, and this is what you find:[6]

**742. Disobedience.—N.** disobedience, insubordination, contumacy; infraction, -fringement; violation, non-compliance; non-observance &c. 773.

revolt, rebellion, mutiny, outbreak, rising, uprising, putsch, insurrection, *émeute*; riot, tumult &c. (*disorder*) 59; strike &c. (*resistance*) 719; barring out; defiance &c. 715.

mutinousness &c. *adj.*; mutineering; sedition, treason; high -, petty -, misprision of- treason; *premunire*; *lèse-majesté*; violation of law &c. 964; defection, secession, revolution, *sabotage*, bolshevism, *Sinn Fein*.

insurgent, mutineer, rebel, revolter, rioter, traitor, *carbonaro, sansculottes*, red republican, communist, Fenian, chartist, *frondeur*; seceder, runagate, brawler, anarchist, demagogue; suffragette; Spartacus, Masaniello, Wat Tyler, Jack Cade; bolshevist, bolshevik, maximalist, ringleader.

**V.** disobey, violate, infringe; shirk; set at defiance &c. (*defy*) 715; set authority at naught, run riot, fly in the face of, bolt, take the law into one's own hands; kick over the traces.

turn -, run- restive; champ the bit; strike &c. (*resist*) 719; rise, - in arms; secede; mutiny, rebel.

**Adj.** disobedient; uncompl-ying, -iant; unsubmissive, unruly, ungovernable; insubordinate, impatient of control; rest-iff, -ive; refractory, contumacious; recusant &c. (*refuse*) 764; recalcitrant; resisting &c. 719; lawless, mutinous, seditious, insurgent, riotous, revolutionary.

disobeyed, unobeyed; unbidden.

**743. Obedience.—N.** obedience; observance &c. 772; compliance; submission &c. 725; subjection &c. 749; non-resistance; passiveness, passivity, resignation.

allegiance, loyalty, fealty, homage, deference, devotion, fidelity, constancy.

submiss-ness, -iveness; ductility &c. (*softness*) 324; obsequiousness &c. (*servility*) 886.

**V.** be -obedient &c. *adj.*; obey, bear obedience to; submit &c. 725; comply, answer the helm, come at one's call; do -one's bidding, - what one is told, - suit and service; attend to orders, serve -devotedly, - loyally, - faithfully.

follow, - the lead of, - to the world's end; serve &c. 746; play second fiddle.

**Adj.** obedient; compl-ying, -iant; law-abiding, loyal, faithful, leal, devoted; at one's -call, - command, - orders, - beck and call; under -beck and call, - control.

restrainable; resigned, passive; submissive &c. 725; henpecked; pliant &c. (*soft*) 324.

unresist-ed, -ing.

**Adv.** obediently &c. *adj.*; in compliance with, in obedience to.

**Phr.** to hear is to obey; as -, if- you please; at your service.

6 By permission. From *Roget's Thesaurus*, copyright 1941, 1947 by Grosset & Dunlap, Inc.

You will notice that the words refer to all kinds of disobedience and give names of people and movements that, in one way or another, were examples of disobedience. The cross references suggest other entries that might be helpful. The words shown here are not synonyms and they are not defined. The advantage of the thesaurus is that it gives you, in one place, a large number of words all related to the same idea. If you do not know how to use these words, you must look them up in your dictionary. The thesaurus is not a substitute for a dictionary, but its purpose and organization help you in a way a dictionary cannot.

## Review Exercises

**A.** From what languages are the following words derived?

| | | |
|---|---|---|
| 1. algebra | 9. devil | 17. nice |
| 2. alcohol | 10. dollar | 18. opera |
| 3. automobile | 11. flannel | 19. pajamas |
| 4. bantam | 12. husband | 20. quixotic |
| 5. boor | 13. inertia | 21. shampoo |
| 6. candy | 14. lemon | 22. skipper |
| 7. caravan | 15. loot | 23. slogan |
| 8. chorus | 16. mosquito | 24. tobacco |

**B.** Which of the following expressions should be italicized as foreign words?

| | | |
|---|---|---|
| 1. anno Domini *in the year of our lord* | 6. en rapport *in relations with* | 11. faux pas *social error* |
| 2. belle *- lovely lady* | 7. enfant terrible *bad child* | 12. in absentia *graduate or el* |
| 3. belles lettres *good writing* | 8. ensemble *- outfit* | 13. matériel |
| 4. debutante *+ speaking* | 9. fiancé *- masculine* | 14. nom de guerre *-name of w* |
| 5. décolleté *- low neckline* | 10. fiasco *- ridiculous end; laughing failure.* | 15. nom de plume *- pen name* |

**C.** What pronunciations does your dictionary give for the following words?

| | | |
|---|---|---|
| 1. abdomen | 13. inquiry | 25. robot |
| 2. acclimate | 14. joust | 26. sagacious |
| 3. alias | 15. massage | 27. schism |
| 4. banal | 16. niche | 28. secretive |
| 5. clandestine | 17. nascent | 29. status |
| 6. data | 18. nuance | 30. technics |
| 7. ennui | 19. obesity | 31. vagary |
| 8. fugue | 20. penalize | 32. vestigial |
| 9. hazard | 21. precedence | 33. victuals |
| 10. heinous | 22. query | 34. Wagnerian |
| 11. impious | 23. quixotic | 35. zealot |
| 12. impotent | 24. rancid | 36. zenith |

**D.** Determine the plural forms of the following:

*ses*  *oes*  *oes*  *Criteria*  *Flower*  *radii*

analysis, buffalo, cargo, court-martial, criterion, crocus, radius, spoonfuls

stratum, thesis, vertebrae

*Strata, theses,*

**E.** Distinguish among the synonyms given in your dictionary for the following words:

| | | |
|---|---|---|
| 1. ambition | 8. examination | 15. melancholy |
| 2. apt | 9. excuse | 16. needful |
| 3. bad | 10. fiendish | 17. oral |
| 4. contention | 11. haste | 18. restive |
| 5. deface | 12. ideal | 19. voracious |
| 6. discover | 13. juncture | 20. wild |
| 7. emergency | 14. luster | |

**F.** Consult the references in Roget's *Thesaurus* for the word *tatters* and describe briefly the kind of information recorded in the first entry.

# 10

## * IMPROVING
## * VOCABULARY

Most students know how important it is to have an adequate vocabulary. They know that diagnostic vocabulary tests are often used to predict the ability to do well in college studies. They quickly see that college lectures and text books will require them to learn many new words. They also know that there is a relationship between vocabulary and success in business or professional life. For these reasons serious students have already answered the question whether increasing vocabulary is desirable. Instead, they are concerned with the question of method — *how* to improve vocabulary. It is with that question that this chapter deals.

### *Improving Your Recognition Vocabulary*

It is useful to distinguish two kinds of vocabulary: *recognition* and *active*. The recognition vocabulary is the total stock of words that a person knows well enough to understand them when he meets them in context. He may not be able to define all these words, and there are many of them that he will never use in his speech or writing, but if he can interpret them correctly when he meets them in context, they are part of his recognition vocabulary. The active vocabulary, on the other hand, is the stock of words that a person actually uses in his own speech or writing. It is, of course, a much smaller stock — perhaps only a third or a quarter the size of the recognition vocabulary.

Not all attempts to increase one's recognition vocabulary are equally profitable. Many ambitious students confuse vocabulary building with the learning of big words rarely met and seldom used, either by the student or by anyone else. Uncritical memorizing of learned words is pretty much a waste of time. So, too, is that old favorite method of learning a new word every day. Even if the daily word is carefully chosen for its usefulness, rather than for its impressiveness, a student following only this method will improve his vocabulary less than one per cent in a year. Such an improvement is trifling. A college student of average ability should increase his recognition vocabulary by at least ten per cent during his freshman year *by doing nothing more than becoming familiar with the words he encounters in his studies.* If, in addition, he deliberately and consistently attempts to cultivate a useful vocabulary, his improvement will be significantly larger.

The one prerequisite for increasing vocabulary is a desire to learn — not just a desire to learn words, but a desire to know more about any subject that comes one's way. Consider how your knowledge of mechanical terms increased as you progressed from kiddie cars to bicycles to automobiles. You did not discover, *rim, spoke, tire, battery, carburetor,* and *piston* in a dictionary. You learned these words because you were interested in bicycles and cars and simply had to have the words to think about and operate your machines. If you have a similar interest in the subjects you study in college, each of them will make its contribution to your vocabulary, even if you do not consciously do anything about vocabulary building. If you do not have that interest or cannot cultivate it, no techniques for vocabulary building will do you much good. A person's vocabulary is a product of his intellectual growth. It cannot be artificially constructed apart from that growth.

For most of us, the great source of new words is the printed page. Therefore anyone who wishes to increase his recognition vocabulary must do a good deal of reading. Your college assignments in all courses will probably require you to read more extensively and more critically than you have done before, but if you wish to make significant increases in your vocabulary you should supplement required reading by a program of voluntary reading. Probably the best way to begin is to develop the habit of reading carefully a daily newspaper and such newsmagazines as *Newsweek* and *Time,* and gradually add some of the excellent inexpensive paper-backed books which provide authoritative but popular explanations of social and scientific subjects and such works of fiction or poetry as suit your taste. This reading should follow your personal interests and needs. It should be regarded as pleasure, not a chore, because what is required is to develop a liking for reading. A student who likes to read will find the things that are most valuable for him, and as his reading experience widens, his taste in books will grow.

Once a student has the desire to learn through reading, he will discover the techniques of increasing his vocabulary — perhaps even without recognizing that they are techniques — in his efforts to understand what he is studying. Let us try to illustrate this point by watching an intellectually curious student at work. Suppose that, as an outside reading assignment in sociology, he is reading the following passage dealing with the Bantu, a primitive tribe living in the forests of the Congo, and that he is meeting for the first time the words in italics.

> What seems to be most relevant [in a study of the relation of the personality and culture of the Bantu] can be stated in more general terms, in terms which also apply to hundreds of small tribes in many parts of the world. . . . We may point out certain aspects of these cultures in a series of words hyphenated with the prefix "pre-," meaning "before," or "not yet." Therefore we can say that they are *preliterate, prescientific, preindustrial,* and *preindividualistic.*
>
> The *Phoenician* alphabet traveled west and north but did not penetrate these isolated regions [the Bantu homeland]. They are preliterate, not only because they cannot learn to read and write but because they have had no opportunity. Now when *scribes* make and preserve books, a profound change comes upon a society and the whole character of their culture undergoes *momentous* alterations. Preliterate people have not added that *increment.* And until they do have it, there are certain important ways in which they differ from those who have letters.[1]

Even though there are eight words in the passage that the student has never seen or heard before, there are only three of them that he will have to look up in his dictionary. He can tell directly from the text what *preliterate* means, because the author explains the prefix *pre-,* and the second paragraph makes it clear that a preliterate people is one that has not yet reached the stage of having an alphabet and therefore has had no opportunity of learning to write or read. Thus, although he has never met the word before, the student will understand it quite clearly from the context. And once he understands *preliterate,* he will not only recognize the meaning of *prescientific, preindustrial,* and *preindividualistic,* but, more important, the principle of putting *pre-* before other words to form new compounds. Thus he will be prepared to interpret correctly *preatomic, precancel, predate, prehistoric, prenatal,* and so on when he first encounters them.

*Phoenician* and *increment,* however, cannot be interpreted from the context. Since the student has no clue to their meaning, he must consult his dictionary. When he does so, he will find that the Phoenicians, an ancient people who lived in what is now Syria, are credited with being the inventors of the alphabet from which all Indo-European alphabets are descended. He will find that *increment* has the same ancestry as *increase* and means an "addition" or "growth" — in this passage an advantage that preliterate peoples have not received. *Momentous alterations* may be recognized as a repetition of the idea expressed in *profound change,* or from the fairly well-known phrase *matters of great moment.* If these associations do not serve as clues, the student will have to consult his dictionary. There he will find that *momentous,*

[1] Ellsworth Faris, "Culture and Personality Among the Forest Bantu," *American Journal of Sociology,* May, 1934.

like *momentum,* a word he may have learned in physics, comes from the same root as *moving* and means in this context "very important."

Since the context of the second paragraph shows that a scribe is one who makes and preserves books, the student may get the meaning of that word directly from its context. Or his familiarity with the related word *scribble* may suggest to him that a scribe is one who writes. Or, if he knows a little Latin, he may recognize *scribe* as a derivative of *scribere,* "to write." In other words, he may recognize the meaning in either of two ways: through the context or through the similarity of the unknown word to other words which he does know. If neither of these methods works, he will have to consult his dictionary.

Here, then, are the three principal techniques for recognizing the meanings of new words: recognition by context, discovery by dictionary reference, and recognition by word analysis. In our illustration the student used these techniques successfully without being conscious that he was using them. His main concern was not to improve his vocabulary but simply to understand what the sociologist was telling him. Let us consider these techniques as procedures which can be used intentionally.

**Recognition by Context.** For a number of reasons, the best way to improve your recognition vocabulary is by watching context. First, it is the method you must use in understanding spoken communications, since you cannot usually stop a speaker to look up his words in a dictionary. Second, it is the method used by lexicographers (makers of dictionaries), and far from being a "lazy" or "guessing" method, it is the only way to become sensitive to educated usage. Third, it is the method you have been using for the last sixteen or seventeen years and by it you have learned nearly all the words now in your recognition vocabulary.

As you acquire skill and confidence in interpreting words from context you will learn to spot the ways in which a speaker or writer helps to make clear the meanings of unusual words. Sometimes he will actually define the new word, as we did with *lexicographers* above and as the sociologist did with *pre-.* Sometimes he will explain the word by showing it in operation, as when we are told that a scribe makes and preserves books. Sometimes he will repeat the meaning in other words of similar meaning, as when the sociologist coupled *profound change* and *momentous alterations.* Sometimes he will use a practical illustration to make the meaning clear, like our imaginary student reader. By learning to look for such aids you will not only become a better reader and listener, but you will begin to use these explanatory techniques yourself and so become a better speaker and writer.

Each of the following passages contains an italicized word, the meaning of which may be obtained from the context. Can you tell without consulting a dictionary what each of these words must mean?

The lawyer said that such newspaper stories were *prejudicial* because they encouraged the public to judge the defendant guilty before he had been tried.

The *pediatrician* examined the baby carefully and recommended a change in formula.

There was an obvious *disparity* in their ages; he looked old enough to be her father.

An Englishman who says that he finds American women homely may not be *disparaging* them. He may just mean that they make him feel at home.

We are often uncertain what punishment to inflict for such offenses. If we are too harsh, we may seem to be seeking vengeance rather than justice; if we show too much *clemency,* we may give the impression that we do not consider the offense a serious one.

**Discovery by Dictionary Reference.** When you look up a word in your dictionary you should try to find out as much as you can about it. You know that when you are introduced to someone your chances of remembering his name or even recognizing him again are influenced by the extent of your first experience with him. If all you learn is his name, you may forget that quickly; but if you talk with him and find out what he does for a living, where he comes from, what his background is, and what his chief interests and hobbies are, you may remember him well months or even years later. The same thing is true of your introduction to new words. The more you find out about them from your dictionary, the better you will remember them; and the better you remember them, the more likely you are to transfer them to your active vocabulary.

The things you most need to know about a new word are its pronunciation, etymology, and meanings. The pronunciation not only helps you to pronounce it conventionally in reading aloud or in speech, but also helps you fix the word in your memory. Since the appearance of a word is often no safe clue to its sound, we have all had the embarrassing experience of making a very obvious mispronunciation when called upon to read an unfamiliar word aloud. Even such fairly common words as *abyss, blatant, caprice, decade, echelon, façade, gauge, impious, impotent,* and *ribald* can be troublesome for a person who has met them only in his reading and has never heard them spoken. The habit of checking pronunciation as you look up a new word greatly reduces the chances of mispronunciation.

The etymology of a word gives you its family history and thus makes your knowledge of it more complete. When you know, for example, that *crucial* comes from the Latin word for *cross,* you can see that in a crucial decision we figuratively stand at a crossroads and decide which way we will go, and you may discover a hitherto unsuspected relationship among *crucial, crucify, crusade,* and *crux.* Similarly, when you learn that *critical* comes from a Greek phrase meaning "able to discern" and was originally used for one who was able to discern the implications of a work or a policy and thus to judge it, you will better understand how the word can be used today in such different senses as: "it is an excellent critical discussion of the problem," "he is a critical user of the dictionary," and "his condition is now critical."

Apart from its usefulness in making you a more discerning or more critical user of words, the study of etymology can be a pleasant hobby. It may not make the study of the *calculus* any easier to know that its name came from the Latin word for a pebble and goes back to the days when the Romans used pebbles to help them with their arithmetic; but it is interesting to be reminded from what primitive origins modern calculating machines have come. It is a testimony to human intolerance that *sinister* originally meant *left-handed* and a *barbarian* was once a *stranger.* And it is amusing to discover that our slang phrase *in the coop* perpetuates the original meaning of *jail,* a cage or coop. It is not surprising that some people find it as much fun to collect etymologies as to collect stamps, and much less expensive.

**Recognition by Word Analysis.** Looking up an etymology inevitably leads to word analysis, the breaking down of a word into its parts and the recognition of the original meaning of each part. Thus we are analyzing *preliterate* when we recognize that it is a compound of the prefix *pre-* and the root *litera,* "a letter"; and we are analyzing *docile* when we see that it is made up of the root *docere,* "to teach," and the suffix *-ile,* "capable of," so that a docile person is literally one who is capable of being taught.

Because so many Latin and Greek words have been borrowed and assimilated by English, a knowledge of the most common Latin and Greek prefixes and roots (the suffixes are less important for our purposes) helps us to recognize, at least in a general way, the meanings of many words. For example, the ability to recognize *-cede* (*-ceed*) and *-cess* as forms of the Latin *cedere,* "to yield" or "go," gives us a partial clue to the meanings of the English words *cede, cessation, cession, accede, access, accession, accessory, antecedent, ancestor, concede, concession, concessionaire, exceed, excess, incessant, intercede, intercessor, precede, precedence, predecessor, procedure, proceed, process, procession, recede, recess, recessive, secede, succeed, succession,* and their inflectional forms. One writer has estimated that a knowledge of fourteen Latin and Greek roots will help us to recognize over 14,000 words.[2]

Common Latin prefixes and roots, their original meanings, and illustrative English words derived from them are given in the following list:

2 James I. Brown in *Efficient Reading* (D. C. Heath and Company, 1952), p. 117.

*ab* (away from, down): abase, abate, abdicate, abduct, abhor, abject, abnormal, abort

*ad* (to, toward): adapt, addict, adduce, adequate, adhere, adjacent, admit, adolescent

*ante* (before): ante-bellum, antecedent, antedate, antemeridien, anterior, anteroom

*bellum* (war): bellicose, belligerent, rebel, rebellion

*bene* (well): benediction, benefactor, beneficent, benefit, benevolent, benign

*bi* (two): biannual, biaxial, biceps, bicuspid, bifocal, bigamist, bilabial

*cap, cept* (take): capable, captivate, capture, concept, deception, intercept, percept

*cide, cis* (cut, kill): decide, matricide, suicide, caesura, concise, incision

*circum* (around): circumference, circumlocution, circumnavigate, circumspect

*cogni* (know): cognition, cognizance, connoisseur, incognito, recognize

*com* (with): command, commence, commend, commission, compact, compare, compass, compeer

*contra* (against): contraband, contradict, contrapuntal, contrary, contrast

*cor* (heart): cardiac, core, cordial, courage, discord, encourage, record

*cult* (care for): cult, cultivate, culture, agriculture, horticulture

*curr, curs* (run): currency, current, curriculum, courier, course, excursion

*de* (off, down, wholly): debase, decapitate, decay, deceive, decline, deduce

*dent* (tooth): dental, dentifrice, dentoid, denture, indent, trident

*dict* (say): dictate, diction, edict, indicate, indict, predict, verdict

*duc, duct* (lead): conduct, deduce, duct, duke, educate, induct, product

*ex* (beyond, from, out): examine, exceed, excel, except, excite, extend

*extra* (outside): extracurricular, extradite, extraneous, extrapolate

*fac, fect* (make): facile, fact, factory, faculty, manufacture, affect, effect

*fin* (end): confine, define, final, finale, finish, infinite, refine

*in* (on, in, toward): inaugurate, incarcerate, incipient, incline, include

*in* (not): inactive, inane, inarticulate, incest, infamous, insensible

*inter* (among, between): interaction, intercede, intercept, interfere

*ject* (throw): abject, dejected, eject, interject, projectile, reject, trajectory

*loqui, locut* (talk): colloquial, eloquent, loquacious, ventriloquist, elocution

*luc* (light): elucidate, illustrate, lucid, pellucid, translucent

*mal* (bad): malady, malcontent, malefactor, malice, malignant, malpractice

*mit, miss* (send): admit, commit, intermittent, remit, transmit, missile

*mor* (dead): morbid, moribund, mortal, mortify, mortuary

*ped* (foot): biped, impediment, pedal, pedestrian, pedicure, pedometer

*pel, puls* (drive): compel, dispel, expel, propel, repel, impulse, pulse

*pon, posit* (place): component, exponent, postpone, preposition, transpose

*port* (carry): deport, export, import, portable, report, support, transport

*post* (after): postdate, posterity, postgraduate, posthumous, postmortem

*pre* (before): preamble, precaution, precede, predict, preface, prefer

*pro* (forward): proceed, procession, produce, profane, profess, proficient

*re* (again, back): react, rearm, reassure, recall, recede, recreate, return

*rupt* (break): abrupt, bankrupt, disrupt, erupt, interrupt, rupture

*scrib, script* (write): circumscribe, inscribe, script, scripture, transcription

*spect* (look): aspect, inspect, perspective, retrospect, spectator, spectrum
*sub* (under): subaltern, subconscious, subject, submerge, subside
*super* (above): superb, supercilious, superfluous, superior, supersede
*tain, ten* (hold): abstain, contain, detain, retain, tenable, tenacious, tenet
*tang, tact* (touch): tangent, tangible, contact, tact, tactical, tactual
*trans* (across, over): transcend, transcribe, transfer, transfuse, transgress
*uni* (one): unicorn, uniform, unify, unilateral, union, Unitarian, unity
*vene, vent* (come): convene, intervene, revenue, adventure, invent
*vers, vert* (turn): verse, version, avert, convert, extrovert, invert, vertical
*vid, vis* (see): evident, provident, revise, supervise, vision, visor, vista
*voc* (call): advocate, avocation, convocation, evoke, provoke, vocabulary

Common Greek forms and their derivatives are shown below:

*anthropo* (man): anthropoid, anthropology, misanthrope, philanthropy
*auto* (self): autobiography, autocracy, autogamy, automobile, autotoxin
*bio* (life): biochemistry, biogenesis, biography, biology, biometry, biotic
*chrono* (time): anachronism, chronic, chronicle, chronological, synchronize
*gen* (birth, race): eugenics, genealogy, genesis, genetics, homogeneous
*gram, graph* (write): diagram, epigram, telegram, graphic, phonograph
*homo* (same): homocentric, homogenize, homograph, homonym
*hydr* (water): hydrant, hydraulic, hydrogen, hydrophobia, hydroplane
*log* (science, speech): biology, cosmology, etymology, epilogue, eulogy
*micro* (small): microbe, microfilm, micrometer, microphone, microscope
*mono* (one): monocle, monogamy, monograph, monolith, monologue
*morph* (form): amorphous, anthropomorphic, metamorphosis, morphology
*pan* (all): panacea, Pan-American, pancreas, pandemonium, panorama
*phil* (friend): Anglophile, bibliophile, Philadelphia, philharmonic
*phon* (sound): euphony, gramophone, phoneme, phonetic, symphony
*poly* (many): polyandry, polychromatic, polygamy, polyglot, polysyllabic
*syn* (together): synonym, syntax, synthesis, sympathy, symposium
*tele* (far): telegraph, telepathic, telephone, telescope, television

## Improving Your Active Vocabulary

Although your active vocabulary is the stock of words you actually use in speaking and writing, we have considered the recognition vocabulary first because we almost always recognize words others use before we begin to use them ourselves. The active vocabulary is expanded chiefly by converting words from the recognition vocabulary. Usually this conversion takes place naturally as we become more and more familiar with a word. For example, some of the words you have met in this book have probably passed over into your active vocabulary — such as *analogy, antonym, coherence, colloquial, context, etymology, idiom, inflection, learned words, standard English, synonym, thesis,* and *transition.* And if you were to write down all the words you have begun to use as a result of your experience in college, you would surely have a long list.

This natural conversion can be extended and accelerated by practice. A student can practice using a word as he looks it up in his dictionary. When he revises his writing he can consider what other words he knows that might fit the context of a particular sentence. He can make a note of words he is quite familiar with but never uses, and begin deliberately to introduce them into his writing and speaking.

The techniques of conversion are less important than the will to do something about it, but of the methods that may be used, four are most worth recommending. The first of these is to explore your recognition vocabulary deliberately for words that might be used for a particular subject. For example, what words can you recall that deal with government? If you start to prepare a list, you will be surprised how rapidly it grows, as you begin to think of all the ramifications of government — *franchise, ballot, election, electorate, nominate, nominee, candidate, canvass, vote, plurality, majority, primary, campaign, issue, returns, caucus, adjournment, recess, amend, veto, repeal, sustain, filibuster, cloture, frank, immunity,* and so on. Probably all or most of these words are in your recognition vocabulary, but how many of them do you use? Recalling them or writing them in a list reminds you that you do know them and can therefore use them if you wish.

The second method is to sharpen your understanding of certain words by distinguishing their meanings from those of similar words — for example, to distinguish among *quick, prompt, ready, apt* — so that you may confidently use them in context. To differentiate clearly among such words, you should consult a dictionary of synonyms, either your own or a library copy. But even if no dictionary of synonyms is handy, you can still do much with a general dictionary. This kind of exercise not only makes you aware of shades of meaning but at the same time helps to convert the words into your active vocabulary.

The third method is a combination of the first two. First, consult a thesaurus for all the words that may be used to express a general idea; next, select from that list all words which are part of your recognition vocabulary only; then look up these words in a dictionary of synonyms or a general dictionary to be quite sure that you know how to use them; finally, use each word in a phrase or sentence that clearly reveals its meaning.

The fourth method — and the best as far as your writing is concerned — is to discipline yourself to seek specific words whenever anything you have written is unnecessarily general. The effort to find the specific word will require you to think of various terms that might be used in place of the general one. Since the new words must come from your recognition vocabulary, you will repeatedly be reviewing part of that vocabulary with a view to conversion. For example, in trying to specify "lacking order," you may think of many words referring to some kind of disorder — *bedraggled, chaotic, confused, dislocated, disoriented, entangled, irregular, jumbled, lawless, muddled, mussed, scrambled, shapeless, slovenly, unsystematic, untidy.* As you turn these words over in your mind, looking for the one that best conveys your thought, you are bringing all of them, not just the one you finally choose, into your active vocabulary.

Two words of caution are necessary before we leave this discussion of conversion. First, new words must be chosen for their usefulness, not for their impressiveness. The real purpose of increasing your vocabulary is to increase your ability to communicate, and communication is not improved by calling a daily newspaper "a diurnal publication" or a sick friend "an incapacitated colleague." Second, the new words must fit the contexts in which they are to be used. Although *glib* means *smooth* in such phrases as *a glib speaker* and *a glib argument,* we cannot talk about *a glib surface* or *a glib texture.* It is better not to use the word at all than to use it in the wrong context. For this reason, it is usually safer to introduce new words in writing rather than in impromptu speech, since the written word may be more easily checked and revised. If these two cautions are observed, deliberate conversion from the recognition to the active vocabulary can be a profitable exercise.

## Review Exercises

**A.** 1. In the following words both the prefixes and the roots are derived from Latin forms. Can you analyze each word and give the literal meaning of its parts? Do not consult your dictionary until you have at least made a considered guess about each word:

| | | |
|---|---|---|
| abduct | except | postpone |
| abstain | excess | produce |
| adjacent | excursive | propel |
| antecedent | expect | recede |
| beneficiary | expedite | recognize |
| bilateral | facsimile | subdue |
| circumstance | induce | subscript |
| contact | inspect | subvene |
| contain | interpose | supersede |
| decide | intervene | transcribe |
| describe | malefactor | transmit |
| effect | postmortem | unilateral |
| eject | | |

2. Both the prefixes and the roots of the following words are derived from Greek forms. Analyze each word and give the meaning of its parts:

|                |              |             |
|----------------|--------------|-------------|
| autobiography  | monologue    | polymorph   |
| bibliophile    | morphology   | symphony    |
| genealogy      | philanthropy | synchronize |
| homogeneous    | phonology    | telegram    |
| monograph      | polygamist   | telephone   |

3. Without consulting the list on pages 220–221, give the meaning of the following Latin prefixes. Then check your answers against the list.

|          |         |         |
|----------|---------|---------|
| ante-    | extra-  | post-   |
| bene-    | inter-  | sub-    |
| circum-  | mal-    | super-  |
| contra-  | pre-    | trans-  |

4. Without consulting the list on page 221, give the meaning of the following Greek forms. Then check your answers against the list.

|          |        |        |
|----------|--------|--------|
| auto-    | homo   | morph  |
| bio-     | log    | poly-  |
| chrono-  | micro- | sym-   |
| graph    | mono-  | tele-  |

5. Choose five Latin and five Greek forms from questions 3 and 4 above and for each choice write as many English words as you can recall containing the Latin or Greek form.

**B.** Using the example of "government" on page 222 as a model, write as many words as you can recall which have some clear relation to each of the following subjects:

|              |             |             |
|--------------|-------------|-------------|
| agriculture  | doctors     | philosophy  |
| architecture | education   | poetry      |
| art          | engineering | radio       |
| astronomy    | factory     | real estate |
| biology      | geology     | scientists  |
| chemistry    | law         | sea         |
| church       | mathematics | war         |
| crime        |             |             |

**C.** Differentiate the meanings of the following sets of synonyms. Use whatever reference works you wish.

1. autocratic, despotic, arbitrary, tyrannical
2. conform, adjust, reconcile
3. bedeck, decorate, embellish, garnish
4. artist, artificer, artisan
5. mean, median, average, norm
6. pithy, terse, succinct, concise

7. perennial, perpetual, constant, incessant
8. balky, restive, perverse, wayward
9. mock, mimic, copy, ape
10. weep, wail, whimper, blubber
11. gnarled, warped, contorted
12. assimilate, embody, incorporate
13. idle, inert, supine, passive
14. damage, harm, hurt, mischief
15. grudge, spite, malice
16. apprentice, probationer, novice
17. ardor, fervor, zeal
18. buff, burnish, polish
19. ascend, soar, surge
20. maudlin, mushy, sentimental

**D.** The following five columns of fifty words each were selected from a book of freshman readings. Check off and ignore those words which are already in your active vocabulary. For those which are in your recognition vocabulary only, prepare a sentence which clearly reveals a correct use of the word. For those which are entirely new to you consult your dictionary. Come to class prepared to demonstrate that you know how to use each word.

| | | | | |
|---|---|---|---|---|
| abyss | affluent | acrid | adroit | abortive |
| accost | agnostic | amplify | apocryphal | abstruse |
| admonish | anonymous | analogous | appraise | affix |
| affront | arrogant | annul | ascertain | amenable |
| alleviate | authentic | bestial | aural | apt |
| amend | bland | chronic | bogus | benign |
| basic | blatant | collaborate | brash | bracing |
| biased | boisterous | colloquial | bullish | brazen |
| boon | caricature | conducive | carping | brusque |
| capitulate | complacent | corroborate | castigate | callous |
| caption | consensus | derive | caustic | cede |
| component | contemporary | discordant | competent | condone |
| concept | covetous | enervating | confront | deficit |
| congenial | cynical | entomology | cursory | delete |
| congested | dextrous | etymology | deluded | deviate |
| context | dialect | fastidious | denuded | ecstasy |
| conversely | diminutive | flippant | dormant | elated |
| corollary | dogmatic | gilded | empirical | elicit |
| decade | dynamic | incentive | espouse | elongate |
| deprive | echelon | inherent | exquisite | eminent |
| diagnosis | enigmatic | insular | feign | felicitate |
| dilate | extol | inter | frugal | fictitious |
| dupe | fabulous | intermittent | fugue | fortify |
| epitaph | fealty | lucrative | gaunt | glib |
| epithet | futile | miniature | haphazard | harried |
| equilibrium | garrulous | mulch | innate | hoary |

| | | | | |
|---|---|---|---|---|
| facile | germinal | nullify | intrinsic | illegible |
| fluent | guise | ostracize | invective | indelibly |
| gist | hapless | panacea | jargon | indolent |
| habitually | hierarchy | philology | jubilant | interminable |
| heresy | humble | pungent | keystone | inveterate |
| hybrid | implicit | regime | kiln | ironic |
| illiterate | imposter | reticent | liaison | laconic |
| illusion | inarticulate | secular | mandatory | linguistic |
| ingenious | integrity | smirk | millenium | odious |
| ingenuous | interlude | tantalize | naive | opaque |
| initiate | interpolate | tenacious | nebulous | optical |
| layman | intransigent | tumult | obsolete | pliant |
| lax | irksome | usurp | omnipotent | putrid |
| mediocre | maudlin | usury | pariah | rampant |
| morose | nucleus | valid | pecuniary | recalcitrant |
| obscure | pediatrician | vandal | replica | ribald |
| periodic | Pollyanna | venomous | rupture | spontaneous |
| pompous | rudimentary | vicarious | status quo | spurious |
| prosaic | rubble | virile | stipulate | staid |
| rebuff | semantics | virtuosity | suppliant | tawdry |
| regress | specious | waspish | terrestrial | toxic |
| specific | tenure | wayward | vapid | trite |
| tangible | thesis | welt | vestigial | wanton |
| ultimate | ubiquitous | writhe | watt | whorl |

**E.** In each line of words select and write out the word closest in meaning to the italicized word. The closest meaning may not be synonymous.

*adamant:* gracious, amenable, unyielding, courageous, stupid, wealthy
*adhere:* ruin, stick to, break off, overhear, wipe out, betray, upset
*anecdote:* poison, cure, malady, rumor, story, lover, opponent, praise
*bedlam:* restaurant, hotel, station, madhouse, garage, resort, store
*bigotry:* narrow mindedness, patriotism, miserliness, immoral love
*clemency:* conviction, payment, proof, weakness, falsehood, mercy, fate
*cogent:* dull, tricky, mean, facetious, wise, empty, flabby, late
*contrite:* gay, optimistic, careful, sorry, overworked, worn out, greedy
*dearth:* debt, scarcity, soil, abundance, mistake, honor, redemption
*doctrine:* literature, paintings, teachings, medicine, refuse, sediment
*dolt:* an old woman, a racehorse, a trained animal, a stupid person, a thief
*edict:* lie, promise, platitude, celebration, proclamation, song, boycott
*excerpt:* rebuttal, addition, exception, law, receipt, fragment, letter
*facet:* error, attitude, water tap, drain, value, surface, cost, labor
*fallacy:* truth, error, virtue, vanity, stimulant, lunacy, fracture
*fiscal:* legal, governmental, new, political, monetary, corrupt, ethical
*gregarious:* fond of company, sulky, merry, confident, not willing, tired
*hackneyed:* incapable, tragic, trite, tawdry, unkempt, swollen, hired
*heinous:* unfinished, out of date, absurd, sharp, heavy, happy, hateful
*impeccable:* hard, metallic, self-righteous, flawless, faint, calm, lazy

*impunity:* without hope, not sullied, not infected, without harm, obsolete
*indigenous:* not edible, sick, salty, robust, nice, native, indiscreet
*inert:* tired, slow, lifeless, weighing nothing, trivial, wet, extra
*inference:* thought, gain, excuse, burden, lament, interlude, clothing
*jeopardize:* endanger, make light of, suppress, buy off, discount, omit
*jibe:* swear, smile, sing, taste, taunt, trip, salute, make friends with
*mitigate:* impress, scorn, esteem, make milder, add to, repair, try again
*mores:* additions, customs, natives, crimes, foods, servants, friends
*mutilate:* ponder, rescue, upbraid, tease, tickle, mix, maim, migrate
*myriad:* a rare volume, a forged document, a large number, a tiny specimen
*nominal:* not known, in name only, not yet elected, subdued, part, regretful
*novice:* artist, artisan, old timer, commanding officer, beginner, culprit
*noxious:* too sweet, difficult to do, pleasant, poisonous, expensive, anxious
*obtuse:* irregular, belligerent, dull, attractive, well padded, innocent
*officious:* authorized, incompetent, official, severe, meddlesome, well done
*opiate:* allowance, quarrel, recitation, decoy, drug, greeting, invitation
*palatable:* sticky, pure, tasty, revolting, cloying, dear, unsupervised
*petulant:* prickly, peevish, prudish, irate, agreeable, modest
*prodigious:* precocious, proud, tardy, wary, clear, enormous, everlasting
*rectify:* receive, return, denounce, cajole, correct, explain, undermine
*restive:* tranquil, impatient, sleepy, angry, tired, frigid, restful
*servile:* cheap, irritable, efficient, eager, slavish, delightful, mad
*sordid:* heavy, dull, gluttonous, dirty, bright, novel, silly, wasteful
*synopsis:* bold attack, happy thought, brief version, clever pun
*tentative:* provisional, fixed, untrustworthy, hasty, inaccurate, partly right
*torpid:* inflammable, exotic, incandescent, slight, cold, sluggish, hot
*ultimate:* unknown, expected, initial, final, revised, brilliant, long
*unique:* old, valuable, broken, queer, saleable, singular, lost, redundant
*verbatim:* genuine, word for word, at long last, without fail, vocal, trivial
*zealot:* criminal, scholar, manager, apprentice, grouch, enthusiast, fraud

# 11

## S Y N O P S E S   A N D

## S U M M A R I E S

PROBABLY the skill most necessary to success in college is the ability to read effectively. College success is largely determined by examinations, and examinations are necessarily concerned with finding out how well the student understands what he has read. The ability, therefore, to restate in one's own words the ideas and information contained in books, articles, and essays is one of the main tests by which academic success is measured. This is true even when an examination is deliberately designed to test a student's evaluation of his reading or what he thinks about it, since he must understand what he reads before he is in a position to evaluate and discuss it.

Any device which helps a student to read more effectively is therefore worthy of his serious attention. You are already familiar with one such device — the outline, which was discussed as a reading aid on pages 64–65. In this chapter we shall consider two other reading aids — the *synopsis* and the *summary*.

## *The Synopsis*

In your literature courses you will be asked to read novels, plays, and stories, on which you will later be examined. Every student knows that after reading a number of plays or stories, it is often difficult to keep the details of each plot clearly in mind and to keep the separate characters distinct. While the pre-examination review helps, there is never time to reread all the original material. What is needed for review is some record of the document short enough to read quickly but detailed enough to give the essentials. For such purposes the synopsis is most useful.

A synopsis is a summary of a plot. When you return from a movie and are asked what it was about, your answer is a synopsis. You identify the main characters and tell what happened to them. By so doing, you review the whole movie in a small fraction of the time required to see it.

The following is a synopsis of a play that you may have read or are likely to read in college. In order to be clear, even to a student who has not read the play, the synopsis has been made fuller than would be required for purposes of one's own review.

## IBSEN, "A DOLL'S HOUSE," 3 ACTS

Characters: Torvald Helmer; Nora, his wife; Dr. Rank; Nils Krogstad; Mrs. Linde

*Act I.* The play opens with a picture of the domestic happiness of the Helmer household. Nora is represented as a pretty, helpless woman, dependent on her husband in all worldly concerns. Torvald is the strong, wise husband who paternally guides his wife's life. *From the man's point of view,* he is the ideal husband, and she the ideal wife. Their home is a doll's house, with Nora the doll.

From Mrs. Linde, a woman who has earned her way in the world, we learn that the tranquillity of the doll's house rests on a deception. At a time when her father was dying and her husband was seriously ill Nora had borrowed from Krogstad enough money to finance a trip to Italy, ostensibly a pleasure trip for her but really a journey to save her husband's life. Rather than worry her dying father, who would have given her the money, Nora forged his name to the security she gave Krogstad. Since then she has been paying the interest by practicing all sorts of domestic economies. Her husband, who knows nothing about the transaction, is always teasing her about her domestic extravagance.

At the moment the play opens the finances of the Helmers are about to improve, for Torvald has been appointed manager of the bank and Nora hopes soon to retire the debt. But the dramatic turn from happiness to disaster is occasioned by Torvald's giving Mrs. Linde the job at the bank now held by Krogstad. Krogstad threatens to reveal Nora's forgery unless she persuades her husband to retain him in his position. Nora tries to do this but fails.

*Act II.* Nora determines to borrow the money to pay Krogstad from Dr. Rank, a good friend of the family. Knowing that he is about to die, Rank visits her and confesses his love for her. Under the circumstances she feels she cannot ask for the loan, although there is no question that she would get it. Krogstad brings pressure on Nora, but she refuses to interfere with her husband's decision, and in her refusal indicates that she is thinking of committing suicide or of leaving her family in order to spare her husband's name. Krogstad leaves a letter for Torvald, explaining the whole transaction. Nora, who wants to postpone the showdown until after the Christmas party, delays her husband's reading of the letter.

*Act III.* While the Helmers are at the party, Krogstad and Mrs. Linde decide to get married. Krogstad says that he will ask Torvald for the letter unread, but Mrs. Linde, who understands that Nora is not happy in her role of doll, tells him it would be better if Torvald read the letter.

The Helmers return from the party, and are visited by Rank, who leaves a marked card which Nora understands as a notice that he is about to die. Torvald later reads Krogstad's letter and bitterly accuses Nora as an immoral woman, unworthy to be the mother of his children. His conduct opens her eyes and she prepares to leave the house. At this time, a second letter arrives from Krogstad, in which he returns Nora's bond and thus frees her from the consequences of her forgery. Torvald is overjoyed and announces his forgiveness of Nora. But the experience has made a serious woman out of her. She reviews for her husband their relationship together and denounces the doll-like status in which she has been kept by both him and her father. They talk it over quietly, with Torvald getting the worst of it. Nora decides to leave him. There is a suggestion that their marriage may be resumed after they prove themselves. Then the door slams as Nora leaves.

The next synopsis will have less meaning for a student who has not read the play, but it would probably be adequate to recall the whole action to a student who had read *Candida* several months earlier.

### G. B. SHAW, "CANDIDA," 3 ACTS

Characters: Rev. James Morell; Candida, his wife; Eugene Marchbanks, a young poet; James Burgess, Candida's father; Proserpine, Morell's secretary; Mill, Morell's assistant.

*Act I.* The main job of this act is to portray the characters of Morell, Candida, and Marchbanks. Morell is drawn by showing: (*a*) the attitudes of Proserpine and Mill toward him; (*b*) the attitude of Burgess toward him; (*c*) his activities in affairs of the church and of socialism; (*d*) the attitude of Marchbanks toward him; and (*e*) his own attitude toward Marchbanks and Burgess. Marchbanks' character is revealed by his own actions and by the attitudes of Morell and Candida toward him. The action of the play during this act sets up the triangle between Morell, Candida, and Marchbanks and develops the theme far enough so that Morell's final defeat is indicated. At the beginning of the act Morell is almost a symbol of the confident and competent master of every situation, while Marchbanks is a symbol of naïve incompetence. During the act Marchbanks succeeds in reversing this judgment.

*Act II.* This act carries on the conflict to the point at which Morell decides to leave Marchbanks and Candida alone while he goes to a meeting. His decision is a desperate attempt to force the issue and find where he stands in Candida's affections.

*Act III.* Marchbanks makes poetic love to Candida while Morell is gone. Morell returns and forces Candida to make a decision between the two men. Marchbanks is horrified at his crudeness. In the auction scene

Candida chooses her husband as the weaker of the two men and therefore the one who needs her most. Marchbanks, who had anticipated her decision, leaves after receiving Candida's final advice.

Although this second synopsis will seem less satisfactory to a student who has not read the play, it is actually more useful to one who has, since it not only identifies the characters and reviews the plot, but also shows the relationship of the separate acts to each other and to the whole drama. A synopsis need not do this, but since the relation of a particular act to the play as a whole may well be asked about on a final examination, this kind of synopsis has an additional merit.

It takes from fifteen to thirty minutes to write an adequate synopsis. A student who feels that he has the details of a play or a novel clearly in mind when he has just finished reading it may see no reason for spending additional time on the assignment. But one test of his reading is not how clearly he knows the work then but how clearly he knows it at the end of the semester. For most students the discipline of making a synopsis as a part of the total reading assignment is rewarded by easier and more accurate recall and hence by better examination grades.

## *The Summary*

The synopsis is useful only for novels, plays, and stories. For all other reading the summary is used. A summary is a condensation of the original. In its simplest form it is nothing more than purposeful note-taking. The student boils down the original passage to the bare facts or ideas which it contains, as illustrated by the following examples:

| *Original* | *Summary* |
|---|---|
| When the site of government was changed to Washington in 1800, there were only one hundred and forty officers and clerks; today there are close to three quarters of a million. | Gov't employees in Washington: In 1800, 140 In 1933, about 750,000 |
| The sun is a fiery, flaming star well toward a million miles in diameter and nearly a hundred million miles from us. Surrounding it is a very deep atmosphere at temperatures running up to 10,000 degrees Fahrenheit, composed of gases and vapors all of which are common on the earth. | Diameter of sun, one million miles Distance from earth, 100 million miles Highest atmosphere temperature, 10,000° |

When comparing the financial success of two business firms of the same kind, we do not simply say that the firm making the greater profit is the more succesful. What we compare is not profits alone, but profits relative to total investment. That is, if $p$ and $i$ represent profit and investment, respectively, the value of the quotient $p/i$ (that is, the percentage of profit) serves to measure relative financial success.[1]

Comparative financial success of two firms not measured by profits alone, but by formula $p/i$, when $p =$ profit, and $i =$ investment.

For many purposes the notes at the right offer the most useful kind of summary. We shall see in Chapter 14 that the use of such notes is recommended in carrying out investigations for a research paper, because this habit of gleaning the facts from a passage encourages alert reading and avoids the possibility of unintentional plagiarism.

However, the kind of summary with which we are principally concerned in this chapter is the *paragraph summary*, in which the reader condenses the content of the whole paragraph into a few sentences. He reads the paragraph, determines what it says, and expresses its essential meaning in short and simplified form. He thus achieves two results: he proves that he understands the paragraph by translating it into his own words, and he reduces it to a more convenient form for review. The following examples illustrate:

### Original

I often wish that this phrase, "applied science," had never been invented. For it suggests that there is a sort of scientific knowledge of direct practical use, which can be studied apart from another sort of scientific knowledge, which is of no practical utility, and which is termed "pure science." But there is no more complete fallacy than this. What people call applied science is nothing but the application of pure science to particular classes of problems. It consists of deductions from those general principles, established by reasoning and observation, which constitute pure science. No one can

### Summary

The attempt to differentiate "pure" and "applied" science misleadingly suggests that "pure" science is not useful. It is useful in two ways: it provides the scientific principles to be applied, and it provides the method which makes application possible.

### Explanation

*The first sentence of the summary expresses in 16 words the idea stated in 50 words in the first two sentences of the original. The second sentence*

[1] From *Introduction to Mathematics,* by Cooley, Gans, Kline, and Wahlert. Copyright, 1949, by Hollis R. Cooley, David Gans, Morris Kline, and Howard E. Wahlert. Reprinted by permission of Houghton Mifflin Company.

safely make these deductions until he has a firm grasp of the principles; and he can obtain that grasp only by personal experience of the operations of observation and of reasoning on which they were founded.[2]

*of the summary restates in 23 words the content of the last four sentences of the original (76 words). The summary, therefore, conveys the basic meaning of the original in less than one-third of the space.*

### Original

Economists write of the "agricultural revolution," of greater productivity per farm worker, of the advantages of farm mechanization and the ability of the farmer to feed more people than he did prior to the nineteenth century. What most of them completely fail to recognize is that production - per - farmer is utterly meaningless divorced from production-per-acre. For a few decades the Western world was able to get along on this assumption — while it still had new lands to open up and while it produced by mining its topsoil. But modern agriculture has not raised the earth's biotic potential; except in very limited areas, it has not reduced environmental resistances. Over most of the earth it has enormously increased them, to the point of destroying hundreds of millions of productive acres. Discussion of the agricultural revolution in terms of increased production-per-farmer — or even in terms of pure agriculture, leaving aside the problem of water tables, forests, nonagricultural lands, fauna and noncrop plants, etc. — expresses a most fallacious and dangerous form of thinking. One man, under an improved technology, might be able to farm a full section; this would not bring into being more sections of agricultural land — nor raise or even maintain productivity on other acres.[3]

### Summary

The belief that improved agricultural techniques will increase the productivity of land is an illusion. Mechanization will allow one man to farm more acres and, hence, get a bigger crop, but it will not produce a greater yield per acre, except in rare instances. On the contrary, by exploiting the natural resources of the soil it may in time decrease the yield per acre.

### Explanation

*The summary reduces the 209-word original to 64 words by picking out the two main reasons why the "agricultural revolution" will not increase the biotic potential of the earth and ignoring the details by which these reasons are explained. In other words, the summary confines the argument to a statement of the thesis and the two factors into which that thesis is broken.*

---

[2] From T. H. Huxley, *Collected Essays.* The Macmillan Company, publishers.
[3] From William Vogt's *Road to Survival.* Copyright, 1948, by William Sloane Associates, Inc. Reprinted by permission of William Sloane Associates, Inc.

*Original*

The object of this Essay is to assert one very simple principle, as entitled to govern absolutely the dealings of society with the individual in the way of compulsion and control, whether the means used be physical force in the form of legal penalties, or the moral coercion of public opinion. That principle is, that the sole end for which mankind are warranted, individually or collectively, in interfering with the liberty of action of any of their number, is self-protection. That the only purpose for which power can be rightfully exercised over any member of a civilized community, against his will, is to prevent harm to others. His own good, either physical or moral, is not a sufficient warrant. He cannot rightfully be compelled to do or forbear because it will be better for him to do so, because it will make him happier, because, in the opinions of others, to do so would be wise, or even right. These are good reasons for remonstrating with him, or reasoning with him, or persuading him, or entreating him, but not for compelling him, or visiting him with any evil in case he do otherwise. To justify that, the conduct from which it is desired to deter him, must be calculated to produce evil to some one else. The only part of the conduct of any one, for which he is amenable to society, is that which concerns others. In the part which merely concerns himself, his independence is, of right, absolute. Over himself, over his own body and mind, the individual is sovereign.[4]

*Summary*

The thesis of Mill's essay *On Liberty* is that society has no right to interfere with the liberty of an individual in matters which concern only himself. He cannot be restrained by penalties or social pressure so long as his conduct does not harm others. The belief that it would be better for him to change may justify persuasion, but not compulsion.

*Explanation*

*The original paragraph takes 80 words to state the thesis and then explains that thesis by seven restatements through 180 words. By stating the thesis in 27 words and restating it only twice in 35 words, the summary boils down the 260-word original to 62 words. Of course, the summary leaves much that has to be inferred, but for a student who had read the original, it would probably be adequate to allow him to restate Mill's position in an essay-type examination.*

The preparation of such digests is more a matter of reading than of writing, and the reading is made easier by an understanding of paragraph construction. As we saw in Chapter 6, most paragraphs

4 From John Stuart Mill's *Essay on Liberty.*

develop a single idea by explanation or illustration. The first task in writing a digest is to find the topic idea of the paragraph. If that idea is not explicitly stated, it must be distilled out of the sentences which come closest to stating it. In the selection from *Liberty,* the introductory phrase, "That principle is," has almost the effect of turning a spotlight on the main idea of the paragraph. The topic ideas of the other two examples are less obvious, since neither is explicitly stated in a single sentence. Both paragraphs have to be read completely before we can be sure of their purpose but, once read, the central thought of each becomes clear.

The second step in preparing a paragraph summary is to eliminate whatever is not essential to a clear understanding of the topic. For ordinary readers a writer must explain his topic sentence to be sure that its implications will not be missed, but a person preparing a summary of a paragraph is not an ordinary reader. He is unusually alert, and so he can dispense with the explanation and illustration which might otherwise be necessary. Therefore, he concentrates on just those sentences which are necessary to explain the topic idea, and ignores the rest. As he does so, he makes up his mind exactly what the paragraph is saying.

The third step is to write the summary. The safest way to do this is to put the original aside and rewrite the paragraph out of the knowledge already obtained. A student who cannot do that has not read the paragraph carefully enough. If he follows it as he writes his digest, he may be tempted to pick out a few sentences in their original form and string them together. If he does this, he is quoting from the paragraph, not summarizing it, and what he produces may distort the meaning of the original. The real value of the summary as a reading device is that it requires the student to master the paragraph and make it his own. This he cannot do by copying selected sentences.

The final step is to compare the digest with the original for accuracy and to make whatever revisions this comparison suggests. Even for students who have had considerable experience writing paragraph summaries this final step often results in further condensation and simplification of the summary.

To summarize:

1. Read the paragraph to determine its basic idea.

2. Read it again to pick out the essentials, summarizing mentally as you read. If necessary, make notes.

3. Without consulting the paragraph, express its content in your own words. If you get stuck, stop writing and repeat step two.

4. Compare your summary with the original and make any necessary revisions.

The technique of the paragraph summary may be applied to a series of paragraphs or to a whole article. In summarizing a selection of many paragraphs, remember that not all paragraphs are equally significant. Some introduce or restate main points; others are transitional; still others give illustrations of a point already made. Since the summary requires you to restate the content, not the paragraphing, you need not summarize each paragraph separately. The best procedure is first to determine the purpose of the selection, then outline the main topics, and finally summarize each of these without being unduly influenced by the original paragraphing. For example, "The Distinction Between War and Peace" (pages 47–49) contains ten paragraphs, yet structurally it consists of three parts — the *legal, political,* and *military* distinctions between war and peace. These three parts would be the real units of the summary, and the essay would be summarized as though it contained three paragraphs instead of ten.

In the illustration that follows, the organization of the article is shown by the outline symbols at the left; the main points are underlined in the text; and the significance of the material is indicated in the notes at the right. In its present form, therefore, the illustration represents the first two steps in preparing a summary of a long article.

LANGUAGE PLANNING FOR A NEW ORDER [5]

OUTLINE
SYMBOLS

NOTES

As far as we can see into the future, there will always be a multiplicity of
I. regional languages for everyday use. Those who advocate the introduction of an international medium do not dispute this. What they do assert is the need for a second language as a common medium for people who speak mutually unintelligible tongues. They envisage a world, of at least federations of what were once

*This paragraph says, in effect, that the proposal of a second language is not impractical.*

A. 1. sovereign states, where people of different speech communities would be bilingual. Everyone would still grow up to speak one or other of existing national languages, but everyone would also acquire a single auxiliary for supranational communication. This prospect is not in-
2. compatible with the mental capacities of

[5] Reprinted from *The Loom of Language,* by Frederick Bodmer, by permission of W. W. Norton and Company, Inc. Copyright, 1944, by W. W. Norton and Company, Inc., New York. Permission to reprint in Canada by courtesy of George Allen & Unwin, Ltd., publishers.

NOTES

ordinary human beings; nor does it involve a total break with existing practice. Bilingualism exists already in Wales, Belgium, South Africa, and many other parts. Throughout the English-speaking world all secondary-school children study at least one foreign language, that is, French, Spanish, or German; and in some countries pupils who leave school with a smattering of a foreign language are in the majority.

*Evidence for IA2.*

In Britain they are not. Most of the children enter the labor market with a knowledge of no language other than their own. Consequently millions of adult workers are excluded from direct communication with their Continental comrades. Postponement of the school-leaving age will provide an opportunity for bringing the curriculum for elementary instruction in Britain into line with that of many other countries. Thus the adoption of an international auxiliary implies no more than regularization of existing educational practice, i.e., universal instruction in a second language and agreement to use one and the same second language everywhere. Creation of conditions for uniformity of educational practice by international agreement, as a prelude to universal bilingualism, as defined above, is not a language problem. It is a political problem.

*This exception to IA2 does not affect author's thesis and may be omitted in summary.*

*Restatement of IA2.*

B.

1.

Many well-informed people still doubt whether the social need for a single universal second language will prove strong enough to override human laziness. At first sight the plight of modern language teaching in Great Britain and elsewhere lends some support to pessimism. Hitherto our schools have produced poor results. After years of travail the British public-school **product** may have mastered enough French to get in Paris what Paris is only too willing to sell without French. This need not make us hopeless. Any society ripe for adopting an inter-

*This support for IB1 may be omitted in summary.*

language will be faced with a new set of problems. Pupils who now take French or German as school subjects rarely have a clear-cut idea of the purpose for which they are learning them and, more rarely still, the chance of using what knowledge they acquire. The future is likely to provide incentives and opportunities hitherto unknown. Fantastic delays, misunderstandings and waste due to the absence of a single common language for international cooperation will impress even those who are not knowingly affected by it at present.

**2.**

A hundred years ago Europe witnessed perhaps less than a dozen international congresses in the course of a whole decade. Delegates were invariably drawn from the upper class. So communication was easy enough. Deliberations were in French. When international congresses became more numerous, they assumed a more gaudy linguistic character. Consequently procedure had often to be conducted in two or more "official" languages. One could choose delegates who were able to compete with the polyglot attendant of an international sleeping car, but the delegate with the best linguistic equipment would rarely be one with the best understanding of relevant issues. This obstacle to international communication becomes more formidable as time goes on. People of new strata and more diverse speech habits discover community of interest, and no single language enjoys the prestige of French during the eighteenth century.

*This paragraph is an illustration of the difference between the past and the future and may be ignored in the summary.*

In short, the prospects for language planning depend on the extent to which the impulse to international co-operation keeps step with the new potential of prosperity for all. Socialist planning, that is planning for the common needs of peoples belonging to different nations or cultural units, will bring about incessant contact between medical officers of

*This paragraph develops IB2. Most of these details may be omitted in the summary.*

health, town-planning experts, electrical engineers, social statisticians, and trade-union representatives. Increased leisure combined with improved traveling facilities will give to a large floating section of the population opportunities to establish new social contacts through the medium of an interlanguage; and its adoption would find a ready ally in the radio. Even those who stay at home perpetually would be tempted to avail themselves of opportunities to learn more of large-scale social enterprise in neighboring communities of the supranational state.

II.

The choice for those of us who cherish this hope lies between a constructed language and an already established medium, either in its existing shape or in some simplified form, such as Basic English. The second involves nothing more than an agreement between educational authorities expressing the will of the people. On account of its grammatical simplicity, its hybrid vocabulary, its vast literature, and, above all, its wide distribution over the planet, the claims of

A.

Anglo-American would undoubtedly exclude those of any other current language which could conceivably have a large body of promoters in the near future; but political objections to such a choice are formidable. It is most unlikely that a socialist Continent would decide for

B.

Anglo-American as its interlanguage if Britain remained hostile to the new order. The chances might improve if a Britain free of its imperial incubus entered into close co-operation with its neighbors next door to build up a world without class, war, and want. Even so there is much to say for the adoption of a neutral medium cleansed from the all too evident defects of existing natural languages.

III. A.

Some linguists meet the plea for a constructed auxiliary with the assertion that language is a product of growth. It is less easy to detect the relevance than to

*Two kinds of international languages, each of which is to be considered.*

*English is the logical choice if a national language is chosen, but political considerations will rule it out.*

*First of two objections against constructed language.*

recognize the truth of this assertion. Admittedly it is beyond human ingenuity to construct a live skylark, but the airplane has advantages which no flying animal possesses. Apple trees and gooseberry bushes are also products of growth, and no reasonable man or woman advances this trite reflection as sufficient reason for preventing geneticists from producing new varieties of fruit by combining inherited merits of different strains or allied species. The work accomplished by pioneers of the science of synthetic linguistics shows that it is also possible to produce new language varieties combining the inherent merits of different forms of natural speech. In the light of their achievements and shortcomings we can now prescribe the essential features of a constructed language which would be free from the conspicuous defects of any natural, or of any previously constructed, language.

*Answer to objection. All this may be reduced to statement that creation of a fully-developed synthetic language is quite possible.*

**B.**  Professional linguists who do not dispute the possibility of constructing a language to meet the requirements of international communication sometimes raise another objection. They say that the adventure would be short-lived, if ever attempted; that no auxiliary could remain intact for long. Even if confined to the territory of Europe itself, it would split into dialects. Each speech community would locally impose its own phonetic habits and its own system of stress; and the Tower of Babel would come crashing down on the builders. Only a perpetual succession of international congresses could thus prevent a new disaster. Such is the gloomy view which Professor Wyld of Oxford takes. There are three sufficient reasons why it need not intimidate us.

*Second objection.*

**C.**

**1.**  To begin with there is nothing inherently absurd in a suggestion for setting up a permanent interlinguistic commission to check the process of disinte-

*First answer to that objection.*

OUTLINE
SYMBOLS

gration. For three centuries the forty immortals of the Académie Française have tried, not without success, to keep literary French in a strait jacket; and Norway has changed its spelling and grammar by three Acts of Parliament in less than forty years. If national governments can control the growth of national languages, an international authority could also maintain an accepted standard for its own medium of communication. Though international committees to supervise scientific terminology, e.g. the International Commission on Zoological Nomenclature, are already in existence, our universities cling to the conviction that intelligent language planning on a world-wide scale is out of the question.

*All this may be reduced to statement that the experience of France, Norway, and the Commission on Zoological Nomenclature shows that prevention of disintegration is possible.*

By the nature of their training academic linguists are unduly preoccupied with times when few people could travel beyond a day's journey on horseback or by cart, when reading and writing, like stenography today, were crafts confined to a few, when there were no mechanical means for distributing news or information. It is true that languages have broken up time and again in the past, because of dispersion over a wide area, geographical isolation, absence of a written standard, and other disintegrating agencies. Those who entertain the hope of international communication by an auxil-

2. iary envisage a future in which these agencies will no longer operate. Indeed, we have experience to sustain a more hopeful view than is customary in academic quarters. During the centuries which have followed the introduction of printing, the gradual dissolution of illiteracy, and revolutionary changes in our means of communication, English has established itself as the language of North America and of Australasia. It is not true

3. to say that the three main Continental varieties of the common Anglo-American language are drifting further apart. It is

*Transition to IIIC2. May be ignored in summary.*

*Second answer to same objection.*

*Third answer to same objection.*

probably more true to say that universal
schooling, the film, and the radio are
bringing them closer together. In any
case, experience shows that geographical
isolation during several centuries has not
made the speech of New England unintelligible to the people of Old England,
or vice versa. Experience should therefore encourage, rather than discourage,
us in pressing for an international auxiliary.

This article presents an argument in favor of creating a synthetic
language as an international auxiliary language. The argument is in
three parts: that an auxiliary language is feasible, that a synthetic
language would be more acceptable than any existing natural language,
and that the old objections against synthetic languages no longer hold
good. It would be logical to summarize each part in a single paragraph,
but since the third part deals with two different objections, it might be
better to devote a paragraph to each of them and to write the summary
as follows:

The hope of a universal auxiliary language, by which people who speak
different national languages may have a medium of international communication, is not an impractical one. In many countries people now use
two languages, and the practice of teaching some foreign language in
secondary schools is generally established. It is true that the level of student achievement in mastering these secondary languages is low, but this
lack of success can be explained by the fact that students of foreign languages have little motivation for learning them and little opportunity to
use them after they have been learned. Those who advocate the adoption of a universal auxiliary foresee a world in which the needs and opportunities of international cooperation will both demand a universal
second language and provide the incentive to make its study efficient.

Whatever auxiliary is chosen must come either from some existing
national language or from a constructed language. Of all existing languages, English, because of its grammatical simplicity, its hybrid vocabulary, its vast literature, and its wide distribution, would seem to have the
strongest claim to become the world language. But political considerations might make it unacceptable to many nations. A constructed language would not be subject to political objections and would be free of
defects which all national languages now show.

There are two common objections to a constructed language. One is
that since language is a product of growth there is no chance of constructing a living language. This objection is hardly significant. The work already done on synthetic languages proves that the creation of a successful constructed language presents no linguistic impossibilities.

The second objection is that, while a constructed language could be made, it would not remain a universal language but would break up into mutually unintelligible dialects. While such disintegration has been common in the past, there are three reasons why we need not fear it: (1) as the experience of France, Norway, and the International Commission on Zoological Nomenclature shows, the tendency towards disintegration can be held in check by an authoritative commission; (2) the agencies of disintegration are less likely to operate in the interdependent world for which the auxiliary language is to be designed; (3) the fact that the common language of Britain, America, Australia, and New Zealand has not broken up into mutually unintelligible dialects proves that the agencies of disintegration can be offset by such integrating influences as universal education and improved means of communication.

If a shorter summary is required, the whole argument may be condensed to little more than its thesis:

The advocates of an international auxiliary language think it possible to make people bilingual and that the needs of the future will make the task easier. They think Basic English would be the best natural auxiliary but that political and linguistic considerations favor a constructed language. The chief objections to a constructed language are that (1) languages cannot be constructed, but must grow; and (2) a constructed language would soon disintegrate. The proponents of a constructed language reply (1) it is now possible to construct a satisfactory synthetic language, and (2) experience shows that, under modern conditions, disintegration need not occur.

This version reduces a 1700-word article to about 100 words. Whether such drastic condensation is wise will depend on the purpose of the summary. If the shorter version gives the content in sufficient detail so that it can be recalled later, it is adequate.

## Exercises

**A.** For each of the following paragraphs, write the shortest possible summary which will still communicate the author's meaning fairly:

### (1)

We do not believe that the objectives of science study in general education are best met by survey courses covering a large area in a limited time. These are too likely to be courses about science rather than courses in science. They are apt to be dogmatic rather than inherently convincing. The student is likely to be taught a great many dramatic contemporary results of science rather than underlying principles and fundamental facts. If a survey course is to be completely outmoded in a few years by new advances, one cannot blame the student for failure to appreciate the basic fundamental truths; science is indeed to him a casual, ephemeral thing. This is not to imply that no advantage should be taken of new applications of science or recent discoveries to stimulate interest and secure motivation; however the cake should not be all frosting. It is usually less confusing and far more satisfying actually to learn and understand the principles behind a group of phenomena and how they bring these phenomena into being than to learn and attempt to remember a large number of superficial facts about the phenomena.[6]

## (2)

It is not possible to depend entirely upon what each nation says of its own habits of thought and action. Writers in every nation have tried to give an account of themselves. But it is not easy. The lenses through which any nation looks at life are not the ones another nation uses. It is hard to be conscious of the eyes through which one looks. Any country takes them for granted, and the tricks of focusing and of perspective which give to any people its national view of life seem to that people the god-given arrangement of the landscape. In any matter of spectacles, we do not expect the man who wears them to know the formula for the lenses, and neither can we expect nations to analyze their own outlook upon the world. When we want to know about spectacles, we train an oculist and expect him to be able to write out the formula for any lenses we bring him. Some day no doubt we shall recognize that it is the job of the social scientist to do this for the nations of the contemporary world.[7]

## (3)

We should know that all the money in the world could not have built an atomic bomb in 1936. Atomic energy was known, and many of its properties were understood. It had been released in small quantities in laboratories, and its release in large quantities in the sun and the stars had been studied. But the critical information and the critical direction to follow for releasing it in large amounts on earth were lacking in 1936, and no one could have used two billion dollars for making an atomic bomb at that time. It is this that is important in understanding the relation of science to industry, to medicine, and to the public. There has to be knowledge before it can be applied. At a certain stage of scientific development, theoretically critical knowledge becomes available. Before that moment — which no one can guarantee in advance — the knowledge cannot be applied. After that moment application is reasonably certain and only the special technics for its utilization need be worked out.[8]

**B.** Write a one-page summary of "The Distinction Between War and Peace" (pp. 47–49).

[6] From Earl J. McGrath and others, *Toward General Education*. Copyright, 1948, by The Macmillan Company and used with their permission.

[7] From Ruth Benedict's *The Chrysanthemum and the Sword*. Copyright, 1946, by Ruth Benedict. Reprinted by permission of Houghton Mifflin Company, publishers.

[8] From Selig Hecht's *Explaining the Atom*. Copyright, 1947, by Selig Hecht. Reprinted by permission of The Viking Press, publishers.

**C.** The following selection is a unit of a longer essay. Study it carefully with a view to purpose and organization, then write a 400-word summary:

### ARE SOCIAL SCIENTISTS BACKWARD? [9]

In discussing the relative difficulties of analysis which the exact and inexact sciences face, let me begin with an analogy. Would you agree that swimmers are less skillful athletes than runners because swimmers do not move as fast as runners? You probably would not. You would quickly point out that water offers greater resistance to swimmers than the air and ground do to runners. Agreed, that is just the point. In seeking to solve their problems, the social scientists encounter greater resistance than the physical scientists. By that I do not mean to belittle the great accomplishments of physical scientists who have been able, for example, to determine the structure of the atom without seeing it. That is a tremendous achievement; yet in many ways it is not so difficult as what the social scientists are expected to do. The conditions under which the social scientists must work would drive a physical scientist frantic. Here are five of those conditions. He can make few experiments; he cannot measure the results accurately; he cannot control the conditions surrounding the experiments; he is often expected to get quick results with slow-acting economic forces; and he must work with people, not with inanimate objects. Let us look at these conditions more closely.

1. Before a physical scientist will admit that his experiment has proved successful, he generally repeats it in his laboratory a great many times, sometimes hundreds of times. The economist, or the political scientist, however, has no laboratory other than the world before him, and its history. An economist who wants to find the effect of war on national income in the postwar period in major nations in modern times can uncover perhaps a score of usable examples. The business-cycle analyst knows that business cycles are a product of only the past century and a half, and that the major business cycles in leading industrial nations are comparatively few in number.

2. Chemists and physicists can weigh and otherwise measure solids, liquids, and gases fairly accurately, but the economist has less effective means of measurement. True, statisticians have devised many ways of correlating figures, determining and eliminating margins of error, and so forth, to the nth decimal point. Unfortunately, this exact mathematics is all too often used to measure units of differing quality or figures collected under uncontrolled conditions. Being able to measure to the nth decimal place has less meaning under such circumstances.

One or two examples will illustrate the point. For the past generation Americans have attached increasing importance to wholesale price indexes and cost-of-living indexes. As you know, in calculating these, a so-called normal year like 1896, 1913, 1926, or 1939 is selected as a base, and prices of several hundred representative goods and services are collected

[9] From "Are Social Scientists Backward?" by Donald L. Kemmerer, in the *American Association of University Professors Bulletin*, Autumn, 1948.

for that year and allotted their proper importance or weight in figuring the index. The prices of these same goods and services are again collected and similarly weighted for each subsequent year. This is done every month now. These indexes have proved extremely useful to social scientists, and I do not want to underestimate their importance. They do have their limitations, however.

According to Bureau of Labor Statistics figures, the cost of living in December, 1947, was 136 per cent higher than it was in 1913. The comparison cannot be so accurate as that. For example, the quality of many of the manufactured goods involved in the 1913 index has improved greatly. Automobile tires cost about the same but will run five times as many miles before wearing out; also gasoline will carry the car farther; and, of course, the cars themselves are greatly improved. Transportation by car or train is faster, thereby saving valuable time; medical knowledge is better so that the average doctor's advice is worth more; fuel for heating homes is cleaner; and so on.

To take a more modern example of difficulties in using indexes, some of you may recall the Battle of the Indexes that raged in 1944. The government maintained that the cost of living had risen only about 23.1 per cent since January, 1941, and did not justify further wage increases, but the AFL and the CIO contended that 43.5 per cent was a more accurate measurement. That was a sizable difference of opinion. The labor statisticians emphasized that some important goods in the index were simply not available at OPA prices and could be obtained only on the black market. All of us had some experience with the poorer quality of numerous wartime goods and learned firsthand that items like white shirts or rented houses were virtually unobtainable at the ceiling prices on which the indexes were based. Under the circumstances, price indexes should be regarded as valuable trend indicators but should not be accepted as highly accurate measuring devices. When someone starts analyzing a price index to explain why it has risen, say 0.45 of 1 per cent, skepticism is in order. Yet it is by such accurate measurements that physical scientists reach significant conclusions.

3. The physical scientist can generally control the conditions surrounding his experiments, whereas the social scientist cannot. As my colleague, Professor Ralph Blodgett, has neatly described the situation, "The student of chemistry, for example, can place a quantity of iron filings in a test tube, cover them with a certain amount of hydrochloric acid under controlled conditions, and be fairly confident of being able to observe and measure the results accurately. The economist cannot place the consumer in a test tube, pour a solution of lowered prices over him, and measure the results. Instead, he must rely on his observations of the consumer in the ordinary business of life where he will react to lowered prices in some way or other, amid a welter of other influences."

Let us take the example of a specific economic experiment. In 1933–34 the government, on advice of certain economists, devalued the gold dollar by 41 per cent. It was expected by the authors of this scheme that it would shortly raise the price level by 69 per cent and thereby restore prices to the so-called normal level of 1926. The purpose was to lighten the debt burden of farmers and others. But the wholesale price level rose only about 21 per cent in the next two years, much less than the experimenters anticipated. Even this disappointing rise could not be definitely ascribed to any single cause. There was good reason for believing some of it was owing to severe droughts, some to the AAA program, some to price increases due to rising wage and other costs under the NRA, and some to normal recovery from the depths of the depression. How much of the price rise was due to each of these? Who can do more than make a rough guess?

4. At this point some thoughtful person may interject, "Ah, but you are asking too much to expect the full results of that experiment to be apparent in so short a time as two years." The objection is well taken. In fact, the matter of time is the fourth difficulty which the social scientists must attempt to solve and yet cannot solve very well. The longer time he allows for his experiment to work out, the more extraneous factors are likely to creep in; and the shorter the time he allows, the more open he is to the accusation that his experiment is incomplete. Yet as the country and the world become more populous and more industrialized, the longer it takes economic and other forces to make themselves felt. At the same time, if the experimenting social scientist is, say, a government economist trying out some plan he has sold the administration, he must be able to show results quickly, convincingly, and on the first try. Otherwise, his theory is tagged as a failure. Would the physical scientists like to make experiments under such conditions?

5. Another reason a government economist's experiment may fail is that people are necessarily the subject of the experiment; they know they are the subject, and they may want the experiment to succeed or to fail. In wartime, by economizing and working harder than usual to help win the war and combat inflation, they may successfully delay the operation of inflationary forces. Or people may sabotage an experiment because they dislike the political and economic philosophy behind it — many persons found the intricate regulations of NRA and OPA distasteful — or because the experiment hurts their pocketbook or the prestige they enjoy in their business, or both. The nature and purpose of any experiment cannot long be kept secret in a democracy. Increased pump-priming by the government in the latter 1930's seems to have made businessmen more distrustful. It slowed down the turnover of currency and the investment of risk capital and partially neutralized just what pump-priming was intended to achieve. As late as 1940 we still had considerable depression left if a figure of ten million unemployed means anything. Professor Joseph Schumpeter of Harvard went so far as to say about that time that recovery from depression had been slowest where the greatest efforts had been made by governments to promote it — in France and in the United States.

Let us take another example. There has been a fairly serious depression in every major nation after every long war in modern times. We have been expecting one almost daily since V-J day in August of 1945. Government economists were especially sure in 1945 that widespread unemployment would follow the war and urged the administration to lay its plans accordingly and the public to prepare for the worst. But the depression has not come yet. It is frequently said that when a depression does come, it will be the best advertised one in history. This may be one important reason that it does not come, or at least that it has been so long delayed. To sum up the situation: the physical scientist does not have to contend with iron filings that resist being dissolved or whose character may change because they expect to be dissolved.

Once you understand the social scientist's difficulties, you will have more patience with him. You will recognize that he can make few experiments, that even history offers him few clear-cut, documentable examples, and that he therefore has to supplement his findings with logic and intangible common sense. That is admittedly to depart from the realm of science and to invade that of judgment. It is at this point that the social scientist is most apt to make mistakes and that disagreements are most likely to arise. You should therefore be most skeptical when he relies on logic alone; yet at the same time you have to admit the necessity for his doing so.

In the past two generations few new principles have been established in the social sciences. This is contrary to the layman's beliefs, but it is true. If you doubt it, name some. True, many interesting theories have been advanced, but most of them have not been widely accepted. The reasons, it may be surmised, lie in the five difficulties just described, namely fewness of experiments, uncontrolled conditions, difficulties of measuring results, concluding experiments at the right time, and resistance by the subject of the experiment. Even if the social scientists eventually accept some of the new theories as principles, it will take many more years before the public and its leaders do likewise.

# 12

\*
\*  **THE ESSAY-TYPE**
\*
\*  **EXAMINATION**
\*

---

THE ESSAY-TYPE EXAMINATION is one of the most practical of all composition assignments. By requiring a student to compose in one or more paragraphs an answer to a specific problem, it calls forth most of the skills which the composition course tries to develop. It tests the student's ability to read accurately and to write purposefully within a rigid time limit. It is thus as much a test of thinking and writing ability as of knowledge.

Failure to recognize this fact usually leads to unsatisfactory answers and poor grades. Instructors frequently complain that the worst student writing is done on essay-type examinations. Of course the pressure under which examinations are written is not conducive to stylistic finish. But the chief weaknesses of examination answers is not that they are ungrammatical or awkward but that they are not *composed* at all. The student does not first plan what he wants to say and then develop his intention into an adequate answer; too often he begins to write without any clear purpose and assumes that as long as he is writing he is answering the question. The result is frequently an answer which is irrelevant, inadequate, unclear, and even self-contradictory.

The purpose of this chapter is to help students get better grades on essay-type examinations by sketching the procedure of taking such a test and by analyzing good and bad answers. This chapter, of course, cannot teach the content of examination answers. A student who does not know his subject will not learn here how to conceal his ignorance. But many of the serious errors in examination papers are caused by careless thinking and writing rather than by ignorance. It is with these faults that this chapter is concerned.

## Recommended Procedure

Listed below are ten recommendations for taking an essay-type examination. There is one other that may be considered a prerequisite for these ten: that is, that a satisfactory answer must first of all be legible. Anything that seriously interferes with ease of reading — careless or crowded handwriting, excessive scoring-out, failure to indicate which question is being answered, or penciled writing which is too faint to read — is bound to affect an instructor's evaluation of the answer. College instructors do not grade on neatness. An occasional erasure or revision between the lines is not objectionable. But an instructor who has difficulty deciphering your answer certainly cannot have a high opinion of it. Therefore, you owe it to yourself and your instructor to see that your paper is reasonably easy to read.

1. **Come Prepared.** The best preparation for an essay-type examination is conscientious attention to the daily assignments followed by a general review before the examination. This review should focus on the major emphases in the course. An essay-type examination is not suited to testing knowledge of a large number of details. Essentially it tests the student's ability to grasp main ideas, form generalizations of his own from the facts, and select and relate details to develop the generalization. It tests thinking, not simply memory. For this reason, a grasp of the major points is more useful than memorizing a host of isolated facts. Indeed, a student who attempts to prepare himself by cramming his mind with detailed information is likely to find himself in the state traditionally described as being unable to see the forest for the trees.

2. **Come Relaxed.** The essay-type examination requires more sustained concentration than does an objective test. A three-hour essay examination is a strenuous intellectual exercise. All things being equal, a student who is fresh and relaxed will do better work than one who is tired and tense; yet the practice of going short on sleep the night before a final examination in order to allow the time for a final review is still a traditional means of preparation. Such a practice is sometimes worse than useless, especially for a student who has a reasonable grasp of the course content. The final preparation for an essay-type examination should be eight hours of sleep.

3. **Before Beginning to Answer Any Part of the Examination, Read It Through, Paying Special Attention to the Directions.** If it serves no other purpose, this act will at least encourage a more deliberate attitude toward the examination. In their eagerness to start writing, some students ignore important directions or confuse the number of questions they are to answer. It is a wise discipline to survey any task before beginning it, and this habit is especially useful when some questions are marked as counting more toward the total grade than others.

4. **If You Are Given a Choice of Questions, Make Your Choice Carefully but Quickly, and Then Stick to It.** Procrastination steals confidence

as well as time. A student who shifts from one choice to another as soon as he strikes a snag is likely to have just as much trouble with his second choice. If any one of a choice of questions is definitely easier, that advantage should be obvious on first inspection.

**5. Determine How Much Time Is Available for Each Question.** This advice is often more necessary for good students than for poor ones. The student who knows the subject well and is eager to demonstrate his knowledge sometimes cannot resist the temptation to let himself go on the first questions and to write four pages where only one was expected. Such a student should remember that examination questions are not opportunities to write all that can be said on the topic; they are invitations to write the best answer possible within the time limit. Usually each question receives a prescribed number of points so that no more can be given no matter how thorough or brilliant the answer. Therefore it is not possible to pile up on some questions extra credit to be used on others. If you feel that you want to say more on a question than time permits, leave a space at the end of your answer. Then, if you have time to spare after finishing all questions, you can make additional comment.

**6. Read Each Question Carefully Before Starting to Answer It.** Unwillingness to heed this advice is probably the greatest single cause of failure. We shall see later in this chapter examples of answers that failed because their authors began to write before they had learned what the question required. You should recognize that if you misinterpret the question your whole answer may be off the point. For that reason it is wise to ask before you begin to write: "What does this question require me to do?" Notice, especially, whether the question asks you to *explain, summarize, evaluate,* or *compare.* These are often key words in an essay-type question and each of them requires a different approach to the answer. Failure to recognize the implications of such key words could cause you to misinterpret the question.

**7. Think Out Your General Answer Before You Begin to Develop It.** Since there is almost no opportunity for rewriting in an essay examination, your answer must be satisfactory as it is put on paper. If a student has the purpose or topic sentence of his answer clearly in mind, explanatory and illustrative details will suggest themselves as he writes. But a student who has not determined what he wants to say before he begins may fall into either of two errors: he may unconsciously veer away from the question or he may write a series of unrelated sentences which do not add up to a unified answer. On some questions, it may be advisable to jot down on the back of the blue book or the mimeographed examination sheet the information you want to work into your answer; on others, framing the topic sentence will be preparation enough.

**8. Remember That Nothing so Annoys a Grader as a Series of Unsupported, Unexplained Generalizations.** Next to irrelevance, vagueness is the chief sin of examination answers, and an answer which is too general is sure to be vague. So far as time permits, give the details which support your generalizations and, if possible, cite or suggest the textual sources for your observations. You will see this procedure repeatedly illustrated in the examination answers presented later.

**9. When You Have Finished Your Answer, Read It Over Critically to See if You Have Done What You Intended to Do.** Even though extensive revision is impracticable, this rereading may suggest specific changes or a comment or illustration which you can insert between the lines or in the margin. It will also give you a chance to correct any obvious errors in grammar, spelling, or punctuation.

**10. Above All, Remember That an Essay-type Question Requires an Essay-type Answer.** If your instructor wanted an answer that could be given in a single sentence, he could have saved himself both time and effort by setting up the question as a completion-type or short-answer question.

### Basic Errors

Given below are contrasted answers to a question on selected poems of Wordsworth and Byron in a sophomore examination in English literature. The students had one hour in which to develop a paragraph for each of the five parts of the question. The answers given on the left are those which the instructor hoped to receive; those on the right are unsatisfactory ones, taken from actual papers. Here is the question:

How do Wordsworth and Byron compare with respect to
A. Their choice of subjects
B. Their attitudes toward their subjects
C. Their appreciation of nature
D. Their attitudes toward the culture of their times
E. Their attitudes toward the French Revolution and Napoleon?

Here are the answers:

### A

*Choice of subjects.* Wordsworth chose as the subjects of his poetry incidents and experiences drawn from rustic life, whether they occurred to himself (*Prelude*) or to others (*Michael*). In general these incidents are undramatic but owe their interest to the poet's treatment of them. Byron preferred dramatic events —

Wordsworth chose incidents and situations from common, rustic life. Byron wrote descriptions of nature, and of his ridicule of sham and his keen insight into the hearts of men. He often wrote of one man and of his many escapades and trials.

COMMENT: The answer lacks spe-

legends of ill-fated lovers (*Bride of Abydos*), the exploits of amorous adventurers (*Don Juan*), or accounts of the travels and reflections of his autobiographical hero, Childe Harold.

cific illustration. It does not identify a single poem by either poet, and the contrast is too general to provide a clear answer to the question. As a result, the student seems to have only a hazy knowledge of the poetry; yet on an objective quiz over the poems mentioned at the left he showed that he was familiar with them.

## B

*Attitudes toward their subjects.* In general Wordsworth adopted a serious, sympathetic, and dignified attitude toward his subjects. He tended to idealize his rustic heroes (*Michael, The Leechgatherer, The Solitary Reaper*) and to see poetic and universal implications in common incidents and people (*My Heart Leaps Up, The Ode*). Byron's attitude varies with his subject. He is sympathetic with the victims of oppression (*The Prisoner of Chillon*), satirical with contemporary writers (*English Bards*) and with social mores (*Don Juan*), and in *Don Juan* he is serious, indignant, satirical, and flippant in different parts of the poem.

Wordsworth generally dealt with humble rustic people because he felt that the character and language of such people were suited to poetry. Byron seldom wrote of humble people. He usually dealt with romantic episodes in the life of one individual. A great deal of his poetry is about himself.

COMMENT: This answer was written by the same student who answered A above. Clearly, he is still answering the previous question. His failure to distinguish between related but separate questions causes him to repeat. He simply has not read the question intelligently.

## C

*Their appreciation of nature.* Both men appreciated nature, but Wordsworth's reactions were more intense. Byron was interested chiefly in impressive or dramatic scenery — the ocean and the mountains. For him the beauty of such scenes was an antidote for world weariness (*Childe Harold*) or a contrast between the insignificance of man and the power of nature ("Roll on thou deep and dark blue ocean"). For Wordsworth, nature is the embodiment of the mystic power which pervades all living things. It not only pleases and refreshes him; it dominates him and becomes his intellectual and moral guide (*Tintern Abbey, The Tables*

Wordsworth says that you will learn more from nature than from all the teachers and books. This was stated in *The Tables Turned*. In *Lines Written in Early Spring* he states that nature has made everything beautiful and in the *Prelude* he tells of his love of nature. Byron's appreciation was less sensitive. He presented nature as he saw it, usually with pictorial realism.

COMMENT: The answer on Wordsworth is not general enough. It cites two pieces of evidence but draws no conclusion. The answer on Byron is too general and vague. The examiner will have to guess what the last

*Turned*). His reactions are essentially religious rather than esthetic.

sentence means. The whole answer shows a paragraph being written one sentence at a time without concern for the relation between sentences. The student has not thought out his answer before beginning to write. So he fails to present a clear-cut contrast.

## D

*Their attitudes toward the culture of their times.* Both condemn their culture, but for different reasons. Wordsworth condemns the materialism and lack of mystery (*The World Is Too Much With Us*); he regrets the indifference to cultural values (Cambridge in the *Prelude*); and he misses the free, dignified, and disciplined spirit which he thought existed in Milton's time. Byron condemns the hypocrisy of social life, the smug and dull standard of virtue represented by Southey, polite education (as represented by the education of Don Juan), and the political autocracy which he found dominant in Britain, France, and Greece (*Childe Harold*).

Wordsworth regarded the culture of his time as superficial. His attitude was that the literature of his time placed too much emphasis on sensational incidents and situations and thus encouraged an artificial culture. Byron regarded the other literary products of his time as being far below the level of his own works. He illustrates this by his denunciation of the work of contemporary poets.

COMMENT: This student has interpreted the question too narrowly. His answer would be much more satisfactory if the question had been confined to literature, but it was not. His answer is incomplete.

## E

*Their attitudes toward the French Revolution and Napoleon.* Both men at first welcomed the French Revolution and the rise of Napoleon; both later turned against them. Wordsworth changed first. He was ready at one time to throw in his lot with the revolutionists (*Prelude*) but their excesses and a conservative inclination made him increasingly unsympathetic. Byron seems to have been less shocked by the terror of the revolution and more shocked by the apostasy of Napoleon. His attack on Napoleon in *Childe Harold* is bitter, all the more bitter because of Byron's appreciation of what Napoleon might have done for Europe.

Wordsworth was opposed to the French Revolution and to Napoleon's tyranny; Byron first admired Napoleon but later denounced him.

COMMENT: While this answer is correct, it is inadequate because the student fails to develop it. It is merely the topic sentence of a satisfactory answer. What the examiner still wants to know is why Wordsworth was opposed, and where he recorded his opposition; and why Byron admired Napoleon and where he denounced him. Since the student had more than ten minutes in which to develop his answer, a single sentence is not enough.

Now here is an important point to notice about all the answers at the right. The students who wrote them were not ignorant of the subject. Most of them, under questioning, could show in class discussion that they knew the poems. They did poorly on the examination because their procedures were bad. Two of the five answers were unsatisfactory because their authors failed to read the question carefully to see what it required. The other three answers were so general that they failed to develop clearly or convincingly the contrast which the question required. In other words, the answers were poor because they were badly composed.

By contrast, the answers at the left are pertinent, adequate, and well illustrated. They do the job required and avoid digressions or irrelevant details. They develop the general answer in enough detail to point the contrast so that it will be clear to a reader. And they illustrate their points by naming particular poems.

A subtler error, one that often separates an average answer from a superior one, is failure to bring the answer to a focus. The student discusses the question but does not quite answer it. He provides a substantial body of factual material, but his facts are not exactly pertinent. Consider, for example, the following contrasted answers to the question: "Illustrate the differences between early and late Renaissance painting by contrasting Fra Filippo Lippi's *Madonna and Child* with Raphael's *Sistine Madonna*."

### C Answer

Filippo's picture is simply designed, and the figures are naturalistic. The Madonna is sweet, gracious, and human, dressed in the mode of the times. The Bambino is a natural, playful child. He is being lifted up by two older boys — undoubtedly Fra Filippo's family posed for the picture. The background is a stylized landscape of rocks and streams, bounded by a frame. The Madonna is seated in a chair with an elaborately carved arm which stands out in the foreground.

Raphael designed the Sistine Madonna in a pyramid with the Madonna herself at the apex. She carries the curly-haired Child, and although she is standing still, her garments swirl as in a strong wind. One's eye is first caught by the figure of Pope Sixtus at the lower

### A Answer

Fra Filippo's picture is a good example of early Renaissance naturalism. The Madonna — his own wife — is wearing a stylish gown, which is painted in faithful detail. Her hair is dressed in the mode of the time. She is seated — as though in her own home — on an elaborately carved chair, with a framed painting of a landscape serving as the background. Her pose and expression are calm, perhaps devout, but neither exalted nor humble. She is an ordinary worldly mother with a chubby baby, who is being lifted to her rather ungracefully by a saucy angel. The entire scene is intimate, personal, and joyous, but hardly reverent. Filippo, pleased with the new-found technical mastery of his age, is content to paint what he sees.

Raphael was able to get above his

left, and through the folds of his garment and his uplifted eyes, drawn toward the central figure of the Virgin. Her garments, billowing to the right, draw the eye downward again to the figure of St. Barbara, kneeling on a cloud. Her eyes are cast down, and the glance follows hers to discover two jaunty cherubs leaning on the lower frame. They look upward, thus deflecting the eyes of the beholder up again, completing the movement of the design. This painting is one of the high points of the development of Renaissance art.

technique and make it expressive of lofty emotion. The figures in the *Sistine Madonna* are monumental and stand out against a subdued background. The Madonna, her feet resting weightlessly on a cloud, wears an expression of sublime dignity. She holds with graceful ease the Child, whose sober eyes reveal the portent of His future. The figures wear classic robes, whose flowing lines give a wonderful, circling movement to the painting. A cloud of tiny cherubs' heads, peeping through the effulgence surrounding the Virgin, completes the heavenly setting. Where Filippo's work is mere copying, Raphael's is imaginative and spiritual. This loftiness of conception combined with grace of design and beauty of execution is the flower of the High Renaissance.

What is the difference between these two answers? Why did one receive an average, and the other an excellent grade? Both are roughly the same length; both are well written; both show an intimate knowledge of the pictures they are contrasting. The difference is essentially one of the selection of details. The answer at the left is unsatisfactory because it drifted away from the question. What the student actually wrote was a description of the *Madonna and Child* and another description of the *Sistine Madonna*. The details she presents describe the pictures effectively, but they do not contrast the differences between early and late Renaissance painting. Therefore her answer does not satisfy the question. The answer at the right selects those details which illustrate the differences between the two periods, and thus gives purpose to the contrast between the pictures. The author is not merely describing two pictures; she is describing the characteristics which make them represent their periods. That is what the question required.

All the errors we have been considering are of three general kinds: (1) failure to read the question carefully enough to see what it required; (2) failure to provide the detailed treatment necessary for an adequate answer; (3) failure to point up the significance of factual information. The first error is a failure to analyze the assignment and is therefore a basic error in determining its purpose, not unlike the purposeless essay we saw on page 4. The other two are errors in composition, failures to see how the writer must go about the task which the assignment requires of him.

## Exercises

**A.** Read the following imaginary case history and write an analysis of John's errors.

John Doe wanted to do a good job in his examination on English literature. He just had to get a C in the course or he would be ineligible for initiation into his fraternity. True, his grade at midsemester had been D, and most of the semester he had known that he had been slighting his work. But he had really studied hard the last two weeks. When he went to bed at two o'clock on the morning of the examination, he was, as he told his roommate, all set for anything old Jonesy could throw at him. But, just to be safe, he set the alarm an hour early and got in a good hour's cramming before examination time. Indeed, he studied longer than he meant to, and though he ran all the way to class, he arrived, out of breath, after the test had begun. He sat down, puffing, sticky, and a little embarrassed.

As soon as he received his copy of the examination he read the first question hastily and began to write. After a few minutes he had an uncomfortable feeling that his answer was getting off the track; so he crossed it out and began over again. His new answer started out confidently, but after three sentences he felt he had said all he had to say on the question. But this was an essay-type test. The directions said "Write at least a paragraph." John restated in different words what he had already said and was relieved to find that his answer now looked like a normal paragraph.

The second question was a pure gift. It dealt with the one part of the course that John knew thoroughly. He had been hoping this question would be asked, and here it was. What a break! He wrote with unusual intensity. From the very first sentence he knew he was writing well. No need to worry about stretching this answer into a paragraph. Of its own accord it grew into a page, then two pages. Midway on the third page John finished, tired but glowing. He re-read his answer with scarcely-decreased enthusiasm. He changed a couple of words and added a clinching sentence which suddenly occurred to him. That made it just about perfect.

He began the third question with a new sense of confidence, but his pen ran dry. He looked around anxiously and finally observed a student three rows away with a bottle of ink on his desk. He was embarrassed at having to disturb several people to fill his pen, and when he returned to his seat his confident mood had disappeared. In an attempt to recapture it he re-read the last page of his second answer, but that did not help, except to catch a couple of misspellings. Mechanically he ground out an answer to question three, hoping the instructor would see what he had in mind.

The fourth question was a difficult one. John started a tentative answer and stopped. The directions said he was to write on six of the eight questions. He would skip four and do five. Unfortunately, the fifth question was as bad as the fourth. After a few preliminary passes at it, John scored out his answer and moved to number six. As he did so, the instructor announced that only ten minutes remained.

For a moment the announcement threw John into a panic. Ten minutes in which to do three questions! He read the remaining questions hurriedly, looking for an easy one; then he went back to question four and wrote whatever came into his head. There was no time now to worry whether the answer was completely satisfactory. The thing to do was to get an answer of any kind. He was perspiring when he moved to question six, but his resolution to put down some kind of answer helped him through. He wrote a fair-sized paragraph before the bell rang. Then, while the papers were being collected, he managed to make a one-sentence stab at question seven.

John left the examination room somewhat shaken in his assurance of getting a C. But the memory of his answer to the second question revived him. And, after all, he had answered all six questions. Even if his last answer was short he would get partial credit for it. On the way to the fraternity house he was enjoying the probability of a B.

**B.** Below are three questions from a final examination in hygiene, and selected student answers. Write a short evaluation of each answer.

Question 1. If someone were now to ask you, "What is good mental hygiene and why is it important?" what answer would you give to help him understand?

*Answer A:* I would say that good mental hygiene is the study wherein we come to know ourselves, our attitudes, the reasons why we react to conditions as we do, and the patterns of our conduct in general. Mental hygiene is important because, if we can recognize the things wrong with our attitudes and personalities, we can work to improve ourselves and thus make ourselves better citizens and better people to live with. Upon recognizing our faults we come to see that everyone has peculiarities, and we can better accept people as they are without criticizing them. It is essential for people to know how to get along with each other. The best way to understand others is to begin understanding yourself.

*Answer B:* Good mental hygiene is the ability to live with people in a clean and happy way. A sufficient knowledge of body care as well as mental care. Knowledge to use one's mind (control it) for the betterment of oneself and those surrounding him.

Question 2. In the film, *Learning and Growth*, the narrator states that "Experience is a good teacher only when you are ready for it." In what way does the film illustrate that statement?

*Answer A:* The film illustrated experience as a good teacher in the case of the baby. When they first gave the baby a toy, he did not know what to do with it. But as he played with it for a while, he began to get familiar with it and see the different things he could do with it. As time went on he knew just what to do with it and how to go about it.

*Answer B:* The narrator in the film explained that the child, though repeatedly shown how to do various little tasks, did not possess nerves and a brain sufficiently developed to comprehend his teacher's actions and instructions. Likewise, though the child was put on his feet and helped to stand, his bones and muscles were not strong enough to make use of the help he was given. He was not ready for the experience of standing or walking.

Question 3. Jane is a sophomore pre-medical student. She has flunked Chemistry and is to be dropped from her pre-med status. She may react in one of these ways:

  a. She may spend the next few weeks complaining that "the instructor was no good; how could I pass?

  b. She may tell everyone that she didn't really want to be a doctor anyway.

  c. She may quit school and return home.

  d. She may say that she just didn't study hard enough and re-register for the course.

Select one of these adjustments, explain what type of adjustment it is, and point out what alternative method she might better have used to solve her problem.

*Answer A:* She may spend the next few weeks blaming the instructor. Such an adjustment will be one of defense. Jane, faced with a situation which exposes her own inefficiency, will defend herself by transferring the blame to someone else. Unfortunately for her, the defense will not prove satisfactory. Jane and others will recognize that under the same conditions other students passed the course. This recognition will force Jane to be more emphatic about the instructor's shortcomings, and the more emphatic she becomes the more obvious it will be to everyone, including herself, that she is creating a scapegoat for her own failure.

A more mature adjustment would be to analyze the failure to find what she had done that was wrong. If she simply has not done enough work in the course, if her methods of studying are poor, if she has little aptitude for chemistry, any one of these factors could explain her failure, and it would be useful for her to know and admit the real cause. Only when she has identified the cause can she know what to do next. If she has no aptitude for medical studies she should change her program. If she has not applied herself or has not worked efficiently she should reform her habits and retake the course.

*Answer B:* She may spend the next few weeks complaining that "the instructor was no good; how could I pass?" Adjustment by defense — alternative might have been (d). She may say that she just didn't study hard enough and re-register for the course.

**C.** Write an analysis of your own procedure in preparing for and taking an essay-type examination. Be as objective as possible. If you have recently taken an essay examination study the answers you submitted and include your judgments of them in the analysis.

**D.** For each of the courses you are now taking write a series of essay-type questions which seem to you to constitute a fair examination for these courses. Word the questions carefully so that a good answer will show both a knowledge of the facts and an ability to draw valid conclusions from them. Discuss your questions with friends or classmates and plan satisfactory answers. Then develop your plan into a finished answer which may be filed as review material for those courses.

# 13

DURING your college years your assignments in all courses will require you to make frequent use of your college library. You will use it more efficiently and with more confidence if, as early as possible, you make yourself familiar with the location of materials you are likely to use frequently. The most important sources for the information you will need are the card catalog, standard reference works, periodicals, and periodical indexes. Most of your library work will be easier if you become acquainted with these sources early in the first semester.

### The Card Catalog

The card catalog is a register of all the books in the library. As each book is purchased, it is "classified."[1] That is, it is given a "call number" which identifies its place in the total library collection. That call number, along with all other pertinent information, is put on a 3 by 5 inch card, and the card is filed alphabetically in one of the series of trays which make up the catalog.

As far as you are concerned, the card catalog is the most important unit in the library. With a few exceptions you will have to consult it for

[1] A general knowledge of the Dewey Decimal Classification, the most popular system of classifying books, will be useful to any student who does considerable library work. That system classifies books according to the following scheme:

| | | | |
|---|---|---|---|
| 000–099 | General Works | 600–699 | Applied Sciences |
| 100–199 | Philosophy and Psychology | 700–799 | Fine Arts and Recreation |
| 200–299 | Religion | 800–899 | Literature |
| 300–399 | Social Sciences | F | Fiction in English |
| 400–499 | Langauges | 900–999 | History, Travel, Collected |
| 500–599 | Pure Sciences | | Biography |
| | | B | Individual Biography |

While it is not necessary for you to know the complete classification, it would be useful to memorize the numbers of particular classes in which your major subjects lie. This is particularly true in those libraries in which students are permitted to go directly to the stacks.

every book you want to withdraw. Unless you learn to use it easily, you will waste time and often fail to get the books you want.

A single tray in the card catalog looks like this:

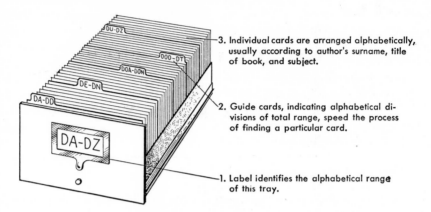

3. Individual cards are arranged alphabetically, usually according to author's surname, title of book, and subject.

2. Guide cards, indicating alphabetical divisions of total range, speed the process of finding a particular card.

1. Label identifies the alphabetical range of this tray.

The catalog contains five kinds of cards:

1. Author cards, a listing according to the author's surname.

2. Title cards, a listing according to the first significant word in the title.

3. Subject cards, a listing according to the subject of the book.

4. Cross-reference cards which refer the reader to other headings under which information may be found.

5. Analytic cards, which analyze a book into its parts and list the parts separately.

A typical author card looks like this:

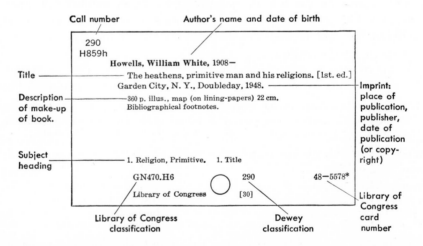

Call number

Author's name and date of birth

```
290
H859h
        Howells, William White, 1908—
          The heathens, primitive man and his religions. [1st. ed.]
        Garden City, N. Y., Doubleday, 1948.
          360 p. illus., map (on lining-papers) 22 cm.
          Bibliographical footnotes.

          1. Religion, Primitive.   1. Title
        GN470.H6                    290
          Library of Congress       [30]        48—5578*
```

Title

Description of make-up of book.

Subject heading

Imprint: place of publication, publisher, date of publication (or copyright)

Library of Congress card number

Library of Congress classification

Dewey classification

Three items of information are of primary importance: the call number, the author's name, and the title. These are the items which you will probably be required to write on the withdrawal slip with which you order the book.

**The Call Number.** In most libraries the call number alone would be sufficient information to allow the librarian to find a required book quickly. Unless the Library of Congress system is being used [2] a call number consists of two lines of figures. The first line is the Dewey classification number, which places the book in its proper class and, therefore, identifies its general location. The second line is the *book number* and consists of the first letter of the author's surname followed by figures which identify the specific location of the book within its class location. In our example, then, the call number will be translated by the librarian as follows:

> 290 (Dewey classification for non-Christian religions)
> H (Surname of author starts with H)
> 859 (Cutter number identifying book within 290 H group)
> h (first letter of first significant word in title, to help distinguish this work from work by same author on similar subject)

Since librarians generally work with call numbers rather than with the names of authors and titles, it is necessary to copy the call number carefully. For example, miscopying the first number as a 5 might send the librarian to the shelf containing books on zoology. If a call line contains a third line or an added abbreviation, copy the whole call number.

**Title and Subject Cards.** Usually, a title or subject card is merely an author card with the title or subject typed above the author's name. Thus the first lines of title and subject cards for the example above would be

> Title card      The heathens, primitive man and his religions.
> Subject card    Religion, primitive (typed in red).

The rest of these cards would be similar to the author card shown above.

When you approach the card catalog with no particular title or author's name in mind but only the subject you wish to investigate, you must begin with subject cards. The more specifically you can identify your subject, the easier your task will be. For example, if you are looking for information about the formation of the Republican Party,

---

[2] In large libraries the Library of Congress classification is often preferred to the Dewey Decimal System, although the latter is generally more popular. In the example given above, GN is the class number, 470 the book number, and H6 the author number. If your library uses the Library of Congress classification, study that system in M. T. Eaton and C. M. Louttit, *A Handbook of Library Usage*, or any similar handbook.

looking for it under "History" would waste time. Begin with "Republican." If you do not find what you want under that heading, try "Political Parties." As you go through the cards on any subject, notice cross references. *See* cards refer you to other common names for the same subject, as "soccer" for "association football." *See also* cards, placed at the end of a subject, refer you to other subjects under which you may find additional information. For example, at the end of the cards on "atomic energy" you may be advised to *See also* "nuclear energy."

**Special Details of Arrangement.** The following points are worth remembering in using the card catalog:

1. When books *by* a writer are listed with those *about* him, the books *by* him are listed first.

2. Abbreviations are listed as though they were written in full. Thus *Mr., Dr., St.,* and *U.S.* are listed as though they were Mister, Doctor, Saint, and United States. Notice, especially, that *Mac, Mc,* and *M',* are listed as though they were *Mac.* Numbers are listed as though they were written out — that is, 50 = Fifty. Thus numbers are filed alphabetically, not numerically ("forty" before "thirty").

3. Prefixes in foreign names (*de, von,* etc.) are not listed as part of the surname. *Paul von Hindenburg* is listed as *Hindenburg, Paul von.*

4. Alphabetizing usually follows the rule of "short before long," which means that a heading with a short word comes before a heading with a longer form or compound as illustrated below:

| | |
|---|---|
| black | blackmail |
| black and tan | blackmail and robbery |
| black and white | blackmailer |
| blackboard | blacksmith |

5. Within like subdivisions of a subject the arrangement is usually alphabetical, but subdivisions of history are arranged chronologically:

| | |
|---|---|
| Dancing | U.S. — History |
| Dancing — Ballet | U.S. — History — Colonial |
| Dancing — Ballroom | U.S. — History — Revolution |
| Dancing — Folk | U.S. — History — Confederacy |
| Dancing — Gymnastic | U.S. — History — Civil War |

6. Titles are listed alphabetically according to the first significant word. Thus, articles (*a, an, the*) and their foreign equivalents are ignored.

## Printed Catalogs

Printed catalogs (in book form) are often useful supplements to the card catalog. Your card catalog is a list of the books in your library, not of all books available. Printed catalogs may give you the titles of other books, quote the price of books you may wish to buy, allow you more easily to compile a bibliography of books on a particular subject, and sometimes provide a *selected* list of books on a subject. The following printed catalogs are standard references and are probably available in your library:

*Books in Print.* Index to *Publisher's Trade List Annual* (see below). Listed by author and title. Gives publisher and price of each book listed.

*Children's Catalog.* Selected list of 4,200 books for children. Published every five years, with annual cumulative supplements.

*Cumulative Book Index.* Index of all books published in English, except government publications. Listed by author, subject, and title. Available in monthly issues, also in annual and five-year cumulative volumes known as the *United States Catalog.*

*Fiction Catalog,* 1941, with cumulative annual supplements. Listed by authors, with subject index. Descriptive note for each entry. Best books are starred; those suitable for young people marked *y.*

*Publisher's Trade List Annual.* A collection of publisher's catalogs, arranged alphabetically by names of publishers. Useful for checking to see if a book is still in print, its present price, and address of publisher from whom to order.

*Standard Catalog for Public Libraries.* List of adult non-fiction books, arranged according to library classification, with index. This catalog, the catalogs of fiction and children's books cited above, and a fourth catalog for high school libraries, comprise a series known as *The Standard Catalog Series.*

*U.S. Catalog.* Annual and five-year volumes of *Cumulative Book Index* cited above. Only American listings given. Fourth edition, 1928, has been supplemented by *Cumulative Book Index.*

*Vertical File Service Catalog.* Subject-index to current pamphlets, with descriptive notes. Annual volumes, with monthly supplements.

In addition to these general catalogs, your library probably contains many specialized printed catalogs. You can obtain the titles of these by consulting the librarian.

## *Reference Works*

Your work on research papers, term papers, and collateral reading assignments for advanced courses will require you to make frequent use of the Reference Room. This is the heart of the library, and it would be worth your while to make a preliminary survey of the works it contains and to memorize the location of the most useful ones. You will not be allowed to take reference books out of the library. But you are at liberty to consult them, and should, as a general habit, turn to them first in any serious study.

It is not possible here to list all the major reference books available in most college libraries. The list that follows is restricted to those fields in which students are generally most interested. If your assignments or interests lead you into other fields, consult Winchell's *Guide to Reference Books* (1951 and supplement) or ask a librarian about the best sources in your field.

### Indexes to Periodical Literature

Periodicals are publications other than newspapers which appear at regular intervals — weekly, monthly, quarterly, and so on. Since much of your reading, especially in advanced courses, will be based on magazine articles, and since these articles are not listed in card or printed catalogs, it will be necessary for you to use indexes to periodical literature. The most important of these are listed below, under the headings of *General* and *Specialized*. A specialized index lists only articles in magazines in the field to which it is confined — engineering, law, and so on. A general index is not restricted in subject matter, though it usually excludes highly specialized or technical material. The most useful general index is *The Reader's Guide to Periodical Literature*, which will be available in your library in annual volumes, with semi-monthly supplements for the current year.

In using any of these indexes, first consult the explanatory material at the front of the volume. There you will find a list of the periodicals cited, thus: *Am City* (*American City*), *Am Econ R* (*American Economic Review*), *Am Hist R* (*American Historical Review*), *Am Home* (*American Home*). You will also find a key to the abbreviations used in the volume. Since every index makes extensive use of abbreviations, this key will be invaluable.

In general, entries in an index to periodical literature are listed alphabetically according to subject matter. Occasionally, as the following excerpt from the *Reader's Guide* shows, particular entries are also listed according to author or title, but the last two entries are more common than the first two.

ABERNETHY, Edgar
    Dogwood winter; poem. Sat Eve Post 219:73 Ap 5 '47

Author listing — author, title, and source of poem.

ABIE'S Irish Rose; drama. See Nichols, A.

Title listing, with cross-reference to author.

ABILENE, Kansas
    Little Ike's home town. J. A. Arndt, C S Mon Mag p 4 My 19 '45

Subject listing. For identification of magazine, see List of Periodicals at beginning of volume.

ABILITY
Inequalities in adult capacity, from military data. W. V. Bingham. bibliog Science 104:147–52 Ag 16 '46; Same abr. Science N L 50:134 Ag 31 '46

Same article published in two periodicals. Original article in first source, abridgement in second.

Limitation of creative years; reply to H. C. Lehman. J. Bjorksten. Sci Mo 62:94 Ja '46

62:94 Ja '46 = volume 62, page 94, January issue, 1946.

*See also*
Efficiency          Musical ability
Great men          Talent
Mechanical ability

Cross-reference to related subjects and specialized abilities.

Since the abbreviated titles used in an index are not conventional in a formal bibliography, it is good practice to expand the magazine title in copying the reference. Thus you should write *Sat Eve Post* as *Saturday Evening Post, Science NL* as *Science News Letter,* and *Sci Mo* as *Scientific Monthly.* If your library requires a withdrawal slip (call slip) for magazines, you will be expected to put the full title on that slip anyway. Remember that index abbreviations are not always self-evident when removed from the explanatory List of Periodicals at the front of the index.

## General Indexes

*International Index to Periodical Literature,* 1907——. In general, confined to the more scholarly magazines in English and foreign languages. Most valuable for serious articles in science and humanities.

*Poole's Index to Periodical Literature,* 1802–1906. First of the magazine indexes and the only one listing articles published before 1890; therefore it should be used to complement *Reader's Guide.* Arranged alphabetically by subject only, except that titles are listed for plays, poems, and stories.

*The Reader's Guide to Periodical Literature,* 1900——. See above.

## Specialized Indexes

The selected indexes below are presented in alphabetical order according to subject fields.

*Agricultural Index,* 1916——. Lists books, magazine articles, pamphlets, and reports dealing with agriculture. Available in annual volumes, with monthly supplements for current year. Listing is by subject, but full index is appended in annual volumes.

*Art Index,* 1929——. Best reference to magazine articles on fine arts and to museum bulletins. Listing by author and subject.

*Book Review Digest,* 1905——. Digests, with excerpts, book reviews on general subjects. Arranged alphabetically by author of book, with subject and title index appended. To use, first find date of book being reviewed, then check author and subject index for that year and the year following. Annual volumes and monthly supplement.

*Debate Index,* 1939————. Subject index of debated questions.

*Dramatic Index,* 1909–1933. Best index of books and articles on the theater, actors, plays, playwrights, and related subjects. Arranged by subject. Since 1933 similar materials available in the Bulletin of *Bibliography.*

*Education Index,* 1929————. Best index of books and articles on education and educational psychology. Listed by author and subject.

*Engineering Index,* 1906————. Lists articles in English and foreign engineering journals and transactions of technical societies. Arranged, since 1919, according to subject, with author index. Before 1919, arranged by subject classes — civil engineering, electrical engineering, mechanical engineering, etc.

*Facts on File,* 1940————. Weekly digest of world events. Available in libraries in annual volumes, with supplements for current year. Arranged by subject divisions.

*Index to Legal Periodicals,* 1908————. Authoritative list of articles in legal journals.

*Index Medicus,* 1879–1926, and *Quarterly Cumulative Index Medicus,* 1927————. Together these indexes, both arranged by author and subject, constitute a bibliography of significant articles on medicine appearing in English and foreign languages.

*Industrial Arts Index,* 1913————. Lists books, magazine articles, and pamphlets on chemistry, commerce, engineering, geology, and physics. Arranged by subject.

*Psychological Abstracts,* 1927————. Contains summaries of current literature on psychology, with subject and author index to publications. Replaces *Psychological Index.*

*Psychological Index,* 1894–1933. An index of the literature of psychology and related subjects in all languages. Arranged according to classified subjects, with author index appended. Since 1933 material available in *Psychological Abstracts.*

*Public Affairs Information Service,* 1915————. Subject index of books, articles, and pamphlets on economics, political science, and sociology. Available in annual volumes, with weekly supplements for current year.

## Other Indexes

*The New York Times* is indexed from 1913 and the London *Times* from 1903. *The New York Times Index* may be available in your library in annual volumes, with monthly supplements for the current year. Since news is usually published in all papers at about the same time, a story may be checked in any paper by first finding when it appeared in *The New York Times* and then consulting the same issue of the paper you are concerned with. Thus *The New York Times Index* can serve as a substitute index for any paper.

The *Document Catalogue* is an index of all government publications from 1893 to 1940. All documents are listed under author and subject, sometimes under title also. For government publications after 1940, the best source is the *Monthly Catalogue,* which is available in annual volumes, with monthly supplements for the current year.

### Yearbooks

Yearbooks are annual publications which digest the year's activities. The following list includes the most generally used yearbooks:

*Britannica Book of the Year.* Annual supplement to *Encyclopaedia Britannica.* Arranged alphabetically by subject, like the *Britannica,* with detailed index.

*Congressional Directory.* Best source of information about Congress, its members, committees, functions, etc. In using, check subjects against alphabetical list of contents; check persons in appended *Individual Index.*

*Information Please Almanac.* A useful source of miscellaneous information. Similar to *World Almanac* below. Either of these inexpensive volumes would be a useful addition to a student's personal library.

*New International Year Book.* Annual supplement to *New International Encyclopedia.* Provides review of major international developments during the year.

*Statesman's Yearbook.* Best general reference for information about government activities in all countries, including such related topics as agriculture, commerce, defense, production, and so on. Fully indexed.

*Statistical Abstract of the United States.* Best source for official statistics on any aspect of American life. Fully indexed.

*Who's Who.* Authoritative, highly-condensed biographies of famous living men and women. Published annually in England. Emphasis is on British citizens. Alphabetically arranged.

*Who's Who in America.* Published every two years; otherwise, the American counterpart of *Who's Who.*

*Who's Who in —.* Many special fields have their own *Who's Who* — for example, *Who's Who in Art, Who's Who in Education.* Whatever such works your library has will be recorded in the card catalog. Check cards following *Who's Who.*

*World Almanac.* A comprehensive source of miscellaneous information. Its general usefulness and low cost justify its purchase as a private reference work. Detailed index in *front* of each volume.

## Dictionaries, Encyclopedias, and Other Reference Works

The following reference works are classified as *General* or *Specialized* on the same basis as the general and specialized indexes listed earlier.

### General

General dictionaries are listed on page 203. Specialized dictionaries and encyclopedias will be given below in their respective subject-fields. The four best-known general encyclopedias are:

*Columbia Encyclopedia,* 1950. A good one-volume reference.
*Encyclopedia Americana,* 30 volumes. Supplemented by *Americana Annual.*
*Encyclopaedia Britannica,* 14th ed., 24 volumes. Supplemented by *Britannica Book of the Year.* For articles on the humanities, the 11th edition enjoys a high reputation.
*New International Encyclopaedia,* 27 volumes, 1922–30. Supplemented by *New International Year Book.*

## Specialized

### Art

Adeline, J. *Art Dictionary,* 1910. A comprehensive dictionary of terms used in fields of art.
Architectural Publishing Society. *Dictionary of Architecture,* 1852–92, 6 vols.
Fielding, M. *Dictionary of American Painters, Sculptors, and Engravers,* 1926.
*Harper's Encyclopedia of Art,* 1937, 2 vols.

### Biography

*Current Biography,* 1940——. Sketches of contemporary celebrities.
*Dictionary of American Biography,* 1928–37, 20 vols. and index. The standard reference work on American biography. Does not list living persons.
*Dictionary of National Biography,* 1912–1921, 22 vols. and supplements. The standard reference on British biography. Also condensed as one-volume *Concise Dictionary of National Biography.* Does not list living persons.
*Webster's Biographical Dictionary,* 1st ed., 1943, and later printings. Contains 40,000 short notices of people of all countries and times. Gives pronunciations of names.
*Who's Who,* etc. See page 269.

### Education

American Council on Education. *American Universities and Colleges,* 6th ed., 1952.
Baird, W. R. *Baird's Manual.* 14th ed., 1949. A standard reference on American college fraternities.
*Education Index.* See page 268.
Monroe, P. (ed.). *Cyclopedia of Education,* 1911–13, 5 vols.
Monroe, W. S. *Encyclopedia of Educational Research,* 1950.
Watson, F. *Encyclopedia and Dictionary of Education,* 1921–22, 4 vols.

### Engineering

*Engineering Encyclopedia* (condensed), 1943, 2 vols.
*Engineering Index.* See page 268.

Glazebrook, Sir R. *Dictionary of Applied Physics*, 1922–23, 5 vols.

*Industrial Arts Index.* See page 268.

Tweney, C. F. and I. P. Shirslov. *Hutchinson's Technical and Scientific Encyclopedia*, 1935–36, 4 vols.

## History

Adams, J. T. and R. V. Coleman. *Atlas of American History*, 1943. 147 maps, indexed.

*Cambridge Histories (Ancient,* 10 vols.; *Medieval,* 7 vols.; *Modern,* 13 vols.). Excellent bibliographies, tables, and indexes.

Channing, E., A. B. Hart, and F. J. Turner. *Guide to Study and Reading of American History*, 1912.

*Dictionary of American History*, 1942, 5 vols. and index.

Dutcher, G. M. and others. *Guide to Historical Literature*, 1949.

*Encyclopedia of the Social Sciences*, 1937, 8 vols.

Handlin, O. and others. *Harvard Guide to American History*, 1954.

Keller, H. R. *Dictionary of Dates*, 1934, 2 vols.

Langer, W. L. *An Encyclopedia of World History*, rev. ed., 1952.

Paullin, C. O. and J. K. Wright. *Atlas of the Historical Geography of the U.S.*, 1932.

Shepherd, W. R. *Historical Atlas*, 8th ed., 1956. Maps, indexed.

## Literature

Baker, E. A. *Guide to Historical Fiction*, 1914.

Baker, E. A. and J. Packman. *Guide to the Best Fiction.* 3rd ed., 1932.

Bartlett's *Familiar Quotations.* 13th edition, 1955.

Brewton, J. E. and S. W. *Index to Children's Poetry*, 1942.

*Cambridge History of American Literature*, 1917–21, 4 vols.

*Cambridge History of English Literature*, 1907–27, 15 vols. Bibliographies superseded by *Cambridge Bibliography of English Literature*, 1940, 4 vols.

*Columbia Dictionary of Modern European Literature*, 1947.

Cook, D. E. *Short Story Index*, 1956.

Eastman, M. H. *Index to Fairy Tales, Myths, and Legends*, 1926. Supplement, 1937.

Firkins, I. T. *Index to Plays (1800–1926)*, 1927. Supplement (1927–34), 1935. Should be supplemented by Ottermiller and West, below.

Hefling, H. and E. Richards. *Index to Contemporary Biography and Criticism.* 2nd edition, 1934.

Moulton, C. W. (ed.). *Library of Literary Criticism of English and American Authors*, 1901–05, 8 vols.

Ottermiller, J. H. *Index to Plays in Collections*, 1951.

Peck, H. T. (ed.). *Harper's Dictionary of Classical Literature*, 1897.

Warner, C. D. (ed.). *Library of the World's Best Literature*, 1917, 30 vols.

West, D. and H. *Play Index, 1949–1952*, 1953.

## Music

Apel, W. *Harvard Dictionary of Music*, 1944.

Baker, T. *Baker's Biographical Dictionary of Musicians*, 1940. Supplement, 1949.

*Grove's Dictionary of Music and Musicians,* 5th ed., 1954, 9 vols.
*International Cyclopedia of Music and Musicians,* 1949.
Kobbe, G. *The Complete Opera Book,* 1954.
*Oxford History of Music,* 2nd ed., 1931–38, 7 vols.
*Pierre Key's Music Year Book,* 1925–38. Annual volumes within this period.
Sears, M. E. *Song Index,* 1926. Supplement, 1934.

## Mythology

Edwardes, M. and L. Spence. *Dictionary of Non-Classical Mythology,* 1923.
Frazer, Sir J. G. *The Golden Bough,* 1907–15, 12 vols. Also one-volume condensation.
Gayley, C. M. *Classic Myths in English Literature and in Art,* 1911.
*Mythology of All Races,* 1916–32, 13 vols. The standard reference work on the subject.

## Philosophy and Psychology

Baldwin, J. M. *Dictionary of Philosophy and Psychology,* 1901–05, 3 vols. Revised edition, 1928.
Drever, J. *A Dictionary of Psychology,* 1952.
Louttit, C. M. *Handbook of Psychological Literature,* 1932.
*Psychological Abstracts,* 1927 ——. See page 268.
*Psychological Index.* See page 268.
Warren, H. C. *Dictionary of Psychology,* 1934.

## Religion

Canney, M. A. *Encyclopaedia of Religions,* 1921.
*Catholic Encyclopaedia,* 1907–22, 15 vols. and 2 supplements.
*Encyclopaedia of Religion and Ethics,* 1908–27, 12 vols. and index.
*Jewish Encyclopaedia,* 1925, 12 vols.
Hastings, J. *Dictionary of the Bible,* 1898–1904, 5 vols. Also independent one-volume edition by the same author.
Mathews, S. and G. B. Smith. *Dictionary of Religion and Ethics,* 1921.
*New Schaff-Herzog Encyclopedia of Religious Knowledge,* 1908–12, 12 vols. and index.
Strong, J. *Exhaustive Concordance of the Bible,* 1894.

## Science

*Atomic Information,* 1946–47, 3 vols. in 1. Monthly publication of National Committee on Atomic Information.
Crane, E. J. and A. M. Patterson. *Guide to the Literature of Chemistry,* 1927.
Flood, W. E. and Michael West. *An Explaining and Pronouncing Dictionary of Scientific and Technical Terms,* 1952.
Glazebrook, Sir R. *Dictionary of Applied Physics,* 1922–23, 5 vols.
Henderson, I. F. and W. D. *Dictionary of Scientific Terms,* 5th ed., 1953.
*International Catalogue of Scientific Literature,* 1902–19, 14 vols. A bibliography of books and articles in all fields of science.

Sarton, G. *Introduction to the History of Science,* 1927–48, 3 vols. Contains good bibliographies.

Thorpe, E. *Dictionary of Applied Chemistry,* 1937–54, 11 vols. and index.

*Van Nostrand's Scientific Encyclopedia,* 2nd ed., 1947.

## Sociology

*Encyclopaedia of the Social Sciences,* 1937, 14 vols. in 8.

Fairchild, H. P. (ed.). *Dictionary of Sociology,* 1944.

*London Bibliography of the Social Sciences,* 1931–37, 4 vols. and supplement. Prepared by British Library of Political and Economic Sciences.

McLaughlin, A. C. and A. B. Hart. *Cyclopedia of American Government,* 1914, 3 vols.

*Palgrave's Dictionary of Political Economy,* 1923–26, 3 vols.

*Political Handbook of the World,* 1927 ——. Annual volumes.

*Social Science Abstracts,* 1929 ——.

## Exercises

**A.** Test your knowledge of the library by marking the following statements True or False. The correct answers are given within this chapter.

F. 1. The Dewey Decimal Classification divides all books into twelve major groups. 10

F 2. This system is also used for classifying magazines.

T 3. The "call number" of a book is its Dewey classification.

T 4. The card catalog lists books but not magazine articles.

T 5. In the card catalog, "Union Pacific" is listed ahead of "U. S. Army."

F 6. "Utopia" is listed before "U. S. Army."

F 7. "San Salvador" is listed before "St. Louis," and "Bluebells" before "Blue skies."

F 8. A student would normally expect a biography of Julius Caesar to be listed under "Julius."

F 9. The *Reader's Guide* is another name for *Poole's Index to Periodical Literature.* 1802–1906

T 10. Listings in the *Reader's Guide* are arranged alphabetically by subject, sometimes also by author and title.

F 11. The *Reader's Guide* lists magazine articles published since 1800. 1900

T 12. Titles of magazines are abbreviated in the *Reader's Guide.*

T 13. The *Book Review Digest* includes excerpts from the reviews it digests.

F 14. *Facts on File* is a statistical abstract. Weekly digest of world events.

T 15. The *Britannica Book of the Year* is a supplement to the *Encyclopaedia Britannica.*

T 16. The *New International Year Book* is a supplement to *The New International Encyclopedia.*

T 17. The *Statesmen's Yearbook* is a good reference for government activities in all countries.

T 18. *Who's Who* is an American publication.

T 19. The *Encyclopedia Americana* is confined to American subjects.

F 20. The *Dictionary of National Biography* contains studies of famous people in all countries. British

T 21. The *Dictionary of American Biography* is confined to the lives of Americans.

T 22. Many specialized fields have their own dictionaries, encyclopedias, and indexes.

F 23. The Cambridge Histories are a series of one-volume histories of several countries. Many volumes

24. The Cambridge History of English Literature is a good reference work on that subject. *Harpers Dict of*

F 25. There is no dictionary of classical literature available.

T 26. One of the best reference books for music is *Grove's Dictionary*.

27. Sir James Frazer's *Golden Bough* is an index to financial literature.

F 28. Reference sources on atomic energy are not yet available.

T 29. The standard reference work on mythology is *Mythology of All Races*.

30. All indexes list books and magazines in complete bibliographical form.

**B.** Test your ability to tell what sources would be best for different subjects by placing in front of the subjects at the left the number corresponding to the best source at the right. If more than one source would be useful, put the number of the preferred source first.

. . . . American pronunciation     1. *Cambridge History of English Literature*

. . . . Oliver Wendell Holmes     2. *Current Biography*

. . . . The date of *Hamlet*     3. *Dictionary of American Biography*

. . . . Eisenhower's re-election     4. *Dictionary of American Painters*

. . . . Photography     5. *Dictionary of National Biography*

. . . . Failure of the Tacoma Bridge     6. *Encyclopaedia Britannica*

. . . . William Pitt the Elder     7. *Engineering Index*

. . . . Grant Wood     8. Firkins' *Index to Plays*

. . . . The labors of Hercules     9. Gayley's *Classic Myths*

. . . . Nineteenth Century plays     10. *The New York Times Index*

. . . . Slang terms derived from animals     11. Kenyon and Knott's *Pronouncing Dictionary of American English*

. . . . Cost-of-living indexes for last ten years

. . . Robert M. Hutchins

.12. Historical development of the meanings of English words

. . . . Ratio of faculty to students in Big Ten universities

. . . . Disputed questions of American written usage

. . . . Volumes of poetry and drama published in U.S. last year

. . . . A bibliography of pamphlets

. . . . College population of the United States

12. *Oxford Dictionary*

13. Partridge's *Dictionary of Slang*

14. *Poole's Index*

15. *Publishers Trade List Annual*

16. *Statistical Abstract of the United States*

17. *Vertical File Service Catalog*

18. *Webster's New International Dictionary*

19. *Who's Who in Education*

20. *World Almanac*

# 14

## T H E    R E S E A R C H

## P A P E R

---

IN ONE FORM or another the research paper is a standard assignment in college classes. It may go under various names, but whether it is called a "research paper," a "term paper," or a "reading report," it is a paper written to present the results of the student's investigation of a topic. In practice the research paper is usually based on printed sources. It is an assignment in *library* research. The student selects a topic, reads about it in books and magazines, takes notes, and writes a long paper based on the information he has uncovered.

## *Types of Research Papers*

In general, undergraduate research papers are of two kinds: *reports* and *theses*. The chief difference between these types is one of purpose. The writer of a report wishes to find out the facts of his subject and present them in a clear, orderly, and detailed account. The writer of a thesis research paper is studying the facts to draw a conclusion from them; this conclusion becomes the thesis of his essay; and he selects and organizes his material to develop his thesis.[1] Both writers seek out the facts of the subject, but their purposes lead to differences in selection and organization.

For example, a student writing a report on Thomas Jefferson's education will be primarily interested in showing what it was like. He will select any material which serves to explain the kind of education Jefferson had: his study of foreign languages, his familiarity with the natural sciences, the extent of his knowledge of classical and European literature, and so on. But the student will feel no obligation to prove that Jefferson's education had important consequences in his later life, or

---

[1] If you have forgotten what a *thesis* is, see pages 24–27.

even that, compared with his contemporaries, his education was in any way unusual. In short, the report writer will not be concerned with evaluating Jefferson's education; he will be trying only to describe it.

But a student whose reading has led him to the thesis that Jefferson's legal education was unusually thorough for his times will ignore everything that has no bearing on Jefferson's study of the law. Instead, he will concentrate on Jefferson's *legal* education and he will study the legal education of several of Jefferson's prominent contemporaries in order to establish the comparison which the thesis requires. This student will be concerned not only with finding the facts but also with evaluating them. His decisions about what material should be included and how it should be arranged will be made to suit the demands of his thesis.

Either type of research paper, if well done, will result in a worthwhile essay. Either type may make a short or a long composition, depending on the scope of the subject and the amount of time available for the assignment. For example, it would be possible, after a few hours' study of selected chapters in Jesperson's *Growth and Structure of the English Language,* Gray's *Foundations of Language,* Laird's *The Miracle of Language,* and particular entries in the *Oxford Dictionary,* to write a good short report on "Changes in the meanings of words" or to develop the thesis that "Changes in the meanings of words tend to follow one of four patterns." With more time and more sources to work from, it would also be possible to develop these same subjects through a much longer paper — two, four, ten thousand words, or even more.

Whether you write a long or a short paper, a report or a thesis, will depend on the particular assignment made by your instructor after he has considered the amount of time the class can give to the research paper. In order to provide adequate instruction for classes which will spend five or six weeks preparing and writing a research paper of 2,000 words or more, we shall assume in the rest of this chapter that the paper is to be a long one. If your needs may be met more simply, your instructor will modify the following discussion to fit his purposes.

## Preview of Research Procedure

Before we consider the separate steps in preparing a research paper, let us preview the whole procedure. Suppose you have been asked to choose a topic, study it, and write a 2,000-word thesis paper. You have five weeks for the assignment. At the end of that time you are to hand in a paper complete with sentence outline, footnotes, and bibliography.

Because you have recently become interested in photography, you choose that as your general subject. You know you will have to restrict that topic, but at present you do not know enough about it to limit it intelligently. You decide that for this subject the first thing to do is to make a preliminary survey of the books listed in the card catalog. As you notice the titles and descriptions of contents, you see how the general subject is broken down into subtopics. You find chapters, even whole books, devoted to the history of photography, the chemistry of photography, celestial photography, commercial photography, color photography, miniature photography, and to studies of developers, lenses, and photographing techniques.

You realize almost at once that each of these limited topics would be enough for a 2,000-word paper and that the first step in restricting your topic is to select one of them. You recognize that some topics require more chemistry or mathematics than you can handle and that others would result in highly technical papers. Miniature photography seems both interesting and possible. With the aid of the card catalog, the *Reader's Guide to Periodical Literature,* and the *Photo-Lab Index,* you draw out the most promising publications, scan them to form a judgment of their usefulness, and begin to prepare a preliminary bibliography of the most useful sources.

Since you know very little about miniature photography, you wisely decide to begin with some introductory reading — books and articles which will give you a general background for more detailed reading later. Accordingly, you begin with the most general and popular works on the subject — perhaps the *Leica Manual,* an elementary textbook on visual aids, and a promising magazine article. Because these works are designed merely to give you an introduction to your subject, you skim them quickly. You have already recognized that even miniature photography is a large topic, and you decide that you had better postpone careful reading and note-taking until you have decided what *precisely* you intend to do with your subject.

At the end of the first week you have a general knowledge of your subject — its history, its popularity, its wide range of uses. You know its advantages and limitations as contrasted with other types of photography, and you see that the topic is still too big for a 2,000-word paper. Already certain specific phases of the subject have begun to suggest themselves as suitable for intensive study. You are particularly impressed by references to the ways microphotography has revolutionized techniques in a wide variety of professions, and you think you would like to write a paper on these developments.

You now discard from your preliminary bibliography all titles which seem to have no relation to your restricted subject. When you see how much has to be discarded, you are glad you did not waste time taking notes on your general subject. But now it is time to take notes; so, as you begin to read intensively on the uses of microphotography, you copy significant evidence on note cards, making sure that the source of the material (author, title, and page number) is shown on *each* card. You use a new card for each note so that you will be able to organize your notes according to whatever scheme you later decide is best.

At the end of the second week you have a respectable pile of note cards and you have become something of an expert on the application of microphotography to industrial and professional uses. Indeed you know so much about the subject that you are beginning to be worried about discussing all these uses in a 2,000-word paper. You begin to think it might be wise to limit your topic still further. As you review your notes with this thought in mind, you see that you could turn your research project into any one of several more specialized studies. With more work, you could show what miniature photography has done for visual aids programs; you could show its uses in banking; you could show how it has revolutionized the techniques of scholarly research; and you could sketch its possibilities in a half-dozen uses which are beginning to emerge. Your material, however, is best suited for a paper on banking or one on scholarly research. After some thought, you decide to show what the miniature camera has done for academic research.

You now discard those notes which no longer have value for your restricted subject, and you spread out your remaining notes to see what kind of pattern they suggest. You will probably experiment with running outlines, as we did on page 61, in an effort to see to what purpose your material lends itself. You find that most of your cards may be grouped under four headings: the quantity of work that photography makes possible, the saving in time, the greater accuracy that exact copies provide, and the saving in total costs to the scholar. After several tries you write as your thesis: "By the use of microphotography, scholars are able to do more work, more accurately, in less time, and at less cost." You even think of a title for your paper — *Streamlined Scholarship*.

It has taken you almost three weeks to see exactly what you wanted to do. Until now, you have been groping toward a decision, but now that your purpose is precise, the rest of your work will move forward rapidly and economically. As you begin to work out trial outlines, you recognize that there are still some gaps in your material. You need more evidence about the development of microfilm libraries in universities. You require estimates of the comparative cost of photostating and microfilming. You need more information than you have about the different types of reading machines. But, at least, you know exactly what you are looking for, and probably you know where to find it. If in the next two weeks you can organize and present your material to develop your final purpose, you will have a superior paper.

The imaginary assignment which we have been considering illustrates the recommended procedure preparatory to writing a research paper. That procedure may be summarized as follows:

1. Make a survey of the material available on your general subject and prepare a preliminary bibliography.

2. Become familiar with the general subject through introductory sources, but postpone note-taking.

3. Restrict the general subject as quickly as you can. Remember that your reading does not become fully pertinent until you have decided the question you wish to answer or the specific phase of the subject that you wish to develop.

4. When you feel that your subject is becoming specialized begin to take notes.

5. Continue to restrict your subject as soon as the results of your specialized reading suggest further restriction.

6. When you feel that restriction of the subject is complete, begin to consider what precisely you intend to do with that subject. Remember that when you decided to show how microphotography had streamlined scholarship, you had a thesis as well as a subject.

7. Begin the preliminary outlining of the paper. You have probably already begun to plan the organization in your head or by means of scratch outlines, but you are now ready for more formal outlines.

8. Fill in by additional investigation the blank spots that remain from your reading.

9. When the research is complete, make a final outline and write the first draft of your paper.

Most of the steps summarized above are preparatory. The total process would be considerably shortened if you knew at the beginning what you know by the time you have reached step 6. The more quickly you arrive at step 6, therefore, the more profitable will be your investigations and the less time they will require. Under favorable conditions you may be able to skip some of the preliminary stages, but even if you cannot, a clear realization that you are looking for a phase of the subject that may be dealt with completely within the limits of your paper will help you to speed up the first steps.

We may now profitably consider the separate stages of carrying out the research assignment.

## Choosing a Subject

The choice of a subject for research depends partly on the purpose of the assignment and partly on your preference. The purpose of the assignment is fourfold: to teach you to use the library efficiently; to help you develop habits of purposeful reading and note-taking; to give you practice in organizing information drawn from a variety of sources and in developing it into a unified essay; and to make you familiar with the conventions of bibliography and footnoting. Since a successful research paper must satisfy all these purposes, the following kinds of topics should be avoided for the reasons noted below:

1. *Topics which would be developed largely from personal experience.* Since such topics do not require library research they would ignore at least three of the four purposes stated above.

2. *Topics which would result in simple descriptions of processes.* Such subjects as "How Plastics Are Made" and "Producing Synthetic Rubber" are undesirable for three reasons: first, all the information necessary may be obtained from a single book or article, thus eliminating the need for consulting various sources; second, since the organization of the paper would inevitably follow that of the source, the paper would offer no real problem in composition; third, the whole assignment could be adequately treated with a few hours' work, and is therefore not worth the time usually allowed for the research paper.

3. *Topics for which no evidence is available.* Such questions as "Are Women More Honest Than Men?" "Do Extroverts Make Good Husbands?" "Who Was the Greater Poet — Chaucer or Milton?" could only be answered by the writer's preference. These topics could be as well treated without research as with it.

4. *Unrestricted topics which could be treated only superficially within the scope of the assignment.* All that was said about restriction in Chapter 2 applies with added emphasis to the research paper. An unrestricted topic offers almost no problem in either research or composition. Since *the most common cause of failure in undergraduate research papers is lack of restriction,* review pages 17–21 carefully before choosing a subject.

5. *Highly controversial subjects, especially those advocating the adoption or rejection of a proposal that calls for action.* Such subjects are objectionable for two reasons: (1) they are too comprehensive to be dealt with thoroughly in a paper of 2,000–3,000 words, and (2) giving reasons for or against a proposal, without careful consideration of all the evidence on both sides of the question, often results in irresponsible and undisciplined argument. For example, such a proposal as, "Congress Should Provide Federal Aid to Education," not only includes many issues, each of which has been argued at length, but also requires a sophisticated understanding of types of reasoning and of the nature of acceptable authoritative testimony. It is therefore hard to avoid a superficial argument which does little more than present unweighed evidence to support the writer's preference. The line between argument and the exposition of a thesis is sometimes a thin one, but a student should consult his instructor before beginning to work on a subject with the intention of persuading his reader that something should or should not be done.

If these five kinds of topics are avoided, almost any subject can yield a satisfactory research paper. Probably your wisest course is to look on the research project as an opportunity to investigate a field which seems to you worth looking into. By the time you have finished your paper you should be, compared with other students, something of an expert on your subject. It is best, then, to choose a subject you *want* to know more about. If, through your work in other courses, you have become interested in history, social science, physics, chemistry, or the fine arts, select from one of these fields a particular topic that you would like to investigate. Sometimes the topic will occur to you as a quite specific question — "What was behind the abdication of Edward VIII?" "Why is English spelling so illogical?" "What are modern painters trying to do?" "Which is the more important — environment or heredity?" "What can be done to help slow readers?" "How does the British Parliament differ from our Congress?" If you would like an answer to any such question, you not only have a subject worth investigating, but, since the answer to the question will give you your thesis, you may be able to skip some of the preliminary steps summarized on page 280. Even if you do not have a specific question to answer, an awareness that the research project provides you with an opportunity to learn more about some phase of a subject that interests you may get you off to a better start and make the whole assignment a rewarding experience.

## Preparing a Bibliography

In the sense in which you will be using the term in your college work a *bibliography* is a list of books, articles and other publications. A *preliminary* bibliography lists the works you expect to use for a paper. A *final* bibliography lists the works you actually did use. A preliminary bibliography is made on 3 × 5 inch cards, with each title on a separate card. A final bibliography is typed or handwritten as a solid list. Both contain the same basic information for each item included — author's name, title of work, and facts of publication (place, publisher, and date).

### The Preliminary Bibliography

In preparing a bibliography, as in other tasks, a few minutes' careful consideration of the problem may save hours of needless work and result in a better product. Many students rush uncritically to the card catalog. Before you begin your actual search for titles, ask yourself two questions: What kind of material do I want? What are the most likely places to find it?

It is wise to ask these questions because different subjects require different approaches to the preparation of a bibliography. If you are dealing with a subject recently developed, the card catalog will be of little use to you. It records only books, and the very latest material in a book is usually at least a year old. For a current topic you must get most of your information from newspapers and recent magazine articles. On the other hand, many subjects — the development of the alphabet, for example — have been thoroughly treated in books, and little of significance will be found about them in current periodicals. The best general sources of information are the card catalog and the *Reader's Guide to Periodical Literature.* For some subjects the best approach will be through an index to technical publications; for others, *The New York Times Index* may yield the required information most readily.

Once you have started to prepare your bibliography, the following advice may be helpful:

1. Try to make your bibliography selective as you prepare it. There is no point in listing three titles which contain the same information, or books which have little to say on your subject. Develop the habit of guessing intelligently whether a book will be useful to you. In some subjects — atomic energy, for example — an old book is likely to be outdated. Usually the best way to guess at a book's usefulness is to draw it out of the library and look at it quickly. Read the preface, or part of it; check the table of contents; see how much space it gives to your subject. With a little practice you will usually be able to tell within three minutes whether the book will be of use to you.

2. Watch for critical bibliographies, which evaluate the works they list and thus tell you what sources are best and for what topics. Many serious studies contain such bibliographies, at the end of chapters or the end of the whole work, and so give you valuable leads to other sources.

3. Study the indexes of books on related subjects. A book on physics may contain a pertinent discussion of atomic energy. But do not begin to read it through merely in the hope that it *may* contain such information. Instead, turn to the index and see how many references are given under *atomic energy* or related headings. Sample the most likely of these references. Similarly, if your study is biographical, check the indexes of memoirs and letters by people acquainted with your subject.

All this advice may be summed up in two words: *act purposefully.* You will save much time, and work with more confidence and enjoyment, if you feel that you are not just drifting around in a library hoping to pick up useful information but are actually following a calculated plan for discovering it.

### The Form of the Bibliography

Each bibliographical card should contain three essential pieces of information: *(1) the name of the author, (2) the title of the work, (3) the facts of publication.* In addition, a card may contain, for the convenience of the student, the library call number and a note concerning the contents of the work. The following card is typical for a book.

```
                                                    428.3
                                                    P822 t

1. Author's name         Pooley, Robert C.

2. Title                 Teaching English Usage

3. Facts of              New York:  Appleton-Century, 1946
   publication
                         Contains chapter on "Evaluation of Usage
4. Annotation            Teaching."  Good bibliography.
```

The form of the entry varies with the kind of publication being cited, and the major variations are illustrated below. Each card must contain all the information needed for a proper footnote citation: the author, the work, and the facts of publication. The forms for a book, a magazine article, and a newspaper article are basic; all others are variations of these.

### 1. A Book by a Single Author or Agency

Gulley, Halbert E.  Essentials of Discussion and Debate.  New York:  Henry Holt and Company, 1955.

*a.* The author's surname comes before his given name or initials for ease in alphabetizing.
*b.* If the book is the work of an agency, committee, organization, or department, rather than of an individual, the name of the agency takes the place of the author's name.
*c.* If no author is given, the citation begins with the title.
*d.* The title of the book is italicized (represented in manuscript by underlining each word separately).
*e.* The facts of publication are the place of publication, the publisher, and the date of publication, in that order.
*f.* If more than one place is given on the title page, use only the first.
*g.* If no date of publication is given, use the last copyright date, usually found on the reverse of the title page.
*h.* The punctuation in the sample above is the preferred form, but accepted variations permit a comma between author and title and between place and publisher, and the omission of the final period.

### 2. A Book by Two Authors

Wellek, René, and Austin Warren.  Theory of Literature.  New York:  Harcourt, Brace and Company, 1949.

*et al.*

n.d. — no date

c.
ci. } about

*a.* The name of the second author is not inverted; otherwise the form is the same as that of Example 1.

*b.* The order of the authors' names is the same as that on the title page. Wellek comes first, even though Warren would be alphabetically earlier.

### 3. *A Book by Several Authors*

Murray, Elwood, and others.  <u>Integrative Speech</u>. New York:  The Dryden Press, 1953.

*a.* <u>The Latin abbreviation *et al.* is a common variation of "and others" and may be used if preferred.</u>

*b.* When there are three authors, but not more than three, it is a common practice to give all three names. Thus the first part of the entry shown above could have been listed:

*et. al (three or more)*

Murray, Elwood, Raymond H. Barnard, and J. V. Garland.

### 4. *A Work of More Than One Volume*

Johnson, Edgar.  <u>Charles Dickens: His Tragedy and Triumph</u>, 2 vols.  New York:  Simon and Schuster, 1952.

*a.* The number of volumes follows the title, is separated from it by a comma, and is always abbreviated as shown.

### 5. *An Edition of an Author's Work*

Robinson, F. N. (ed.).  <u>The Works of Geoffrey Chaucer</u>, 2nd ed.  Boston:  Houghton Mifflin Company, 1957.

*a.* If the edition is by more than one person, the names of the editors are arranged as in Example 2 or 3, whichever form is appropriate.

*b.* If the work is a revised or later edition, the appropriate description (rev. ed., 2nd ed., 7th ed.) is placed immediately after the title and separated from it by a comma.

### 6. *An Edited Collection or Anthology*

Commins, Saxe, and Robert N. Linscott (eds.). <u>The World's Great Thinkers</u>, 4 vols.  New York: Random House, 1947.

*(sic.) — word was misspelled in actual work.*

### 7. A Translation

Gouzenko, Igor. The Fall of a Titan, trans.
Mervyn Black. New York: W. W. Norton & Company, 1954.

### 8. A Pamphlet

Because there is considerable variation in the bibliographical information given in pamphlets, they are sometimes difficult to cite. Whenever
possible, treat them like books, with or without an author (Example 1).
If the bibliographical information is so incomplete that you cannot
confidently describe the pamphlet, show it to your instructor and get
his advice. Following are three variant forms:

Chafee, Zechariah, Jr. Freedom of Speech and
Press. New York: Carrie Chapman Catt Memorial
Fund, 1955.

Bureau of the Budget. The Federal Budget in
Brief: Fiscal Year 1954. Washington, D.C.:
U.S. Government Printing Office, 1953.

Your Library: A Guide for Undergraduate Students,
University of Illinois (n. d.).

a. The last example is intended to show a difficult pamphlet, since the
only bibliographical information given is the title.
b. The symbol [n. d.], meaning "no date," is used to show that no date
of publication or copyright is given and that the omission is not an
oversight. Parentheses are used in our example because most type-
writers do not have brackets.

### 9. An Essay in an Edited Collection

Highet, Gilbert. "The American Student as I See
Him," Patterns in Writing, ed. Robert B. Dore-
mus and others. New York: William Sloane
Associates, 1950.

a. This entry requires two titles and both an author and an editor.
b. The title of the essay (or story or poem) is in quotation marks, and
the title of the book is italicized.
c. The comma separating the two titles comes *inside* the final quotation
marks.

### 10. An Article in an Encyclopedia

Macauley, Thomas Babington. "Samuel Johnson,"
Encyclopaedia Britannica (11th ed.), XV, 463-
71.

*publisher not used*

"Navigation Acts," The Columbia Encyclopedia
(1950), pp. 1367-68.

*a.* Some encyclopedia articles are initialed, and the authors are identified in a list at the beginning of the volume. The article on Johnson is signed *M*, Macauley's initial.
*b.* The British spelling *Encyclopaedia* is often bothersome to American students. Copy the title exactly as it is given on the title page.
*c.* Either the edition number *or* the date of publication may be used. Thus (1911) could have been used instead of (11th ed.) in the first example, and (2nd ed.) instead of (1950) in the second.

### 11. *A Magazine Article*

Faust, Clarence. "Main Currents of General Education," Basic College Quarterly, 1:15-23
(Fall, 1955).

Wolf, A. V. "Thirst," Scientific American, CXXIV
(January, 1956), 70-76.

*a.* Two titles, separated and differentiated as in Example 9.
*b.* No place of publication or publisher is given, but volume, date, and page numbers are shown. The volume number may be in Roman numerals preceding the parenthetical date, as in the second sample, or in Arabic numerals preceding the page numbers and separated from them by a colon, as in the first sample. Thus the first sample could have been written: I (Fall, 1956), 15-23 and the second sample: 124:70-76 (January, 1956). Because Roman numerals are cumbersome in large numbers, the newer system of using Arabic numerals is becoming increasingly popular.
*c.* The words *volume* and *page* (or their abbreviations, *vol.* and *p.*) are not used.

### 12. *A Newspaper Article*

Rutter, Richard. "New Attitudes Made to Order,"
The New York Times, December 31, 1955, p. 19,
col. 2.

"Council Seen Voting Down Manager Now," Champaign-Urbana Courier, January 4, 1956, p. 3,
col. 8.

*a.* The two samples illustrate signed and unsigned articles.
*b.* In both samples the name of the city has been italicized because it

p. 15-16 ff. (spread over magazine)

is part of the title. If it is not, it is given but not italicized, thus: the Champaign-Urbana *News-Gazette*. The definite article is capitalized and italicized only when part of the official title, as in the first sample.

c. Unlike the form for a magazine article, the date is *not* placed in parentheses.

d. Although column numbers are sometimes omitted, they are often so helpful to a reader that it is good form to include them.

In order to get practice as quickly as possible with the various forms illustrated in this discussion, convert the following information into conventional bibliographical form. Since the number of each item corresponds to the number of a preceding illustration, you can check your answer against the appropriate illustration.

1. A book by John R. Reinhard called Medieval Pageant, copyrighted in 1939 and published by Harcourt, Brace and Company in New York.

2. A book called The Reader Over Your Shoulder, written by Robert Graves and Alan Hodge, and published in New York by The Macmillan Company in 1944.

3. A book published by the University of Illinois Press at Urbana, Illinois, in 1952. The book was written by Gordon N. Ray, Carl J. Weber, and John Carter and is called Nineteenth Century English Books.

4. A two-volume edition of Selected Works of Stephen Vincent Benét, prepared by the author and published by Farrar and Rinehart of New York in 1942.

5. John M. Manley's edition of Chaucer's Canterbury Tales, copyrighted in 1928 and published in New York by Henry Holt and Company.

6. British Poetry and Prose, a two-volume work edited by Paul Robert Lieder, Robert Morss Lovett, and Robert Kilburn Root, and published in Boston by Houghton Mifflin Company in 1938. This is a revised edition.

7. A translation by Dorothy Bussy of a novel by André Gide. The translation, called Lafcadio's Adventures, was published by Alfred A. Knopf, Inc. of New York in 1928.

8. A pamphlet entitled Memo: The Citizen and International Trade prepared by the League of Women Voters and printed in Washington, D.C. in 1952.

9. Charles Lamb's essay on Old China, reprinted in Literary Masters of England which was edited by Nelson S. Bushnell, Paul M. Fulcher, and Warner Taylor and was published in 1950 by Rinehart & Company, New York, as a revised edition.

10. An article by M. S. Fisher on pages 573–76 of volume XI of the Encyclopedia of the Social Sciences. The article is entitled Parent Education.

11. An article entitled, Present Status of Advanced Composition and Rhetoric, on pages 177–79 of volume 16 of College English. The article was written by Tyrus Hillway and appeared in December, 1954.

12. A newspaper story headed Spanish Students Opposed to Franco

in the St. Louis Post-Dispatch. The story was written by Camille M. Cianfarra and appeared on the first column of page 13A of the issue for January 5, 1956.

## The Final Bibliography

The final bibliography will be typed from the bibliographical cards and will follow the forms already discussed. It should contain a citation for each work mentioned in the footnotes. It may also contain a few works which you found to be useful background references, even though you neither cited nor quoted them in your paper. But padding a bibliography to make it look imposing is more likely to annoy than to impress an instructor. If your instructor prefers, your bibliography may be annotated — that is, it may contain a brief statement explaining the significance of each item or of selected items. See the annotated bibliography on pages xiii–xiv of this book.

In typing or writing your bibliography, observe the following conventions unless your instructor recommends modifications.

1. If the bibliography is long, group the publications according to type: books, magazine articles, newspaper articles, etc. When the bibliography consists of a single page, this grouping is less necessary. If in doubt whether grouping is desirable, consult your instructor.

2. Within each group list items alphabetically by author's surname or, if the author is not given, by the first letter of the title (not counting "A," "An," or "The").

3. If more than one book by the same author is being listed, you may substitute a 7-space line for the author's name after you have once given it:

```
Baldwin, T. W.  William Shakespeare's Five-Act
     Structure. . . .


-------.  William Shakespeare's Petty School. . . .
```

4. Single space each item and double space between items.

5. In each item, indent two spaces for all lines after the first.

The bibliography of the sample research paper on page 323b illustrates all but the first of these conventions.

## *Introductory Reading*

For most research studies the reading may be divided into three stages — introductory, intensive, and supplementary. The introductory reading gives the background needed in order to begin the investigation intelligently. The intensive reading provides the bulk of the information from which the paper will be written. The supplementary reading fills in gaps and provides added information needed to make your paper complete.

Thus, in our imaginary assignment on pages 277–279, all reading done before the decision to restrict photography to the uses of microphotography in industry and the professions was introductory. All reading done after the final decision to write on "Streamlined Scholarship" was supplementary. That in between was intensive. Of course, it would have been more economical if no introductory or supplementary reading had been required, if you had known from the beginning that you were going to write on "Streamlined Scholarship." But few research papers actually develop that way. Even so, a careful concern with purpose can greatly reduce the introductory and supplementary reading.

Once the function of the introductory reading is understood, it will be clear that note-taking at this stage is not profitable. The information obtained from this reading is probably not going to appear in your paper, or if it does, it will probably be so general that notes are not needed. This reading should therefore be done quickly. Indeed, the early accumulation of miscellaneous notes may actually be confusing, since a student who has notes on every aspect of his subject is likely to have a harder time deciding which phase of it to concentrate on. Again, as in the preliminary bibliography, the test is usefulness, not quantity. And it is therefore wise to take no notes until you are reasonably sure you will use them.

Usually the best sources for introductory reading are general works — articles in encyclopedias, chapters in elementary textbooks, histories, biographical references, and specialized dictionaries. For example, a student setting out to answer the question, "How Did English Spelling Become So Illogical?" might profitably begin with the article on the English Language in a good unabridged dictionary, the *Encyclopaedia Britannica,* or such textbooks as Baugh's *History of the English Language* or Jesperson's *Growth and Structure of the English Language.* These works would not only refer him to more specialized studies but would also provide him with the background necessary to profit from such studies.

For some subjects a good popular article is the best introduction. A student investigating the development of the atomic bomb might profitably begin with an article in *The New York Times, Newsweek,* or *Time,* and then move through other magazine articles and reprints or round-table discussions to Selig Hecht's *Explaining the Atom* and finally to the *Smyth Report.* In such a study he will find that the last two works include almost everything he first found in the magazine articles, but by the time he reaches the *Smyth Report* he will be better prepared to appreciate this document than if he had come to it first. Reading — intensive as well as introductory — should be from the general to the specialized and from the popular to the scholarly.

## Note-Taking

Once you begin intensive reading it will be necessary to take notes. The results of your preliminary reading may be carried in your head, but you are now beginning to collect the actual evidence from which your paper will be written, and it is important to the success of all the rest of your work that both the form and the content of your notes be satisfactory.

### The Form of the Notes

All notes should be written on cards [2] and should contain two kinds of information: (1) the fact or opinion being noted, and (2) the exact source from which you took it. This second item is absolutely necessary, since you will be required to identify the sources of your material in the footnotes to your paper. Usually that means you must identify the author, title, and page of the book or article from which the note was taken. Here is a typical note made from a book:

Morison, Samuel E.
Admiral of the Ocean Sea, p. 7

Columbus born in Genoa, 1451,
between Aug. 25 and October, of
family of woolen weavers
who had lived in Genoese
Republic for at least 3 generations.

If you are making a number of notes from the same source, the complete identification given above may be abbreviated. Thus, if you are using no other work by this author, "Morison, p. 7" would be enough, since your bibliographical card would provide the full title. Or you may give each of your bibliography cards a separate identification symbol and use that symbol and the page number on every note card made from that work.[3] Thus, if the bibliographical card for Morison's *Admiral of the Ocean Sea* bore the symbol A and Danzig's *Number* the symbol B, then A7 on the note card would tell you that the note came

[2] Some instructors prefer 4 × 6 inch cards in contrast with the 3 × 5 inch bibliographical cards.

[3] This use is illustrated in the notes on pages 314a–322a.

from page 7 of Morison's work, and B40 would tell you the second note came from page 40 of Danzig's work. But no matter what system is used, each card must be accurately identified. To avoid any possibility of a slip, *always write the identification before you begin the note.*

The practice of using note cards instead of notebooks has grown out of the experience of thousands of research workers. To be really useful your notes must be so flexible that you can shuffle them to suit whatever order you finally decide upon and can discard useless notes easily. Notes written solid in a notebook cannot conveniently be rearranged or edited. They are fixed in the order they had in the source from which they were taken, whereas the order which suits your final purpose may be entirely different. Recording information in a notebook is therefore inefficient, no matter how easy it may seem at first glance.

Only one note should be placed on a card. Two notes on one card are inseparably bound together. Since you must be free to shuffle your notes, to discard useless ones and add supplementary ones, the only satisfactory method is to use a separate card for each.

It is wise to leave enough space at the top of each card so that you may write in a subject heading when you group your cards and develop your outline, thus:

Because these subject headings may be changed as your organization develops, it is wise to enter them in pencil.

### The Content of Notes

Your notes may contain statements of fact or of opinion, in your own words or in the words of the author from whose work they came. *If the wording as well as the content is taken from a source, be extremely careful to use quotation marks, both on your note card and, later, in your paper.* Failure to use quotation marks on the note card may later lead you to think that the information is expressed in your own words and thus may trap you into unintentional plagiarism.[4] The cards shown below contrast a quoted opinion and the same opinion stated in the student's words.

*Danzig, p. 35*

"In the history of culture the discovery of zero will always stand as one of the greatest single achievements of the human race."

*Danzig, p. 35*

Discovery of zero one of greatest cultural accomplishments.

Whenever possible your notes should be summaries of the source material, not direct quotations. Too many quotations result in wordiness and give the impression that the student has merely strung together statements made by others without digesting these statements or doing any thinking about them. The technique of summarizing is discussed in Chapter 11 and it might be wise to read over that chapter before you begin intensive reading for the research assignment.

If the information you are noting is factual, confine yourself to a bare statement of fact; do not copy out the whole paragraph in which the facts are embedded. Most students need practice in this discipline, for it takes less thought to copy a paragraph verbatim than to thresh out the significant facts. But the threshing has to be done some time before the paper is written, and it might as well be done as the notes are taken.

---

[4] Plagiarism is the representation of another's writing as one's own. Both socially and academically, it is considered a form of dishonesty. Few college students will deliberately plagiarize, but in the research paper naive practices often lead to unintentional plagiarism.

Even if the job seems at times like extracting a needle from a haystack, remember that taking home the whole haystack does not help at all.

Long statements of opinion or of fact and opinion combined should nearly always be summarized. Nothing is more irritating to an instructor or more detrimental to the purpose of the research assignment than the habit of padding the paper with several long quotations, each of which could have been summarized in two or three sentences. The accompanying cards show economical but effective summaries of extensive passages. The first note is a digest of a three-paragraph passage containing about 480 words; the second condenses the material of five paragraphs totaling about 500 words.

Morison, pp. 190-191

According to Morison, Columbus overestimated distance sailed by about 9%. Intentional underestimate of "phony" reckonings designed to allay fears of crew actually more accurate, therefore, than secret reckonings which he believed true.

Danzig, pp. 1-3

Says number sense not to be confused with counting. Counting confined to humans, but some animals, birds, insects have remarkable sense of number.

Illustrations:

Crows and "Solitary Wasps"

Notice that these cards are identified just as carefully as if they contained direct quotations. The material was taken from the work of another and must be acknowledged in footnotes.

In making notes, the student must be careful that what he writes is consistent with the meaning of the whole source. If what is put on the notecard is qualified by something said in a preceding sentence or paragraph, the student should record that qualification. All notes must honestly and accurately reflect the content of their sources.

What we have said about note-taking may be summarized as follows:

1. Put notes on cards, not in notebooks, with one note to a card.

2. On each card identify the exact source of the note, including the page number. Abbreviations may be used only if there is no danger of ambiguity.

3. The actual words of an author must be placed in quotation marks, regardless of whether the notes are statements of fact or opinion.

4. Summarize extensive quotations if possible, but still identify the source.

5. Digest factual information out of a long passage before making the note.

6. Be careful that your notes — whether direct quotations or digests — do not distort the meaning when taken out of the original context.

7. Finally, remember that these conventions governing note-taking are designed to teach you good research habits as well as to protect you from beginners' mistakes. Follow the conventions at all times, even when a home-made system might seem more convenient.[5]

Suppose you were writing a research paper to show that social scientists work under more difficult conditions than do physical scientists and one of your sources was Kemmerer's "Are Social Scientists Backward?" (pages 245–248). From that source make whatever notes you think you might use and hand them in for your instructor's inspection.

## Stating the Thesis

Before you formulate your thesis, be sure to review pages 24–27. The following observations supplement that discussion and are confined to four kinds of difficulties that students encounter at the thesis-writing stage.

The most serious difficulties have their origin in faults which occurred long before the thesis is written. If a student has chosen a subject about which no thesis can be formulated, or if he has failed to restrict his general subject and so has gathered only a miscellany of information, he cannot write a satisfactory thesis, and there is nothing at this late date that his instructor can do to help him. The only solution is to start over from the beginning, and there is not time for that. The student simply has to accept the consequences of his failure to understand the assignment and to work purposefully toward carrying it out.

[5] It might be wise at this point to study the set of student notes provided with the research paper on pages 314a–322a.

Many students create trouble for themselves by trying to avoid the discipline that writing a thesis normally imposes. Faced with the task of expressing a controlling idea in a single sentence, they take one of two escapes: they write a thesis which is so general that it exerts no control over the development of the paper, or they write one which looks good but has no relation to the material in their notes and therefore does not represent the idea they intend to develop. Faulty theses are usually exposed if there is time to discuss them in class, through the collective criticism of twenty students exploring the meaning of a sentence on the blackboard.

Some students have trouble with the thesis because they still have a conflict of purposes in their minds. For example, the student who wrote the paper on Jefferson (page 311) was unsure — without realizing it — whether she was more interested in Jefferson's intellectual habits as a student or in what she called his "independent thinking." Only after class criticism and several revisions of preliminary theses, did she discover that she was really interested in the relation between these two topics — the conclusion that Jefferson's characteristic approach to a problem reflected the intellectual habits he developed as a law student. This kind of difficulty is normal. If the student does not worry unprofitably about it, he will learn how to resolve it.

Still other students find it hard to phrase an idea in precise and simple language. This also is a normal problem among people who care about making a sentence say what they intend it to say. You should not run away from this difficulty, but neither should you magnify it or imagine that it is unique.

Each of the following numbered excerpts contains the thesis and the main statements of a student outline. To be satisfactory, an excerpt should give you at least a clear hint of what the student proposes to do in his paper and how he proposes to do it. In each excerpt, study the thesis and the relation of the main statements to that thesis. If the excerpt is satisfactory in both respects, mark it O.K. If it is not satisfactory explain why.

1. Quaker education is essentially a religious education.
   I. Family life is oriented around the belief that parents must set a moral example for the children.
   II. The school program, in its curriculum, conduct, choice of teachers, and texts, emphasizes religious instruction.
   III. The Meeting, to which children are admitted at an early age, establishes a pattern of silent worship.

2. Adolph Hitler's rejection as an artist led him to develop psychological complexes which resulted in the destruction of his beloved Germany.
   I. As a boy Hitler rebelled against his father's wish to make him a civil servant.

II. Hitler's failure to graduate from high school kept him from being admitted to art school in Vienna.

III. During his Vienna years, opera was Hitler's chief passion.

IV. While in Vienna, Hitler first conceived of himself as a political leader.

3. It is possible to defend against a nuclear attack.

    I. The development of nuclear bombs is getting out of hand.

    II. A description of the bomb's characteristics.

    III. The nuclear bomb and its application to warfare.

    IV. An analysis of the bomb's characteristics show that it can be defended against.

4. The potentialities of many gifted children are left undeveloped because of certain social pressures.

    I. The parents create strong pressure to force the child to be "normal."

    II. Teachers often are unaware of, neglect, or overemphasize the child's potentialities.

    III. Other children put tremendous pressure on a gifted child to conform to the practices and preferences of his age group.

5. The best way to achieve a perfect life on earth is through the perfect contemplation of the Trappist monks.

    I. Perfect contemplation is the giving over completely of one's life to God, thus giving Him the worship He most desires.

    II. The life of a monk is kept as simple as possible so that he may keep his mind on God and his duty.

    III. Justification of monasticism may be found in its ability to survive and flourish in spite of constant persecution.

6. A better knowledge of the facts of the disease is bringing new hope to lepers and a new understanding of leprosy to others.

    I. Down through history all cultures have had erroneous beliefs about leprosy.

    II. This fear can be driven out of men's minds only by a knowledge of the facts concerning leprosy.

7. The popular conception of a schizophrenic as a person with a "split personality" is inaccurate.

    I. The "split personality," as popularly conceived, is a symptom of amnesia, not schizophrenia.

    II. The split which actually is present in schizophrenia is the separation of a person from his social and physical environment.

## Outlining

We pointed out in Chapter 3 that the need for a formal outline will depend largely on the length and complexity of the material to be organized. Since the research paper is usually one of the longest and most complex papers written by college students, it nearly always requires a careful outline. Indeed, many instructors make the writing of a detailed outline a critical stage in the preparation of the paper and do not allow students to begin actual composition until the outline is approved.

The best preparation for outlining your research paper is a careful review of Chapter 4, with special attention to pages 69–73, which discuss shaping and testing the organization. Most good students begin to develop the outline mentally while they are doing their intensive reading. From time to time they spread their notes on a table and study ways of grouping them. When they find them falling into logical groups, they begin to write the subject label on each card in the group. Students who work this way actually tackle outlining in three stages: (1) classifying information by subject groups while the information is still in the notes, with periodic attempts to work the groups into a running outline; (2) preliminary outlining to discover a thesis or to test one which is beginning to take shape in the mind; (3) final outlining, in which the structural pattern which has been developing through the two earlier stages is given its finished form.

The final outline, then, is merely a refinement of the organization already suggested by the study of your notes. But observe that the notes will suggest a pattern only if they have been efficiently made — that is, if each note is on a separate card, if useless cards are discarded with each restriction of the subject, if the content of the note cards is economically stated so that you can see at a glance what information each card contains. If the notes have not been efficiently taken — if they are long, undigested excerpts crowded together on both sides of the pages of a notebook — they will suggest neither a thesis nor an outline. The student who makes such notes must expect to have a hard time with his outline.

## Composing the Paper

All that has been said about composition in Part One of this book applies to the research paper. But in addition the research assignment has its special problem — the relationship between borrowed material and the use that is made of it. The research paper is admittedly and necessarily written from information derived from printed sources. But that information has to be woven into an essay which is essentially the student's own work. A student who has worked purposefully will not have too much difficulty reconciling these two conditions, for he will have selected his material with a view to using it in support of a purpose he has been forming as he reads. In a sense he is like a man who is building a house with bricks obtained from others. The bricks are not his, but the design and construction of the house are. *Writing a research paper, then, is not just stringing together statements from books and magazines. It is a complete reorganization and reworking of the source material into an original composition.*

Failure to recognize this sometimes results in a paper which is merely a transcription of the information in the note cards. The following excerpt from a student research paper reveals this weakness:

Article 123 of the Mexican Constitution has the sole purpose of solving the labor problem. It is looked upon as the declaration of the rights of the workmen.[1]

The workers' hours have a maximum limit of eight hours for a day's work. At least one day's rest for every six days' work is to be enjoyed by everyone.[2]

Children over twelve and under sixteen years of age can work only six hours a day, and children under twelve are not permitted to be made the subject of a contract.[3]

The minimum wage that can be received by a workman should be considered sufficient according to the conditions of life prevailing in the workman's particular region of the country. This same compensation is to be paid without regard to the sex of the worker.[4]

Wages are required to be paid in legal currency rather than by any other representative token with which it is sought to substitute money.[5]

---

[1] Tannenbaum, op. cit., p. 529
[2] Ibid.
[3] Ibid.
[4] Ibid.
[5] Ibid., p. 530.

Obviously, all this student is doing is setting down the contents of five note cards, all from the same source and four from the same page. He has not organized his material to develop any judgment of his own.

The noticeable inequalities of style suggest to a reader that he has occasionally copied the actual wording of his source without using quotation marks. At any rate, there is nothing in the excerpt to suggest any contribution of the student's own. The same facts built into a paragraph which the student has actually created himself might come out like this:

Article 123 of the Mexican Constitution attempts to standardize labor conditions by setting up basic principles governing hours and salaries. It provides a maximum work-week of six eight-hour days, prohibits the contractual hiring of children under twelve years of age, and limits the employment of children between twelve and sixteen to six hours a day. It requires that all wages be paid in legal currency, thus eliminating company script and other cash substitutes. It provides for a minimum wage scale which takes into account differences in the standard and cost of living in various parts of the country. It abolishes discrimination against women by making the wage rate the same for both sexes. In general, therefore, it seeks to establish a uniform code which will provide the general pattern of labor-management relations throughout the country.[1]

---

[1]Tannenbaum, op. cit., pp. 529-530.

The first of these two versions is a series of raw notes; the second is a unified paragraph created by the student. Both contain exactly the same facts, but the revised version rearranges and rewords the facts to make them develop the idea stated in the opening sentence. It also avoids the overdocumentation of the first version by acknowledging the two pages of Tannenbaum's book as the source for all the information in the paragraph. If an instructor were to compare the second version with the notes from which it was written, he would clearly see that the writer had mastered the information he was using and had shaped it to suit his own purpose. This point has already been illustrated by an assignment in paragraphing on pages 121–122.

Because of the importance of the research paper and because it is not always easy to weave factual material into a finished essay in one try, the composition should usually be done in three stages: writing the rough draft, preparing the final revision, and proofreading the finished paper. No two of these stages should be completed at a single sitting; indeed, it is best to allow a day between the completion of one and the beginning of the next.

How a student should compose the rough draft will depend partly on his work habits and partly on the nature of his material. For the average student the best advice is to break the total job into the main units of the outline and to tackle these units in order. A paper so developed is likely to be a bit stiff, to proceed rather mechanically from one step to the next, and to lack the qualities that make for an interesting or effective style. But these are not serious weaknesses if careful revision is to follow.

Footnotes and any graphic illustration being used should be written into the rough draft so as to avoid difficulties with spacing in the final version. Even though footnotes are finally placed at the foot of the page, it is often convenient in the first draft to insert them between ruled lines within the text immediately after the line containing the footnote marker. Not all research papers need or are suited to graphic illustrations — tables, graphs, charts — but since these aids present complex or cumbersome data compactly and thus make the reader's task easier, they should be used when they are appropriate.

The revision should turn the rough draft into a finished essay. It should provide smooth transitions between units — a more difficult task in a long composition than in a short one. It should polish the diction and sentence structure and remove any awkward constructions. It should check the relationship of detailed information to the topic idea. It should make sure that direct quotations are clearly marked and that indirect quotations and summaries actually serve the purpose of a paragraph and are not merely strung together without any purpose other than to get *something* written.

When the paper has been revised, the final bibliography should be added. This will be a list of the sources actually used in preparing the paper. It should include all sources cited in the footnotes and may contain one or two works which were valuable as background material even though not actually cited in the paper. The form of this bibliography was discussed on page 289.

Finally, the paper should be proofread at least twice to detect any errors which survived the revision. These readings should be mainly concerned with mechanical matters — doubtful spellings, punctuation, usage, and typographical errors. The proofreadings should include both the footnotes and the bibliography, and it is wise at this stage to check these against the recommended forms. Proofreading should be done slowly — more slowly than reading for content. Some students find it helpful to read the paper aloud slowly so as to concentrate on the appearance of each word.

## Documenting the Evidence

As we have said, all information taken from a specific source must be identified in a footnote.[6] That is, the evidence must be *documented*. The purpose of this convention is twofold: (1) to avoid the appearance of representing somebody else's work as yours; (2) to let the interested reader consult your sources and so check the accuracy of your investigation or carry on his own. This convention is so important in research writing that inaccurate documentation — or none at all — is regarded as a serious offense. For the research writer it is both good manners and good morals to acknowledge sources fairly and accurately.

**When to Footnote.** Inexperienced research writers often have difficulty in deciding what statements require documenting. The general principle is that you should cite the source of any statement for which you are indebted to the work of another. For most student research this general principle can be broken down into six conditions. You should provide a footnote whenever:

1. You use a direct quotation.
2. You copy a table, chart, or other diagram.
3. You summarize a discussion in your own words.
4. You construct a diagram from data provided by others.
5. You paraphrase an opinion which you have read rather than reached independently.
6. You present specific evidence which cannot reasonably be considered common knowledge.

The first four of these conditions are sufficiently definite to require no discussion. Difficulties, if any, will come from the last two, and these difficulties are better resolved by experience than by definition. By the time you have got well into any research project, you will have reached conclusions you did not have when you began your study. Unless these conclusions came specifically from one of your sources, they need not be documented. They are products of your total reading, not borrowings from any specific source.

Similarly, as you become familiar with a subject, you will find that

---

[6] The kind of footnote discussed here is called a "reference footnote." Footnotes may also qualify, explain, or comment on statements made in the text when it would be awkward to include such matters in the main discussion. Such footnotes may be called "explanatory footnotes." This footnote is explanatory. It provides an explanation which, though necessary, would be awkward to include in the body of the text.

facts of which you at first were ignorant are so well known that they must be considered common knowledge. For example, you probably do not now know the dates of Matthew Arnold's life. But if you were writing a research paper on Arnold you would find them common knowledge to all the writers you were reading. It would be unnecessary, and a little naive, to footnote these dates. This does not mean that no factual information need be footnoted. If you were recording the number of fatalities at Gettysburg, the tonnage and dimensions of the *Santa Maria*, or the population of London in 1450, you would be expected to cite your source in a footnote.

It is often asked how many footnotes a freshman research paper should have. Despite the popularity of this question, it cannot be answered specifically. The number will vary with the length of the paper and the nature of the data. Most student papers have from two to five footnotes on a page, but that is an average estimate only. Some pages may require no footnotes; others may need seven or eight. If you understand the purpose of footnotes and the six requirements discussed above, you should be able to make your own decisions. If by the time you come to write your paper you are still uncertain, submit a sample of your work to your instructor and get his advice.

**How to Footnote.** A footnote consists of two parts: the footnote marker, a number placed in the text at the end of the statement to be documented and slightly above the level of the typed or handwritten line; and the footnote proper, which usually comes at the foot of the page and is numbered to correspond with the marker, as illustrated in the sample paper on pages 313–322b.

The purpose of the footnote is to identify as precisely as possible the source to which the statement in the text is indebted. Although no one form is universally preferred, the minimum information required is a clear reference to the author, title, and page. If the author's work appeared in a magazine, an edited anthology, a reference book, or a newspaper, additional information is needed. In general, a footnote reference is similar in form to a bibliographical citation, *but there are noteworthy differences.* The following summary presents the most important conventions of footnoting.

1. Author
   a. In a footnote the author's name is given in its normal order — John Smith — not inverted as in a bibliography.
   b. When more than one author is to be named, the form is the same as that used in a bibliography (page 284) except that the first author's name is not inverted.
   c. In a reference to an edited work, the editor's name, in normal order,

goes in place of the author's name and is followed by (ed.), as in the bibliographical form.

d. After the first reference to a work in a footnote, the author's or editor's name may be shortened to surname only.

e. If there is no author's or editor's name, the footnote begins with the title.

## 2. Title

All titles follow the forms used in bibliography, but after the first footnote reference to a work, a convenient shorter form of the title or certain conventional abbreviations may be used (see uses of *ibid.* and *op. cit.*, in the following pages).

## 3. Facts of Publication

a. In the most formal style, such as is common in doctoral dissertations, the first footnote reference to a work contains a full identification of the facts of publication (place, publisher, and date). In the least formal style, the facts of publication are omitted entirely. Since the student research paper is short and contains a bibliography from which the facts of publication may quickly be determined, the examples used in this chapter will usually be given without the facts of publication. The choice, however, depends on personal preference, and since it is your instructor's preference that counts, you should consult him before writing your footnotes.

b. If any reference is made to place, publisher, and date of publication, it is made only in the first footnote reference to a work and it is enclosed within parentheses between the title and the page number. (See first sample entry, page 306.)

c. The facts of publication for a magazine article do not include place and publisher, but do include: (1) the title of the magazine (italicized to contrast with the title of the article, in quotation marks), (2) the volume and page numbers (see heading 4 below), (3) the date of issue — month (not abbreviated), day (if the magazine is published oftener than once a month), and year. The date is enclosed in parentheses.

d. The facts of publication of a newspaper article consist of: (1) the title of the newspaper (see page 288), (2) the month, day, and year, *not in parentheses,* (3) the page and column numbers.

## 4. Volume and Page Numbers

a. In references to a one-volume work, the abbreviation *p.* is used for *page* and *pp.* for *pages.*

b. When the reference is to a work of more than one volume, both the volume number and the page number must be given.

*c.* When both volume and page numbers are given, the abbreviations *vol.* and *p.* (or *pp.*) are *not* used. Instead, use Roman numerals for the volume and Arabic numerals for the page (CXV, 48) or Arabic numerals for both with the volume number first and followed by a colon (115:48).

## 5. Use of *Ibid.*

*Ibid.* (an abbreviation for *ibidem,* "in the same place") is used to refer to a work cited in the *immediately preceding* footnote. If the second reference is to the same volume and page of the work, *ibid.* alone is sufficient. If the second reference is to a different volume or page of the work, then *ibid.,* must be followed by the new volume and page numbers.

*Ibid.* cannot be used to refer to a preceding footnote if a reference to another source intervenes. The following contrasted references illustrate correct and incorrect uses of *ibid.*

| *Correct Uses of Ibid.* | *Incorrect Uses of Ibid.* |
|---|---|
| [1] Edgar Johnson, <u>Charles Dickens: His Tragedy and Triumph</u>, I, 24. | [1] Edgar Johnson, <u>Charles Dickens: His Tragedy and Triumph</u>, I, 24. |
| [2] <u>Ibid</u>. | [2] <u>Ibid</u>., I, 24. (Omit I, 24.) |
| [3] <u>Ibid</u>., p. 27 | [3] <u>Ibid</u>., II. (New page number required.) |
| [4] <u>Ibid</u>., II, 95. | [4] Charles Dickens, <u>Bleak House</u>, p. 87. |
| [5] <u>Ibid</u>., I, 28. | [5] <u>Ibid</u>., p. 26. (This is correct if it refers to *Bleak House,* but not to Johnson's work because of the intervening reference to *Bleak House.*) |

Notice that *ibid.* is italicized and followed by a period. It is capitalized when it begins a footnote.

## 6. Use of *Op. cit.*

*Op. cit.* (an abbreviation for *opere citato,* "in the work cited") may be used to refer to a work which has already been cited, but not in the *immediately* preceding footnote. It serves as a substitute for the title only, and must be preceded by the author's name and followed by the volume and page numbers. If more than one work by the same author is being cited, *op. cit.* cannot be used, since a reader could not tell which work by that author was being cited. The following footnotes show the correct use of *op. cit.*

[1] Edgar Johnson, <u>Charles Dickens</u>: <u>His Tragedy and Triumph</u>, I, 24.
[2] Charles Dickens, <u>Bleak House</u>, p. 87.
[3] Johnson, <u>op</u>. <u>cit</u>., I, 26.
[4] Dickens, <u>op</u>. <u>cit</u>., p. 88.

You will observe that when the title is a long one, as in footnote 1, the use of *op. cit.* is a real convenience. But when the title is short, as in footnote 2, little is saved by the use of *op. cit.* For this reason, many writers prefer to avoid *op. cit.* and to use the original title or a shorter form of it when little is gained by the Latin abbreviation.

## 7. Punctuation

The punctuation of the footnote need present no problem, since, except for periods after abbreviations and at the end, commas may be used throughout. Even the period at the end is optional, though its use or omission should be consistent.

The following footnotes illustrate the preceding discussion and may be used as models against which to check your own footnotes.

*First Reference to a Book*

*Formal:* [1] William Flint Thrall, and Addison Hibbard, <u>A</u> <u>Handbook</u> <u>to</u> <u>Literature</u> (Garden City, N.Y.: Doubleday, Doran and Company, 1940), p. 15.

*Informal:* [2] Thrall and Hibbard, <u>A</u> <u>Handbook</u> <u>to</u> <u>Literature</u>, p. 15.

*Second Reference Following Immediately After First*
[3] <u>Ibid</u>., p. 22.

*Second Reference Following Reference to Another Book*
[4] Thrall and Hibbard, <u>op</u>. <u>cit</u>., p. 22.

*Reference to an Essay in an Anthology*
[5] André Maurois, "Private Universes," <u>Modern Essays</u>, p. 213.

*Reference to a Magazine Article*

6 Hugh L. Dryden, "The International Geo-
physical Year," The National Geographic
Magazine, CIX (February, 1956), 289.
     or 109:289 (February, 1956).

*Reference to an Article in an Encyclopedia*

7 "Mississippi Scheme," The Columbia Encyclopedia (2nd ed.), p. 1294.

*Reference to a Newspaper Article*

8 Dudley McAllister, "Heating Bill Up?
Company Explains Why," Champaign–Urbana
Courier, Friday, January 27, 1956, p. 2,
col. 1.
9 "Salt Treatment of Trees Described," St.
Louis Post–Dispatch, Thursday, January 5,
1956, p. 4C, col. 1.

## Miscellaneous Abbreviations

In addition to those already used, the following abbreviations are in
common use in footnotes:

*cf.*, "compare."
*chap*(s)., "chapter(s)."
*ff.*, "and the following pages." (p. 17 ff.).
*l.*, "line." (l. 10).
*ll.*, "lines." (ll. 6–12). Same pages.
*loc. cit.*, "in the place cited." Not a synonym for *op. cit.*, but used to refer
    to a source already cited, regardless of whether another footnote inter-
    venes. Commonly used to refer to collections of material, often unpub-
    lished collections. Seldom used in undergraduate papers.
*passim*, "in various places in the text." Used to indicate a number of scat-
    tered references to a subject.
*sic*, "thus." Used in brackets (or in parentheses if typed) to indicate that an
    apparent error is not a miscopying but appeared thus in the source.

Assume that the following footnotes appeared in this order in a student
paper. If you think the footnote is acceptable, mark it O. K. If you think
it needs revision, revise it.

1 Morris L. Ernst and David Roth, Report on the
American Communist (New York: Henry Holt and
Company, 1952), p. 28.
2 Ernst and Roth, ibid., p. 28.

3 Morris R., and Angell, E., "Should Congress Investigate?" <u>Sat</u>. <u>Review</u>, vol. 38, pg. 9, Feb. 26, 1955.

4 Morris and Angell, <u>op</u>. <u>cit</u>., p. 10.

5 <u>Ibid</u>., pg. 10.

6 Eugene Lyons, "Red Decade," <u>American Mercury</u>, 38 (April 29, 1955), 66.

7 Ibid.

8 <u>Ibid</u>., 67.

9 Lyons, <u>ibid</u>., p. 68.

### Presenting the Finished Assignment

The assignment has not been fully met until the paper has been presented to the instructor in the form which he has stipulated. Your paper should look like the sample on pages 311–323b. A typical student research paper consists of the following parts:

1. A title page containing at least the title of the paper and the student's name and section number.

2. A detailed sentence outline of the paper.

3. The body of the paper, typed if possible, each page numbered and adequately footnoted. If the paper is typed, the text should be double spaced. Quotations of five or more lines should be indented and single-spaced without quotation marks.

4. Conventional footnotes with corresponding footnote markers at appropriate points in the text.

5. A bibliography of works used in preparing the paper.

6. The note cards used in writing the paper, arranged in the order in which they were used, labeled with outline symbols to show their relation to the outline, and tied together or sealed in an envelope. The purpose of handing in the notes is to allow the instructor to trace the development of your paper from outline and notes to finished composition.

If your instructor wishes to modify these requirements, he will notify you. Make sure that you understand clearly what is wanted. If you are uncertain, consult your instructor well in advance of the deadline.

## Review Exercises

**A.** From the following list of subjects:

> The abdication of Edward VIII
> The Scopes trial
> The contemporary reputation of George Washington
> Is weather-predicting just a guess?
> In what order were the first five books of the Bible written?

The drafting of the Constitution
Proportional representation
The development of the A-bomb
Do animals "think"?
Any subject chosen by you and approved by your instructor

1. Select one subject and explain briefly what procedure you would follow in preparing a preliminary bibliography for it.

2. Following the procedure you have explained, prepare a bibliography of ten sources for the subject you have chosen. Do not include any source until you have examined it briefly, and indicate on each bibliographical card the features for which you selected that work. Do not spend more than two hours on this part of the assignment, but try to get the best sources available in your library.

**B.** As preparation for a short paper to be entitled, "Colloquial Usage, What It Is and Is Not," study both the pertinent introductory material and the dictionary entry "Colloquial" in the sources that follow. Make notes on your reading on 3 × 5 or 4 × 6 inch cards, whichever your instructor prefers. Following the model shown on page 61, organize your notes as a first step towards an outline; then write a sentence outline and label each card with the outline symbol which it would develop. Hand in both the outline and the cards.

The American College Dictionary.
Kennedy, Arthur G. Current English (check index for page references).
Kenyon and Knott. A Pronouncing Dictionary of American English.
The Oxford English Dictionary.
Webster's New International Dictionary, Second Edition.
Webster's New World Dictionary.

**C.** As preparation for a short paper to be entitled, "Do Antihistamines Cure Colds?" consult and make notes on the following periodical articles:

"Allergy Drug for the Cold," Newsweek, 30:53 (December 1, 1947).
"The Antihistamines," Consumer Reports, 15:7–10 (January, 1950).
"Antihistamines," Consumer Reports, 15:127–129 (March, 1950).
"Antihistamines," Scientific American, 182:28 (May, 1950).
"The Cold Tablet War," Newsweek, 35:53 (May 15, 1950).
"Deadly Evidence," Time, 55:83–84 (February 12, 1950).
"The Failure of Antihistamines," Consumer Reports, 15:315–317 (July 5, 1950).
"Stopper Story Stayed," Newsweek, 34:54 (November 20, 1949).
"Unproved Plum," Time, 55:63 (March 6, 1950).

Organize your notes to outline an answer to the question you are studying. Write a sentence outline from the notes, and label each note card with the outline symbol which it would be used to develop. Hand in both the outline and the labeled note cards.

**D.** The following student research paper, complete with outline, notes, text, footnotes, and bibliography, is presented as an exhibit for detailed study. It is chosen because its restricted purpose, its organization, notes, paragraph development, and educational value to the student author all make it a profitable paper to study. If you analyze it carefully, you will have a helpful review of the process of writing a research paper.

First, study the outline, paying particular attention to the relationships among the sentences. Do the Roman numeral statements show a clear relation to the thesis? Do the subordinate parts clearly relate to the main units? Challenge every statement to test its relation to the idea it is being used to develop.

Second, study the text for structure alone. Is there a clear relation between successive parts of the paper and the outline? Does every paragraph play a part in advancing the purpose of the thesis, or are there any irrelevant paragraphs? Is there adequate transition between the paragraphs? Check the relation of text and outline by inserting the outline symbols in the margin opposite appropriate units of the text.

Third, study the notes as notes, to see what kind of material they contain and how it is expressed. These notes have been organized to develop the outline and contain three kinds of information, in this order: (1) the outline symbol showing the place the note occupies in the organizational scheme, (2) the material content, (3) the identification of the source from which the note was taken. The identification of the source consists of two parts: a Roman numeral keyed to the bibliography, so that I refers to the first item in the bibliography, II to the second item, and so on; and an Arabic numeral indicating the page reference.

Fourth, study the relation of notes and text. Are the paragraphs merely strings of notes in the same form they had in the note cards or is the author *composing* from the notes? If the author is more successful sometimes than others, notice where she is successful and why. If there are paragraphs which contain information not in the notes, try to determine whether such information would normally be part of the background a student would build during such a study. If there are notes that were not used, should they have been used, or was the author wise in omitting them? Try to see the development of the paper from the notes so that you will be better prepared to handle this problem when you come to it in your own paper.

Fifth, check the footnotes and bibliography. Do the forms used in this paper agree with your understanding of the conventions?

Finally, evaluate the whole paper in terms of: (1) the purposefulness of the author's procedure as it is revealed in notes, outline, and text, (2) the thoroughness of the development of the paper within the limits of a 2,000-word assignment, (3) the success of the author in communicating to you, as a reader, the results of her study.

THE PATTERN OF JEFFERSON'S SCHOLARSHIP [7]

by

BETTY BLACK

ENGLISH 101, SECTION **L**

MR. WALTERS

February 25, 1957

[7] Printed by permission of the author, Mrs. Betty Black. Not all instructors require a title page, but if one is required the form above may be used as a model.

311

# The Pattern of Jefferson's Scholarship

Thesis:   As a law student Thomas Jefferson developed
the scholarly habits of thorough study and
independent thinking which were characteristic of his later writings.

I. As a law student Jefferson developed the habit
of reading extensively and evaluating independently what he read.
A. His scholarly habits were established during
his study of the law.
B. His reading at this period was unusually extensive.
1. Although not required to, he studied law
for five years before seeking admission to
the bar.
2. His reading covered the whole history of
legal literature.
3. He read widely and carefully outside the
field of law.
a. His advice to a friend shows the kind
of reading program he thought advisable
for a lawyer.
b. His notebooks show the extensiveness of
his own reading.
C. His entries in his notebooks reveal his independent evaluation of what he read.

II. Jefferson's later writings reflect the scholarly
pattern which he developed as a law student.
A. His Summary View of the Rights of British
America shows extensive reading and independent thinking.
1. It is based on a thorough knowledge of
English history.
2. His opinions about the rights of the colonies were original, not a reflection of
prevailing contemporary opinion.
B. His Notes on Virginia provides another example of his scholarly workmanship.
1. The accurate and detailed answers it pro-

**312**

vided to a series of questions reflect the thoroughness with which he had collected his data.
2. His opinions are often at variance with those of his environment.
   a. Although a member of a slave-holding society, he was opposed to slavery.
   b. Although religious conformity was mandatory in his society, he defended the right of individuals to believe what they pleased.
C. His <u>Life</u> <u>and</u> <u>Morals</u> <u>of</u> <u>Jesus</u> <u>of</u> <u>Nazareth</u> is an excellent illustration of Jefferson's scholarly procedures in writing.
   1. It was undertaken in a spirit of scholarly curiosity.
   2. It was dominated by a concern for the facts as they were revealed through reason.

Thesis

Jefferson said he had "canine appetite" for reading

IX-13

I A

Jefferson would procrastinate about doing lessons as a boy, caught up with work during holidays

I-12

I A

J. impressed with gay social life during freshman year

VI-2

I A

In letter home, J. confessed to spending more time and money on social events than he thought wise

VI-22

I A

"Jefferson was an expert violinist, a good singer and dancer, proficient in outdoor sports, and an excellent horseman."

VIII-301

I A

Speaking of years as law student, J. said: they were "a time of life when I was bold in the pursuit of knowledge, never fearing to follow truth and reason to whatever results they led, and bearding every authority which stood in their way."

I-33

# THE PATTERN OF JEFFERSON'S SCHOLARSHIP

The habits of careful research and independent
thinking characteristic of Thomas Jefferson's writings in his adult life were established when he was
a student of law.  It was during his student years
that Jefferson developed what he termed his "canine
appetite"[1] for reading.  It was also during this
time that his almost belligerent demand to the right
to do his own thinking and his habit of freely ex-
ercising that right were formed.

As a boy, at the Reverend Dr. Maury's school,
Jefferson was considered a superior student, although he sometimes got behind in his assignments
and had to depend on occasional holidays to allow
him to catch up.[2]  During his first year at William
and Mary he allowed social activities to take more
of his time, attention, and money than he later
thought wise.[3]  Since he was an ardent horseman, a
competent violinist, a good dancer, and an easy and
pleasant conversationalist who was popular with the
young ladies of Williamsburg, he might have been
expected to continue his college career as he had
begun it, but in his second year he reduced his
social activities and devoted himself more intensively to his studies.  The following year, at the
age of nineteen, he began to read law under George
Wythe, one of the ablest lawyers in the colonies.
Under Wythe's influence his scholarly habits were
firmly established.  Jefferson himself described
these years as "a time of life when I was bold in

---

[1]Karl Lehmann, Thomas Jefferson:  American Humanist,
    p. 13.
[2]Claude G. Bowers, The Young Jefferson, p. 12.
[3]The Encyclopedia Americana (1950), XVI, 2.

**314b**

*I B 1*

J. studied law for 5 years before applying for admission to bar

*VI-1*

*I B 1*

Chinard says Patrick Henry studied for six months

*II-29*

*I B 1*

*Americana* says P. H. read law for "a few weeks."

*I B 1*

In The Head and Heart of Thomas Jefferson (p. 120), John Dos Passos says that P. H. read law for 6 weeks, then talked several prominent lawyers into signing his admission papers by promising to do more reading.

*I B 1*

Wythe considered J. his best student; W. also taught John Marshall and Henry Clay

I-31

*I B 2*

J.'s Commonplace Book of legal studies contains 556 articles analyzing special cases from the Reports of Cases in the King's Bench — George Andrews, Robert Raymond, Wm. Salkeld, and Coke's Institutes of the Laws of England.

II-28

315d

the pursuit of knowledge, never fearing to follow
truth and reason to whatever results they led, and
bearding every authority which stood in their way."[4]

Some indication of the thoroughness of Jefferson's study of the law may be seen from the fact
that he studied under Wythe for five years before
he applied for permission to practice before the
General Court of Virginia.[5] In his day no such
period of study was required or expected. Many men
passed their bar examinations after a very superficial reading of the law. Patrick Henry, for example, studied law for less than six months before
he was licensed to practice.[6] When we realize that
Jefferson's normal study day was fifteen hours long
and that Wythe, who numbered among his distinguished
pupils John Marshall and Henry Clay, considered
Jefferson his favorite student, the thoroughness of
his legal preparation becomes evident.[7]

In his reading of law Jefferson covered every
major work in this field from the beginning of English law during the reign of Alfred the Great up to
and including eighteenth century authors.[8] The
commonplace book he used to record his notes on
legal and political subjects is still in existence.
It contains no less than 556 entries in which he
analyzes special cases from the Reports of Cases in
the King's Bench and passages from the legal writings of George Andrews, Robert Raymond, William
Salkeld, and from the classic Coke's Institutes.[9]
At times, though, his enthusiasm for the Institutes

---

[4] Bowers, op. cit., p. 33.
[5] The Encyclopedia Americana (1950), XVI, 1.
[6] Gilbert Chinard, Thomas Jefferson: The Apostle of
    Americanism, p. 28.
[7] Bowers, op. cit., p. 31.
[8] Chinard, op. cit.. p. 28.          [9] Ibid.

I B 2

Concerning use of Commonplace Book, J. wrote: "In
reading the Reporters, enter in a commonplace book
every case of value, condensed into the narrowest
compress possible, which will admit presenting
distinctly the principles of the case. This operation is doubly useful, insomuch as it obliges the
student to seek out the pith of the case, and
habituates him to a condensation of thought, and
to the acquisition of the most valuable of talents,
that of never using two words when one will do."

III-81-82

I B 2

In letter to John Page, J. says: "Well, Page,
I do wish the Devil had old Coke, for I am sure
I never was so tired of an old dull scoundrel
in my life."

VIII-78

I B 3a

Study plan recommended for law students based on
his own schedule:
    dawn--8 o'clock, read books about agriculture,
        chemistry, astronomy, zoology, botany,
        ethics or national religion
    8-12, read law
    12-1, politics
    afternoon, history
    sunset--bedtime, literature, criticism, rhetoric,
        and oratory

I-32

I B 3b

Passages assumed to have been written in the
"Literary Bible" while J. was studying law
include: Herodotus (in Greek), Bolingbroke (30pp.
in Chinard's book), Cicero (in Latin. J. admired
his philosophy), Euripides (in Greek), Homer (Greek,
also some of Pope's translation), Virgil (Latin),
Ovid (Latin), Pope's Essay on Man, Milton's Paradise Lost, Shakespeare (no comedies or love stories),
English drama (Dryden, Jonson, Otway, Rowe)

IV-4ff

I B 3b

Chinard says, "His knowledge of
Greek literature was more than a
superficial one that would have
enabled him to shine in
learned society... Through constant use and systematic study
he really lived in the commerce
of the Greeks."

IV-11

316a

seems to have flagged.  Once, in a letter to his
friend John Page, he wrote: "Well, Page, I do wish
the Devil had old Coke, for I am sure I never was
so tired of an old dull scoundrel in all my life."[10]
Despite this reaction against the dusty law books,
he persevered in his studies until he had completed
the program he had set for himself.

During this time Jefferson did not confine his
studies to the law alone.  Shortly after he was
admitted to the bar a friend who was beginning his
own law studies wrote asking Jefferson's advice on
how to budget his time.  The schedule of reading
which Jefferson sent in reply is generally considered to be the one which he himself followed: from
dawn until eight o'clock, the study of agriculture,
chemistry, anatomy, zoology, ethics, and natural
religion; from eight until noon, the law; from noon
until one, politics; in the afternoon, history; and
from sunset until bedtime, literature, criticism,
rhetoric and oratory.[11]

Along with this schedule he included a list of
books for each subject.  There can be no doubt that
Jefferson read these books, since references to them
appear in his letters, his later works, his commonplace book, and in another notebook which Dr. Chinard has called "The Literary Bible of Thomas Jefferson," in which Jefferson made notes on his reading
outside the fields of law and government.  That
notebook contains passages from Homer, Herodotus,
and Euripides in Greek, and excerpts from Virgil,
Cicero, Horace, and Ovid in Latin.  It also contains
references to the writings of European philosophers

---

[10] Marie Kimball, _Jefferson_: _The Road to Glory_, p. 78.
[11] Bowers, _op_. _cit_., p. 32.

**316b**

IC

In commonplacing Homer, J. ignored all passages concerning mythology and battles. Collected verses expressing poet's views on life and human destiny.

IV-5-6

IC

J. copied passages from books because he agreed with them. Example: passage from Euripides stressing man's natural aversion to crime

IX-44

IC

While studying with Wythe, J. said he "was in the habit of abridging and commonplacing what I read, meriting it, and sometimes mixing my own reflections on the subject."

II-84

IIA

Summary View established J. as a leader in America.

I-95

IIA

Adams said J. was chosen to write Declaration of Independence because he had "the reputation for a masterly pen."

I-146-7

317a

and essayists and to the works of such English
writers as Shakespeare, Jonson, Dryden, Otway, Rowe,
Pope, and Bolingbroke.[12]

The "Literary Bible" reveals not only the extent
of Jefferson's reading but also something of his
independent evaluation of what he read. He often
passed over much-quoted selections to record or make
reflections on less well known excerpts. For example, he made no notes on descriptions of the war
in the Iliad, nor on Greek mythology, nor on any of
the famous examples of Cicero's oratory. Instead,
he abridged passages which expressed the philosophy
of the authors and "merited" or evaluated those
passages, sometimes adding his own thoughts on the
subject.[13]

In 1774 Jefferson, then a member of the House
of Burgesses, was elected a delegate for his county
to a convention at Williamsburg to consider the
state of the colony and to elect the Virginia representatives to the First Continental Congress. As
preparation for the work of the convention Jefferson
wrote the Summary View of the Rights of British
America, a pamphlet which established him as a
writer and a revolutionary leader, and later led to
his selection as the man to frame the Declaration
of Independence. His preparation for the writing
of the Summary View, like his preparation for the
law, was both thorough and thoughtful and illustrates the pattern of extensive reading and independent thinking which he had established during
his student days.

The Summary View is an analysis of the relations

---

[12] Gilbert Chinard (ed.), The Literary Bible of
Thomas Jefferson, p. 6.
[13] Chinard, Thomas Jefferson: The Apostle of
Americanism, p. 84.

## II A 1

In S-V J. draws a parallel between Saxon and
Dane migration to England and English migration
to America

## II A 1

J's Commonplace Book shows evidence of a
great deal of research into history of Celts
and Gauls as preparation for writing the
Summary View

VIII-241

IX-49

## II A 1

The opinions of S-V result of study of English
history, especially Dalrymple, Molesworth, and
Pelloutier

II-48

## II A 1

Chinard says J. tackled Summary View "with
the methods used by a lawyer to prove title
to a piece of property."

II-51

## II A 1

S-V respectfully received by English liberals.
Burke published and used it to put pressure
on Lord North

I-94

318a

between the colonies and the mother country.  In it
Jefferson drew an analogy between the settling of
the American colonies by British citizens and the
settling of England during the fifth to tenth centuries by German and Scandinavian adventurers, and
from that analogy he advanced the thesis that the
claims of the British government to authority over
the American colonies were no more valid than would
be similar claims by German and Scandinavian governments to authority over Great Britain.[14]  In order
to develop this thesis he read extensively and made
notes in his commonplace book on the history of
colonizing in general and of the Anglo-Saxon migrations to England in particular.  He consulted law
books for legal precedents for establishing the
ownership of property during the early days of English history.  The entries in his commonplace book
at this time show that he studied Sir John Dalrymple's Essay Towards a General History of Feudal
Property in Great Britain and the works of other
British legal and historical writers[15] in his
thoroughgoing effort to cite the facts of British
history to refute the British claims with respect
to the colonies.  As a consequence of the thoroughness of his work, the Summary View, although it was
a revolutionary document, was received with respect
even among British lawyers and liberal statesmen,
and Burke, after making a few alterations in the
text, published and used it in support of his own
efforts to force Lord North to undertake conciliation with America.[16]

The Summary View must be considered the result

[14] Kimball, op. cit., p. 241.
[15] Gilbert Chinard, Thomas Jefferson: The Apostle of
Americanism, p. 48.
[16] Bowers, op. cit., p. 94.

**318b**

**II A 2**

Bowers says that what J.
was asking for was status
now held by members of
British Commonwealth.
Such a suggestion extremely
radical in J's time

I - 87

**II A 2**

J. wrote S-V as instructions to be read to delegates at Virginia Convention.  J. took sick and
could not attend.  Text exhibited at Convention,
but considered too radical to be used as
instructions.  Looked at by some, but not formally presented to Convention

XI-5-6

**II A 2**

Difference between S-V and
Fairfax Resolution is that
J. maintained complete independence of the country
from Great Britain

II - 46-7

**II A 2**

J. said that at time he
wrote S-V only Wythe
agreed with him

VIII - 241

**II B 1**

Notes on Va. contained answers
to 23 queries sent J. by
Barbé-Marbois, secretary of
French legation.

II - 118-9

**II B 1**

List of native plants
and animals

II - 121

319a

of Jefferson's independent thinking about the relationship between the colonies and the Crown. In a
sense, he anticipated by nearly two centuries the
relationship between Britain and her colonies that
now exists in the British Commonwealth.[17] The proposal of such a relationship in 1774 was considered
radical, even by those who agreed that the British
government had far exceeded its authority with respect to the American colonies; for, although many
Americans protested the British taxation policies,
most of them acknowledged Britain's right to some
control over the colonies. Jefferson's argument,
therefore, was far in advance of even the most advanced American opinion. As he himself said later,
when he wrote the Summary View he could find no one
who agreed with him except George Wythe.[18]

Another example of Jefferson's thorough and independent scholarship is his Notes on Virginia, a
book written in answer to a questionnaire received
by Jefferson from Barbé-Marbois, the secretary of
the French legation, concerning the physical, political, and social characteristics of Virginia. To
each of the twenty-three queries Jefferson provided
extensive, detailed, and accurate answers from a
mass of data which he had been accumulating about
his native state over the years. In reply to questions about the government he supplied a record of
events up to that time along with an analysis of the
present situation and frequent expressions of his
views on what the future might hold. He also included a complete list of the plants and animals
native to Virginia with detailed descriptions.

Although Notes on Virginia was primarily a re-

---

[17]Bowers, op. cit. p. 87.
[18]Kimball, op. cit., p. 241.

319b

## II B2a

J. says slave-holding injures white man. Owner
teaches his children cruelty when child sees
him mistreat a slave

X-99-100

## II B2a

J. attacks slave-holding and says of Negroes,
"The opinion that they are inferior in the
faculties or reason and imagination must be
hazarded with great diffidence."

X-99-100

## II B2b

In Notes on Va. J. says that
though there is no statutory
oppression of religious belief,
there is still oppression
under common law

XI-674

## II B2b

J. says, "The legitimate powers of
government extend to such acts
only as are injurious to others. But
it does me no injury for my neighbor to say that there are twenty
gods, or no God. It neither picks
my pocket nor breaks my leg."

XI-675

320a

port of the state, it does contain evidence of
Jefferson's ability to free his thinking from the
customs and conventional points of view of his environment. This is especially true of his remarks
on slavery. He was born into a society in which he
and his associates were slave holders. Slavery was
not only an established institution; it was the
foundation of the agricultural economy on which the
prosperity of the state and the privileges of the
aristocracy, of which Jefferson was a member, depended. Yet, in Notes on Virginia he attacked
slavery as a moral wrong that would one day prove
injurious to the country. He could not even accept
the prevailing assumption that Negroes were a lesser
breed. "The opinion," he said, "that they are inferior in the faculties of reason and imagination
must be hazarded with great diffidence."[19]

Another example of his independent thinking in
Notes on Virginia was his attitude towards religious
conformity. In Virginia at the time of Jefferson's
birth and childhood the Church of England was the
established church. He grew up in a culture in
which it was considered a crime to fail to attend
church services or to disparage an article of faith.
Even after the revolution the belief in complete
religious freedom was not widely held. Yet, in
Notes on Virginia Jefferson maintained the right of
the individual to believe, or not to believe, what
he pleased. He felt there was no compelling reason
for religious conformity. ". . . it does me no injury," he wrote, "for my neighbor to say there are
twenty gods, or no God. It neither picks my pocket

---

[19] Saul K. Padover, Thomas Jefferson on Democracy,
    pp. 99-100.

320b

II C 1

Early in life J. copied passage
(a sign of approval) from one
of Locke's books saying that
the words of Jesus were only
true basis of Christianity but
present sources were historically
conditioned

IX-89

II C 1

Jefferson and Priestly attempted to unearth the
"original sources" of the words of Jesus. The
"Jeffersonian Bible" was the result of this
search

IX-89

nor breaks my leg."[20]

Perhaps the best illustration of Jefferson's scholarly approach to a subject is The Life and Morals of Jesus of Nazareth. Although he was attacked many times during his political career for his religious beliefs, Jefferson's ideas about religious freedom were not a result of indifference to religion. In some of his earliest entries in his notebooks there is evidence that he was reading and giving thought to religious matters. At one time he copied a passage from Locke to the effect that the words of Jesus are the only true foundations of Christianity but that the present sources of Christ's teachings have been affected by traditional beliefs.[21] Because Jefferson found himself in agreement with this opinion and because he appreciated the difficulty of translating from one language to another without losing significant shades of meaning, he set out to discover for himself just what were the words of Jesus. The Life and Morals of Jesus of Nazareth, more popularly the "Jefferson Bible," was an attempt to provide an answer.

The actual writing of the book was controlled by two disciplines: careful collection and comparison of the evidence, and the acceptance or rejection of it on the basis of reason rather than authority. To compare the evidence, Jefferson pasted texts from the New Testament in Greek, Latin, French, and English in columns side by side.

To be guided by reason rather than authority, he followed his own advice to his nephew, that the Bible be read critically, like any other book:

---

[20] Saul K. Padover (ed.), The Complete Jefferson, p. 675.
[21] Lehmann, op. cit., p. 89.

*II C 2*

J.'s advice to nephew: "Read the Bible, then, as
you would read Livy or Tacitus. The facts which
are within the ordinary course of nature, you will
believe on the authority of the writer, as you do
those of the same kind in Livy or Tacitus. . . . But
those facts in the Bible which contradict the laws
of nature must be examined with more care, and under a variety of faces. Here you must recur to the
pretensions of the writer to inspiration from God.
Examine upon what evidence his pretensions are
founded, and whether that evidence is so strong, as
that its falsehood would be more improbable than a
change in the laws of nature, in the case he
relates."

XI-1058

*II C 2*

J. wrote in a letter to Adams: "I think that
every Christian sect gives a great handle to
atheism by their general dogma that, without
revelation, there would not be sufficient proof
of the being of God."

X-168

*II C 2*

J. wrote: "Of all the systems of morality,
ancient or modern, which have come under my
observation, none appears to me so pure as
that of Jesus."

X-119

## 9

> Read the Bible, then, as you would read Livy or
> Tacitus. The facts which are within the ordi-
> nary course of nature, you will believe on the
> authority of the writer, as you do those of the
> same kind in Livy or Tacitus. . . . But those
> facts in the Bible which contradict the laws of
> nature must be examined with more care, and un-
> der a variety of faces. Here you must recur to
> the pretensions of the writer to inspiration
> from God. Examine upon what evidence his pre-
> tensions are founded, and whether that evidence
> is so strong, as that its falsehood would be
> more improbable than a change in the laws of
> nature, in the case he relates.22

Accordingly, he accepted those stories which revealed the teachings of Jesus and rejected stories
of miracles, which, he felt, had no real relation to
these teachings. He also rejected those passages
which had to be supported by revelation. "I think,"
he wrote in a letter to Adams," that every Christian
sect gives a great handle to atheism by their general dogma that, without revelation, there would not
be sufficient proof of the being of God."[23] The
result was a work which emphasized what Jefferson
considered the purest system of morality known[24] and
toned down or omitted incidents of the supernatural.

The three works that are cited in this paper to
illustrate the pattern of Jefferson's scholarship
could be supplemented by his other writings and by
activities other than writing -- for example, his
agricultural studies and experiments. He was, perhaps by disposition, but certainly by training, a
scholar, and the foundations of his scholarship were
laid in the habits of thorough study and critical
evaluation which, under Wythe's stimulation and
supervision, he developed in his student days at
Williamsburg.

---

[22] Padover, The Complete Jefferson, p. 1058.
[23] Padover, Jefferson on Democracy, p. 168.
[24] Ibid., p. 119.

NOTE that while this bibliography looks comparatively brief, it represents the rather thorough reading of nine books and two encyclopedia articles which were of actual use to the student in the preparation of her paper. She unquestionably examined a number of other sources, some of which she found of general help; but she did not list any of these in her final bibliography because they were not of immediate and specific use to her. For details of the form in which the bibliography is set up, see pages 283–287.

## 10

## Bibliography

Bowers, Claude G. The Young Jefferson, 1743-1789. Boston: Houghton Mifflin Company, 1945.

Chinard, Gilbert. (ed.). The Commonplace Book of Thomas Jefferson. Baltimore: The Johns Hopkins Press, 1926.

_____ (ed.). The Literary Bible of Thomas Jefferson. Baltimore: The Johns Hopkins Press, 1928.

_____. Thomas Jefferson: The Apostle of Americanism, 2nd ed. Boston: Little, Brown & Co., 1948.

"Jefferson, Thomas," The Encyclopaedia Britannica, (1911), XV, 301-307.

"Jefferson, Thomas," The Encyclopedia Americana, (1950), XVI, 1-14.

Jefferson, Thomas. The Life and Morals of Jesus of Nazareth. St. Louis: N. D. Thompson Publishing Company, 1902.

Kimball, Marie. Jefferson: The Road to Glory, 1743-1776. New York: Coward-McCann, Inc., 1943.

Lehmann, Karl. Thomas Jefferson: American Humanist. New York: The MacMillan Company, 1947.

Padover, Saul K. (ed.). Thomas Jefferson on Democracy. New York: D. Appleton-Century Company, 1939.

_____ (ed.). The Complete Jefferson. New York: Duell, Sloan & Pearce, Inc., 1943.

*Same author*

*Same author*

323b

# 15

* * ARGUMENT
* *
* AND
* *
* PERSUASION
*

IN GENERAL, the term "argument" means to give reasons for or against a belief. In popular usage the word is often used to mean giving reasons to others in order to convince or persuade them, as when we compare costs to persuade dad that it would be cheaper to buy a new car than to maintain the old one. In this chapter, however, we shall make a distinction between "argument" and "persuasion." The distinction is this: argument is the process of *reaching* conclusions; persuasion is the art of *getting others to accept* these conclusions. As we shall see, persuasion usually relies on argument, since one way of persuading others is to show them the reasoning by which we reached our conclusions. But argument need not be limited to offering reasons to others. The word may be used, as it is in logic and in this chapter, for the reasoning process by which we draw conclusions from evidence. In this sense, argument is a form of thinking. We have constructed an argument when we have "thought out" a problem and reached a conclusion about it.

## The Structure of Argument

In Chapters 3 and 4 we dealt with informal and formal organizational patterns of exposition. There we were concerned with the relation of the parts of an essay. We factored a thesis into its subtheses and provided explanatory information to make each factor clear. In dealing now with the structure of argument we are still dealing with the relations of parts; we are making a special application of the general lesson learned earlier. Instead of *thesis* we will now use the term *conclusion;* instead of *explanation* or *illustration* we will say *proof.* But essentially we are going to be studying the relation between a general statement and the specific statements which develop it.

324

In its simplest form an argument consists of two statements, one of which is a conclusion drawn from the other. Thus

*He is a careless driver.* He has been involved in four automobile collisions within the past year.

is an argument in which the italicized conclusion is drawn from the other statement, which we call a *premise.* In its simplest form, therefore, an argument is a conclusion, drawn or *inferred* from a premise. *Whenever we have two statements so related that one is inferred as a conclusion from the other, we have an argument.*

Since this premise-conclusion relationship is the basic unit of argument, let us fix it in mind by contrasting statements which are related as premise and conclusion with statements which are not so related. Below, the paired statements at the left consist of a premise and an italicized conclusion inferred from that premise — the beginning and end points of an inference. In contrast, the paired statements at the right are not the beginning and end points of an inference. They are logically independent of each other. In these examples we shall use the symbols P–C as an abbreviation for premise-conclusion.

| *P–C Relationship* | *No P–C Relationship* |
|---|---|
| Steam is coming from the kettle. *The water must be boiling.* | Will you have some tea? The water is boiling. |
| *He has a weakness for blondes.* Every girl he has dated has been a blonde. | He has a weakness for blondes. He also likes brunettes and redheads. |
| Final examinations cause unnecessary hardships for both students and instructors. *Final examinations should be abolished.* | Final examinations cause unnecessary hardships for both students and instructors. Final examinations encourage cramming. |
| *Bill Smith is sure to make the All-Conference team;* he is the leading scorer in the conference. | Bill Smith is the leading scorer in the conference. He is only a junior. |
| Judges are college graduates with much legal experience; therefore *a board of judges would be better qualified than a jury to decide law suits.* | Judges are college graduates with much legal experience. Many judges are elected to office. |

Each of the paired statements at the left is an argument, because each pair consists of a premise and a conclusion inferred from the premise. Notice that we do not say that these arguments are "good" or "convincing." Not all people will "accept" them. Some may deny that the premises are "true"; others may refuse to accept the conclusions as logical inferences from the premises; still others may want additional premises or "proof." But whether acceptable or not, the paired statements at the left are related as premise and conclusion, while those at the right are not.

So far we have been considering arguments of the most rudimentary structure — a single premise and a single conclusion. In practice most arguments are more complex. They may consist of several premises from which a single conclusion is inferred — for example: Final examinations should be abolished because (1) they are detrimental to student health, (2) they place undue emphasis on memorizing facts, (3) they encourage last-minute cramming instead of daily preparation, (4) they penalize the nervous student. Or a conclusion from one or more premises may be used as a premise for another conclusion, as one unit of argument is built on another. In the following series the parenthetical comment identifies the P–C relations among the statements:

1. The adoption of the 13-month calendar would create serious disadvantages. (Conclusion from all other statements.)

2. It would require large-scale conversions to the new system. (Premise for 1, but conclusion from 3 and 4.)

3. All dates in existing books would have to be changed. (Premise for 2.)

4. Existing contracts and leases would have to be redated. (Premise for 2.)

5. It would be expensive. (Premise for 1, but conclusion from 6, 7, and 8.)

6. The cost of redating documents would be expensive. (Premise for 5.)

7. The cost of operating a business would increase. (Premise for 5, but conclusion from 8.)

8. Monthly statements and payrolls would have to be prepared thirteen times a year instead of twelve times. (Premise for 7.)

If we set up these statements in outline form, the outline symbols help us to see the structure of the argument, which is also indicated by the P–C symbols at the left:

| | | |
|---|---|---|
| C | *Conclusion:* | The adoption of the 13-month calendar would create serious disadvantages. |
| P–C | I. | It would require large-scale conversions to the new system. |
| P | | A. All dates in existing books would have to be changed. |
| P | | B. All contracts and leases would have to be redated. |
| P–C | II. | It would be expensive. |
| P | | A. The cost of redating documents would be expensive. |
| P–C | | B. The cost of operating a business would increase. |
| P | | 1. Monthly statements and payrolls would have to be prepared thirteen times a year instead of twelve times. |

An outline of an argument, then, is a P–C outline. It is an arrangement of premises and conclusions into a structure which reflects the author's thinking. Traditionally, the outline begins with the conclusion and moves down to the premises, though the direction of the author's thinking is usually from the premises to the conclusion.

**Assumptions.** Literally, an assumption is something that is taken for granted. If we are planning to buy an expensive article — say an air conditioner — and a friend tells us that he can get us the model we want at a 20 per cent discount, he does not usually ask if we would like to save 20 per cent of the normal price; he assumes or takes for granted that we would.

Whenever we go from a premise to a conclusion some kind of assumption is implied in our inference. A student who solves an algebra problem and gets the same answer as the one in the textbook assumes that the textbook answer is correct. We might structure his reasoning this way:

*Premise:* My answer agrees with the one in the textbook.

*Assumption:* The textbook answer is correct.

*Conclusion:* My answer is correct.

Actually, though, the assumption is seldom stated as part of the argument. The student may not even be conscious that he is making an assumption. Yet the assumption is implied in his inference, since it would not be logical to believe that an answer that agrees with the textbook is correct unless one first believed that the textbook is correct.

Because assumptions are seldom clearly stated, or made explicit, it is sometimes difficult to identify them. Yet a recognition of the assumption in an argument is necessary in any evaluation of the argument. The following additional illustrations should give you enough experience with assumptions so that you can detect those that are implied in later exercises.

| *Argument* | *Assumption* |
|---|---|
| Better pass that car; the driver is a woman. | It is dangerous to follow a woman driver. |
| There goes the bell; I'm late for class. | The bell is working properly — that is, it is on time. |
| I guess she's no longer angry; she smiled at me. | A smile is a friendly sign. |
| A careful study at thirty widely-scattered colleges shows that the heights and weights of entering fresh- | A conclusion derived from these thirty colleges will hold true for the country as a whole. |

| *Argument* | *Assumption* |
|---|---|
| men are greater than they were thirty years ago. This indicates that young men and women are both taller and heavier than they were a generation ago. | |
| Just as a citizen cannot take the law into his own hands but must settle his differences with others through the courts, so must a nation be required to renounce war as a means of settling international disputes. | With respect to settling their differences, nations are like individuals, and a procedure that works well among individuals will work well among nations. |
| The fact that so many young men failed the army physical tests when called in the draft shows that the general health of the nation is poor. | The tests provide a reasonable measurement of general health and the draftees are a fair sample of the whole population. |

## Exercises

The following exercises are designed to increase your familiarity with the premise-conclusion relationship so that you can better perceive the structure of arguments. The exercises become progressively complex. Since all we are concerned with now is the relationship between premise and conclusion, do not bother about the truth or soundness of the conclusions.

**A.** In each pair of statements, one is a conclusion inferred from the other. For each pair write the letter ( *a* or *b* ) which labels the conclusion and state the assumption implied in each inference.

1. *a.* A board of judges would be better than the jury system.
    *b.* Judges can distinguish between emotional appeals and facts.
2. *a.* Judges would be better qualified than a jury to decide complex questions.
    *b.* Judges are college graduates with much legal experience.
3. *a.* Judge Knott says, "Because of the inefficiency of the jury system, the United States is the safest place in the world in which to commit murder."
    *b.* The jury protects the criminal.
4. *a.* The average juror ignores the facts in arriving at a decision.
    *b.* Questions put to the jurors by a correspondent of the *New York World* after the Sinclair-Doheny trial revealed the jury's ignorance of the fundamental facts of the case.
5. *a.* England has been gradually discarding the jury system.
    *b.* The tendency to discard the jury system is growing.
6. *a.* Children's Court in New York may now try felonies of the highest degree without a jury.
    *b.* The jury system is gradually being discarded in the United States.

7. *a.* Americans need not fear injustice if the jury system is replaced by a board of judges.
   *b.* Judges are elected by the people.
8. *a.* A jury is inefficient in determining and judging the facts.
   *b.* No educational qualifications are required for jury service.
9. *a.* There is a great deal of dissatisfaction with the jury system.
   *b.* We should replace the jury by a board of judges.

**B.** In each set of three statements, the first is a conclusion inferred from *one* of the other two. For each set write the letter (*a* or *b*) which identifies the premise.

1. The 12-month calendar fails to divide the year into consistent units.
   *a.* The months are of unequal length.
   *b.* The 12-month calendar is called the Gregorian calendar.
2. The 12-month calendar is not satisfactory.
   *a.* It is about 200 years old.
   *b.* It causes inconvenience and expense in keeping business statistics.
3. The proposed 13-month calendar is more consistent than the present one.
   *a.* The 13th month would not be an unlucky one.
   *b.* Each of the 13 months would have 28 days.
4. In the 13-month calendar days and dates are perfectly correlated.
   *a.* In the 13-month calendar Monday always falls on the 2nd, 9th, 16th, or 23rd.
   *b.* In the 13-month calendar there is no need for leap year.
5. There would be no great inconvenience in a change to a 13-month calendar.
   *a.* There is a slight inconvenience even in the most desirable changes.
   *b.* Tables for converting from a 12- to a 13-month calendar are simple and accurate.
6. The 13-month calendar is not an untried proposal.
   *a.* Many businesses are now using the 13-month calendar.
   *b.* Religious opposition to the 13-month calendar is expected.

**C.** In each set of three statements, one is the conclusion, one is the premise, and the remaining one has no P–C relation with the other two. We can call it an irrelevant statement. Mark the conclusion C, the premise P, and the irrelevant statement X.

1. Final examinations foster bad study habits.
   Final examinations encourage cramming as a substitute for daily preparation.
   Final examinations penalize the nervous student.
2. Final examinations are all crowded within a two-week period.
   Final examinations do not provide a fair test of what a student knows.
   Final examinations cannot cover all the work of the course.
3. Final examinations create student-faculty antagonism.
   Final examinations force students to compete with each other.
   Final examinations force students to compete with the faculty.

4. Students seldom get enough sleep during final examinations.

College students generally do not get enough physical exercise.

Final examinations are detrimental to student health.

5. Most college students have very poor memories.

Final examinations give excessive credit for the ability to memorize.

Most examination questions are questions of fact.

**D.** In each set of three statements one is a conclusion from both the others, one is a conclusion from one statement and a premise for the other, and one is a premise only. Mark the conclusion C, the combined premise and conclusion P–C, and the premise only P.

1. We should adopt Federal Aid to Education to provide uniform educational standards in all states.

The amount spent on education by different states is unequal.

New York spends much more on each child's education than does Mississippi.

2. Federal support for Land Grant colleges has resulted in compulsory ROTC.

Federal Aid to education would bring federal control over the curriculum.

The University of Illinois, a Land Grant college, is required to have an ROTC program.

3. Federal Aid to Education is necessary to raise teachers' salaries.

Compared with doctors and lawyers, teachers have less real income now than they had in 1920.

Teachers' salaries have failed to adjust to the increased cost of living to anywhere near the extent that salaries in other professions have increased.

4. Arkansas pays a higher percentage of its income for education than does Ohio.

The Southern States especially need Federal Aid to Education.

The Southern States are making a greater effort to improve their educational systems than are the Northern States.

**E.** In each set of four statements, any statement may be: (1) a conclusion only, (2) a premise only, (3) a combined premise-conclusion, or (4) an irrelevant statement. Mark each statement in the set P, C, P–C, or X to identify its relation to the others in the set. Do not assume that there must be an X or a P–C in each set.

1. The office of the Presidency is made more exacting than is necessary.

The President has many obligations that could easily be discharged by an assistant.

The President must sign every commission in the armed services.

The annual tour dates of the marine band must be approved by the President.

2. Most European countries compress their highly intensified pre-college activities into 10 years compared to 12 years in the United States.

School children in Europe work harder and play less than those in the United States.

Technical training in European schools is based on the needs of individual countries.

For the European student extracurricular activities are rare.

3. Our antiquated "child labor" laws promote delinquency by denying jobs to young people.

Unionization of labor has resulted in limitation of employment for minors.

One expert has stated that he has yet to see a really serious delinquent who was kept busy by a job.

A study of case histories reveals that many delinquents have fallen into gang activities because they could not secure work permits.

4. The relation between doctor and patient would be damaged by a compulsory national health program.

The American Medical Association does much to improve the doctor-patient relationship.

Doctors, regardless of individual ability, would be placed on the same professional plane by a compulsory program.

A compulsory national health scheme would lower the standards of the medical profession.

5. In reversing convictions, judges too often show greater concern with the behavior of the police than with the prevention of crime.

In one out of three cases in which the defendant is convicted an appeal is made to a higher court.

Our present legal system often permits the guilty to escape just punishment.

Charging the police with unreasonable arrest is a common dodge used by lawyers when evidence of guilt is undeniable.

**F.** The following ten statements represent a scrambled version of a student outline of an argument that the adoption of Universal Military Training would hinder the cause of democracy. Reconstruct the outline by studying the P-C relations among the statements and ordering them in conventional outline form. Then state whatever assumptions are implied in the argument.

1. Compulsory training in Germany resulted in the indoctrination of the youth, and through them their families, with militaristic ideas.

2. Dr. Einstein says, "If the United States introduces UMT it will intensify the conviction everywhere that in the foreseeable future the problems of the world will be decided by brute force, instead of by supranational organization."

3. In Japan, military conscription did away with the warrior class and extended to all Japanese the military psychology which once characterized the few.

4. The adoption of UMT would hinder the cause of democracy by militarizing the minds of the people of the United States.

5. Ex-congressman Bruce Barton says, "It means putting the education of our boys into the hands of thousands of men whose professional background is — Don't argue. Don't talk. Don't think. Do what you're told."

6. A *New York Post* editorial says that our adoption of compulsory military training would be interpreted abroad as a renunciation of our faith in a peaceful world and our hope of restoring the world's economic health.

7. The adoption of UMT would hinder the cause of democracy internationally by creating a fear of the United States and by acknowledging a lack of faith in the democratic system.

8. In France, the continued practice of peacetime conscription and the resultant increase in civilian reliance on military leadership and thinking helped produce the sense of false security which proved fatal.

9. The experience of other nations indicates that the practice of compulsory military training over a period of years results in the militarization of the nation.

10. Mr. Devan asserts that the adoption of UMT would confirm the suspicion of other nations that we are an imperialistic power seeking domination by war.

### Types of Premises

The most common types of premises are statements of fact, judgments, and expert testimony. *Statements of fact* may be verified by checking them against the facts which they report. If the statement corresponds to the facts it is "true"; if it does not, it is "false." Since the facts lie outside the mind of the person making the statements and are presumably the same for all people, the truth or falsity of a factual statement does not depend on the opinion of the writer or speaker.

Statements of fact make the most reliable premises. Among intelligent people the authority of facts is decisive; hence the common saying, "the facts speak for themselves." This saying is something of an exaggeration, since different conclusions can sometimes be inferred from the same factual premise, but controversies tend to dissolve when they are reduced to questions of fact. For this reason, the best preparation for argument is a diligent search for the facts.

*Judgments* are conclusions inferred from the facts. The inference may be so obvious that the judgment hardly differs from a statement of fact, or the judgment may go so far beyond the facts that we have trouble seeing what the facts were. For example, consider these judgments:

> The cost of a new car in 1957 is more than double what it was in 1937.
> All things considered, a new car in 1957 is a better buy for the money than a new car was in 1937.

The first statement is a conclusion from a contrast of the prices, but the inference involves nothing more than a simple computation. The inference of the second statement includes a consideration of the relative purchasing power of the dollar in 1937 and 1957, a consideration of the improvements available in modern cars, and a decision that the increase in value of the 1957 car more than offsets the increase in cost. This kind of value judgment depends as much on an *evaluation* of the facts as on the facts themselves, and since evaluation may differ with different people, such a judgment will often be less reliable than a statement of fact.

*Expert testimony* is a statement by a person presumed to be an authority on the subject. His statement may be factual, as when a doctor describes the conditions revealed by an autopsy; or it may be a judgment, as when a psychiatrist testifies that in his opinion a defendant is insane. Since expert testimony is always a statement of fact or a judgment, it could be dealt with under those two categories. It is here considered separately (1) because factual statements by an expert are often extremely difficult for a nonexpert to verify (for example, ordinary citizens cannot usually check the facts to determine whether a swimmer's death was caused by heart failure or by drowning); and (2) because the qualifications of the expert require special consideration.

Expert testimony is often abused. It is too easy to assume that the testimony of any prominent person is reliable, though most of us — if we stop to think — realize that a man may be distinguished in one field but not in another, or may be expert in one phase of a subject and still know little about another phase of it. To be reliable, expert testimony must meet two requirements: the expert must be an authority on the particular point at issue, and there must be no reasonable probability that he is biased. Thus the testimony of a college president might be more reliable on the organization of his college than on the needs of the public schools or on the wisdom of deferring college students from the draft. For he might not be expert on public school matters, and his position might prejudice him toward keeping young men in college.

## Exercises

In the following arguments,[1] identify the premises as statements of fact, judgments, or expert testimony. If the premise is testimony, consider its reliability.

1. "If English speaking people will streamline their spelling . . . they will soon save enough money to pay the entire cost of World War II. George Bernard Shaw repeatedly states this opinion in letters to the London *Times*."

2. "Our attempts to make a foreign alphabet of twenty-six letters do the work of forty-two are pitiable. We write the same vowel twice to give it

[1] Adapted from "Should Spelling Be Streamlined?" by Falk Johnson in *The American Mercury* for September, 1948. Reprinted by special permission of *The American Mercury* and the author.

a different sound . . . or make two consonants represent simple sounds for which the alphabet does not provide."

3. "As a result of these discrepancies between alphabet and pronunciation, most letters represent different sounds. The Merriam-Webster dictionary, for example, lists eight different pronunciations for the letter *a* and illustrates them by the following words: *ale, chaotic, care, add, account, arm, ask,* and *sofa.* (The *a* in *ale* is accented, that in *chaotic* unaccented.)"

4. When we realize that fifty per cent of all words in English are not spelled as they are sounded, we see what a mess English is.

5. "On this side of the Atlantic, too, the demand for reform in spelling is strong. For example, in the *Journal of the National Education Association,* Dr. Frank C. Laubach, who has developed at Columbia University a new system known as "Basic Spelling," declared . . . 'I have asked several hundred audiences how many favored reformed spelling and three-fourths of them have raised their hands.'"

6. The confusion of English spelling has been encouraged by misguided attempts to "correct" what seems like faulty spelling. Caxton's Dutch typesetters put the *h* in *ghost* to make it conform to Dutch spelling, although there never was an *h* in the Old English *gast* from which our *ghost* is descended. Then Dr. Johnson, the great eighteenth century lexicographer, inserted the *h* in *ghastly* and *aghast.*

7. There is a tremendous lack of agreement between sound and spelling in English. "A single one of the eight *a* sounds is represented by at least fourteen different symbols: *a* in *ale, ae* in *maelstrom, ai* in *bait, ao* in *gaol* (pronounced jail), *au* in *gauge, ay* in *day, aye* in *aye* (meaning always), both *e* and *ee* in *melee, ea* in *break, eh* in *eh, ey* in *prey, et* in *beret,* and *eigh* in *weigh.*"

8. English is full of silent letters. "Of the 604,000 words in the Merriam-Webster unabridged dictionary, over 400,000 have at least one silent letter; and many, of course, have more than one."

9. The spelling of college students is worse today than it ever was. According to an editorial in the local newspaper, two out of every five college graduates consistently misspell such common words as *Britain, committee, duly, niece, professor, tragedy,* and *weird.*

10. English spelling is sadly in need of revision. It is not a system, but a jumble of historical accidents overlaid with well-intentioned but erroneous "corrections."

### Types of Inference

Inferences are traditionally classified as of two main types: *inductive* and *deductive,* and the processes as *induction* and *deduction.* In induction we start with facts and try to see some pattern in them. In deduction we start with a general judgment and try to discover more specific implications or particular instances of it. For example, if we polled a number of Iowa voters and inferred from their answers (the facts) that Iowa will vote Republican in the next election, we would be making an inductive inference — reasoning from facts to a general conclusion. But if we began with the judgment that farm states usually vote Republican and reasoned that since Iowa is a farm state it will vote Republican, we would be making a deductive inference — reasoning from a general statement to a particular implication of it. Because of the direction of the reasoning, induction is often described as particular-to-general reasoning and deduction as general-to-particular reasoning. It can also be said that induction is reasoning from examples and deduction is reasoning from general principles.

## *Induction*

Induction may be divided into three subtypes: *generalization, causal relation,* and *analogy.*

**Generalization.** A generalization is a conclusion about a whole class or group based on a study of individuals in it. Thus if we measured 2,000 American soldiers and 2,000 British soldiers and found that the average height of the Americans was greater, we might infer that American soldiers as a group are taller than British soldiers. We would be studying a sample of each group and, on the basis of the sample, drawing a conclusion about the whole class of American soldiers as contrasted with the whole class of British soldiers.

The fact that a generalization is based on a study of only some members of the class is both its usefulness and its potential weakness. Obviously, if we measured every American and every British soldier we would scarcely have to make an inference at all; the reasoning would be confined to computing the average height of both classes and recognizing that one was greater than the other. But the amount of measuring required could easily discourage anyone from making the study. The great advantage of a generalization is that it allows us to predict the characteristics of the part of the class which has not been examined and thus permits us to extend our knowledge beyond what we have actually experienced.

Obviously, a generalization based on a few samples, all things else being equal, is riskier than one based on many samples. The measurements of twenty American and twenty British soldiers would be too few to warrant any conclusion. But the mere size of a sample is not by itself a trustworthy test of a generalization. Thus if we measured 10,000 British soldiers, all members of crack regiments with minimum height requirements of six feet, we could draw no reliable conclusions about the average height of all British soldiers, since we would have no reason to assume that the sample was representative — indeed, we might conclude that it was not. The members of the crack regiments are not *typical* in height.

It is important to understand this distinction, because hasty assumption that samples are typical is the chief cause of unsound generalization. It is often very difficult — sometimes impossible — to be sure a sample is typical, and much useful reasoning is based on samples which can only be presumed so. But for any serious generalization, all possible care should be taken to see that the samples probably are typical. Certainly, any sample which tends to be "loaded" — that is, more likely true for part of a class than all of it — should be rejected. The following samples all contain factors which make them unacceptable bases for the generalizations they are used to support:

A study of college hospital records to determine how many days a semester a student is likely to be sick. (The sample will exaggerate because it ignores the healthiest part of the student population — those who did not need hospitalization.)

A study of students who received failing grades while working their way through college to determine the effect of outside employment on academic success. (The sample should include students at all grade levels since low scholastic aptitude as well as employment will affect college grades.)

A study of the drinking habits of divorced couples to determine whether the use of alcohol is detrimental to married life. (By limiting the study to unsuccessful marriages the sample has been loaded.)

A contrast of unemployment figures in Michigan in June and January to determine whether unemployment is increasing. (A comparison between two Junes would be safer, since the January figures may be increased by "seasonal unemployment.")

An analysis of all automobile accidents reported in a state during a year to determine whether men or women are the safer drivers. (If there are more men drivers than women drivers, or if men drive more frequently for longer distances or under adverse conditions, one would expect more men to be involved in accidents. The sample is likely to be loaded.)

The commonest safeguard against "loading" is to choose samples at random. A random sample is one in which the selector has no control over which items are selected but most choose them by chance, as in a lottery, or by some other procedure so arbitrary that it is almost the same as a chance selection — for example, choosing the first word on every twentieth page of a dictionary. The assumption behind random selection is that any inference made from a sample so selected would be equally valid for any other sample also selected at random. If a random sample meets this test it is probably typical of the whole class.

If you were making a serious study of the relation between reading the comics and juvenile delinquency, which of the following samples would seem suitable?

Everyone arrested for a delinquent act in your home town during the last three months.

All boy scouts in the Los Angeles area.

All students named Smith in junior high schools in New York City.

All teen-age volunteers in boot training at Great Lakes Naval Training Center.

Two hundred Chicago high school seniors selected at random.

All teen-agers buying comics from a large Detroit drugstore during one week.

All teen-agers in families listed in the first five pages of your telephone directory.

All teen-agers in your home town whose parents have been divorced for more than three years.

All teen-age children of inmates of a state penitentiary.

**Causal Relation.** Probably the most common kind of inductive reasoning is that which relates two events and concludes that one is the cause of the other. Such a conclusion reflects an underlying assumption called the *principle of causation*. According to this principle, every event has a cause, so that whenever we discover that event *B* always must follow event *A*, we may describe their relationship by saying that *A* is the cause of *B* and *B* the effect of *A*.

Causal reasoning may go from cause to effect or from effect to cause. Either way, we reason from what we know to what we are trying to determine. If what you know is a cause, the reasoning is cause to effect. If what you know is an effect, the reasoning is effect to cause.

Sometimes we reason from an effect to a cause and then on to another effect. Thus, if we reason that because the lights have gone out the refrigerator won't work, we first relate the effect (lights out) to the cause (power off) and then relate that cause to another effect (refrigerator not working). This kind of reasoning is called, for short, *effect to effect*. It is quite common to reason through an extensive chain of causal relations. For example, if when the lights go out we take the milk out of the refrigerator, we reason in the following causal chain: lights out — power off — refrigerator not working — temperature will rise — milk will sour. In other words, we diagnose a succession of effects from the power failure, each becoming the cause of the next.

Causes are classified as necessary, sufficient, or contributory. A *necessary cause* is one which must be present for the effect to occur, as the presence of a spark is necessary for combustion in a gasoline engine. A *sufficient cause* is one which can produce an effect unaided, as a dead battery is enough to keep a car from starting. A *contributory cause* is one which helps to produce an effect but cannot do so by itself, as running through a red light may help cause an accident, though other factors — the presence of pedestrians or other cars in the intersection — must also be present.

Most of our concern with causal relations arises from a need to discover causes. Something happens, and immediately we ask "Why?" In attempting to answer that question — to find the cause — we usually go through one or more of the following stages in our thinking:

1. *Whatever the cause is, it must exist in the situation and it must be sufficient to produce the effect.* This assumption requires us: (1) to check the situation carefully in order to identify possible causes, and (2) to consider which of the possible causes is sufficient to produce the effect. In making this analysis we are influenced by our past experience with similar situations. If we have repeatedly observed that event *B* follows event *A*, we incline to infer that *A* is the cause of *B*. But we should remember that, although a cause always precedes an effect, one event can regularly precede another without being its cause. Eight o'clock classes always come before nine o'clock classes, but the first do not cause the second.

2. *If a sufficient cause is eliminated from the situation, the effect will also be eliminated, unless other causes are also operating.* At this stage in our reasoning we are ready to test the possible causes to see if there is any connection between them and the effect. If the effect ceases when we remove a possible cause, this possible cause is the actual one. Thus we can often test a possible cause by experiment. If we suspect that a light failure is caused by a faulty bulb, we can substitute a new bulb and see whether the effect (no light) is removed. If it is, we need look no further for the cause. But if the new bulb does not give light, we cannot infer that the original bulb was all right, since the effect could have been produced by any of several sufficient causes or a combination of them — for example, a defect in the bulb, the wiring, the outlet, or a defect in more than one of these.

3. *If the cause is introduced into a similar situation it will produce a similar effect.* This is an additional way to test possible causes. If we suspect that a light failure is due to a faulty bulb, we can predict that the bulb will not light when placed in a socket where another bulb has been burning. If the bulb does light, we must reject the hypothesis that it was faulty and caused the light failure. If the bulb does not light, we have additional support for our belief that it is the cause we are seeking.

Whether we go through all three of these stages to discover a cause will probably depend on how important finding the cause is to us. To find our faulty bulb we need not go beyond the second stage, once we find that changing bulbs removes the difficulty; but a laboratory scientist attempting to establish the cause of a disease would perform every experiment he could think of before reaching a final conclusion.

**Correlation.** The preceding causal analysis works best with a single event which we can separate into parts and test each part separately as a possible cause. It is essentially an experimental method in which we analyze the facts, invent a hypothesis to explain them, predict other effects which will occur if the hypothesis is correct, and test for these effects.

Not all problems permit such a procedure. We cannot test cigarette smoking as a cause of lung cancer by forcing thousands of people to smoke or not to smoke cigarettes for twenty years in order to compare the results. Neither can we eliminate dust, fumes, and other impurities from the air in order to limit the cause to tobacco smoke. The most we can do is to show that one factor is probably a contributory cause of the effect. Usually we attempt to do that by establishing a "correlation" between the effect and the alleged cause.

In establishing a correlation we are combining generalization and causal relation in what is sometimes called a "causal generalization." We select samples and try to see in them a pattern which relates them in a manner similar to causal relation. We must not say, however, that a correlation *is* a causal relation. For instance, we might average a particular student's high school grades and then his college grades. Even if we observed that both averages were low, we would not ordinarily say that his low high school grades were the cause of his low college grades. At most we could infer that both sets of grades had a common explanation.

We can illustrate the method of correlation in terms of this example. Suppose we want to discover whether there is any relation between high school and college grades. From a class of 1000 college sophomores, we can select at random fifty who graduated in the bottom half of their high school class and fifty who graduated in the top half. If we find that forty of the second fifty made better than average grades in college, we can say that there is a *positive correlation.* Conversely, if forty of the upper high school group received lower than average grades in college, we can say that there is a *negative correlation.* And if twenty-five in each group ranked above average in college and twenty-five ranked below, we can say there is no correlation, or *zero correlation.*

What is significant in a correlation is its direction and its extent. A positive correlation may range from 0 to 1, a negative correlation from 0 to –1. If the correlation is positive we incline to infer that there is some relation between the two factors, and the higher the correlation is — the closer it approaches 1 — the stronger the inclination to make an inference.

But we must be cautious. We do not know what factors other than grades are involved in our study, and we do know from experience that some students who get good grades in high school flunk out of college. All that a high positive correlation between high school and college grades can do is to suggest a contributory causal relation — that, all things being equal, a student who does well in high school is likely to do well in college, perhaps because his high school record reflects aptitude, industry, and motivation, all of which contribute to success in college. Such a causal generalization may be useful for large numbers of students and still be unreliable for any particular student.

As a test of your understanding of what has been said so far about inferences, first read the following selection carefully; then discuss it in class with special reference to:

1. The qualifications of the author as an expert on the subject. (You may, if you wish, look him up in *Who's Who in America*.)

2. The type of causal-relation reasoning predominately used in the selection: cause to effect, effect to cause, effect to effect?

3. The method by which the author identifies the cause, and the potential weaknesses of that method.

4. The question whether the cause is necessary, sufficient, or contributory.

5. The number and nature of the samples used by the author.

6. The correlation that the author seems to find in his samples between reading the comics and juvenile delinquency.

7. The inference that you would draw from the evidence presented in the selection.


## The Comics . . . Very Funny [2]

An anxious mother consulted me some time ago. Her four-year-old daughter is the only little girl in the apartment house where they live. The boys in the building, from about three to nine years old, hit her, beat her with guns, tie her up with rope whenever they get a chance. They hit her with whips which they buy at the circus. They push her off her bicycle and take her toys away. They handcuff her with handcuffs bought with coupons from comic books. They take her to a vacant lot and use her as a target for bow and arrow. They make a spearhead and scare her. Once, surrounding her in this way, they pulled off her panties to torture her (as they put it). Now her mother has fastened the child's panties with a string around her neck so the boys can't pull them down.

What is the common denominator of all this? Is this the "natural aggression" of little boys? Is it the manifestations of the sex instinct? Is it the release of natural tendencies or the imitation of unnatural ones? The common denominator is comic books.

I examine in the clinic a boy of eleven, referred because he fights in school and is inattentive. He says:

I buy comic books every week. They kill animals, sometimes they kill people. One of the girls is the best fighter. Sometimes they tie her up and sometimes they put her in a snake cave so that the snakes would kill her.

[2] Condensed from Frederic Wertham, M.D.: "The Comics . . . Very Funny," *The Saturday Review of Literature,* May 29, 1948. Reprinted by permission of *The Saturday Review of Literature.*

I examine a boy of fourteen referred to the clinic for stealing. I ask him: "Do you think your stealing had anything to do with the comic books? He answers: "Oh, no. In the comic books it is mostly murder." This is like the arguments used by the experts under subsidy from the comic-book industry.

A boy of seventeen is referred to me by the Juvenile Aid Bureau because in an argument he stabbed a boy of thirteen in the right arm "with full intent." He says: "I don't read many comic books — only about ten a week. I like crime comics. Sometimes they kill the girl. In one of the books the girl wanted more money so they stabbed her in the back." Was it "full intent," or was it perhaps imitation that motivated him in his own actions? . . .

A boy of fifteen took a boy of twelve up a fire escape and threatened to push him down if he didn't give him a quarter. He says: "I read two comic books a day." A thirteen-year-old boy is referred to me by the State Charities Aid Association. He was caught stealing five dollars. When asked why he took it he confided to me that the older boys in school got up a gang and threatened him. If he did not get them the money they would beat him up. So he stole the money and gave it to them. (I verified this later.) . . .

Think of the many recent violent crimes committed by young boys and girls. A twelve-year-old boy who kills his younger sister; a twelve-year-old boy who kills his older sister; a thirteen-year-old burglar who operates with a shotgun; a seventeen-year-old boy who kills a thirteen-year-old boy and leaves a note signed "The Devil"; a public school in New York City where two police officers circulate on the grounds and in the corridors to prevent violence; a mathematics teacher who has to give examinations with a policeman present in the classroom; a thirteen-year-old who shot a nurse and was sent to a reformatory (where, incidentally, he will read more comic books); a gang of adolescent bandits led by a fifteen-year-old girl; two twelve-year-old boys and one of eleven stopping a man on the street and shooting him with a semi-automatic; a fifteen-year-old boy third-degreed as a suspect in a murder case; three sixteen-year-old boys killing a fourteen-year-old "for revenge"; a New York City school where the older pupils threaten the younger ones with violence and with maiming them, robbing them of their money, watches, and fountain pens. The young victims don't dare tell the names of their tormentors. When two of them were asked by a teacher, they refused to answer: "We don't want our eyes cut out." Actually one sixteen-year-old boy in this school was beaten with a broken bottle from behind and cut so severely that seven stitches had to be taken around his eyes. Adults are horrified at this attack. They don't know that this is old stuff for comic-book readers. In one of the "good" comic books (*Classics Illustrated*) in a rendering of the novel by Eugene Sue, *The Mysteries of Paris*, there is a picture of a man tied down in a chair — a man whose eyes have been gouged out and whose blood runs down from beneath the bandage. . . .

All these manifestations of brutality, cruelty, and violence and the manner in which they are committed — that is the folklore of the comic books. . . .

My own clinical studies and those of my associates of the Lafargue Clinic, the first carried out independently from the comic-book industry, and the first leading to their condemnation, have convinced me that comic books represent systematic poisoning of the well of childhood spontaneity. Many children themselves feel guilty about reading them.

Having read Dr. Wertham's arguments, now read the following excerpts from a reply made by a teen-age critic. What method is Mr. Wigransky using to refute Wertham's inferences?

### CAIN BEFORE COMICS [3]

Sir: *And it came to pass, when they were in the field, that Cain rose up against Abel his brother, and slew him.*

The brothers Cain and Abel lived in a world of ideal tranquility, a world that had never before known violence or crime, a world completely devoid of comic books. How then does Dr. Frederic Wertham account for this brutal fratricide told within the pages of the Bible, the only book in the history of man more widely read and more widely attacked than American comic books?

Or, if Cain's slaying of Abel seems far-off and far-fetched, let us take the Leopold-Loeb case, which took place in early 1924, just five years before publication of the first independently produced comic book. Nathan Leopold and Richard Loeb, eighteen and seventeen years old respectively, were accused of brutally murdering fourteen-year-old Robert Franks, thereby committing what has been acknowledged by some as the most brutal crime in United States history. Both boys were of well-to-do and cultured families and were readers of "good" books. How then could Dr. Wertham possibly account for even the remotest thought of murder or violence entering the minds of either?

Dr. Wertham cites some two dozen gruesome and horrible cases of juvenile delinquency from his files. These crimes were committed recently by weak-minded children and adolescents, who, Dr. Wertham implies, would never have considered crime had not they been comic-book readers. In none of these cases was it proved that reading comic books was the cause of the delinquency. A good many of the delinquents mentioned happened to be readers of comic magazines just as are 69,999,975 perfectly healthy, happy, normal American boys and girls, men and women, who also read the comics. It is just as ridiculous to suppose that 69,999,-975 people are law-abiding citizens just because they are comic-book readers as it is to suppose that twenty-five others are depraved criminals due to the same reading habits.

[3] From David Pace Wigransky's "Cain Before Comics," *The Saturday Review of Literature,* July 24, 1948. Reprinted by permission of *The Saturday Review of Literature.*

Capable as Dr. Wertham may be in the psychoanalyzation of adults, I certainly do not believe him able to deal equally as well with children, due to his fanatic hatred and prejudice toward comic books. From reading his article I get the impression that this feeling colors all of his investigations and reports. It appears that his $64 question to a child being psychoanalyzed is, "Do you read COMIC BOOKS, my little man?" Of course the juvenile delinquent being a normal child in at least that way, will answer, "Yes."

"Ah ha," says Dr. Wertham. "This child is a juvenile delinquent. This child reads comic books. Therefore it is because he reads comic books that he is a juvenile delinquent." This is enough for Dr. Wertham. . . .

The child, having never been an adult, cannot be expected to understand the adult point of view. The adult, on the other hand, was once a child, and should therefore realize that this craving for horror is not for actual physical violence, but for imaginary violence in the form of comics, radio, movies, or a good game of "Cops 'n' Robbers," the last of which I am sure was enjoyed many years before the other three had even been thought of. If all the Dr. Werthams in the world would realize this, the greatest barrier between parent-child mutual understanding would be automatically removed.

If let alone by the Dr. Werthams and John Mason Browns, I think the comic-reading kids will turn out all right, as did the present generation, the first brought up on comic books. Let any who starts to raise his voice in protest to this generation, first compare it with any preceding one. I am certain that he will discover the cards are stacked in favor of the comic-book readers of the present age.

**Analogy.** Analogy is the type of reasoning in which we compare two things known to be alike in some respects and infer that they will also be alike in certain other respects. The following famous Shakespearian analogy illustrates this type of inference:

I am a Jew. Hath not a Jew eyes? hath not a Jew hands, organs, dimensions, senses, affections, passions? fed with the same food, hurt with the same weapons, subject to the same diseases, healed by the same means, warmed and cooled by the same winter and summer as a Christian is? If you prick us, do we not bleed? If you tickle us, do we not laugh? If you poison us, do we not die? And if you wrong us, shall we not revenge? If we are like you in the rest, we shall resemble you in that.
—Shylock, in *The Merchant of Venice*.

We can better see the structure of this analogy by setting up the compared characteristics in parallel columns, matching each characteristic of a Christian with similar characteristic of a Jew, the whole combining to form a series of premises leading up to the conclusion that, like the Christian, the Jew will seek revenge if wronged.

|  | Christian | | Jew |
|---|---|---|---|
| P | 1. Has hands, organs, dimensions, etc. | →| 1. Has hands, organs, dimensions, etc. |
|  | 2. Is affected in specific ways by food, weapons, disease, etc. | →| 2. Is affected in the same specific ways by food, weapons, disease, etc. |
|  | 3. If pricked, he bleeds. | →| 3. If pricked, he bleeds. |
|  | 4. If tickled, he laughs. | →| 4. If tickled, he laughs. |
|  | 5. If poisoned, he dies. | →| 5. If poisoned, he dies. |
| C | 6. If wronged, he seeks revenge. | →| 6. If wronged . . . |

In Chapter 3 we saw the use of analogy to provide explanatory detail. In exposition and description analogy can often make abstract ideas concrete or explain the unfamiliar by likening it to the familiar. In argument, however, analogy can be both useful and misleading. It is helpful in suggesting hypotheses for further investigation. For example, if we have found that the best protection against one virus disease is to isolate the virus and prepare an immunizing serum from it, we can predict that the same method will work with another virus disease. If the prediction proves true, the analogy has given us a useful hint toward solving our problem. If the prediction proves false, the suggested solution will be quickly rejected and no great harm will have been done.

Analogy is also useful when we have no other means of reaching a conclusion. For example, we cannot descend to the bottom of the ocean deeps and collect evidence about the kinds of life, if any, existing there, but we can infer by analogy that the characteristics we observe in the depths we can penetrate will hold true in those we cannot reach. But such inferences are, at best, tentative, and we replace them by more reliable evidence as soon as possible.

When analogy is used as the sole proof of a conclusion it is even less reliable. It may be more persuasive than it should be and lead us to a conclusion which is not valid. For it is easy to assume that because two things are alike in some respects they will be alike in others, whereas in fact the similarities may be only superficial. Even if the two things seem fundamentally alike, a single difference can render the whole analogy false. For example, domesticated skunks reared as pets are like their wild brethren in every respect but one: the domesticated animals have been deactivated. It would be unfortunate to assume that because one can handle a pet skunk with impunity, one can take similar liberties with a wild one.

The test of an analogy, then, is the question, *Are the two things analogous for the purpose for which the analogy is being used?* They need not show perfect correspondence; they may have many differences which are unimportant to the inference based on the analogy. But they must not be different in any detail which is essential to that inference. Thus the analogy that a motherless baby ape could be reared by feeding it as if it were a human baby would be sound because, despite many differences, young apes and human babies have similar digestive systems. But to reason that because mushrooms and toadstools look much alike, toadstools will be good to eat, is to indulge in a false analogy, since the fact that toadstools are poisonous is a crucial difference — in this case a fatal one.

Reasoning by analogy is sometimes treacherous, and it is wise to be suspicious of any argument that depends largely or wholly on such reasoning. Analogy can safely illustrate a point already made or introduce an argument which will finally be proved by other means. For both writer and reader such expository analogies are helpful. But any analogy which carries the brunt of an argument should be examined most carefully for any essential differences between the things being compared.

The following selections offer additional examples of analogies. Are they used as hypotheses or as proof? If proof, consider whether there are essential differences between the two things being compared.

### (1)

We often wonder whether or not Mars is inhabited. At present there is no service, regular or irregular, which will transport us to the surface of Mars so that we can find out for certain. And our best telescopes do not bring us near enough to determine the question. But we do employ analogy. Did you ever ask yourself why it is *Mars* that interests us so much in this connection? It is because Mars is so similar to the earth in major respects. It has a similar history, a comparable temperature, an atmosphere, is subject to similar solar seasons; it revolves around the sun, it gets light from the sun, it is subject to the law of gravitation, etc. May it not also be similar in respect to harboring life? If Mars were without water, like the moon, or experienced great extremes of temperature, like Mercury, we should not be so much interested in it. But we entertain the idea because Mars is so similar in many respects to the earth *and life has evolved on the earth!* [4]

### (2)

Bagehot suggests that the English people are protected against any such violent upheavals as a French revolution by their superior stupidity. He compares the English to the Romans as a great political people. Of the Romans he says: "Is not a certain dullness of mind their most visible characteristic? What is the history of their speculative mind? A blank. What their literature? A copy. They have not left a single discovery in any abstract science, not a single perfect or well-formed work of high imagination." He points out that the Greeks, in contrast, who invented almost everything worth inventing, succumbed to the Romans at last, and that in

[4] From *The Rhyme of Reason,* by Roger W. Holmes. Copyright, 1939, by Appleton-Century-Crofts, Inc.

general the stupid people win and the clever people lose. Such are the attractions of stupidity.[5]

### (3)

At the end of an address on the evils of alcohol the lecturer said, "Now, I am going to demonstrate that actions speak louder than words. I am going to show you what happens to a living organism when it is exposed to alcohol, and I am going to let you be the judges of the experiment." He then dropped a live worm into a glass of water. When it had wriggled vigorously for a minute he took it out and dropped it into a glass of whiskey. The worm curled up and died. The town drunk, sitting in the front row, watched as though fascinated. Noticing his obvious interest, the lecturer turned to him and asked, "Well, sir, what does this prove?"

"Why," said the drunk, "it proves that them as has worms ought to drink whiskey."

### (4)

*Soldier.* But if the cause be not good, the king himself hath a heavy reckoning to make, when all those legs and arms and heads, chopped off in battle, shall join together at the latter day. . . . I am afraid that there are few die well that die in a battle; for how can they charitably dispose of anything, when blood is their argument? Now, if these men do not die well, it will be a black matter for the king that led them to it; whom to disobey were against all proportion of subjection.

*King.* So, if a son that is by his father sent about merchandise do sinfully miscarry upon the sea, the imputation of his wickedness, by your rule, should be imposed upon the father that sent him: or if a servant, under his master's command transporting a sum of money, be assailed by robbers and die in many irreconciled iniquities, you may call the business of the master the author of the servant's damnation: but this is not so; the king is not bound to answer for the particular endings of his soldiers, the father of his son, nor the master of his servant; for they purpose not their death, when they propose their services. . . . Every subject's duty is the king's; but every subject's soul is his own.[6]

## Deduction

Deduction is the type of inference in which we start from a given statement and reach a conclusion which was implied in that statement. If we start with the statement that a straight angle measures 180°, a right angle 90°, an obtuse angle more than 90° and less than 180°, and

---

[5] From *The Attractions of Stupidity*, by Howard Mumford Jones. A commencement address at Tufts College, June 1944. Copyright, 1944, by *The Tuftonian*. Reprinted by permission of *The Tuftonian*.

[6] Shakespeare, *King Henry V*, Act IV, Scene i.

an acute angle less than 90°, we can draw the following conclusions: that if a straight angle is divided equally, each new angle will be 90°; that if a straight angle is divided unequally, one new angle will be obtuse, the other acute; that we cannot get more than two right angles or one obtuse angle in a straight angle; that we can get any number of acute angles in a straight angle.

To draw these conclusions we do not have to measure the angles, or construct a straight angle and divide it. If we know the definitions of the terms we are using, we can simply *deduce* these conclusions from the given statement, which is another way of saying that the conclusions were implied in the given statement. Deduction, then, is "thinking out" the implications of a statement. We lead out, or deduce, the conclusions from it.

**The Syllogism.** The form of deduction that is most important for our purposes is the *syllogism*. This is an argument consisting of three statements: a *major premise,* a *minor premise,* and a *conclusion.* Each statement contains two *terms* (underlined in the following example) connected by a verb. Each term occurs twice in the syllogism, so that the whole contains three terms, each used twice.

| | |
|---|---|
| *Major Premise:* | All college students are high school graduates. |
| *Minor Premise:* | Joe Smith is a college student. |
| *Conclusion:* | Joe Smith is a high school graduate. |

Such a syllogism is *reliable* if it satisfies three conditions: (1) it must have just three terms (each used twice) and they must not be ambiguous, (2) the premises must be true, and (3) the syllogism must be valid. Let us consider these conditions in order.

To be unambiguous a term must have precisely the same meaning both times it is used. Here is a syllogism with an ambiguous term:

| | |
|---|---|
| *Major Premise:* | No superior student receives less than average grades. |
| *Minor Premise:* | Three-letter men are superior students. |
| *Conclusion:* | No three-letter man receives less than average grades. |

In the major premise the term "superior student" is used to mean "academically superior," and in the minor premise to mean "athletically superior." The phrase therefore actually represents two different things so that the argument has four terms, not three, and is not a syllogism but only looks like one. Do you recognize the ambiguous terms in the following?

Cats have nine lives.
His wife is a cat.
His wife has nine lives.

All Americans live under a republican form of government.
Canadians are Americans.
Canadians live under a republican form of government.

Anyone who graduates from college receives a college degree.
Apprentice barbers graduate from a college.
Apprentice barbers receive a college degree.

The words "true" and "valid," as applied to a syllogism, mean quite different things. The premises are true if they accord with the facts; if they do not, they are false. Thus if there is no exception to the statement that all college students are high school graduates, the major premise of our earlier example is true; if there is an exception, the premise is false. Similarly, the minor premise may be true or false, depending on whether Joe Smith is, in fact, a college student. If either premise is false, no conclusion will be reliable. The truth or falsity of the premises, therefore, is a major test of a syllogism.

A syllogism is valid if the conclusion logically follows from the premises, even though one or both of the premises may be false. This is another way of saying that a syllogism is valid if its conclusion is implied in the premises and that, given the premises, the conclusion *must* follow. Thus if all college students are high school graduates and Joe Smith is a college student, Joe Smith *must* be a high school graduate. That conclusion is implied in the premises, which identify Joe Smith as a member of a group, all of whom are high school graduates.

Validity and truth, then, are not the same thing. Validity has to do with the logical relationship of statements to each other; truth has to do with the relationship of statements to the facts. The statements in a syllogism may be true without the syllogism's being valid, and the syllogism may be valid although the statements in it are not true. *For a syllogism to be reliable, however, the statements which compose it must be true and the inference drawn must be valid.*

There are several types of syllogisms and each has its own tests of validity. To consider all the types and their technical tests would require more space than we can afford, but we can learn most of what we need to know about validity by analyzing representative syllogisms to see what conclusions may validly be inferred from the premises. Since we will be concerned only with validity, we need not worry about whether the premises are true or false.

*Major Premise:* All college professors are absent minded.
*Minor Premise:* Father is absent minded.

What conclusion may we validly infer from these premises? The major premise identifies a characteristic of a class, college professors. We can deduce that what is true of all college professors will be true of any one of them. But the major premise tells us about "all college professors," not about all absent-minded people; therefore we cannot deduce anything about a particular absent-minded person, but only about a particular college professor. Since all we know about father is that he is absent minded, we can draw no valid conclusion about him. The conclusion that father is a college professor certainly does not follow from the premises. But if the minor premise had identified him as a college professor we could validly conclude that he was absent minded.

*Major Premise:* If Jones gets an A in history he will be off probation.

If Jones gets an A in history, what conclusion may we draw? The conclusion is implied in the major premise — he will be off probation. But if he does not get an A in history, we can draw no conclusion, because the major premise tells us what will happen if he *does* get an A, not what will happen if he does *not* get an A. Jones may get off probation by other means, by getting a B in history and A's in all his other subjects. Had the major premise read, "Only if Jones gets an A in history, will he get off probation," we could conclude that if he did not get that particular A he would remain on probation.

*Major Premise:* Either the plugs are not sparking or the fuel line is clogged.

With this major premise we can draw a valid conclusion from either of two minor premises. If the plugs are sparking, the fuel line must be clogged, because we know that one of the stated conditions must exist. And if the fuel line is not clogged, the plugs must be failing to spark. But what can we conclude ( *a* ) if the plugs are not sparking, ( *b* ) if the fuel line is clogged? We can draw no valid conclusion from either of these minor premises because all that the major premise tells us is that if one is not the cause of the trouble the other is. It does not exclude the possibility that both conditions may exist at the same time, though it would have done so had it read:

> Either the plugs are not sparking or the fuel line is clogged, but not both at the same time.

*Major Premise:* She cannot love me and tell such scandalous stories about me.

If the minor premise is, "She loves me," we can conclude that she does not tell the scandalous stories. If the minor premise is, "She does tell scandalous stories about me," we can conclude that "She cannot love me." But what conclusion may be drawn from the minor premise "She does not love me" or "She does not tell scandalous stories about me"? We can draw no valid conclusion from these premises because all that the major premise tells us is the relationship between "loving me" and "telling scandalous stories about me." The relationship is that if she does the first she cannot do the second. What will happen if she does not do the first (love me) we do not know; or what is the case if she does not do the second (tell scandalous stories) we do not know. The answers to these questions are not implied in the major premise.

In the analysis of these syllogisms the question we are dealing with is: what can we validly deduce from the premises? The general answer is: we can deduce nothing that is not already implied in the premises. That means that deductive inference is the process of seeing what the premises imply. The best way to get experience with that process is to use it. Therefore we will give you a series of premises and ask you what conclusions may be inferred from them. If you compare your answers with those of your classmates you will be getting a valuable experience with deduction; but remember that validity is not the same as truth, and do not let your willingness or unwillingness to accept the premises as true interfere with your attempts to draw valid conclusions from them. The major premise is indicated by the abbreviation *MP*, the minor premise by *mp*, and the conclusion by *C*.

1. *MP*   All independent voters voted for X.
   *mp*   Mr. B voted for X.
   *C*

2. *MP*   All independent voters voted for X.
   *mp*   Mr. C did not vote for X.
   *C*

3. *MP*   If you are an independent voter you will vote for X.
   *mp*   You are not an independent voter.
   *C*

4. *MP*   Either you vote for Y or you are an independent voter.
   *mp*   You do not vote for Y.
   *C*

5. *MP*   Either you vote for Y or you are an independent voter.
   *mp*   You vote for Y.
   *C*

6. *MP*   You cannot vote for Z and be an independent voter.
   *mp*   You vote for Z.
   *C*

7. *MP*   You cannot vote for Z and be an independent voter.
   *mp*   You are not an independent voter.
   *C*

8. *MP*   You cannot vote for Z and be an independent voter.
   *mp*   You are an independent voter.
   *C*

9. *MP*   All A is B
   *mp*   C is B
   *C*

10. *MP*   All A is B
    *mp*   C is A
    *C*

11. *MP*  No A is B
    *mp*  C is A
    *C*
12. *MP*  No A is B
    *mp*  C is not A
    *C*

We constantly come upon "hidden" syllogisms, which we may not recognize because they occur in abbreviated form. For example, the syllogism about Joe Smith may be presented in one of the following forms:

Joe Smith is a college student; so he must be a high school graduate.

Joe Smith must be a high school graduate because he is a college student.

Since all college students are high school graduates, Joe Smith must be a high school graduate.

From your knowledge of the complete syllogism you will recognize that the first two forms omit the major premise and the third form omits the minor premise. To test the validity of such abbreviated syllogisms it is usually necessary to expand them into their complete forms. But abbreviating a syllogism by omitting a premise does not affect its validity, since the omitted premise is understood.

## Combined Induction and Deduction

For convenience we have been considering induction and deduction as two entirely separate types of inference. Actually, the two are often combined in a single argument. Deduction usually depends on a prior induction, since the major premise is usually a generalization from experience and the minor premise a statement of fact. And the practical decisions made from an induction often result from an accompanying deduction. Thus an insurance company, having found inductively that men in Mr. X's age group have an average life expectancy of so many years and that Mr. X's physical condition is better than average for his age, deduces that he is a fair risk and issues him a policy. Can you construct the syllogism which leads to this decision?

The combined use of induction and deduction, which has proved so fruitful in science, is a common pattern in everyday thinking. We observe fact A (that the lights in our home have gone out) and fact B (that all the other houses on the street are dark) and we relate these two facts with previous experience and make an inductive inference that the power is off. We do not really know the power is off, but our inference offers a possible explanation, a hypothesis. From this hypothesis we deduce certain other consequences that must follow if the power is off, and we therefore predict (*a*) that the refrigerator, the radio, and other electrical appliances will not work, (*b*) that we must wait until the power comes on again — that is, there is nothing we can do about the situation. If any of these predictions proves untrue, there is something wrong with our hypothesis. Thus, if a light comes on across the street, but not at our house, we change our opinion and say, "The power is on; a fuse must have blown out." We have substituted a new hypothesis which, in turn, suggests a new prediction, that if we insert a new fuse the power will go on again.

The reasoning process may be diagrammed as follows:

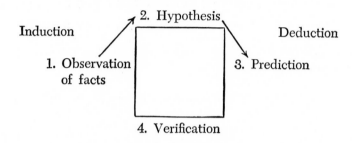

If the reasoning is sound, all four sides of the square are completed. If the prediction fails, there is a flaw in one side: we may have misobserved the facts, drawn a faulty hypothesis, predicted something that does not logically follow from the hypothesis, or tested the prediction inaccurately. Since there are many chances for error, we cannot assume that our reasoning is sound until we have tested it to the best of our ability.

To gain experience with the types of inferences, identify the type used in the following examples. When more than one type is used in an example identify all the types used.

1. An income-tax clerk checks every tenth return coming into his office and concludes that the average citizen is weak in arithmetic.

2. A doctor listens to a patient's symptoms, takes a blood test, and concludes that the patient needs his appendix removed.

3. A government official tells newspaper reporters that a proposed policy will be a good one because it has worked well in large business corporations.

4. Canaries are taken into mines to warn miners of the presence of poisonous gas.

5. A freshman wants to make up with a girl he has offended. His roommate tells him that, where girls are concerned, he can't go wrong sending flowers.

6. At midsemester a freshman writes to her older sister that male college students are wolves.

7. A famous statistician of the twenties was fond of comparing the average salary of college graduates with that of high school graduates who never went to college and concluding that a college education soon repaid its cost.

8. A study of the educational background of people whose names were included in *Who's Who in America* led the investigator to conclude that the sons of ministers had the best chance of being successful.

9. An American tourist in London was asked by an Englishman, "Are all women in America as beautiful as they are in the movies and do they all speak so atrociously?"

10. A Director of Admissions in a state university checked an applicant's high school transcript and observed that the boy graduated 11th in a class of 68. He issued the boy a permit to enter the university.

11. A student opposed to compulsory health insurance in this country cited figures from Britain, Sweden, and New Zealand to show that the costs of such programs in those countries were much higher than had been anticipated. He then accused the proponents of the proposal of seriously underestimating the costs of their plan.

12. In a bridge game South has nine hearts to the ace, king, jack, ten; he also has the king and queen of clubs and the ace and eight of diamonds. He opens the bidding with two hearts, his partner responds with three spades, and the opponents pass. South then bids four no trump to discover how many aces his partner has. Partner indicates two aces by bidding five hearts. South bids and makes seven hearts.

13. In preparing his annual budget a college president finds through a statistical study that (*a*) a steadily increasing number of students transfer to his college in the junior year, and (*b*) the cost of instruction in junior and senior classes is markedly higher than in freshman and sophomore classes. The president decides that, even if there is no increase in total enrollment, he will need more money to run the college.

14. Although your car has been driven only 7000 miles the engine has developed a disturbing knock. You consult a mechanic. He listens to the engine and says, "Either you need a new ring job or the elevators are sticking. If the rings are bad I'll have to take the engine apart and the cost will be about $150. If the trouble is with the elevators it can often be fixed by using a special kind of oil." You have him change the oil and the knock ceases.

## *Fallacies*

A fallacy is an error in reasoning. The following fallacies occur most frequently, and should be studied so that you can recognize and refute them.

**Begging the Question.** A question is said to be "begged" when one or more of the premises by which it should be proved are assumed to be true without proof. A classic example is the juror who had no doubts about the evidence against a woman but argued, "I have such a respect for motherhood that I cannot conceive of any mother committing this crime." In other words, the woman must be innocent since she belonged to a class of which it is assumed that no member (including the defendant) could be guilty. The best defense against begging the question is to show clearly how the begging takes place. The following examples illustrate such arguments:

| *Examples* | *Analysis* |
| --- | --- |
| Dad, you don't need to worry about lending me the money for this business. Just as soon as the profits come in I can pay you back with interest. | *This argument begs the question of the advisability of the loan by assuming that the profits will be sufficient to pay off the debt. That, however, is a major part of dad's doubt, and cannot be assumed to be true.* |
| Much of this talk about spending millions for slum clearance is based on the essential fallacy that if we provide fine homes for people who live in the slums they will suddenly become responsible and productive citizens. This argument puts the cart before the horse. The basic trouble is with the people who live in the slums. These people are thoroughly shiftless and irresponsible. The conditions under which they live prove this. If they had any initiative or industry they would not be living under slum conditions. | *This is an argument in a circle. The thesis that slum-dwellers are responsible for slum conditions is supported by asserting that if they were not responsible they would not be living in slums. The writer assumes that what he has to prove is true, and his argument goes round in the following circle: Slums are caused by shiftless tenants; this is true because shiftless tenants cause slums.* |
| Resolved: That the farce of the Honor System be abolished. | *This assumes the truth of the affirmative position in the resolution, whereas the affirmative should prove that the Honor System is a farce.* |
| "There is bound to be life on other planets."<br>"Can you prove it?"<br>"Well, can you prove there isn't?" | *This example shifts the burden of proof. In arguments both inside and outside law courts, "He who asserts must prove." We cannot prove an assertion by defying the opposition to disprove it.* |

**Ignoring the Question.** To ignore the question is to digress into an irrelevant argument. The digression may be a result of inability to keep the issues clearly in mind and to distinguish what is and is not pertinent, or it may be a deliberate attempt to distract attention from the real issues by drawing a red herring across the trail. The best rebuttal is to point out the digression, refuse to follow it, and insist that the discussion return to the main issues. The following examples illustrate various means of ignoring the question:

*Examples*

My opponent asks me to tell him what is wrong with this proposal of compulsory medical insurance. I'll tell him what is wrong with it. It is a half-baked plan cooked up by him and other Fellow-Travelers who are more interested in socializing a great profession than they are in providing better medical care. These men will sacrifice everything to their bigoted faith in a system of regimentation that is abhorrent to the American people. They want to begin by socializing medicine; they will not rest until they have made over the whole American economy into the image of the dictatorship to which their secret allegiance is pledged.

*Analysis*

*This argument attempts to refute a plan by making an attack on the character of the people who support it. It is an argument against the man, not against the plan, and is usually called* argumentum ad hominem. *The character of the proponents of compulsory medical insurance is not an issue in this question. The speaker is ignoring the question to indulge in personal abuse. This fallacy is not uncommon in political oratory in which argument by abuse is a colorful and traditional way of confusing the voters.*

The professor says that two negatives do not make an affirmative in English. Well, professors, like other people, are entitled to their opinions, no matter how eccentric they may be. But in this case the facts are against the professor. Any high school freshman could tell him that two negatives do make an affirmative. When you multiply minus *a* by minus *b*, the result is a plus or positive quantity. That is not just the freshman's opinion, or my opinion, or the opinion of educated people everywhere. It is a mathematical law. And it holds true whether it is written in English, Latin, Greek or Hindustani.

*This is an example of ignoring the question by shifting to another question. The point at issue is whether two negatives make an affirmative in English usage. There is no dispute about what happens in mathematics. This fallacy is sometimes called the device of the straw man. Instead of tackling one's real opponent, one sets up an easy substitute and puts on an effective demonstration of tearing it to pieces.*

*Closely related to the "straw man" is the device of extension, in which an argument is extended beyond its author's intention and attacked in its extended form, as when the statement that spanking a child sometimes does as much harm as good is represented as being an argument that children should never be spanked.*

What was good enough for the Founding Fathers is good enough for us.

If God had meant women to have red toenails He would have made them red in the first place.

Now, son, when I was a boy . . .

Mother knows best!

Why, whoever heard of such a thing!

*Statements like these are often used to ignore the question by appealing to the customs of the past — the appeal to antiquity — or by an uncritical appeal to authority. Although tradition and authority must receive serious consideration in our reasoning, since they represent the accumulated thinking of the past, new practices and proposals should be judged on their own merits. Tradition should be a supplementary, not a sole, consideration; otherwise all new proposals would be automatically rejected.*

**Hasty Generalization.** A hasty generalization jumps to a conclusion from insufficient evidence. Unless a group of samples are probably typical, a small number of samples proves nothing. The fact that three students cheated on a final examination would not justify the generalization that college students are dishonest; the fact that a few children out of many thousands contracted polio after receiving a Salk injection would not warrant the conclusion that the injections were too dangerous to use. The hasty generalization is a popular form of argument in fraternity and sorority "bull sessions," in which sweeping generalizations about the other sex are made from the very limited personal experience of the speakers. Fortunately, no one really believes these generalizations, not even the people who make them; at least the relationship between the sexes seems to proceed normally despite the hasty generalizations that each makes about the other.

A related fallacy is the *exaggerated generalization,* which overstates a conclusion that might, if more modestly worded, be acceptable. For example, studies on the relation between the incidence of lung cancer and heavy cigarette smoking over a long period of time justify the generalization that a significantly higher percentage of cigarette smokers than nonsmokers contract lung cancer, or even that, statistically, one's chances of developing lung cancer are likely to be increased by continued cigarette smoking. But a newspaper headline, *Research Proves Cigarettes Cause Cancer,* would exaggerate the generalization by claiming more than the evidence warrants. This tendency to state a conclusion more dramatically than it should be stated is not confined to headline writers. There is a common temptation to magnify the results of a study by saying "all" instead of "some," "prove" instead of "suggest," and "causal relations" instead of "correlation." The following statement is an exaggerated generalization:

. . . college students, at least American college students, are different from all other people on this planet; they are the only people who try to get as little as possible for their money.

They will spend the most valuable years of their lives, thousands of dollars of their parents' money and some of their own if they can get any, in trying to derive as little as possible out of their college courses, provided only that they will receive their coveted diploma at the end of four years of such efforts.

The label, *college students,* is a class name for more than two and a half million people. Some of them are men; some are women. Some are on their own for the first time in their lives; others are veterans who are well acquainted with other lands and peoples. Some have all their expenses paid by their parents; others earn their own way; still others are married and are supporting a family while they study. Some came to college simply because their parents sent them; some came hoping to find themselves — or husbands; some want to prepare for a profession; and some came out of a conviction that a college education offered the best introduction to the wisdom and culture of the ages. These people are of all sizes, shapes, colors. They differ in their moral, economic, and political philosophies, in their tastes, customs, and habits as much as a similar number of other people would differ. Obviously these two and a half million individuals are so diverse that it is difficult to make any responsible statement that will apply to all of them, and easy to make a statement that applies to some of them. The statement that *some* college students seem to be concerned only about a degree may be true but, when so stated, it is not dramatic or arresting. The temptation to drop the "some" and to imply that the description fits "all" or "most" college students is often hard to resist, and so the generalization gets exaggerated.

**Stereotype.** The fallacy of stereotyping is the mistake of paying too much attention to characteristics or traits which members of a group are supposed to have in common and not enough attention to individual differences within the group. We begin with a number of individuals who have at least one thing in common (let us say that they all have married children); we group them into a class (mothers-in-law); we develop an attitude towards that class (mothers-in-law are interfering); then we apply that attitude to individual mothers-in-law without waiting to see whether or not they are interfering.

Individual members of a class always have more differences than similarities. Fathers have little in common except the authority and responsibility that go with fatherhood. All that freshmen have in common is that they have not yet completed their first year in college. All that redheads have in common is red hair. To develop an attitude about these classes (fathers are stern, freshmen are naive, redheads are hot-tempered) is to indulge in hasty generalization. But to go further and to infer that these characteristics will be true of individual members of the class without examining the individuals is to behave unintelligently. We can find out by experience whether this particular father is stern, that particular freshman is naive, and yon redhead is hotheaded. There is no need to deduce these conclusions from a hasty generalization.

Stereotype thinking is frequent in our reactions to members of national groups. All Germans, Frenchmen, Scotsmen, Irishmen are thus and so; therefore we know without checking that any particular German, Frenchman, Scotsman, Irishman will be thus and so. To help us avoid this fallacy some students of language advise us to use index numbers after the class names to remind us that each member of a group has his own personal characteristics — that $German_1$ is not $German_2$ that college $professor_A$ is not college $professor_B$, that $freshman_{1957}$ is not $freshman_{1927}$. Whether we actually write these index numbers or merely think them, they are useful reminders that it is unintelligent to assume that individuals with a common class name will be alike in all respects.

**Mistaken Causal Relation.** We frequently assume the relation between two events to be causal when it is not so at all. The test of such an assumption has already been discussed. It is to ask whether the relationship regularly and necessarily exists. If both conditions cannot be answered affirmatively, the assumption of a causal relation is discredited.

| *Examples* | *Analysis* |
|---|---|
| In giving a blood transfusion, doctors must be sure that the donor and the recipient are of the same race; otherwise, the recipient may acquire the racial characteristics of the donor. This is why the Red Cross used both white and colored blood banks during the war. | *This assumes that an effect (racial characteristics) will be produced by the cause (transfusion of blood from a member of a different race). In this reasoning the cause is mistaken. Racial characteristics are transmitted by the genes, not by blood. The differences in blood types have nothing to do with race, since members of different races may have the same type, and members of the same race may have different types.* |
| I failed the course because the instructor had a prejudice against me. | *Even if we assume that the prejudice existed, it must be the effect of some cause. This reasoning therefore mistakes a possible effect for a cause. A more probable reason is that the student's conduct caused both the alleged prejudice and the failure.* |

Careful research shows that the most successful men have the largest vocabularies. This proves that the development of an extensive vocabulary is a cause of success.

*Since success and large vocabularies may both be results of native intelligence, the evidence that the two regularly appear together is not proof that one is the cause of the other.*

**Oversimplification.** Questions may sometimes be profitably simplified by pruning out irrelevancies, but any attempt to make a question seem easier than it is may keep us from finding a useful answer. When we brush aside a serious criticism on the grounds that the critic is prejudiced or "never satisfied," we are using the *argumentum ad hominem* (page 355) to oversimplify the problem. In effect we are ignoring the criticism by minimizing its significance. Similarly, the student who explained his failure by asserting that his instructor was prejudiced, oversimplified his problem.

Although oversimplification may occur in any type of inference — generalization, causal relation, analogy, or deduction — it occurs most frequently in causal relations. The following inferences illustrate.

|  | |
|---|---|
| *Examples* | *Analysis* |

I know my spelling is terrible. All the members of my family are poor spellers.

*Family environment may be a contributing factor to poor spelling, but it is not the sole cause. The student has oversimplified the cause of his deficiency by failing to consider other causes, about which he could do something.*

We would not have all these wars, strikes, riots and dissension if people would only return to religion.

*This is an attempt to find a single cause for a complex of effects. A return to religion is being offered as a panacea for all the world's ills. Some people substitute "education" for "religion," and get the same kind of oversimplification.*

On the question whether the husband should be the boss in the household, there are only two alternatives: either the man will be the boss or the woman will. Any man who lets himself be dictated to by a woman is a sorry specimen and probably deserves what he will get. But most of us will not make that mistake. We will make it known at the start, gently but

*This is an example of ignoring the question by ignoring a significant part of it. There are three positions in this question: the husband should be boss; the wife should be boss; nobody should be boss. This argument overlooks the third possibility; therefore it is not true that if the husband does not dominate, the wife will. Essentially the example oversimplifies the*

| *Examples* | *Analysis* |
|---|---|
| firmly, that we intend to be masters in our own homes. The sooner the little lady gets that idea through her head, the better for everybody. | *question by unnecessarily limiting the alternatives. This kind of oversimplification is sometimes called the either-or fallacy.* |

**False Analogy.** As we have seen, an analogy is false when the two things being compared may be shown to be different in some respect essential to the purpose of the analogy.

| *Examples* | *Analysis* |
|---|---|
| The argument that fooball is a dangerous sport is disproved very simply by showing that the death rate among high school, college, and professional players combined is much less than the death rate of the total population. | *Football may not be dangerous, but this analogy does not prove it. The total population includes old people, invalids, and men engaged in hazardous occupations. Football players are selected for youth and health as well as ability. The essential difference of selectivity keeps the two groups from being analogous.* |

**Faulty Deduction.** As was pointed out earlier, a sound deduction must meet three conditions: none of the three terms may be ambiguous, the premises must be true, and the inference from the premises must be valid. If the truth of the premises is not self-evident, it has to be established before any inference from the premises will be accepted. The following are faulty deductions.

| *Examples* | *Analysis* |
|---|---|
| No cat has two tails; this cat has one more tail than no cat; therefore this cat has three tails. | *The term "no cat" is ambiguous. In the major premise it is used to mean "No member of the class called cats"; in the minor premise it is used to refer to a particular kind of cat, "the no-cat," which is presumed to have two tails. Playing fast and loose with the meanings of words, while common as a humorous device, makes any serious deduction impossible.* |
| Of course she's selfish; she's a woman, isn't she? | *This cynical deduction proceeds from the major premise that all women are selfish to the conclusion that this particular woman must be selfish. The reliability of the deduction depends on the truth of the generalization that all women are selfish. Certainly that truth is not self-evident.* |

| *Examples* | *Analysis* |
|---|---|
| Both major parties are indifferent to the will of the people.<br><br>The Socialist Party is not a major party.<br><br>The Socialist Party is not indifferent to the will of the people. | *The major premise is questionable, but even if true, it could yield a conclusion only about a major party. If the Socialist Party is not a major party the major premise does not apply to it. The conclusion does not follow from the premises.* |
| All men prefer blondes.<br>Gentlemen prefer blondes.<br>All men are gentlemen. | *Both premises are hasty generalizations, but even if they are accepted as true, it does not follow that all men are gentlemen simply because both classes prefer blondes.* |

**Statistical Fallacies.** Statistics often contain fallacies which are difficult to detect without an expert knowledge of the data on which they were based and of the statistical procedures used. Usually, therefore, the reliability of statistical evidence must be determined by the tests already given for expert testimony. But, as the following examples show, there are certain common misuses of statistics which an alert student can detect.

| *Examples* | *Analysis* |
|---|---|
| Statistics show that the average age of college students at the time of graduation is 21. They also show that superior students graduate before the average age and less capable students graduate after the average age. Now, since Jones was almost 30 when he graduated, we must assume that he is not very bright. | *Statistical averages are misused when applied to individuals. No conclusion about Jones's scholastic ability may be drawn from these data. For a dozen possible reasons — including military service — his graduation may have been delayed.* |
| The grades of the ten students who took the test were 94, 66, 64, 62, 61, 60, 59, 58, 56, 56. An analysis of these figures shows that the average score is 63.6 and that 70% of the students made less than average scores. This is a discouraging result. | *This is the fallacy of overrating the significance of an average. In this test the score of 94 distorted the average so that it was not descriptive of the results. Had that score been ignored, the average would have been 60 and the lowest score would have come within 4 points of this average — not nearly so discouraging a result. In such figures the median grade (the grade which has as many scores above it as below it) is a more significant figure.* |

| *Examples* | *Analysis* |
|---|---|

When the average percentage score of each group was determined it was found to be as follows: Group A, 80%; Group B, 70%; Group C, 60%. From these figures it can be seen that the average of all three groups was 70%.

*This is the fallacy of averaging percentages without considering the numbers involved in each percentage. The conclusion stated will be true only if each group contains the same number of people. If, for example, the three groups contain 20, 30, and 50 people respectively, the average for all groups will be*

$$\frac{(20 \times 80) + (30 \times 70) + (50 \times 60)}{100} = 67\%$$

In 1932 a young instructor, with a Ph.D. but no teaching experience, could expect a salary of about $1500. In 1956 an instructor with the same qualifications could expect a salary of $4000. This increase of 167% is encouraging evidence of the improved economic position of college teachers.

*This is the fallacy of comparing units which are not comparable. The purchasing power of a dollar in the depression year of 1932 was much greater than in the boom year of 1956. In order to determine whether the teacher's economic position had improved, salaries for both years would have to be translated into "real wages" and compared on that basis.*

Can you identify the fallacies in the following arguments?

1. Girls just aren't any good at logic. Although there are twelve girls to ten men in our logic section, the four highest scores on the final examination were made by men, and the four lowest scores by girls.

2. If students won't study there's nothing the instructor can do. After all, you can lead a horse to water but you can't make him drink.

3. The team will be more successful this year than last, for all its regulars are back and it has a better coach.

4. The professor pointed to the rising rate of failure in his freshman course as evidence of the deterioration of high school instruction.

5. Their son has no business going to college; he barely graduated from high school.

6. If we do not attack the Russians, they will attack us. Ten years from now they will surpass us in all kinds of armaments. We ought to take care of them now while we still have the upper hand.

7. If the University allows men to live in unsupervised houses and keep whatever hours they please, it should extend the same privileges to coeds. Failure to do so implies that women students are less responsible or less moral than men students.

8. I hear that their first-string quarterback has an A-minus average. Can you imagine that?

9. A study of the characteristics of great historical figures shows that they were predominantly right-handed. This indicates that a right-handed person is more likely to become famous than is a left-handed one.

10. I was pleasantly surprised when I met my professors for the first time. Some of them were quite young and none was bald.

11. There are only two kinds of men: those who care for nothing but themselves, and those who care for nothing. Your young man doesn't seem to be conceited; so he must be shiftless.

12. It is a waste of public funds to send a girl to a state university. All that a girl wants from college is a husband. A good matrimonial agency would meet her needs at less cost to the taxpayer.

13. Our basketball team hasn't lost a game since the coach started wearing those red socks. I hear that the football coach is going to borrow them next fall.

14. A survey of college presidents shows that they smoke Coffin Nails twice as frequently as the next most popular brand. Among men who know what's what, it's Coffin Nails two to one.

15. Final examinations should be abolished because they encourage cramming.

16. This boy will some day be a great football player, for his father was an All-American halfback.

17. The papers say that Senator Blank won by a landslide. There's something fishy about that. I have checked with all my neighbors and associates and I have found only two who voted for Blank.

18. Habitual drunkards lack will power; that is why they are habitual drunkards.

19. A French Minister of Education is reputed to have told a visitor that at that moment every Fourth Grade pupil in all France was studying exactly the same lesson. In France the national government controls education. If we adopt the proposed federal aid to education bill we will bring about federal control of our schools and get the same kind of regimentation that exists in France.

20. The fact that no national fair employment law has been passed is proof that the people will not accept such laws. If the people would accept them, these laws would have been passed long ago.

21. If you want to find what the costs of national health insurance will really be, take the average cost of caring for a patient in the veterans' hospitals and multiply it by the whole population. The results will stagger you.

22. She cannot be both his wife and his sister; she is not his wife; therefore she must be his sister.

23. The senator said that the testimony of so many college presidents that trained intelligence is the country's greatest natural resource had convinced him that college students should be exempted from the draft.

24. Every rule has exceptions; this is a rule and therefore there are exceptions to it; therefore there are some rules that have no exceptions.

25. He: If God had intended women to be men's equals he would have made them equally strong. By giving men the more powerful physique He intended them to have authority over women.

She: Oh Yeah? Then if God thought man was so special, why did He assign the important job of bearing children to women?

26. Dad, I think you will be making a mistake if you take out a big insurance policy now. The mortality tables show that you have a life-expectancy of 69 and you are only 44 now. That means that you have a reasonable expectation of living 25 more years. In four years both Joe and I will be through college and will be self-supporting. If you postpone the insurance until then we won't have to skimp to pay the premiums.

27. Add together two facts — that there are as many men as there are women, and that the movie queens get married as often as they please — and you see that the only reason some girls don't get married is that they don't make themselves attractive to men.

28. It stands to reason that students brought up in a home where both English and a foreign language are spoken will have an inferior command of English. The effective use of English is largely a matter of experience, and these students have less experience with English because half of the time their parents are speaking a foreign language.

29. A Scottish king once performed an interesting linguistic experiment. In order to discover which language a child would naturally speak if taught no other language by his elders, he arranged for a baby to be reared without ever having experience with human speech. It is reported that at the conclusion of the experiment the king was satisfied that under these conditions a child will speak only Hebrew.

30. When a certain Colonel Johnson, a distinguished citizen of Salem, New Jersey, announced in 1830 that he would eat a tomato on the Court House steps, the townspeople thought that either he had lost his reason or he was engaging in a sensational publicity stunt. Everybody knew that the tomato, or love apple, was poisonous. It had always been regarded as poisonous; it was known to be related to the deadly nightshade; and the highest medical authorities were agreed that it contained enough oxalic acid to kill a man.

31. In a recent experiment several feeble-minded babies were fed, bathed, and tended exclusively by a group of feeble-minded teen-age girls. Subsequent tests showed that the intelligence of both the girls and the babies improved significantly. This proves (a) that all feeble-minded girls ought to get married, and (b) that feeble-minded girls make good mothers.

32. These figures which my opponent has used to show that there is an increase in unemployment certainly do not fit the facts in our town. I have checked the payrolls of the ten largest industries in town. Only four of them show any reduction in the number of employees over the same period last year and the average decrease of these four is about 6 per cent. Two of the ten show increases of 10 per cent, and 14 per cent respectively, or an average increase of 12 per cent. I don't know how my opponent arrives at his fancy figures, but elementary arithmetic shows that employment in this town is increasing, not decreasing.

33. If we consider the number of marriages per thousand of girls who did not continue their education beyond high school and of girls who, after completing college, continued with graduate or professional studies, we find that statistically the girl with less education has a better chance

of marriage. This is something that every girl who thinks a college education will get her a husband should stop to consider.

34. Determine which of the following statements can be deduced from the data in the table and which statements require us to make assumptions which are not given.

*Percentage Distribution of Students*

|  | 1946 | 1947 | 1948 |
|---|---|---|---|
| Freshman | 40 | 25 | 20 |
| Sophomore | 20 | 30 | 25 |
| Junior | 15 | 15 | 20 |
| Senior | 10 | 15 | 15 |
| Graduate | 15 | 15 | 20 |
| Total | 100 | 100 | 100 |

*a*. The shift during the three-year period was toward heavier enrollment in advanced courses.

*b*. During the three-year period average freshmen enrollment amounted to slightly more than 28 per cent of total enrollment.

*c*. In 1946 there were two sophomores enrolled for each senior.

*d*. There were the same number of juniors in 1947 as in 1946.

*e*. Taking the three-year period as a whole, the total number of juniors equalled the total number of graduate students.

*f*. The average age of students was higher in 1948 than in 1946.

*g*. In 1946 the number of freshmen equalled the number of juniors, seniors, and graduate students combined.

*h*. In 1947 about one out of every two students on campus was either a freshman or a sophomore.

*i*. Assuming that the cost of instruction increases in advanced courses, the cost of instruction per student was lower in 1946 than in 1948.

*j*. Assuming that classes must be kept smaller in advanced courses and that total enrollment did not increase, more classrooms were used in 1948 than in 1946.

35. Mark statements *a* to *j* as follows:

A if the statement is a valid inference from the data in the tables;
B if the statement exaggerates or overstates the data;
C if the statement minimizes or understates the data;
D if the statement has no relation to the data.

| Car Speed miles per hour | Reaction distance feet | Braking distance feet | Car Speed miles per hour | Gasoline miles per gallon |
|---|---|---|---|---|
| 30 | 33 | 40 | 30 | 24 |
| 40 | 44 | 70 | 40 | 21.6 |
| 50 | 55 | 109 | 50 | 19 |
| 60 | 66 | 156 | 60 | 16 |
| 70 | 77 | 240 | 70 | 12.5 |

a. Reaction distance varies with individuals.

b. Doubling the speed doubles the reaction distance.

c. Doubling the speed doubles the braking distance.

d. Increasing the speed decreases the life of the tires.

e. To avoid hitting a roadblock, a driver travelling 60 mph must see it more than 200 feet away.

f. The legal speed limit should not exceed 60 mph.

g. The greater the speed, the less control the driver has over the car.

h. Increase in gas consumption is directly proportional to increase in speed.

i. The total distance required to bring a car to a stop is almost three times as great at 70 mph as it is at 40 mph.

j. Doubling the speed doubles the gas consumption.

## Evaluating Controversy

So far we have been concerned with understanding the structure of argument, recognizing assumptions, distinguishing different types of premises and inferences, and detecting fallacies. We are now ready to combine all these considerations in an evaluation of controversy.

When we evaluate a controversy we are trying to determine how well each party to the dispute does what he is trying to do. Our main concerns are with the pertinence and persuasiveness of arguments, but we can best proceed by asking three questions: (1) What are the issues in the controversy? (2) What are the arguments used to resolve them? (3) How persuasive are these arguments?

The *issues* are those points in a controversy at which disagreement becomes crucial. In any debate there may be points at which both sides agree; there may be others at which there is trivial disagreement; finally there are a few points at which the disagreement is so fundamental that the whole debate hinges upon them. These are the main issues. If the debate is efficiently conducted most of the argument should be concentrated on these issues.

To illustrate the difference between trivial and fundamental disagreements, let us analyze a question which is perennially popular — the question of compulsory military training. The analysis that follows is not concerned with taking either side on this question. It is concerned only with pointing out the issues.

Generally, those who support the proposal affirm that compulsory military training will produce the following results:

1. It will help preserve peace by discouraging potential aggressors.

2. In the event of war, it will significantly increase our chances of victory.

3. It will improve national health by a program of physical education, medical care, and scientific diet.

4. It will provide educational opportunities for many who could not otherwise obtain them.

5. It will develop the characters of the trainees by teaching them discipline and responsibility.

6. It will train them for technical positions in industry.

7. It will make them better citizens.

On each of these assertions the affirmative and the negative may disagree. It is therefore easy to infer that all seven points are important issues. But a little reflection shows that if the affirmative could prove its first two assertions, it would win the debate no matter how badly it was defeated on the others, and that if it failed to prove the first two, it would lose regardless of the other five. Since compulsory military training is really proposed as a means of preserving peace and securing national defense, the debate will be won or lost at these two points. These are the basic issues. Whether compulsory training does or does not improve health, character, citizenship, educational and employment opportunities are not decisive questions. If they distract attention from the main issues, they are positively harmful.

In any debate on the adoption of a new policy, the controversy is likely to pass through three stages. There will be disagreement, first, about whether there are evils in the present system serious enough to require a change; second, about whether the proposed change will remove these alleged evils; and third, about whether the proposed change will introduce serious new evils. These questions are called the *stock issues*. On compulsory military training, the stock issues would be stated in some such manner as this:

I. Are there serious evils in our present system of national defense?
   A. Is there a serious threat to world peace?
   B. Are our present defense measures inadequate to meet that threat?
II. If compulsory military training were adopted, would it offer us better protection?
   A. Would it lessen the danger of war by discouraging an aggressive power?
   B. If war became inevitable, would compulsory military training offer the best assurance of victory?
III. Would compulsory military training introduce serious new evils?
   A. Would it be a serious drain on our resources of manpower, material, and money?
   B. Would it weaken our democracy by encouraging militaristic attitudes in the civilian population?

The identification of arguments used in a controversy requires nothing more than what we have been doing in most of this chapter. It is important, however, to distinguish between argument and assertion. As we have learned, an argument is a relation between one or more premises and a conclusion, and it requires both elements, just as the father-son relationship requires both a father and a son. If there is no premise, there is no conclusion. A statement of opinion without a supporting premise is not a conclusion and does not constitute an argument, not even an abbreviated one. It is merely an assertion, like the 'Tis — 'Tain't of childish quarrels. And do not forget, *assertion is not argument.*

It is of course much easier to make an assertion than to formulate an argument. Getting the facts and making valid inferences from them takes intellectual discipline. A person accustomed to this discipline is likely to develop the habit of speaking and writing responsibly. On the other hand, continued indulgence in assertion is likely to encourage more confidence in one's own statements than their truth and validity warrant and may also beget the habit of repeating what one has read or heard without checking it against experience. The following extract from a student essay shows this fault.

> The comics which are sold at our newsstands should be censored before they are sold to our boys and girls. These comics are, for the most part, detrimental to the characters of the children who read them.
>
> A child goes to the newsstands today and rather than buy "Donald Duck" or "Mickey Mouse" comics he looks for crime or horror comics and buys the one with the most gruesome or gory cover. The child is developing the habit of enjoying things because they are gruesome or horrible and he unconsciously develops a sadistic attitude.
>
> Most of the characters in crime and horror comics are sadists. The authors have these characters do the most horrible things possible to torture the other characters. From these comic characters a child sees how these methods of torture are performed and before long he may be slowly burning his little sister or tying his best friend to a tree and shooting him so that he can see the facial expression and have the satisfaction of being the "big boss" and hurting others.
>
> The child does not even learn that "Crime does not pay." The bad guy in the comics is made to be clever and able to outsmart the good guy. The child takes the part of the bad guy and begins to steal and to do things to see how clever he can be and how long he can keep the good guy from finding this.

Except perhaps for one statement in the third paragraph and one in the fourth, there are no premises in this essay. The author simply asserts that children prefer undesirable comics and become delinquent through their influence. Yet in a conference with her instructor after writing the paper the author admitted that she and all her friends read comics consistently as children and still read them occasionally, and that she could not recall a single member of her group performing a vicious act suggested by the comics. As preparation for this essay she had read Dr. Wertham's article, quoted on pages 340–342, and she had simply taken over Wertham's conclusions without checking them against her own experience. In Wertham's article these statements were conclusions, because he supported them with premises drawn from his experience in courts and clinics. But the girl had no premises to offer; therefore in attempting to pass on Wertham's arguments she simply presented assertions.

At the beginning of this chapter we defined persuasion as the art of getting others to accept conclusions. Its success depends on two factors: the reliability of the argument and the trustworthiness of the person who presents it.

A reliable argument is one that draws valid inferences from true premises. Its premises (even when they are judgments or expert testimony) must accord with the facts, and all of the facts; its assumptions must be acceptable; and its inferences, whether inductive or deductive, must be free from fallacies (pages 353–362). When the reliability of an argument is clear, a reader is likely to accept it. So persuasion succeeds when reliable arguments are presented in such a way that the reader will recognize their reliability.

But often a reader cannot directly perceive whether an argument is reliable. He may be uncertain whether all pertinent evidence has been presented in the premises; he may not be sure that the premises, especially those dealing with expert testimony, are true; he may even feel that he is not competent to pass on the validity of an inference. Whether he accepts or rejects the argument is then likely to depend on his trust in the person presenting it.

Trustworthiness refers to the character or personality of the arguer. No writer is persuasive if his readers do not trust him, or if they develop a distrust for his method or manner of argument. Trustworthiness, then, is the sum of those traits of character or personality by which the writer wins confidence. The chief traits are honesty, knowledge, unselfishness, and fairness. No writer will be trusted if he is suspected of distorting the facts to suit his convenience, if he is ill-informed about his subject, if he is suspected of attempting to persuade his readers for selfish purposes, or if he is obviously biased or unfair. On the other hand, a writer whose arguments are not as sound as they might be will often be read sympathetically if his readers feel that he is honest and careful about his facts, unselfish in his motives, and fair and reasonable in his presentation.

Two devices often give a sophisticated reader an impression of unfairness in a writer. One of these is *slanting* — intentionally distorting facts by presenting only those which support the writer's inference and ignoring others which would suggest a contrary inference. The other device is *loaded diction* — the use of words chosen because they will evoke a favorable or unfavorable emotional response. Illustrations follow.

### Slanting

Everett Watson is short, stocky, almost bald. His skin is coarse, his teeth irregular and tobacco-stained. His suits are cheap, ill-fitting, and usually unpressed. At a party he is self-conscious and ill at ease. He has no knack for social conversation and on such occasions when he has to dance with a woman his efforts are embarrassing both to himself and to his partner. Although his association with business and civic leaders frequently requires him to eat in public, he has never learned to do it with any grace.

Everett Watson has taken an active part in almost every worthwhile community enterprise sponsored during the last ten years. His usefulness to the city is best revealed in the success of the Community Chest drive which he organized last fall, and in the recent report of the Citizen's Committee, of which he is chairman. Although his health is a matter of concern to all his friends, he has never hesitated to spend his strength and energy on any project which promised to be of service to the community.

The passage at the left is slanted to create an unfavorable impression, the one at the right, a favorable impression. Both descriptions may be in accordance with the facts, but each accords with only some of the facts. A complete and fair picture of the subject would include both kinds of information.

### Loaded Diction

This talk of sincerity, I confess, fatigues me. If the *fellow* was sincere, then so was P. T. Barnum. The word is *disgraced* and *degraded* by such uses. He was, in fact, *a charlatan, a mountebank, a zany without shame or dignity*. His career brought him into contact with the first men of his time; he preferred the company of *rustic ignoramuses*. It was hard to believe, watching him at Dayton, that he had traveled, that he had been received in civilized societies, that he had been a high officer of state. He seemed only *a poor clod* like those around him, *deluded* by *childish* theology, full of an almost *pathological hatred of all learning, all human dignity, all beauty, all fine and noble things*. He was a *peasant* come home to the *barnyard*. Imagine a *gentleman,* and you have imagined everything that he was not. What animated him from end to end of his *grotesque* career was simply ambition — the ambition of a common man, to *get his hand upon the collar of his superiors,* or, failing that, *to get his thumb into their eyes*. He was born with a *roaring* voice, and it had the *trick of inflaming half-wits*. His whole career was devoted to raising those half-wits against their *betters,* that he himself might shine. His last battle will be grossly misunderstood if it is thought of as a mere exercise in *fanaticism* — that is, if *Bryan the Fundamentalist Pope* is mistaken for one of the *bucolic fundamentalists*. There was much more in it than that, as everyone knows who saw him on the field. What moved him, at bottom, was simply *hatred* of the city men who had laughed at him so long, and brought him at last to so *tatterdemalion an estate*. He *lusted for revenge* upon them. He yearned to lead the *anthropoid rabble* against them, to punish them for their execution upon him, by attacking the *very vitals of their civilization.* He went far beyond the bounds of any merely *religious frenzy,* however inordinate. When he began denouncing the notion that man is a mammal even some of the *hinds* at Dayton *were agape.* And when, *brought upon Darrow's cruel hook,* he *writhed* and *tossed* in a very *fury* of *malignancy, bawling against the boldest elements of sense and decency* like a man *frantic* — when he came to that tragic climax of his striving there were *snickers* among the *hinds* as well as *hosannas.*[7]

The italicized words in this selection are so loaded with unfavorable connotations that they amount to "name calling." Such terms as *fellow, charlatan, mountebank, rustic ignoramuses, poor clod, anthropoid rabble* — to select the most obvious — are chosen for their unfavorable connotations, and are so obviously emotional that a fair-minded reader will rather interpret them as a reflection of Mencken's attitude than as a fair description of Bryan. Carried to excess, loaded diction and name calling often work against a writer. Instead of making the reader share his view of the subject, they weaken his trust and may even create sympathy for the opposite view. No writer can afford to let his readers feel that he is immoderate and irresponsible.

As an exercise in evaluating a controversy, first read the following debate carefully and then follow the procedure suggested.

### SHOULD COMMUNISM BE STUDIED IN OUR SCHOOLS?

#### YES [8]

I assume that the word "Communism" means Russian Communism, and not the philosophical Communism which has been the subject of theoretical speculation since ancient times. I assume that the word "studied" means careful, comprehensive, systematic, and critical examination of facts for the purpose of achieving understanding, and not the inculcation of political doctrines. I assume that the word "schools" means secondary schools, colleges and universities, and not kindergartens and elementary schools.

The answer to the question, as thus interpreted, is in my judgment an emphatic "yes." In fact, failure to provide for the serious study of Russian Communism at the upper levels of our educational system would be enough to convict the older generation of either stupidity or violation of trust. In the world as it is today, any person who does not have at least an elementary knowledge of Russian Communism — its controlling ideas, its institutions and practices, its impact on the world, its powerful outward thrust, and its challenge to our democracy — must be regarded as politically illiterate. The Russian revolution of 1917 and the development of the Soviet state

[7] From *Prejudices: Fifth Series,* by H. L. Mencken. Copyright, 1926, by Alfred A. Knopf, Inc.

[8] George S. Counts in *Talks,* October, 1947. Copyright, 1947, by Columbia Broadcasting System, Inc. Reprinted by permission of CBS and the author.

together constitute perhaps the outstanding political event of this century. It can no more be ignored with safety than the atomic bomb.

To those who think that the young can be shielded from the ideas of Russian Communism by prohibiting their study in the schools, the answer is they do not understand American society. Our youth hear about Communism daily in the discussions of their elders, on the platform, and over the radio. They read about it in newspapers and magazines. Moreover, they are sure to encounter it in any study of recent history, of world geography, of comparative governments and social systems, and even in any honest and complete study of our American society. Indeed, they encounter it in their own organizations and their informal relations with one another. Only by abandoning our political liberties and by establishing a system of thought control on the pattern of Russian Communism itself, or any other totalitarian state, could we hope to keep the young in complete ignorance on this question. Certainly, few Americans would want to follow this course and thus insure without a struggle the triumph of totalitarianism in the United States.

It is my conviction that knowledge — accurate and balanced — is the only secure foundation of human liberty. Therefore, instead of leaving the young to the mercies of the organized and unorganized propaganda of the home, the street, the marketplace, the radio, and the movie, we should do everything possible to acquaint them, through scholarly study under the guidance of well-trained teachers, with Russian Communism in all of its aspects. By pursuing such a course, we shall prepare our youth to discharge intelligently the responsibilities of citizenship and defend the cause of freedom in the difficult period ahead. If informed men and women are faced with the choice between democracy and dictatorship, they will, I am confident, choose democracy. To deny this is to repudiate the faith that sustains and inspires our system of government.

The study of Russian Communism should be projected on a background of understanding of and loyalty to the principles of democracy. From the earliest years of formal education, children should be reared by both precept and practice in those principles. There is needed here a profound reorganization of our entire school system from the bottom to the top. At no time in our history have we faced squarely the task of developing an educational program carefully and imaginatively designed to cultivate in the young the loyalties, the knowledges, and the understandings essential to the guarding and the strengthening of the great tradition of American liberty. If we undertake this task successfully, we shall not have to worry about shielding our youth from the doctrines of any totalitarian system. We shall equip them, also, to correct all weaknesses and deficiencies in our democracy and thus add greatly to its strength and guarantee its indefinite perpetuation.

## No 9

"Know the enemy" is the first law of self-preservation. Communism is the self-styled enemy of the American way of life. Therefore, in the interest

9 Ruth Alexander in *Talks*, October, 1947. Copyright, 1947, by Columbia Broadcasting System, Inc. Reprinted by permission of CBS and the author.

of national survival, every American adult should study the aims of Communism and the methods by which it proposes to achieve these aims.

But today's discussion is limited to whether or not young people should be taught Communism in our schools. I believe not, for what is wise for adults is often unwise for young people. Whether they fancy themselves to be fully grown or not, there are certain qualitative differences between maturity and immaturity. These are primarily differences in judgment, and the law itself recognizes them by denying minors certain privileges and protecting minors from certain responsibilities. The law should provide similar safeguards in the field of ideas. Therefore, Communism should *not* be studied until intellectual and emotional maturity is reached and the individual is competent to take it or leave it on the basis of experience with human nature and knowledge of history.

There are three major counts against teaching Communism in our schools.

First, adolescence ranges in age roughly from 14 to 21, the seven crucial school years. One of the by-products of adolescence is emotional instability and a tendency towards sentimentality. Whenever youth sees poverty and delinquency its natural sentiment is to try to remedy these tragedies. But youth lacks the experience of age which tempers impulse with judgment. Youth observes the effects of poverty and delinquency, but is unable or unwilling to see clearly the causes. Communism cunningly proclaims the cause to be purely social. It willfully ignores or covers up the historic fact that the predominant cause lies in the ancient universal and durable evils of human nature. And it vigorously denies the historic fact that the American system of civil liberty, voluntary enterprise, and private property has humanized human nature and evolved a finer, higher scale of living than any society known to mankind.

Second, whenever Communism is taught in our schools, it is seldom taught objectively, although there are exceptions, of course. Instruction too often degenerates into indoctrination. It does not confine itself to a rational portrayal of Marxist doctrine, but seeks rather to convert the young student to the Marxist point of view. Masquerading under the cover of academic freedom, many teachers propagandize Communism which, if adopted, would suppress not only academic freedom, but all other freedoms as well. It does not make sense.

Frankly, there is considerable reason for wide-spread academic sympathy toward Communism. Teachers are notoriously underpaid in view of long and costly preparation for their noble profession. But the remedy is not Communism. The remedy is to pay our teachers the highest wage of all civil servants. Until that fortunate day, a study of Communism in our schools would put the young pupil at the mercy of those whose viewpoint is warped by poverty and discontent and who favor any system that promises a phony utopia. Many teachers are innocent of intent to further Communism. Others in high places who teach teachers what and how to teach youth, boldly proclaim a Soviet challenge to America and dare the schools to build a new social order, behind the smoke screen of academic freedom.

Third, Communism is a dangerous dose for youth because it is more than a politico-economic doctrine. Its explosive emotional content amounts to religious fanaticism. It despises and represses orthodox religions as the so-called "opiate of the people." At the same time it substitutes itself as both an opiate and a stimulant. Communists seduce the minds and souls of youth by the prospect of a perfectly functioning "planned economy" wholly at variance with the inescapable laws of economics. They cunningly neglect to mention that their self-styled welfare state is a slave state, achieved and maintained by the firing squad and the concentration camp.

It would sound ridiculous to ask, "Should robbery be studied in our schools?" Yet, if academic freedom is the sole issue rather than national survival, such a question is consistent and in order. If carpentry, why not burglary? Both are ways and means of getting a living. But carpentry is socially constructive and robbery is socially destructive. Communism is likewise socially destructive for its methods frankly include robbery, murder, arson, lying, and incitement to violence. These it defends and advocates on the basis of its working slogan that the "ends justify the means."

We protect our young people from harmful epidemic diseases of a physical nature such as smallpox, by quarantining them. We expose our young people to harmful epidemic diseases of an ideological nature, such as Communism, by a false suicidal interpretation of academic freedom. What youth does when it reaches maturity is something else again. At that time, in the interest of national survival, adults should study Communism to be able to recognize it and fight it for dear life whenever and under whatever disguise it rears its hideous head.

1. In order to be sure that you understand the debate that you are evaluating, summarize both speeches as briefly as possible without distorting their content. If your summary is efficient, each speaker would accept your statement as a fair condensation of his speech.

2. Next determine the issues by deciding to what extent and at what points the speakers disagree. Begin with the definitions. Do both speakers agree on what they mean by *Communism, studied,* and *schools?* To what extent do they agree that Communism should be studied? What is their basic disagreement? This is the main issue. Can it be subdivided into subordinate issues?

3. What are the chief arguments used by Mr. Counts? (Distinguish between argument and assertion.) What types of inferences are used in these arguments? What assumptions does he make? Are there any fallacies in his reasoning? To what extent do you find his arguments persuasive, and why?

4. Follow the same procedure with Miss Alexander's speech.

5. Finally, discuss both speeches in class and work out a common evaluation which represents a class criticism of the debate.

# 16

# THE CRITICAL

# REVIEW

A CRITICAL REVIEW is an appraisal. The subject of the appraisal may be almost anything — a historical movement, an election, a philosophy, a work of literature, a movie, a radio program, a football game, or a date. In composition classes, however, the subject is usually a book, an essay, or a poem; and it is with reviews of such subjects that this chapter is concerned.

## The Requirements of the Review

A good critical review communicates to a reader the critic's evaluation of a book or essay in such a way that the reader can then make his own estimate of the work. To do this the critic must meet three requirements: he must report what the book does; he must judge how well it does it; and he must provide enough evidence from the book itself to support or illustrate his judgment.

Each of these obligations is important. To the extent that the reviewer slights any of them, the usefulness of his review decreases. If his report of what the book does is inadequate for a reader who does not know the book, that reader will have difficulty following the critic's analysis. If, on the other hand, the reviewer tells only what the book does, and not how well it does it, he is writing a synopsis, not a critical review. Finally, if he fails to support or illustrate his judgments from the book itself, he gives the reader no opportunity of forming his own judgment. No reviewer has the right to assume that his unsupported opinions will be accepted as facts. If he says the book is badly organized, that its style is turgid, or that it is full of inaccuracies, he should present evidence for these assertions.

A fourth obligation is taken for granted, that the reviewer will be fair to the work he is judging. He must not allow his prejudices on a subject to influence his appraisal unduly. He has no right, for instance, to condemn a history of capitalism or trade-unionism simply because he dislikes capital or labor. He must not allow his own preferences to blind him to the merits or demerits of the work he is reviewing.

Observe how the following student review meets these requirements.

## AGE OF THUNDER [1]

Frederic Prokosch's *Age of Thunder* is ample evidence that beautiful writing is not enough. Few living writers can handle the English language with more distinction than this poet turned novelist. Even Thomas Mann has paid tribute to the Prokosch prose. But, I think Prokosch's isolated talent of turning exquisite sentences or fashioning fabulously beautiful passages (sometimes several pages in length) actually destroys his chances of achieving greatness. His character development, plot construction, and even intellectual honesty tend to disappear in a purple mist of liquid syllables.

Prokosch's novel pictures the life and death struggles of the maquis in the Haute-Savoie during the years of French underground resistance. Jean-Nicolas, a loyal parachutist spy, dropped for vague reasons of collecting information, dreams his way toward the Swiss border on a magic carpet of Prokosch philosophizing. Later, Jean-Nicolas is betrayed to a German officer by a shadowy caricature named Robinson. That this Robinson or the German commandant would entertain and edify this obvious spy with long and rather juvenile philosophical essays sounded unreal to me.

I do not believe that three mountain gangsters who waylay Allied sympathizers would talk like three versions of Prokosch while planning the murder of Jean-Nicolas. And I do not believe that Susanna, the convenient virgin who tosses the conventions aside like the "winter garment of repentance" upon meeting Jean-Nicolas, would talk or act as she did. In fact, the whole novel is Prokosch any way you cut it.

Incidentally, logical readers who have an eye for detail will want to know why the Swiss border was always a line of hills as these poetic escapists approached it, and how it suddenly became a river when they reached it. But Prokosch, in his illogically slap-happy approach to the problem, undoubtedly thinks such matters are beneath his attention. Personally, I think Prokosch had better stick to poetry.

The only good points I can see about the whole book are the beautifully written passages and the romantic backdrops. However, the reader wants to know how the maquis operated, how the Germans and the collaborationists countered their efforts, and what men would do, think, and say under such circumstances. It is here that Prokosch evades the issue and covers it up with his philosophizing.

This is an unfavorable review. A little more restraint on its author's part might have made it even more convincing, for such expressions

[1] Miriam Graham, "Age of Thunder." Reprinted with permission from *The Green Caldron*, a magazine of freshman writing (University of Illinois), November, 1945, p. 38.

as "even intellectual honesty tend to disappear" and "illogically slap-happy approach" suggest that the reviewer is overstating her objection to the book. And a reader may wonder if, in condemning Prokosch's work for its lack of realism and its failure to explain how the resistance movement actually operated, the reviewer has not missed the author's real purpose. But within the limits of a 400-word assignment the reviewer has done ably what was required of her. She has described the book, passed a clean judgment upon it, and given us samples, though not enough, of the evidence which dictated that judgment.

Special conditions governing a particular assignment will often modify the requirements of a review. For example, students are often asked to write a critical review of an essay which the whole class is reading. In this situation the readers of the review are as familiar with the subject as the reviewer is. There is no need, then, for him to devote any considerable space to what the essay says. What is required of him is his critical estimate of its contents and style. This point is made because instructors are often, and with reason, annoyed to find that an assignment intended to test students' ability to appraise the value of a piece of writing turns out to be largely a report of the essay's contents. Too much attention to a report of content is generally a weakness in a critical review. That weakness is increased when the readers are thoroughly familiar with the work under discussion.

### Reading for the Review

The preparation of a good review requires careful reading as well as careful writing. Lazy or uncritical reading will nearly always result in a poor review; therefore, you should begin to read the book *with the intention of reviewing it.* An awareness of this intention will help to point your reading, just as the intention of outlining or summarizing an essay helps you to read it more purposefully. This does not mean that one should make up his mind about a book in the first thirty pages and then skim the rest merely to find additional evidence to support a hasty judgment. Except in rare cases, an honest reviewer will not make a final judgment until he has read the whole book. But if he reads alertly, he will begin to formulate tentative judgments as he goes along.

In beginning to read, always pay special attention to the introductory or prefatory material. The opening paragraphs of an essay usually reveal the purpose and may even summarize the organization. The preface of a book is often the clearest statement of what its author proposes to do. It may also contain explanations which will affect your review. For example, if the author of a biography of Franklin Delano Roosevelt states in his preface that he has limited himself to a study of Roosevelt's political life, it would be embarrassing to miss that statement and condemn the book on the ground that it failed to present an adequate picture of Roosevelt's personal life. A reviewer has a right to point out, even regret, the limitations the author has imposed on himself. But he does not have the right to condemn a writer for not doing what he never intended to do.

For most books it will be wise to take notes as you read. These notes should contain at least a clear statement of the purpose of the book, some hints about its organization, and references to pages and passages which illustrate the author's style or which deserve special mention in the review. These notes will serve a double purpose: they will help to keep your reading alert and so give you a keener insight into the success or failure of the work, and they will reduce or eliminate the time required to go back and find what you remember as good evidence to support your observations.

## Writing the Review

The writing of a critical review presents no special problems of composition. As long as you satisfy the three requirements discussed earlier, you are free to organize and present your material in whatever way best suits your purpose. The writing of a critical review, therefore, is merely the application to a particular assignment of the principles of composition which were discussed in Part One of this book.

As always, the first step is a concern with purpose. Before you begin to write, you must be clear about two things: your obligations to your readers and your over-all judgment of the book. If you are sure of these things, the organization of your paper should present no unusual difficulty. But if you begin without understanding what is expected of you or what you want to do, your review may be hard to write and even harder to read. Therefore, if you have no clear opinion of the work when you finish reading it, you should review your notes and analyze your impressions in order to form a judgment.

For most students the most difficult part of the review is the opening paragraph. It is quite reasonable, of course, to plunge at once into your final judgment of the book and then devote succeeding paragraphs to the reasons for that judgment. But if you feel that this is too abrupt — and it often is — there are various other ways of beginning, such as:

1. With an introduction of the author, telling the reader who he is, what other books he has written, or how he came to write this one.

2. With a summary of the problem which the author is discussing. Thus, a review of a book on juvenile delinquency might begin with a brief report on the growth of juvenile delinquency and the attempts being made to curb it.

3. With an anecdote or an illustration, either to suggest the mood of the review or to introduce the author's attitude toward his subject.

4. With a quotation that sums up the purpose of the book.

5. With a description of the book in general terms in order to give the reader a brief, comprehensive picture of it.

6. With a classification of the book to show how it resembles or differs from others of the same kind.

7. With a combination of two or more of these openings.

Study the organization of the following student review, paying particular attention to the function of the first paragraph.

## I, Claudius [2]

In the history of the Roman Empire, Emperor Claudius holds a rather obscure place. It is a historical fact that he once wrote an autobiography which was lost centuries ago. In *I, Claudius,* Robert Graves attempts to rewrite that story as the Emperor himself might have dictated it. The result is an elaborate canvas of the history of Rome from the reign of Augustus in the first century B.C. through the elevation of Claudius himself to the throne in A.D. 41.

*I, Claudius* is not a formal history, but resembles a family chronicle written in a conversational style. By writing the story in the first person, the author succeeds in maintaining a certain pleasing informality throughout the book. Graves assembles his work with careful reference to two of the principal Roman authorities, Suetonius and Tacitus. He includes interesting minor touches such as the pretense of writing in Greek, the amusing soldier's jests, and the frequent use of colloquial verse.

In this book, Claudius, a rather decent fellow, unfolds the story of the corruption and degeneracy of the Roman Empire during the period when Rome was a place of extravagance, violence, and evil. He tells of the growing impotence of the upper class as the group tried to preserve the illusion of power. That society is subtly portrayed in the fascinating character of Livia, whom Claudius calls "both admirable and abominable." Obsessed with an uncanny lust for power, she encouraged the poisoning of a potential candidate for the throne so that her husband, Augustus, might ascend as the emperor. During his reign, Livia, the grandmother of Claudius, gained such a hold over her husband that she literally ruled Rome for more than sixty years.

Although the story deals essentially with the collapse of the Roman Empire, in effect it has a much deeper significance. The reader finds himself comparing the Roman times with our own troubled era. Certainly Livia can be compared with recent and contemporary world leaders who have shown that they value power and material wealth above common decency and respect for the individual. *I, Claudius* is filled with such parallels, both subtle and obvious.

Even an attempt to write about a time of such historical dispute is an act of courage. Robert Graves nobly succeeds in painting a vivid portrait of Rome in its glory and in its eventual downfall. Especially remarkable is his ability to combine fascinating history with an interesting narrative,

---

[2] Eleanor Sifferd, "I, Claudius." Reprinted with permission from *The Green Caldron,* a magazine of freshman writing (University of Illinois), December, 1948, p. 11.

into which are injected deep and significant questions to challenge the reader. *I, Claudius* is a book which is well worth reading.

In her first paragraph the author of this review does three things: she introduces the subject (Claudius), she states in general terms the author's purpose, and she gives an introductory description of the book. Thereafter, in successive paragraphs, she analyzes the way the book is developed, summarizes its basic plot, points out the significance of the work to modern readers, and gives her final judgment of its success. To do that in less than five hundred words is a respectable accomplishment. The reviewer has to sacrifice illustrative details which might have made the paper still more convincing, but enough evidence is given in paragraphs 2, 3, and 4 to keep the review from being a presentation of unsupported judgments.

As you develop your review be on guard against these common weaknesses:

1. Taking up a disproportionate space to explain the action or content of the book so that the review is essentially a digest instead of a criticism.

2. Picking out parts for review instead of reviewing the book as a whole. It is justifiable to criticize particular parts in relation to the whole, but a student who concentrates on particular sections is likely to produce a distorted picture of the whole book.

3. Drifting into digressions which better illustrate the reviewer's philosophy than the merits or demerits of the book.

4. Allowing the style of the review to dominate the reviewer's purpose, thus creating an exaggerated or biased treatment.

5. Keeping the review at too general a level by failing to provide specific illustration of general statements.

The first four of these weaknesses result from failing to keep the purpose of the review clearly in mind. The last comes from a failure to remember that the reader cannot see into the reviewer's mind and hence can never be quite clear about what these general judgments mean unless he is shown. In the critical review, as in all writing except summaries, the writer must elaborate his general observations in order to make them convincing.

## Exercises

**A.** The three reviews of *Language in Thought and Action* that follow were written in a class in which everyone was required to read the book. The reviews illustrate varying degrees of success and failure. First read the three reviews, then write a paper in which you rate them in order of merit and explain the good or bad points on which you base your rating.

## (1)

"Much of this book may have sounded like warnings against words. Such has not been its purpose. Words are, as has been said from the beginning, the essential instruments of man's humanity. This book only asks the reader to treat them as such."

In the author's own words, this is the thought that is emphasized in *Language in Thought and Action*. Mr. Hayakawa attempts to establish his idea by breaking down and analyzing different aspects of the words of the English language. Many of his observations he has presented in a philosophical way which may be cause for discussion on the part of some readers. In several cases the reader was given new definitions for some of the qualities of words which probably emphasized something that he already knew. This is best illustrated in the section on the habit of confusing what is inside of us and what is outside in respect to the meaning of words. The words "Jew" and "criminal" were used as examples in the illustration.

The highlight of the book was Chapter 8 which was titled "How We Know What We Know." This chapter deals with the relation of words with what they stand for or, in other words, definition. People often complain about words meaning different things to different people, but meanings of words are not within the words, but within us.

When defining "Two-valued Orientation," Mr. Hayakawa says that there is a tendency to see things in terms of two values only, affirmative and negative, good or bad, and hot and cold. In many of his suppositions, he goes against himself in that he uses extremities when analyzing some of the qualities of words. Perhaps this should be over-looked, however, in view of the fact that the author may have used this device for emphasis.

In the concluding chapter of the book, the author stresses that some of his ideas may have sounded like warnings against words and this was not the purpose. However, I believe it would be hard for any reader to finish the book and not be a little skeptical of the world of words around him. Maybe if the reader does have this feeling after finishing the book, in reality, the author has been successful in getting his thought across to the reader.

## (2)

When I first began to read *Language in Thought and Action* I was quite surprised to find that I liked the book. Since we are to use it as a supplementary textbook, I expected to find it dull and uninteresting, a book which would be difficult to read and comprehend. Instead, I found most parts of the book easy to read and understand.

The purpose of the book is to give the reader a general system for clearing the mind of harmful obstructions to thought. Professor Hayakawa attempts through 15 short chapters to apply his scientific study of meaning (semantics) to the thinking, speaking, reading, and writing done in every day life. Some of the points he makes are common knowledge. Others are vaguely understood but seldom practised. Most of them open up to us an entirely new view of language and of the use and abuse we make of it.

The stories which the professor has used to illustrate his meaning throughout the book are rather peculiar. Usually, a writer who wishes to convert readers to his way of thinking stays away from controversial topics because of the difficulty of handling these topics without antagonizing some readers. Mr. Hayakawa, however, repeatedly deals with the three most controversial topics in the world today: religion, race, and politics. In the opinion of some people this would obviously class him as a radical. I believe, however, that he is actually interested in the disagreements between people which result from a discussion of these subjects. These disagreements so often produce "loaded words," "intensional orientation," "slanting," and other semantic errors that they offer exceptionally striking examples of the misuse of language.

Throughout his book the author uses a vocabulary of terms which are common to studies of semantics. I suppose these terms are necessary, but they are often very difficult to understand, and many times I had difficulty seeing the distinction between some of them. The terms "extensional and intensional orientation" were clear, but the "affective," "directive," and "presymbolic" uses of language seemed to overlap so much that Mr. Hayakawa can sometimes use a single word or expression to illustrate all three. It would have been helpful if he had provided a dictionary of technical terms at the end of the book so that a student could turn to it and clear up his confusion.

On the whole, though, I think the author has succeeded in doing what he set out to do, and he has done it in an interesting and lively fashion. I am sure that my whole attitude toward language has changed as a result of reading this book.

### (3)

A story with a moral is told in the beginning. It is a story about how differently two people consider an act when one of them calls it "insurance" and the other calls it "relief." The sum total of the story shows the misconceptions and various viewpoints which arise from the words we use in our everyday language.

The importance of language is stressed as an aid to cooperation with our fellow humans. It is also stressed as a factor in permitting facts and observations to be handed down from generation to generation, thus eliminating the necessity of rediscovering or observing the same things again. The point is made of warning the reader against planning life by imaginary maps or false ideas.

The fact that words have no meaning in themselves, but are merely symbols of meanings is a point worth considering. The people of the world live by symbols. Good clothes, ornaments, comfortable homes are symbols of wealth. Rags and shacks symbolize poverty. Many people who misunderstand language try to explain things in terms of themselves or on the same levels of abstraction. Since education is largely a matter of learning facility in the manipulation of words, it is necessary to filter them correctly. The term linguistic naïveté means that many people show ignorance in interpreting things they hear or read.

In writing reports a person must guard against the addition of judgments or implications of judgments or opinions. The use of inferences should be excluded in writing reports, while the process of slanting one's judgments in one direction should be replaced by judgments both for and against.

The definition of a word is arrived at by the use given it by writers in the past. We learn the definition by repeated association with its use in language. In addition much of the meanings of words are conveyed in the tone with which they are spoken or used. The context of what is said is often sufficient to convey the intended meaning even if what is actually said is entirely different.

Symbolic language is both informative and affective upon the hearer. Most advertising is symbolically written for the purpose of affecting the reader. These symbolic writings are called affective connotations and are used extensively by politicians. In directive language these connotations may contain implied promises, as in the speeches of politicians or the claims of advertisers.

The process of abstracting is illustrated by cows, it being that one cow is not another cow although they possess things in common. They cannot be explained in terms of one another on the same levels of abstraction, but must be explained on a higher level of abstraction using characteristics common to both. The main point stressed is that $COW_1$ is not $COW_2$.

**B.** The following condensation of a much longer review is confined chiefly to the climax of the movie, *Henry V* — the Battle of Agincourt. Study the review and decide how well it meets the three requirements discussed earlier. Then write a 300-word paper in which you explain and illustrate your judgment.

### MASTERPIECE [3]

The movies have produced one of their rare great works of art. . . . At last there has been brought to the screen, with such sweetness, vigor, insight and beauty that it seems to have been written yesterday, a play by the greatest dramatic poet who ever lived. It had never been done before. For Laurence Olivier, 38 (who plays Henry and directed and produced the picture), the event meant new stature. For Shakespeare, it meant a new splendor in a new, vital medium.

As Shakespeare wrote it, *The Cronicle History of Henry the fifth* is an intensely masculine, simple, sanguine drama of kinghood and war. Its more eloquent theme is a young king's coming of age. Once an endearingly wild Prince of Wales, Henry V (at 28) had to prove his worthiness for the scepter by leading his army in war. He invaded France, England's longtime enemy. He captured Harfleur, then tried to withdraw his exhausted and vastly outnumbered army to Calais. The French confronted him at Agincourt. In one of Shakespeare's most stirring verbal sonnets, Henry urged his soldiers on to incredible victory. English mobility (un-

---

[3] Courtesy of *Time*. Copyright, Time, Inc., 1946.

armored archers) and English firepower (the quick-shooting longbow) proved too much for the heavily armored French. Casualties (killed): English, 29; French, 10,000. . . .

The Battle of Agincourt is not realistic. Olivier took great care not to make it so. To find the "kind of poetic country" he wanted, and to avoid such chance anachronisms as air raids (the picture was made in Britain during the war), Olivier shot the battle sequence in Ireland.

Making no attempt to overresearch the actual fight, he reduced it to its salients — the proud cumbrousness of the armored French chevaliers, and Henry's outnumbered archers, cloth-clad in the humble colors of rural England. A wonderful epitomizing shot — three French noblemen drinking a battle-health in their saddles — is like the crest of the medieval wave. The mastering action of the battle, however, begins with a prodigious truck-shot of the bannered, advancing French chivalry shifting from a walk to a full gallop, intercut with King Henry's sword, poised for signal, and his archers, bows drawn, waiting for it. The release — an arc of hundreds of arrows speeding with the twang of a gigantic guitar on their victorious way — is one of the most gratifying payoffs of suspense yet contrived.

But the most inspired part of Shakespeare's play deals with the night before the Battle of Agincourt. It is also the most inspired sequence in the film. Olivier opens it with a crepuscular shot of the doomed and exhausted English as they withdraw along a sunset stream to encamp for the night. . . .

The invisible Chorus begins the grandly evocative description of the night camps:

> Now entertain conjecture of a time
> When creeping murmur and the poring dark
> Fills the wide vessel of the universe.

The screen sustains this mood with a generalized shot of the opposed camps, their fires like humiliated starlight. There are no creeping murmurs, neighing steeds, crowing cocks, clanking armorers. Instead, William Walton's score, one of the few outstanding scores in movie history, furnishes subdued, musical metaphors. Midway through the Chorus, the film boldly breaks off to interpolate, to better effect, a scene in the French camp which in Shakespeare's version precedes it.

This scene itself also improves on Shakespeare. His Frenchmen, the night before their expected triumph, were shallow, frivolous and arrogant. By editing out a good deal of their foolishness, by flawless casting, directing and playing, and by a wonderfully paced appreciation of the dead hours of rural night, Olivier transforms the French into sleepy, over-confident, highly intelligent, highly sophisticated noblemen, subtly disunified, casually contemptuous of their Dauphin — an all but definitive embodiment of a civilization a little too ripe to survive.

The hypnotic Chorus resumes; the camera pans to the English camp and strolls, as if it were the wandering King himself, among the firelit tents.

And here poem and film link the great past to the great present. It is unlikely that anything on the subject has been written to excel Shakespeare's short study, in *Henry V*, of men stranded on the verge of death and disaster. The man who made this movie made it midway in England's most terrible war, within the shadows of Dunkirk. In appearance and in most of what they say, the three soldiers with whom Henry talks on the eve of Agincourt might just as well be soldiers of World War II. No film of that war has yet said what they say so honestly or so well.

Here again Olivier helped out Shakespeare. Shakespeare gave to a cynical soldier the great speech: *But if the cause be not good,* etc. Olivier puts it in the mouth of a slow-minded country boy (Brian Nissen). The boy's complete lack of cynicism, his youth, his eyes bright with sleepless danger, the peasant patience of his delivery, and his Devon repetition of the tolled word *die* as *doy,* lift this wonderful expression of common humanity caught in human war level with the greatness of the King.

*Henry V* is one of the great experiences in the history of motion pictures. It is not, to be sure, the greatest: the creation of new dramatic poetry is more important than the recreation of the old. For such new poetry movies offer the richest opportunity since Shakespeare's time, and some of them have made inspired use of the chance. But *Henry V* is a major achievement — this perfect marriage of a great dramatic poetry with the greatest contemporary medium for expressing it.

**C.** Write a 300-word critical review of the following review.

### THE LONG SHIPS PASSING [4]

In the three centuries that the white man has been sailing them, the Great Lakes have recapitulated the whole long history of maritime commerce. They have seen the exploitation of their waters increase from the primitive but adventurous navigation of Indian warriors and trappers to the busy traffic of one of the great trade routes of the world, and in that short time they have witnessed almost the entire evolution of transport by water. They have seen the paddle give way to sail, and sail to steam. They have seen the craft propelled by those forces grow from birch canoes to steel freighters over 600 feet in length and over 14,000 in net tonnage. They have watched arduous and sometimes prohibitive portages circumvented by canals so that the once inaccessible ports of Lake Superior have been opened to the commerce of the seven seas. And they have seen those canals, in turn, fitted with everexpanding locks, until over the passage between Huron and Superior (a passage which less than a hundred years ago was a decisive barrier to navigation unless, like the 50-ton schooner *Algonquin,* ships were placed on rollers and inched along by land at a speed of five lengths a day) more than three quarters of a million tons of freight have passed in a single day.

The story of Great Lakes navigation, then, is a story of man's persistent and ingenious efforts to exploit the greatest inland waterway in the world

4 From "The Long Ships Passing," *Quarterly Bulletin,* Historical Society of Northwestern Ohio, January, 1943. Reprinted by permission of the Society.

for his own needs and ambitions. Call it the romance of the lakes or the romance of those men who have made the lakes a highway to empire, it is a dramatic story, and considering the variety of its appeal, one that has received less than its share of attention in the literature of our expanding frontiers.

In *The Long Ships Passing* Mr. Havighurst has dealt with that story, sketching the development of the lakes from the explorations of the earliest voyageurs to the controversy over the present Seaway proposal. His book is not a history, if we are to understand by history the organization and synthesis of all the evidence that is relevant to an understanding of the development of the Great Lakes. Rather it is a collection of stories and legends, each complete in itself, the whole forming a series of episodes that reflects the changes the lakes have seen and accentuates the romance that has attended these changes.

Such a controlling purpose, of course, limits the appeal of the book, and probably Mr. Havighurst's work will have a greater attraction for the layman than for the professional historian. Moreover, it always runs the risk of producing a book which, because of its lack of any unifying theme, is merely another book *about* the subject with which it deals. There are, indeed, moments when one feels that Mr. Havighurst has not sufficiently resisted the temptation to add another story merely because it is a good story, without concerning himself too much about the relationship of the story to the theme that he is developing. Thus the chapter dealing with Strang's kingdom on Beaver Island hardly escapes being an eight-page digression, since it has no other claim to being an integral part of the story of the development of the Great Lakes than the fact that Beaver Island happened to be located in Lake Michigan. The story, of course, is interesting, but, like a cuckoo in a sea-gull's nest, it would be more at home in other quarters.

Such intercalations, however, are rare in *The Long Ships Passing*, for Mr. Havighurst is dealing with the vicissitudes of life on and about the Great Lakes, and he has no trouble in selecting episodes to illustrate those vicissitudes. Thus all sorts of stories are grist to his mill, whether they be tales of shipwrecks from fire or storm, reports of conflagrations that destroyed whole areas of lumber towns, glimpses of immigrants embarking at Buffalo to find new homes in a new country, exposition of the steps leading up to the building of the Soo Canal and of the difficulties that beset its builders, or the story of Charlie Mott's squaw, Angelique, who escaped the starvation that killed her husband on Isle Royal by weaving rabbit snares from the hair of her head.

The material from which the author selected his illustrations is abundant. That material — for example, the freezing to death of the *Mataafa's* crew on the rocky beach at Duluth while 40,000 people stood on the pier impotent to help them — is dramatic in itself. The author has seen to it that none of the drama is lost in the telling. His accounts of the burning of Menominee and of the relief of Marquette from starvation — to cite two episodes out of hundreds — are little masterpieces of dramatic narrative. His style — if style and story can be separated — is the style of the novelist, with careful attention to the details that give his picture reality. Adequate quotation is impossible, but two small excerpts will perhaps help the reader to form his own judgments. The first is from the account of the *Independence's* first voyage on Lake Superior:

> In her main cabin people listened grimly to the smashing seas and the wind's high whistle. Then the stove broke loose from its foundation and went skidding across the cabin. Sparks streamed out of the broken smokepipe and burning embers strewed the deck. While they fought fire in that cabin all the faces were grim and set, but a few were haunted. A few of them had seen the fifty kegs of blasting powder stored beneath the hatches.

The second excerpt is from a chapter entitled "Smoke Clouds Blowing":

> Frontier towns burned like tinder. The board streets and sidewalks, the open frame buildings, the lack of water pressure and of fire-fighting apparatus made them terribly vulnerable. . . . The very ground they rested on, built up of sawdust, slabs and refuse from the mills, was inflammable. The drying yards, with lumber stacked and open to the air, could quickly roar into acres of flame. . . . Sawdust towns lived violently, with the rumble of logging, the snarl and scream of the buzz saw, and the tumult of the loading wharfs. And mostly they died violently.

If stories of sinking ships and burning towns, of killing cold and wind-lashed waves, of reckless men engaged in dangerous pursuits make up the warp of *The Long Ships Passing*, the woof is formed by the pressure of an expanding economy in an era becoming increasingly mechanized. Throughout the book there is constant illustration of the economic forces that opened and developed the great inland waterway. The need for the grain and lumber and minerals of the Great Lakes regions, the stream of immigrants from the Old World, providing the man power to harvest those resources, and the mechanical improvements that facilitated the transporting of the products — markets, men, money, and machines, all these are pictured as coming together to keep the long ships passing.

**D.** Select any volume of fiction or non-fiction that you have recently read and write a 500-word critical review of it.

# 17

*
*   **T H E   B U S I N E S S**
*
*   **L E T T E R**
*

---

THE WRITING of a business letter as a college assignment serves a double purpose: it makes students familiar with the conventional forms of business correspondence and it provides a practical application of the principles of effective composition. Of the two purposes, the latter is the more important. The conventions of business correspondence should be understood and followed, but it should also be understood that a good business letter is primarily a good composition. Indeed, the writing of a convincing letter of application is often a more exacting test of a student's ability to select, organize, and present pertinent information than many of the more usual composition assignments.

### The Form of a Business Letter

All business letters follow a relatively standardized form which is illustrated by the example given below. For convenience, the various parts of the letter have been numbered.

```
                                    115 Ohio Street          1
                                    Galesburg, Illinois
                                    December 28, 1949         2
        Fisher Paint Company
   3    212 West Madison Street
        Chicago 7, Illinois

   4    Gentlemen:

        In your advertisement of Colopake in recent
        issues of Time you say that the superiority
        of Colopake over other paint products is
        achieved by reducing the size of the pigment
   5    particles.  Since I am making a comparative
        study of various paints I should like to have
        more information on this point.  Would it be
        possible for me to obtain a copy of the compara-
```

tive data which were the basis of your advertising statement?

*6*

Yours truly,

*John A. Baker*

*7*

John A. Baker

As our illustration shows, a business letter consists of at least seven parts:

**1. The Return Address.** This part will be omitted, of course, if stationery containing a printed letterhead is used, since the letterhead itself is the return address. The form used in our example is called a *block* heading with *open* punctuation. In a block heading the lines are not indented; each line begins flush with the one preceding. In open punctuation no marks are used at the ends of lines, but elements within the lines are separated in accordance with the usual conventions. Alternative forms — *indented* headings and *closed* punctuation — are common and accepted but not preferred. In indented headings each line is indented a few spaces to the right of the line preceding. In closed punctuation a comma is used after the street and the state. Addresses should be written in full, though figures are generally used for numbered streets, and *North, South, East* and *West* are often abbreviated — *42nd Street, 15th Avenue, 212 W. Madison Street;* but *300 Fifth Avenue.*

**2. The Date Line.** The date line is written as part of the first heading and takes the same form as the return address — flush or indented, with open or closed punctuation, depending on the style used in the return address.

**3. The Inside Address.** This heading consists of three or more lines and follows the form established in the first heading. Abbreviations such as *Co.* and *Inc.* are used only if these terms are abbreviated in the letterheads of the companies being addressed. When the title of the addressee is given, it is usually placed after his name on the first line; but if this practice would result in an awkwardly long line, the title may be given as a separate line.

> Dr. David D. Henry, President
> University of Illinois
> Urbana, Illinois
>
> Dr. Robert B. Downs
> Director of the Library School
> University of Illinois
> Urbana, Illinois

Names which would be awkward or impossible in a single line are written in two lines:

```
North Carolina State College
of Agriculture and Engineering
University of North Carolina
Raleigh, North Carolina
```

**4. The Salutation.** When an individual is being addressed, the salutation usually takes one of the following forms: *Dear Mr.* (or *Mrs.*) *Blank, Dear Sir* (or *Madam*). Such an informal salutation as *Dear Bob* is acceptable only in writing to a personal friend. The form, *My dear Mr.* (or *Mrs.*) *Blank* may be used in distinctly formal letters. When the letter is addressed to a company, rather than to an individual, the accepted salutation is *Gentlemen;* the form *Dear Sirs* is seldom used in modern business letters. If the company is known to consist of women, the salutation may be either *Mesdames* or *Ladies.* A colon follows the salutation.

**5. The Body.** The body of the letter usually consists of one or more paragraphs of single-spaced text, with double spacing between paragraphs. There is a growing preference for starting all paragraphs at the left margin so that no indention is used to mark the opening of a paragraph. However, the older style of starting the first paragraph under the colon of the salutation and thereafter indenting the first line of each paragraph seven spaces from the margin is still common. The opening lines of paragraphs may be indented even when no indention is used in the headings.

**6. The Complimentary Close.** The most common endings are *Yours truly, Yours very truly, Very truly yours, Yours sincerely,* or *Sincerely yours.* Such closes as *Cordially,* or *Cordially yours,* are used only when the writer is on familiar terms with his addressee. *Respectfully* is a formal close used chiefly in submitting a formal report to a superior. A comma is used at the end of the complimentary close.

**7. The Signature.** The signature consists of two parts: the written signature, and below this the writer's name and official position, if any, typed in. Both parts are necessary. The written signature is the legal identification of the writer; the typed name is a safeguard against misreading of the signature. Since it is conventional in business to address a woman as *Miss* unless she signifies that she is married, married women enclose *Mrs.* in parentheses before their typed signatures.

*Helen White*

```
(Mrs.) Helen White
  or (Mrs. John White)
```

When an individual writes a letter in the name of his company, it is frequent practice to place the company name before his written signature, thus:

Very truly yours,
Main Motor Sales Company

*W. R. Smith*

Webster R. Smith, Secretary

When a letter is typed by someone other than the author, the typist puts first the author's initials, then her own (with a colon between them) flush with the left margin and below the author's signature:

WRS:HW.

## The Appearance of the Letter

The appearance of a business letter is extremely important. As much as possible the letter must be centered on the page and framed by adequate margins. The various parts of the letter should be separated from each other by extra spacing — usually at least two spaces between the first and second headings, between the inside address and the salutation, between the salutation and the body, and between the body and the complimentary close. Single-spacing is used within the headings. Within reasonable limits, the margins may be adjusted to get a long letter on a single page or to keep a short letter in the center of a page. A letter, of course, may consist of more than one page, but the spacing should be so contrived that the second page does not consist of only two or three lines. It goes without saying that the typing must be neat and accurate.

## The Letter of Application

The rest of this chapter will be devoted to the letter applying for a position. This is the kind of business letter which students are most likely to write, and of all business letters it probably presents the problem of composition at its most difficult level. A student who can write an effective letter of application has had a useful introduction to the art of business correspondence.

Although some variation is possible, letters of application generally follow a standardized organization. The body of the letter usually consists of five parts: the lead, the record of education and experience, the references, the request for further communication (usually an interview), and the data sheet. These parts are illustrated by the following letter.

2223 Edgewood Avenue
New York, New York
April 22, 19—

Robertson and Rand, Inc.
Public Accountants
410 Lexington Avenue
New York, New York

Gentlemen:

*Lead*

Because I am deeply interested in Public Accounting, I want to secure a position with an organization carrying on this kind of work. Professor F. H. Higbee, in charge of the Accounting Department of the Manchester Business Institute, speaks highly of your firm. At his suggestion I wish to apply for a position with you.

I completed my high school course in May, 19—, and entered the Manchester Business Institute. I am now a senior and will be graduated from the four-year course next June.

*Education*

In my work I have always specialized in accounting, taking every course offered. Among the courses I have taken are Auditing, C.P.A. Problems, Income Tax Accounting, Cost Accounting, Accounting Systems, and Governmental Accounting. In addition I have studied courses allied to accounting and have read extensively from books and periodicals devoted to the subject. I have detailed these readings and other personal information on the attached sheet.

*Experience*

During the past two years I have been doing accounting work for three small companies. With them I have had complete charge of the books and income tax returns. I feel that this experience has been valuable to me in broadening my point of view.

*References*

Mr. F. H. Higbee, who is, as you no doubt know, the senior partner of a local firm of public accountants, has kindly allowed me to use his name as a reference in regard to my character and abilities. I am also permitted to use the names, on the attached sheet, of men who have known me as a student or employee.

If you will communicate with me, I shall be glad to furnish you with further particulars of my experience or any personal information you may wish.

Sincerely yours,

*George N. White*

George Neilson White

(*Separate Enclosure*)

## PERSONAL DATA

PERSONAL
Name –– George Neilson White
Present Address –– 2223 Edgewood Avenue, New York
Permanent Address –– 3213 Riverside Avenue, Springfield, Mass.

Height –– 5' 11"          Weight –– 170
Age –– 24                 Place of Birth ––
                             Springfield, Mass.
Nationality –– Scotch
Not married and have no dependents
Religion –– Member Presbyterian Church
Physical Condition –– No defects of any
                             kind

EDUCATION
High School –– Springfield, Massachusetts
Manchester Business Institute
Accounting Courses Studied
   Elementary Accounting
   Applied Accounting
   Cost Accounting
   Advanced C.P.A. Problems
   Income Tax Accounting
   Accounting Systems
   Auditing
   Governmental Accounting

Courses Allied to Accounting Studied
   Mathematics of Investments
   Theory of Economics
   Corporation Finance
   Investments

Money and Banking
Commercial Law
Corporation Law
Credits and Collections
Factory Administration
Commercial Correspondence
Marketing Methods
Sales Administration

Books Read on Accounting and Allied
    Subjects
Kester, Theory and Practice of Ac-
    counting
Nicholson and Rohrbach, Cost Accounting
Regulations 45 and 19 -- Income Tax Law
Montgomery, Auditing Theory and Practice
Oakey, Principles of Governmental
    Accounting
Cole, Accounts -- Their Construction
    and Interpretation
Copeland, Business Statistics
The Duties of a Junior Accountant

EXPERIENCE
Two years bookkeeping, The Central
    Pharmacy

Accounting work, 1947 to 1949, with three
    Bronx stores

REFERENCES
Prof. F. H. Higbee, Manchester Business
    Institute, New York
Prof. Jas. H. Mundt, Manchester Business
    Institute, New York
Theo. Rau, The Central Pharmacy, New York
V. C. Brown, Vice-Pres., Commonwealth
    Bank, Springfield, Mass.[1]

Each of these five parts has its own special role in developing the
total purpose of the letter. These functions may be stated briefly.

1. The Lead. The lead is an introductory statement in which the
applicant establishes contact with the potential employer and declares
himself a candidate for a position. The source of the lead is usually an
advertisement or, as in our sample, the recommendation of a friend or
an employee of the company. If the writer is applying for a specific
job, he usually indicates in the lead his knowledge of the requirements
of that position — for example:

Mr. Bruce Benedict, Senior Accountant in
your office, tells me that you intend to
hire an additional secretary at the begin-

[1] From Robert Ray Aurner, *Effective English in Business.* Copyright, 1935. Reprinted by permission of Professor Aurner and the South-Western Publishing Company.

```
ning of the year.  I understand that the
position requires someone who has had both
bookkeeping and secretarial experience.
Since I am qualified in both fields I should
like to be considered as a candidate.
```

When the applicant is writing an unsolicited letter the lead might take such form as this:

```
I wonder if, within the next few weeks, you
intend to add an additional typist to your
staff.  I find that in order to finance my
college education it will be necessary for
me to seek a full-time position and, since I
live on the campus, I should particularly
like to work for the University.
```

**2. Education and Experience.** This section is the main part of the letter, since candidates are selected for interviews chiefly on the strength of their education and experience. If either of these is slight, the other should compensate for it. The writer of our sample letter has had only limited experience, so he wisely detailed the nature of his training. A man with considerable experience would give a much briefer account of his education, but he would not pass hurriedly over *both* his education and his experience. As we shall see in the next section, one of the most serious weaknesses of student letters is that they do not adequately develop this important part of the application.

**3. References.** The references are the names and addresses of people who can do for the applicant what he cannot, with any modesty, do for himself — testify to his abilities, accomplishments, and desirable characteristics. It is both wise and courteous to obtain permission to use names as references before writing the letter.

**4. Request for Further Communication.** The conventional ending of a letter of application is a request for an interview. This request should be neither obsequious nor demanding but should be stated something like this:

```
I should appreciate a personal interview at
our mutual convenience.  I am free after five
o'clock every day and all day Saturdays.  My
home telephone number is Fairfield 0172.
```

Of course the best way to obtain an interview is to write the kind of letter that will make the employer eager to arrange a personal meeting. But even in the best of letters it is wise to ask for an interview unless distance makes one impracticable.

**5. The Data Sheet.** Many applications are written without a data sheet, in which event the most significant data is worked into the body of the letter. The advantages of the data sheet, however, are obvious, since it presents in the shortest possible space a complete outline of the candidate's qualifications and permits convenient reference if the employer wishes to re-check particular items.

### Analysis of Failing Letters

The sample letter on page 392 is a most effective application. It is attractively arranged, logically organized, detailed in its treatment of education and experience, free from immodest judgments about the writer's qualifications, and clearly and correctly written. Such a letter is sure to make a good impression. Indeed, this particular letter was referred to the president of the company who personally wrote to the applicant with a view to offering him a position.

The following are examples of unsuccessful letters. To save space, the headings and signatures have been omitted:

```
Dear Personal Manager:

It was my ambition to be associate with a
progressive firm like yours where my talents
are appreciated.

I am graduating from college in June.  The
major pursued here is industrial management.

I would like a job as soon as possible.

                         Yours Respectively;
```

The natural response of an employer receiving such a letter would be to forward it to the college from which the writer claims to be graduating with a note asking if this boy was a typical product of the college. The letter is not only stylistically impossible; it fails completely to present any information (other than the questionable statement that the writer is about to graduate with a major in industrial management) which would be useful to a prospective employer. The only picture it presents is that of a person with no qualifications whatsoever, not even a sense of tact.

The next letter is only slightly better:

```
Dear Sir:

You have a vacancy in your accounting de-
partment according to my adviser, Mr. O. R.
Strabe of Branch College.  I am prepared
to fill it.  My qualifications are of the
best.

Your prompt reply will gratify me.  I am so
anxious to work for you.

                         Yours sincerely,
```

If this writer really wants serious consideration he should present the evidence which makes him feel that he is well qualified. Judgments about one's own qualifications are always open to question, but unsupported judgments are flatly objectionable. The chief purpose of an application letter is to show why the applicant merits serious consideration. The way to do that is to present the *facts* of education and experience. This applicant has done Mr. Strabe and himself a disservice by his naïve assumption that he need not take the time to present a detailed picture of his qualifications. The letter says almost nothing.

The following paragraph illustrates an error that was discussed in pages 141–142 — the error of overreaching oneself in an attempt to achieve a dignified literary style:

It is understandable that your highly respected firm is exceedingly anxious to
secure the valuable services of competent
young men who have undergone specialized and
detailed training in the outstanding educational institutions of our day — and let
me say in a patriotic aside, our noteworthy
institutions are indeed comparable in
prowess and achievement and dignity to the
most heralded universities and colleges of
any nation, bar none! — and thus it is my
earnest conviction that, when you go far
afield in search of promising prospects for
your dominant organization, you will proceed eventually to the hallowed college from
which I send forth this missive.

This kind of writing is more likely to be amusing than annoying, but the purpose of an application is not to amuse; it is to get a job. An applicant cannot afford to make himself ridiculous; yet that is what this applicant does. What he has to say need not be said at all. Certainly it should not be said in such a wordy and preposterous way.

The next letter deserves special attention, since it is more representative than any already given of the kind of inadequate letter which competent college students are inclined to write:

Gentlemen:

Will one of your research laboratories
need an assistant next year?

Education: I am a graduate of Nelson High
School and will graduate from
Midwest College this June with
a B. S. degree and a major in
chemistry.

Experience:     During my summer vacations I
have worked in the labora-
tories of A. N. Weir and Company. During the fall of 1949
I worked in the plating department of the Maddox Hard-
ware Company where I had some
experience with metallurgy.

References:     The following people have
kindly allowed me to use their
names as references:

        Professor William Linbeck
        Department of Chemistry
        Midwest College

        Mr. Thomas Norton
        Weir Laboratories
        Dunsan, Iowa

    I should appreciate the opportunity of
an interview any Saturday that is convenient
to you.

                Yours sincerely,

At first glance this may seem a satisfactory letter. But if it is compared with the sample letter given earlier, its inadequacies will be
obvious. Assuming that most of the candidates for this position are
college graduates with majors in chemistry, what has this letter to
recommend it? It is little more than an outline. The applicant should
at least have shown what kind of work he did in the Weir laboratories
and what kind of metallurgical experience he has had. By failing to
give details, he keeps his letter from offering a convincing picture of
his qualifications. None of the other qualified applicants could do less
than he has done, and the chances are that most of them will do more.

We can sum up this analysis of unsatisfactory letters by saying that
the errors to avoid in a letter of application are:

1. Stylistic and grammatical imperfections.
2. Inadequate development of one's qualifications.
3. Unsupported judgments of one's abilities.
4. Statements which are arrogant, naïve, or in bad taste.
5. Unattractive appearance of the letter.

For the kind of position which requires a good letter of application,
the employer is probably going to require an interview. If there are
twenty or thirty candidates for the position, probably only three or four

will be invited for interviews. The immediate purpose of the letter, then, is to get an interview. The best way to do that is to present the facts of one's qualifications clearly and fully. This can best be done in a well-organized data sheet and an accompanying letter which is clear, concise, and in good taste. The importance that will be attached to the application justifies the time and effort required to make it a good one.

### The Letter Declining a Job

In one sense, a letter declining a job is an easy one to write. If all that the writer wants to do is to say "No," any courteous refusal will do. Thus he may merely say, "Thank you for offering me the position. It is in many ways an attractive one; but I have accepted an appointment with the W. F. Brenning Company and am therefore no longer available." Such a reply will meet the writer's minimum obligations to the company that offered him a position.

There are three considerations, however, that suggest something more than a minimum reply. First, if an employer has paid an applicant's expenses for an interview and has spent valuable time showing him around the plant and discussing with him the position and its possibilities, a minimum reply is an ungracious return for this hospitality. It is true that the employer has been acting in his own interests, but he has probably made a greater expenditure of time and money to fill the position than most applicants realize, and an abrupt refusal, even though politely expressed, is a disappointing return for his efforts.

Second, an offer of a position is the best kind of evidence that an employer thinks well of an applicant. That good will is a business asset and should, if possible, be preserved. There may later be more attractive opportunities in the company, or the employer may sometime be in a position to be helpful. The applicant therefore owes it to his own future to consider these possibilities before writing his letter of refusal.

Third, it often happens that for one of several reasons a position that looked most promising when it was accepted becomes less attractive later. A man may change his mind about the kind of work he wants to do; he may decide that a smaller company in a smaller town offers satisfactions that he had not previously appreciated; or he may find that the climate or the social environment to which his job commits him is not to his liking. In short, he may want to reconsider an offer which he had previously declined.

For these reasons, it is often wise to consider the letter declining a position as one which preserves a favorable business contact. How this should be done will depend on circumstances. There can be no one pattern to fit all conditions, but the following suggestions may be modified to suit particular situations.

1. Do not, even by the faintest suggestion, belittle the offer. It may

be inferior to other offers you have received, but do not say or imply so.

2. Suggest that your refusal is not a hasty one but is carefully and reluctantly made.

3. Express appreciation of the offer in more than general or perfunctory terms. If possible mention details that you found especially attractive.

4. If any one officer of the company spent considerable time with you during your interview, express your appreciation of his efforts, with specific reference to any actions of his that showed more thoughtfulness than mere duty required of him.

5. There is no objection to describing briefly an alternative offer which you have accepted, if your experience suggests that the person you are writing to is genuinely interested in what you are going to do. But keep such description short and allow nothing in its tone to suggest bragging or gloating.

6. Keep the letter short but not abrupt.

The following letter illustrates the content and tone of a letter of refusal. To save space the heading and close have been omitted.

Dear Mr. Root:

I have spent several days thinking over and talking over with my wife your letter of May 27. The position you offer me is most attractive, and what I saw of Ruston and the plant makes me feel that Mary and I would have a congenial and satisfying future with the company and in the community.

But I feel that for my own professional training I need the experience of working in a large company in a metropolitan area. I have therefore decided to accept a position with Bowen-Revelson in Chicago. I will be working on public relations techniques in large industrial areas. I think it likely that Mary and I will finally want to settle and bring up our family in a smaller town, and that consideration made Ruston most attractive. But at this stage of my professional development I think the Chicago position offers me the experience I most need.

I want to thank you for all your many kindnesses to me during my visit to Ruston and for the very helpful overview you gave me of the public relations problems which new industry in the South is posing. I will be grateful for a copy of any article you write on that subject.

## Exercises

**A.** Study each of the following student letters carefully. Then write a report in the form of a business letter to your instructor telling him how you would grade these letters and why. Since your report will itself be graded, be sure to detail the evidence for your judgments. To save space all headings have been omitted.

### (1)

Dear Sir:

Your newspaper ad about wanting an ex-, perienced, capable man to fill position of office manager in your company interests me. Provided the job pays enough, of course.

Rest assured I can handle your office staff. Write me at once so an interview can be arranged.

Confidently yours,

### (2)

Dear Sir:

In two weeks I will receive my Bachelors Degree in Architectural Engineering, and I am very anxious to enter the Construction field. I believe I am amply qualified to begin my career in your field, and I am looking forward to working for your concern.

During my four years at the University of Illinois, I have maintained a numerical average of 3.86. I have been subjected to Construction business all my life, and during semester breaks I have built up my experience with actual field estimating. I have taken every University estimating course available. In view of this, I believe I am capable of fulfilling an estimators position. I consider $350.00 per month an ordinary salary for this position.

During the period from June 23 to June 30, I will be at the Mammoth Hotel in downtown Indianapolis. I can be contacted at any hour of the day, and I would appreciate an interview at your convenience. I will have my letters of recommendation and I will provide you with any information I may have neglected in the enclosed data sheet.

(3)

Dear Sir:

| | |
|---|---|
| HONESTY | EFFICIENCY |
| RESOURCEFULNESS | ADAPTABILITY |
| LEADERSHIP | COURAGE |
| RESPONSIBILITY | INITIATIVE |
| NEATNESS AND CLEANLINESS | INTELLIGENCE |

Would you employ a person if he possessed the above qualities? You would, no doubt.

But unfortunately, the perfect is seldom obtained. Then the next best thing is the object of your search. I can offer you the services of a person who is, altho far from perfect, far above average in all of the above fields and excels in many.

I will promise you one thing-----that you will realize that you selected the right man for the job. I will serve you faithfully and efficiently.

I can come to Chicago any week-end you may desire for an interview. I will be glad to serve you.

(4)

Dear Sir:

This is an application for a position.

For months I have been investigating different firms interested in hiring college graduates that have majored in foreign economics and export trade. In the course of my investigation I have found there is a place in your organization for a man of my talents and education.

Your firm is interested in men who have majored in economics, with particular stress on foreign trade. I have studied every phase of economics and am well prepared.

I have not yet had any job -- I'm still young -- but I am confident I can meet your requirements.

The college officials will recommend me, if
you will write them.

I shall be glad to have an interview with
you. Any time will do.

(5)

Dear Mr. Jones:

In Tuesday's Sun I noticed your advertisement for a private secretary and correspondent. May I be considered an applicant for this position?

It is my understanding that you want a
young man with a working knowledge of
office methods. He must also be able to
take dictation rapidly and accurately, and
he must have a background of general business training.

I am a graduate of Larchmont High School,
Springfield, Illinois, class of 1953.
Here I took the four-year commercial
course. During the past four years since
graduation I have been private secretary to
Mr. James A. Parker, executive director of
the Illinois State Commerce Commission.

My work with Mr. Parker has been widely
varied. I have taken much dictation,
both by transcription from notes, and also
direct to the typewriter. I have handled
on my own responsibility much of the
routine correspondence and have found this
experience highly valuable in broadening my
general business and secretarial ability.
I have become thoroughly familiar with commercial and legal forms.

I believe I have developed the ability to
handle your position. My training and
experience have been of the type necessary
to the consistent handling of the duties
you require. I enjoy this kind of work. My
reason for making a change is to improve my
position. Mr. Parker now tells me I have
reached the maximum salary permitted by the
commission, and he fully understands and
approves my wishes for further advancement.

Mr. Parker has kindly permitted me to use his
name as a reference. On the enclosed data

```
sheet you will find further references and
data in regard to my general qualifica-
tions.

May I have a personal interview?  My tele-
phone is Grandview 4177, Springfield, if
you wish to make an appointment.  My mailing
address is 36 North Avenue, Springfield,
Illinois.
```

**B.** Assume that you are about to graduate from college and have had no more experience than you might reasonably obtain during your summer vacations. Clip from a newspaper or magazine an advertisement of a position for which you might reasonably expect to compete. Write your letter of application and hand it in to your instructor with the advertisement attached.

**C.** Suppose that, having written letters of application and having been interviewed, you have received two offers of positions and have accepted one of them. Write a letter refusing the other position.

PART THREE ✳ HANDBOOK OF GRAMMAR AND USAGE

# A Point of View Toward Grammar

ENGLISH, like all languages, has developed a great many conventions popularly and generally known as "the rules of grammar." The nature of these rules is widely misunderstood, and because of this misunderstanding, the study of the conventions of educated usage is often less profitable than it might be. The first step toward using your native language with confidence is to acquire a sensible attitude toward these rules. We shall attempt to foster such an attitude by showing you what we mean when we talk about rules of grammar, how these rules have grown up and are still growing, and how you can use this knowledge to solve your own language problems. A point of view from which you can see particular questions of usage in perspective will help you to judge for yourself which usages are acceptable, and when.

## The Evolution of English

The language that Americans speak and write is descended from the language spoken by the English, Scottish, and Irish immigrants who founded the British colonies in America. Their language, in turn, was descended from the dialects of Germanic tribes which, during the fifth and sixth centuries, invaded Britain and settled there. One of these tribes, the Angles, later became known as the Englisc (English) and thus gave their name to a country and a language, both of which they shared with other peoples — the Saxons, the Jutes, and, later, the Danes and the Normans.

All these racial groups were the Founding Fathers of the English language, but other peoples, too, have made their contribution to its development. As England grew in political, economic, and cultural importance, the language borrowed from various sources the words it needed to name the things and ideas that Englishmen were acquiring. Today the vocabulary of the English language is international in origin, and to talk, as some people do, of "pure" English is to use an adjective that is as inappropriate as it is misleading.

Needless to say, the language which has come down to us through some fifteen centuries has undergone great changes. A modern college student could understand, not without difficulty, the speech of any ancestors of his who came over on the *Mayflower*. But the English that Chaucer wrote is something of a puzzle to him. And before Chaucer's time — well, judge for yourself. Here are the opening lines of the Lord's Prayer in the English of nearly a thousand years ago:

> Fæder ūre,
> þu þe eart on heofonum,
> sī þīn nama gehālgod.
> Tōbecume þīn rīce.
> Gewurþe ðīn willa on eorðan swā swā on heofonum.

A contrast of this version of the Lord's Prayer with the modern version offers a brief but revealing impression of the changes that have occurred in the language during its development from an insignificant Germanic dialect to the mightiest language the world has ever known. It is important to recognize that these changes were the product of evolution rather than of revolution. True enough, there were times when so many basic changes occurred so rapidly that they must have seemed revolutionary to those who witnessed them. But, by and large, the language changed slowly as it reflected gradual and unprompted shifts in the speech habits of those who spoke English. Often the old and new forms persisted together in competition for centuries, and sometimes an older form which was threatened with extinction enjoyed a renewal of popularity and survived at the expense of its rival. But the process of evolution always put a premium on survival value. The test of competing usages was not which was the more logical, the more beautiful, or the more "correct," but which one was more *used*. Usage has always been, as it still is, the ultimate maker of rules.

It is important also to recognize that the changes which occurred during the development of the English language were not always made painlessly. Whenever any two usages compete for popularity there is a tendency on the part of speakers to be confused about which one to accept. And the closer the competition, the greater the confusion. There must have been a time, for example, when our ancestors were perplexed whether to call a certain garment a *shirt* or a *skirt*, since both forms of the word were applied to the same garment and both were popular. That particular difficulty was resolved by using one form for a man's garment and the other for a woman's. This solution was not a deliberate one. It was not laid down by any authority, and it was not reached overnight. It just happened that people gradually drifted into the habit of using the two forms in different ways and thus established a new usage.

Finally, it is important to recognize that this evolutionary process is still going on. Any one of us can notice hundreds of examples of it in our own experience. We can hear the older pronunciations of *penalize* (peenalize), *status* (staytus) and *detour* (de *toor*) being challenged by pronunciations which were at first labeled "uneducated" but which have gradually become more common, even in the speech of highly educated people. We can observe words acquiring new meanings. And we can watch grammatical distinctions which once were generally observed falling more and more into disuse as substitutes take over their work. Like our ancestors puzzling over *shirt* and *skirt,* we will fluctuate between the old usage and the new until one or other triumphs. Then all the uncertainty will be forgotten, and we will use the new form with confidence.

## The Rules of Grammar

Contrary to popular belief, the rules of grammar do not determine how the language should be spoken and written. Grammar is a science, and it follows the general scientific method of reporting not what *ought to be* but what *is.* Except for differences of subject matter, the rules of grammar are exactly like the laws of physics and chemistry: they are scientific generalizations about the facts. In grammar, as in physics, these generalizations must be verifiable. If the rule does not fit the facts, or if it ceases to fit them, it must be revised or discarded.

Ideally, the grammar of a language is a description of the speaking and writing habits of the people who use it. Since there are some 300,-000,000 users of English, widely separated geographically, politically, economically, and socially, the task of drawing a picture of their common linguistic habits is not easy. The grammarian simplifies his task by restricting himself chiefly to the printed language. He collects samples of printed usage, studies them, finds patterns in them, and generalizes these patterns into a system. The description he produces by this method is necessarily abstract. It necessarily leaves out much. It is necessarily a simplification. It bears a relation to the language habits of 300,000,000 people similar to the relation that a map of the United States bears to the 3,000,000 square miles it portrays. Indeed, a grammarian could be called a linguistic cartographer, a maker of language maps.

In making his maps, the grammarian depends on printed sources, and this fact has two results. First, it tends to slight spoken usage, since very little of all that is spoken gets printed. Second, it tends to limit the study of usage to educated usage, since usually only educated people publish what they write. Grammar, therefore, is almost exclusively a description of educated written usage, which we call the *standard* dialect. If a particular construction does not commonly occur in educated usage, it is called *nonstandard.*

This description of the limited nature of the grammarian's methods does not discredit the usefulness of his work. Without his painstaking study of usage and his periodic reports on it, we could have no comprehensive picture of current English. If all grammarians were to stop work tomorrow we would soon know as little about the facts of usage as we would about the facts of population if census-taking were abolished.

But while nearly everyone understands that the census reports of one hundred years ago would give a false picture of the population today, few people realize that grammatical reports must likewise be kept up to date. Consequently, while nobody blames the census-taker for reporting a change in the population, many people seem to want to condemn the grammarian for reporting a change in our speech habits. This is an occupational hazard of being a grammarian. Language is such an <u>intimate</u> and important subject that many people have strong <u>preconceptions</u> of what it *ought* to be like, and they do not like to have these notions shattered.

The rules of grammar, then, are not "Thou shalt not's"; they say "This is how it is done." They are an explanation of the conventions which have grown up between writers and readers. Learning to use one's language is learning to use these conventions. A writer who ignores the conventions will not be doomed for a civil offense or damned for a moral one. He will simply be dismissed as not deserving attention, on the assumption that if he has not learned how to use his native language he is not likely to write anything worth reading. That judgment may be harsh, but it is the judgment which prevails in our society.

The conventions, however, are not so restrictive as many students believe them to be. It is true that a writer has little leeway in spelling, since, with few exceptions, there are no alternative spellings. In punctuation, however, he may choose between a "closed" style, which generally observes all the conventional uses of commas, and an "open" style, which omits commas that can be left out without confusing the structure of the sentence — that is, it omits commas which are conventional but not functional. In diction, he can usually choose among many accepted words or phrases, any one of which will serve his purpose, and his selection is often controlled less by the conventions than by a subtler criterion, his own sense of what is appropriate in a particular situation. He can also choose among various sentence patterns. All the conventions require of him is that he stay with the pattern he has chosen and not confuse two patterns in one sentence.

In a sense, then, a writer is like a man going to visit a friend in another part of town. He is not completely free to go as he pleases; he cannot go "as the crow flies." He must follow an established path or street, but he has a choice of routes, any of which will take him where he wants to go. Within the general frame of the conventions, the writer has a great deal of freedom to express himself in the way he feels most efficient or most natural.

## On Being Your Own Authority

Socially, a sophisticated person is one who is familiar with social conventions and observes them naturally and comfortably. Linguistically, a sophisticated person is one who observes language conventions naturally and comfortably. One aim of the composition course is to encourage the student to develop linguistic sophistication, to make him aware how things are done in English and to help him do them habitually, without having to stop and puzzle over them.

There are two reasons why this aim cannot be met by viewing grammar as a set of arbitrary rules which must be learned and practiced. First, this view distorts the relationship between purpose and technique. Just as the Sabbath was made for man, not man for the Sabbath, so the conventions of usage should serve, not be served by, the writer's purpose. A student whose main thought is to get his spelling, punctuation, and grammatical forms "correct" is in no condition to communicate. For him, writing will be a frustrating exercise, to be done only under compulsion and to be avoided whenever the compulsion is removed. This is why some students believe that all their linguistic worries will be over as soon as they "pass" the composition course.

Second, memorizing the conventions of usage is at best a poor substitute for working with them. All we know about learning tells us that memorized facts are soon forgotten unless they are clearly related to life goals and put to use outside the classroom. A student who conscientiously learns the rules of spelling or punctuation *in order to please or pacify his instructor* will soon forget them, and the progress that he and his instructor worked so hard to achieve will largely be lost. This is one reason why student writing so often deteriorates after completion of the composition course.

To accomplish the purpose of the course, at least with respect to the conventions of usage, a student must realize two things: he must recognize that following the conventions of language may help him communicate better and so make him a more powerful person; and he must understand that, while dictionaries and handbooks are helpful reference works, he must often make his own decisions about usage, when these books are not available or are not decisive.

This second requirement may seem like a tall order, since, in effect, it asks the student to become his own authority on language. But there is no alternative. To use a language well, one must use it confidently. No one can speak or write with confidence if he continually depends on the crutch of a handbook. It is only a temporary aid, useful for those linguistic questions which cannot yet be answered from experience, but to be dispensed with as soon as possible.

How is this confidence to be won? In the long run, it is gained, as are so many things, by observation. That is how the grammarian learns grammar and how the editors of dictionaries learn the meanings of words — by observing how educated people use their language. An intelligent curiosity about language is therefore the first requirement for using it effectively. A student who has or develops that curiosity will seldom be seriously bothered by the "rules," because he has discovered them through his own observation of language practices.

All this may seem a strange introduction to a handbook which often arbitrarily says, "Do this; don't do that." But this advice is merely a supplement to your own experience. It presumes to tell you what the conventions are. If you know what they are, you do not need the advice. If you do not know, the advice will provide you with information to solve some of your immediate writing problems. It is assumed that your instructor will decide from your writing which conventions you need to study and will refer you to the section or sections dealing with them. It is hoped that you yourself will care enough about your own writing to make a special point of mastering, by observation as well as by handbook exercises, whatever conventions are now conspicuously ignored in your writing.

# S1

## Sentence Elements

A SENTENCE is a conventional pattern of expression which serves as the basic unit of spoken or written communication. The pattern may make a statement (*Tomorrow will be Sunday.*), ask a question (*What is his name?*), express a command or a wish (*Speak quietly! Oh, if she could only cook!*), or utter an exclamation (*Of all the nerve! What a ridiculous statement!*). It may range in length from one word to more than a hundred; it may refer to a preceding statement or may anticipate one to follow; but it is grammatically independent of other sentences and is therefore considered as a unit in itself.

As a family consists of related members, so a sentence consists of related elements. These elements are **subject, verb, complement, modifier,** and **connective.** If we use the letters *S, V, C, M,* and *K* respectively, to label these elements, we can see the nature of their relationship in the following sentence:

*S   K   S   V   C   M*

Dad and mother liked her at once.

The key word in this sentence is the verb *liked.* The nouns, *Dad, mother,* tell us who did the liking, and are joined by the connective *and.* The pronoun *her* tells who was the object of the liking. The phrase *at once* tells when the liking took place. In our example all the elements except the connective are in one way or another related to the verb.

Trouble with sentence structure is generally considered to be among the most serious errors in student writing, and faults in structure usually result from failure to recognize the elements of a sentence and to see how they are related. The following discussion is therefore fundamental.

**a. The subject and the verb are related as actor and action.**

The subject identifies the actor by telling who or what performs the action of the verb; the verb identifies the action by making an assertion about the subject. This actor-action sequence is the basic relationship in the sentence, and without it no sentence is complete, though a sentence with nothing more than a subject and a verb can be complete. In the following sentences the subject is italicized and the verb set in capitals.

> *John* SMILED.
> The *money* HAS BEEN FOUND.
> The *chair* WILL DO.

413

A subject may be a single word, as we saw; it may be a compound (*Dad* and *Mother* LIKED her at once); it may be a series (*Fred, Mary, Bill,* and *Jane* ARE GOING); it may even, as we shall see later, be a subordinate clause. Although most subjects are nouns or pronouns, any part of speech may be a subject if it is so related to the verb in a sentence.

Verbs are usually classified as *transitive, intransitive,* or *linking.* A transitive verb needs an object to complete the statement of action performed by the subject — She ASKED an embarrassing **question;** He WANTS **sympathy;** I WROTE the **letter.** An intransitive verb needs no object, but by itself makes a complete statement of the action performed by the subject — The girls HAVE LEFT; Tomorrow our vacation BEGINS; The evidence HAS VANISHED. A linking verb, sometimes called a "copula," connects the subject to a noun or adjective — Smith IS a **sophomore;** They WERE **ill;** He FELT **sick;** The audience BECAME **restless.** The most common linking verb is the verb *to be.*

### b. Complements are completing constructions.

If the subject-verb sentences used earlier had been written:

> John *said*
> The money *ruined*
> The chair *needs*

we should feel that they were incomplete. We should want to ask — Said *what?* Ruined *what?* Needs *what?* In other words, we should want something to complete the assertions made by the verbs — perhaps something like this:

> John said *nothing.*
> The money ruined their *friendship.*
> The chair needs a *leg.*

In these sentences the words in italic type are complements.[1] The function or job of the complement is to complete other constructions, usually to answer *what?* or *whom?* when the construction is so incomplete as to pose these questions. While the most common use of the complement is to complete a verb which makes an incomplete assertion about its subject (a transitive or a linking verb) it may complete a variety of constructions. If you are bothered by the grammatical terms in the parentheses below, you can check them in the Glossary (pages 557–597), or you may ignore them, since at present we are more concerned with the function of complements than with the names for them.

---

[1] As it is being used here, the term *complement* is more general than the term *object.* It includes all constructions which serve a completing function: objects of verbs, verbals and prepositions, and predicate nouns and adjectives.

Mays caught the *ball*. (Object, completes transitive verb *caught*.)

His father is a *doctor*. (Predicate noun, completes linking verb *is*.)

My roommate became *ill* (Predicate adjective completes linking verb *became*.)

She wants to be *boss*. (Completes infinitive *to be*.)

Learning *to drive* the new cars is *easy*. (*To drive* completes the gerund *Learning; easy* completes the verb *is*.)

I got *to know her*. (Infinitive *to know* completes the verb *got;* pronoun *her* completes the infinitive.)

In the following sentences identify all subjects, verbs, and complements.

1. That man is her father.
2. I have no time.
3. The girls are giving a party.
4. Who is that girl? I'd like to meet her.
5. Did you get the tickets?
6. This is my raincoat; yours has a rip over the pocket.
7. We are having a dance to celebrate homecoming.
8. While we were watching the program, the telephone rang.
9. Nothing has been done. They are still at the beginning of the project.
10. He was offended by her criticism of his conduct.

**c.** Any word or group of words which describes or qualifies another element in the sentence is a modifier of that element. The modifier may be a single word, a phrase, or a subordinate clause.

In general, a modifier describes a subject, a complement, or another modifier, or tells how, where, when, why, under what conditions, or despite what conditions the action of the verb took place. The italicized modifiers in the following sentences illustrate these characteristics:

*Old* soldiers never die. (Modifies subject.)

Honesty is the *best* policy. (Modifies complement.)

It was a *most* unlikely story. (Modifies the modifier *unlikely*.)

He arrived *late*. (Modifies the verb — tells when.)

He arrived *at the party*. (Modifies the verb — tells where.)

He went *for my sake*. (Modifies the verb — tells why.)

I will go, *if you pay my way*. (Modifies the verb — tells under what conditions.)

I will go, *even if I'm not invited*. (Modifies the verb — tells despite what conditions.)

Identify the modifiers in the following sentences.

1. My bicycle is a black one with white trim.
2. It was an oppressively hot day.

3. There is something strangely familiar about his face.
4. She lives in the brick house at the end of the block.
5. The new car was damaged beyond repair.
6. Go sit under that tree while I change the tire.
7. I'll go if you will wait till I get back.
8. Worried by his failure to write, his mother telephoned him.
9. Unless we get there by noon we won't have time for shopping.
10. Having studied the map at the last gas station, I knew we were on the wrong road.

**d. Connectives join other elements in a sentence. They are of three types: coordinating, subordinating, and transitional.**

A **coordinating connective** joins two similar, or coordinate, elements:

Tom *and* I will go. (Connects two subjects.)
Bill grumbled *and* sulked for days. (Connects two verbs.)
He fought cleverly *and* courageously. (Connects two modifiers.)
I'll do it *but* I won't like it. (Connects two main clauses.)
*Either* Bert *or* I will do it. (*Either — or* connect two subjects.)
We have *neither* the money *nor* the time. (Connect two complements.)
You pretend to be her friend, *yet* you gossip about her. (Connects two main clauses.)

A **subordinating connective** does two things: it joins two clauses and subordinates one to the other. If we take two main clauses

He is cross. He is tired.

and join them with *because* — *He is cross because he is tired* — we not only connect the two clauses but we subordinate the second to the first. In this example *because* is a subordinating connective. In the following examples the subordinate clauses are in parentheses and the connectives in italics:

I don't know (*why* he did it).
He did not say (*when* he would return).
I won't do it (*if* you seriously object).
You may go (*whenever* you please).

In these examples the subordinating connective comes between the clauses it joins. But a subordinate clause may precede the main one, and the connective may come at the beginning of the sentence:

(*If* you seriously object), I won't do it.
(*Because* I flatter him), he likes me.
(*Since* you are in a hurry), I won't bother you about it.

A **transitional connective** joins two sentences by providing a transition between them. See "Transitional Markers," pages 112–113, and "Conjunctive Adverbs," page 452.

In the following sentences, identify coordinating and subordinating connectives.

1. Smile when you say that.
2. I have no idea what he wants.
3. When the right time comes, I will tell you.
4. I would do it if I could, but I cannot.
5. His only faults are that he has neither looks nor money.
6. She has had nothing to eat or drink since she came home.
7. Although he is taller, he weighs less.
8. While I want to be pleasant and agreeable, I cannot do what you ask.
9. Neither Helen nor Jean has the book you want.
10. Although he brings me nothing but trouble, I must do what I can for him.

**e.** Occasionally, an element in a sentence has no clear grammatical relationship to any other element yet clearly belongs. We call it an *absolute construction.*

Consider the following sentences:

*Nonsense,* it is all a hoax!
*Good heavens,* is it that late?
*Mr. Hughes,* may I talk to you for a moment?
*No,* I won't do it!
I wish, *madam,* you would make up your mind.
She said — *as if I cared* — that she was through with me.

The italicized expressions serve useful purposes, but they are not grammatically related to other sentence elements. They are absolute constructions.

Using the symbols, *S* — Subject, *V* — Verb, *C* — Complement, *M* — Modifier, *K* — Connective, and *A* — Absolute, identify the underlined elements in the following sentences. For your convenience, subordinate clauses have been placed in parentheses. Occasionally an element and its modifier have been underlined as a single element.

1. The woman offered no explanation.
2. Henry, you are impossible!
3. Bill's father will retire next year.
4. My parents are moving tomorrow.
5. Mother wore a blue skirt and a white blouse.
6. She is irritable (when she is tired).
7. (When she feels well) she is a pleasant person.
8. He likes to wrestle and he wrestles well.
9. The governor was re-elected by a narrow margin.

10. The defeated candidate resumed his law practice.
11. Because of the wind, the mountain climbers abandoned the attempt.
12. He will try to speak (whenever he gets a chance).
13. Everyone hopes (that the worst is past).
14. The answer to that question is unknown.
15. The doctor will see you now, Mr. Brown.

**S 2** | *Phrases and Clauses*

---

**a. A phrase is a group of two or more words acting as a single element in a sentence but not having a subject and verb of its own.**

In the following sentences the phrases are italicized.

She stood *by the door*. (Phrase modifies verb.)
He *has been calling* you. (Phrase is verb.)
*Hunting big game* is expensive. (Phrase is subject.)
A page *near the end* is missing. (Phrase modifies subject.)
No → Her brother is a *medical student*. (Phrase is complement of verb.)
*My dear woman*, I never said that! (Phrase is absolute.)

*Nouns of Address*

**b. A subordinate clause is a group of words acting as subject, complement, or modifier, but having a subject and verb of its own.**

In the following sentences the subordinate clauses are italicized.

*Whoever did that* is foolish. (Clause is subject of verb *is*.)
You may ask *whatever you want*. (Clause is complement of verb *may ask*.)
The people *who lived there* have moved. (Clause modifies subject.)
I will go *wherever you send me*. (Clause modifies verb.)
This is the book *that I want*. (Clause modifies complement.)

In each of these sentences the subordinate clause is introduced by a subordinating connective. This connective may sometimes be omitted without changing the subordinate nature of the clause:

This is the book *I want*.
The plumber *you sent for* is here.

**c. A main clause has a subject and verb but does not act as a subject, complement, or modifier.**

It may be a complete sentence in itself; it may be part of a compound sentence; or it may be an absolute in a larger sentence.

*I cut the lawn.*  (Main clause in a simple sentence.)
*I cut the lawn,* and *Joe raked it.*  (Two main clauses forming a compound sentence.)
He said — *wasn't it mean of him?* — that I was an irresponsible adolescent. (Italicized main clause is an absolute in a complex sentence.)

Distinguish between main and subordinate clauses in the following sentences by underlining main clauses once and subordinate clauses twice.

1. I will do whatever you say.
2. What he said is nobody's business.
3. The book that I bought cost a dollar.
4. The dress I bought is too tight.
5. If that is how you feel, you go your way and I'll go mine.
6. The man who is wearing the plaid shirt is his brother-in-law.
7. We don't want your advice; we just ask to be left alone.
8. Get a good night's sleep.  That is the best preparation I know for the examination.
9. He said that he was terribly embarrassed.  If I had been he, I would have been sick.
10. He said there was nothing he could do.

## Review Exercises

In the following passages certain constructions have been underlined and numbered. Copy the numbers and opposite each write *Main Clause, Subordinate Clause,* or *Phrase,* whichever is appropriate.

**A** (1) It was a bright sunny day (2) when we left Columbus (3) in a tightly packed car (4) for Sparrow Lake, Canada. (5) Along the way (6) we stopped at Niagara Falls (7) to see one of nature's beautiful creations, and then (8) continued to drive (9) what seemed to be an endless distance. (10) At last (11) we arrived in Orillia, Canada, (12) bought a few necessary supplies, and (13) drove down a typical washboard road (14) till we arrived (15) at our destination.

**B** The relationship (1) between a writer and a reader may be illustrated (2) by an analogy with dancing. Anybody (3) who has danced knows (4) that both partners move (5) in accordance with patterns (6) which both understand and take for granted. The man, (7) by his leading, indicates which pattern (8) he wishes to set; (9) the girl follows. (10) If the man leads his partner (11) to expect one kind of movement and then switches to another, (12) the girl will have difficulty following.

(13) The relationship between the writer and reader is similar. Each as-

sumes (14) that the other is familiar with the basic patterns of sentence structure. The reader, (15) like the girl in the dance, must follow the writer's lead, and (16) as long as the writer follows an accepted pattern (17) the reader has no trouble. But (18) if the writer sets one pattern in the first half of a sentence and (19) then shifts to another, (20) the reader is likely to be confused.

   C (1) One day a girl brought me a composition (2) that had been corrected and returned. (3) On the two pages (4) that it occupied there was (5) a total of 127 corrections. (6) I could not get any coherent picture from (7) such a complete mess, (8) so I tabulated the errors (9) according to type. (10) Out of the 127 mistakes, (11) 92 came from wrong punctuation. There were no errors (12) of capitalization or grammar. (13) Two sentences were incomplete, (14) 19 were far too long and involved, (15) 8 contained wrong references, and (16) 6 lacked parallelism. The girl had another composition (17) to write at once. (18) I told her (19) to go to work on it, but (20) to concentrate on the avoidance of a single error — the long, loose-jointed sentences. In fact, (21) I was so sure from the analysis (22) that her key mistake was mere length (23) that I instructed her (24) to use not over fifteen words per sentence. (25) She promised to keep within this limit. . . . (26) The total length of this second composition was (27) about twenty words more than the first, but (28) when it came back there were only eight errors — one incomplete sentence, three errors in spelling, and four unnecessary commas. All of the mistakes (29) the girl had made earlier had been pyramided upon the single error of (30) trying to write sentences that were too long.[2]

# S 3 | *Verbs and Verbals*

MOST TROUBLE with verbs comes from failure to distinguish verbs from verbals. A **verbal** is derived from a verb but does not act as a verb in a sentence. For example, in the sentences

> *Wrestling* IS a body-building sport.
> *To wait* IS not easy.
> He SPOKE in *threatening* terms.

the verbs are in capital letters. The words *wrestling, to wait,* and *threatening* may look like verbs but they do not act as verbs. *Wrestling*

---

  [2] From Luella Cole's *The Backgrounds for College Teaching.* Copyright, 1940, by Farrar & Rinehart, Inc. Reprinted by permission of Rinehart & Company, Inc.

and *To wait* are the subjects of their sentences; *threatening* modifies *terms*. These words are verbals, not verbs.

Verbals are of three types: **infinitives, participles,** and **gerunds.**

**a. Such verbals as *to do, to choose, to be seeking, to have said,* and *to have been invited* are called infinitives.**

Usually, but not always, they have the infinitive marker *to*. They often serve as subjects (*To do* that is not easy; *to be excused* from class is a rare treat) or as complements (They asked *to go;* we expected *to be called*), but they occasionally act as modifiers (I bought it *to read;* we have no time *to spare*).

Identify the infinitives in the following sentences.

1. Nobody wants to tell him.
2. He is said to have refused an offer to settle out of court.
3. I'd like to do good work and have fun, too.
4. We tried to call them and explain the difficulty.
5. To play as well as he does takes more time than I can afford to give.
6. You should be able to analyze and evaluate the information and reach sound conclusions from it.
7. She seems to be looking for an excuse to pick a quarrel with him.
8. He is said to have done the same thing in several states and to be wanted by the police in Texas.
9. Not to have invited her would have caused trouble.
10. He is thought to be willing to sell at a low price in order to settle the estate quickly.

**b. A participle is a word or phrase which is derived from a verb but acts as a modifier.**

The present participle ends in -ing (*crying, smiling, sulking*). The past participle most frequently ends in -ed (*disgusted, excused, inspired*) but many are irregular (*chosen, grown, kept, slung*). The following sentences illustrate forms and uses of participles.

His *fighting* days are over. (Present participle modifies subject.)
He is a *fighting* fool. (Present participle modifies complement.)
*Having fought* all challengers, he retired. (Past participle modifies subject *he.*)
Goldsmith wrote a poem about a *deserted* village. (Past participle modifies the complement of *about.*)
*Having been deserted* by her husband, she supported the family. (Passive form of past participle modifies subject *she.*)

Identify the participles in the following sentences.

1. She is a clinging vine.
2. A broken watch is of little use.

3. The metal is now near the breaking point.
4. This is a thrilling story.
5. Thrilled by the movie, we stayed up too late.
6. A drunken man is usually a bore.
7. Disappointed by the results, he gave up the experiment.
8. With screeching brakes the car came to a jarring stop.
9. They have forgotten that they called him the forgotten man.
10. The play having been called back, it was now third down and seven.

c. Gerunds, or verbal nouns, have the same form as the present participle but are used as subjects and complements in a sentence, not as modifiers.

The only difference between a gerund and a present participle is one of function.

> Thinking is hard work. (Gerund is subject of verb is.)
> That will take some thinking. (Gerund is complement of verb will take.)
> Looking innocent won't help you. (Gerund is subject of won't help.)
> She can't stop crying. (Gerund is complement of can't stop.)

Distinguish between the participles and gerunds in the following sentences by identifying each verbal and explaining its function in the sentence.

1. Bacon said that reading makes a wise man.
2. During the semester his reading speed increased significantly.
3. This course requires too much reading.
4. They were looking for an abandoned mine.
5. Abandoned by her allies, Czechoslovakia was forced to yield.
6. Tired by the long hike, we took a nap before dinner.
7. Looking for trouble is the quickest way to find it.
8. Becoming angry will not help; try smiling for a change.

## Review Exercises

Copy and turn in to your instructor the following sentences. Distinguish between verbs and verbals by underlining all verbs once and all verbals twice.

1. Swimming is fun. I would like to swim well. I was swimming yesterday. My brother has been swimming since he was four.

2. They say that a rolling stone gathers no moss; they could just as truthfully say that a stone that is rolling isn't gathering anything but momentum.

3. It is easier to win a letter in college than to receive a Phi Beta Kappa key. That is a point worth remembering when we are tempted to make fun of serious students.

4. The statement that a watched kettle never boils is not true. Water in a kettle boils just as quickly watched or unwatched. But you are more conscious of time when you are watching the kettle and therefore the time seems to be longer.

5. I am tired of having to be told what I may and may not do. My parents seem to have forgotten how they resented too much supervision when they were my age.

6. Discouraged by his grades, he was thinking of quitting school. But the dean persuaded him to revise his habits of studying and finish the semester before making a decision.

7. Leave him alone! Let him do it his own way. He has to learn some day to discover his own mistakes and correct them, and he might as well make a beginning now.

8. Having tried everything to get good grades without studying, we reluctantly decided to give that method a try.

9. Weakened by hunger and exposure, the old couple were in serious condition.

10. He said nothing would interfere with his ambitions, but he has found that it is easier to profess ambitions than to achieve them.

---

# S4 | *Fragmentary Sentence and Period Fault*

**a. A full sentence is grammatically complete.**

In its simplest form the full sentence consists of only a main clause (see page 419) but it may contain more than one main clause and one or more subordinate clauses.

**b. A fragmentary sentence is not grammatically complete, although in context it may make as complete a statement as is needed.**

It may simply be an exclamation: *Oh! Nonsense! Wonderful! Good Heavens!* It may serve as a question: *Cigarette? Lemon or sugar? Anything else?* It may be a phrase or clause uttered in response to a question: *Maybe. Not at all. If you wish. Whenever it is convenient.* Or it may be a stereotyped expression, such as: *The more, the merrier. First come, first served. Like father, like son. Easy come, easy go.* When it is used in these ways, the fragmentary sentence is sometimes called a minor sentence.

The use of such fragmentary sentences is conventional in conversation and in writing which imitates the patterns of speech, such as dialogue in narration. As we saw in Chapter 8, sentence fragments are not uncommon in colloquial expository writing, and are sometimes, though not often, used in informal expository writing. There is, however, a strong objection to their use in most college expository papers. The objection is not to the fragment as a sentence pattern as much as it is to the uncritical use of fragments in contexts in which they are not appropriate.

**c. Most unwarranted fragments in student essays result from confusion of main and subordinate clauses or confusion of verbs and verbals.**

The writer thinks that two parts of a sentence are different sentences, and so separates them with a period. This use of the period is usually called a **period fault.** In the first three of the following examples a subordinate clause has been confused as an independent statement and separated from its main clause by a period. In the next three a verbal phrase has been cut off from its main clause by a period.

| *Fragmentary Sentence Structure* | *Explanation* | *Full Sentence Structure* |
|---|---|---|
| He made a point of entering each misspelled word in a notebook. *Which he kept for that purpose.* | *Italicized subordinate clause modifies* notebook *and is not an independent statement.* | He made a point of entering each misspelled word in a notebook which he kept for that purpose. |
| I refused to go to the show. *Because I had been up late last night and needed sleep.* | *The italicized clause explains the refusal and is therefore a modifier of* refused. | Because I had been up late last night and needed sleep, I refused to go to the show. |
| He is always complaining about his grades. *Although he does nothing to improve them.* | *The italicized clause is a modifier, not an independent statement.* | He is always complaining about his grades, although he does nothing to improve them. |
| The Tigers made two runs in the ninth. *Thus tying* the score. | Tying *is not a verb, but a present participle modifying the main clause.* | The Tigers made two runs in the ninth, thus tying the score. |
| It was difficult to decide which choice to make. *To return to* school or *to accept* the job. | *The italicized infinitives modify* choice; *therefore they do not act as verbs.* | It was difficult to decide whether to return to school or to accept the job. |
| It was a wonderful week. *Fishing* and *swimming* every day and *dancing* every night. | *The italicized words are gerunds. They should either be made into verbs or should serve as complements of another verb.* | . . . We fished and swam every day and danced every night. (or) We went fishing and swimming every day and dancing every night. |

As the revisions at the right indicate, period faults may be corrected either by changing the faulty period to a comma, thus incorporating the separated phrase or subordinate clause within the sentence to which it belongs, or by expanding the fragment into a main clause so that it can stand as an independent sentence.

In the following sentences correct the period faults.

1. He refused to answer the question. Despite the fact that he knew his silence would be interpreted as guilt.

2. The author of such books or magazine articles writes to appeal to the general public. Not just to a few.

3. The judge said that the court was not inclined to show mercy. This being the third time the defendant had been convicted of that offense.

4. I refused the job. Although I could have used the money.

5. I think I would do as I did then. Conditions remaining the same.

6. The same procedure is used in the running of wind sprints as was used in the long runs. Twenty minutes of exercises. Two warm-up turns around a quarter-mile track. Followed by several fast sprints of 220 yards.

7. The technique of the Communists was to publicize every act of oppression and intolerance and at the same time to assure minority groups that the Communists were concerned about their plight. Thus exaggerating the failures of Democracy and implying that Communism was a philosophy of brotherly love.

8. He died alone and in poverty. Deserted by those who had once sung his praise and borrowed his money.

9. This has been one of those days that we all have once in a while. When, no matter how careful we are, everything seems to go wrong.

10. He said that all this talk about security puzzled him. That he knew no way of guaranteeing that his investments would turn out as he had planned them. Or even of being sure that he would live to know how they did turn out.

11. What he wants to know is. Will you date him?

12. After filling out the necessary papers and making a deposit. I was assigned to my room.

13. I am answering your advertisement expressing need of experienced draftsmen. Which appeared in a recent issue of the *Toledo Blade*. I should like to apply for one of those positions. And submit the following credentials.

14. The student of English grammar should recognize that there is likely to be some shuttling about between regular and irregular principal parts. That principal parts which were unacceptable a generation ago may have become established usage. While forms which were previously acceptable have passed out of fashion.

15. This spring my father had to make a very difficult decision. Whether to sell his business and move to California. Or to remain here where all his friends are. He finally decided to go to California. Which pleases me very much.

16. Two of the most unforgettable characters in my life are my parents.

Unforgettable not only because of our common bond but also because of the striking differences in their personalities.

17. You should take into consideration whether such a marriage would force John into a type of work he dislikes. Instead of giving him the opportunity to look around for the kind of work he really likes.

18. The greatest struggle in the world today is caused by two opposing ways of life. The Communistic way being characterized by government control. And the American way which is characterized by liberty, freedom, and Christian principles.

19. The possible solution to the problem of juvenile delinquency could be more and better recreational facilities. Facilities that would fill the spare time of the teen-ager and keep him occupied.

20. It is an important question, Jane. One which cannot be answered without much thought.

*epitome – boiled down*

## S 5 | *Fused Sentences* -

When two sentences are run together without any separating punctuation or without an intervening connective, they are said to be fused.

Unless such sentences are separated they will create difficulty for a reader or will, at least, irritate him because they do not observe convention.

| *Fused Sentences* | *Separated Sentences* |
| --- | --- |
| I want that boy how I want it. | I want that. Boy, how I want it! |
| I knocked on the door when the lady came I gave her my most ingratiating smile. | I knocked on the door. When the lady came I gave her my most ingratiating smile. |
| Why should I apologize when he insulted me he did not apologize. | Why should I apologize? When he insulted me he did not apologize. |
| It is difficult to believe that he said that what could he have been thinking of? | It is difficult to believe that he said that. What could he have been thinking of? |
| Why do you ask what concern is it of yours? | Why do you ask? What concern is it of yours? |

Separate the following fused sentences.

1. I will not object on the other hand don't expect me to contribute.
2. It could have been anyone I know of no way of finding out who did it.

3. The first couple of years will be difficult after that much of the work will be routine.

4. The Northern Pike is the gamest fish in these waters pound for pound he will outfight a muskie every time.

5. The sheriff's office is not willing to carry out the ruling of the court even though the evictions are legal they are afraid of public sympathy with the tenants.

6. Because of its involved forms for case and gender German is a difficult language for most students it is the most difficult language in college.

7. I wrote to mother when she answered I knew that the story had been exaggerated since then I have learned that the newspaper printed a retraction.

8. Informative lectures bore me when information is available in books I would rather read it than listen to it.

9. In situations such as this one there is no way of reaching a compromise unless both sides are willing to make concessions the dispute will become a stalemate.

10. At Roosevelt's death Truman succeeded to the Presidency without any real executive experience, without previous training, and without a unified party to direct him, he was called on to fill the most exacting job in the world.

---

**S 6** | *Comma Splice*

---

The use of a comma, instead of a period or semicolon, between two main clauses not joined by a connective is called a comma splice or comma fault.

For example:

It's a beautiful day, the park will be crowded.

A comma splice will trouble a reader most when a modifying phrase or clause comes between the two main clauses, since he may not be able to tell which main clause the modifier relates to. On page 131 we saw that a doctor's use of a comma splice made it impossible for an insurance company to decide whether the applicant's sister had or had not had tuberculosis. The following illustrates the same difficulty:

He has never before been suspected of theft, *to the best of my knowledge,* he has been employed by his present firm since he graduated from high school.

To which main clause does the italicized modifier belong? Which statement is the writer qualifying, that the man has never before been suspected of theft, or that he has always worked for the same company? The reader is free to guess, but he will get no help from the sentence. This comma splice brings about a real failure of communication, the worst kind of sentence error.

Because the comma splice sometimes causes this kind of confusion, many teachers strongly condemn all comma splices, even though some cause no real break in communication, and even though comma splices are not rare in the writings of some competent professional writers. It would better accord with the facts to say that, at its best, the comma splice is unconventional and, at its worst, it makes communication impossible. The sometimes indiscriminate condemnation of comma splices by college instructors is a result of painful experience with the latter type.

**b. Comma splices may be corrected by one of three methods.**

The simplest way is to change the faulty comma to a period or a semicolon, whichever is more appropriate:

| *Comma Splice* | *Revision* |
|---|---|
| His chances of election are not good, because the independents do not like him, it would be safer to nominate another candidate. | His chances of election are not good, because the independents do not like him. It would be safer to nominate another candidate. |
| This is the best book I have ever read, it kept me up all night. | This is the best book I have ever read; it kept me up all night. |

A second method of revision is to provide a coordinating connective between the two main clauses, thus making the comma conventional punctuation:

| | |
|---|---|
| She says she does not like football, I doubt that she has seen two games in her whole life. | She says that she does not like football, but I doubt that she has seen two games in her whole life. |
| It will cost a great deal of money, there is no guarantee that the plan will succeed. | It will cost a great deal of money, and there is no guarantee that the plan will succeed. |

The third method is to subordinate one main clause to the other:

| | |
|---|---|
| It is a beautiful day, the park will be crowded. | Because it is a beautiful day the park will be crowded. |
| He is discouraged about flunking, I think he will quit school. | He is so discouraged about flunking that I think he will quit school. |

When two main clauses are joined by a transitional connective (conjunctive adverb) — *consequently, however, moreover, nevertheless, therefore* — the conventional punctuation between them is a semicolon, though a period is not unusual:

I admit that he is honest and conscientious; nevertheless, I will not vote for him.

When two main clauses are felt to be closely related, informal usage sometimes prefers a comma to a semicolon:

I passed, Mary doubled.
The women like him, the men don't.

Using whatever method seems best, revise the comma splices in the following sentences.

1. The two days preceding the Spring Carnival are filled with much excitement, all the houses and organizations try to create interest in their floats.

2. There is still plenty of opportunity in this country, if a young man really cares about building a career, his chances of success are as good today as ever.

3. There are two wires sticking out from two small holes in the center of the dash, they have to be crossed to turn on the ignition.

4. The school had an attendance of 1500 students, this number included night school enrollment.

5. Do you believe that children should never be spanked, or do you believe that moderate spanking helps them to develop self-discipline, this is a question on which many parents disagree.

6. The difficulties are great, but not insuperable, although the answer is not in sight, it can be obtained by patient and persistent work.

7. It has been observed that the average youth in America reads at least one of the many different types of comics, the most popular kinds are the comics that are based on sensationalism and fantasy.

8. There are too many students for each teacher, no one receives any direct help or attention.

9. There is a great amount of detrimental reading material on the magazine shelves, most of this cannot be defended, even by the most liberal-minded person.

10. When in high school a week-end meant two days of nothing to do, in college it means two days in which you have to work to catch up.

11. In all three of these bills there is free choice of doctors, dentists, and hospitals, the only requirement is that they must be participants in the plan.

12. I remember how I used to spend hours living in a dream world as I sat in my room and followed the adventures of men who had super-human powers, some of them stopped bullets which bounced off their

bodies, others jumped over buildings and flew through space under their own power.

13. Their vocabularies seem to be made up of twenty-letter words, their sense of humor, if they have one, is very dry.

14. I had to fight temptations which led me away from my music, much to my dismay, the temptations quite often won.

15. The wages are low and the work is monotonous, moreover, the job offers little chance of promotion.

## S7 | Faulty Parallelism

PARALLEL SENTENCE structure was discussed in some detail on pages 134–136. If you have difficulty with this kind of sentence pattern, review those pages before studying this section.

**The convention of parallelism is that elements of equal importance should, as far as possible, be expressed in similar grammatical form.**

Thus two or more sentence elements arranged in a series or joined by a coordinating connective should have the same form: a phrase should be followed by a phrase, a clause by a clause, a noun by a noun, and a verb by a verb. The following sentence contains a series which enumerates the powers of a commission:

> The Commission has the power *to investigate, to conciliate, to hold* hearings, *to subpoena* witnesses, *to issue* cease-and-desist commands, *to order* reinstatement of a discharged employee, and *to direct* the hiring of a qualified applicant.

Notice that, grammatically, most of the sentence is a series of infinitive phrases, each identifying one of the powers of the commission and therefore modifying the noun *power*. Since each element in the series has the same modifying function, it is given the same infinitive form. It would have been possible to use a form other than the infinitive, as long as the same form was used throughout — (The Commission has the power *of investigating, of conciliating, of holding*, etc.). What is not acceptable is to mix forms. Notice how the following student sentence shifts from nouns to verbs and thus disrupts the parallel structure which the series demands.

The Commission has the power of investigation, conciliation, holding hearings, subpoena witnesses, issue cease-and-desist commands, order the reinstatement of a discharged employee, and direct the hiring of a qualified applicant.

| Faulty Parallelism | Explanation | Acceptable Structures |
|---|---|---|
| Few people understood the full extent of his disappointment or *how angry* he really was. | *Compound complement of* understood. *The first complement is a phrase, the second a subordinate clause. The two should be in parallel form.* | Few people understood the full extent of his disappointment or *the degree of his anger.* |
| Because he has always been wealthy *and with indulgent parents,* he has never been forced to accept responsibility. | *Compound modifier consists of a subordinate clause and a phrase. Should be two clauses or two phrases.* | Because he has always been wealthy and *has been protected by indulgent parents,* . . . (or) Because of *his wealth* and *his indulgent parents,* . . . |

Rewrite the following sentences to revise faulty parallelism.

1. Many of our laws are descended from old Roman laws, but ~~being~~ ^are^ changed to fit our modern needs.

2. A decision must be made as to whether the acres of grass surrounding the university buildings are more important from a standpoint ~~of~~ ^for^ landscaping or ~~to be converted into~~ ^more^ practical ^for^ parking lots open to all personnel, staff, and students.

3. For a settlement I will accept either twelve new blinds or ~~having~~ the old ones ~~perfectly repaired~~ ^repaired^.

4. She is inclined to be giggly and ^to^ always embarrass~~ing~~ her escort.

5. My two ambitions are to have my own business, thus being my own boss, and ~~having~~ ^to have^ enough money to provide my children with a good home and education.

6. There is no happy ending such as occurs in most novels, but rather ~~how~~ ^that^ people ~~that~~ ^who^ sin usually do not have a happy life as they grow older.

7. These discoveries may have been thought of back in the seventeenth century and ~~being used~~ ^are in use^ now.

8. A recent shipment consisting of Venetian blinds was found damaged and ~~for which~~ some adjustment should be made.

9. He continued his work, without hope, without pleasure, and ~~having no~~ ^without^ assurance that people would understand the significance of what he was trying to do.

10. For the sake of your parents, your friends, and ~~in the interests of~~ your future, I hope you will reject the offer.

11. The closeness of a family relationship is brought out and ~~how~~ typical family problems ~~can be worked out.~~ *(the solution of)*

12. Each of my courses has contributed in several ways to ~~my~~ being a *(help me be)* more intelligent person to talk with, and to help me read efficiently.

13. Your main aims in life are to settle down and having a home and *(to have)* children.

14. Uncle John taught me such things as honesty, faith in God, ~~to be~~ considerate and ~~making progress~~ but never at the expense of others. *(progress)*

15. My requirements for an ideal wife are honesty, intelligence, pleasantness, ~~being able~~ to cook and do housework, and ~~to have~~ confidence in me. *(ability)* *(possession of)*

# S 8 | Dangling Modifiers

DANGLING MODIFIERS were discussed in detail on pages 137–138. If you have more difficulty with such modifiers than can be removed by the following exercises, review the earlier discussion.

**A dangling modifier is one which has nothing in the main clause to modify and is thus left dangling.**

For example, in the sentence

*By going to the various sorority houses on campus and meeting hundreds of new girls,* my conversation, manners, and poise became more polished.

there is nothing in the main clause for the italicized modifying phrase to modify. When the author began to write that sentence she was unquestionably thinking of herself as the subject of the main clause — she was going to make a statement about herself. Had she finished with "I polished my conversation, manners, and poise," she would have had a satisfactory sentence, because the introductory phrase would then have modified the subject "I." But by inadvertently making "conversation" the subject of the main clause she spoiled what she started to do and invited the ludicrous interpretation that it was her conversation that visited the sorority houses.

The dangling modifiers most frequent in student essays begin, like the one above, with a **verbal phrase** — participle, gerund, or infinitive — and are left hanging because the originally-intended subject is not retained in the main clause. The best precaution against this kind of error is to make sure that the opening verbal clearly modifies the subject of the main clause. A sentence written with a dangling verbal phrase

*dangling elliptical clauses — dangling dependent sent.*
*Elliptical clause to be used correctly in a sentence must be followed by an independent clause; its omitted subject must*

may be revised either by rewording the main clause or by expanding the opening phrase into a subordinate clause. Notice how the italicized dangling modifiers in the left column are revised at the right.

| Dangling Modifiers | Explanation | Revised Version |
|---|---|---|
| *Walking downtown,* a streetcar jumped the tracks. | *In the absence of anything else to modify,* walking *seems to modify* streetcar. *The revised version contains a subject which the participle can logically modify.* | Walking downtown, I saw a streetcar jump the tracks. |
| *After recording the information required of me,* my adviser checked my card to see that I had followed instructions. | *It was the student, not the instructor, who did the recording, yet the gerund* recording *seems to modify* adviser. *If the opening phrase is changed to a clause, this possible misinterpretation will be avoided.* | When I had recorded the information required of me, my adviser checked my card to see that I had followed instructions. |
| *To qualify for the position,* a rigorous examination must be passed. | *While there is no ambiguity in this example, the dangling infinitive phrase creates an unnecessary shift in the sentence pattern. This shift can be avoided by keeping the whole sentence in the active voice.* | To qualify for the position you must pass a rigorous examination. |
| *Impressed by the newspaper stories,* war seemed inevitable. | *Who was impressed? The opening phrase needs something to modify. The revised version gets rid of this difficulty by making* we *the subject of the main clause.* | Impressed by the newspaper stories, we felt that war was inevitable. |

Other revisions of these dangling modifiers are possible:

*While I was walking downtown, I saw a streetcar jump the tracks.* (This revision combines both methods suggested earlier.)

*I recorded the information required of me; then my adviser checked my card to see that I had followed instructions.* (This revision avoids the dangling modifier by changing the opening phrase to a main clause.)

*You may qualify for the position by passing a rigorous examination.* (This revision changes the phrase to a main clause and reduces the original main clause to a phrase. Since the final phrase modifies the verb, it does not dangle.)

*Because we were impressed by the newspaper stories we felt that war was inevitable.*

(or)

*become the subject of the sentence.*
*A verbal phrase that begins sent. must refer to sub. of ind. clause or*
*clar.*

*We were so impressed by the newspaper stories that we felt war was inevitable.*

Sometimes a dangling modifier begins with an **elliptical clause** — a subordinate clause some elements of which are not expressed. The simplest revision of a dangling elliptical clause is to supply the necessary elements and complete the clause.

| *Dangling Modifier* | *Revised Version* |
|---|---|
| *When only five years old,* my mother died. | When I was only five years old my mother died. |
| *While still of preschool age,* my father began daily batting practice with me. | While I was still of preschool age my father began daily batting practice with me. |
| *Although working full time on an outside job,* my grades remained good. | Although I was working full time on an outside job, my grades remained good. |

As all these examples suggest, the most troublesome dangling modifiers are those beginning with an introductory verbal phrase or an elliptical clause. A dangling modifier at the end of a sentence is more likely to be awkward or unemphatic than ambiguous.

| *Dangling Modifier* | *Explanation* | *Revised Version* |
|---|---|---|
| He took a full program of studies during each summer session, *thus graduating in three years.* | *The main idea in this sentence is that the student graduated in three years. Since a main clause is grammatically more important than a phrase, the main idea should go in the main clause.* | By taking a full program of studies during each summer session he was able to graduate in three years. |

Improve the following sentences by revising the dangling modifiers.

1. Upon hearing a sharp click the suds subsided and the dial on the top of the washing machine read "drain."
2. Working in a drugstore, several professors chat with me every day.
3. After signing for all your classes, the next place to go is the finance office.
4. When in high school, classes were dull and monotonous.
5. When placing these men under arrest, comic books were usually found in their possession.
6. By getting your purpose clearly in mind at the beginning, the actual writing will be easier.
7. Without expecting a reply, a letter was written to the President.
8. Being very tired, the walk home took much too long.
9. By improving the English Department a student would not only be prepared for college English but for any subject.

10. After rushing to get to the station on time the information clerk said that the train would be more than an hour late.

11. Completely unaware that the landing gear had been damaged and that a crash landing at the end of the flight was inevitable, the plane, with its carefree passengers, sailed confidently through the night.

12. After having made all these plans and preparations and having such high expectations, the party was pretty much of a dud.

13. The car failed to observe the curve sign, thus losing control and going over the embankment.

14. Oddly enough, school was no more a drudgery, resulting in better grades.

15. I believe that, by delaying marriage until after your college graduation, the chances of happiness are much better.

---

## S9 | *Shifts in Subjects and Verbs*

ON PAGES 134–139 we saw that English sentences follow certain conventional patterns and that unintentional shifting from one pattern to another results in awkward, inconsistent structures. The following kinds of inconsistencies arise from awkward shifts in the form of the subject or verb.

**a. Awkward shifts in subject usually take one of two forms: unnecessary shift of subject within a paragraph, and shifts between personal and impersonal pronoun subjects within a sentence.**

In the examples below, the grammatical subjects are italicized.

| *Shifted Subjects* | *Explanation* | *Revised Version* |
|---|---|---|
| When *one* gets through with a three-hour examination *you* are exhausted. | *The subject shifts from the impersonal pronoun* one *to the second personal pronoun* you. *A shift from* one *to* he *is conventional but the shift to* you *is not. Any of the three revisions at the right would be an improvement.* | When *one* gets through . . . *one* is exhausted. When one gets through . . . *he* is exhausted. When *you* get through . . . *you* are exhausted. |

| *Shifted Subjects* | *Explanation* | *Revised Version* |
|---|---|---|
| The *worries* about entrance examinations leave the minds of the students before *they* leave for the campus. The last *days* are spent shopping for clothes during the day and gallivanting with friends at night. Their *families* receive little attention, and entrance *examinations* are no longer thought of. | *Although these three sentences all deal with the same logical subject (the students' activities before leaving for college), the paragraph has five grammatical subjects. This unnecessary shifting of the subject weakens the unity of the paragraph. The revision at the right reduces the subjects to two forms; the noun* students *and the pronoun* they. | During the last week before leaving for campus, *students* spend their days shopping for clothes and their nights attending farewell parties with their friends. *They* have little time to spend with their families and no longer worry about entrance examinations. |
| I did not like to refuse his invitation, but a *person* can't spend all their time going to shows. | *Although the writer is the logical subject of both clauses, the grammatical subject shifts from* I *to* person, *and the pronoun* their *shifts the second clause from singular to plural. The author would have been wiser to use the first personal pronoun throughout.* | I did not like to refuse his invitation, but *I* can't spend all my time going to shows. |

**b.  Avoid unnecessary shifts in the forms of the verbs.  Keep the tenses consistent and especially avoid shifting from active to passive voice.**

In the following examples the verb forms are in italics.

| *Shifted Verb Forms* | *Explanation* | *Consistent Verb Forms* |
|---|---|---|
| The older girls *had* a coke party to get us acquainted and it *was* deeply *appreciated* by me. | *The shift from active voice in the first clause to passive in the second is unnecessary and awkward. The revision subordinates the second clause and keeps both verbs in the active voice.* | I *appreciated* the coke party which the older girls *gave* to get us acquainted. |
| As centuries *passed,* the dress patterns *become* more and more complicated. | *The tense changes from past to present. Since the changes in dress were taking place while the centuries were passing, the verbs in both clauses should be in the same tense.* | As centuries *passed,* the dress patterns *became* more and more complicated. |

| Shifted Verb Forms | Explanation | Consistent Verb Forms |
|---|---|---|
| He *said* he *will* call for me at eight. | The author is confusing the tenses for direct and indirect discourse. Either form at the right will serve. | He *said* he *would* call for me at eight. He *said,* "I will call for you at eight." |

Revise the following student sentences to remove the awkward shifts in subjects or verbs.

1. It often makes one shudder at the sights you see.

2. You know it's really very odd how a person can have so many different feelings about something they plan to do.

3. I have experienced the strange sensation of losing one's wallet. When something like this happens you do not know what to do.

4. Upon completion of my program I'm informed that all the sections I wanted have been closed.

5. I was told to hurry over to Civil Engineering Hall or I may not get what I wanted.

6. My high school days taught me the value of learning to get along with others. As you worked with others you learned to accept responsibilities and to be a good follower. We were supposed to learn to be both followers and leaders.

7. There I was with a stack of papers, cards, envelopes, a time table, and a catalog, and he wants me to stop and sign my name.

8. I asked dad if I may borrow the car for the evening.

9. They had known hardship at first hand, for the dangers and misery of war had been experienced by them.

10. To do the author justice, a good job of exposing the foolishness of the English aristocracy was done in several instances in the book.

11. Faith means to have complete confidence in someone, even if they are under suspicion.

12. He said that we would be late anyway, so let's go ahead and not worry.

13. We talked over the problem for an hour but no decision was reached.

14. One way of judging the maturity of a person is to find out how well they are able to govern themselves.

15. I have been making these medallions since I was a junior in high school and I found it a satisfying hobby.

16. In choosing a mate for the rest of one's life certain qualities are searched for according to your individual preferences and standards.

17. There are a great many socially timid students on the campus. The University tries to help them. They are urged to join a group with similar interests. With the variety of possibilities offered, success is inevitable. An adjustment of this kind is every bit as important as academic success.

18. After paying my tuition and having my picture taken, an invitation to subscribe to the *Daily* was extended to me.

19. After an hour we came up with what my roommate called the per-

fect program. It looked awfully difficult to me, but if she said it was good what can a new freshman do but accept it?

20. To me dependability means simply what the word itself says — being able to depend on a person, whether it be simply to remember to pick up a loaf of bread at the grocery store, or whether it is depending on them to provide a home and love for your children.

---

## S 10 | *Incomplete Constructions*

The omission of words necessary for a clear understanding of the thought often results in a difficult or unidiomatic sentence.

Careless omissions often occur in making a clean copy of a paper, since copying is a mechanical task which takes little attention to meaning. For this reason, the final copy should be carefully reread before it is turned in.

Other omissions are the result of confusion about the structure of a sentence. The constructions most likely to be incompletely written are illustrated below.

| *Incomplete* | *Explanation* | *Complete* |
|---|---|---|
| We searched through all our pockets, but no money. | *Incomplete main clause. The conjunction* but *requires a main clause to balance the sentence. The verb* found *cannot be omitted.* | We searched through all our pockets, but *found* no money. |
| I don't like the crowd which he associates. | *Omitted preposition. With a choice of two forms of the subordinate clause —* with which he associates *or* he associates with — *the writer has failed to supply* with *in either position.* | I don't like the crowd *with* which he associates. (or) I don't like the crowd he associates *with*. |
| Statistics show that college men like their studies better than women. | *Omitted verb resulting in a possible ambiguity. What is being compared is not* studies *and* women, *but* men *and* women. *To avoid ambiguous comparison, the clause having* women *as the subject must be given a verb.* | Statistics show that college men like their studies better than women *do*. |

| *Incomplete* | *Explanation* | *Complete* |
|---|---|---|
| Their hope is the child has wandered off with some older companions who will take care of him. | *Omitted subordinating connective. While such connectives may often be omitted without causing difficulty, an omission which allows the subject of the subordinate clause to be misread as the complement of the verb in the main clause should be avoided.* | Their hope is *that* the child has wandered off with some older companions who will take care of him. |
| Today is as hot, if not hotter, than any day this summer. | *Confused comparison. This construction confuses two idioms — as hot as and hotter than. Since these idioms take different prepositions, than will not serve for both. Possibly the best way to express this comparison is to avoid this construction entirely by using one of the substitutes shown at the right.* | Today is one of the hottest days of the summer. (or) Today is at least as hot as any day we have had this summer. (or) Today may be the hottest day we have had this summer. |

Revise the following sentences to complete the incomplete constructions.

1. He is as old, if not older, than I.
2. He understands German better than his brother.
3. She is as proud of the choir as the students are.
4. I advertised my car in the papers, but no response.
5. I have and always will say that he is innocent.
6. The state he wants to live in his old age is California.
7. The trouble was the fuel pipe was clogged.
8. He was patient and tolerant of the children's bickering.
9. It made her mother from a girl to a wrinkled old woman in twelve short years.
10. Nowadays glasses often add rather than detract from a girl's looks.
11. He is as good, if not better, than any guard in the conference.
12. Having eaten and my schedule once again altered, I went back to finish registration.
13. She would rather live in a large city than the country.
14. When at a party a man should show respect and attention to his wife.
15. Azaleas are easier to grow in the South than the Midwest.

## Excessive Coordination

COORDINATION and subordination were discussed on pages 148–149. The following exercises supplement that discussion.

**a. Avoid excessive use of main clauses by subordinating less important ideas.**

| *Excessive Coordination* | *Explanation* | *Revision* |
|---|---|---|
| (1) I had only a single paddle and (2) I was not used to handling a canoe in rough water. (3) I could not hold its nose into the waves. (4) The canoe tacked from side to side. (5) I expected every moment to capsize. | *The most important ideas are those in clauses 3 and 5. The revision keeps them as main clauses and subordinates the rest, thus achieving variety, emphasis, and economy in the passage.* | Unaccustomed to handling a canoe in rough water with a single paddle, I could not hold its nose into the waves. As the canoe tacked from side to side I expected every moment to capsize. |

Revise the following extract from a student paper to get rid of excessive coordination.

There were new motives encouraging Benedict Arnold to commit treason. First, there were the repeated slights of Congress. In Philadelphia Arnold presented his accounts to Congress. They in turn appointed a committee to audit and investigate them. The committee took its time in reporting its findings and Congress failed to act. Arnold petitioned Congress a second time. They turned his petition down.

When Joseph Reed presented charges against Benedict Arnold, Congress took its time in settling them. The investigation dragged out over a period of several months. This began to cause Arnold to develop a persecution complex. It seemed whenever Congress was called upon to settle charges presented against Arnold it took them a long time to come to a decision.

Second, there was his need for ready cash with which to pay his debts. Arnold lived in a style of splendor and extravagance which was far beyond his means. He contracted more debts than he was able to pay. Rather than lower his standard of living he continued to go farther in debt. The people to whom he owed money finally asked him to pay up. This was of course impossible because he had no money. He petitioned Congress to settle his accounts, but they turned him down. He was confused and highly irritated. He finally resorted to all forms of acquiring money with which to pay his creditors. Some of the methods he resorted to were not in keeping with the rank he held.

**b. Avoid excessive use of coordinating connectives, especially *and* and *so*.**

| *Excessive coordination* | *Revision* |
|---|---|
| I did not know how mother would feel about my accepting such an invitation, *so* I called her on the phone *and* she said it was all right, *so* I accepted. | I did not accept the invitation until I had called mother on the phone and obtained her consent. |

Remove the excessive coordination in the following examples.

1. The game went into extra innings and we had to go home and get dressed or we would be late for the party, so we had to leave at the end of the ninth.

2. I was standing by the window and looking into the street and two cars suddenly crashed together. So I ran down the stairs and joined the crowd that was beginning to collect.

3. He said that thousands of draftees could not pass the army physical tests and were rejected and that most of their deficiencies could have been cured by proper medical attention and that this proved that the health of the nation was bad and something should be done about it.

4. Cliff Mercer is very popular in my home town and I attribute his popularity to his personal attitude toward his listeners. He creates a feeling of closeness with his audience and this makes his program one of the best on the network.

5. I believe the most valuable quality a woman can have is the ability to be a good cook. Meals are a very important part of everyday life, and a man's whole day may depend on the kind of breakfast he has and the way it is served. So every girl should be taught to cook a good meal and serve it attractively and her chances of making a successful marriage will be increased.

# S 12 | *Illogical Subordination*

**Main ideas in a sentence should be expressed in main clauses and less important ideas in subordinate clauses or phrases.**

If this practice is reversed and important ideas are placed in subordinate constructions, the sentence may be unemphatic, awkward, or even ludicrous.

| *Illogical Subordination* | *Explanation* | *Logical Subordination* |
|---|---|---|
| On his third try at the qualifying height, Bragg's pole fell against the crossbar, thus eliminating one of the world's greatest polevaulters from the Olympic trials. | *This construction makes the pole, rather than the man, the subject of the main clause and leaves the most important idea — Bragg's elimination — dangling in a phrase at the end of the sentence.* | Bragg, one of the world's greatest pole vaulters, was eliminated from the Olympic trials when his pole fell against the crossbar on his third try at the qualifying height. |
| The workman stepped on a live wire when he was electrocuted. | *The important idea is the electrocution, not the means by which it occurred. The subordination is backwards.* | The workman was electrocuted when he stepped on a live wire. |
| Because he had no money with him and could not pay the fine he had to spend the night in jail. | *The sentence consists of two subordinate clauses and one main clause. The second subordinate clause is more important than the first. It should be given greater grammatical rank by making it a main clause.* | Because he had no money with him he could not pay the fine and had to spend the night in jail. |
| There was a great deal of excitement in the neighborhood caused by the attempts to capture the escaped bull. | *The sentence is made wordy and undramatic by relegating the main idea — the attempts to capture the bull — to a final phrase and putting unimportant material in the main clause.* | The attempts to capture the escaped bull caused great excitement in the neighborhood. |

Revise the following sentences to make the subordination more logical.

1. The manager called me on the telephone, offering me the job.
2. It was a beautiful Sunday in May when they were married.
3. While my pocket was being picked I was waiting in line at the theater.
4. He fell from a ladder, which resulted in a brain concussion.
5. It was a great surprise when the governor was defeated for re-election.
6. The search party combed the area for five hours before finding the child unharmed at the bottom of a dry well.
7. We pulled out of the lot as our jalopy hooked the back fender of the Cadillac.

8. Sime pulled a thigh muscle at the start of the 100 meters, causing him to withdraw in pain from the race.

9. Mantle took a terrific cut at the ball when he drove it over the stands 550 feet from home plate.

10. Because the wild life service has built fish ladders as detours around impassable locks, the salmon are able to swim upriver to spawn.

# WO 1 | Conventional Word Order *  *  *

In English, word order is grammatically meaningful. To a large extent, we interpret the grammatical function of a word by its position in the sentence. Thus, *Dog bites man* will be given a quite different meaning if we interchange the positions of *dog* and *man*.

A writer must therefore know what word order is normal in English, what departures from this order are generally accepted, and what ones are undesirable. This section deals with normal order and with acceptable variations from it; the following five sections deal with variations that often cause trouble in college writing.

The normal order of elements in an English sentence is as follows:

**a. Subjects ordinarily precede their verbs.**

We write, "*Robert* has gone," except in questions: "How tall is *he?*" "Are *you* going?" and in sentences beginning with an expletive "There is a *ring* around the moon."

**b. Complements generally follow their verbs.**

Thus, "We lost *them.*" When the complement contains both a direct and an indirect object, the latter comes first if it is a single word (We gave *him* the book), but not if it is a phrase (We gave the book *to him*).

**c. Single adjectives precede the nouns they modify.**

Thus, "The *old* man was here." But modifying phrases follow their nouns: "He is a man *of the people.*"

**d. Adverbs modifying verbs usually follow the verbs.**

"He fought *desperately.*" But adverbs modifying adjectives or other adverbs usually precede the words they modify (He is *very* old. They dance *remarkably* well).

**e. Main clauses usually precede subordinate clauses.**

The following exceptions, however, are common:
  1. Adjective clauses follow immediately the nouns they modify (The man *who did that* should be whipped).
  2. Adverbial clauses, especially conditional clauses, often precede the main clause (*If you do that,* you'll be sorry).

3. Noun clauses may serve as subjects or complements of the verb in a main clause (*That he will accept* is taken for granted. He says *that you are afraid*).

## f. Closely related elements are kept as close together as possible.

Thus prepositions immediately precede their objects except when modifiers of the object intervene (This is *for* you. This is the top *of* the highest mountain); modifiers remain close to the constructions which they modify (The girl *with the red hair* was absent; NOT The girl was absent *with the red hair*); and subject-verb, verb-complement, and pronoun-antecedent combinations are not separated unless the special needs of the sentence require.

To sum up, in declarative statements the basic order of an English sentence is subject — verb — complement, with modifiers kept close to the elements they modify, and with all related parts of speech united as closely as possible. The order of the elements in a sentence should clearly reveal their relationships.

## Accepted Inversions

Any inversion of normal word order tends to attract attention and to emphasize the inverted expression. If this emphasis is desirable and if the departure from normal order is not outlandish or unidiomatic, a writer may gain interesting variety in sentence structure by moderate use of inversion. The commonest inversions for emphasis are as follows:

## a. If it does not create misinterpretation or awkwardness, an element may be transposed from its normal order for emphasis.

| *Normal Order* | *Emphatic Inversion* |
|---|---|
| The skies cleared *slowly*. | *Slowly* the skies cleared. |
| No leaf stirred *in all the forest*. | *In all the forest* no leaf stirred. |
| He threw *out* the runner. | He threw the runner *out*. |
| That is a good country *from* which to come. | That is a good country to come *from*. |
| There is no excuse *for him*. | *For him* there is no excuse. |

## b. For stylistic reasons, a normal sentence may be inverted into a periodic sentence.

For a more detailed discussion of the periodic sentence see page 137.

| *Normal* | *Periodic* |
|---|---|
| Think only this of me *if I should die*. | *If I should die*, think only this of me. |
| I broke the window *in order to unlock the car door*. | *In order to unlock the car door*, I broke the window. |

c. If no vagueness or awkwardness results, related elements, which normally would not be separated, may be interrupted by absolute or modifying constructions.

| Interruption | Explanation |
|---|---|
| These, *I am told,* were his last words. | Absolute between subject and verb. |
| Their conduct *in this situation* was heroic. | Modifying phrase between subject and verb. |
| Related elements, *which normally would not be separated,* may be interrupted. | Nonrestrictive modifying clause between subject and verb. This particular interruption is normal order. |
| He answered, *with obvious annoyance,* that the story was false. | Modifying phrase between verb and complement. |
| Don't *under any conditions* make such a promise. | Modifying phrase between parts of a verb. |

# WO 2 | *Ambiguous Modifiers*

The relationship between a modifying word, phrase, or clause and the element it modifies must be clear.

If a modifier is so placed that it could modify either of two elements, its reference will be ambiguous. (See also "Confused Pronoun Reference," pages 132–133, and "Misleading Word Order," pages 133–134.) If the ambiguity is complete, as in the extract from the doctor's letter quoted on page 131, the reader will be unable to tell which meaning was intended. More frequently he will be able to make the correct interpretation but will be conscious of the writer's ineptitude. The following examples supplement those given in Chapter 7.

| Ambiguous Order | Explanation | Revised Order |
|---|---|---|
| They talked about going on a second honeymoon *frequently,* but they never did. | Frequently *is closer to* going *than to* talked *and could modify either. It thus looks both ways, or "squints." Placing it immediately before or after* talked *removes the ambiguity.* | They talked *frequently* about going on a second honeymoon, but they never did. |

| *Ambiguous Order* | *Explanation* | *Revised Order* |
|---|---|---|
| The car is in the garage *which he smashed.* | *Since conventional order places adjective clauses after the nouns they modify, a reader is tempted to take* garage *as the antecedent of* which. *Putting the modifying clause immediately after* car *removes this possibility.* | The car *which he smashed* is in the garage. |
| There is a lecture tonight about juvenile delinquency *in the student lounge.* | *The italicized phrase was intended to modify the main clause but its position suggests that it locates the scene of the delinquency rather than of the lecture.* | Tonight there is a lecture *in the student lounge* about juvenile delinquency. |

Remove possible ambiguities in the following sentences by changing the position of faulty modifiers.

1. Fortunately, the fire was put out before any serious damage was done by the volunteer firemen.
2. A car came down the street decked with ribbons.
3. I listened while he talked attentively.
4. Everyone stared at the girl who was dancing with the dean in the low cut gown.
5. There was a noisy disturbance when the speaker said that at the back of the hall.
6. Humphrey Bogart played the part of the man who was corrupted by gold superbly.
7. He looked at the boy with sad eyes.
8. My roommate brought me the book from the library that I wanted.
9. At one time his neighbors said he had been in jail.
10. No one would treat his father like that unless he was irresponsible.

# WO 3 | *Vague Pronoun Reference*

In speech, a pronoun often refers to an unspecified or implied antecedent, but in college writing it is desirable to make pronoun references as specific as possible.

A pronoun which refers to a whole clause rather than to an explicit antecedent sometimes puts an additional strain on the reader by requiring him to do something which is really the writer's responsibility. The following examples illustrate pronoun references which, because they are unnecessarily vague, make the writing less precise than it should be.

| Vague Reference | Explanation | Revision |
|---|---|---|
| They have agreed to have a formal church wedding *which* pleases their parents. | *The pronoun* which *has no explicit antecedent but refers to the whole idea expressed in the main clause. The vague reference may be improved by supplying an antecedent as in the first revision or, better, by recasting the sentence as in the second revision.* | They have agreed to have a formal church wedding, *a decision* which pleases their parents. (or better) Their decision to have a formal church wedding pleases their parents. |
| The bigger car will be expensive to operate. Not only will its repairs cost more but its gasoline consumption will be greater. You should take *this* into account. | *The demonstrative pronoun* this *has no explicit antecedent, is singular in form, and refers to two different costs. In the revised version, the phrase* these added costs *removes the difficulties.* | The bigger car will be expensive to operate. Not only will its repairs cost more but its gasoline consumption will be greater. You should take *these added costs* into account. |
| The crash is being investigated. At present *they* think that the planes must have collided. | *The antecedent of* they *is not identified. The writer, of course, is thinking of the investigators. The sentence would be improved by dropping the pronoun entirely.* | At present the investigators think that the planes must have collided. |
| If he does not get to work on his research assignment pretty soon *it* is going to be difficult for him to get it finished on time. | *The first* it *is impersonal but looks at first glance as if it should refer to* research assignment — *particularly unfortunate because the second* it *does have this reference. The sentence would be improved by keeping* he *the subject of both clauses.* | If he does not get to work on his research assignment pretty soon he may not get it finished on time. |

Revise the following sentences if necessary to make the pronoun references clear.

1. When you advance to the upper grades — fifth, sixth, seventh, and eighth — there are two grades in each room, which allows you to become acquainted with more pupils.

2. She hasn't a good word to say for anybody. Her parents are old-fashioned, her girl friends are catty, her boy friends are conceited, and her instructors are sarcastic. This makes me discount anything she tells me about a person.

3. I expect to receive a D in History and, at best, another D in Accounting, which means that I will be on probation next semester.

4. In high school they always told us exactly what we were to do and how we were to do it.

5. In the book it says that the meanings of words are determined by the ways people use them, which surprised me.

6. In college I like the way they treat you as an adult and call you Mister and Miss. This is a pleasant change from the way it was in high school.

7. My parents are divorced, which means that I see very little of my father.

8. At the Student Counseling Bureau they told me I should make an effort to get to know other girls better and be more active in outside activities, but that is easier to tell than to do.

9. Dayton, Ohio, adopted this plan in 1914 and they have kept it ever since, which is a good example of the success of the council-manager form of municipal government.

10. To have a decent job, a nice home and family, good friends, and enough money for a few luxuries. Such is my ambition.

# WO 4 | *Awkward Separation of Elements*

Although related elements in a sentence may be separated (see page 446), there should usually be no *unnecessary* separation of subject and verb, verb and complement, modifier and its referent, or preposition and its complement.

Unnecessary separation of such closely related elements distorts the sentence pattern and interferes with ease of reading.

| Awkward Separation | Explanation | Revised Order |
|---|---|---|
| My *father*, after considering what the trip would cost and how long it would take, *refused* to go. | *Awkward separation of subject and verb. The unnecessary interruption of the main clause by a phrase and two subordinate clauses distorts the structure of the main clause.* | After considering what the trip would cost and how long it would take, my father refused to go. |

| Awkward Separation | Explanation | Revised Order |
|---|---|---|
| The evidence shows, if you examine it carefully and impartially, *that the best baseball is played in the National League.* | *Awkward separation of verb and its complement. The reader has to leap over the if-clause to find the complement of shows.* | A careful and impartial examination of the evidence shows that the best baseball is played in the National League. |
| He gave the sweater to his girl *that he had won in track.* | *Awkward separation of noun and its modifying clause. This kind of separation resembles the ambiguous modifiers discussed on page 446.* | He gave the sweater that he had won in track to his girl. (or) He gave his girl the sweater that he had won in track. |
| We *have* since then *had* no more trouble. | *Awkward separation of two parts of verb by modifying phrase.* | Since then, we have had no more trouble. |
| I am neither in support *of* nor opposed to *the bill.* | *Awkward separation of preposition of and its complement. The revision at the right is the best way of expressing the idea.* | I neither support nor oppose the bill. |

The **split infinitive** often provokes criticism in college writing. An infinitive phrase is "split" when an adverb separates its parts (*to almost laugh, to have never tried*). In some sentences (I decided *to almost quit*) the split infinitive gives a wrong emphasis and is awkward. In others (The prosecution failed *to completely demolish* the alibi), the intervening modifier gives a more precise emphasis or is more idiomatic than if the position of the modifier were changed. Although neither the facts of usage nor the judgment of grammarians justifies blanket condemnation of split infinitives, the safest practice for a college student is to place the modifier before or after the infinitive, whichever position gives the emphasis he wishes. For example:

| Split Infinitive | Revision |
|---|---|
| He tried *to* quickly *retreat.* | Quickly he tried *to retreat.* (or) He tried *to retreat* quickly. |

Revise the following sentences to eliminate any unnecessary separation.

1. Her father, even, admits that she is extravagant.
2. Dad promised that he would in plenty of time get the tickets.
3. I was until yesterday of that opinion.

4. Herself more than others she will hurt by her conduct.

5. He is reported to recently have denied the story.

6. He had no desire to or expectation of getting married.

7. Every one of my instructors, I am firmly of the opinion, acts as though his course was the only one I am taking.

8. Although some kinds of extra-curricular activities are overrated for some students, those are often socially valuable that give a shy girl experience in working with both men and women.

9. I was so surprised that I forgot what I intended to say to her when she smiled.

10. He said while he did not object to our going that he would like to stay home.

# WO 5 | *Misplaced Emphasis*

SINCE THE EMPHASIS on any sentence element often depends on its position, a writer must be careful not to give too much or too little emphasis by placing an element in a wrong position. The following precautions should help you to avoid the most frequent faults of emphasis in student writing.

### a. Do not place minor ideas at the ends of sentences.

The most emphatic position in an English sentence is the end; the next most emphatic position is the beginning; the least emphatic is the middle. Unimportant ideas coming at the end of a sentence will be made unduly conspicuous by their position, and the sentence will seem to run down hill. Notice the contrast in effectiveness in the following sentences.

| *Unemphatic Order* | *Emphatic Order* |
|---|---|
| He was accused of cheating and was expelled at a hearing by the discipline committee after lunch yesterday. | He was accused of cheating and, at a hearing by the Discipline Committee after lunch yesterday, he was expelled. |
| Last night someone stole our car while we were in the theater. | Last night, while we were in the theater, someone stole our car. |
| She is innocent in my opinion. | In my opinion she is innocent. |
| Nothing can be done, however. | Nothing, however, can be done. |
| He is going to propose, I think. | I think he is going to propose. |

| *Unemphatic Order* | *Emphatic Order* |
|---|---|
| In a magnificent stretch run Needles overtook six horses and won by a nose, thrilling the crowd. | Needles thrilled the crowd by a magnificent stretch run in which he overtook six horses and won by a nose. |

The order in the last revised example is sometimes called the order of climax, or climactic order. The sentence moves toward the climax of Needles' victory through a succession of increasingly dramatic events. Not all sentences permit such order, and it would be a mistake to force a climactic order which the events themselves did not contain. When the sentence permits, it is a good maxim to start strong, finish strong, and put less important material in the middle.

**b. Do not weaken the force of an important concluding statement by reducing it to a participial phrase.**

Many a good sentence ends with a participial phrase, but to use such a phrase for an idea which is important enough to deserve a main clause often creates a lame ending. For example, in

> He fell from the roof, *thus breaking his neck.*

the italicized phrase is at least as important as the main clause, yet it is grammatically subordinate and trails off weakly. The idea in the phrase is important enough to come at the end of the sentence, but it deserves the dignity of a stronger grammatical form:

> He fell from the roof and *broke his neck.*

**c. Do not place a conjunctive adverb at the beginning of a sentence unless you deliberately wish to emphasize it.**

Conjunctive adverbs — *however, moreover, nevertheless, therefore,* etc. — serve in a double capacity. As conjunctions they connect; as adverbs they modify. But they are relatively weak modifiers referring to the whole sentence rather than any element of it, and consistently placing them at the start of the sentence may give them too much emphasis. If they deserve emphasis, as the third example below may do, they may be used to start the sentence; but they are usually better near, not at, the beginning.

> I am willing to advise you. I will not, *however,* accept responsibility for what you do.
> He thinks she deceived him deliberately; he is *therefore* in no mood for a reconciliation.
> We have repeatedly tried to make friends with them and have been consistently repulsed; *nevertheless,* I shall try again.

**d. Do not misrepresent meaning by putting a modifier in the wrong position.**

Since a modifier usually seems to refer to the nearest referent, be careful that the position of modifiers gives the meaning you want to convey. The following sentence can mean quite different things depending on the position of the adverb.

They *secretly* intend to be married.     They intend to be married *secretly*.

In the first sentence the position of the modifier emphasizes the intention; in the second, it emphasizes the nature of the ceremony. Either meaning is possible, but the one expressed depends on the position of the modifier.

The following contrasts also show how much the position of a modifier can affect meaning.

| | |
|---|---|
| John *just* made it. | *Just* John made it. |
| Mary knows *only* the date. | *Only* Mary knows the date. |
| *Until today* they promised to stay. | They promised to stay *until today*. |
| *Even* mother is annoyed with him. | Mother is *even* annoyed with him. |

**e. Do not overindulge in inversion as a shortcut to a "literary" style.**

Inexperienced but ambitious writers sometimes try to create a literary style by using a great many self-conscious inversions. While unusual word order is arresting, strained or distorted inversion that does little but call attention to itself is more a vice than a virtue. Inverted order is exceptional order. It should be used deliberately and with restraint.

| *Affected* | *Natural* |
|---|---|
| Pleasant were those days. | Those were pleasant days. |
| Little cared I what my parents said. | I cared little what my parents said. |
| Learn he must to appreciate his own deficiencies. | He must learn to appreciate his own deficiencies. |

Revise the following sentences to avoid misplaced emphasis.

1. The chairman said that the committee would continue in session until all business had been dispensed with, if there was no objection.

2. He scored through center after two unsuccessful plunges, thus tying the game.

3. I would have liked to take her to a movie but I did not even have a dollar; moreover, my only decent suit was at the cleaners.

4. I almost read the whole novel last night. I could have finished it had I started an hour earlier, I believe.

5. Time for my assignments I never seem to find, thus being always behind.

6. Neither of the candidates intends to speak here, as far as I know.

7. I have never been away from home before, and I find it both exciting and frightening.

8. He said that I could come over and listen to his records tonight, if I had time.

9. She graduated in three years with highest honors from the University.

10. The express plunged into the rear of the freight train and 37 people were injured as the result of a faulty signal.

**WO 6** | *Use and Abuse of the Passive Voice*

ENGLISH VERBS have two voices, active and passive, which show whether the subject performs or experiences the action indicated by the verb:

| *Active (Subject acts)* | *Passive (Subject is acted upon)* |
|---|---|
| The man scolds the boy. | The boy is scolded by the man. |
| The attendant washed the car. | The car was washed by the attendant. |

Most verbs are active, since the normal pattern of our thought is to assert that some person or thing did or does something. In the sentences above, the active forms are much more normal and expected idiomatic expressions than the passive.

**a. Use the passive voice when the subject is obvious or unknown.**

Sometimes, when the subject is not known, is obvious, or is unimportant, the passive form is more natural.

| *Idiomatic passive* | *Vague or distorted active* |
|---|---|
| The President was elected by a huge majority. | They elected the President by a huge majority. |
| | (or) |
| | A huge majority elected the President. |
| | (or) |
| | The people elected the President by a huge majority. |
| We were driven around old Quebec in an open carriage. | A man drove us around old Quebec in an open carriage. |

Everyone knows who elects Presidents (in the United States at least) and nobody knows or cares who drove us around Quebec. In such sentences the active voice would be strained or unidiomatic.

**b. Use the passive voice when it gives more accurate emphasis.**

Notice that the object of a verb in the active voice becomes the subject when the verb is passive. Since the subject position in a sentence is more emphatic than the object position, changing a noun from object to subject gives it greater stress. Therefore when the object is the more important, a change from the active to the passive voice puts the emphasis where it belongs.

We see a fine illustration of what can be gained by such a shift if we contrast a common misquotation of Churchill's famous tribute to the Royal Air Force with the correct version. Churchill wished to express three ideas: (1) the greatness of the service performed by the RAF; (2) the small number of men who performed it; and (3) the large numbers who benefited by it. If you keep in mind that the sentence is about the wonderful work of the RAF, you will agree that the greatness of the service and the few men who provided it are more important than the number who benefited. Yet the misquotation puts the least important idea in the important subject position:

"Never . . . have so many owed so much to so few."

In his actual words Churchill put the verb in the passive voice and thus made grammar more precisely show the emphasis he wanted:

"Never . . . was so much owed by so many to so few." [1]

In the following contrasted examples the passive voice permits a more fitting emphasis than does the active.

| *Active* | *Explanation* | *Passive* |
|---|---|---|
| Although *Moby Dick* is Melville's greatest novel, the critics ignored it when it first appeared. | *Making* critics *the subject of the main clause takes the emphasis away from the novel and unnecessarily shifts the subject. Both defects are removed in the revision.* | Although *Moby Dick* is Melville's greatest novel, it was ignored by the critics when it first appeared. |
| The legislature founded the University ninety years ago. | *Unless the context deals with the work of the legislature ninety years ago, the important noun is* University. *The passive form makes it the subject.* | The University was founded by the legislature ninety years ago. |

[1] The complete quotation is: "Never in the field of human conflict was so much owed by so many to so few." The modifying phrase is here omitted to simplify analysis.

**c.** Do not use the passive voice if it weakens the emphasis on an important noun or pronoun.

| Weak Passive | Explanation | Preferred Active |
|---|---|---|
| The car was not driven by me. | *The writer is more concerned about himself than about the car; so he should put himself in the subject position.* | I did not drive the car. |
| A final examination was failed by both starting halfbacks. | *The only importance of the examination is that the halfbacks failed it. They should be placed in the subject position.* | Both starting halfbacks failed a final examination. |

**d.** Above all, do not use the passive voice when it results in an awkward shift in sentence structure.

| Awkward Shift to Passive | Explanation | Active Form |
|---|---|---|
| Looking through the binoculars, the ship was sighted. | *Awkward shift to passive leaves the modifying phrase dangling. See* **S8.** | Looking through binoculars, I sighted the ship. |
| The women talked, the men pitched horseshoes, and tag was played by the children. | *The pointless shift to passive in the third clause spoils the parallelism of the series. See* **S7.** | The women talked, the men pitched horseshoes, and the children played tag. |

Many awkward shifts are a result of switching from an active to a passive construction within a sentence. For this reason, most of the following exercises ask you to identify and correct this abuse of the passive.

Determine whether the sentences would be improved by any changes in voice and make necessary revisions.

1. The judge said that the verdict would be given by him later.
2. After the carpenters had finished, work was begun by the bricklayers.
3. There was a big attendance at the dance and a good time was had by all.
4. In writing to his father, requests for more money ~~were frequently made.~~ he frequently
5. The building, which is sixty years old, has been condemned.
6. When the band stopped for the intermission they served cold drinks.
7. He was not prepared for the test. Consequently, only half of the questions were answered.
8. According to the press reports, the announcement was released in Washington.
9. In a fit of temper his clubs were thrown in the lake.
10. It was not expected by us that we would win.

# Grammar: Parts of Speech

IN ORDER to study English grammar we must have some system of classifying words. The traditional scheme divides all words into eight categories called **parts of speech**. These, you remember, are *nouns, pronouns, verbs, adjectives, adverbs, prepositions, conjunctions,* and *interjections.* These terms are usually defined as follows:

1. A **noun** is the name of a living being (*John Brown, woman, horse*), a place (*New York, prairie, desert*), an object (*stone, tree, bullet*), a quality (*happiness, honesty, hate*), or a collection (*herd, flock, army, team*).

2. A **pronoun** is a word used as a substitute for a noun or another pronoun. (Don't wait for John; *he* won't be here.)

3. An **adjective** is a word used to modify a noun or a pronoun. (He is a *ruthless* man. You have the *wrong* one.)

4. A **verb** is a word or a phrase that asserts action, state, or being. (He *has run* away. They remained standing. He *is* ill).

5. An **adverb** is a word that modifies a verb, an adjective, or another adverb. (He fought *furiously.* She is *very* young. I talked *most* bluntly.)

6. A **preposition** is a word showing the relationship between a noun (or pronoun) and some other word in the sentence. (We stood *at* the door. Sue lives *with* her aunt. They ran *to* the window.)

7. A **conjunction** connects words, phrases, or clauses. (You *and* I. To be *or* not to be. I'd like to *but* I can't.)

8. An **interjection** is a word or phrase used to express an emotion or feeling. (*Oh! Rot! Hurrah! Thank goodness!*)

These definitions presume to define the ways the parts of speech are used, but in practice any part of speech may be used in a variety of ways. The noun *man,* for example, serves as an adjective in *man child,* a verb in *man the boats,* an adverb in *man crazy,* and an interjection in *Man, I'm tired!* When, therefore, we are talking about the way words are used within a sentence, as we were in "Sentence Elements" (pages 413–417), it is more convenient to use terms which show sentence relations — *subject, verb, complement, modifier,* and *connective.* When we are talking about the grammatical forms of words (changes in the form of a word to show number, gender, case, tense, etc.), the parts of speech provide a more satisfactory classification.

**Nouns**

The whole class of nouns is often subdivided as follows:

**Proper nouns** — those which name particular persons, places, or events (*Dwight D. Eisenhower, New York City, the Battle of the Bulge*).

**Common nouns** — all nouns other than proper nouns.

**Abstract nouns** — those common nouns which name qualities or characteristics of things or people (*anger, bravery, hardness, mercy, thickness*).

**Collective nouns** — those common nouns which refer to groups or collections (*army, clergy, crowd, electorate, flock, mass*).

The inflection of English nouns presents very few problems. Except for a relatively few words which have both masculine and feminine forms (actor-actress, fox-vixen, duke-duchess, master-mistress, etc.), the basic form of a noun is changed only to show plural number and possessive case.

**Number.** Most English nouns have singular and plural forms. Since perhaps 95 per cent of all nouns form their plurals by adding -*s* or -*es* to the singular form [1] and since irregular plural forms are given in a dictionary (see page 206), the simplest method of deciding about troublesome plurals is to consult your dictionary. Nouns which do not take -*s* plurals usually belong to one of the following classes:

*a.* **-en Plurals** (*children, oxen*).

*b.* **Vowel-Changing Plurals** (*foot-feet, goose-geese, louse-lice, man-men, mouse-mice, tooth-teeth, woman-women*).

*c.* **Unchanged Plurals** (*deer, sheep, swine*).

These irregular plurals are relics of Old English plural inflections which once were common but which, during the evolution of the language, have been superseded by the -*s* plural.

*d.* **Foreign Plurals** (*agenda, alumnae, bacilli, data, synopses*).

Words borrowed from foreign languages bring with them their foreign methods of forming the plural. If these words pass into popular speech there is a strong tendency to ignore their foreign plurals and to treat them like the great majority of English nouns. However, until that change has become accepted, it is conventional to use the foreign plural. If you have had Latin or Greek you will remember that:

1. Latin nouns ending in -*a* take -*ae* in the plural (*alumnae, antennae, larvae, nebulae, vertebrae*).

2. Most borrowed Latin nouns ending in -*us* take -*i* in the plural (*alumni, bacilli, loci, radii*).

---

[1] The conditions under which the -*es* plural is used are essentially a matter of spelling and are summarized on pages 536–537.

3. Latin nouns ending in -*um* take -*a* in the plural (*agenda, bacteria, data, dicta, errata, residua, strata*).

4. Greek nouns ending in -*is* take -*es* in the plural (*analyses, crises diagnoses, emphases, hypotheses, oases, parentheses, synopses, syntheses*).

But since no law requires modern Americans to follow the speech habits of the Greeks and Romans, the fact that certain plural endings were used in Latin or Greek is not proof that they are used in English. Therefore, when you are in doubt about foreign plurals, consult your dictionary.

**The Plurals of Compounds.** Nouns which are compounds of two or more words form their plurals in different ways. Most compounds (like *billiard balls, blackboards, class reunions, footballs, fountain pens, girl scouts, heartbreakers, pick-ups, policemen, seamen, wall-flowers*) merely use the plural form of the last word in the compound. But exceptions are so numerous that when you are not sure you should consult your dictionary. The following exceptions are worth noting:

1. Compounds which inflect the first word (*brothers-in-law* [or any other relative-in-law], *commanders-in-chief, editors-in-chief, justices-of-the-peace, lookers-on, passers-by*).

2. Compounds which inflect more than one word (*men servants, men-shoppers, women students, women teachers*). Notice that these have two characteristics in common: (1) in the singular form, the first word is either *man* or *woman;* (2) the gender of the whole compound is indicated by the first word. Only when both these characteristics are present, are both elements of the compound inflected. Contrast *woman haters* with *women workers* and *man-eaters* with *men-patients.*

3. Compounds ending in -*ful* signifying a unit of measure add -*s* (*cupfuls, handfuls, mouthfuls, spoonfuls*). In such sentences as *I left two cupfuls of coffee in the pot* and *I left two cups full of coffee on the table,* the terms *cupfuls* and *cups full* have different meanings. Whether or not *cups full* should be classified as a compound is open to dispute.

## Pronouns

The classes of pronouns that most require attention are the personal, relative, demonstrative, reflexive, and indefinite pronouns.

**Personal Pronouns.** Personal pronouns are inflected for gender, number, and case, and also for person. The complete inflection of the personal pronouns follows.

| NUMBER | CASE | 1ST PERSON | 2ND PERSON | 3D PERSON | | |
|---|---|---|---|---|---|---|
| | | | | *mas.* | *fem.* | *neut.* |
| | *Subjective* | I | you | he | she | it |
| Singular | *Possessive* | my (mine) [2] | your(s) | his | her(s) | its |
| | *Objective* | me | you | him | her | it |
| | *Subjective* | we | you | they | | |
| Plural | *Possessive* | our(s) | your(s) | their(s) | all genders | |
| | *Objective* | us | you | them | | |

**Relative Pronouns.** The pronouns *who, which, that, what,* with their compounds, *whoever, whosoever, whichever, whatever,* and *whatsoever,* are often used to relate a subordinate clause to its main clause. When so used, they are called **relative pronouns.** The only relative fully inflected for case is *who,* which has the forms: *who* (subjective), *whose* (possessive), *whom* (objective). This pronoun is not inflected for number or gender. The compounds *whoever* and *whosoever* have no distinct forms for the possessive, but become *whomever* and *whomsoever* respectively in the objective case — thus:

> *Whoever* did this should be horsewhipped.
> I'll take *whomever* I can get.
> *Whosoever* believeth in me shall not perish.
> To *whomsoever* it may concern.

**Demonstrative Pronouns.** When *this* and *that* are used as pointing words they are called **demonstrative pronouns.** When so used, they are inflected for number. Their plural forms are *these* and *those* respectively — thus:

> *This* is mine; *these* are yours.
> *That* was the seventeenth; *those* records were lost.

**Reflexive Pronouns.** In such sentences as *He corrected himself, You will hurt yourself, They are deceiving themselves,* we call *himself, yourself,* and *themselves* **reflexive pronouns** because the object refers to the same individual or group as the subject. Reflexive pronouns are inflected as follows:

| | *Singular* | *Plural* |
|---|---|---|
| 1st person | myself | ourselves |
| 2nd person | yourself | yourselves |
| 3rd person | himself, herself, itself | themselves |

[2] The forms in parentheses are used in such constructions as *These papers are mine* (*ours, yours, hers, theirs*) — that is, when the pronoun alone is used after the verb to complete the verb and to modify the antecedent.

Indefinite Pronouns. When followed by a noun, such words as *any, each, every, no, some* act as modifiers (Is there *any* hope? We tried *every* way). When used without a noun as subjects or complements, these words, and their compounds with *one, body, thing,* are pronouns. Since their antecedent is not specified, they are called **indefinite pronouns.** The commonest indefinite pronouns are *all, any, both, each, every, few, many, much, no, one, several, some,* and their compounds with *one, body,* or *thing.*

## Verbs

On pages 413–414 we considered the verb as a sentence element and were then exclusively interested in how it functions in a sentence, how it is related to other sentence elements, especially the subject and the complement. Here we are considering the verb as one of eight parts of speech and are primarily interested in its different forms, its inflection or conjugation.

Inflection. English verbs are said to be inflected to show number, person, voice, mood, and tense. Theoretically, we can tell from its ending whether the verb is singular or plural (number), whether it describes an action performed by the person speaking (first person), the person spoken to (second person), or the person spoken about (third person). But, except for the highly irregular verb *to be,* the only inflection for number and person is the final *-s* in the third person singular form of the present tense (I walk, he walk*s*). In all other tenses, and in the other persons of the present tense, no change occurs in the basic form of the verb to show number or person. For the most part, we identify the number and person of a verb by the number and person of its subject. Inflection for mood and voice is almost as simple. Most problems with verb forms arise from the changes required to show tense.

Principal Parts. All tenses are made by taking certain forms of the verb and using them either alone or in combination with other verbs. Thus, all tenses of the verb *to talk* are made from the forms: *talk, talking, talked* (I *talk,* I am *talking,* I do *talk,* I *talked,* I have *talked,* I have been *talking,* I will *talk,* etc.). Similarly, all tenses of the verb to *speak* are made from the forms: *speak, speaking, spoke, spoken.* These forms are called the **principal parts.**

As the last example shows, we recognize four principal parts: the present and past tense forms, and the present and past participles. Thus, for the verbs *to come, to see, to conquer,* the principal parts are:

| Present Tense | Present Participle | Past Tense | Past Participle |
|---|---|---|---|
| come | coming | came | come |
| see | seeing | saw | seen |
| conquer | conquering | conquered | conquered |

The great majority of English verbs form both the past tense and the past participle by adding *-ed* or *-d* to the first principal part (*talk, talked, talked; blame, blamed, blamed*). Such verbs have two characteristics: the vowel remains unchanged in all principal parts; and the forms for the past tense and the past participle are identical. Verbs which do not have both these characteristics are said to be **irregular**.[3]

**Tense.** Although it is possible to recognize some thirty different tenses, not counting idioms which do the work of tenses, six tenses are considered basic. These are

Simple present: They object

Simple past: They objected

Simple future: They will object

Present perfect: They have objected

Past perfect: They had objected

Future perfect: They will have objected

The uses of these tenses and their full conjugations are shown on pages 471–472.

**Mood.** Of the three moods of English verbs — the **indicative, imperative,** and **subjunctive** — the indicative is by far the most common. A verb is in the indicative mood unless:

1. It expresses a command or entreaty (*Sit down! Please listen to me!*), in which case it is in the imperative mood.

2. It is used in one of the following ways, in which case it is in the subjunctive mood:

    *a.* To express a condition contrary to fact (If I *were* you, I would go).

    *b.* To grant a concession (*Be* it as you say).

    *c.* To state an improbability (If this *were* the end of the matter, I'd be happy).

    *d.* To conduct certain parliamentary proceedings (I move that the committee *go* on record; it is moved and seconded that this measure *be* adopted).

The form used for the imperative mood is always the same as the first principal part. The subjunctive, once fully inflected, is so little used in modern English that we need consider only the forms for the simple present and past tenses of the verb *to be*. These are *be* for all persons in the singular and plural of the simple present and *were* for all the persons in the singular and plural of the simple past.

### Adjectives and Adverbs

Adjectives and adverbs cannot always be distinguished from each other by their form. Most adverbs end in *-ly,* but so do some adjectives

[3] For a selected list of irregular verbs, see page 466.

(*silly* and *manly,* for example). Some adverbs (*clean, far, fast, straight,* etc.) do not have *-ly,* and some have two forms, one with and one without that ending (*late-lately, loud-loudly, slow-slowly,* etc.). For these reasons, adjectives and adverbs are best recognized by the work they do in the sentence: adjectives modify nouns or pronouns; adverbs modify verbs, adjectives, or other adverbs.

When an adjective precedes the noun or pronoun it modifies (a *blue* gown), it is called an **attributive adjective.** When it both completes a verb and modifies its subject (The man is *lazy*), it is called a **predicate adjective.** Adverbs do not serve as complements, but in addition to their chief function of modifying verbs, adjectives, and adverbs, they are frequently used in the following ways:

1. As interrogative adverbs to introduce a question (*Where* were you? *When* did he go? *Why* did you say that?).

2. As sentence modifiers to modify a whole sentence rather than a single element (*Maybe* he is ill. *Incidentally,* that answer is wrong).

3. As conjunctive adverbs (or transitional connectives) to join two sentences and modify the second one (The men did not complain; they were, *however,* rather sullen for the rest of the evening. His wife was not hostile; *on the contrary,* she seemed most friendly).

**Comparison.** Modern English adjectives and adverbs have sloughed off all the inflectional endings they had in Old English except those which show **degree of comparison.** There are three such degrees: positive, comparative, and superlative.

There are three methods of indicating comparison in adjectives and adverbs: (1) by adding *-er* for the comparative and *-est* for the superlative; (2) by prefixing *more* for the comparative and *most* for the superlative; (3) by using different words for each degree. The following comparisons illustrate all three methods:

| *Positive* | *Comparative* | *Superlative* |
|---|---|---|
| strong | stronger | strongest |
| beautiful | more beautiful | most beautiful |
| good | better | best |

Of the three methods, the first two are considered regular. In general, words of one syllable take the *-er -est* endings, and words of more than two syllables use *more* and *most.* The usage in two-syllable words is divided, though words common in popular speech tend to retain *-er -est.*

The third method is called irregular comparison. Several words that are irregularly compared have the same form for adjective and adverb. Here are the most common irregular comparisons:

| Positive | Comparative | Superlative |
|---|---|---|
| bad, ill | worse | worst |
| far | farther, further | farthest, furthest |
| good, well | better | best |
| little | less, lesser | least |
| much, many | more | most |

## Prepositions

Such words as *after, around, at, behind, beside, for, in, into, of, on, to, with* are called **prepositions** when they precede a noun or pronoun and show its relation to some other word in the sentence, usually a verb, adjective, noun, or pronoun:

He is good *at* tennis. (Relates the noun *tennis* to the adjective *good.*)
They live *in* Detroit. (Relates the noun *Detroit* to the verb *live.*)
I am the head *of* the house. (Relates the nouns *head* and *house.*)

As these examples indicate, the preposition and its object (*tennis, Detroit, house*) make up a phrase, called a **prepositional phrase,** which acts as a unit in the sentence. Prepositional phrases function as modifiers of nouns and verbs and as complements:

Peace *with honor.* (Functions as adjective modifying noun *Peace.*)
They play *for money.* (Functions as adverb modifying verb *play.*)
He told *of finding them.* (Functions as complement of intransitive verb *told.*)

Since many words may be used as prepositions or as adverbs, and since prepositional phrases often act as adverbial modifiers, it is sometimes hard to decide whether a word is being used prepositionally or adverbially. Fortunately this distinction is seldom important. If it has to be made, see whether the word relates a noun or pronoun to some other word in the sentence or whether it modifies only one element, a verb. For example, in "The birds flew off," *off* indicates the direction of flight. It is therefore an adverb, similar in meaning to the adverb *away.* But in, "He fell off the ladder," *off* relates *fell* and *ladder.* It is a preposition, similar in meaning to the preposition *from.*

## Conjunctions

Conjunctions also join, but unlike prepositions, which are always part of a phrase and therefore not complete elements in a sentence, conjunctions are sentence elements and, as such, were discussed in **S1** (page 416). Their function is to connect two or more grammatical units. These units may be words, phrases, subordinate clauses, main clauses, or even sentences. Most conjunctions fall into two main classes.

Coordinating Conjunctions. These words join parallel elements by connecting two or more units of equal grammatical importance such as nouns, phrases, or clauses. Such conjunctions are *and, or, but, yet, for, as well as, both . . . and, either . . . or, neither . . . nor, whether . . . or.* Coordinating conjunctions in pairs, like the last four examples, are called **correlative conjunctions.**

Subordinating Conjunctions. These words introduce subordinate clauses and connect them with main clauses. Examples are *although, as, because, how, if, since, that, what, where, which, while,* and compounds with *ever* (*whatever,* etc.). Since subordinate clauses may come before, after, or within main clauses, the subordinating conjunction does not always come between main and subordinate clauses.

Also, certain adverbs are used to connect two sentences and thus provide a transition between them. These adverbs modify either the whole sentence which they introduce or some element in it. Examples are *accordingly, again, at the same time, consequently, furthermore, however, indeed, moreover, nevertheless, still, therefore.* Because of their double function these words are called **conjunctive adverbs.**

### Interjections

Interjections are words used at or near the beginning of a sentence to express emotion or to emphasize the content of the sentence. Examples are *Ah! Bah! Bravo! Dear me! Hurrah! Well!* These words may be used outside a sentence to form sentence fragments or minor sentences by themselves (*Good Heavens! What a mess!*) or they may be included in a sentence and separated from the rest by a comma (*Oh,* it hurts dreadfully). When so included they are absolutes — that is, they have no grammatical relationship with any element in the sentence, though they may be classified as sentence modifiers.

# G 2 | *Wrong Principal Part*

### a. Use the accepted principal part.

The use of the wrong principal part (*blowed* for *blew* or *seen* for *saw*) is often an advertisement of nonstandard speech habits. As we pointed out on page 462, the great majority of English verbs form the past tense and past participle by adding *-ed* to the first principal part. All exceptions are specifically listed in a good dictionary (see page 206). The following list contains the principal parts of irregular verbs which cause most trouble in college writing.

| *Present* | *Past* | *Past Participle* |
|---|---|---|
| am, is, are | was, were | been |
| bear | bore | borne |
| beat | beat | beaten |
| begin | began | begun |
| bite | bit | bitten |
| blow | blew | blown |
| break | broke | broken |
| bring | brought | brought |
| burst | burst | burst |
| cast | cast | cast |
| choose | chose | chosen |
| come | came | come |
| deal | dealt | dealt |
| do | did | done |
| draw | drew | drawn |
| drink | drank | drunk |
| eat | ate | eaten |
| fall | fell | fallen |
| fly | flew | flown |
| forsake | forsook | forsaken |
| freeze | froze | frozen |
| give | gave | given |
| go | went | gone |
| grow | grew | grown |
| hang [4] | hung | hung |
| have | had | had |
| know | knew | known |
| lay | laid | laid |
| lie | lay | lain |
| ride | rode | ridden |
| ring | rang (rung) | rung |
| rise | rose | risen |
| run | ran | run |
| see | saw | seen |
| shake | shook | shaken |
| shoe | shod | shod |
| shrink | shrank (shrunk) | shrunk |
| sing | sang (sung) | sung |
| sink | sank (sunk) | sunk |
| slay | slew | slain |
| slink | slunk | slunk |
| speak | spoke | spoken |

[4] Notice that the verb *to hang,* meaning execute, is regular: *hang, hanged, hanged.*

| Present | Past | Past Participle |
|---|---|---|
| spin | spun | spun |
| spring | sprang (sprung) | sprung |
| steal | stole | stolen |
| strive | strove | striven |
| swear | swore | sworn |
| swim | swam | swum |
| take | took | taken |
| teach | taught | taught |
| tear | tore | torn |
| throw | threw | thrown |
| wear | wore | worn |
| weave | wove | woven |
| win | won | won |
| write | wrote | written |

**b. Distinguish between the forms for the past tense and the past participle.**

In verb phrases the past participle, not the past tense form, should follow an auxiliary verb (is *done*, has *been*). Except when the verb is acting as an auxiliary (*had* gone, *was* crying), its past tense form is not used in combination with another verb.

| *Confusion of Forms* | *Conventional Forms* |
|---|---|
| It is *broke*. | It is *broken*. |
| These tires are *wore* out. | These tires are *worn* out. |
| He has *began* all over again. | He has *begun* all over again. |
| I *seen* him do it. | I *saw* him do it. |
| The river is *froze* solid. | The river is *frozen* solid. |
| Everybody has *went* home. | Everybody has *gone* home. |
| Have you *wrote* to him? | Have you *written* to him? |
| They *come* back yesterday. | They *came* back yesterday. |

Write out and hand in to your instructor the conventional verb form in each of the following sentences:

1. They said they had (went, gone) home.
2. I was told that you had (come, came) to an agreement.
3. Prices have (fell, fallen) considerably.
4. As soon as I had (wrote, written) the letter I mailed it.
5. They must have (chosen, chose) their own way.
6. I (seen, saw) him yesterday.
7. Landy has (run, ran) the mile several times under four minutes.
8. One of the prisoners was (hung, hanged).
9. That is the best horse I have ever (rode, ridden).
10. She is reported to have (drunk, drank) poison.
11. The wind (blew, blowed) all night.
12. I would have (swore, sworn) that he was innocent.
13. This is the third time he has (broken, broke) that arm.

14. All the tomato plants were badly (froze, frozen).
15. I would have called if I had (knew, known) you were sick.
16. I have never (saw, seen) anything so vicious.
17. After a while we (begun, began) to get tired.
18. It was a good fight. He was (beaten, beat) fairly.
19. He was (bit, bitten) by the dog.
20. The plane has (flew, flown) out of sight.

c. **Distinguish between the uses and forms of** *lie, lay, rise, raise, sit, set.*

The principal parts of these verbs are:

| Present | Present Participle | Past | Past Participle |
|---------|--------------------|------|-----------------|
| lie     | lying              | lay  | lain            |
| lay     | laying             | laid | laid            |
| rise    | rising             | rose | risen           |
| raise   | raising            | raised | raised        |
| sit     | sitting            | sat  | sat             |
| set     | setting            | set  | set             |

As grouped above, these verbs can be seen to be three pairs, each pair having principal parts which are similar, though not the same, in form and general meaning. The chief difference in each pair is that the first verb is intransitive, the second transitive; that is, the first needs no complement to complete the action of the verb; the second does need a complement. Thus, whether we *lay* a rug, *raise* an alarm, or *set* a bone, we always *lay, raise,* or *set something.*[5] But we never *lie, rise,* or *sit* anything. Determining the accepted form, therefore, depends on the answers to two questions: (1) Does the sentence require the transitive or the intransitive verb? (2) What are the principal parts of the required verb?

In the examples that follow, the unacceptable forms at the left are revised at the right.

| *Unacceptable* | *Explanation* | *Accepted* |
|----------------|---------------|------------|
| We *laid* breathless with suspense. | *The sentence contains no complement; therefore the intransitive verb is wanted. The past form of* lie *is* lay. | We *lay* breathless with suspense. |
| It was *setting* on the table. | *No complement; therefore intransitive form* sitting *is required.* | It was *sitting* on the table. |
| They have *lain* the carpet. | *Carpet is a complement; therefore transitive* laid *is required.* | They have *laid* the carpet. |

[5] Notice, however, that *The sun sets early now* is an exception to this generalization. In this sentence *sets* is used intransitively.

| *Unacceptable* | *Explanation* | *Accepted* |
|---|---|---|
| It has been *laying* there all night. | *No complement; therefore intransitive* lying *is required.* | It has been *lying* there all night. |
| After a while he *raised* up and walked to the bench. | *No complement. Intransitive* rose *is required.* | After a while he *rose* and walked to the bench. |

Write out and hand in to your instructor the conventional verb form in each of the following sentences:

1. They were (sitting, setting) the chairs in a circle.
2. The hat was (lying, laying) in the corner.
3. We (lay, laid) the money on the counter and left.
4. We (lay, laid) on the pier and dozed.
5. I have (laid, lain) out your new suit.
6. I would like you to (rise, raise) my wages.
7. Go out and (rise, raise) the flag.
8. Finally, the curtain (raised, rose).
9. They (raised, rose) the curtain promptly.
10. I could (sit, set) here all day.
11. It was (sitting, setting) there a minute ago.
12. (Sit, set) down and rest for a while.
13. (Sit, set) the book on the table.
14. These tools have been left (lying, laying) in the rain.
15. They were (laying, lying) in wait for us.
16. He (raised, rose) himself on his elbow.
17. (Sit, set) up and take this.
18. She has (laid, lain) down for a rest.
19. Clothes were (lying, laying) all over the room.
20. He is out (rising, raising) the money.

# G 3  Tense Forms

## Use of Tenses

In theory, verbs are inflected to show the time at which an action occurs. In practice, the tense of an English verb sometimes has little relation to the time of the action. The present tense may refer to past, present, or future actions, or to actions that run through past, present, and future, as the following sentences show:

While Sharkey *is claiming* a foul, Dempsey *knocks* him out. (Tense, present; time, 1927.)

This summer he finally *gets* a chance at the title. (Tense, present; time, future.)

At the moment he *objects*. (Tense, present; time, present.)

History always *repeats* itself. (Tense, present; time, past, present, and future.)

Moreover, English has ways of indicating time by idiom rather than by tense. For example, in the following sentences the events have not yet occurred, yet not once is a future tense used. The "progressive" present, various uses of the infinitive, and adverbs of time are used instead.

I am going to do it tomorrow.
We are to see them next week.
They are to be married this summer.
I expect to hear from him in a day or two.
Be sure to call me when you come to town.

The uses of the six basic tenses are as follows:

**Simple Present.** The chief uses of the simple present tense are to indicate present action, action which occurs at all times (the timeless present), and past action which, for dramatic purposes, is described as occurring in the present (historical present).

Present time:

Bill *is* absent; his father *is* ill.

Timeless present:

The rain *falls* alike on the just and the unjust.
Nature *abhors* a vacuum.
The sum of the angles in a triangle *equals* 180 degrees.

Historical present:

Finally, Caesar *makes* his decision. He *gives* the order, and his troops *begin* the fateful march to the Rubicon.

**Present Perfect.** The present perfect tense indicates that the action has recently been completed.

She *has broken* her engagement.
They *have built* a new house.
He *has moved* to New York.

**Simple Past.** The simple past tense is used to indicate an action which may have occurred at any time in the past. It therefore is not so close to the present as the present perfect.

She *broke* her engagement.
They *built* a new house.
He *moved* to New York.

Notice that the use of an adverb of time along with the simple past tense achieves the same effect as the use of the present perfect:

She broke her engagement yesterday.
They recently built a new house.

**Past Perfect.** The past perfect is used to indicate that, of two past actions, one took place before the other.

He *had been* sick only a few days when he died.
I *had left* before she arrived.
We *had expected* little, but we received nothing.

**Simple Future.** The simple future is used to indicate an action still to occur.

He *will sail* tomorrow.
They *will try* to persuade you.

**Future Perfect.** The future perfect is used to indicate that, of two future actions, one will occur before the other.

By the time you get there they *will have gone.*
He *will have spent* all his allowance by the end of the week.

The inflection (conjugation) of the indicative mood of typical regular and irregular verbs is given below:

| | Regular verb, *to talk* | | Irregular verb, *to write* | |
|---|---|---|---|---|
| | *Singular* | *Plural* | *Singular* | *Plural* |
| *Simple Present* | 1. I talk | 1. we talk | 1. I write | 1. we write |
| | 2. you talk | 2. you talk | 2. you write | 2. you write |
| | 3. he talks | 3. they talk | 3. he writes | 3. they write |

*Method of forming:* Use first principal part unchanged for all forms except to add *s* in third person singular.

| | | | | |
|---|---|---|---|---|
| *Present Perfect* | 1. have talked | 1. have talked | 1. have written | 1. have written |
| | 2. have talked | 2. have talked | 2. have written | 2. have written |
| | 3. *has* talked | 3. have talked | 3. *has* written | 3. have written |

*Method of forming:* Add past participle to simple present tense of verb *to have.* Except for third person singular, forms are the same throughout.

|  |  |  |  |  |
|--|--|--|--|--|
| *Simple* | 1. talked | 1. talked | 1. wrote | 1. wrote |
| *Past* | 2. talked | 2. talked | 2. wrote | 2. wrote |
|  | 3. talked | 3. talked | 3. wrote | 3. wrote |

*Method of forming:* Third principal part unchanged throughout.

|  |  |  |  |  |
|--|--|--|--|--|
| *Past* | 1. had talked | 1. had talked | 1. had written | 1. had written |
| *Perfect* | 2. had talked | 2. had talked | 2. had written | 2. had written |
|  | 3. had talked | 3. had talked | 3. had written | 3. had written |

*Method of forming:* Add past participle to simple past tense of *to have.*

|  |  |  |  |  |
|--|--|--|--|--|
| *Simple* | 1. will talk | 1. will talk | 1. will write | 1. will write |
| *Future* | 2. will talk | 2. will talk | 2. will write | 2. will write |
|  | 3. will talk | 3. will talk | 3. will write | 3. will write |

*Method of forming:* Add first principal part to *will.* In formal usage *shall* is sometimes used instead of *will* in the first person singular and plural.[6]

| *Future* | will have talked (same form in all persons and numbers). |
|--|--|
| *Perfect* | will have written (same form in all persons and numbers). |

*Method of forming:* Add past participle to *will have.* In formal usage *shall* is commonly used instead of *will* in the first person singular and plural.[6]

## a. Avoid illogical or unconventional sequence of tenses.

### 1. Keep the tenses of main clauses consistent.

Do not shift needlessly from present to past or from historical present to simple past.

| *Inconsistent* | *Explanation* | *Consistent* |
|--|--|--|
| She laughed, and I asked her what she knew about him. She *laughs* again, this time much louder. | *In the first sentence all verbs are in the past tense, but* laughs *is present. There is no reason for the shift.* | She laughed, and I asked her what she knew about him. She *laughed* again, this time much louder. |
| For five rounds the young challenger danced and ducked and jabbed and piled up points. Then the champion found an opening – and Bam! The fight *is* over. | *All the verbs except the last are in the past tense. The last sentence shifts to historical present tense. Either that tense or the simple past should have been used throughout.* | For five rounds the young challenger danced and ducked and jabbed and piled up points. Then the champion found an opening – and Bam! The fight *was* over. |

[6] For comment on the *shall-will* distinction, see page **476**.

**2. Keep the tense of a subordinate clause in logical sequence with that of the main clause.**

| Illogical Sequence | Explanation | Logical Sequence |
|---|---|---|
| They *have made* so much money last year that they bought a second store. | *The present perfect* (have made) *suggests a more recent action than the simple past* (bought); *it is illogical to use the present perfect for the earlier action.* | They *made* so much money last year that they *have bought* a second store. |
| Before I was introduced to her I *heard* rumors of her unsavory reputation. | *Since the rumors came before the introduction, the past perfect tense should be used in the main clause.* | Before I was introduced to her I *had heard* rumors of her unsavory reputation. |
| By that time they will be married and *will have gone* on their honeymoon. | *Will have gone is future perfect and implies a time preceding that of the simple future. Since people usually get married before they go on honeymoons, the tenses at the left reverse the natural order of events. Either revision at the right is logical.* | By that time they *will have been married* and *will be* on their honeymoon.<br>(or)<br>. . . *will have been married* and *will have gone* on their honeymoon. |

**3. In converting direct discourse to indirect discourse observe the conventional change in tense.**

Direct discourse reports the actual words of the speaker, and quoted verbs should be in the tense the speaker used. When direct discourse is converted to indirect discourse, the tenses of the original quotation are, whenever possible, pushed one stage further into the past. Thus an original present tense form becomes past and an original past becomes past perfect. Since there is no tense more past than past perfect, an original verb in that tense does not change.

| Direct Discourse | Explanation | Indirect Discourse |
|---|---|---|
| He said, "I *want* to read that novel." | *Change simple present to simple past.* | He said that he *wanted* to read that novel. |
| He said, "I *wanted* to read that novel yesterday." | *Change simple past to past perfect.* | He said that he *had wanted* to read that novel yesterday. |

| Direct Discourse | Explanation | Indirect Discourse |
|---|---|---|
| He said, "I *had wanted* to read that novel until I *saw* the movie." | *Leave the verbs as they are. There is no way to make* had wanted *more past than it is, and to change* saw *to* had seen *would destroy the sequence of tenses.* | He said that he *had wanted* to read that novel until he *saw* the movie. |

The following examples contrast faulty and accepted conversion from direct to indirect discourse.

| Direct Discourse | Faulty Conversion | Accepted Conversion |
|---|---|---|
| I said, "He *is* a good financial risk." | I said he *is* a good financial risk. | I said he *was* a good financial risk. |
| I asked, "*Have* you *consulted* your physician?" | I asked if he *consulted* his physician. | I asked if he *had consulted* his physician. |

**4. Observe the conventional tense relationships between verbs and verbals.**

The tense of a verbal is not determined by the tense of the verb in the main clause. Regardless of the tense of the verb, a present participle is used to express an action occurring at the same time as that of the verb. A perfect participle expresses time before that of the verb. A present infinitive indicates the same time or a time later than that of the verb. A perfect infinitive suggests time before that of the verb.

| | |
|---|---|
| *Rounding* the last turn he *was* ahead by two yards. | The present participle (*rounding*) and the past tense verb refer to simultaneous actions. |
| *Having finished* housecleaning she *washed* her hair. | The perfect participle (*having finished*) refers to an action before that of the verb (*washed*). |
| I *tried to telephone* you. | The verb (*tried*) and the present infinitive (*to telephone*) refer to actions occurring at the same time. |
| I *expect to hear* from him tomorrow. | The expectation is now; the hearing has yet to occur. Therefore the present infinitive refers to a time later than that of the verb. |
| They *are reported to have adopted* a child. | The perfect infinitive points to a time before the reporting. |

| Unconventional Sequence | Explanation | Conventional Sequence |
|---|---|---|
| *Asking* the blessing, we began to eat. | *Since the blessing was asked before the eating began, the perfect participle is required.* | *Having asked* the blessing, we began to eat. |
| *Having faced* the spectators, the referee signalled a holding penalty. | *Since both actions took place at the same time, the present participle is required.* | *Facing* the spectators, the referee signalled a holding penalty. |
| We meant to *have told* you earlier. | *The perfect infinitive suggests that the telling occurred before the intention. The present infinitive is the required form.* | We meant *to tell* you earlier. |
| I am sorry *to overlook* that fact. | *Since the overlooking occurred before the regret, the perfect infinitive should be used.* | I am sorry *to have overlooked* that fact. |

Revise the following sentences to correct any illogical sequence of tenses:

1. There is little chance of promotion in that job unless you had a college degree.
2. While the outlook wasn't hopeless, it is discouraging.
3. We wanted to have reported the robbery earlier, but we thought we had better wait until we are sure.
4. Before I arrived they had a serious quarrel.
5. I asked if she has seen him recently.
6. She answered, "I had not seen him for more than a year."
7. We wondered what they are thinking now.
8. Finishing the job, he put away his tools.
9. For years now they had been good friends but they disagree more and more frequently.
10. He asked if I consider him a good teacher.
11. I said that I thought he is better than average.
12. Meeting Bill's wife I have asked her when he would be home.
13. She said that he had been coming next Saturday.
14. I intended to have ignored the gossip, but I could not.
15. They sat up all night studying, having hoped to get at least a B on the final examination.
16. They have worked so hard on the farm that they lost weight.
17. Before I heard her story I thought she was the first to give offense.
18. Committing himself to this extent, John could not be indifferent about the trial.
19. I asked if she bought the car she had been talking about.
20. I would have liked to have seen that movie.

**b. In the future tense indicate either by context or by the appropriate auxiliary whether you imply simple futurity or determination.**

## 1. Shall–Will

Whether to use *shall* or *will* in the future tense is a vexed question, partly because usage is divided, and partly because many people have an allegiance to the *shall-will* distinction that transcends the evidence of usage. Hence teachers and textbooks (including this one) often devote more attention to this question than it warrants.

The distinction is generally stated as follows: when the verb is intended to express only the idea that an action will occur in the future (simple futurity) *shall* is used in the first person, singular and plural, and *will* in the other two persons (I *shall* write tomorrow; they *will* probably be home next week). When the verb is intended to express determination, resolve, or compulsion, as well as futurity, *will* is used in the first person and *shall* in the other two (We *will* go regardless of the consequences; they *shall* pay for their negligence).

Although many careful users of English observe this distinction, many equally careful ones do not. For example, Winston Churchill, speaking on a most formal occasion (an address in the House of Commons after the evacuation of Dunkirk in World War II) consistently used *shall* in the first person to express determination:

> . . . we shall not flag or fail. We shall go on to the end, we shall fight in France, we shall fight in the seas and oceans, we shall fight with growing confidence and growing strength in the air, we shall defend our island, whatever the cost may be, we shall fight on the beaches, we shall fight on the landing-grounds, we shall fight in the fields and in the streets, we shall fight in the hills; we shall never surrender . . .[7]

The distinction between *shall* and *will* is further obscured by the following facts:

1. American, English, Scottish, and Irish uses of these auxiliaries sometimes differ, and the "rule" tends to emphasize English usage at the expense of the others.
2. The context is often a better clue to the writer's purpose than is the form of the auxiliary. In speech the distinction between simple and emphatic future is indicated more by the speaker's stress on the auxiliary verb than by its form.
3. Both simple and emphatic futurity are often expressed by idiomatic constructions rather than by a future tense (see page 470).
4. *Shall* is predominantly used in statements of laws (Congress *shall* have the power . . . ), in military commands (The regiment *shall*

[7] From *Their Finest Hour*, by Winston S. Churchill. Copyright, 1949, by Houghton Mifflin Company.

proceed as directed), and in formal directives (All branch offices *shall* report weekly to the home office).

5. In questions, *shall* is often used in the third person as well as in the first ("Where *shall* he be tomorow?" But also, "Where *will* he be tomorow?").
6. The popularity of the contracted forms (*I'll, she'll,* etc.) in the conversation of educated speakers tends to weaken, or even nullify, any distinction between *shall* and *will* in speech, and these colloquial contractions are often carried over into informal writing.

In view of this diversity of usage, any concise statement is bound to oversimplify, but the following summary should fit most of the needs of American college students:

1. To express simple futurity only, *will* is used in the second and third persons and either *will* or *shall* in the first person, *shall* being the more formal. *Shall* in the second and third person is not acceptable when the sentence implies futurity only.
2. To express determination, resolve, or compulsion, *shall* is used in the second and third persons and either *shall* or *will* in the first person. But if the context clearly implies determination rather than futurity only, the form of auxiliary becomes less significant.

## 2. Should—Would

These words are used as the past forms of *shall* and *will* respectively and follow the same pattern (I *would* [*should*] be glad to see him tomorrow; he *would* welcome your ideas on the subject; we *would* [*should*] never consent to such an arrangement). They are also used to convert a *shall* or *will* in direct discourse into indirect discourse.

| *Direct Discourse* | *Indirect Discourse* |
|---|---|
| "Shall I try to arrange it?" he asked. | He asked if he *should* try to arrange it. |
| I said, "They *will* need the money." | I said that they *would* need the money. |

In addition, *should* and *would* have specialized uses:

*Should* is used:

1. To express obligation, necessity, or duty (I really *should* go to her tea; the two sides of the equation *should* balance).
2. To express probability (She *should* be home by then; these tires *should* be good for another 5,000 miles).
3. In a subordinate clause, to express a supposition (If I *should* be late, will you hold dinner for me?).

*Would* is used:

1. To express a customary action in the past (During those years he *would* write once or twice a year and send a card at Christmas).
2. As a synonym for "were willing" in conditional clauses (He could do it, if he *would*).
3. As a polite form in requests or commands (*Would* you mind making three copies of this letter?).

c. **Avoid the overuse of the auxiliary *would*.**

Repeating *would* in a compound sentence is often awkward or wordy.

| *Awkward* | *Revised* |
|---|---|
| If they *would have done* that earlier, there *would have been* no trouble. | If they *had done* or (*Had* they *done*) that earlier, there *would have been* no trouble. |
| He *would have been nominated*, if he *would have been* at the meeting. | If he *had been* (or *Had* he *been*) at the meeting, he *would have been nominated*. |
| We *would want* some assurance that they *would accept* before we *would make* such a proposal. | We *would want* some assurance of their acceptance before we *made* such a proposal. |
| If I *would be* in your place I *would apologize*. | If I *were* in your place, I *would apologize*. |

d. **Use the subjunctive form of *to be* in conditional clauses contrary to fact.**

This use of the subjunctive is discussed on page 462. The last revised example in c above illustrates the construction. Other examples:

If she *were* my daughter, I would spank her. (She is not the speaker's daughter.) *Were* I ten years younger, I'd propose to her. (He is not ten years younger.) What would Lincoln say about that if he *were* alive today? (He is not alive.)

Some of the following sentences are quite acceptable; others contain faulty or undesirable verb forms. On a sheet of paper write down the number of each sentence. Opposite that number place a check ( ✓ ) if the verb forms need no revision. If they do need revision, write the appropriate forms. Then hand in the sheet to your instructor.

1. I am sure you shall be very happy together.
2. He said he shall be home late for dinner.
3. They shall probably get here right after you leave.
4. It shall be the duty of the treasurer to collect dues, to keep an accurate record of all monies received and spent, and to submit a monthly report of the club's finances.
5. If I would miss that bus I'll come on the next one.

6. Every night when I left the office she would be waiting for me.

7. If they would have come, the family reunion would have been complete.

8. If I would have difficulty, may I call you?

9. Was there any alternative, I should refuse.

10. I think that you should know within a week.

11. It should be awkward, would they refuse.

12. Was I the judge, I'd be lenient in a case like that.

13. If I would have known you were coming I would have baked a cake.

14. It is a safe prediction that they shall feel ashamed of themselves tomorrow.

15. The law reads that no one shall be placed in jeopardy twice for the same offense.

16. She said that she will be busy for the rest of this week.

17. When they were children they should be at our house most of the time.

18. If you should do it, I should be grateful.

19. There should still be some money in the account.

20. It would be a relief, would they be pleasant for a change.

# G 4 | *Case*

CASE IS A SYSTEM of inflection to show the relation of nouns and pronouns to other words in the sentence. English has three cases: *subjective*, *possessive*, and *objective*. In general, a word is in the subjective case when it acts as a subject, in the objective case when it acts as an object, and in the possessive case when it modifies a noun (*his* bicycle).

English nouns, pronouns, and adjectives were once fully inflected to show case, but word order and idiomatic constructions have largely replaced case endings in modern English. Adjectives are no longer inflected; nouns are inflected only in the possessive case (the boy's cap); only pronouns (and chiefly the personal pronouns) still make any considerable use of case forms. The study of case in modern English, therefore, is pretty much restricted to the case of pronouns.

**a. The case of a pronoun is determined by its function in its own clause.**

If a pronoun is the subject of its clause, it takes the subjective case; if it is an object (a complement receiving the action of the verb or following a preposition), it takes the objective case; if it is a modifier, it takes the possessive case. There are two modifications of this practice: (1) a pronoun subject of an infinitive takes the objective case (I want *him to see* it); and (2) the complement of the verb *to be* takes the subjective case in formal writing (It was not *I* who said that).

The general convention stated above may be broken down as follows:

*Pronouns take the subjective case when:*

1. They are subjects of verbs (*I think* that *he missed*).
2. They are in apposition with subjects (Three men — Fred, Roy and *I* — were elected delegates).
3. They are complements of the verb *to be* (I am sure it *was he*).

*Pronouns take the objective case when:*

1. They are objects of verbs (Mother *likes her*).
2. They are objects of prepositions (They pointed *at me*).
3. They are in apposition with objects (They gave *us* — Dave and *me* — the money).
4. They are subjects or objects of infinitives (I want *her to go.* Wouldn't you like to be *me?*).

*Pronouns take the possessive case when:*

1. They modify a noun or a pronoun (Those are *my* six *children;* this is *his one*).
2. They precede and modify a gerund (What's wrong with *his swimming? His winning* was a surprise).

The following sentences illustrate the general convention that the case of a pronoun is determined by its function in its own clause:

> Please don't misunderstand *me.* (Objective case, object of *don't misunderstand.*)
> Try to be nice to *her.* (Objective case, object of preposition *to.*)
> I asked *him* to write. (Objective case, subject of infinitive *to write.*)
> Find out *who* did it. (Subjective case, subject of *did.*)
> *Whoever* wrote that was a genius. (Subjective case, subject of *wrote.*)
> Tell *whoever* will listen. (Subjective case, subject of *will listen.*)
> I wish it were *he.* (Subjective case, complement of *were.*)
> I like *his* dancing. (Possessive case, modifier of gerund *dancing.*)
> We can't stop *his* drinking. (Possessive case, modifier of gerund *drinking.*)
> The terrible thing is *his* having lost all that money. (Possessive case, modifier of gerund *having lost.*)
> *His* hopes are shattered. (Possessive case, modifier of noun *hopes.*)
> *He whom I* love is dead. (He, subject of *is dead;* I, subject of *love;* whom, object of *love.*)

**b. Most errors in case occur in a few constructions.**

In general, errors in case occur for two reasons: (1) because the construction is such that the student does not readily see the function of a pronoun; and (2) because the case which is inappropriate in writing is so often used in speech that the colloquial form seems more natural than the more formal one. Often these two reasons merge. That is, the construction requires more deliberate analysis than speakers have time to give it and so begets a colloquial usage which competes with the formal one.

The following constructions create most of the "case" troubles in college composition:

1. *Parenthetical constructions.* Any construction which interrupts the normal pattern of a clause is likely to obscure the function of a pronoun in the clause. In the following sentence it is quite clear that *who* is the subject of *won* and takes the subjective case:

That is the man *who* won the prize.

But if we introduce a parenthetical clause — *they say* — into the original sentence, the function of *who* becomes less clear:

That is the man who they say won the prize.

There is now a tendency to assume that *who* is the object of *say* and to put it in the objective case. But grammatically its function has not changed. The parenthetical clause is an absolute and has no grammatical relationship to any element in the sentence. Yet the faulty analysis suggested by the interrupting construction often leads to the selection of the wrong case form, as in the sentences at the left below.

| Wrong Case | Explanation | Correct Case |
|---|---|---|
| The man *whom* they think did it has been arrested. | *Pronoun is subject of* did *and should be subjective.* | The man *who* they think did it has been arrested. |
| A girl *whom* I hear is her sister is being sought. | *Pronoun is subject of* is *and should be subjective.* | A girl *who* I hear is her sister is being sought. |
| She introduced me to a man *whom* she said was her employer. | *Pronoun is subject of* was *and should be subjective.* | She introduced me to a man *who* she said was her employer. |
| He is the general *whom* the reporters agree was most popular with the troops. | *Pronoun is subject of* was *and should be subjective.* | He is the general *who* the reporters agree was most popular with the troops. |

2. *Complement of "to be."* In formal usage the complement of the verb *to be* takes the subjective case (It is *I.* Was it *she?*). In colloquial usage the objective is more common in the first person (It's *me*). The

choice, therefore, between *It is I* and *It's me* is not a choice between standard and nonstandard usage but between formal and colloquial styles. This choice seldom has to be made in college writing, since the expression, in whatever form it is used, is essentially a spoken rather than a written sentence. Its use in writing occurs chiefly in dialogue, and then the form chosen should be appropriate to the speaker.

The use of the objective case in the third person (That was *her*) is less common even in colloquial usage and should probably be avoided in college writing except when dialogue requires it. The use of the objective case in a clause containing a subjunctive form of *to be* is especially to be avoided, because the subjunctive is a fairly formal construction, and the contrast between formal and colloquial usage points up the inappropriateness of the pronoun form:

| *Inappropriate* | *Appropriate* |
|---|---|
| If I were *him,* I should resign. | If I were *he,* I should resign. |
| Would you do it, if you were *her?* | Would you do it, if you were *she?* |

But notice that when the infinitive form of *to be* is used, its subject and complement both take the objective case:

> She wants *me* to be there. (Pronoun is subject of infinitive.)
> I wouldn't want to be *her.* (Pronoun is complement of infinitive.)

**3.** *"Whoever" and "whomever."* These two pronouns follow the rule that the case of a pronoun is determined by its function in its own clause, but because they often follow a transitive verb or the preposition *to,* they are often mistaken as objects when they are not.

| *Confused* | *Explanation* | *Revised* |
|---|---|---|
| Give it to *whom-ever* wants it. | *Pronoun is subject of* wants; *its whole clause is the object of* to. | Give it to *who-ever* wants it. |
| Invite *whomever* will come. | *Pronoun is subject of* will come; *whole clause is object of* invite. | Invite *whoever* will come. |
| Send it to *whom-ever* you think would like it. | *Pronoun is subject of* would like. *The preposition* to *and the absolute* you think *do not affect its case.* | Send it to *who-ever* you think would like it. |

**4.** *Comparative with "than" or "as."* The case of a pronoun following *than* or *as* in a comparison often causes difficulty. Such comparisons as

He is at least ten years older than *she*.
I am about twenty pounds lighter than *he*.
The judge liked us better than *them*.

are considered as contracted statements which in full would be

He is at least ten years older than *she is*.
I am about twenty pounds lighter than *he is*.
The judge liked us better than *he liked them*.

*Than* and *as* are connectives joining two clauses, and the pronouns are the subjects of the italicized clauses. The convention is that the pronoun in the contracted comparison takes the case it would have if the comparison were fully expanded. That is, it takes the subjective case if it is the subject of the unexpressed verb, and the objective case if it is the object of that verb.

There is often a difference between colloquial and formal usage in such constructions. In colloquial usage, *than* and *as* tend to be interpreted as prepositions, and the pronouns are often in the objective case even when they are actually subjects. Unless the assignment permits a colloquial style, the more formal usage is expected in college writing.

5. *Possessive with a gerund.* We have seen (page 480) that a pronoun preceding and modifying a gerund takes the possessive case (I am opposed to *his going*). In a formal style, a noun modifying a gerund also takes the possessive case (Imagine *John's saying* that!). Colloquial usage, which usually ignores this convention and puts the modifier in the objective case (Imagine *John* saying that!), has influenced both speech and informal writing.

The following sentences further illustrate the use of the possessive case when a noun or a pronoun modifies a gerund:

There is really no excuse for *his failing* the course.
I resent *David's trying* to influence her.
We are embarrassed by *their* continual *begging*.
They object to *my having dated* you.
*Mary's interrupting* annoys him.
*Their believing* that doesn't surprise me.

In observing this convention it is necessary to distinguish between a verbal used as a gerund and one used as a modifier. For example, in *Can you imagine him kissing a girl?* the event to be imagined is *him* in the act of *kissing* a girl. *Him* is considered the object of the verb, and *kissing* a modifier of the object. This distinction, it must be admitted, is often subtle. The following contrast may illustrate it:

| Verbal as a Modifier | Verbal as a Gerund |
|---|---|
| It was painful to see *him weeping*. | *Her weeping* is a triumph of art over nature. |
| We found *him sleeping*. | He gave up Sunday-morning golf because it interfered with *his sleeping*. |
| I want to see *him killing* the hog. | *His killing* that hog was a slick job of butchering. |
| You will see *them working* till all hours of the night. | We must put a stop to *their working* till all hours of the night. |

## Exercises

**A.** In the following sentences some of the italicized case forms are conventionally acceptable in college writing and some are not. Write out and turn in to your instructor a report on the acceptability of each form. If the acceptable case has been used, merely write the word "Acceptable" opposite the number of the sentence. If the wrong form has been used, write the acceptable form opposite the number of the sentence and justify your revision.

1. Between you and *I*, she is asking for trouble.
2. I think I am a little older than *him*.
3. Was it really for mother and *I*?
4. She wants you and *I* to get married.
5. I am as much to blame as *her*.
6. All the men went fishing, *him* along with the others.
7. A group of *we* girls are planning a party.
8. I want *him* to be notified.
9. Can you imitate *his* singing?
10. I would like to catch *him* doing that.
11. The instructor was disappointed by *us* doing so badly.
12. Helen, *who* I dislike, is coming with her.
13. *Whom* can you imagine did such a thing?
14. He was the kind of man *whom* everybody said would have made a wonderful father.
15. There is a girl *whom* I admire.
16. *Whoever* you are, come out.
17. Tell it to *whomever* will listen.
18. I shall marry *whoever* I please.
19. We can play as well as *them*.
20. *His* refusing our offer was a serious disappointment.
21. We were all relieved by *him* leaving early.
22. They asked the Johnsons as well as *we* to come.
23. He means *us* two, you and *I*.

24. Communism does not appeal to *we* Americans.
25. The prize should go to *whoever* has the highest score.
26. That is the man *who* they say used to be married to her.
27. There are few men more capable than *he*.
28. That was the last of *me* running for office.
29. If you were *me*, would you take this job?
30. Select *whomever* you wish.
31. She does not care *who* she gets the money from.
32. I don't know whether I can do it as well as *him*.
33. We had trouble finding out *whom* the thief was.
34. Let's keep this a secret between *we* two.
35. He said he liked us both, but *me* better than *her*.

**B.** Rewrite the following selection to revise any case forms unacceptable in college writing:

When Dude Nissen turned down the nomination there was nothing for *we* sophomores to do but find someone *who* we could count on to represent our interests and *who* the sorority girls would vote for. Ted Newsome seemed to be our best bet. He was a good speaker, and we had no doubts about *him* attending meetings regularly or about his following our advice. It was generally agreed that it was *him* who was most responsible for the success of the freshman formal last year, and the fact of *him* dating June Hallison would win sorority votes, both for him and for *whomever* served as his running mate. His grades were so low that there was some risk of *him* not being eligible next semester, but he was the only man *who* we could win with; so we agreed to nominate him.

---

# G 5     *Agreement (Subject–Verb)*

---

IN GRAMMAR the term **agreement** is used to describe the relationship between the inflectional forms of different elements within a sentence. When two related elements (subject and verb, pronoun and antecedent) show the same kind of inflection, they are said to agree. Thus a verb agrees with its subject if its form shows the same number and person as the subject. A pronoun agrees with its antecedent if both show the same gender, number, and person.

*The fundamental convention of agreement is that the inflectional endings of two related elements should agree as far as possible.* Since different parts of speech are inflected for different purposes (verbs for person, number, and tense, not for gender or case; nouns for number and possessive case, not for person or tense), related elements can agree only in those qualities which they have in common. If they agree in these, complete agreement is taken for granted. Therefore, the general rule might be more usefully stated in the negative: *There should be no grammatical disagreement between the inflectional endings of related elements within a sentence.*

**Verbs agree with their subjects in number and person.**

A singular subject requires a singular form of the verb, a plural subject a plural form. If the subject is a personal pronoun, inflected for person, the verb agrees in person. If the subject is a noun it is always considered to be in the third person, and takes the third person form of the verb. The following sentences illustrate this agreement:

> *I am* late. (Subject first person singular; verb first person singular.)
> *He is* sorry. (Subject third person singular; verb third person singular.)
> The *man works* slowly. (*Works* is third person singular to agree with *man.*)

Most troubles in agreement arise in the constructions that follow.

**1. When two or more singular subjects are connected by *and,* a plural form of the verb is required.**

> He and his brother *are* identical twins.
> Tom, Joe, Graff, and I *make* a good foursome.
> Both the bull and the calf *have won* prizes.
> A fool and his money *are* soon *parted.*

There are three modifications of this convention. First, when each of the singular subjects is considered individually, the singular form of the verb is used. This usage is most frequent after *each* or *every:*

> Here, every man and woman *works* for the good of the organization.
> Each boy and girl *makes* a separate report.

Second, when the two singular subjects refer to the same person or thing, the singular verb is used.

> My wife and boss *has* something to say about that.
> Grapejuice and ginger ale *is* a good drink.

Third, mathematical computations may take either a singular or a plural verb.

> Five and five *is* ten.　　　　　　Two times three *is* six.
> Five and five *are* ten.　　　　　Two times three *are* six.

**2.** When two or more singular subjects are connected by *or, nor,* or *but,* a singular form of the verb is required.

> Mason or Dixon *is* to be elected.
> Neither Bill nor Hugh *has* a chance.
> Not Sue but Betty *was invited.*
> Neither the Giants nor the Dodgers *is* the team to win.
> Not only his wife but even his mother *finds* him selfish.

**3.** When one of two subjects connected by *or, nor,* or *but* is singular and the other is plural, the verb agrees in number with the nearer one.

> Neither Lewis nor his lawyers *were* there.
> Not only the boys but also their father *encourages* it.

**4.** When two subjects connected by *or* or *nor* differ in person, the verb agrees with the nearer.

> Jean or you *are* to go.
> Either Red or I *have won.*

When conforming to this rule creates an awkward sentence, we usually restate the idea in a form which is both correct and natural. For example, rather than write

> Neither Mary nor I am to blame.
> You or he is the leading contender.

we would restate these sentences as follows:

> Mary is not to blame; neither am I.
> You and he are the leading contenders.

**5.** A singular subject followed immediately by *as well as, in addition to, including, no less than, with, together with,* or a similar construction, requires a singular verb.

> The husband as well as the wife *needs* advice.
> The coach together with his assistants *was praised.*
> The president no less than the secretary *is* responsible.
> The store in addition to the farm *was sold.*

Because this convention sometimes seems illogical (since more than one person or thing is included in the subject phrase), there is a tendency to avoid the construction altogether and to write:

> Both the husband and the wife *need* advice.
> The coach and his assistants *were praised.*
> The president *is* just as responsible as the secretary.
> The store and the farm *were sold.*

**6. A singular subject followed by a plural modifier requires a singular verb.**

> The *attitude* of these men *is* definitely hostile.
> The *leader* of the rebel forces *has* been captured.
> *One* of the women in the back row *looks* sick.
> A *list* of the names of all survivors *is* available.

In speech, a plural modifier immediately before a verb often leads to a plural verb. This is particularly true in a sentence like the fourth above, in which the subject is followed by a long modifier containing two plural nouns. This colloquial usage has less justification in writing, since the more deliberate nature of writing and revision makes it easier to use the conventional form.

**7. Such indefinite pronouns as** *anybody, anyone, each, either, everybody, neither, nobody, no one,* **and** *somebody* **generally require a singular verb.**

> *Anybody* who does that *is* just reckless.
> *Does* anyone want to split this with me?
> *Each* of them *makes* fifty dollars a week.
> *Somebody has been using* my shaving soap.
> *Nobody* in town *admits* seeing him.
> *Everybody* does as he pleases.

**8. The pronouns** *any* **and** *none* **take either singular or plural verbs.**

> *Are any* of you *going* to the show?
> *Any* of these times *is* satisfactory.
> *None works* so faithfully as he.
> *None are expected* from that district.

In general, the preference is for the singular verb after these pronouns in a formal style, and for the plural verb in an informal one. Either form, however, is generally acceptable in college writing.

**9. When the subject is a relative pronoun, the verb agrees with the antecedent of that pronoun.**

> He is one of the *men who act* as advisers.
> This is one of those *problems which have* two solutions.
> *One* of the *girls who sing* in the choir *is being married.*

The last example is rather tricky. Its construction may be better seen if we enclose the modifier in parentheses:

> *One* (of the *girls who sing* in the choir) *is being married.*

**10. When a sentence is introduced by the expletive** *There* **or the adverb** *Here,* **the verb agrees with the following subject, not with the introductory word.**

> Here *is* your *money.*
> Here *are* the *receipts.*

There *are* no second *chances.*
There *are* a *man* and a *boy* in that boat.
*Is* there a *chance* of his winning?
*Were* there many *people* present?

This convention is not strictly observed in spoken usage, because we often begin a sentence with an expletive followed by a single subject and then add more subjects before we finish the sentence. For example:

Did you see anyone there that I know?
Well, there was Joe Botts, and Ray Carrell, and Dan Snader.

In speech, we cannot conveniently revise the verb to take care of these additional subjects. But we do have such an opportunity in writing, and hence a plural verb is more common in such sentences.

**11. When a sentence is introduced by the expletive *It*, the verb is always singular, regardless of the number of the subject.**

It *is* the *Johnsons.*
It *is we* whom they want.

**12. The complement of the verb *to be* does not affect the number of the verb.**

*Books are* her chief source of enjoyment.
The one *thing* you must be ready for *is* their attempts to disguise the play.
*What annoys me* about them *is* their constant complaints.
Her chief *source* of enjoyment *is* books.

If the demands of this convention result in an awkward sentence the wisest thing to do is to recast it.

| *Conventional but Awkward* | *Revised* |
| --- | --- |
| The amusing *thing* about campaign speeches *is* the attempts that both sides make to represent themselves as the only friends of the people. | In campaign speeches, it is amusing to see how both sides attempt to represent themselves as the only friends of the people. |

**13. A collective noun takes a singular verb when the class it names is considered as a unit, a plural verb when the members of the class are considered individually.**

| *Singular* | *Plural* |
| --- | --- |
| The jury *is* finally complete. | The jury *were* divided in their opinions. |
| The family *holds* an annual reunion. | My family *have* never been able to agree. |
| The clergy *is* wretchedly underpaid. | The clergy *are* supporting this proposal from their pulpits. |

This convention also applies to such nouns as *number, part,* and *rest.*

A large number *is* expected.

A number of errors *have* been found.

Only part of the order *was* delivered.

A great part of the people *have* no opinion on the question.

The rest of the page *is* illegible.

The rest of the votes *are* about equally divided among the three candidates.

**14. Titles of books, magazines, movies, newspapers, plays, and the like take a singular verb.**

*The Good Companions* is a fine novel.
*The Outcasts* was not a success at the box-office.
*The New York Times* is his bible.
*The Little Foxes* was a smash hit.

**15. Plural numbers take a singular verb when they are used in a phrase to indicate a sum or a unit.**

A million dollars *is* a great deal of money.
Ten years *is* too long to wait.
Five per cent *is* good interest.
A thousand yards *is* more than a half mile.
Forty hours *is* the regular work week.

**16. Certain nouns which are plural in form but singular in meaning generally take a singular verb. The most common of these are *economics, ethics, dynamics, mathematics, news, physics, semantics, statics, whereabouts.***

Economics *has* been called the dismal science.
No news *is* good news.
Semantics *is* the study of meanings.

## Exercises

**A.** Write out and turn in to your instructor the form in parentheses which would be preferred in college writing:

1. All hope of finding the victims alive (has, have) been abandoned.
2. One of the two girls (is, are) going.
3. Neither of my uncles (have, has) any children.
4. There (is, are) plenty to go around.
5. There (is, are) two mistakes in your work.
6. There (is, are) an apple and an orange for each child.
7. Five hundred dollars (is, are) more than I can afford.
8. Either Mary or Jean (was, were) here.
9. Neither Roy nor his dad (have, has) seen it.
10. The gangster, with all his henchmen, (were, was) arrested.
11. The father no less than the children (is, are) to blame.
12. The parents no less than the children (is, are) to blame.

13. Every one of the group (are, is) here.
14. Here (is, are) a piece of cake and a glass of milk.
15. (Is, are) there two pictures like that?
16. Two hundred pounds (were, was) his best weight.
17. The engine in addition to the body (was, were) in bad shape.
18. Bacon and eggs (are, is) the favorite breakfast.
19. It (is, are) the Thompsons.
20. There (is, are) one for each couple.

**B.** Revise the following sentences to remove any subject-verb disagreements or any awkward constructions caused by following the conventions too closely. Some sentences may be satisfactory as written.

1. Neither of the applicants are fully qualified.
2. The cost of food, clothing, and household goods have risen considerably.
3. He is one of those men who votes against any measure that costs money.
4. Don't tell me that; it don't make sense.
5. There is two or three things that you ought to know about him.
6. What they are looking for is girls who can swim.
7. Not only his clothes but even his appearance were shabby.
8. The money, including the day's receipts, were stolen.
9. The extent of his injuries have not yet been determined.
10. Milwaukee led the league at the beginning of the season and are now in second place.
11. Either Helen or I am going to the convention.
12. One of the girls who work in the office is wearing a ring.
13. That he will be elected by a large plurality is almost certain.
14. The works of such a poet contains something for each of us.
15. Investment in government bonds is a secure way of saving.
16. One of the things I like best about summer is the attractive dresses the girls wear.
17. What I would like to know is the costs of the program.
18. There has never been any reports made public.
19. This is one of those questions that has two answers.
20. Languages are difficult for me; so are economics.

# G 6    *Agreement (Pronoun–Antecedent)*

**Pronouns agree with their antecedents in gender, number, and person.**

If the antecedent is a masculine singular noun, the pronoun should be the masculine singular third person pronoun (*he, his,* or *him*). A pronoun does not necessarily agree with its antecedent in case, since its case is determined by its function in its own clause (see page 479).

| *Examples* | *Explanation* |
|---|---|
| The *men* got *their* wages. | *Their* is third person plural to agree with *men.* The plural form of the pronoun is the same for all genders. |
| The *girl* found *her* watch. | *Her* is third person feminine singular to agree with *girl.* |
| The *boy* misses *his* dog. | *His* is third person masculine singular to agree with *boy.* |
| The *ship* changed *its* course. | *Its* is third person neuter singular to agree with *ship.* |

### Troublesome Constructions

Most troubles with agreement of pronouns occur in a half-dozen constructions, and arise because of conflict between formal and colloquial usage. In general, formal usage insists that the *form* of the antecedent, not its *meaning*, determines the number of the pronoun, whereas colloquial usage tends to be governed by *meaning*. For example, *everybody* is singular in form but plural in meaning, since it refers to more than one person. Formally, *everybody* requires the singular form *his;* colloquially, it often is followed by the plural form *their.* In general, this colloquial usage is discouraged in college writing, so that *his* rather than *their* is the safer form.

**1. When two or more antecedents are connected by *and,* a pronoun referring to them is plural.**

> *Bill* and *Ted* are looking for *their* girls.
> *Helen* and *I* are buying *our* tickets today.
> That *man* and his *partner* have ruined *themselves.*

**2. When the antecedent is *each, either,* or *neither,* followed by a plural modifier, a singular pronoun is preferred.**

> *Each* of the girls is sure *she* is going to win.
> *Neither* of the men would admit *his* mistake.
> *Either* of these women may lose *her* temper at any time.

In colloquial usage, the plural modifier often leads to a plural pronoun, *they* or *their.*

**3. When the antecedent is *everybody, each, either, everyone, neither, nobody,* or *a person,* a singular pronoun is preferred.**

> *Each* has *his* own group of supporters.
> *Everybody* had *his* work in good shape.
> *Nobody* had *his* speech ready today.

*Everyone* was keeping *his* fingers crossed.

*A person* finds *himself* in trouble if he begins to cut classes.

Notice that the masculine form of the pronoun is generally used when the sex of the antecedent is unknown or when the antecedent refers to both sexes, thus:

*Everyone* should vote for the candidate of *his* choice.

The boys and girls have been told that *everybody* must do *his* share of the work.

But if the context clearly shows that the antecedent is feminine, the feminine pronoun is used:

When we girls have a picnic *everyone* brings *her* own utensils.

**4. When the antecedent is the impersonal one, the third person pronoun is generally used, unless the style is very formal.**

*One* must watch *his* step with that girl.

*One* can't really blame *himself* for that.

If *one* had a second chance, how much wiser *he* might be.

In a very formal style the impersonal pronoun is sometimes used throughout.

Under such conditions *one* laments *one's* utter incapacity to be of any genuine service.

*One* finds *oneself* wishing that the evidence were more convincing.

**5. When the antecedent is a collective noun, the pronoun may be either singular or plural, depending on whether the group is considered as a unit or as a number of individuals.**

| *Singular* | *Plural* |
|---|---|
| The *family* keeps pretty much to *itself*. | The *family* may have *their* private quarrels but *they* always agree in public. |
| The judge reprimanded the *jury* for *its* disregard of the evidence. | At the request of the defense attorney, the *jury* were polled and *their* individual verdicts recorded. |
| The *team* had *its* back to the wall. | The *team* are electing *their* captain. |

**6. The relative pronoun who is used when the antecedent is a person; which is used when the antecedent is a thing; that is used to refer to persons, animals, or things.**

This is the *man who* drove the car.

The *girl who* found it is here.

The *woman that* I mean had brown hair.

Here is the *parcel which* (or *that*) she left.
This is the *cow that* jumped the fence.

The possessive form *whose* is theoretically confined to persons, but in practice is often used when the more formal *of which* seems awkward.

The *nation whose* conscience is clear on that score is exceptional.
The newspaper *whose* reporters are most alert gets the most scoops.

Write out and turn in to your instructor the form in parentheses which would be preferred in college writing:

1. A person has to decide for (himself, themselves).
2. Neither of them will promise (their, his) support.
3. Everyone must bring (his, their) own food.
4. A person must do (one's, his) best.
5. Each of the boys tried as hard as (they, he) could.
6. One must do (one's, their) utmost.
7. The team was cheered for (its, their) courage.
8. Nobody in the room (were, was) willing to give up (their, his) (seat, seats).
9. He would just as soon insult a person as look at (them, him).
10. One must work twenty years to be eligible for (their, one's, your) pension.
11. There is the man (which, that) lost the money.
12. Each girl must contribute (their, her) share of the expenses.
13. Every boy and girl in the class (were, was) awarded a certificate for (their, his, her) work.
14. The car (with the broken fender, whose fender is broken) is mine.
15. Give this to the lady (which, who) lost it.
16. The committee (has, have) always voted according to (its, their) consciences.
17. Has everyone got (his, their) own coat?
18. After Ohio State won the title (they, it) went on to play in the Rose Bowl.
19. He is the instructor (which, who) told me my English was weak.
20. The nation to (whom, which) I am referring is not Russia.

**G7**

| | |
|---|---|
| | *Faulty Complement* |

**a. Avoid an illogical or awkward construction as the complement of the verb to be.**

The verb *to be* is most frequently used either as an auxiliary verb (I *am* learning) or as a linking verb (Honesty *is* the best policy). When used as a linking verb, it links its complement to its subject and thus acts as a kind of equals sign (Honesty = best policy). A reader who is familiar with the conventions of English sentence structure expects two things of this linking verb: (1) that it will be followed by a complement, (2) that the complement will be such that it can be logically equated with the subject. If either of these expectations is denied him, he will be bothered. Thus, if he encounters the sentence, "Honesty is in the little details of everyday life," he will feel that the promised linking relationship has not been provided. He will want to revise the sentence to read, "Honesty is best expressed in the little details of everyday life," thus changing *is* from a linking to an auxiliary verb (*is* expressed).

Similarly, a reader who meets the sentence, "Honesty is what you do in such a situation," will feel that the complement throws the equation out of balance, since it equates the abstract noun "Honesty" with a statement of action. He will want to revise the sentence to read, "What to do in such a situation is to tell the truth," so that both sides of the equation refer to an action (*to do* and *to tell*).

In order to avoid such annoying constructions, a writer should make sure that the complement of *to be* can be logically equated with the subject. If it cannot, or if the equation results in a wordy or awkward sentence, the writer should either revise the form of the complement or rewrite the sentence to get rid of the misleading linking verb.

| *Illogical or Awkward Complement* | *Explanation* | *Revised Sentence* |
|---|---|---|
| Before I built the house all I had learned about carpentry was *watching my dad.* | *The equation requires some statement of knowledge, not a statement of how the knowledge was obtained. Of the various possible revisions, perhaps the best is to substitute a more active verb, which does not promise an equation.* | Before I built the house all that I knew about carpentry I had learned from watching my dad. |

| *Illogical or Awkward Complement* | *Explanation* | *Revised Sentence* |
|---|---|---|
| The chief disadvantage of weeping willows is the branches are brittle and break easily. | *The sentence has two faults. Logically, it is the brittleness that constitutes the disadvantage, not the branches; grammatically, the plural noun* branches *following* is *sounds like a subject-verb disagreement. The sentence may be saved very simply, by providing a subordinate conjunction so that the final clause is revealed as a complement.* | The chief disadvantage of weeping willows is that the branches are brittle and break easily. |
| The most unusual food I ever had was when I ate a serving of boiled snails. | *The reader expects the food to be identified immediately after the linking verb. The adverbial clause stresses time, instead, and is wordy.* | The most unusual food I ever ate was a serving of boiled snails. |

**b.** Avoid the use of *is when, is where,* and *is if* when the complement of *to be* is intended to describe or define the subject.

This advice is a special application of the more general statement given in **a.** The use of an adverbial clause instead of a noun or noun phrase is one kind of illogical complement which occurs frequently in student definitions. This error and its revision are illustrated by the following examples.

| *Faulty Complement* | *Explanation* | *Revision* |
|---|---|---|
| Plagiarism is *when* you represent another person's writing *as your own.* | *The reader expects to find what plagiarism is, not when it is. The construction calls for a noun phrase similar to the italicized phrase at the right.* | Plagiarism is *the representation of another's writing as one's own.* |
| Manslaughter is *where a person is killed deliberately but without premeditation.* | *Again, the construction requires a definition of manslaughter, not where it is.* | Manslaughter is *the deliberate but unpremeditated killing of a person.* |
| A comma splice is *if a comma is used to separate two independent sentences which are not connected by a coordinating conjunction.* | *The complement should tell what a comma splice is, not how a comma splice is made. Use a noun such as* use *at the right.* | A comma splice is *the use of a comma to separate two independent sentences which are not connected by a coordinating conjunction.* |

**c.** Use the appropriate case for a personal pronoun acting as the complement of *to be.* (See G4.)

**d.** Use the adjective form for the complements of sensory verbs.

A sensory verb is one which identifies some action of the senses — seeing, hearing, feeling, etc. Since the complements of these verbs usually describe the subject rather than the action of the verb, they are adjectives, not adverbs. Their adjectival function can be illustrated by expressing the complement as an attributive adjective, as in the parenthetical phrases at the ends of the following sentences:

> Your hands feel rough. (rough-feeling hands)
> This tire looks good. (good-looking tire)
> That dog smells awful. (awful-smelling dog)
> This water tastes bitter. (bitter-tasting water)

To use an adverb after these verbs would have the effect of describing the manner in which the feeling, looking, smelling, and tasting were performed. Compare

> He looked *hungry.*
> He looked *hungrily* at the steak.

In the first sentence, *looked* is a linking verb which joins an adjective to a pronoun to indicate a hungry look. In the second, the verb indicates an action performed by the subject, and the adverb describes the manner in which the action was performed (He looked at the steak in a hungry manner). Unless the modifier completing a sensory verb is clearly intended to describe the action suggested by the verb, an adjective is the correct form.

Revise the following sentences to remove the faulty complements.

1. The source of his fortune was from real estate.
2. The reason I failed the course was I missed a third of the lectures.
3. A hybrid is when you cross two different types of plants.
4. Whatever is in the oven smells deliciously.
5. The chief merit of the play was in its humor.
6. I read in this morning's paper where there has been another airplane crash.
7. Technically, a sophomore is having 26 hours of credit.
8. What annoys me about him is the practical jokes he plays.
9. Conduct unbecoming a student is if you do something you shouldn't and get caught.
10. Half an hour after dinner he became quite sickly.
11. One of his greatest assets is how well he can tell a story.
12. The thing I most regret about working my way through college was the dates I never had time for.

13. After that kind of experience I can't help feeling bitterly about her.

14. The most embarrassing thing that can happen to you on a trip is when you run short of money and try to cash a personal check at a gas station.

15. The reason they were divorced was not supporting his family.

16. The thing that troubled me most was cats all over the place.

17. An Act of God is when something happens, like a flood, which nobody is really to blame for.

18. The difference between an amateur and a professional is when an athlete is paid for playing a sport.

19. An honor student is if you have a straight B average.

20. The only money he has is his grandfather left him a small inheritance.

---

## G 8 | *Faulty Modifier*

FAULTY MODIFIERS which are a result of word order are discussed in **WO2** and **WO3**. This section is limited to errors in the form of the modifier.

### a. Distinguish between the uses and forms of adjectives and adverbs.

Adjectives are used to modify nouns and pronouns; adverbs are used to modify verbs, adjectives, and other adverbs.

### 1. Do not use an adjective to modify a verb.

| *Adjective Misused for Adverb* | *Correct Form* |
|---|---|
| The old car still runs *good*. | The old car still runs *well*. |
| Do it as *careful* as you can. | Do it as *carefully* as you can. |
| Listen *close* to what I tell you. | Listen *closely* to what I have to tell you. |

### 2. Do not use an adjective to modify an adverb or another adjective.

| *Adjective Misused for Adverb* | *Correct Form* |
|---|---|
| He is *considerable* better this morning. | He is *considerably* better this morning. |
| It was a *real* difficult decision. | It was a *really* difficult decision. |

3. Do not use an adverb as the complement of a sensory verb unless you clearly intend to modify the verb, not the subject. (See G7)

4. When a modifier could modify either a noun or a verb, indicate by the form which you intend.

| *Adverb* | *Adjective* |
|---|---|
| Tie the knot *tightly* and *securely*. | Tie the boat *tight* to the dock. |
| Her husband held her *firmly*. | He kept his resolutions *firm*. |
| John spoke out *forthrightly*. | His answers seemed *forthright*. |

**b. Avoid excessive use of intensive modifiers.**

Certain modifiers such as *awful(ly)*, *extremely*, *much*, *real(ly)*, *terrific(ally)*, *tremendous(ly)*, etc., are called **intensives** because their chief function is to stress or intensify the words they modify. Intensives are common in conversation. Discreet use of them in writing is legitimate, but overuse causes wordiness, vagueness, and a gushy "schoolgirl style." In the following sentences the italicized intensives could profitably be deleted.

It was a *very, very* congenial group, and everybody had a *tremendously* good time.

We were *awfully* tired and *terrifically* hungry from the *extremely* long trip.

Do you ever have that *real* tired feeling when it is *such* an effort to do even the *very* simplest things?

Rewrite the following sentences to revise or delete faulty modifiers.

1. He plays every shot so easy that it looks simple.
2. The way you put it, it sounds ~~pretty~~ well.
3. She near fainted when he told her.
4. We ought to treat everybody fair and square.
5. It was obviously a cheap made dress.
6. Let's divide the work equal among the three of us.
7. The nightwatchman had been gagged and tied tight in a chair.
8. It was a ~~simply~~ tremendous show, with such lovely costumes and many, many really terrific songs.
9. The work had been done so sloppy that I spoke real sharp to him.
10. We were considerable wiser after that experience.

<table>
<tr><td>

**G 9**

</td><td>

## *Faulty Connective*

</td></tr>
</table>

**a. Discriminate among the uses of different conjunctions.**

A careful choice of conjunctions often sharpens the meaning of a sentence. Sometimes two or three conjunctions have similar meanings yet differ enough so that one is clearly a better choice than the others in a given sentence. The right choice may mean the difference between saying precisely what the writer means and roughly what he means.

$$\text{The critics were enthusiastic about the book} \begin{Bmatrix} \text{and} \\ \text{while} \\ \text{but} \end{Bmatrix} \text{I found it trivial.}$$

Clearly the sentence calls for a contrast of two opinions. *And* connects without contrast; *while* expresses contrast but de-emphasizes the second opinion by subordinating it to the first, and also suggests that both opinions were formed at the same time. *But* expresses contrast and nothing else. Since contrast is the only purpose of the conjunction, *but* is the best choice for this sentence.

Similarly in

$$\begin{Bmatrix} \text{When} \\ \text{Because} \\ \text{As} \end{Bmatrix} \text{I missed the test, I had to take a makeup.}$$

the idea to stress is the causal relation between missing the test and having to take a makeup. *When* suggests time rather than cause, and *As* denotes cause but also suggests time. Hence in this sentence it is vaguer than *Because,* which indicates only the causal relation.

**b. In college writing, avoid *like* as a conjunction.**

At all levels of style, *like* is used as a preposition (She looks *like* her mother). In speech and colloquial writing, it is also often used as a conjunction:

It happened *like* I said it would.
It looks *like* it would rain.

Most college assignments do not lend themselves to a colloquial style, and many people object to *like* as a conjunction. So in writing, use *as* or *as if* instead of *like* as a conjunction:

> It happened *as* I said it would.
> It looks *as if* it would rain.

But, straining to avoid *like* as a conjunction, some students use *as* as a preposition:

> She looks *as* her mother.

instead of

> She looks *like* her mother.

This overcorrection is worse than the use it is trying to avoid.

In the following sentences change the conjunction when a different one would give a more precise or acceptable sentence. When there is a choice, choose the conjunction that most clearly expresses the intended meaning.

1. While I have no money, my credit is good.
2. He'd like to be on the first squad and he hasn't the talent.
3. He acts like I was responsible for his failing the course. *Subjunctive Mood*
4. When dad was ill I decided to stay out of college for a year.
5. She could handle the job, yet she doesn't have a degree.
6. (While, When, Since) there was nothing else to do, I went to the library.
7. Being as you are only seventeen you are too young to be thinking of getting married.
8. (Since, Because, As) my brother was married and had three children to support we did not ask him to help.
9. He could do A work in school (yet, but, still) he doesn't like to work.
10. It begins to look (like, as how, as if) the Yankees will win again.

---

# G 10

*Faulty Comparison*

---

**a. Avoid redundant comparison.**

As we saw on page 463, there are two regular methods of comparing adjectives and adverbs (tall, tall*er*, tall*est* and quickly, *more* quickly, *most* quickly) and an irregular method (good, better, best). Thus words like *taller* and *better* are already inflected to show comparison. If *more* or *most* is used with these words, the result is a double or redundant comparison (*more better, most tallest*). This kind of double comparative or superlative was once standard usage (compare Shakespeare's "That was the most unkindest cut of all"), but it is no longer acceptable. In the following sentences the redundant *more* has been struck out.

> Altogether it was a ~~more~~ smoother performance.
> The damage done was ~~more~~ worse than I had expected.

Closely related to redundant comparison is the comparison of words such as *opposite, perfect,* and *unique* which logically do not have comparative and superlative degrees. Thus if a specimen is *perfect,* it can hardly become more perfect; *opposite* poles are already as opposite as they can be; and a *unique* object — the only one of its kind — is not *very* unique, it is completely so.

**b. Avoid such nonstandard comparisons as *all the farther, all the faster,* etc.**

| Nonstandard | Standard |
|---|---|
| Is that all the farther you can throw it? | Is that as far as you can throw it? |
| This is all the larger they come. | This is as large as they come. |
| That is all the higher he can jump. | That is as high as he can jump. |

**c. In college writing, generally avoid using the superlative form when only two things are being compared.**

The superlative in such sentences as "Jim is the oldest of Mr. Brown's two sons" is common in speech and in colloquial writing, and some grammarians consider it occasionally appropriate even in a formal style.[8] But most instructors object to this usage in college writing.

| Questionable | Revised |
|---|---|
| I like both boys, but I think John is the nicest. | I like both boys, but I think John is the nicer. |
| It may not be the best of the two but it's certainly the cheapest. | It may not be the better of the two but it's certainly the cheaper. |

**d. Avoid incomplete or confused comparisons.**

The kinds of awkward comparison illustrated below have already been discussed as "Incomplete Constructions" in **S10.**

[8] See Marckwardt and Walcott, *Facts About Current English Usage,* p. 42, for the judgment that "of the two disputants, the warmest is usually wrong" is "literary English."

|                           *Incomplete*                            |                           *Revised*                            |
| --- | --- |

*Incomplete*

Father likes Shakespeare better than mother.

He is as courteous, if not more so, than any other boy I have dated.

*Revised*

Father likes Shakespeare better than mother does.

I don't remember dating a more courteous boy.

Revise the following sentences to make the forms for comparison acceptable in college writing:

1. It was the ~~most worse~~ *worst* storm I have ever seen.
2. He said that, although there was little to choose between both major political parties, he liked the Democrats ~~best~~. *better*
3. Two weeks is ~~all the~~ longer *as* I can afford to be gone.
4. The two speakers had ~~the most~~ opposite points of view.
5. Is that ~~all the~~ tighter *that* you can tie the knot?
6. Bill is the ~~more perfect~~ *better* gentleman of the two.
7. I think languages can be as difficult, ~~if not more difficult~~, *if not more so* than *as* mathematics.
8. Although I ran ~~all the~~ *as* faster *I* could, he beat me easily.
9. Between Washington and Lincoln most historians would say that Lincoln was the ~~greatest~~. *greater*
10. The temperature was the ~~most low~~ *lowest* of this winter.

7

# Punctuation: Uses of the Comma

In English there are about a dozen common marks of punctuation: *period* [ . ], *comma* [ , ], *semicolon* [ ; ], *colon* [ : ], *question mark* [ ? ], *exclamation mark* [ ! ], *quotation marks* [ " " or ' ' ], *apostrophe* [ ' ], *dash* [ — ], *parentheses* [ ( ) ], and *brackets* [ ]. Most of these marks have highly specialized functions and once these are understood, it is easy enough to use them conventionally. The chief exception, perhaps, is the comma, which is at once the most common mark of punctuation and the one with the most complex uses.

The comma is used to make the internal structure of the sentence clear. It does so in three general ways: (1) by separating elements which might otherwise be confused, (2) by setting off interrupting constructions, and (3) by marking words out of normal order. This section will specify and illustrate these three uses.

**a. Use commas to separate elements which might otherwise seem to run together.**

**1. To prevent a confused, ambiguous, or awkward reading.**

We saw on pages 131–132 that a major cause of confused sentence structure is inadequate punctuation. The most important use of the comma is to prevent a confused, ambiguous, or awkward reading. All other uses are subordinate to this one. Notice how the confused sentences at the left are made clear at the right by the use of commas.

| *Confused* | *Explanation* | *Clear* |
|---|---|---|
| Mr. Smith our milkman has been hurt. | *Is this a statement to or about Mr. Smith?* | Mr. Smith, our milkman has been hurt. |
| | | (or) |
| | | Mr. Smith, our milkman, has been hurt. |
| I do not care for money isn't everything. | *Lest* money *seem to complete* care for, *a comma should be inserted after* care. | I do not care, for money isn't everything. |
| A hundred yards below the bridge was flooded. | *Comma necessary to avoid misreading of* bridge *as the object of* below. | A hundred yards below, the bridge was flooded. |

| *Confused* | *Explanation* | *Clear* |
|---|---|---|
| When we had finished eating the cigarettes were passed around. | *Comma necessary to show that* cigarettes *is not the object of* eating. | When we had finished eating, the cigarettes were passed around. |

**2. To separate two main clauses joined by a coordinating conjunction (*and, or, nor, but*).**

The real purpose of this convention is to prevent possible misinterpretation on first reading, specifically to keep the subject of the second main clause from being misread as a second complement in the first clause. Consider the following sentences:

> He sprained his ankle and his temper was ruined.
> He traded his car and his wife was angry.

In both these sentences the noun following the conjunction appears, at first reading, to be part of a compound object of the first verb. The comma before the conjunction shows clearly that the two nouns are in different clauses:

> He sprained his ankle, and his temper was ruined.
> He traded his car, and his wife was angry.

When there is no possibility of a confused reading, the comma becomes less necessary and is often omitted. But even when it is not functionally necessary, careful writers insert a comma between two connected main clauses if the subject of the second differs from that of the first, as in the following examples:

> I tried to sleep, but the neighbor's radio made that impossible.
> The huge elm had been cut down, and a garage now covered the spot where it once stood.

But notice that a comma is not used when the subject of the first clause is understood as the subject of the second:

> I discussed the question with the family and then made my decision.

**3. To separate elements in a series.**

> He promised them only *blood, sweat, toil,* and *tears.*
> *Reading, swimming,* and *dancing* are my favorite recreations.
> It was said of Washington, that he was *first in war, first in peace,* and *first in the hearts of his countrymen.*
> *North passed, East bid two spades, South bid three hearts,* and *West doubled.*
> We were *tired, hungry,* and *disconsolate.*

As these illustrations show, the series may consist of single words, phrases, or clauses. The items in the series may be nouns, pronouns, verbs, verbals, adverbs, or adjectives, though within a single series they must not shift from one part of speech to another. The comma before the conjunction joining the last two items is optional. Its use is largely a matter of personal preference, though it is more likely to be omitted in an informal style than in a formal one.

> She is small, dark, and vivacious.
> (or)
> She is small, dark and vivacious.

**4. To separate contrasted elements in a *this, not that,* construction.**

> He is sick, not drunk.
> We are disgusted, not angry.
> The German schools became institutes of propaganda, not of education.
> This is a problem which must be handled with sympathy, not harshness.

**5. To separate direct quotation from such constructions as *He said, She answered, We replied,* etc.**

> He said, "You are only half right."
> "This," I said, "is the last straw."
> "Nobody asked you, sir," she said.
> "But," he asked, "what if they refuse?"

Since the quotation marks themselves set off the quoted material, no confusion would result if the comma were omitted; but convention requires the comma. Whether the punctuation should come *inside* or *outside* the quotation marks is discussed in Section **P9**.

**6. To separate elements in dates, addresses, and place names.**

> January 1, 1940; Dec. 25, 1910. (Comma between day and year.)
> 875 Main Street, Galesburg, Illinois. (Comma between street and city and between city and state.)
> Chicago, Illinois, is the second-largest city in the country. (Notice the comma before and after the state.)
> He was born in London, England. (Comma between city and country.)

**7. In the following miscellaneous constructions:**

> In figures — 22,745; 1,000,000; 150,743,290.
> In names followed by titles — R. W. Leeds, M.D.
> At the end of the salutation in informal letters — Dear Joe,
> After an introductory *Yes* or *No* — Yes, I'll do it.

In the following sentences insert commas where they are needed for ease of reading or are conventionally required. Some of the sentences may be satisfactory as they are.

1. This summer our family tried a split vacation. Dad went fishing in Minnesota with Bill and me and mother took my sister to New York.

2. Below the town glittered with a million lights.

3. My roommate learned about the deal and wrote a story about it for the *Daily*.

4. The correct quotation is "And malt does more than Milton can to justify God's ways to man."

5. The author was Housman not Pope. He was born on March 26 1859.

6. Will you please forward my mail to 1620 Third Avenue Anoka Minnesota?

7. I expect to be there as long as the fishing is good.

8. The correct sum is 4530 not 4350.

9. I'll take orange juice ham and eggs and coffee.

10. He praised the food and the waitress seemed pleased.

11. He married Helen and her sister served as bridesmaid.

12. "I wonder" he said "if she still lives in Geneva Illinois."

13. "I think not" I answered. "She was living in Kansas City Missouri when I last heard of her."

14. Throughout the ceremony was inspiringly conducted.

15. The room was a clutter of discarded clothing strewn books and newspapers overflowing ash trays and dirty dishes.

16. After all their hopes were too ambitious.

17. We tried to look in the cellar windows but someone had placed cardboard rectangles against them on the inside.

18. I cannot stay longer for mother will be expecting me to meet her at the station.

19. The students sat tensely while the test papers were being distributed and then began to write feverishly.

20. The letter should be addressed to A. D. Jones M.D. Christie Clinic Champaign Illinois.

**b. Use commas to set off an interrupting construction.**

Any construction which comes between subject and verb, verb and complement, or between any two elements not normally separated, may be called an interrupting construction. If the interruption is awkward, it should be avoided; but many interrupters are necessary and conventional. They should, however, be set off by commas so that a reader can recognize them and still see the basic pattern of the sentence.

We must distinguish, however, between constructions which actually interrupt and those which come between related elements without interrupting them. For example, in

The girl, *you say,* has gone.

the italicized clause comes between subject (*girl*) and verb (*has gone*). The interrupter need not occupy this position. The sentence could have been written:

> You say that the girl has gone.
> The girl has gone, you say.

But in the sentence

> The girl *you want* has gone.

the italicized clause identifies the particular girl and cannot be moved without weakening the sentence. Although the clause modifies the subject, it so closely identifies it that we consider *The girl you want* as the "whole subject" of *has gone*. A modifying phrase or clause which is so closely related to another element that it is felt to be a part of that element should not be set off with commas, since the commas would distort the relationship, not clarify it. The italicized modifiers in the following sentences are so necessary that they are not considered interrupting constructions:

> The man *with him* is his brother.
> The girl *at the piano* is his wife.
> The leader *of the revolt* has been captured.

As you study the following uses of commas to set off interrupting constructions, notice this about all of them: *an interrupting construction between subject and verb or verb and complement requires two commas to enclose it.* These commas act like mild parentheses and are always used in pairs.

### 1. To set off an appositive.

An *appositive* is an identifying word or phrase (a noun or pronoun and its modifiers) which is considered grammatically equivalent to the noun or pronoun it identifies:

> Marciano, *the champion,* has retired.
> His father, *the president of the company,* will be responsible.
> They want us, *you and me,* to go.
> I want to see Dr. Roberts, *the English professor.*

The first three examples show that the appositive is often a particular kind of interrupter. The fourth appositive does not interrupt the main clause, but is conventionally separated from the rest of the sentence by a comma.

### 2. To set off nouns of address.

A noun of address is a proper or common noun used to name the listener when we are speaking to him directly (I wish, *dad,* you would reconsider your decision. I understand, *Mrs. Ellison,* that you are now a grandmother). Such nouns may occupy the beginning, middle, or end of a sentence, so that strictly speaking they are not always interrupters. But they are always set off from the rest of the sentence by commas.

I would like to ask you, *Mr. Jones,* for your opinion.
I think, *madam,* that you had better leave.
*Sir,* I'd like to ask a question.
Listen, *chum,* I've had enough of you!
I wish I were going with you, *Ted.*

### 3. To set off conjunctive adverbs and other transitional markers.

Conjunctive adverbs (*however, moreover, therefore,* etc.) are adverbs which double as connectives between sentences. Usually they provide a transition between two sentences and usually they come *near,* and occasionally *at,* the beginning of the second sentence (see pages 452 and 514).

We thought, moreover, that we could get away with it.
There was a chance, on the other hand, that prices would go up.
You must try, first of all, to consider it objectively.

In informal usage the commas around common conjunctive adverbs are omitted if the writer feels that they would provide more separation than he desires (I am therefore cancelling the order).

### 4. To set off a nonrestrictive modifier.

A modifier is said to be *restrictive* when it specifies a particular member or members of a group. Thus in "The President *who succeeded Roosevelt* came from Missouri," the italicized modifier selects from the whole class of Presidents a particular one. When a modifier does not limit a class to a particular group or individual but modifies the whole class, it is said to be *nonrestrictive.* Thus in "The President of the United States, *who is both the chief of state and the leader of the majority party,* holds one of the most powerful offices in the world," the italicized modifier refers to all Presidents of the United States and does not restrict the statement to any particular one. It is a nonrestrictive modifier.

The following examples include restrictive and nonrestrictive modifiers. We should recognize that context often determines how a modifier is to be interpreted and that it might be possible to place the sentences at the right in contexts which would make the modifiers restrictive.

| *Restrictive* | *Nonrestrictive* |
|---|---|
| All students *who were absent* will be required to do an additional assignment. | College students, *who represent a superior intellectual group,* must be asked to accept the responsibility of leadership. |
| Soldiers *who have flat feet* had better stay out of the infantry. | Soldiers, *who are selected by physical fitness tests,* should show a lower sickness rate than that of the total population. |

Restrictive modifiers are so much a part of the whole subject that they cannot be omitted without changing the basic meaning of the sentence. Nonrestrictive modifiers on the other hand, can be omitted without significant change in basic meaning. Compare the following revisions with the originals.

All students . . . will be required to do an additional assignment. (This is not what the original statement meant.)

College students . . . must be asked to accept the responsibility of leadership. (This is substantially what the original statement meant.)

Soldiers . . . had better stay out of the infantry. (Not the original meaning.)

Soldiers . . . should show a lower sickness rate than that of the total population. (The original meaning has not been substantially changed.)

Restrictive modifiers are not set off by commas, because they are felt to be an essential part of the element they modify. Nonrestrictive modifiers are felt to be similar to the interrupting constructions shown earlier and are therefore enclosed by commas. The examples already given illustrate this difference in punctuation.

In the following sentences provide commas to set off appositives, nouns of address, conjunctive adverbs, and nonrestrictive modifiers. Some sentences may require no additional punctuation.

1. Mr. Ludovic the new German instructor was born in Berlin.
2. The man wearing the Stetson is his uncle.
3. The tall man who happened to be wearing a Stetson said he had never been west of Chicago in his life.
4. Do you think Bill that we could play a round after work?
5. Are these your gloves Mrs. Davidson?
6. The suit that he bought two years ago fits him better than the one he bought last winter.
7. The doctor looking very grave came towards us.
8. I thought however that things would be different this time.
9. The girl evidently on the edge of tears could hardly finish her story.
10. Sir may I trouble you for a light?
11. My girl's mother who used to be an English teacher helps me with my themes.
12. The dog which had evidently been trained sat beside the table and begged charmingly for food.
13. First turn on the gas and oil; second set the choke; third pull the rope.
14. I had a talk with her father who is not so crotchety as you led me to believe.
15. I had a talk with the man who witnessed the accident.
16. The elm tree disease is killing off most of the old elms; consequently the people in our neighborhood are planting maples.

17. No, I mean the Mr. Brown who lives over on Florida Avenue.

18. I hear that Abelson, the fire marshal, was badly hurt last night.

19. A scientist called Fermi was chiefly responsible for the success of the Chicago experiment.

20. Mr. Welch, our next door neighbor, has a daughter who placed second in a national beauty contest. There is some talk that she will be given a movie contract. That, however, may be merely rumor.

## c. Use commas to mark an inversion.

### 1. To emphasize an inverted element.

Any word, phrase, or clause transposed from its normal position is said to be *inverted*.

> *Myself*, I will vote in favor of it.
> *Except for physics*, my courses are not difficult.

But if the inversion is so common as to seem normal, the comma is usually omitted. No commas would be used in the following inversions:

> *Yesterday* I had a bad time of it.
> *In 1913* the concept of total war was unknown.
> *In the following sentences* the verbs are underlined.

### 2. To cut off a long introductory phrase or an adverbial clause preceding the main clause.

When a sentence opens with a long phrase or adverbial clause, it is conventional to use a comma between this element and the main clause:

> *Pulling over to the curb at the first opportunity*, I waited for the fire engines to pass.
> *If there is going to be any difficulty about this request*, I would rather withdraw it.
> *Being ignorant of the facts of the situation*, I could say nothing.
> *If I go*, you'll be sorry.
> *To be sure of getting up in time to catch the train*, I left a call with the switchboard operator.
> *When you say that*, smile.

This convention is not universal, for writers sometimes feel that a particular introductory construction is so closely related in meaning to the main clause that the separating comma is undesirable. The comma is generally used when, as in the last example, the introductory construction is clearly an inversion, when an introductory phrase contains a verbal (examples 1, 3, 5), and when the subordinate and main clauses have different subjects (example 4). The comma should always be used if it makes the sentence pattern clearer and the reader's job easier.

In the following sentences insert commas to set off inversions and introductory constructions where desirable.

   1. Dissatisfied with our blocking the coach announced an extra session on defense.

   2. In a last desperate effort to score the team went into a spread formation.

   3. If you want it take it.

   4. On learning that his wife had never formally renounced her share of the property and could still block its sale we told the real estate agent that we were no longer interested.

   5. As far as I know that is the answer.

   6. Just the other day I saw his mother.

   7. Whoever he is he should be punished.

   8. If he objects tell him to talk with me.

   9. Knowing that he had a tendency to make a ten-minute speech in five minutes Hugh timed his delivery with a stop watch.

   10. Angry my roomate threw the tickets in the fireplace.

---

# P 2     *Misuse of the Comma*

TOO MANY COMMAS are often more annoying than too few. The following "don't's" should be carefully observed.

**a. Do not use a comma instead of a period between independent sentences.**

Such a use may cause serious misinterpretation. (See "Comma Splice," **S6.**)

| *Comma Splice* | *Conventional Punctuation* |
| --- | --- |
| He spoke very quietly, as I listened, I had the impression that he was speaking to himself. | He spoke very quietly. As I listened, I had the impression that he was speaking to himself. |
| There was nothing more to be said, when they took that attitude, further negotiation was impossible. | There was nothing more to be said. When they took that attitude, further negotiation was impossible. |

**b. Do not use a comma between closely related elements except to mark an interrupting construction.**

The comma should reveal the structure of a sentence, not disguise it. Closely related elements (subject-verb, verb-object, verb or noun and modifier) are unnecessarily separated if a single comma is placed between them. If, however, these elements are interrupted, a pair of commas to enclose the interrupting construction helps to bridge the interruption.

| *Misuse of Comma Between Related Elements* | *Correct Use of Comma Between Related Elements* |
|---|---|
| My car, is at the service station. | My car, which is at the service station, needs a thorough overhauling. |
| He said, that he would try. | He said, when I asked him, that he would try. |
| The student who lost this money, may need it badly. | The student, who had lost money on other occasions, was reprimanded for his carelessness. |

The last illustration contrasts a restrictive with a nonrestrictive clause (see page 509). The comma is misused in the version at the left because the subordinate clause is not an interruption but a necessary part of the whole subject. It is a restrictive modifier.

## c. Do not use commas excessively.

The modern tendency, especially in informal writing, is to keep punctuation to a minimum. Hence it is usual to avoid commas which serve no recognizable purpose. Moreover, it should not be assumed that a comma *must* be used in a particular sentence because convention recommends its use in sentences of that type. The conventions are statements about general practice. There are times when slavishly following the rules will chop a sentence to pieces by commas. In such cases, either revise the sentence or ignore the strict letter of the convention. The following examples illustrate excessive and adequate punctuation:

| *Excessive* | *Adequate* |
|---|---|
| However, it is not, in my opinion, desirable. | However, it is not in my opinion desirable. |
| Yesterday, a little, old lady, in a dilapidated, old Ford, picked me up, and brought me home. | Yesterday a little old lady in a dilapidated old Ford picked me up and brought me home. |
| Sometimes, she would appear in an elaborate beach outfit, sometimes, she wore a simple, white suit, and, occasionally, she put on a red, white, and blue bathing suit, with a detachable skirt. | Sometimes she would appear in an elaborate beach outfit, sometimes she wore a simple white suit, and occasionally she put on a red white and blue bathing suit with a detachable skirt. |

# P3    *Uses of the Semicolon*

**a. Use a semicolon to separate closely related independent clauses not connected by a conjunction.**

> Try this one; it seems to be your color.
> His mother won't let him; she is afraid he might get hurt.
> Your car is new; mine is eight years old.

In each of these sentences a period could be used instead of the semicolon. But the clauses, even though grammatically independent, are felt to be so closely related that a period makes too sharp a separation.

The semicolon provides a more emphatic separation than the comma; it affords an easier transition between statements than the period; it is, therefore, the most appropriate punctuation to balance two contrasted ideas parallel in form:

> Take care of the children; the adults can take care of themselves.
> It was not the hours or the wages that discouraged me; it was the constant monotony of the work.

**b. Use a semicolon before a transitional connective (conjunctive adverb) between two main clauses.**

The most common transitional connectives are *also, besides, consequently, furthermore, hence, however, likewise, moreover, nevertheless, in addition, since, so, then, therefore, yet.*

> It won't work; *therefore* there is no sense in buying it.
> His argument has some merit; *however,* he goes too far.
> His eyes went bad; *consequently,* he had to resign his position as a proofreader.

**c. Use a semicolon to separate elements in a series when they contain internal punctuation.**

> Among those present were Dr. Holmes, pastor of the First Methodist Church; A. C. Levitt, superintendent of schools; B. L. Rainey, manager of the Benson Hotel; and M. T. Cord, vice-president of Miller and Sons.

Had commas been used between the elements in this series they might be confused with the commas which set off the appositives.

P 4     *Misuse of the Semicolon*

**a.** Do not use a semicolon as the equivalent of a colon.

Although their names suggest a close relationship, semicolons and colons have quite different uses and are not interchangeable. The colon (see **P7**) is used chiefly to indicate that something is to follow, usually a series of items; the semicolon is never used between an independent clause and a subordinate construction. In the following sentences the faulty semicolon is followed by the correct colon in parentheses.

> My records show that the following students have not handed in the assignment; (:) Mr. Andrews, Mr. Richardson, Mr. Smith, and Miss Wallace.
> Dear Sir; (:) May I call your attention to an error. . . .

**b.** Do not use a semicolon as the equivalent of a comma.

A comma is internal punctuation and is used only *within* a sentence; a semicolon is a stronger mark and, as we have seen, is used between grammatically independent statements. A semicolon may be substituted for a comma between main clauses joined by a conjunction when more emphatic punctuation is desired (My old job paid higher wages; but the new one offers a brighter future); but a semicolon cannot be substituted for a comma between a main clause and a subordinate construction. In the following examples the faulty semicolon is followed by the correct comma in parentheses.

> Although I seldom have trouble with grammar or spelling; (,) I never seem to use the right punctuation.
> We stayed up until two o'clock in the morning; (,) hoping that they would arrive.
> We could come to only one conclusion; (,) that his mother had changed his mind.

**c.** Avoid indiscriminate substitution of semicolons for periods.

Using a semicolon for a period will do less harm than using a semicolon for a colon or a comma. Yet the semicolon and the period have different functions and should not be used interchangeably. The normal punctuation between independent statements is the period. Between sentences this is the conventional mark to use; but if a writer wishes to relate the two sentences more closely than a period would permit, he may use a semicolon. This specialized substitution, however, does not abolish the distinction between the two marks. In the following passage the parenthetical periods are preferable to semicolons. The first word following the period would, of course, be capitalized.

> Today it is easy to smile at such superstitions and to assume that they are the products of an uncivilized age, but the close association of words and things which is the basis of word magic is a subtle association which persists even in the thinking of highly civilized societies; (.) some of the opposition to daylight-saving time illustrates this confusion of word and thing;(.) people uneasily suspect that if they turn the hands of the clock ahead, they have dropped an hour out of their lives; (.) often the best argument for such people is not to deny that they will have "lost" an hour, but to promise that they will get it back in the fall; (.) the common practice of skipping thirteen in numbering the floors and rooms of a hotel is another illustration of the lingering belief in word magic.

## P 5  The Period

**a. A period is used to mark the end of a declarative sentence.**

Unless a sentence is intended as a question, a command, or an exclamation, it is declarative and is closed by a period:

Today is Tuesday.
We have three days to go.

Even when a sentence is mildly imperative or exclamatory, modern usage often prefers a period to an exclamation mark:

Be careful of the step.
Let's forget the whole matter.
How pleasant it would be to be there now.

**b. A period is used to mark an accepted abbreviation.**

*Titles:* Col., Dr., Hon., Mrs., Rev.
*Degrees:* B.A., B.S., M.D., Ph.D.
*Names:* John A. Jones; Chas. W. Brown.

*Months:* Jan., Feb., Aug., Nov.
*States:* Ala., Ga., Me., Ill., Wash.
*Miscellaneous:* Ave., St., vol., p., U.S.A., B.C., A.D.

Notice, however, that when usage has sanctioned the dropping of the period, it is no longer required — *exam, gym, prom, 1st, 2nd, 3rd, percent.* Periods are usually omitted in abbreviations of government agencies — *USNR, TVA, AEC, FBI.*

**c. A period is used before a decimal and between dollars and cents.**

The error is less than .01 of an inch.
The correct answer is 57.39.
The price tag read $11.98.

# P 6

## Question and Exclamation Marks

**a. The question mark is used almost entirely to indicate that a sentence is to be understood as a question.**

Whose is this?
You mean he's ill?

It is sometimes used in parentheses to question the accuracy of the preceding word:

These amateurs (?) make a comfortable living out of sports.

As a device for irony, however, it is generally weak.

His funny (?) remarks were more than I could bear.

**b. The exclamation mark is used to show that a statement is imperative or that it is spoken with strong emotion.**

Be quiet! Attention!
Leave the room at once! Good Heavens!
Oh, you fool! God help us!

Like the question mark, the exclamation mark is generally considered a poor way of expressing irony or humor.

Arabella was so beautiful (!) that everybody gasped.

## P7    *The Colon*

THE MAIN USES of the colon are:

**a. To indicate that something is to follow, especially a formal series.**

Here are the facts: The money was there five minutes before he entered the room; it was missing immediately after he left; the next day he bought a new suit, although he had previously spent all of this month's allowance.

The slogan goes like this: Look sharp! Feel sharp! Be sharp!

**b. In place of a comma before long or formal direct quotations.**

In that speech Bryan said: "You shall not press down upon the brow of labor a crown of thorns; you shall not crucify mankind upon a cross of gold."

This is his statement as reported in the papers: "I have never advocated such ideas; I do not advocate them now; I do not approve of them; and I have no reason for believing that I ever will approve of them."

**c. Before a clause which is intended to restate in different form the idea of the preceding clause.**

*Henry V* is one of the great experiences in the history of motion pictures. It is not, to be sure, the greatest: the creation of new dramatic poetry is more important than the recreation of the old.

Except for differences of subject matter, the rules of grammar are exactly like the laws of physics and chemistry: they are scientific generalizations about the facts.

In each of these examples the clause following the colon says, in another way, what was already said in the clause preceding the colon. The restatement, however, is not needless repetition: it serves to illustrate or amplify the content of the preceding clause.

## Quotation Marks

THIS SECTION is limited to the use of quotation marks. The troublesome question of the position of other punctuation with respect to quotation marks is treated separately in the next section.

Quotation marks may be double (" ") or single (' '). Double quotation marks have the following uses:

**a. To enclose the actual words of a speaker (direct discourse).**

> I said, "That's your worry."
> "Bob," he said, "you can't do that!"
> "What is the matter?" she asked.

Notice that since all the words of a speaker are enclosed in quotation marks an interrupting *he said, she replied,* etc. requires two sets of quotation marks in the sentence. Notice also that when direct discourse is reported as indirect discourse the quotation marks are not used.

> She asked what was the matter.

**b. To identify words which are being discussed as words.**

> The word "garage" comes from the French; the word "piano" comes from the Italian.
> "Buxom" originally came from the Old English verb meaning "to bend."
> "To be" is the trickiest verb in the language.

This use is sometimes extended to include slang terms (According to her story her brother "socked" her in the eye and "beaned" her with a ruler). This usage, though occasionally appropriate, is often overdone in student writing. Quotation marks do not make a slang term appropriate. If it is appropriate it can usually stand without quotation marks; if it is not appropriate, it should not be used.

**c. To enclose the titles of short stories, poems, songs, etc. (but not books).**

> I think Kipling's best short story is "Without Benefit of Clergy."
> Have you read Emerson's "Self-Reliance"?
> It was Cole Porter who wrote "Begin the Beguine."
> "The Trouble With Harry" is the funniest picture Hitchcock has made.
> He says that Da Vinci's "Mona Lisa" is a portrait of an Italian noblewoman.

**d.** In bibliography, to distinguish the title of a selection from that of the whole book in which the selection is printed.

> Faulkner, William. "Two Soldiers," *Collected Stories of William Faulkner.* New York: Random House, 1950.

For additional examples of this use see pages 286–287. Notice that titles of books are set in italics rather than in quotation marks.

Single quotation marks are used:

**a.** To mark quotations within quotations.

When it is necessary to include one set of quotation marks within another, the internal quotation is placed in single quotation marks, the longer quotation in double quotation marks:

> Here is an excerpt from my brother's letter: "Today in class Mr. Blair quoted Wordsworth's line, 'A three-months darling of a pigmy size,' and said it appeared in one edition as, 'A three-months darling of a pig my size.' "

> When the director said, "Let's try that passage again, beginning with, 'Once more into the breach,' and remember that this is a battle, not a declamation contest," there was an audible bronx cheer from one of the soldiers.

**b.** In print, as a substitute for double quotation marks to improve the appearance of the page.

When it is necessary to place quotation marks around a great many single words on a page, an editor will sometimes attempt to improve the appearance of the page by substituting single marks for double marks. The need for this substitution almost never exists in college writing.

---

**P 9** | *Punctuation with Quotation Marks*

---

WHETHER PUNCTUATION should be placed *inside* or *outside* quotation marks is often a problem. Practice is not uniform, but the following excerpt from *The MLA Style Sheet* — a respected authority among English instructors — states the prevailing procedure succinctly:

For the sake of appearance put all commas or periods *inside* quotation marks. . . . Other punctuation goes inside quotation marks only when it is actually part of the quoted matter.[1]

This convention may be stated in detail as follows:

**a. When the quoted words are followed by a comma, put the comma *inside* the quotation marks.**

"If you insist," I said, "I'll do it."

The word "skirt," for example, has both standard and slang meanings.

"But," Bill objected, " 'Knabe,' in German, doesn't mean 'knave'; it means 'boy.' "

Notice that this convention applies only to quoted material. It does not mean that a comma after *he said, she replied,* etc. should be placed inside the quotation marks.

**b. The period, like the comma, always goes inside the quotation marks.**

That is not the way to spell "eclectic."

He said, "You can always count on Tom to muddle the issue."

**c. If the quotation is a question, the question mark goes inside the quotation marks; otherwise, it goes outside.**

Somebody yelled, "Why don't you go home?" (What was yelled was a question.)

Did he actually say, "Let Williams do it"? (The quotation is not a question, but the whole sentence is; therefore the question mark goes outside the quotation marks, and no other punctuation is used at the end of the sentence.)

Well, how *do* you spell "eclectic"? (The whole sentence is a question, not the word "eclectic.")

**d. The exclamation mark, like the question mark, goes inside if the quoted part is an exclamation; otherwise, it goes outside.**

"Get out of my sight!" he yelled. (The quoted part is an exclamation.)

I did, too, say "Friday"! (The whole sentence is an exclamation; "Friday" is not.)

His only answer was "Nonsense!" (Only the quoted word is an exclamation.)

[1] From *The MLA Style Sheet,* Revised Edition, p. 9. Compiled by W. R. Parker, for the Modern Language Association of America, 1947–56. By permission. The omitted material indicated by the ellipsis refers to exceptions which almost never occur in freshman writing.

e. Since the semicolon and the colon almost never occur as part of quoted material, the practice is always to place them outside the quotation marks.

> He said, "You can be confident that I'll do it"; but I was by no means confident.

If the sentence ended with the quotation, there would be a period inside the quotation marks. The semicolon is used to provide contrast between the two main clauses, not to end the first one.

> "There are three parts," she said; "we have two of them."

Although the semicolon would be included in the quotation if it were written — She said, "There are three parts; we have two of them." — the semicolon is always placed after *she* (*he*, etc.) *said* when it interrupts such quotations.

f. Since the dash stands for an omitted part of the quotation, it is always included within the quotation marks.

Occasionally a speaker is interrupted or for some reason fails to finish what he has begun to say. When this happens, a dash is used to show that the quotation is not finished.

> "But Mary said — " she began, then stopped suddenly.
> Nicholson said loudly, "In my opinion, our instructor is —" Just then the instructor walked into the room.

Notice that a concluding period is not used after the dash.

# P 10 | *The Apostrophe*

THE APOSTROPHE (') has three general uses:

a. Use an apostrophe to indicate the possessive case of a noun.

An apostrophe followed by *s* is added to the common case of the following types of nouns:

*Both singular and plural nouns, neither of which ends in* s:

boy's, girl's, ox's, mouse's, tooth's, antenna's
men's, women's, oxen's, mice's, teeth's, antennae's

*Singular nouns ending in* s:

James's, Charles's, Keats's, Burns's

Usage for the latter group varies. Some writers omit the final *s*
(James', Charles', etc.). When a noun already contains two *s* sounds,
there is a greater reluctance to add a third one (Massachusetts', mistress',
Jesus'), but since most written communications are not read aloud the
repetition of *s* sounds is usually not so objectionable as it might seem
to be. With such nouns, follow your own preference.

*Indefinite pronouns:*

anybody's, anyone's, everybody's, one's, nobody's, someone's

An apostrophe without an *s* is added to plural nouns ending in *s:*

babies', boys', brothers', fathers', dogs', horses'

**b. Use an apostrophe to indicate the omission of letters or figures.**

I've, can't, hasn't, isn't, '48 (1948), the class of '39

**c. Use an apostrophe to indicate the plural of letters or figures.**

Let's begin with the A's; look under the K's; the S's look like 8's.

## P 11     *Ellipsis and Dash*

## *Ellipsis (...)*

**The basic use of the ellipsis (three periods) is to mark an incomplete construction:**

Usually the ellipsis indicates that one or more words have been
omitted from a quotation. It is also used to indicate that a progression
of numbers continues beyond the last figure given (1,4,7,10,13,16 . . .).

If an ellipsis occurs at the end of a sentence, a fourth period is usually added:

| *Original Quotation* | *Elliptical Quotation* |
|---|---|
| Death is at all times solemn, but never so much as at sea. A man dies on shore, his body remains with his friends, and "the mourners go about the streets," but when a man falls overboard at sea and is lost, there is a sadness in the event and a difficulty in realizing it, which gives it an air of awful mystery. | Death is at all times solemn, but never so much as at sea. A man dies on shore, his body remains with his friends, . . . but when a man falls overboard at sea and is lost, there is a sadness in the event, and a difficulty in realizing it. . . . |

## Dash

The dash should not be used as a general utility mark to substitute for a comma, period, semicolon, or colon. It is a specialized punctuation mark which serves the following purposes:

**a. To stress a word or phrase at the end of a sentence.**

In the whole world there is only one person he really admires — himself.

And now it is my pleasure to present a man whom we all know and admire and to whom we are all deeply indebted — the Reverend Dr. Mason.

Absence makes the heart grow fonder — of somebody else.

**b. To sum up or complete an involved sentence.**

To live as free men in a free country; to enjoy, even to abuse, the right to think and speak as we like; to feel that the state is the servant of its people; to be, even in a literal sense, a trustee and a partner in the conduct of a nation — all this is what democracy means to us.

**c. To mark an interrupted or unfinished quotation.**

"I'd like to," he said, "but I'm — "

"You're what?" I asked.

"Well, I'm — I — you see, I've never done anything like that before."

**d. When used in pairs, to set off a pronounced interruption.**

There will never again be — you may be sure of this — so glorious an opportunity.

This answer — if we can call it an answer — is completely meaningless.

## P 12 | Parentheses and Brackets

## Parentheses

The three most common uses of parentheses, in order of importance, are:

**a. To enclose an explanation, qualification, or example:**

His wife (he married about a year ago) is a member of a very fine New England family.

*Nice* (in the old sense of discriminating) has almost fallen out of use.

Foreign words (*data,* for example) slowly become naturalized and lose their foreign characteristics.

**b. To enclose cross-references:**

(*See* Appendix A), (*See page 271*), (*Consult* Webster's Biographical Dictionary).

**c. In formal business transactions, to repeat a sum previously stated in words:**

I enclose three-hundred dollars ($300.00) to cover my share of the costs.

## Brackets

Brackets are used chiefly to enclose an editorial explanation or comment within a passage being edited or reported. The words within the brackets are supplied by the editor; the rest is the work of the author.

According to the Associated Press, Mrs. Henry Thall [the former June Wexler of this city] was a passenger on the missing plane.

I have written to [name of correspondent illegible] that I will not be a party to that transaction.

Brackets are occasionally used to enclose symbols which cannot conventionally be left without some enclosing device. The identification of the various punctuation marks on page 504 is an example of this use.

## Review Exercises

**A.** Rewrite and hand in to your instructor the following sentences, inserting as you write any punctuation clearly required by the conventions.

If no punctuation is necessary, do not copy the sentence. To make your insertions obvious, use red ink or red pencil for punctuation which you add.

1. He said I propose to transfer at the end of the semester.
2. He said he would transfer at the end of the semester.
3. I expect he said to transfer at the end of the semester.
4. Dr J A Frazer was born on March 18 1901
5. Dr Koch a German scientist discovered the tuberculosis bacillus.
6. The lecturer was the Rev Nelson Laird D D
7. Have you read his latest book
8. The cars in that series were as follows Aerosedan Fleetline Fleetmaster and Stylemaster.
9. The manuscript was dirty blotched and unevenly typed.
10. I have not seen him since his wife left he has been keeping to himself.
11. Mr. Reynolds the insurance man called.
12. She is quite inexperienced and has never worked in an office before.
13. See the new revolutionary car of the year the Ford.
14. She said, when I asked his opinion, he answered, I don't give advice on such questions.
15. I am enclosing eighty-five dollars $85.00 for the semiannual premium.
16. This meaning See *The American College Dictionary* is now established usage.
17. He looked at it enviously. Its a beauty he exclaimed.
18. However I still have five payments to make.
19. That she wont like it may be taken for granted.
20. Do you think he will accept she asked.

**B.** Distinguish between restrictive and nonrestrictive modifiers by inserting commas around the nonrestrictive modifiers in the following sentences. Use red ink or red pencil for inserted commas.

1. Girls who hate cooking are poor matrimonial risks.
2. Girls who are physically less rugged than boys should not be subjected to strenuous athletic programs.
3. The man driving the Maxwell is Jack Benny.
4. Benny driving a Maxwell was charged with obstructing traffic.
5. Salesmen who don't argue with customers make more money.
6. Salesmen most of whom are young men lead an unsettled life.
7. The pilot realizing his plight radioed for instructions.
8. The pilot who radioed for instructions does not answer.
9. His wife satisfied with these concessions wisely kept quiet.
10. His wife resentful of his extravagance asked for an increased allowance.
11. They questioned the man who reported the robbery.
12. The man who reported the robbery cannot be found.
13. The man at the back of the room was told to leave.

14. The man evidently seriously hurt was taken to the hospital.
15. The fighters who were quite obviously stalling were disqualified.
16. Their wives who needed the money were indignant.

**C.** The best way to develop a confident knowledge of the conventions of punctuation is to observe how punctuation marks are actually used in modern writing. In the following selection, which is fairly formal, particular punctuation marks have been numbered. Write down each number and describe the purpose for which the punctuation is being used.

Turning to the more modern theories,[1] which agree at least that language is of human rather than divine origin,[1] we encounter first what is best known by its nickname,[2] the "bow-wow" theory. This asserts that primitive language was exclusively *"echoic"*;[3] that is,[3] that its words were directly imitative of the sounds of nature or of animals. All the word-stock is thought to have originated in a way parallel to the child's calling a dog "bow-wow"[4] or a duck "quack-quack."[4] The great objection to this theory is that it has not been demonstrated that early or primitive languages are composed exclusively or in great part of onomatopoetic words; on the contrary,[5] it is clear that the primitive languages of savage tribes are largely made up of words that are quite as conventional as those of civilized peoples. At best,[6] the "bow-wow" theory can explain the origin of but a part,[7] and not the largest part,[7] of language. Yet it seems fair to add that the theory has in the past been somewhat unjustly derided. Words that are imitative or at least partly so —[8] for there are many gradations between the purely imitative and the purely conventional —[8] do form an appreciable part of the vocabulary of most languages. There are many words that we instinctively feel to be symbolic, or semi-echoic. Thus,[9] such English words as *battle*,[10] *roar*,[10] and *thunder* have not perhaps a completely imitative quality, certainly not as compared with *hiss*,[11] *whistle*,[11] *bang*,[11] and *crash;* yet they approach echoism in a way that the conventional words of language do not. If,[12] then,[12] the "bow-wow" theory does not solve the riddle of the origin of language,[13] it does at least help to account for the sounds of many words.[2]

**D.** In the following selections all punctuation has been omitted, except the periods at the ends of the sentences. Copy the selection, adding all necessary punctuation in red.

The Bible is written in very poor English isnt it remarked a grade school child to his father as they walked home from church.

What makes you say that inquired the astonished parent for whose ears the musical dignity of the King James Version approached the perfection of English prose.

Well our teacher said it was bad English to begin sentences with and. But almost every sentence the minister read this morning began with and replied the child.

[2] Reprinted by permission of Prentice-Hall, Inc., from *The Development of Modern English*, by Stuart Robertson. Copyright, 1934, 1938, by Prentice-Hall, Inc.

The father smiled as he recognized the accuracy of the childs observation. The reading had been from the eighth chapter of the Gospel according to St Matthew it was true enough that almost every sentence began with and. He thought a moment longer before he spoke. Your teacher has made a natural mistake he began. In trying to give good advice to boys and girls just learning to write she has made a rule about and. The rule is too big. People who know how to write well use and correctly and effectively at the beginning of sentences. On the other hand boys and girls in schools use and too much. Your teachers purpose in trying to help you was good but the rule she stated is untrue.

In this trifling episode may be found the epitome of the problem of correctness in English. It lies in the recurrent conflict between rule and practice. Rules of usage are usually made to cover specific situations to govern the use of language at a certain time for a certain purpose. Gradually as the rule is taught and applied the specific purpose for which it was created is forgotten and the rule is applied universally often in defiance of a language custom centuries old. Take for example the much taught but erroneous rule that a sentence must not end with a preposition. Or as one grammar is supposed to have stated it A preposition is a bad thing to end a sentence with. In certain types of formal literary English the terminal preposition is considered undesirable because of the rhetorical looseness it gives to the style. Because certain formalists disliked the construction the rule was created. It was repeated copied placed in school books. Teachers unaware of the reason behind the origin of the rule taught that a sentence must never end with a preposition. Teachers are still teaching this rule. Yet English for centuries has been idiomatically and correctly expressed in such sentences as Where are you from I didnt know whom to give it to. John will go but I dont expect to. What city has he lived in To apply the rule to such sentences as these which are characteristic of informal or colloquial English is to make an absurdity of a caution. Many such absurdities have been created and are being perpetuated through honest but misguided zeal.[3]

**E.** The following exercise is to be taken up orally in class. Before coming to class, study the passage and insert any punctuation which you feel is required. You should be able to explain orally in class why the punctuation is necessary.

A current attitude toward science is reflected in a recent cartoon which depicts two solicitous parents saying to their precocious son But what on earth do you want to be a scientist for Robert Isn't there enough trouble in the world already New and sensational developments in science and technology are usually accompanied by fears that we have created a monster that may devour us Even scientists appalled at the possible social consequences of their handiwork sometimes join in the hue and cry for a moratorium on science More frequently however the idea is

[3] From *Teaching English Usage*, by Robert C. Pooley. Copyright, 1946, by the National Council of Teachers of English. Reprinted by permission of Appleton-Century-Crofts, Inc.

advanced by a small group of romantics who are oppressed with their urban existence as contrasted with a dream world which they vaguely think of as the "simple" life. The most eloquent deprecators of the technological age often are "writers" living in New York apartments who would not know how to get downstairs if the elevators stopped running

Actually very few people seriously question the importance and the promise of the advancement of science Nearly everyone agrees that whatever troubles the advancement of science may have brought in its wake it has released us from some age-long fears and insecurities The natural sciences have undoubtedly given us a large measure of control over many of our traditional enemies although we may not always exercise this power

Even when we cannot do anything directly about averting natural events science is still invaluable in two principal ways First science forewarns us of certain events and thus enables us to avoid their more serious consequences If rain is predicted we carry an umbrella Ships are warned that a hurricane is likely to follow a certain path We may protect ourselves from certain diseases by proper inoculations and so forth Second the mere possession of scientific knowledge and scientific habits of thought regarding the natural universe relieves us of a world of fears rages and other unpleasant dissipations of energy Scientific knowledge operates as a sort of mental hygiene in the fields where it is applied If the morning paper reports an earthquake an eclipse a storm or a flood these events are immediately referred to their proper place in the framework of science in which their explanation i e their relationship to other events has already been worked out Hence each new event of this character calls for very little if any "mental" or "emotional" strain upon the organism so far as our intellectual adjustment to it as an event is concerned.[4]

**F.** The punctuation in the following student papers is unsatisfactory. First, go through each paper and mark the errors successively 1, 2, 3, 4, etc. Then, for each number, write down the revision you would make. Be prepared to explain and justify your revision in class. Your instructor will probably not object to your improving the grammar as you study the punctuation.

## (1)

Probably sometime in everyone's life, there has been the urge to travel, to see the sights of the world. The many booklets and leaflets describing and picturing ocean cruises winter vacationlands, western deserts; and other ideal sight-seeing tours encourage that ambition that has so long been held close to the heart. But not all of us can afford the luxury of travel. That is the reason that reading is such an ideal substitute.

Reading is available to the majority of the people. While traveling at least of any distance takes from a week or two to several months reading need only occupy a few hours or an evening at a time. It can be done in the leisure hours of the busiest and most tiring day. The man, who

[4] From *Can Science Save Us?*, by George A. Lundberg. Copyright, 1947, by George A. Lundberg. Reprinted by permission of Longmans, Green & Co., Inc.

since childhood has dreamed of making an ocean voyage around the world, can fulfill that dream by spending an evening in his easy chair reading a good book.

Reading not only takes less time; but less money. There are undoubtedly thousands of people who long to go abroad to Paris and London, or south to Mexico and even to South America, but they know that their incomes will not stretch far enough for such luxuries. Here again reading fulfills the hopes of many! Good books can be found by the hundreds in public libraries. Book clubs have flourished because so many people have chosen this substitute for travel. No longer as in Lincoln's day do people have to hunt for books to read. There is neither a lack of books, nor a lack of funds to buy books.

While traveling can occupy a lifetime, a book requiring only a few evenings rapid reading can cover a period of a year or two. The vast areas in this world would take even more than a lifetime to explore. Yet reading makes it possible to travel continually and accomplish it in much less time. Though one may never see the Grand Canyon or the famed sidewalk cafés of Paris, the vivid descriptions found in books can keep his imagination alive with these scenes forever.

It would be impossible for the most of us to explore the mountain peaks of the Alps or the cold tundra of Siberia. It would be out of the question to attempt to make a daring trip down the Mississippi in a canoe. But we can live and experience these adventures in remote places merely by reading the accounts, both true and fictional, that have been written by others, who enjoy traveling as much as we.

Though travel is said to be broadening and educational, it lacks these qualities somewhat when compared to reading. Reading, because it can include many finer details that are lost in traveling and sightseeing, is factual. Though a story of a missionary's life in South Africa may be fiction, the setting and surroundings may be so accurately described that, were you to go there you could actually point out the landmarks mentioned in the story. Likewise, from a fictional story of the cliff-dwellers of Arizona and New Mexico, the true story of their lives, customs and practices could be derived.

Books contain many facts that would be overlooked in traveling. Traveling is usually spent to gain pleasure and enjoyment. On the other hand, while reading, one can also gain knowledge and further his understanding and education.

Reading is definitely a substitute for travel — an ideal substitute. For all of us who don't have the opportunity to travel, books have helped make life worth-while! Our traveling can be done in our own living room with a good book.

## (2)

### What I Expect of Marriage

I do not believe that my parents have made too much of a success of their marriage because there has always been quarreling strife and dissatisfaction among our family members. I don't doubt but what there is a feeling of love and affection between my mother and father, but they have never learned to adjust themselves to each others individual lives. My father is powerful possessive and over-bearing while my mother is weak submissive and unable to go ahead and think for herself. I hope to learn from the example my parents have set before me, and I shall not make the same mistakes that they have.

I intend to give all that I am capable of giving to my marriage and my family. There will be no time for a career or excursions into the business world; unless the money I could earn was essential for the welfare of the marriage. Nevertheless, I want a good liberal education to prepare me to take my place as the wife and mother in a happy family unit. Such an education should teach me to get along with other people to understand their ways and beliefs and thus, to understand and know better my husband and his individual characteristics. Certainly, it would help in understanding and guiding my children through childhood or until they were capable of caring entirely for themselves.

I think it best if I marry a man from my own social financial and religious class. Then, if there were any changes to be made we would make them together. However, regardless of his standing in the world, I intend most of all to marry a man I can love and respect and one who is a Christian with the idea of raising his children to be Christians in a good Christian home.

From my marriage, I want children who will serve as a living part of me here on earth after my death. In those children I hope to mold all of the good traits of their parents, but undoubtedly some of the bad ones will also show up. To them I shall try to give every advantage for an easier, and happier life but not at the expense of having them lose the determination, and will power that comes from facing and overcoming hardships.

I expect an equal amount in return for the things I try to give my marriage. I want love, companionship, and devotion from a faithful husband in whom I can believe and trust. Our companionship through the years should include working together to own a home of our own. Also, it should include many compromises as to the training of the children, the balancing of the budget, and the deciding of whose family we spend holidays and vacations with.

I expect to face long years of hard work with probably a small income, but I also expect to be rewarded by a home of our own, a family, and a well-provided-for retirement in old age. With all of these things I could truly say I would be happy, but there is one last item I feel I must mention.

From all of these things I have discussed, I also need a feeling of contentment and satisfaction within myself along with the knowledge that I have tried to make my marriage a success and that it will not exist as an unhappy arrangement such as my parents failure.

I want to know when I die that I have a companion beside me forever and that my unfinished work will be carried on by our followers.

# *Spelling*

ONE REQUIREMENT of standard English is that words be spelled as they are spelled by educated writers and recorded in dictionaries. Colleges and universities are held responsible by society for ensuring that their graduates have a reasonable mastery of standard English. It is for this reason that college instructors insist that all college writing — even the most informal — show a decent regard for accepted spelling. The real purpose of this insistence is to protect the student; for conspicuously bad spelling is generally considered a clear sign of illiteracy. Socially and professionally, a student who cannot spell is at a disadvantage. It is easier to judge a man's spelling than most other things about him; and, whether rightly or not, people do jump to conclusions about a person's education and intelligence on the evidence of his spelling. A student who refuses to make a serious and sustained effort to cure major spelling deficiencies penalizes himself in college and out of it.

Students who spell poorly usually act on one of three assumptions: (*a*) that spelling is not important, (*b*) that nothing much can be done to improve one's spelling, or (*c*) that the only way to learn is to spend hours memorizing spelling lists. None of these assumptions is sound. Spelling *is* important. Provided that misspelling is not a result of an organic or psychological disorder, there is no reason why any student cannot train himself to be a reasonably good speller within a single semester. And an uncritical memorizing of spelling lists is not conspicuously effective.

### How to Improve Your Spelling

The first step in improving your spelling is to take an inventory of your errors. Keep a record of those words *which you actually misspell in your writing*. The best way to begin such an inventory is to take a standard spelling list, such as the one on pages 538–542, and check those words which cause you difficulty, ignoring those you seldom use or never misspell. The checked words then become your basic, private spelling list. You should copy their correct spellings in alphabetical order into a special notebook, leaving space for later additions. Your basic list probably will not exceed fifty words. Even an unusually poor speller could probably correct ninety per cent of his spelling errors by concentrating on a carefully selected list of 100 words.

You should keep your basic list up to date by scoring out words you have mastered and adding new words you have misspelled. This step is most important. Your original list was merely an estimate of your spelling weaknesses, but actual misspellings are a record of errors. Remember, it is the errors you have made that you are really interested in correcting, and the more accurately your list records them, the more useful it will be. Also, because the frequency with which you misspell a word is part of your spelling record, you should indicate repeated misspellings of the same word by adding a check mark each time you misspell it.

Keeping such a list will of itself help a great deal, but the list should be reviewed regularly. Any normal student who conscientiously studies such a list for ten minutes a day should be able to eliminate all his common spelling errors within a single semester. If you think this statement is an exaggeration, put it to the test. The experiment may give you a lasting sense of confidence in your spelling ability that will more than justify the time spent.

In studying your list, concentrate on the *part* of the word which you misspell. Generally we do not misspell words but syllables. For example, most students who misspell *secretary* interchange the second and third vowels; most misspellings of *tragedy* are a result of placing an extra *d* before the *g*; and misspellings of such words as *receive, belief,* and *friend* come from reversing the *i* and *e*. Identifying your specific errors allows you to concentrate on the syllable in which the error occurs.

For words which prove unusually troublesome it is often helpful to learn or invent some memorizing device: a rule, a slogan, a jingle — anything, no matter how absurd, which will remind you of the correct spelling of a particular syllable. The rule of *i* before *e* except after *c,* which is stated as a jingle on page 536, and the rules for prefixes and suffixes, are generally useful memorizing devices. Unfortunately some rules have so many exceptions that they are hardly worth learning. It is therefore often wise to invent your own memorizing device. Some students find it extremely helpful to remember statements like *A good secretary keeps a secret, Remember the gum in argument,* and *Every cemetery has a "meter" in the middle.* Other students are helped by capitalizing the danger spots during spelling practice — tRAGedy, main-TENance, desPERate. If these devices help you, use them; if not, invent your own.

Finally, a concern with spelling during composition should, so far as is practicable, be postponed until revision. If you break off the writing of a paragraph to consult a dictionary, you may lose a thought you can not recapture. If you keep a record of your misspellings, you will be conscious of troublesome words, so that when you are uncertain of a spelling, you can place a check in the margin and go on. Then, when the first draft is finished, look up the correct spelling of all checked words. Indeed, a student with severe spelling troubles will be wise to proofread his whole paper at least once for spelling alone.

In short, then: (1) Keep a spelling record, (2) study it at regular periods, (3) identify the trouble spot in the word, (4) devise a means of remembering the correct spelling, and (5) check your spelling when proofreading. If this procedure is followed conscientiously, spelling will soon cease to be a problem.

### The Most Common Traps in Spelling

Although any word which is not spelled phonetically (as it sounds) may give trouble, six types of words are especially likely to cause errors. These are:

1. Words containing a "colorless" vowel.
2. Words with *ie* or *ei*.
3. Words with similar sounds but different meanings.
4. Words with irregular plural forms.
5. Words which double the final consonant before a suffix beginning with a vowel.
6. Common exceptions to general rules.

**1. The Colorless Vowel.** Vowels in unstressed positions (*a*go, *a*gent, awkw*a*rd, maintenance, incred*i*ble, bachel*o*r) are likely to be pronounced as a very weak *uh*. This sound is called the colorless or neutral vowel.[1] Because it is quite common in English and because its sound gives no indication of its spelling, the colorless vowel is responsible for many spelling errors. There is nothing to guide one in spelling this sound. The only solution is to memorize the vowel in any word which repeatedly causes trouble. The best help is a memorizing device, such as magnifying the syllable in question — *baLANCE, indepenDENT, eli-gIBLE, sponSOR, foREIGN, chauffEUR.*

**2. The *e-i* Combination.** Words like *niece, receive,* and *friend* are frequently misspelled through the interchanging of the *e* and the *i*. Most of these errors may be easily removed by following Rule 4 below and memorizing the ten exceptions.

**3. Words with Similar Sounds but Different Meanings.** Such words as *altar, alter; peace, piece; weak, week; weather, whether* are easily confused. A list of troublesome contrasted pairs is given on pages 542-543. You should study that list and copy into your personal spelling record any pairs which you tend to confuse.

**4. Irregular Plurals.** Since most English nouns take *s* plurals, all plurals formed in any other way may be considered irregular. The most troublesome plurals to spell are those of nouns ending in *o* or *y*. Such

---

[1] Students using *The American College Dictionary* or Webster's *New World Dictionary* should notice that in these dictionaries the colorless vowel is represented by the phonetic symbol called the *schwa*, and written ə, like an inverted *e*.

nouns have regular *s* plurals when the *o* or *y* immediately follows a vowel (*cameo, cameos; key, keys; studio, studios*), but are generally irregular when the *o* or *y* follows a consonant (*cargo, veto, lady, torpedo*). See Rules 6 and 7 on pages 536–537.

**5. Doubling a Final Consonant.** Some words double a final consonant before adding a suffix beginning with a vowel (*refer, referred*), while others (*benefit, benefited*) do not. This lack of consistency causes many spelling errors, and the "rule," is so cumbersome and has so many exceptions that students often prefer to study the individual words which cause them trouble. The more useful part of the rule concerning doubled consonants is given as Rule 9 on page 537.

**6. Exceptions.** Any exceptional spelling is likely to be difficult because of the tendency to make it conform to the regular pattern. For example, a student who is not sure how to spell *seize* is likely to interchange the *e* and *i* because of the *ei* rule. Similarly the rule that a silent *e* at the end of a word is retained in adding a suffix beginning with a consonant leads many students to misspell *argument*. Words like these are exceptions to general rules and cause many spelling errors. The only safe procedure is to *memorize the exceptions along with the rule*. Whenever a rule is given in the following pages the common exceptions are noted. Study these as carefully as you study the rule itself.

## Rules of Spelling

The rules given here are those which are most generally useful.

**1. The prefixes un-, dis-, mis- do not affect the spelling of the root.**

Thus, *unafraid* but *unnecessary; disappoint* but *dissatisfy; misrepresent* but *misspell.*

| | | |
|---|---|---|
| unable | disable | misbehave |
| unknown | disorder | misconduct |
| unopened | disregard | misguided |
| *but* | *but* | *but* |
| unnatural | disservice | misshapen |
| unnerved | dissimilar | misspent |
| unnoticed | dissolve | misstatement |

**2. When a suffix beginning with a consonant is added to a word ending in silent e, the e is retained.**

Examples: *absolutely, achievement, extremely, indefinitely, sincerely.*

Exceptions: *argument, awful, duly, ninth, probably, wholly.*

Three common words have alternative spellings:

*abridgment, abridgement; acknowledgment, acknowledgement; judgment, judgement.*

**3.** When a suffix beginning with a vowel is added to a word ending in silent e, the e is dropped unless it is required to indicate pronunciation or to avoid confusion with a similar word.

Examples: *accumulating, achieving, boring, coming, grievance, icy.*

Exceptions:

| To Keep<br>a c or g Soft | To Prevent<br>Mispronunciation |
|---|---|
| advantageous | canoeist |
| changeable | eyeing |
| courageous | hoeing |
| manageable | mileage |
| noticeable | shoeing |
| outrageous | |
| peaceable | *To Prevent . Confusion* |
| serviceable | *with Other Words* |
| singeing | |
| tingeing | dyeing |
| vengeance | |

**4.** The order of the vowels in the *ie* combination (*ceiling, niece*) is explained in the jingle:

> Write *i* before *e*
> Except after *c*
> Or when sounded like *ay*
> As in *neighbor* and *weigh.*

Exceptions: *counterfeit, either, foreign, forfeit, height, heir, leisure, neither, seize, sovereign.*

**5.** Words ending with the sound *seed* are usually spelled -cede.

Examples: *accede, concede, intercede, precede, recede, secede.*

Exceptions: There are only four exceptions. Three of them end in *-ceed* (*exceed, proceed, succeed*); the fourth is the only word that ends in *-sede* (*supersede*).

**6.** Singular nouns ending in a consonant plus *y* form their plurals by changing the *y* to *i* before adding -es.

This rule also applies to the third person singular of verbs.

Examples: *ally, allies; baby, babies; city, cities; cry, cries; try, tries.*

Exceptions: The plurals of proper names often add *s* immediately after the *y*: *the Kellys, the Marys, the Sallys.*

Notice that singular nouns ending in a vowel plus *y* are regular and simply add -*s* to form the plural:

> *attorneys, donkeys, valleys.*

**7.** Singular nouns ending in a consonant plus o generally form their plurals by adding -es.

There are, however, so many exceptions that it may be safer to dispense with the rule and learn troublesome words individually.

Examples:*buffaloes, cargoes, echoes, heroes, potatoes, torpedoes, vetoes.*

Exceptions: The chief exceptions are musical terms: *altos, bassos, oratorios, pianos, solos, sopranos.* Others are *autos, cantos, dynamos, Eskimos, halos, mementos, provisos, quartos.*

Notice that singular nouns ending in a vowel plus *o* are regular and simply add -*s* to form the plural:

*cameos, folios, radios, studios.*

**8.** Most singular nouns ending in -s, -ss, -sh, -ch, -x, or -z, form their plurals by adding -es.

Examples: *Jameses, Joneses, ashes, bushes, matches, pitches, foxes, taxes, buzzes.*

Exceptions: *bass, fish, perch, six's, Swiss,* and borrowed Greek nouns ending in -*is* (*ellipsis — ellipses, thesis — theses,* etc.).

**9.** Words of one syllable double the final consonant before adding a suffix beginning with a vowel if (1) they end in a single consonant, and (2) they contain a single vowel.

Notice that the rule holds only if both conditions are satisfied. Thus a word of one syllable ending in two consonants does not double the final consonant before a suffix beginning with a vowel (a*cting,* a*sked,* pa*rting,* si*fted,* etc.). And a one-syllable word containing two vowels does not double the final consonant (bea*ring,* cree*ping,* dea*ling,* ree*ling,* soa*ring,* etc.).

This rule is extended to words of more than one syllable, provided that the accent falls on the last syllable (thus prefér — preferred, but bénefit — benefited; confér — conferring, but cónference). This part of the rule, however, has so many exceptions that students sometimes find the rule more confusing than helpful.

## Review Exercises

**A.** Following is a list of words frequently misspelled by college students. When two spellings are given for the same word, both are correct and the first is preferred.

As you read through the list underline those words which you recognize as being part of your writing vocabulary and which you have had trouble spelling. Then copy the correct spelling of the underlined words into a special notebook so that you will have a preliminary record of your spelling difficulties. Revise this list periodically by adding the correct spelling of any word which you misspell in subsequent papers and scoring out words which you no longer misspell. Check, also, the list given in Exercise B.

| | | |
|---|---|---|
| abbreviate | analysis | beggar |
| absence | analyze | beginning |
| absolutely | annual | believe |
| absurd | antecedent | beneficial |
| accelerate | anxiety | benefited |
| accidentally | apartment | biscuit |
| accommodate | apparatus | boundaries |
| accomplish | apparent | breathe |
| according | appearance | brilliant |
| accumulate | appropriate | Britain |
| accustom | arctic | Britannica |
| achievement | argument | Briton |
| acoustics | arising | bulletin |
| acquaintance | arithmetic | buoyant |
| acquitted | arouse | bureau |
| across | arranging | buried |
| address | article | burying |
| adoption | artillery | business |
| advice (noun) | ascend | busy |
| advise (verb) | association | cafeteria |
| adviser, advisor | athlete | calendar |
| aggravate | athletics | candidate |
| aggression | attempt | can't |
| airplane | attractive | carburetor |
| alleviate | audible | carrying |
| alley | audience | casualties |
| allotted | authorities | causal |
| allowed | automobile | ceiling |
| all right | auxiliary | celebrity |
| ally | awkward | cemetery |
| already | bachelor | certain |
| although | balance | changeable |
| altogether | balloon | changing |
| always | barbarous | characteristic |
| amateur | barring | chauffeur |
| ambiguous | battalion | chief |
| ammunition | bearing | choose |
| among | because | choosing |
| amount | becoming | chose |
| analogous | before | chosen |

clause
climbed
clothes
colloquial
colonel
column
coming
commission
commitment
committed
committee
companies
comparatively
compel
compelled
competent
competition
complaint
completely
compulsory
concede
conceivable
conceive
condemn
condescend
condition
conjunction
connoisseur
conqueror
conscience
conscientious
considered
consistent
contemptible
continuous
control
controlled
convenient
co-operate, coöperate
copies
corner
coroner
corps
corpse
costume
countries
courteous
courtesy
cozy

cries
criticism
criticize
cruelty
cruise
curiosity
curriculum
custom
cylinder
dealt
debater
deceitful
deceive
decide
decision
defendant
deferred
deficient
definite
definition
democracy
dependent
descendant
describe
description
desirable
despair
desperate
destruction
develop, develope
developed
development
device (noun)
devise (verb)
diaphragm
diary
dictionary
dietitian
difference
digging
diphtheria
disappearance
disappoint
disastrous
discipline
discussion
disease
dissatisfied
dissipate

distribute
divine
doctor
doesn't
dominant
don't
dormitories
dropped
drunkenness
echoes
ecstasy
efficiency
eighth
eligible
eliminate
embarrass
eminent
emphasize
employee
encouraging
encyclopedia
enthusiastic
equipment
equipped
equivalent
erroneous
especially
eventually
exaggerate
exceed
excel
excellent
exceptional
excitement
exercise
exhaust
exhilaration
existence
experience
explanation
extensive
extracurricular
extremely
exuberance
fallacious
fallacy
familiar
fascinate
February

fiery
finally
financial
financier
forehead
foreign
foremost
forfeit
forty
frantically
fraternities
freshman
friend
fulfill, fulfil
furniture
gaiety
generally
genius
genuine
glorious
government
grammar
grandeur
grievous
guarantee
guard
guardian
guerilla, guerrilla
guess
guidance
handicapped
handkerchief
harass
hearse
height
heinous
heroes
hesitancy
hindrance
hoarse
hoping
horde
human
humane
humorous
hundredths
hurries
hygiene
hypocrisy

hysterical
illiterate
illogical
imaginary
imagination
imitative
immediately
implement
impromptu
inadequate
incidentally
incredible
indefinitely
independent
indicted
indispensable
inevitable
influential
innocent
inoculate
intellectual
intelligence
intentionally
intercede
interested
interpret
interrupt
irrelevant
irreligious
irresistible
irreverent
itself
judgment, judgement
judicial
khaki
kindergarten
knowledge
laboratory
laid
later
latter
legitimate
leisure
library
lightning
likable, likeable
likely
literature
loneliness

losing
magazine
magnificent
maintain
maintenance
maneuver
manual
manufacture
mathematics
mattress
meant
medicine
medieval
messenger
millionaire
miniature
minute
mischievous
misspelled
modifies
modifying
momentous
mortgage
mosquitoes
mottoes
mountainous
murmur
muscle
mysterious
naïve, naive
naturally
necessary
necessity
Negroes
neither
nervous
nevertheless
nickel
niece
ninety
ninth
noticeable
notorious
nowadays
obedience
obliged
obstacle
occasionally
occur

occurred
occurrence
o'clock
official
officious
omission
omit
omitted
oneself
opinion
opportunity
optimistic
organization
original
orthodox
ought
outrageous
overrun
paid
pamphlet
parallel
parliament
participle
particularly
partner
pastime
peaceable
perceive
perform
perhaps
permissible
perseverance
persuade
Philippines
phrase
physical
physician
picnicked
piece
planed
planned
playwright
pleasant
politics
possess
possessive
possible
potatoes
practice

prairie
precedence
precedents
preceding
predominant
prefer
preference
preferred
prejudice
preparation
prevalent
primitive
privilege
probably
professor
prominent
pronounce
pronunciation
propaganda
propeller
protein
psychology
pursue
pursuing
putting
quantity
quarantine
quarter
questionnaire
quizzes
realize
really
recede
receipt
receive
receiving
recognize
recommend
refer
reference
referred
referring
regard
regional
relevant
religion
religious
remembrance
reminiscence

rendezvous
repetition
replies
representative
reservoir
resistance
restaurant
reverent
rhetoric
rheumatism
rhythmical
ridiculous
sacrifice
sacrilegious
safety
salary
sanctuary
sandwich
scarcely
scene
scenic
schedule
scrape
secretarial
secretary
seized
sense
sensible
sentence
sentinel
separate
sergeant
severely
shining
shriek
siege
sieve
similar
sincerely
sincerity
skeptical
slight
soliloquy
sophomore
source
specifically
specimen
sponsor
spontaneous

statement
statue
stature
statute
stomach
stopped
strength
strenuously
stretched
struggle
studying
subordinate
subtle
succeed
success
successful
suffrage
superintendent
supersede
suppress
surely
surprise
suspense
swimming
syllable
symmetry
synonym
synonymous
taboo, tabu
tangible
tariff
tasting
technical

technique
temperament
tenant
tendency
than
therefor
therefore
they're
thorough
though, tho
thought
till
tired
together
tournament
toward, towards
traffic
tragedy
transferred
tremendous
tries
truly
Tuesday
twelfth
typical
tyranny
unanimous
undoubtedly
unnecessary
until
usage
useful
using

usually
vacancy
vacuum
valuable
vengeance
victorious
view
vigilant
vigorous
village
villain
volume
warrant
warring
weird
welfare
where
which
whole
wholly
whom
wiry
woman
women
won't
worried
worrying
writing
written
yacht
your
you're (you are)
zoology

**B.** Errors in the following words may be classified as errors in spelling or errors in diction, since both meaning and spelling are involved in the correct usage. Study these words carefully. Check those which you have confused in the past or of which you are uncertain and look them up in alphabetical order in the Glossary.

accept, except
access, excess
adapt, adopt
adaptation, adoption
affect, effect
all together, altogether
altar, alter
angel, angle

berth, birth
born, borne
canvas, canvass
capital, capitol
censor, censure
cite, sight, site
coarse, course
complement, compliment

conscience, conscious
council, counsel
dairy, diary
decent, descend, descent
desert, dessert
dining, dinning
dying, dyeing
elicit, illicit
emigrant, immigrant
euphemism, euphuism
fare, fair
formally, formerly
forth, fourth
hear, here
holy, wholly
instance, instants
irrelevant, irreverent
its, it's
knew, new
know, no
later, latter
lead, led
loath, loathe
loose, lose
luxuriant, luxurious

moral, morale
past, passed
peace, piece
plain, plane
precede, proceed
presence, presents
principal, principle
prophecy, prophesy
quiet, quite
respectively, respectfully
right, rite
shone, shown
sleight, slight
speak, speech
staid, stayed
stationary, stationery
straight, strait
suit, suite
threw, through
to, too, two
troop, troupe
vain, vein, vane
weak, week
weather, whether
who's, whose

**C.** All of the following words have a single consonant enclosed in parentheses. In some words, that consonant should be doubled; in others, it should not. First, check the words that should have the double consonant; then write them out in their correct form.

| | | | | |
|---|---|---|---|---|
| di(s)appear | di(s)atisfied | di(s)ect | di(s)ervice | di(s)locate |
| di(s)mantle | di(s)pel | di(s)turb | mi(s)pent | di(s)olve |
| mi(s)guided | mi(s)tatement | mi(s)take | mi(s)rule | mi(s)believe |
| u(n)known | u(n)ecessary | u(n)oticed | u(n)kempt | u(n)done |

**D.** Some of the following words should have an *e* in the blank space; some should not. Write out the correct spelling of the words in which an *e* should be inserted:

achiev_ment, argu_ment, blam_ing, brak_ing, cano_ing, chang_ing, choos_ing, clos_ing, desir_able, develop_ing, du_ly, knif_ing, manag_able, mil_age, nin_th, notic_able, outrag_ous, prepar_ing, servic_ing.

**E.** The blank spaces in the following words should contain -*ie* or -*ei*. Write out the complete spelling of those words which require *ei*:

bel__ve, exper__nce, h__ght, for__gn, fr__nd, ch__f, h__r, l__sure,

misch_ _f, n_ _ce, p_ _ce, rec_ _ve, c_ _ling, w_ _gh, w_ _rd, y_ _ld, th_ _r,
s_ _ze, repr_ _ve, gr_ _vous.

**F.** Some of the following words form their plurals by adding -*s* to the
singular form, some by adding -*es*. Write out the plurals which take -*es*:

alto, analysis, auto, ditch, dynamo, echo, Eskimo, fox, hero, piano, radio,
solo, synopsis, tobacco, tomato, veto.

**G.** Write the plural forms of the following nouns:

alley, alumna, alumnus, attorney, axis, baby, basis, belief, category, crisis,
half, key, lady, loaf, major general, mother-in-law, ox, quantity, study, tax,
taxi, try, 5, 7, A.

**H.** Write the simple past tense form of the following verbs:

act, annul, benefit, confer, crop, defer, develop, drip, drop, equip, excel,
gas, kidnap, occur, propel, quiz, reap, rebel, refer, regret, rip, rob, scar,
slip, stop, strap, worship, wrap.

**I.** In some of the following words the parenthetical consonant should
be double; in some it should be single. Write out the words which require a single consonant:

acco(m)odate, a(c)ross, a(p)arent, begi(n)ing, emba(r)ass, exa(g)erate,
i(m)agination, i(m)ediate, incidenta(l)y, ma(r)iage, ne(c)essary,
occa(s)ion, perso(n)el, po(s)ess, pro(f)essor, re(c)ommend, roo(m)ate,
su(c)eed, tyra(n)y, wri(t)ing.

**abr** | *Abbreviations*

IN GENERAL, abbreviations should be used in college writing only if
they satisfy two conditions: they must be standard abbreviations recognized by dictionaries, and they must be appropriate to the context. The
first condition rules out such slang abbreviations as *b. f.* (boy friend),
*hon.* (honey), and *n. g.* (no good). The second requires students to
recognize that many standard abbreviations (*advt., Ave., Feb., Xmas*)
are inappropriate in a formal style and that abbreviations of certain

titles (*Col., Dr., Mr., Rev.*) are used only when followed by the name of the person to whom the title applies.

The following is a summary of the most common standard abbreviations. For the correct form of abbreviations not included in this list, consult your dictionary.

Bibliographical terms: *cf., op. cit., vol., pp.* (For these and others, see pages 305–307).

Names of days: *Sun., Mon., Tues., Wed., Thurs., Fri., Sat.* (Used only in dates).

Names of months: *Jan., Feb., Aug., Sept., Oct., Nov., Dec.* (Used only in dates).

Names of organizations: *A.F.L. ,C.I.O., D.A.R., U.S. Steel, W.C.T.U.*

Names of government agencies: *AAA, ERA, FBI, SEC, TVA* (Notice that abbreviations of government agencies generally do not require periods).

Names of states: *Calif., Del., Mass., N.Y., Ill.* (Used chiefly in addresess).

Signs: When the context permits, the following signs are used as abbreviations: & (ampersand: see *Glossary*), $ (dollar), £ (British pound sterling), % (per cent), " " (ditto marks, used in tabulations to repeat the item immediately above the marks).

---

# caps | *Use of Capital Letters*

---

**a.** Capitalize the first word of each sentence and of each line of regular poetry.

Ask for Mr. Lane. He is in charge of service.
Too bad! Better luck next time.

> Earth has not anything to show more fair;
> Dull would he be of soul who could pass by
> A sight so touching in its majesty:
> — Wordsworth, "Composed Upon Westminster Bridge"

**b.** Capitalize the first word of a direct quotation.

The President's answer was, "No comment."
"If you will give me a receipt," I said, "you can have the money now."

**c.** Capitalize proper nouns.

Sergeant York was one of the great heroes of World War I.
She works for the National Broadcasting Company.
Laurence Olivier was knighted after his production of *Henry V.*

I find French easier than German.
The *Saratoga* was sunk at Bikini.
The Amazon is longer than the Mississippi.

*Note:* Words which were originally proper nouns but have taken on more general meanings are regarded as common nouns and are not capitalized: *boycott, calico, china, port* (wine), *tweed.*

**d. Capitalize adjectives formed from proper nouns.**

They seem to be ignorant of the *American* point of view.
There is a *Miltonic* quality in this verse.
The *Renaissance* period was Italy's second hour of glory.
The inductive method has been called the *Baconian* method.
He is studying the *Pauline* doctrines.

*Note:* Words originally derived from proper nouns cease to be capitalized when they are used as allusions rather than as direct references to the original noun. For example, *colossus, gargantuan, herculean, meandering,* and *panic* do not take capitals. *Philippic* is capitalized when it refers directly to the orations made by Demosthenes, but not when it is used to describe some other denunciatory speech.

**e. Capitalize nouns or pronouns referring to the deity:**

*God, Lord, our Father, Savior, Messiah, Trinity, Holy Ghost, He, His, Him.*

**f. Capitalize names of offices only when they are used as titles:**[1]

| *Capitalized* | *Not Capitalized* |
|---|---|
| States-Attorney Johnson | Tell it to the states-attorney. |
| Prime Minister Macmillan. | Eden was prime minister. |
| Dr. A. L. Street, Chairman of the Civic Betterment Committee. | He was made chairman of the committee. |

*Note: President, Presidential,* and *Presidency* are capitalized when they refer to the office of President of the United States: *One of these men will be our next President; the Presidency is at stake.*

[1] The convention stated here is a simplification of actual practice. The usage of newspapers varies: some capitalize important offices when they are not used as titles; others omit capitals even in titles.

**g.** Capitalize *north, south, east,* and *west* and their derivatives only when they refer to geographical areas.

| *Capitalized* | *Not Capitalized* |
|---|---|
| We found the South charming. | Next year we are going south. |
| Her parents live in the East. | New York is east of Chicago. |
| They live on the West Side. | The west side of the field is wet. |
| The Southern armies fought gallantly. | The house has a fine southern exposure. |

**h.** Capitalize titles of books, magazines, plays and the headings of chapters or sections of a work.

The preferred practice is to capitalize all significant words in a title, including the first word:

*A Child's History of the United States*
*The Return of the Native*
*Mourning Becomes Electra*

Some publishers, however, capitalize every word in the title:

*A Child's History Of The United States*

Either form is acceptable in college writing, but be consistent.

**i.** Capitalize the names of days, months, and holidays.

New Year's Day will fall on Thursday.
Next Sunday is Mother's Day.
The favorite vacation months are July and August.

**j.** Avoid unnecessary capitalization.

In general, do not use capitals unless they are required by one of the conventions stated above. The modern tendency is to use a small letter whenever the conventions permit. Especially avoid unnecessary capitalization of the names of the seasons, of family relationships (*father, mother, sister, uncle*), and of such words as *army, college, freshman, navy, sophomore, university* unless they are being considered as proper nouns.

| *Capitalized* | *Not Capitalized* |
|---|---|
| He is a captain in the Army of the United States. | In foreign affairs an army is a political instrument. |
| Whom do you pick in the Army-Navy game? | The senator said we must have an army and a navy second to none. |

| *Capitalized* | *Not Capitalized* |
|---|---|
| Sanford Junior College | He wants a college education. |
| The University will have a strong team next year. | He is a university professor. |
| Are you going to the Freshman Hop? | Are you a freshman or a sopho-more? |
| The Summer Festival starts next week. | I like summer best and winter least. |
| He belonged to The Society for the Prevention of Cruelty to Animals. | He belonged to a society for the prevention of cruelty to animals. |

# hyph | *Hyphenation*

HYPHENS are used for two purposes: to divide a word at the end of a line, and to join two words as a compound.

**a. Use a hyphen to break a word.**

The use of a hyphen to break a word at the end of a line is less frequently necessary in manuscript copy than it is in print. In student writing, words should be broken at the ends of lines only when failure to hyphenate would result in obviously awkward spacing. If hyphenation seems necessary, the following conditions should be observed:

**1. Do not break words of one syllable.**

If there is not room at the end of a line for such words as *burst, change, drink, through,* carry the whole word over to the next line.

**2. Do not separate a suffix of less than three letters from the rest of the word.**

An *-ing* may be separated, but single letters or *-al, -le, -ly,* and *-ed* endings should not.

**3. Break words only between syllables.**

When in doubt about syllables, consult your dictionary.

adver-bial, ab-surd, al-ready, pre-tend

**4. Hyphenate compound words between the elements of the compound.**

*arm-chair, black-bird, sail-boat, white-caps.*

**5.** Subject to the limitations stated in (2), hyphenate between prefix and root or between root and suffix.

| Between Prefix and Root | Between Root and Suffix |
|---|---|
| ante-cedent | adapt-able |
| be-loved | back-ward |
| com-mit | depend-ent |
| con-tagious | ego-ism |
| dis-appear | kitchen-ette |
| inter-rupt | lemon-ade |
| intro-duce | mile-age |
| per-suade | racket-eer |
| trans-late | trouble-some |

**b. Use a hyphen between elements of a compound.**

Hyphenation of compounds varies so much that college students should keep two points in mind: (1) for any particular word, the only safe authority is a reliable, up-to-date dictionary; (2) whenever usage is uncertain, a writer is allowed a choice between competing usages.

Some compounds (*applesauce, blackboard, steamship*) are written solid; others (*dirt cheap, place kick, wedding ring*) are nearly always written as separate words; still others (*father-in-law, ready-made, up-to-date*) are usually hyphenated. There is an increasing tendency to write compounds solid, especially in an informal style, but in general a hyphen is preferred in the following types.

**1. Hyphenate a compound modifier preceding a noun.**

| | |
|---|---|
| A self-made man | An off-the-cuff judgment |
| A well-dressed woman | A tear-jerking movie |
| A pay-as-you-go tax | A Sunday-morning golf game |
| A round-by-round report | A dog-in-the-manger attitude |

Notice that compound numerical modifiers fall into this class: *Twenty-seven dollars, one hundred and twenty-five pounds, a two-thirds majority.* However, whole numbers below twenty-one are not hyphenated: *Her nineteenth birthday; the sixteenth of the month.* Notice also that a compound modifier following a noun is usually not hyphenated: *The woman was well dressed; the machine is worn out.*

**2. Hyphenate a compound consisting of a prefix and a proper noun.**

Pro-Russian, un-American (also unAmerican), anti-Hitler.

**3. Hyphenate compounds of ex ("former") and a noun.**

ex-wife, ex-sweetheart, ex-President.

**4. Hyphenate most compounds beginning with *self*.**

*self-satisfied, self-government, self-conceit.*

But *selfless* and *selfsame* are written solid.

**ital** *Use of Italics*

WORDS IN PRINT are made to stand out by using a special kind of slanting type called *italic;* they are similarly set off in manuscript by underlining. Italics or underlining is used for the following purposes:

**a. To indicate that a word is still considered a foreign element in the language.**

*en rapport, in absentia.* (See "Foreign Words," page 208.)

**b. To mark titles of publications, movie and stage productions, songs, and the names of airplanes, ships, and trains.**

Mencken's *The American Language*
The *Saturday Evening Post*
Beethoven's *Eroica*
Berlin's *White Christmas*
Da Vinci's *Last Supper*
The New York Central's *Twentieth Century Limited*
Lindbergh's *Spirit of Saint Louis*
The *Queen Elizabeth*

Notice that, except for books, this use of italics is an alternative for the use of quotation marks. See page 519.

**c. To call attention to a word being named.**

The word *judgment* has two spellings.
What does *discriminate* mean?
A good example is the phrase, *to go scot free.*

In handwritten work or typescript quotation marks are more common than italics (see page 519). Both, however, are standard.

**d. To emphasize a word.**

Not *Angles* but *angels.*
That is *precisely* the point.

This last device should be used sparingly. Overused, it becomes a poor substitute for emphatic diction.

# no | *Forms of Numbers*

**no**

WHETHER NUMBERS should be written in words or figures depends partly on the nature of the writing. Scientific, statistical, and technical writing uses figures whenever possible. In essays and literary publications numbers are more frequently written out, and the more formal the style, the less figures are used. The following advice holds good for the kind of writing you will do in a composition class.

**a. Figures are used in writing dates, hours, or street numbers.**

| | | |
|---|---|---|
| January 22, 1949 | 5:00 A.M. | 17 Main Street |
| January 1 | 6:15 P.M. | 417 Fifth Avenue |
| The year 1860 | 0430 | 1021 Third Street |

Notice that figures are used for street numbers but that street names, even when they are numbers, are written out to avoid confusion.

**b. Figures are used in recording sums of money other than round sums.**

$2.75; 98 cents; but a hundred dollars; thirty cents

If the style is informal, even round sums may be expressed as figures.

100 dollars; 30 cents; 40,000 spectators

**c. Use figures for large numbers that would be awkward to write out.**

365 days; 1760 yards; 14,320 students

**d. Use figures in citing volume, chapter, and page references.**

This whole question is discussed in Volume 2 of Brand's work.
II, 132–134. (In footnotes and bibliographical citations, the abbreviations *vol.* and *p.* or *pp.* are not used when both volume and page are cited. See pages 304–305 above.)
Now turn to page 37.
Our topic is discussed in Chapter 5.

**e. Do not use figures at the beginning of a sentence.**

Sixty per cent is a passing grade.
*Not:* 60% is a passing grade.

**f. Generally avoid figures when a number can be conveniently expressed in one word.**

one, five, third, quarter, twelve

But in an informal style, numbers over ten are frequently expressed in figures.

**g.** Do not use figures in a formal invitation or reply.

> . . . on Saturday the twenty-third of June
> at seven-thirty o'clock in the evening

This most formal usage is an exception to the practice recommended in a above.

**h.** Roman numerals are used chiefly as volume and chapter numbers in some books and as page numbers in the front matter of books.

Because Roman numerals are so little used, they are often confusing to students. Most of this confusion can be eliminated by first recognizing the key numerals and then understanding the principle by which these are combined.

The key numerals are i (1), v (5), x (10), l (50), c (100), d (500), m (1000), which may be written in capitals: I, V, X, L, C, D, M. The basic principle is that higher numbers are created by adding another unit to a lower number — i, ii, iii, vi, xi — or by subtracting a unit from a higher number — iv, ix, xl, xc.

| | *Units* | *Tens* | *Hundreds* |
|---|---|---|---|
| 1 | i | x | c |
| 2 | ii | xx | cc |
| 3 | iii | xxx | ccc |
| 4 | iv | xl | cd |
| 5 | v | l | d |
| 6 | vi | lx | dc |
| 7 | vii | lxx | dcc |
| 8 | viii | lxxx | dccc |
| 9 | ix | xc | cm |

## *Review Exercises*

**A.** Rewrite the following sentences to substitute abbreviations and figures where permissible in college composition:

1. Have you seen the new professor? He has a Doctor of Philosophy degree from Cornell.
2. Mister Thompson is not here, but you can telephone him at Main five-seven-five-two.
3. My sister graduated from the University of Illinois with a Bachelor of Arts degree in February nineteen hundred and forty-eight.
4. She was married on the twenty-first of October, nineteen hundred and forty-nine.

5. Her husband is Doctor William Reid, a research economist with the American Federation of Labor.

6. Look on page one thousand, four hundred and seventy.

7. He was born on January thirty-one at five minutes after eleven post meridian.

8. The date of the battle of Hastings is anno Domini 1066.

9. Send this letter to Colonel Donald Andrews, care of the Thirty-third Division at Fort Sam Houston.

10. Fifty-four people were hurt in the wreck, including the three top executives of the Columbia Broadcasting System.

**B.** Rewrite the following sentences to remove any abbreviations or figures which would be undesirable in college composition:

1. The speaker was a prof. from the U. of Indiana.
2. I saw her downtown this a.m.
3. 10 days later, the man died.
4. The candidate spoke as often as 8 times in a single day.
5. Somebody said to me "Mr., this man needs a Dr."
6. The party consisted of Brig. Gen. T. A. Smith, a Col., and two Lt. Cols.
7. The math exam will be held in Rm. 511 at 2:00 P.M.
8. He paid $20; he could have bought a good second-hand one for $5.

**C.** In the following sentences, change lower case letters to capitals wherever the conventions require such a change:

1. She asked, "what makes it spin?"
2. it is one of the best of the english movies.
3. Some of his activities are alleged to be unamerican.
4. The words are, "our father which art in heaven, hallowed be thy name."
5. The greeks called their chief god *zeus;* the romans called him *jupiter.*
6. The king James bible is called the authorized version. It was translated by a committee of biblical scholars.
7. The title is *20,000 leagues under the sea.*
8. F. D. Roosevelt is the only president who won the presidency four times.
9. What did you get your mother for mother's day?
10. The bowl games are played chiefly in the west and south. The winter weather in the north and east is not suitable for post-season football.

**D.** In the following sentences remove unnecessary capitalization:

1. He is a Four Star General in the U. S. Army.
2. Our Navy is twice as large as that of the British.
3. This course is required for all Freshmen. Sophomores who are transfers from another University may also be required to take it.
4. My Father wants me to be a University Professor but I prefer a better-paying Profession.

5. Spring may be the most beautiful Season, but I prefer Fall.

6. Go East for three blocks and then turn North.

7. It will soon be time for the birds to start their Southern migrations.

8. Her Uncle is a Rear-Admiral in the Navy and an authority on Naval strategy.

9. He studied for the Ministry before going to Law School.

10. "I will do it," She said, "If you will help me."

**E.** Rewrite the following letter to revise any unconventional use of abbreviations, capitals, hyphens, or numbers:

Twenty–five Main Street
Ridgeville, Minnesota
Aug. 17, 1957

Doctor L. P. Wright
English Dept.
U.of M.

Dear Dr. Wright:

When I entered the University in Feb. I was notified that because of a one–Unit deficiency in High School english I would have to take a non credit course called remedial english.   I took the course, but because I was ill most of the Semester I missed the Final Examination and received a Final Grade of f.   My instructor, Mister Larsen, told me it would be possible to remove my failure by petitioning for a Make Up Examination.

If possible I would like to take the Exam before School starts in Sept. so that I can begin the regular comp. course this coming Semester.   Would that be possible?   I must complete 15 credit–hours next term to be eligible to join a Fraternity and therefore cannot afford to take a 3 hour non credit course.   I could take the Make Up anytime before the 15th of Sept., preferably between the 5th and 10th.

Yrs. Sincerely

*Geo A Jones*

**F.** Write the following figures as Arabic numerals:

| | | |
|---|---|---|
| ix | xcv | cml |
| xiv | cxv | cmxc |
| xl | cccix | mclx |
| xlvi | cd | md |
| lxxi | dcx | mcml |

Write the following figures as Roman numerals:

| 3 | 10 | 50 | 400 |
|---|----|----|-----|
| 4 | 14 | 80 | 550 |
| 5 | 19 | 90 | 1776 |
| 9 | 30 | 154 | 1948 |

# ✳
# ✳
# ✳ **GLOSSARY**
# ✳
# ✳

---

THIS IS A reference section. Its main purpose is to list those words and constructions which frequently cause trouble in composition and to advise you whether particular usages are acceptable in college writing and, if they are, under what conditions. A secondary purpose is to explain grammatical terms which may not have been adequately discussed elsewhere in the text. Since this book has a separate index giving page references for all subjects discussed in the text, the Glossary usually does not duplicate these references.

The judgments recorded here about usage are based primarily on *The American College Dictionary* (referred to throughout as the *ACD*), the Merriam-Webster dictionaries (referred to as *Webster's*), and the *New World Dictionary* (referred to as the *NWD*). These sources have been supplemented by other dictionaries and by individual studies of modern usage,[1] but the emphasis given to the dictionaries cited above necessarily makes the judgments conservative. These dictionaries sometimes record as colloquial, or fail to record at all, usages which other reputable studies accept as literary English, and which one's experience suggests are common in the careful writings of educated authors. It was shown in Chapter 9 that the conservative bias of a good dictionary is often unavoidable. That bias, however, should be kept in mind while consulting this Glossary.

Since the dictionaries do not distinguish between formal and informal usage — other than colloquial — it has seemed wise to indicate whether particular usages would be more appropriate to a formal than to an informal style, and whether certain colloquialisms would be generally

---

[1] Chiefly *The Oxford English Dictionary*, Fries's *American English Grammar*, Horwill's *Dictionary of Modern American Usage*, Kennedy's *Current English*, Marckwardt and Walcott's *Facts About Current English Usage*, Perrin's *Writer's Guide and Index to English*, and Pooley's *Teaching English Usage*, all of which are fully identified in the Bibliography following the Preface of this book.

acceptable in informal writing. In careful writing, the choice of diction is often subtle, and the really significant choices are not between standard and nonstandard expressions; they are choices within the standard vocabulary. The final answer in such questions depends less on the dictionary than on the style of the paper being written. Whether a particular colloquialism is desirable in a particular paper is a decision for the student and his instructor to make. You should bear in mind, therefore, that although all judgments in this Glossary about the status of a usage are the judgments of authoritative dictionaries, all judgments concerning the acceptability of an informal usage in college writing are the opinions of this author. The basic assumption behind these opinions is that the stylistic level appropriate for college writing is informal rather than either colloquial or formal.

**accept — except**   Words frequently confused because of similar sound.

*Accept* is roughly synonymous with *take* [I will accept your thanks, but not your money]. *Except,* as a verb, means roughly *to leave out* or *exempt* [Present company is excepted].

**access — excess**   The second syllable of both words comes from a Latin root meaning "to go." Etymologically, *access* means "a going toward," hence "approach" or "admission" [The auditor has access to the records]. *Excess* originally meant "going out or beyond," hence its present meaning of "beyond what is necessary or desirable" [He worries to excess; a tax on excess profits].

**Accusative case**   In modern English, the objective case. See page 479.

**ad**   Clipped form of *advertisement.* Colloquial. Appropriate in college writing only when style is colloquial. Generally inappropriate in business correspondence — especially in letters applying for a position — in which the word should be written in full.

**A. D.**   Abbreviation for Latin *Anno Domini* (in the year of our Lord). Opposite of B. C. (before Christ). Used to distinguish dates before and after the beginning of the Christian era [He lived from 31 B. C. to A. D. 12; from 100 B. C. to A. D. 100 is 200 years].

**adapt — adept — adopt**   *Adapt* means "adjust to meet requirements" [The play was adapted for the movies; the human body can adapt itself to all sorts of environments]. *Adept* means "skilled" or "proficient" [He is adept at various sports]. *Adopt* means "to take as one's own" [We are going to adopt a child; he immediately adopted the idea] or — in parliamentary procedure — "to accept as a law" [The motion was adopted].

**adaptation — adoption**   *Adaptation* is the act of adapting. See **Adapt** [This play is an adaptation of a popular novel]. *Adoption* is the act of adopting [The adoption will not be legal until all the papers have been signed].

**affect — effect**   Words often confused because of similarity of sound. When used as a noun, *effect,* meaning "result," is the word wanted [His speech had an unfortunate effect; the treatments had no effect on me]. Both words may be used as verbs, though *effect* is the more common. As a verb, *affect* means "impress," "influence," or "disturb" [His advice affected my decision; does music affect you that way?]. As a verb, *effect* is rarely required in student writing, but may be used to mean "carry out" or "accomplish" [The aviator effected his mission; the lawyer effected a settlement]. For students who have chronic difficulty with these words, a useful rule is to use *affect* only as a verb, and *effect* only as a noun.

**affective — effective**   See **affect — effect.**   The common adjective is *effective* [an effective argument], meaning "having an effect." The use of *affective* is largely confined to technical discussions of psychology and semantics, in which it is roughly equivalent to "emotional."

**aggravate**   The word has two levels of meaning. In formal English it means to "make worse" or "intensify" [His shoe aggravated the sore; his attitude aggravated the hostility of the audience]. Colloquially it is used to mean "irritate" or "annoy" [Her silly remarks aggravated me beyond endurance].

**ain't**   Nonstandard contraction for "is not" and "are not." Some grammarians would accept it as colloquial in the form of "ain't I" on the grounds that it is historically and logically a suitable contraction of "am I not." But unless a student is attempting to record nonstandard speech, the use of *ain't* is not acceptable in college speech or writing.

**alibi**   In formal English the word is a legal term used to indicate that a defendant was *elsewhere* when the crime was committed. Colloquially *alibi* is used to mean excuse [I'm not worried about being late, I have a good alibi]. This usage is becoming increasingly common in informal writing.

**all the farther, further, quicker**   Nonstandard usage for "as far as," "as quick as." Write: "That is as far as I have read;" "this is as quickly as I can do it."

**all together — altogether**  Distinguish between the phrase [They were all together at last] and the adverb [He is altogether — i. e. entirely — to blame]. *All together* means "all in one place;" *altogether* means "entirely" or "wholly."

**Alliteration**  Repetition of the same consonant, especially an initial consonant, in several words within the same sentence or line of poetry. Alliteration is a common device in poetry and in slogans, but it should be used with restraint in ordinary prose since its overuse or inappropriate use may seem affected.

The *m*ur*m*uring of i*mm*e*m*orial el*m*s.
*T*ippecanoe and *T*yler *t*oo.

**allow**  When used to mean "permit" [No smoking allowed on the premises] *allow* is acceptable. Its use to mean "think" [He allowed it could be done] is nonstandard and is not acceptable in college writing.

**allusion — illusion**  Words sometimes confused because of similarity of sound. An *allusion* is a reference [The poem contains several allusions to Greek mythology]. An *illusion* is an erroneous mental image [Rouge on pallid skin gives an illusion of health].

**alright**  An established variant spelling of *all right.*

**altar — alter**  The first word is a noun [They stood before the altar]; the second is a verb [We will alter the coat without charge]. If you confuse the two spellings, try associating the *a* in *sacred* with the alt*a*r of a church.

**altho**  Now accepted as a variant spelling of *although.*

**A. M., P. M.; a. m., p. m.**  Abbreviations for the Latin phrases *ante meridiem* (before noon), *post meridiem* (after noon). A. M. is used to indicate the period from midnight to noon; P. M., from noon to midnight. These abbreviations are used only when a specific hour is named [The first watch on a ship is from 12 P. M. to 4 A. M.]. The use of these abbreviations to stand for *morning* and *afternoon* when no hour is named [He gets up late in the a. m. and goes back to bed early in the p. m.] is a slang use not acceptable in college writing.

Notice that either capital or small letters may be used in these abbreviations.

**among** See **between.**

**amount — number** The occasional confusion of these words in college writing creates awkwardness. *Amount* is roughly synonymous with "deal" or "quantity" [He has a great amount of money; we collected a considerable amount of scrap iron]. *Number* is used for groups, the individual members of which may be counted [He has a large number of friends; there is a number of letters to be answered].

**Ampersand** The sign &, an abbreviation for *and*, is used in some company names [Harper & Brothers] and in various types of notations. Except in statistical tabulation it is not acceptable in college writing.

**an** Variant of indefinite article, *a*. Used instead of *a* when the following word begins with a vowel sound [an apple, an easy victory, an honest opinion, an hour]. When the following word begins with a consonant sound, including *y*, the article should be *a* [a yell, a unit, a history, a house]. Such constructions as *a apple, a hour* are nonstandard usage. The use of *an* before *historical* and *humble* is an older usage which is dying out.

**and etc.** *Etc.* is an abbreviation of the Latin phrase *et cetera* (and so forth). *And etc.* is therefore redundant. Use either *and so forth* or *etc.* in an informal style but only *and so forth* in a formal style.

**angle** The use of *angle* to mean "point of view" [Let's look at it from a new angle] is acceptable, but the word is so over-used in college writing — and so often used inaccurately — that many instructors object to it. Use it sparingly, and do not confuse its spelling with that of *angel*.

**Antonym** A word opposite in meaning to a given word [Love is the antonym for hate].

**any = every** Many people object to this use of *any* [Any high school student knows that; as any fool can plainly see]. This usage, however, is accepted by all dictionaries consulted.

**anybody's else** An old form of *anybody else's*. It is no longer conventional.

**anywheres** A nonstandard variant of *anywhere*.

**Apposition** In grammar, two constructions are in apposition when the second follows and identifies the first, as in "Mr. Botts, *the chemistry instructor,* has resigned." Most frequently the appositive is treated as a nonrestrictive modifier (see pages 508–510) and is therefore set off by commas, as above. When, however, the appositive word or phrase is felt to be so closely related to the construction with which it is in apposition that the two cannot be separated, it is treated as a restrictive modifier and written without commas [*Secretary of State* Dulles, *Commander-in-Chief* Dwight D. Eisenhower].

**apt** See liable.

**Arabic numerals** The numbers 1, 2, 3, etc. as contrasted with Roman numerals [i, ii, iii].

**around** The uses of *around* to mean "about" [He arrived around four o'clock], "near" [That is how they pronounce it around Brooklyn] and "throughout" [We traveled around the country] are colloquial. They are acceptable in an informal, though not in a formal, style.

**as . . . as** The use of *as . . . as* in a negative statement [I am not as old as she is] is sometimes censured on the assumption that this construction should be used only for affirmative statements and that the correct negative form is "not *so* old as." In a very formal style the "not so . . . as" form may be preferable; but both forms are educated usage, and either is appropriate in college writing. In an affirmative statement, use *as . . . as.*

**as = because** Although it is accepted standard English, *as* is weaker than *because* to show causal relation between main and subordinate clauses. Since *as* has other meanings, it may in certain contexts be confusing [As I was going home, I decided to telephone]. Here *as* may mean *when* or *because.* If there is any possibility of confusion, it is wise to use *because* or *while* — whichever is appropriate to the meaning.

**as if = as though** Synonymous constructions. The first is slightly less formal, but either is appropriate in college writing.

**as = that** The use of *as* to introduce a noun clause [I don't know as I would agree to that] is colloquial. This usage would be hopelessly inappropriate at a formal level and would be rejected by most college instructors at an informal level. Unless you are deliberately aiming at a colloquial style, use *that.*

**as to = with respect to** Although *as to* is unquestionably standard usage, many instructors object to it on the ground that it is jargon (see page 578). Certainly its overuse should be avoided, and in an informal style *about* would be more appropriate than either *as to* or *with respect to*. For example, "I am not concerned as to your father's reaction" sounds stilted. It would be more natural to say "I am not concerned [or I do not care] about your father's reaction."

**Assonance** The similarity of vowel sounds in words which do not rhyme [we — weep, fine — white].

**Asterisk** The sign *. A single asterisk is sometimes used as a footnote marker or to indicate items in a list which deserve special attention. A row of asterisks is sometimes used to indicate that the action of a story has been broken off or to suggest an interval of time.

**at** Avoid the use of the redundant *at* in such sentences as: "Where were you at?" "Where do you live at?"

**auto** A clipped form of *automobile*. Inappropriate in formal writing, but appropriate in an informal or colloquial style.

**Auxiliary verb** A "helping" verb which combines with another to form a verb phrase [I *am* going; he *has been* talking]. The most common auxiliaries are *be, can, do, may, must, ought, shall, will*.

**awful, awfully** The real objection to *awful* is not that it is colloquial but that it is worked to death. It is inappropriate in a formal style unless used to mean "awe-inspiring." As a utility word it has become almost indispensable in informal speech, but the more deliberate nature of writing and the opportunities it allows for revision make the overuse of this word objectionable.

**back of = behind** Although this idiom is usually considered colloquial, it is recorded without reservation in Webster's *International*. Inappropriate in a formal style, but acceptable in any writing which is trying to capture the tone of informal American idiom.

**bad** The ordinary uses of *bad* as an adjective cause no difficulty. Its use as a predicate adjective [An hour after dinner I began to feel bad] is sometimes confused with the adverb *badly*. After the verbs *look, feel, seem*, you will almost never have occasion to use the adverb. Say, "It looks bad for our team;" "I feel bad about that quarrel;" "She seemed bad this morning." But do not use *bad* when an adverb is required, as in "He played badly;" "A badly torn suit."

**badly = very much**   *Badly* is used in informal and colloquial writing as an intensifying word [I wanted badly to be asked. He was badly in need of a shave]. When it is used in this way care should be taken to avoid misleading word order. In "I wanted to play very badly" the adverb may be interpreted as a modifier of *to play*, which the writer did not intend. In college writing it would be safer to avoid this use of *badly* and to use one of various possible synonyms. For example:

He was obviously in need of a shave.
I was eager to play.

**balance = rest of, remainder**   This usage was formerly considered colloquial, but the *ACD* and *NWD* now accept it without qualification. In most college writings it will probably be acceptable.

**bank on**   A colloquial synonym for "rely on."

*Colloquial:* I wouldn't bank on him. He has let me down too many times.
*Formal:* I would not rely on him. He has too frequently disappointed me.

In college writing the formal usage is preferred.

**because**   See   **reason is because.**

**being as**   The use of *being as* for "because" or "since" in such sentences as "Being as I am an American, I believe in democracy," is nonstandard and is not acceptable in college speech or writing. Say, "Because I am an American, I believe in democracy."

**berth — birth**   Do not confuse the spelling of *berth* [The man in the lower berth was ill. The tugs pushed the liner into its berth] and that of *birth* [The birth of the prince was celebrated for days].

**between, among**   In general, *between* is used of two people or objects and *among* for more than two [We had less than a dollar between the two of us] but [We had only a dollar among the three of us].
   The general distinction, however, should be modified when insistence on it would be unidiomatic. For example, *between* is the accepted form in the following examples:

He is in the difficult position of having to choose between three equally attractive girls.
A settlement was arranged between the four partners.
He decided to build the house between the trees, at a spot roughly equidistant from all of them.

**Bible**   When used to refer to the Scriptures, "Bible" is always capitalized, but not italicized. When used metaphorically [*Das Kapital* is the bible of the Communists], the word is not capitalized.

**blame on**   This usage [He blamed it on his brother] is accepted without reservation by some dictionaries but labeled colloquial by others. The more formal usage would be "He blamed his brother for it."

**born — borne**   Although both words come from the verb *to bear,* the form without the *e* (*born*) is restricted to the bearing of children or other young [He was born lame]. The form with the final *e* (*borne*) has the more general meaning of being supported or carried [The ship was borne on the waves; the troops were airborne].

**broke**   When used as an adjective, *broke* is a slang synonym for "bankrupt" or "out of funds." This usage is common in informal, educated speech, but in college writing it should be restricted to papers clearly colloquial in style. The use of such circumlocutions as "financially embarrassed" is generally more objectionable than the slang itself. Simply say, "I had no money."

When used as a verb, *broke* is the simple past tense of *break* (past participle, *broken*). Do not confuse the past tense with the past participle. Say "He has broken his leg," not "He has broke his leg."

**bunch**   Avoid the overuse of *bunch* as a general utility word. In formal English it is used to refer to a cluster of objects [bunch of grapes, a bunch of carrots]. Colloquially, it is used as a synonym for *group,* as in "A fine bunch of friends you have." This colloquial use is overworked in college writing. The following contrasted synonyms illustrate more discriminating choices:

| | |
|---|---|
| A bunch of material | A collection of material |
| A bunch of money | A quantity of money |
| A bunch of enemies | A host of enemies |
| A bunch of examples | Several examples |
| A bunch of Radicals | A clique of Radicals |
| A bunch of lumber | A supply of lumber |
| A bunch of errors | A number of errors |

**bunk**   A slang synonym for *nonsense.* Seldom appropriate in college writing in this sense.

**bust**   At a formal level *bust* is used as a synonym for *bosom* and to represent the sculptured head and shoulders of a person. The use of *bust* to mean "failure" [The party was a complete bust] is colloquial. The use of *bust* to mean "burst" [The pipes have bust again] is nonstandard and not acceptable in college writing.

**but that, but what** *But what* [I can't doubt but what he said it] is nonstandard. *But that* [I don't doubt but that he is married] is accepted educated usage, but redundant. It is perfectly clear to write:

I can't doubt that he said it.
I don't doubt that he is married.

**can = may** The distinction that *can* is used to indicate ability and *may* is used to indicate permission [If I can do the work, may I have the job?] is a stylistic distinction. It is not generally observed in informal usage but is still observed in a formal style.

**can but** A formal variant of *can only* [I can but hope you are mistaken].

**cannot but** A formal variant of *cannot help* or *must* [We cannot but accept the verdict]. In most college writing "We must accept the verdict" would be preferred.

**cannot (can't) help but** While this construction is accepted in informal usage, it represents a confusion between the formal *cannot but* and the informal *can't help*. In college writing, the form without *but* is preferred.

**can't hardly** A confusion between *cannot* and *can hardly*. The construction is unacceptable in college writing. Use *cannot, can't,* or *can hardly*.

**can't seem** A colloquial shortcut for "I seem to be unable." Acceptable at informal levels.

**canvas —canvass** The form with one *s* is a heavy cloth [a canvas tent, a canvas bag]; the form with two *s*'s means generally *to solicit* [I am canvassing for the Red Cross; he canvassed every voter in the precinct].

**capital — capitol** The form *Capitol*, used only to designate the building which houses the seat of government, takes a capital letter when it refers to the building in which the U.S. Congress meets. When it refers to the building in which a state legislature meets it is sometimes spelled with a small letter [The Capitol and the White House are the most famous buildings in Washington, D.C.; our state capitols are not always models of the best architecture; he has an office in the Capitol in Columbus].

The form *capital* has a variety of meanings, the nucleus of which is "chief" or "first-rate" [The capital city, capital punishment, a capital letter, a capital idea]. Unless you are referring to a building, the form you want is *capital*.

**Caret**   The symbol ( ∧ ) used to identify the place in a printed, typed, or written line at which something is to be inserted.

**case = instance, example**   There is no question that this usage [In the case of John Jones . . . ] is established, but a widely read essay labeling it jargon (see page 578) has created some objection to it. Like most utility words, *case* (meaning *instance*) may be overused, but its restrained use in college writing should be acceptable.

**censor — censure**   Both words come from a Latin verb meaning to "set a value on" or "tax." *Censor* is used to mean "appraise" in the sense of appraising a book or a letter to see if it may be made public [All outgoing mail had to be censored] and is often used as a synonym for "delete" or "cut out" [That part of the message was censored].

*Censure* means "to evaluate adversely," "to find fault with" or "rebuke" [The editorial writers censured the speech; such an attitude will invoke public censure].

**Circumlocution**   Literally, "round-about speech." An attempt to avoid a direct statement by a circuitous reference. See page 144.

**cite — sight — site**   *Cite* means "to refer to" [He cited chapter and verse]. *Sight* means spectacle or view [The garden was a beautiful sight]. *Site* means "location" [This is the site of the new plant].

**claim = assert *or* maintain**   The *ACD* and *NWD* accept this usage [I claim that the assignment was never announced] as established. There would seem to be no valid objection to the construction in informal college writing.

**Cliché**   A synonym for "trite expression": an overused or threadbare word or expression (see page 190), or an idea or observation which lacks originality.

**Clipped words**   Shortened forms [auto, exam, gym, plane] which are considered whole words rather than abbreviations of the longer form. Clipped words do not require a period to mark abbreviation and are more appropriate to informal than to formal styles.

**coarse — course**  The central meaning of *coarse* is "rough" [a coarse skin, coarse talk, coarse cloth]. The word *course* originally came from a French word for *run* and then became the area or path in which the running was to take place. This is the core of its meaning in such uses as "a golf course," "a course in mathematics," "the ship's course," "the course of time." It is easiest to remember that unless the word means *rough* it is spelled *course*.

**Coherence**  The quality of being logically integrated. In composition, chiefly used to refer to the integration of sentences within a paragraph. See page 109.

**combine = combination**  This use of *combine* [Several fraternities have formed a combine which will present its own slate of candidates] is colloquial. It is acceptable at informal levels of college writing. The more formal statement would be "Several fraternities have combined to present a common slate of candidates." *Combine* is also the accepted term for a machine used in harvesting.

**compare, contrast**  *Contrast* always implies differences; *compare* may imply either differences or similarities. When they are followed by a preposition, both verbs usually take *with* [Contrast the part of the lawn that has been fertilized with the part that has not; the handwriting on the lease compares with this signature; if you compare the old leaves with the new you will see that the old leaves are darker]. However, the past participial form, *compared,* usually takes *to* as its preposition [Compared to her mother, she's a beauty].

**complected**  Nonstandard form of *complexioned.* Not acceptable in college writing.

**Complement**  Literally, a completing construction. Used in grammar chiefly to refer to the construction which completes a linking verb. In this book, especially in sections dealing with sentence structure, *complement* is often used in its larger sense to identify any construction which serves a completing function. When so used, it includes direct and indirect objects of verbs, objects of prepositions, and any construction which completes a linking verb. (See pages 413–415.)

**complement — compliment**  The confusion of these two words lies entirely in the middle vowel. If you remember that *complement* means "to complete" you may associate the *e* of *complement* with the *e* of *complete* [a complement of troops, complementary angles].

A *compliment* is a word or gesture of praise [My compliments to the cook; the line between compliment and flattery is often a faint one].

**Complex, compound sentences**  Sentences are usually classified as follows:

*simple:* containing only one clause, and that a main clause.

*compound:* containing two or more main clauses but no subordinate clauses.

*complex:* containing a main clause and one or more subordinate clauses.

*compound-complex:* containing two or more main clauses and at least one subordinate clause.

**conscience — conscious**  *Conscience* is a noun indicating a sense of right conduct [Let your conscience be your guide]. *Conscious* is an adjective meaning "to be capable of sensations" or "to be aware of" [It will be some time before he is conscious; I am conscious of having done wrong].

**considerable**  The use of *considerable* as a noun [I have spent considerable on this enterprise] is acceptable at a colloquial level. In a formal style, the preferred usage would require a noun after *considerable* [I have spent considerable money on this enterprise].

**contact = communicate with**  This usage [We will contact you by letter or telephone within a week] is established and is standard usage in business communications, but there is considerable objection to its use in college writing. *Communicate with* would be safer usage.

**Contractions**  The use of contractions [I'll, can't, couldn't, didn't, he's, shouldn't] is appropriate in informal and colloquial styles but not in a formal style. See page 173.

**could of = could have**  Although these two constructions have almost the same sound in informal speech, *of* for *have* is not acceptable in college writing. In writing, *could of, should of, would of* are nonstandard.

**council — counsel**  A *council* is an advisory group [He was elected to the council]. *Counsel* means "advice." In law, a *counsel* is one who gives legal advice [My friend counseled me to take this course; he refuses to testify without advice of counsel].

**couple**  The use of couple to mean "two" [The tickets will cost a couple of dollars] is informal or colloquial but should be avoided in formal writing.

*Informal:* Joe, I'd like you to meet a couple of my friends.
*Formal:* Mr. Smith, may I present two of my friends?

**cute** A utility word used colloquially to indicate the general notion of "attractive" or "pleasing." Its overuse in writing shows haste or lack of discrimination. A more specific term will generally improve communication.

His girl is cute. [lovely? petite? of a pleasant disposition?]
That is a cute trick. [clever? surprising?]
The baby is cute. [charming? endearing?]
She has a cute accent. [pleasant? refreshingly unusual?]
She is a little too cute for me. [affected? juvenile? demonstrative? clever?]

**dairy — diary** Pronunciation offers the best clue to the spelling of these words. The *a* comes first in the *ay*-sound, as in *maid*. *Diary* comes from the same root as *dial* and means a record of daily activities.

**data** Since *data* is the Latin plural of *datum* (given or admitted as a fact) it has long taken a plural verb or pronoun [These data have been double-checked]. This requirement is beginning to be ignored so that in informal English "This data has been double-checked" is acceptable. Data is thus losing its foreign characteristics and being made to fit the general pattern of English nouns. The requirement of a plural verb is still observed, however, in scientific writing and in a formal style. For alternative pronunciations, see dictionary.

**Dative case** In Old English, generally the case of the indirect object.

**decent — descent** Most students who misspell *descent* (downslope) have no trouble with the verb *descend*. Associate the *s* in descend with that in *descent*.
　　*Decent* — without the *s* — means "fitting" or "proper" [the decent thing to do].

**Demonstrative** *This, that, these, those* are called demonstratives when they are used as pointing words [This is the man. That coat is mine].

**desert — dessert** The word used for the final course of a meal has two *s*'s. The word with one *s* designates a wasteland [The Sahara Desert] or the action of running away from something [He deserted his wife; they deserted from the Army].

**Dialect** A pattern of speech habits shared by members of the same geographic area or social level. See page 166.

didn't ought   Nonstandard for *ought not* [You didn't ought to have told her] and not acceptable in college writing or speech. Say, "You ought not to have told her" or "You should not have told her."

different than   The preferred construction is *different from* [He is different from his brother], though *Webster's*, the *ACD*, and the *NWD* all accept *different than* as established usage. *Different to* is essentially a British usage.

Digraph   Two letters pronounced as a single sound, as in bl*ee*d, b*ea*t, *th*in, sti*ck*, *p*sychology, gra*ph*.

dining — dinning   In general, a double consonant shortens the vowel preceding it. That is why the *i* in *dine* is long and the *i* in *dinner* short.

| Long *i* [pronounced *eye*] | Short *i* |
|---|---|
| dining | dinning |
| mining | pinning |
| whining | winning |
| writing | written |

Diphthong   A combination of two vowel sounds run together to sound like a single vowel. Examples are the *ah-ee* sounds combining to form the vowel of *hide, ride, wide* and the *aw-ee* sounds combining in *boy, joy, toy.*

don't   As a contraction for "do not" it is appropriate in informal and colloquial styles, but not acceptable in college speech or writing as a contraction for "does not."

*Acceptable:* They don't want to go; we don't need help.
*Not acceptable:* It don't make sense; he don't like you.

Double negative   The use of two negative words or particles within the same construction. In certain forms [I am not unwilling to go] the double negative is educated usage for an affirmative statement; in other forms [I ain't got no money] the double negative is uneducated (nonstandard) usage for a negative statement. The fact that the latter usage is an obvious violation of the conventions of standard English justifies its censure in high school and college speech and writing, but the objection that "two negatives make an affirmative" in English usage is a half-truth based on a false analogy with mathematics.

dove = dived    Informal standard usage. *Dived* would be preferred in a formal style.

drunk    A respectable word for an unrespectable condition. *Intoxicated* might sometimes be preferred in a formal style, but attempts to avoid the use of *drunk* by such circumlocutions as "under the influence" or "in an inebriated condition" are usually prudish. Simply say, "The man was drunk." Avoid the numerous slang terms for this condition.

due to    The use of *due to* to mean "because of" or "owing to" in an introductory adverbial phrase [Due to the icy roads, we were unable to proceed] is an established usage to which there is a strong objection in the schools. It would be out of place in a formal style. You will generally encounter less criticism if you use "because of."

dying — dyeing    When dye is used to color clothes the process is called *dyeing*. Normally the *e* would be dropped before *ing*, but it has been retained in *dyeing* to avoid confusion with the common *dying* — about to die.

The girls are dyeing their hair.
The noise is dying away.

economic — economical    *Economic* refers to the science of economics or to business in general [This is an economic law; economic conditions are improving]. *Economical* means "inexpensive" or "thrifty" [That is the economical thing to do; he is economical to the point of miserliness].

effect    See    affect.

either    Used to designate one of two things [Both hats are lovely; I would be perfectly contented with either]. The use of *either* when more than two things are involved [There are three ways of working the problem; either way will give the right answer] is not generally accepted. When more than two things are involved, use *any* or *any one* instead of *either* [There are three ways of working the problem, any one of which will give the right answer].

elicit — illicit    The first word means to "draw out" [We could elicit no further information from them]; the second means "not permitted" [an illicit love affair].

Elliptical constructions    A construction which is literally incomplete but in which the missing terms are understood [I *am taller than he* (is tall); Who told him? (It was) *Not I* (who told him)].

**emigrant — immigrant**  An emigrant is a person who moves *out* of a country; an immigrant one who moves *into* a country. Thus, refugees from Europe who settled in the United States were emigrants from their native countries and immigrants here. A similar distinction holds for the verbs *emigrate* and *immigrate*.

**enthuse**  Colloquial for "to be (become) enthusiastic." Unless the style is colloquial, the more formal phrase is preferred in college writing. Say, "He was enthusiastic about the plan."

**equally as**  In such sentences as "He was equally as good as his brother," the *equally as* is a confusion of *equally* and *as good as*. Say, "He was his brother's equal," "He was as good as his brother," or "Both brothers were equally good."

**etc.**  An abbreviation for *et cetera* (and so forth). Should be used only when the style justifies abbreviations and then only after several items in a series have been identified [The data sheet required the usual personal information: age, height, weight, religion, etc.]. Avoid the redundant *and* before *etc.* See *and etc.*

**Etymology**  The study of the derivations of words. See pages 207 and 219.

**euphemism — euphuism**  A *euphemism* is a word or phrase used as a substitute for an expression which is felt to be crude, improper, or vulgar. Examples are "retire" for "go to bed," "a lady dog" for "a bitch," "pass away" for "die." *Euphuism* is a name given to an ornate and affected literary style which was popular in England at the end of the sixteenth century and to any modern style which shows the same characteristics.

**exam**  A clipped form of *examination.* Although classified as colloquial by the dictionaries, it is accepted at all but the most formal levels of college writing.

**except**  See **accept.**

**expect = suppose or suspect**  This is a colloquial usage. In college writing, use *suppose* or *suspect* [I suppose you have written to him? I suspect that we have made a mistake].

**Expletive**   In such sentences as "There are two answers to the question" and "It seems to me that you are mistaken," the words *There* and *It* are called *expletives*. In such sentences the order is expletive, verb, and real subject, the expletive occupying the normal position of the subject. In written usage an expletive has no influence on the number of the verb, except that the expletive *It* always is followed by a singular verb.

**extra**   The use of *extra* to mean "unusually" [It was an extra fine performance] is often condemned, though accepted by all the dictionaries consulted in preparing this glossary. It would be wise to avoid this usage in formal writing.

**famous, notorious**   *Famous* is a complimentary and *notorious* an uncomplimentary adjective. Well-known people of good repute are famous; those of bad repute are notorious (or infamous).

**fare — fair**   *Fare* comes from the OE verb *faran* (to travel) and is related to the expression *fare you well*. It is most commonly used today to indicate the cost of transportation [The fare to Chicago is $10.40]. *Fair* has a variety of meanings [a fair decision, a fair copy, a fair skin, just fair, fair weather, a fair profit].

**farther, further**   The distinction that *farther* indicates distance and *further* degree is now less widely observed than it used to be. All dictionaries consulted recognize the two words as interchangeable. But to mean "in addition," only *further* is used [Further assistance will be required; we need further information on that point].

**feature (verb)**   The use of *feature* to mean "give prominence to" [This issue of the magazine features an article on juvenile delinquency] is established standard usage and is appropriate in informal college writing. But this acceptance does not justify the slang use of *feature* in such expressions as "Can you feature that?" "Feature me in a dress suit," "I can't feature her as a nurse."

**fellow**   As a noun, *fellow* is colloquial for "man" or "person." It is appropriate only in colloquial and informal styles. As an adjective [fellow students, a fellow traveler] *fellow* is acceptable at all levels.

**Figures of speech**   Metaphors, similes, personifications, allusions, and similar devices are grouped under the general name, *figures of speech*. See page 186.

**Fine writing**   In college, often used as an uncomplimentary term for writing which, because of its attempts to be "literary," is artificial, pretentious, or wordy. See page 141.

**fix**   As a noun, *fix* is colloquial for "predicament" [Now we *are* in a fix!]. As a verb, it is colloquial for "repair" or "adjust" [My pen is broken and I can't fix it; will you help me fix this desk?]. This second usage is appropriate in an informal style. The verb *fix*, meaning "to make fast," is acceptable at all levels.

**flunk = fail**   Colloquial. Not suited to a formal style, but so commonly used in college that there would seldom be objection to its use in an informal paper.

**folks**   Colloquial for *people*, especially relatives. Generally acceptable in college writing.

**formally — formerly**   *Formally* means "in a formal manner" [They dressed formally]. *Formerly* means "previously" [He was formerly with A. C. Smith and Company].

**forth — fourth**   The common word is *fourth* [I was *fourth* in line]. Associate *fourth* with *four* to remember the *ou*. *Forth* generally means "forward" [They went forth to battle].

**funny**   The use of *funny* as a utility word [She gave me a funny look; it was a funny observation to make] is greatly overused in college writing. Although appropriate at informal and colloquial levels, its constant use makes for vague diction. Select a more exact synonym:

> She gave me a funny look. [hostile? alarmed? annoyed? scathing? perplexed? baffled?]
> It was a funny observation to make. [comical? humorous? astounding? puzzling? unusual?]

**gentleman, lady**   These are good words, but avoid their use as synonyms for "man" or "woman" in expressions in which the latter terms are normal [manservant, man of the house, women's building, League of Women Voters]. Also avoid their euphemistic use to designate the sex of animals [bull, tomcat, mare, ewe].

**get**   The use of *get*, either as a single verb or in combination with infinitives, adjectives, or adverbs, is extremely popular and varied in colloquial and informal styles. It should be used discreetly in a formal style, but this fact should not lead the student always to seek a more formal or pretentious synonym, such as *acquire* or *obtain*.

**good**   The use of *good* as an adverb [He talks good; he played pretty good] is not acceptable in college writing. Even though it is classified as colloquial by the *ACD*, this usage is discouraged in college speech. In both writing and speaking, the accepted adverbial form is *well*.

This discussion does not apply to the use of *good* as an adjective after verbs of hearing, feeling, seeing, smelling, tasting, etc. See **bad**.

**good and**   Used colloquially as an intensive in such expressions as: "good and late," "good and sleepy," "good and ready," "good and tired." The more formal the style, the less appropriate these intensives are.

**got**   See **get**.

**gotten**   Leading dictionaries now accept *gotten* without comment as one of two past participles of *get*. The other one is *got*.

**guess**   The use of *guess* to mean "believe," "suppose," "think" [I guess I can be there on time] is accepted by all three dictionaries on which this glossary is based. There is still considerable objection to its use in formal college writing, but it should be acceptable in an informal style.

**Hackneyed diction**   See **Cliché**.

**had have, had of**   Neither form is appropriate in college writing. Use *had*.

*Unacceptable.* If he had have (of) come . . .
*Acceptable.* If he had come (had he come) . . .

**had (hadn't) ought**   Nonstandard for *ought* (*ought not*). Not acceptable in college writing or speech.

**hanged, hung**   Alternative past participles of *hang*. When referring to an execution, *hanged* is preferred; in other senses, *hung* is preferred.

**hardly**   See **can't hardly**.

**healthful = healthy**   The distinction that *healthful* means "conducive to health" but *healthy* means "possessing or characteristic of health" is no longer recognized by the dictionaries. The two words may now be used interchangeably.

**heap**  In formal usage the noun *heap* means a "pile" or "accumulation" of things [a heap of stones, a heap of junk]. Colloquially, the noun is used to mean "a great deal," "a considerable amount" [He made a heap of money. It takes a heap of living to make a house a home]. This colloquial usage is usually acceptable in an informal style, but is not appropriate in a formal style.

**hear — here**  Associate *hear* with *ear* as a means of remembering the *-ea* combination of vowels in the verb [I hear a noise; he heard, but did not answer]. The adverb *here* (in this place) has no *a*.

**height — heighth**  The form *heighth* is nonstandard, probably caused by confusion with the final *th* in *breadth* and *width*.

**high school**  Do not capitalize unless you use it with the name of a particular high school [He attended high school for three years; he graduated from Lincoln High School].

**Historical present**  Also called *dramatic present*. The use of the present tense in narrative style to record action in the past [His friends try to persuade him to escape but Socrates reasons with them and shows them he must die]. See page 470.

**holy — wholly**  *Holy* means "sacred" [The Holy Bible, the holy city of Jerusalem]. *Wholly* comes from the same root as *whole* and means "completely" [He is wholly well again; it is wholly my fault].

**home**  Used colloquially and informally for "at home" [We have been home all afternoon; if you arrive too late, we will not be home]. In a formal style say "at home."

**Homonyms**  Words which are pronounced alike [air, heir; blew, blue; plain, plane; sail, sale].

**human**  The use of human as a noun [He is a congenial human; they are the most sordid humans I have ever encountered] is generally accepted by authoritative dictionaries. The phrase *human being(s)* is still preferred and should be used in a formal style.

*Informal:* Humans are a queer lot.
*Formal:* Human beings have an inherent capacity for self-delusion.

**idea**  In addition to its formal meaning of "conception," *idea* has acquired so many supplementary meanings that it must be recognized as a utility word. Some of its meanings are illustrated on the next page:

The idea [thesis] of the book is simple.
The idea [proposal] he suggested is a radical one.
I got the idea [impression] that she is unhappy.
It is my idea [belief, opinion] that they are both wrong.
My idea [intention] is to leave early.

The overuse of *idea*, like the overuse of any utility word (see page 183), makes for vagueness. Whenever possible, prefer a more precise synonym.

**if = whether, though**  Dictionaries generally agree that the use of *if* with the meaning *whether* is established; they do not clearly agree on the use of *if* to mean *though*. Both uses would be more appropriate in an informal than in a formal style.

> *Informal:* We will go, even if you stay home.
>    I don't know if I should go or not.
> *Formal:* We will go, even though you stay at home.
>    I do not know whether or not I should go.

**in back of**  See  **back of.**

**individual**  Although the use of *individual* to mean *person* [He is a fascinating individual] is accepted by the dictionaries, college instructors generally disapprove of this use, probably because it is overdone in college writing. In its formal uses *individual* signifies "single" or "separate" [We are all Americans but we are also individuals; the instructor tries to give us individual attention].

**inferior than**  Possibly a confusion between *inferior to* and *worse than.* Say "inferior to" [Today's workmanship is inferior to that of a few years ago].

**in regards to**  The only acceptable form is *in regard to.* The *-s* ending is not uncommon in speech but it is not acceptable in college writing.

**inside of**  The use of *inside of* to mean "within" [I'll be there inside of an hour] is accepted as established usage, but in a formal style *within* would still be preferred.

**instance — instants**  An *instance* is an example, illustration, or case in point [That is just one instance of his attitude]. *Instants* is the plural of instant, meaning "moment."

**Intensives**  Such modifiers as *much, so, too, very* merely add emphasis to the words they modify [much obliged, so tired, too bad, very good].

The pronouns *myself, yourself, himself, herself* and their plurals may also be used as intensives [I will do it myself]. The overuse of intensives, especially *very*, is more likely to result in wordiness than in emphasis.

**irrelevant — irreverent** *Irrelevant* means "having no relation to" or "lacking pertinence" [That may be true, but it is quite irrelevant]. *Irreverent* means "without reverence" [Such conduct in a church is irreverent].

**its — it's** The confusion of these two forms causes frequent misspelling in college writing. *It's* always means "it is" or "it has." The apostrophe is a sign of contraction, not of possession [The dog wagged its tail; it's (it is) too difficult a problem; it's (it has) been raining all night].

**it's me** This construction is essentially a spoken one. Except in dialogue, it rarely occurs in writing. Its use in educated speech is thoroughly established. The formal expression is *It is I.* See page 481.

**Jargon** A name applied to diction which is wordy and unnecessarily abstract. The name is also applied to the technical vocabulary and usages of special groups — the jargon of the medical profession, legal jargon.

**kind of, sort of** Use a singular modifier and a singular verb with these phrases [That kind of people is always troublesome; this sort of attitude will get us nowhere]. In colloquial usage, *kind of* or *sort of* followed by a plural noun is felt to be plural in idea, even if singular in form, and is often given a plural verb and modifier [Those kind of mushrooms are poisonous].

**kind (sort) of = somewhat** This usage [I feel kind of tired; he looked sort of foolish] is colloquial. It would be inappropriate in a formal style and should be used sparingly in an informal style.

**knew — new** The misspelling arising out of a confusion of these two common words is usually a result of carelessness. *Knew* comes from OE *cunnan* and is related to *ken* and *cunning;* hence the *k*, which remains in the written form although it is not pronounced. *New* [a new hat, a new leaf] has historically no reason for being spelled with a *k*.

**lady** See **gentleman.**

later — latter   The confusion of these two words in college writing is probably a spelling error. *Later* is the comparative of *late* [It is later than you think]. *Latter* is the opposite of *former* and is used either as a synonym for second [The latter choice seemed the better] or as a reference to the second of two things previously mentioned [World War I and World War II were both global wars, but the latter involved civilians to a much greater extent than the former].

lead — led   The principal parts of *lead* are *lead, led, led.* Do not confuse the spelling of the past tense, *led,* with the spelling of the name of the metal, *lead.*

learn = teach   The use of *learn* to mean "teach" [He learned us arithmetic] is nonstandard and is not acceptable in college speech or writing. Say, "He taught us arithmetic."

leave = let   The use of *leave* for *let* [Leave us face it] is never acceptable in college speech or writing. Say, "Let us face it," "Let ( *not* leave) us be friends."

let's   A contraction of *let us.* The expression *let's us* is redundant and not acceptable in college writing.

liable, likely, apt   *Liable* to mean "likely" or "apt" [It is liable to rain; he is liable to hit you] is a colloquial usage to which instructors often object. *Liable* means "subject to" or "exposed to" or "answerable for" [He is liable to arrest; you will be liable for damages]. In formal usage *apt* means "has an aptitude for" [He is an apt pupil; she is apt at that kind of thing]. The use of *apt* to mean "likely" is accepted colloquially [She is apt to leave you; he is apt to resent it].

like = as, as though   The use of *like* as a conjunction [He talks like you do; it looks like it will be my turn next] is colloquial. It is not appropriate in a formal style and many people object to it in an informal style.

likely   See   liable.

line   The use of *line* to indicate a type of activity or business [What's your line? His line is drygoods] is accepted as established usage; its use to indicate a course of action or thought [He follows the party line] is also accepted. However, the overuse of *line* in these senses often provokes objection to the word.

loan, lend   Both forms of the verb are accepted in educated American usage.

**loath — loathe** The form without -*e* is an adjective meaning "reluctant," "unwilling" [I am loath to do that; he is loath to risk so great an investment] and is pronounced to rhyme with "both." The form with -*e* is a verb meaning "dislike strongly" [I loathe teas; she loathes an unkempt man], and is pronounced to rhyme with "clothe."

**locate = find** This usage [I cannot locate that quotation] is established, but its extension to mean *remember* [Your name sounds familiar, but I cannot locate your face] is not acceptable in college writing.

**locate = settle** This usage [He and his family have located in San Francisco] is colloquial. In college writing *settled* would be preferred.

**loose, lose** The confusion of these words causes frequent misspelling. *Loose* is most common as an adjective [a loose button, a loose nut, a dog that has broken loose]. *Lose* is always used as a verb [You are going to lose your money; don't lose your head].

**Loose sentence** The term used to describe a sentence in which the main thought is completed before the end. The opposite of a *periodic sentence*. See page 148.

**lot(s) of** The use of *lot(s)* to mean a considerable amount or number [I have lots of friends; they gave us a lot of excuses] is colloquial. This usage is common in informal writing.

**Lower case (l. c.)** Printer's terminology for small letters as contrasted with capitals. Frequently used by college instructors in marking student papers.

**luxuriant — luxurious** These words come from the same root but have quite different connotations. *Luxuriant* means "abundant" and is used principally of growing things [luxuriant vegetation, a luxuriant head of hair]. *Luxurious* means "luxury-loving" or "catering to luxury" [He finds it difficult to support so luxurious a wife on so modest an income; the appointments of the clubhouse were luxurious].

**mad = angry or annoyed** This is colloquial [My girl is mad at me; his insinuations make me mad]. In formal and informal styles, use *angry, annoyed, irritated, provoked,* or *vexed,* which are more precise.

**Malapropism** A humorous, though unintentional, confusion of words similar in form and sound [Henry VIII died of an *abbess* on his knee; one of the most momentous events in early English history was the invasion of the *Dames*]. The error is named for Mrs. Malaprop, a character in Sheridan's play *The Rivals,* who was much addicted to this sort of thing.

**math** A clipped form of *mathematics.* Appropriate in a colloquial or informal style but not in formal writing.

**may** See **can.**

**maybe = perhaps** Both usages are established; *perhaps* is the more formal.

**mean = petty, nasty, vicious** These uses of *mean* [It was mean of me to do that; please don't be mean to me; that dog looks mean] are colloquial. They are appropriate in most college writing, but their overuse sometimes results in vagueness. Consider using one of the suggested alternatives to provide a sharper statement.

**Metaphor** See page 187.

**might of** See **could of.**

**mighty = very** This usage [I'm mighty fond of her; that's a mighty big house] is colloquial. It could be used discreetly in informal college writing, but it is often an unnecessary intensive.

**moral — morale** Roughly, *moral* refers to conduct and *morale* refers to state of mind. A *moral* man is one who conducts himself according to the conventions of society or religion. People are said to have good *morale* when they are cheerful, cooperative, and not too much concerned with their own worries.

|   *Moral*   |   *Morale*   |
| --- | --- |
| Socrates said that a wise man was a moral man. | A pat on the back now and then is good for any man's morale. |

**most = almost** This usage [I am most always hungry an hour before mealtime] is colloquial. In college writing *almost* would be preferred in such a sentence.

**movie** Although "movie" is the predominant usage in newspapers, newsmagazines, and magazines, the dictionaries still record this word as "colloquial." If it is good enough for the *Saturday Review* it should be good enough for a composition course. The formal term is "motion picture."

**muchly** There is no such word. Say *much* [I am much pleased by the news].

**must (adjective and noun)**   The use of *must* as an adjective [This book is must reading for anyone who wants to understand Russia] and as a noun [It is reported that the President will classify this proposal as a must] is accepted as established usage by the dictionaries.

**must of**   See   **could of.**

**myself = I**   This usage [John and myself will go] is not generally acceptable. Say, "John and I will go." Myself is accepably used:
(1) as an intensifier [I saw it myself; I myself will go with you];
(2) as a reflexive object [I hate myself; I can't convince myself that he is right].

**myself = me**   This usage [He divided it between John and myself] is not recognized by the dictionaries, though Professor Marckwardt considers it "fully established in literature and current English" (*Scribner Handbook*, p. 241). The preferred usage would be "He divided it between John and me."

**naive, naïve**   Both spellings are now accepted.

**neither**   See   **either.**

**nice**   A utility word much overused in college writing. Avoid excessive use of it and, whenever possible, choose a more precise synonym.

It was a nice dance. [enjoyable? exciting? genteel? popular successful? well-organized?]
That's a nice dress. [attractive? becoming? fashionable? well-tailored?]
She's a nice girl. [agreeable? beautiful? charming? virtuous? friendly? well-mannered?]

**nice and**   See   **good and.**

**nickel**   Unlike *fickle, sickle, trickle,* and most words ending with the syllable pronounced *ul, nickel* ends in *el.* This exception often causes misspelling.

**Nominative absolute**   An introductory participial phrase which is grammatically independent of the rest of the sentence [*All things being considered,* the decision is a fair one; *the interview having been ended,* the reporters rushed to the phones]. This construction is common in Latin but should be used sparingly in college writing, partly because it is sometimes unidiomatic, and partly because it may result in a dangling modifier. The first example given above is idiomatic English; the second would normally be written, "When the interview was ended, the reporters rushed to the phones."

**Nominative case**   Another name for the Subjective case.

**none**   *None* may be followed by either a singular or a plural verb. See page 488.

**not . . . as, not . . . so**   See   **as . . . as.**

**nowhere near = not nearly**   Established usage, but *not nearly* is often preferred.

**nowheres**   Nonstandard variant of *nowhere.*

**Object**   In this book an object is considered one of a larger class of completing constructions, called *complements* (see page 414). An object is a noun or pronoun which completes the action of a transitive verb [We bought the *car;* I asked *her*] or completes a preposition [She smiled at *me;* it is lying on the *table*]. An *indirect object* identifies the recipient of the action indicated by a verb-object combination [We bought *dad* a car; the children gave *her* a party].

**off of**   In such sentences as "Keep off of the grass;" "He took it off of the table," the *of* is unnecessary and undesirable. Omit it in college speech and writing.

**OK, O.K.**   Its use in business to mean "endorse" is generally accepted [The manager OK'd the request]. Otherwise, it is colloquial. It is a utility word and is subject to the general precaution concerning all such words: do not overuse it, especially in contexts in which a more specific term would give more efficient communication. For example, contrast the vagueness of OK at the left with the discriminated meanings at the right.

| | |
|---|---|
| The garagemen said the tires were OK. | The garagemen said the tread on the tires was still good. |
| | The garagemen said the pressure in the tires was satisfactory (OK). |

**one . . . he, his**   The feeling that the repetition of *one . . . one's* [One must do what one can to ensure one's family a decent standard of living] makes for a stilted style has led to the permissible shift from *one, one's* to *he, his* [One must do what he can to ensure his family a decent standard of living]. In general a shift in the number or nature of pronouns is undesirable, but this particular shift is established usage. See page 435.

only   The position of *only* in such sentences as "I only need three dollars" and "If only mother would write!" is sometimes condemned on the grounds of possible ambiguity. In practice, the context usually rules out ambiguous interpretation, but a change in the word order would often result in more appropriate emphasis [I need only three dollars; If mother would only write].

out loud = aloud   This usage is colloquial. In a formal style, prefer *aloud*.

outside of = aside from, except   This usage [Outside of his family, no one respects him; outside of that, I have no objection] is colloquial. It would be inappropriate in a formal style, but not objectionable in an informal one.

over with = completed, ended   This usage [Let's get this job over with; she is all over with that romance] is colloquial. It should be avoided in a formal style, but could be used in informal writing.

part, on the part of   This usage [There will be some objection on the part of the students; on the part of businessmen, there will be some concern about taxes] often makes for a wordy and flabby style. Simply say, "The students will object;" "Businessmen will be concerned about taxes."

party = person   Colloquial, and generally to be avoided in college writing. In telephone usage, however, party is the accepted word [Your party does not answer].

past — passed   Although both forms may be used as past participles of the verb *to pass, past* is primarily used as an adjective or a noun [in days past, the past tense, she is a woman with a past]. *Passed* is a past tense or past participial form [They have passed the half-way mark; he passed all his examinations].

peace — piece   Associate *peace* with *calm* as a reminder that *peace* is spelled with an *a* [a peaceful sleep, an hour of peace]. Associate *piece* with *bit* as a reminder that *piece* is spelled with an *i* [a piece of chalk, a piece of news, in small pieces].

per = a   This usage [You will be remunerated at the rate of five dollars per diem; this material costs $1.50 per yard] is established. As the second illustration shows, the *per* need not be followed by a Latin noun. This use of *per* is most common in legal and business phraseology. For most purposes, "five dollars a day" and "$1.50 a yard" would be more natural expressions.

**per = according to, concerning**  This usage [The order will be delivered as per your instructions; per your inquiry of the 17th, we wish to report] is business slang which is unacceptable in college and in business. Say "according to" or "concerning."

**per cent, percent**  Originally an abbreviation of the Latin *per centum*, this term has been Anglicized and is no longer considered a foreign word. It may be written as one or two words and no longer requires a period to indicate abbreviation [There is a ten percent markup; interest is at three per cent].

**Periodic sentence**  A sentence in which the main thought is not completed until the end. The opposite of a *loose* sentence. See page 137.

**Personification**  A figure of speech in which animals, inanimate objects, and qualities are given human characteristics [Death cometh like a thief in the night; the breeze caressed her hair]. See page 188.

**phone**  Clipped form of *telephone*. Appropriate at informal and colloquial levels. In a formal style use the full form.

**Phonetics**  The science dealing with the sounds of language. These sounds are represented by phonetic symbols which ignore the appearance of a word and record only its pronunciation [Phonetically, *schism* is transcribed sɪzəm]. When words are spelled as they are pronounced the spelling is said to be phonetic.

**photo**  Colloquial clipped form of *photograph*. In a formal style, use the full form.

**Plagiarism**  The offense of representing as one's own writing the work of another. The use of unacknowledged quotations. See page 293.

**plain – plane**  *Plain* means "simple," "unadorned," "easily seen" [a plain dress, the plain truth, as plain as the nose on your face]. *Plane* means "level" [a plane surface, all on the same plane, he planed the board]. The short form of *airplane* is *plane*.

**plan on**  When *plan* is used in the sense of "arrange" [I plan to be in Columbus on the seventh], the accepted idiom is *plan to*. When, however, *plan* means "intend" or "hope" [I plan to see that picture whenever it comes to town; they are planning on saving enough money to buy a new car], either *plan to* or *plan on* is acceptable. The safer usage is *plan to.*

plenty   The use of *plenty* as a noun [There is plenty of room] is acceptable at all levels. Its use as an adverb [It was plenty good] is colloquial and would not be appropriate in college writing.

precede — proceed   The basic distinction in the use of these words is that *precede* means to "go before" and *proceed* means to "go forward." Thus ladies precede gentlemen in entering a vehicle or leaving a sinking ship. But a car proceeds along a road and one proceeds with one's plans.

Précis   A summary which preserves the organization and principal content of the original.

Predicate   That part of a sentence which states the action performed by or upon the subject. The predicate may consist of an intransitive verb, with or without modifiers, or of a transitive verb and its complement, with or without modifiers.

Predicate adjective   An adjective completing a linking verb, hence one kind of complement [His mother is *sick;* oh, it is *beautiful!*].

Predicate noun   Same function as *predicate adjective* above [His mother is a *writer;* her brother became a successful *lawyer*].

Prefix   A word or syllable placed before the root of another word to form a new word [*anti*bodies, *mono*syllabic, *un*natural].

presence — presents   *Presence* is the opposite of *absence* and ends in *-ce* [Your presence is requested; his presence at the meeting is essential]. *Presents,* when used as a noun, is the plural of *present,* meaning "gift." Associate the *t* in *gift* with the *t* in *presents* [He bought presents for everyone]. *Present* (accent on the second syllable) may also be used as a verb [Present arms; present your credentials].

principal — principle   The confusion of these words is a common source of misspelling. For the purpose of college writing it might be useful to oversimplify the distinction between their uses and say that *principal* is always an adjective unless it means "the principal (officer) of a school" and that *principle* is always a noun.

> *Principal:* The principal point is this . . .
> He is one of the principal offenders.
> He is a principal stockholder.
> One school has a new principal.

*Principle:* He is a man without principles.
I object to the principle of the thing.
Principles are nice; but profits are necessary.

**prof**  A clipped form of *professor.* In college writing use it only at a colloquial level.

**prophecy — prophesy**  *Prophecy* is always used as a noun [The prophecy came true; the prophecies of the Bible]. *Prophesy* is always a verb [He prophesied another war; don't be too eager to prophesy].

**proposition**  The use of *proposition* as a verb [They propositioned us to buy the car] is slang and is not acceptable at any level of college writing. Its use as a noun, meaning "proposal" [I have a proposition I'd like to make to you] is a colloquialism much overused in college writing. Say, "They proposed that we buy the car;" "I have a proposal I'd like to make to you."

**proven**  Alternative past participle of *prove.* The preferred form is *proved,* but *proven* is permissible.

**providing = provided**  This usage [I will go, providing you accompany me] is established. Either form is acceptable in college writing, though *provided* is more common and more widely accepted.

**quiet — quite**  Although pronunciation is often a doubtful guide to English spelling, the careful pronunciation of *qui-et* as a two-syllabled word would help eliminate the confusion of the spelling of these two words [The orchestra played quietly; quiet please! I am quite tired; that is quite proper].

**quite**  In formal English *quite* is used to mean "entirely" or "wholly" [The statement is quite in accordance with the facts]. The use of *quite* as an intensive [The news was quite a shock to us] is colloquial. It would be acceptable in an informal style.

**raise — rear**  The use of *raise* meaning to *bring up* [She raised a large family] is recognized by the dictionaries, though *rear* would be preferred in a formal style.

**real = really (very)**  At formal and informal levels of college writing use *really* [It was a really (not real) difficult assignment; she can be really (not real) annoying when she talks that way].

**reason is because** This is a colloquial idiom [The reason I did it was because I was angry]. Although some authorities classify it as established literary usage (see *Facts About Current English Usage,* p. 30) there is still considerable objection to it in college writing. In general, a better sentence may be obtained by omitting "The reason . . . was" and simply saying, "I did it because I was angry."

**Redundancy** Repetitious wording. For an example, see next entry.

**refer back** A confusion between *look back* and *refer.* This usage is objected to in college writing on the ground that since the *re* of refer means "back," *refer back* is redundant. *Refer back* is acceptable when it means "refer again" [The bill was referred back to the committee]; otherwise, say *refer* [Let me refer you to page 17; from time to time he referred to his notes].

**Referent** The *thing* as contrasted with the symbol which refers to it. The person, object, event or idea to which a word refers.

**respectfully — respectively** *Respectfully* means "with respect" [He spoke respectfully; Respectfully submitted]. *Respectively* means roughly "each in turn" [These three papers were graded respectively A, C, and B].

**Reverend** *Reverend* is used before the name of a clergyman and in formal usage is preceded by *the* [I met the Reverend Alexander White]. It is not used immediately preceding the surname [the Reverend White], but must be followed by Dr., Mr., or a Christian name or initials [Rev. Dr. White, Rev. Mr. White, Rev. A. L. White]. In informal usage, the *the* is often omitted and the word *Reverend* abbreviated.

|  *Formal* |  *Informal* |
|---|---|
| The Reverend Alexander L. White | Rev. A. L. White |
| 2472 Bancroft Street | 2472 Bancroft Street |
| Toledo, Ohio | Toledo, Ohio |

**right — rite** A *rite* is a ceremony or ritual. This word should not be confused with the various uses of *right.*

**right (adv.)** The use of *right* as an adverb is established in such sentences as: "He went right home;" "It served him right;" "Please try to act right;" "I will go right away." Its use to mean *very* [I was right glad to meet him; that's a right pretty girl] is colloquial and should be used in college writing only when the style is colloquial.

**role, rôle**   The preferred spelling is now *role,* without the circumflex.

**Run-on sentence**   Independent sentences separated by a comma instead of a semicolon, period, or other end mark of punctuation. Also called a *comma splice.* See page 427.

**said (adj.)**   The use of *said* as an adjective [said documents, said offense] is restricted to legal phraseology. Do not use it in college writing.

**same as = just as**   The preferred idiom is *just as* [He acted just as (not the same as) I thought he would].

**same, such**   Avoid the use of *same* or *such* as a substitute for *it, this, that, them* [I am returning the book, since I do not care for same; most people are fond of athletics of all sorts, but I have no use for such]. Say "I am returning the book because I do not care for it;" "Unlike most people, I am not fond of athletics."

**scarcely**   In such sentences as: "There wasn't scarcely enough;" "We haven't scarcely time," the use of *scarcely* plus a negative creates an unacceptable double negative. Say, "There was scarcely enough;" "We scarcely have time."

**scarcely than**   The use of *scarcely than* [I had scarcely met her than she began to denounce her husband] is a confusion between *no sooner . . . than* and *scarcely . . . when.* Say "I had no sooner met her than she began to denounce her husband," or "I had scarcely met her when she began to denounce her husband."

**seldom ever**   The *ever* is redundant. Instead of saying, "He is seldom ever late;" "She is seldom ever angry," say, "He is seldom late;" "She is seldom angry."

**self, selves**   The plural of *self* is *selves.* Such usages as "They hurt themselfs;" "They hate theirselfs," are nonstandard and are not acceptable in college speech or writing. See **myself.**

**Semantics**   The science of the meanings of words as contrasted with phonetics (pronunciation) and morphology (form).

**sensual — sensuous**   Avoid confusion of these words. *Sensual* has unfavorable connotations and means "catering to the gratification of the senses" [He leads a sensual existence]. *Sensuous* has generally favorable connotations and refers to pleasures experienced through the senses [The sensuous peace of a warm bath; the sensuous imagery of the poem].

**Series**  Parallel constructions arranged in succession [He was *tall, tanned,* and *terrible*]. The elements of a series may be single words, phrases, subordinate clauses, or main clauses, but all elements must be in the same grammatical form. See page 430.

**shape = condition**  This usage [Both fighters are in good shape; the house has been neglected for years and is now in wretched shape] is colloquial. It would be appropriate in an informal style, but *condition* would be more appropriate in a formal style.

**sharp = attractive, handsome**  Slang, generally unacceptable in college writing.

**shone — shown**  *Shone* is the past tense and the past participle of *shine* [The sun shone; her eyes shone with happiness]. *Shown* is the past participle of *show* [You have shown it to me before; that rookie hasn't shown a thing all season]. The form *showed* is an alternative past participle for *shown.*

**should of**  See **could of.**

**show = chance**  This usage [Give him a fair show] would be appropriate only in a colloquial style. In formal and informal style use *chance* or *opportunity.*

**show = play, motion picture**  Colloquial. Acceptable in an informal or colloquial style.

**show up**  The uses of *show up* to mean "expose" or "appear" [This test will show up any weaknesses in the machine; I waited for an hour, but he didn't show up] are established. The use of *show up* to mean "prove much superior to" [The girls showed up the boys in the spelling bee] is colloquial.

**sic**  The Latin word *sic,* pronounced *sick,* is used in brackets to indicate that an error in a quotation appeared in the original source and was not made by the person copying the quotation. Example: "The significant words in the paragraph are these: 'No person will be allowed on the premises unless he is duely [*sic*] authorized.'"

**sick = disgusted**  This usage [All these pious platitudes make me sick] is now recognized by the dictionaries. It should be acceptable in most college writing, but not in formal style.

**sleight — slight** *Sleight* comes from the same root as *sly* and is usually associated with a clever trick [sleight of hand]. The more common word *slight* means "slender," "flimsy" [a slight girl, slight hope, a slight protection]. It is also used as a verb to mean "treat disdainfully" [They consistently slighted their opponents; he was quite obviously slighting his wife].

**so (conj.)** The use of *so* as a connective [She refused to exchange the merchandise, so we went to the manager] is thoroughly respectable, but its overuse in college writing is objectionable. There are other good transitional connectives — *accordingly, for that reason, on that account, therefore, for example* — which could be used to relieve the monotony of a series of *so's*. Occasional use of subordination [When she refused to exchange the merchandise we went to the manager] would lend variety to the style.

**so . . . as** See **as . . . as.**

**some** The use of *some* as an adjective of indeterminate number [Some friends of yours were here; there are some questions I'd like to ask] is acceptable in all levels of writing. Its use as an intensive [That was some meal] or as an adverb [She cried some after you left] is slang and should be avoided in college writing.

**somebody's else** Say, "somebody else's." See **anybody's else.**

**somewheres** Nonstandard variant of *somewhere.* Not acceptable in college speech or writing.

**sort (of)** See **kind (of).**

**speak — speech** The difference in vowels between the verb *speak* and the noun or adjective *speech* causes frequent misspellings. The only solution is to memorize the spelling and uses of these words [a long speech, a speech impediment; speak honestly; the ability to speak effectively].

**staid — stayed** *Staid* means "sedate" or "decorous" [a staid old woman]. The more common word *stayed* is the past tense form and the past participle of *stay* [We stayed a week; he stayed where he was].

**stationary — stationery** *Stationary* means "fixed," "unchanging" [The front was stationary; his opinions are so stationary they have taken root]. *Stationery* means "writing materials" [a box of stationery; stationery and other supplies].

**straight — strait**  The more frequent word is *straight* [a straight line, straight talk, straight from the heart]. *Strait* is a common name for a narrow water passage [the Strait of Gibraltar] and is extended to mean any difficult condition [in financial straits, straitened circumstances, in desperate straits].

**Strong verb**  A verb which uses a change in the vowel rather than inflectional endings to distinguish between present and past tenses [sing, sang, sung]. *Weak verbs* [walk, walked, walked] are regular, strong verbs irregular. See page 462.

**suit — suite**  The common word is *suit* [a suit of clothes, follow suit (in cards), suit yourself, this doesn't suit me]. *Suite* means "retinue" [The President and his suite arrived late], "set" or "collection" [a dining room suite, a suite of rooms]. Check the pronunciation of these words in your dictionary.

**sure = certainly**  This usage [I sure am annoyed; sure, I will go with you] is colloquial. Unless the style justifies colloquial usage, say *certainly* or *surely*.

**sure and**  See **good and.**

**swell = good, fine**  This usage [It was a swell show; we had a swell time] is slang. It is generally unacceptable in college writing above the colloquial level.

**Symbol**  A word, signal, or sign. The word as contrasted with what it stands for. See **Referent.**

**Synonym**  A word having the same meaning as a given word [When used as a noun, *cab* is often a synonym for *taxi*]. See page 208.

**Syntax**  The relationships of words within a sentence. The chief units of syntax are the subject, verb, complement, and modifiers.

**take and**  This usage [In a fit of anger he took and smashed the bowl] is slang. Simply say *smashed* [In a fit of anger he smashed the bowl].

**take sick**  *Webster's* calls this usage [He took sick and died] dialectal, but the *ACD* accepts it as established. It would be appropriate in an informal style, but in a formal style *became ill* would be preferred.

taxi  Used either as a noun [We took a taxi to the station] or as a verb [The big plane taxied to a stop] the word is now acceptable at all levels of style.

terrible, terribly  An overused colloquialism for *very* [She was terribly nice about it]. Its restrained use in informal papers is not objectionable.

terrific  Used at a formal level to mean "terrifying" and at a colloquial level as an intensive. The overuse of the colloquialism has rendered the word almost useless in formal writing. For most students the best thing to do with this word is to forget it.

that there, this here  This usage [That there Stalin caused a lot of trouble; this here nut won't fit] is nonstandard and is not acceptable in college speech or writing. Omit the *there* or *here*.

Theme  Used in two ways in college composition courses: (1) The dominant idea of an essay [The theme of this essay is that self-deception is the commonest of vices]. (2) A general name for a composition assignment [Write a 500-word theme for Monday]. The first meaning is synonymous with *thesis* as it is used in this book.

there — their  The confusion of these words causes one of the commonest errors in spelling. *Their* is the possessive form of the pronoun *they* [They have their money; where are their things?]. *There* is the adverbial form contrasted with *here* [Put it there; it fell over there]. *There* is also used as an expletive to begin a sentence [There used to be a man . . . ; there were once three bears . . .].

these kind  See  kind.

Thesis  As used in this book, the dominant idea or purpose of an essay. The most restricted form of the purpose statement. See page 24.

tho  A variant spelling of *though*. The longer form is preferred in formal usage.

threw — through  Distinguish between the verb *threw* [He threw quickly to first base; he threw away his money] and the preposition *through* [through the woods, through the window, down through the years].

through = finished  This usage [Aren't you through with that story yet?] is classified as colloquial by *Webster's* but accepted without comment by the *ACD*. It would be appropriate in an informal style.

In a formal style "Haven't you finished that story" (not "finished with") would be preferred.

**to — too — two**   Distinguish the preposition *to* [Give it to me] from the adverb *too* [That is too bad] and the number *two* [Two chickens in every pot].

**tough**   The uses of *tough* to mean "difficult" [a tough assignment], "hard fought" [It was a tough game], "hard to bear" [It was a tough blow for all of us] are accepted without qualification by reputable dictionaries.

**toward, towards**   Both forms are acceptable. *Toward* is more common in America, *towards* in Britain.

**troop — troupe**   Both words come from the same root and share the original meaning, "herd." In modern usage *troop* is used of soldiers and *troupe* of actors [a troop of cavalry, a troop of scouts; a troupe of circus performers, a troupe of entertainers].

**try and**   *Try to* is the preferred idiom. *Try and* would generally be acceptable in informal and colloquial styles.

**Understatement**   The opposite of exaggeration. The device of deliberately saying less than one means, as in Winston Churchill's comment, "My life so far has not been entirely uneventful." Understatement is often used for ironic or humorous effect.

**unique**   The formal meaning of *unique* is "sole" or "only" [Adam had the unique distinction of being the only man who never had a mother]. The use of unique to mean "rare" or "unusual" [Spinal anesthetics allow the patient the unique experience of being a witness to his own appendectomy] has long been popular and is now accepted. But unique in the loose sense of uncommon [a very unique sweater] is generally frowned upon, especially when modified by an intensive adverb.

**up**   The adverb *up* is idiomatically used in many verb-adverb combinations which act as a single verb [break up, clean up, fill up, get up, tear up]. Often *up* adds a note of thoroughness to the action of the verb. Compare "They ate everything on their plates" with "They ate up everything on their plates." Avoid unnecessary or awkward separation of *up* from the verb with which it is combined, since this will have the effect of making *up* seem to be a single adverb modifying the verb rather than combining with it. For example,

"They held the cashier up" is subject to misinterpretation; "She made her face up" is simply awkward. Say "They held up the cashier;" "She made up her face;" "They filled up the front rows first."

**used to**   Notice the final *d* in *used*. We do not pronounce it in informal speech because it is elided before the *t* of *to*. But the phrase is written *used to*, not *use to*.

**used to could**   Nonstandard for *used to be able*. Not acceptable in college speech or writing.

**vain — vane — vein**   *Vain* means "useless" [a vain hope] or conceited [a vain woman]; a *vane* is a marker which is moved by wind or water [a weather vane]; a *vein* is a bloodvessel [the jugular vein] or a seam of ore [a rich vein of gold].

**very**   A common and useful intensive, but avoid its overuse in any one paper.

**vice — vise**   Distinguish between these words. A *vice* (compare *vicious*) is an evil [Virtues when carried to excess may become vices]. A *vise* is a tool [I put the board in a vise and sawed it].

**Vulgate**   Synonymous with *nonstandard*. Any usage characteristic of uneducated speech.

**wait on**   *Wait on* means "serve" [A clerk will be here in a moment to wait on you]. The use of *wait on* to mean "wait for" [I'll wait on you if you won't be long] is a colloquialism to which there is some objection. Say *wait for* [I'll wait for you if you won't be long].

**want for**   The use of *for* or *should* after *want* in such sentences as: "I want for you to come;" "I want you should come," is not acceptable in college speech or writing. After *want* in this sense use the objective case plus an infinitive [I want you to come; I want them to go at once]. When the sentence does not require an object, the infinitive is used immediately after *want* [I want to go home; he wants to return next week].

**want in, out**   This usage [The dog wants in; I want out of here] is classified as dialectal (nonstandard) by the *International* and is not recognized by the *ACD*. Although the *Oxford* calls it colloquial, it has not yet received dictionary recognition in America. Write, "The dog wants to come in;" "I want to get out of here."

**want = ought**  This usage [You want to save something every month; they want to be careful or they will be in trouble] is colloquial. *Ought* is the preferred idiom and *want* would be inappropriate in a formal style.

**ways**  Colloquial for *way* in such sentences as: "You must have come a long ways from home;" "They walked a long ways this morning." Except in a colloquial style the accepted form in college writing is *way* [You must have come a long way; they walked a long way].

**weak — week**  Distinguish between the adjective *weak* (without strength) and the noun *week* [the days of the week].

**weather — whether**  The word referring to the condition of the atmosphere is spelled *weather* [good weather, stormy weather]. *Whether* usually introduces alternatives [She doesn't know whether to marry Bill or Fred].

**well**  See **good.**

**when**  In college writing avoid the use of a *when*-clause in defining a term [A comma splice is when you put a comma between two separate sentences]. Instead of *when* use a noun phrase or clause [A comma splice is the use of a comma between two separate sentences]. See page 496.

**where (in definitions)**  See **when.**

**where . . . at, to**  The use of *at* or *to* after *where* [Where was he at? Where are you going to?] is redundant. Simply say, "Where was he?" "Where are you going?"

**where = that**  The use of *where* in such sentences as: "I heard on the radio where there was a violent storm in Chicago;" "I see in the paper where that bandit was caught," may be occasionally acceptable in a colloquial style, but it is inappropriate in formal or informal writing. Use *that* [I heard on the radio that there was a violent storm in Chicago; I see in the paper that the bandit was caught].

**which**  *Which* is not used to refer to persons. It is used to refer to things [The house which he built]. When referring to persons use *who, whom,* or *that* [The man who is talking, the girl whom I love, the doctor that I called].

**who — whom**  In informal and colloquial writing *who* is often used instead of *whom* when the pronoun is in subject territory — that is, when it comes near the beginning of the sentence [Who is she marrying? Who are you looking for?]. This is the colloquial and informal usage of educated people, but in a formal style *whom* would be required [Whom is she marrying? For whom are you looking?].

**who's — whose**  *Who's* is a colloquial and informal contraction for *who is* [Who's there? See who's at the door]. *Whose* is the possessive case of *who* [The man whose car he took; whose is this?].

**whose**  In informal and colloquial writing *whose* is a popular substitute for the formal and awkward *of which* [The nation whose army is occupying the territory will exert the greatest influence]. No good writer would be so concerned about the demands of formal grammar as to revise this sentence to read "The nation the army of which is occupying the territory . . . " Instead he would dodge the *of which* construction by saying "The nation which occupies the territory . . ." or "The army which occupies the territory will exert the greatest influence."

**wire**  The use of *wire* as a noun to mean "telegram" [Your wire arrived this morning] and as a verb to mean "telegraph" [Wire me when you arrive] is colloquial. It is appropriate in informal writing but *telegram* and *telegraph* would be preferred in a formal style.

**wood, woods**  The use of the plural form *woods* in the sense of "forest" [He went for a walk in the woods] is accepted by the dictionaries. The metaphorical use of *woods* [Paying off that debt has been a tough struggle, but we are out of the woods at last] is colloquial.

**would have**  The use of *would have* for "had" [If he would have told me I would have helped him] is generally unacceptable in college writing. Say, "Had he told me . . . " or "If he had told me . . . " See page 478.

**would of**  See  **could of.**

**you = one**  The use of *you* as an indefinite pronoun instead of the formal *one* is characteristic of an informal style, but be sure that this impersonal use will be recognized by the reader; otherwise he is likely to interpret a general statement as a personal remark addressed to him.

Do not use this impersonal *you* in a formal style, and avoid any arbitrary shifts from *one* to *you* [One must learn these things from your own experience]. Say either "One must learn these things from one's own experience" or "You must learn these things from your own experience."

# 604 INDEX

Parallel sentence: defined, 134; examples 134–135; requirements of, 136, 430

Parallel structure, convention in outline, 68–69

Parallelism, faulty, 430–431

Parentheses: uses of, 525; in outline, 67–68

Parenthetical constructions: errors in case due to, 481

Participial phrase, as dangling modifier, 137–138, 432–434

Participle: defined, 421; as verbal, 421. *See also* Past participle *and* Present participle

Particular-to-general, in paragraph development, 104–105, 108

Parts of speech: dictionary information on, 206; listed, 457–465

Passive voice: for emphasis, 455; uses of, 454–455; misuses of, 456

Past participle, 461; dangling, 137–138, 432–434; misuse of, 465–469

Past perfect tense, 471

Past tense (simple), 461, 470–471; misuse of, 465–469

Pattern, recognizable in parallel sentences, 135. *See also* Organization

Period: at end of declarative sentence, 516; with abbreviation, 516–517; with decimals and money, 517; position with quotation marks, 521

Period fault, 424

Periodic sentence, 137–139, 580, 585; can be overdone, 148; inversions in, 445

Periodical literature, indexes to, 266–269

Personal observation, main source of details for composition, 88

Personal pronoun, 459; as complement of "to be," 497

Personification, 188–189, 573; defined, 585

Persuasion, by argument, 324

Phonetics, 585, 589

Phrases, 418–420; infinitive and participial, 137–138; defined, 418; prepositional, 464

Plagiarism, 293; defined, 585

Planning: value in writing, 9–10, 13–14

Planning a composition. *See* Organization, Outlining, *and* Purpose

Plurals: foreign words, 458; regular and irregular, 458, 534; of compounds, 459; of letters and figures, 523

Popular words, contrasted with learned, 167–168

Positive degree, 463

Possessive case, 479; designated by apostrophe, 522–523

Précis, defined, 586

Precise thesis, 24, 26

Predicate, 586

Predicate adjective, defined, 463, 586

Predicate noun, defined, 586

Prefixes: Latin and Greek, 219–221; spelling rule for, 535; use of hyphen with, 549; defined, 586

Premises: common types of, 332–333; major and minor, 347

Preposition, defined, 457, 464

Prepositional phrase, 464

Present participle, 461; dangling, 137–138, 432–434

Present perfect tense, 470

Present tense (simple), 461, 470, 576; misuse of, 465–469; progressive, 470

Pretentious diction, 141–143

Progressive present tense, 470

Pronoun: vague reference, 447–448; defined, 457; kinds of, 459–461; inflection of, 459–461; personal, 459–460, 497; relative, 460, 493–494; demonstrative, 460; reflexive, 460; indefinite, 461; agreement with antecedent, 491–493; determining case of, 479–480

Pronoun reference, coherence through, 112; confused, 132–133; inconsistent, 139–140

Pronunciation, dictionary as guide to, 206, 218

Proper noun, 458

Punctuation: inadequate, 131–132; in bibliography, 284–288, 520; in footnotes, 306; comma, 504–513; semicolon, 514–515; period, 516–517; question and exclamation marks, 517; colon, 518; quotation marks, 519–520; apostrophe, 522–523; ellipses and dash, 523–524; parentheses and brackets, 525

Purpose: effective writing controlled by, 3; factors in achieving, 3–14; failures of, 4–13; clarifying and restricting, 21–23; stating the, 24–28; outlining as help in determining, 59–62; selection of details to fit writer's, 88–89; need of paragraph for, 98

Purpose statement: the thesis, 24–27; other forms, 27–28; in outline, 67; test of a satisfactory, 71–72

Purposeful details, use of, 80–97

Question, begging the, 353–354

Question, ignoring the, 354–356

Question mark, 517

Question to answer, in paragraph development, 107–109

Quotation marks: with titles, 519; uses

# CORRECTION SYMBOLS

| | |
|---|---|
| adj | Use adjective instead of adverb (p. 499) |
| adv | Use adverb instead of adjective (p. 498) |
| agr | Make circled words agree (subject-verb, pp. 485-491; pronoun-antecedent, pp. 491-494; tenses, pp. 469-479) |
| apos | Use apostrophe (pp. 522-523) |
| bib | Check form of bibliography (p. 283-288) |
| cap | Use capital letter(s) (pp. 545-548) |
| case | Use correct case form (pp. 479-484) |
| cs | Remove comma splice (pp. 427-429) |
| det | Provide details (pp. 89-91) |
| det? | Details not pertinent (pp. 88-89) |
| d | Indicated diction needs revision (162 ff.) |
| gen | Diction or statement too general (pp. 181-186) |
| i | Illegible word |
| id | Diction is not idiomatic (pp. 168-170) |
| lev | Confusion of stylistic levels (pp. 179-181) |
| lc | No capital. Use small letter(s) (pp. 545-548) |
| no ¶ | No paragraph |
| no p | No punctuation needed |
| ns | Nonstandard usage (pp. 166-167) |
| no | Use numbers (pp. 551-552) |
| om | Something omitted |
| ¶ | Begin new paragraph |
| p | Punctuation needed |
| ref | Clarify reference of pronoun (pp. 447-448) or modifier (pp. 446-447) |
| rep | Undesirable repetition |
| sp | Consult dictionary for correct spelling |
| t | Use correct tense form (pp. 469-478) |
| wo | Revise word order for clarity (pp. 444-446) |
| wordy | Reduce wordiness (pp. 140-146) |
| wr | Write out. Do not abbreviate or use numbers |
| ww | Wrong word (pp. 166-171) |
| / | Remove word, letter, or punctuation so slashed |
| x | Careless error |
| ./;/ | Provide punctuation indicated |